Visual InterDev™ 6 Bible

Visual InterDev™ 6 Bible

Richard Mansfield and Debbie Revette

IDG
BOOKS
WORLDWIDE

IDG Books Worldwide, Inc.
An International Data Group Company

Foster City, CA ✦ Chicago, IL ✦ Indianapolis, IN ✦ New York, NY

Visual InterDev ™ 6 Bible

Published by
IDG Books Worldwide, Inc.
An International Data Group Company
919 E. Hillsdale Blvd., Suite 400
Foster City, CA 94404
www.idgbooks.com (IDG Books Worldwide Web site)

Copyright © 1998 IDG Books Worldwide, Inc. All rights reserved. No part of this book, including interior design, cover design, and icons, may be reproduced or transmitted in any form, by any means (electronic, photocopying, recording, or otherwise) without the prior written permission of the publisher.

Library of Congress Catalog Card Number: 98-073337

ISBN: 0-7645-3135-2

Printed in the United States of America

10 9 8 7 6 5 4 3 2 1

IB/RX/QZ/ZY

Distributed in the United States by IDG Books Worldwide, Inc.

Distributed by Macmillan Canada for Canada; by Transworld Publishers Limited in the United Kingdom; by IDG Norge Books for Norway; by IDG Sweden Books for Sweden; by Woodslane Pty. Ltd. for Australia; by Woodslane (NZ) Ltd. for New Zealand; by Addison Wesley Longman Singapore Pte Ltd. for Singapore, Malaysia, Thailand, Indonesia, and Korea; by Norma Comunicaciones S.A. for Colombia; by Intersoft for South Africa; by International Thomson Publishing for Germany, Austria, and Switzerland; by Toppan Company Ltd. for Japan; by Distribuidora Cuspide for Argentina; by Livraria Cultura for Brazil; by Ediciencia S.A. for Ecuador; by Ediciones ZETA S.C.R. Ltda. for Peru; by WS Computer Publishing Corporation, Inc., for the Philippines; by Unalis Corporation for Taiwan; by Contemporanea de Ediciones for Venezuela; by Computer Book & Magazine Store for Puerto Rico; by Express Computer Distributors for the Caribbean and West Indies. Authorized Sales Agent: Anthony Rudkin Associates for the Middle East and North Africa.

For general information on IDG Books Worldwide's books in the U.S., please call our Consumer Customer Service department at 800-762-2974. For reseller information, including discounts and premium sales, please call our Reseller Customer Service department at 800-434-3422.

For information on where to purchase IDG Books Worldwide's books outside the U.S., please contact our International Sales department at 650-655-3200 or fax 650-655-3297.

For information on foreign language translations, please contact our Foreign & Subsidiary Rights department at 650-655-3021 or fax 650-655-3281.

For sales inquiries and special prices for bulk quantities, please contact our Sales department at 650-655-3200 or write to the address above.

For information on using IDG Books Worldwide's books in the classroom or for ordering examination copies, please contact our Educational Sales department at 800-434-2086 or fax 317-596-5499.

For press review copies, author interviews, or other publicity information, please contact our Public Relations department at 650-655-3000 or fax 650-655-3299.

For authorization to photocopy items for corporate, personal, or educational use, please contact Copyright Clearance Center, 222 Rosewood Drive, Danvers, MA 01923, or fax 978-750-4470.

is a trademark under exclusive license to IDG Books Worldwide, Inc., from International Data Group, Inc.

ABOUT IDG BOOKS WORLDWIDE

Welcome to the world of IDG Books Worldwide.

IDG Books Worldwide, Inc., is a subsidiary of International Data Group, the world's largest publisher of computer-related information and the leading global provider of information services on information technology. IDG was founded more than 25 years ago and now employs more than 8,500 people worldwide. IDG publishes more than 275 computer publications in over 75 countries (see listing below). More than 90 million people read one or more IDG publications each month.

Launched in 1990, IDG Books Worldwide is today the #1 publisher of best-selling computer books in the United States. We are proud to have received eight awards from the Computer Press Association in recognition of editorial excellence and three from *Computer Currents'* First Annual Readers' Choice Awards. Our best-selling *...For Dummies*® series has more than 50 million copies in print with translations in 38 languages. IDG Books Worldwide, through a joint venture with IDG's Hi-Tech Beijing, became the first U.S. publisher to publish a computer book in the People's Republic of China. In record time, IDG Books Worldwide has become the first choice for millions of readers around the world who want to learn how to better manage their businesses.

Our mission is simple: Every one of our books is designed to bring extra value and skill-building instructions to the reader. Our books are written by experts who understand and care about our readers. The knowledge base of our editorial staff comes from years of experience in publishing, education, and journalism — experience we use to produce books for the '90s. In short, we care about books, so we attract the best people. We devote special attention to details such as audience, interior design, use of icons, and illustrations. And because we use an efficient process of authoring, editing, and desktop publishing our books electronically, we can spend more time ensuring superior content and spend less time on the technicalities of making books.

You can count on our commitment to deliver high-quality books at competitive prices on topics you want to read about. At IDG Books Worldwide, we continue in the IDG tradition of delivering quality for more than 25 years. You'll find no better book on a subject than one from IDG Books Worldwide.

John Kilcullen
CEO
IDG Books Worldwide, Inc.

Steven Berkowitz
President and Publisher
IDG Books Worldwide, Inc.

Eighth Annual Computer Press Awards ➣ 1992

Ninth Annual Computer Press Awards ➣ 1993

Tenth Annual Computer Press Awards ➣ 1994

Eleventh Annual Computer Press Awards ➣ 1995

IDG Books Worldwide, Inc., is a subsidiary of International Data Group, the world's largest publisher of computer-related information and the leading global provider of information services on information technology. International Data Group publishes over 275 computer publications in over 75 countries. More than 90 million people read one or more International Data Group publications each month. International Data Group's publications include: **ARGENTINA:** Buyer's Guide, Computerworld Argentina, PC World Argentina; **AUSTRALIA:** Australian Macworld, Australian PC World, Australian Reseller News, Computerworld, IT Casebook, Network World, Publish, Webmaster; **AUSTRIA:** Computerwelt Österreich, Networks Austria, PC Tip Austria; **BANGLADESH:** PC World Bangladesh; **BELARUS:** PC World Belarus; **BELGIUM:** Data News; **BRAZIL:** Annuário de Informática, Computerworld, Connections, Macworld, PC Player, PC World, Publish, Reseller News, Supergamepower; **BULGARIA:** Computerworld Bulgaria, Network World Bulgaria, PC & MacWorld Bulgaria; **CANADA:** CIO Canada, Client/Server World, ComputerWorld Canada, InfoWorld Canada, NetworkWorld Canada, WebWorld; **CHILE:** Computerworld Chile, PC World Chile; **COLOMBIA:** Computerworld Colombia, PC World Colombia; **COSTA RICA:** PC World Centro America; **THE CZECH AND SLOVAK REPUBLICS:** Computerworld Czechoslovakia, Macworld Czech Republic, PC World Czechoslovakia; **DENMARK:** Communications World Danmark, Computerworld Danmark, Macworld Danmark, PC World Danmark, Techworld Denmark; **DOMINICAN REPUBLIC:** PC World Republica Dominicana; **ECUADOR:** PC World Ecuador; **EGYPT:** Computerworld Middle East, PC World Middle East; **EL SALVADOR:** PC World Centro America; **FINLAND:** MikroPC, Tietoverkko, Tietoviikko; **FRANCE:** Distributique, Hebdo, Info PC, Le Monde Informatique, Macworld, Reseaux & Telecoms, WebMaster France; **GERMANY:** Computer Partner, Computerwoche, Computerwoche Extra, Computerwoche FOCUS, Global Online, Macwelt, PC Welt; **GREECE:** Amiga Computing, GamePro Greece, Multimedia World; **GUATEMALA:** PC World Centro America; **HONDURAS:** PC World Centro America; **HONG KONG:** Computerworld Hong Kong, PC World Hong Kong, Publish in Asia; **HUNGARY:** ABCD CD-ROM, Computerworld Szamitastechnika, Internetto online Magazine, PC World Hungary, PC-X Magazin Hungary; **ICELAND:** Tolvuheimur PC World Island; **INDIA:** Information Communications World, Information Systems Computerworld, PC World India, Publish in Asia; **INDONESIA:** InfoKomputer PC World, Komputek Computerworld, Publish in Asia; **IRELAND:** ComputerScope, PC Live!; **ISRAEL:** Macworld Israel, People & Computers/Computerworld; **ITALY:** Computerworld Italia, Macworld Italia, Networking Italia, PC World Italia; **JAPAN:** DTP World, Macworld Japan, Nikkei Personal Computing, OS/2 World Japan, SunWorld Japan, Windows NT World, Windows World Japan; **KENYA:** PC World East African; **KOREA:** Hi-Tech Information, Macworld Korea, PC World Korea; **MACEDONIA:** PC World Macedonia; **MALAYSIA:** Computerworld Malaysia, PC World Malaysia, Publish in Asia; **MALTA:** PC World Malta; **MEXICO:** Computerworld Mexico, PC World Mexico; **MYANMAR:** PC World Myanmar; **NETHERLANDS:** Computer! Totaal, LAN Internetworking Magazine, LAN World Buyers Guide, Macworld Netherlands, Net, WebWereld; **NEW ZEALAND:** Absolute Beginners Guide and Plain & Simple Series, Computer Buyer, Computer Industry Directory, Computerworld New Zealand, MTB, Network World, PC World Centro America; **NICARAGUA:** PC World Centro America; **NORWAY:** Computerworld Norge, CW Rapport, Datamagasinet, Financial Rapport, Kursguide Norge, Macworld Norge, Multimediaworld Norge, PC World Ekspress Norge, PC World Nettverk, PC World Norge, PC World ProduktGuide Norge; **PAKISTAN:** Computerworld Pakistan; **PANAMA:** PC World Panama; **PEOPLE'S REPUBLIC OF CHINA:** China Computer Users, China Computerworld, China InfoWorld, China Telecom World Weekly, Computer & Communication, Electronic Design China, Electronics Today, Electronics Weekly, Game Software, PC World China, Popular Computer Week, Software Weekly, Software World, Telecom World; **PERU:** Computerworld Peru, PC World Profesional Peru, PC World SoHo Peru; **PHILIPPINES:** Click!, Computerworld Philippines, PC World Philippines, Publish in Asia; **POLAND:** Computerworld Poland, Computerworld Special Report Poland, Cyber, Macworld Poland, Networld Poland, PC World Komputer; **PORTUGAL:** Cerebro/PC World, Computerworld/Correio Informático, Dealer World Portugal, Mac*In/PC*In Portugal, Multimedia World; **PUERTO RICO:** PC World Puerto Rico; **ROMANIA:** Computerworld Romania, PC World Romania, Telecom Romania; **RUSSIA:** Computerworld Russia, Mir PK, Publish, Seti; **SINGAPORE:** Computerworld Singapore, PC World Singapore, Publish in Asia; **SLOVENIA:** Monitor; **SOUTH AFRICA:** Computing SA, Network World SA, Software World SA; **SPAIN:** Communicaciones World España, Computerworld España, Dealer World España, Macworld España, PC World España; **SRI LANKA:** Infolink PC World; **SWEDEN:** CAP&Design, Computer Sweden, Corporate Computing Sweden, Internetworld Sweden, it.branschen, Macworld Sweden, MaxiData Sweden, MikroDatorn, Natverk & Kommunikation, PC World Sweden, PCaktiv, Windows World Sweden; **SWITZERLAND:** Computerworld Schweiz, Macworld Schweiz, PCtip; **TAIWAN:** Computerworld Taiwan, Macworld Taiwan, NEW ViSiON/Publish, PC World Taiwan, Windows World Taiwan; **THAILAND:** Publish in Asia, Thai Computerworld; **TURKEY:** Computerworld Turkiye, Macworld Turkiye, Network World Turkiye, PC World Turkiye; **UKRAINE:** Computerworld Kiev, Multimedia World Ukraine, PC World Ukraine; **UNITED KINGDOM:** Acorn User UK, Amiga Action UK, Amiga Computing UK, Apple Talk UK, Computing, Macworld, Parents and Computers UK, PC Advisor, PC Home, PSX Pro, The WEB; **UNITED STATES:** Cable in the Classroom, CIO Magazine, Computerworld, DOS World, Federal Computer Week, GamePro Magazine, InfoWorld, I-Way, Macworld, Network World, PC Games, PC World, Publish, Video Event, THE WEB Magazine, and WebMaster; online webzines: JavaWorld, NetscapeWorld, and SunWorld Online; **URUGUAY:** InfoWorld Uruguay; **VENEZUELA:** Computerworld Venezuela, PC World Venezuela; and **VIETNAM:** PC World Vietnam.   5/7/98

Credits

Acquisitions Editor
John Osborn

Development Editors
Denise Santoro
D.F. Scott

Contributing Authors
Evangelos Petroutsos
D.F. Scott

Technical Editors
Jim Sally
Debbie Zelten

Copy Editors
Suki Gear
Richard H. Adin
Robert Campbell
Marcia Baker
Barry Childs-Helton

Project Coordinator
Tom Debolski

**Graphics and
Production Specialists**
Mario Amador
Sue DeFloria
Mark Yim

Quality Control Specialists
Mick Arellano
Mark Schumann

Illustrator
Donna Reynolds

Proofreader
Jenny Overmyer

Indexer
Infodex Indexing Services, Inc.

Cover Design
Murder By Design

Cover Coordinator
Andreas Schueller

About the Authors

From 1981 through 1987, **Richard Mansfield** was editor of *COMPUTE!* magazine. During that time, he wrote hundreds of magazine articles and two columns. From 1987 to 1991 he was editorial director and partner in Signal Research. Richard began writing books full-time in 1991. He's written 21 computer books. Of those, four became bestsellers: *Machine Language for Beginners, The Second Book of Machine Language, The Visual Guide to Visual Basic,* and *The Visual Basic Power Toolkit* (with Evangelos Petroutsos). His most recent titles include *Discover ActiveX* from IDG Books Worldwide. Overall, his books have sold more than 500,000 copies worldwide, and have been translated into nine languages.

Debbie Revette has been involved with software development for more than 20 years as a consultant, programmer, and manager. In 1995, she was bitten by the WWW bug and is now focused exclusively on helping businesses use the Internet. Prior to that, she was Director of Product Development Management at a division of Dun & Bradstreet that produced a suite of OLAP tools marketed worldwide by Nielsen Marketing Research and IMS. She has designed and developed software for Hewlett-Packard, MDG.org, Kraft Foods, Nielsen Media Research, ADP, Tymshare, and the U.S. Department of Commerce's Atlantic Oceanographic and Meteorological Laboratory. Debbie holds a BS degree in Applied Math/Computer Science from Florida State University. She currently resides in San Francisco, California, with her husband, dog, and two birds. Debbie can be reached at drevette@sprynet.com.

To Jim Coward, for his friendship.

— Richard Mansfield

To my mother, Jean Revette, for her love and support.

— Debbie Revette

Preface

Visual InterDev is the leading data-driven Web application development environment available today, and version 6, released in the Fall of 1998, includes many significant new features. This book covers in-depth all the utilities, tools, and features included in the Visual InterDev 6 (VI) package. VI is more than a fine-tuned, feature-packed HTML editor. It's a rich integrated design and development environment, boasting a graphical Site Designer, powerful editors (WYSIWYG Page editor, SQL editor, Cascading Style Sheets editor), IntelliSense script statement completion, excellent debuggers (that work seamlessly on both client- and server-side scripts as well as Microsoft SQL Server stored procedures), instant preview of your client-side work, support for cutting-edge technology such as scriptlets and DHTML, and much more. If you're experienced with VI 1.0, you'll find this book invaluable. Not only will it bring you up to speed on the many new features in VI 6, but it's also packed with ideas and shortcuts, tips and techniques.

This book's authors have years of experience with project management, data and process analysis, database management, site design, and programming. Throughout this book, you'll find the information you need to minimize your labor and maximize your results when building logical, attractive, professional Web applications.

Who Should Read This Book

This book is written for developers at all levels of expertise in Web application construction, though the chapters on scripting and connecting databases to Web pages assume some experience with computer programming and databases. We do briefly define basic concepts such as loops and arrays, but this book isn't designed to teach elementary programming. The programming primarily explored here is scripting, writing code that is executable in an Internet browser. Both VBScript and JavaScript are covered, along with techniques for creating stand-alone components. Nevertheless, beginners with an aptitude for programming should be able to follow and understand the many step-by-step examples. The book isn't riddled with computer jargon; obscure concepts and terminology are thoroughly explained in clear, plain language.

How This Book Is Organized

The book is divided into seven parts:

       I. Visual InterDev Fundamentals

       II. Creating Web Pages

       III. Working on the Client Side

       IV. Working with Active Server Pages

       V. Using the Visual Database Tools

       VI. Using Databases in a Web

       VII. Managing Web Applications

In addition, *Visual InterDev 6 Bible* offers these reference resources:

+ Appendix A describes the physical design of the Register Database.

+ Appendix B serves as a reference to HTML 4.0.

+ Appendix C describes the contents of the accompanying CD-ROM.

+ A glossary supplies definitions for important terms.

Note   Please check the IDG Books Worldwide Web site at www.idgbooks.com for any significant Visual InterDev updates.

The categories addressed in the book's seven parts cover the entire range of VI's features. This book can be read sequentially by those wanting a thorough education in the uses and features of Visual InterDev. Just as profitably, you can read topics here and there to satisfy an immediate interest. Some chapters are paired tutorials, intended to be read sequentially unless the basics of the topic are familiar to you. For example, Chapter 12 introduces scripting and Chapter 13 explores advanced scripting. Chapters 14 and 15 are similarly structured: 14 covers the basics of DHTML and 15 goes into cutting-edge techniques. However, for the most part, the book's chapters are self-contained tutorials. Brief descriptions of this book's seven categories follow.

Part I: Visual InterDev Fundamentals

In this section you find out what, precisely, Visual InterDev can do for you. All the main features are described in an overview in Chapter 1, and then Chapter 2 gets you up to speed on the process of creating software for the Web. Once you've reviewed each phase in the development process and where Visual InterDev fits in, we take a more detailed look at what's involved in the first phase: planning a Web project. You then learn about the four basic architectural components of Visual InterDev: the Web browser client, the VI client, the Web server, and the database server.

Part II: Creating Web Pages

Now that you've learned to design and spec your site, you're ready to get down to the business of generating professional, effective Web pages. This second section begins with a survey of VI's IDE (Integrated Design Environment). We assume you understand the basics common to most computer applications — we don't explain what the Save As option on the File menu means. We do explain features unique to VI, or features that the average computer user might not easily understand. We also show you how and when to use FrontPage, VI's companion application. You also start actually creating Web pages at this point in the book.

Part III: Working on the Client Side

Now you go down into the engine room and get going with some programming. You find out what tools to use to create objects — reusable components — and how to use script to add computing power to the inherently static and limited page-description capabilities of HTML. Among other issues, you see how to use script to manipulate objects — Java applets or ActiveX components. You'll also understand the differences between JavaScript and VBScript — you can translate between them or choose which scripting language most appeals to you. This section concludes with an introduction to the basics, then the advanced features, of DHTML.

Part IV: Working with Active Server Pages

Now it's time to switch sides and see how to create Web pages that run on the Web server rather than in the user's browser. Until recently, the development of pages with which the user could interact and submit information to the server meant programming in Perl, or other programming languages. With Active Server Pages (ASP), the situation has changed drastically and everyone who can write a client script with VBScript or JavaScript can also write programs that work on the server. As you learn in this section, however, the server is a more complicated environment than a client workstation.

Part V: Using the Visual Database Tools

One of Microsoft's goals in producing the Visual Database Tools, consisting of Data View, Database Designer, Query Designer, and SQL Editor, was to create a single user interface to manage the data objects of every ODBC-compliant database. You'll see as you work with each of these tools that Microsoft has achieved this goal. You learn how to use VI's Project Explorer and Data View — which operate like the familiar Windows Explorer — to find and access each of the database objects in your project. You work with example projects to create data connections and manage the Data View window, which reflects a live connection to a database. You'll go on to work with database diagrams, tables, views, queries, stored procedures, and triggers.

Part VI: Using Databases in a Web

To help developers build robust, data-driven Web applications, Microsoft has defined the Windows Distributed Internet Applications Architecture (DNA). In this section of the book, you'll understand the three-tiered architecture supported by VI tools and distributed operating environments. Universal Data Access is a key component in this architecture because it accesses relational and nonrelational data in place. This capability is of tremendous interest to corporations that have zillions of bytes of data disbursed throughout the organization, in legacy systems, e-mails, and Excel spreadsheets, to name just a few backwaters where data accumulates. As you see in the hands-on chapters in this section of the book, Visual InterDev is one of the first Microsoft tools that delivers on the capabilities envisioned by DNA. You learn more about Microsoft's vision and the associated architectural components in this section. You'll also learn how to connect your Web application to your database and how to use data commands and Design-Time Controls (DTCs) to display data and automatically generate the necessary client or server-side script for you.

Part VII: Managing Web Applications

This section wraps up the job of creating a Web application by examining several important issues. First, you learn to use Link View to maintain a sophisticated, complex site, and to repair links. You also see how VI's built-in features make it easy to transfer a finished Web site from the design location to a public (or intranet) server. Deployment — including re-registration of dependencies and components — has never been this easy. You'll also find out how VI handles the various security concerns that you have on the server side as well as the legitimate concerns of Internet surfers that they might download viruses. You'll see what security features can be adjusted, and how they help reduce the serious fear that a system can be corrupted by a random and senseless act of cyber violence.

This book concludes with Appendix A, which describes the physical design of the sample Microsoft SQL Server database called Register, which you use in the hands-on examples in Chapters 18 through 23. Appendix B is a complete reference to the latest version of HTML, version 4.0, which is supported by Internet Explorer 4.0. Appendix C describes the contents of the book's CD-ROM.

Conventions Used in This Book

Throughout the book, you'll notice text set off by one of the following icons:

Sections marked *Note* contain additional explanatory information.

Tips provide useful information that is not immediately obvious and that will make the task easier and/or save you time.

The *Caution* sections are warnings of possible problem situations and how to avoid them.

System Requirements

The minimum requirements to run Visual InterDev are as follows:

✦ Pentium 90

✦ Windows 95, windows 98, or Windows NT 4.0

✦ 24 MB of RAM (32MB recommended)

✦ 81MB hard disk space (98MB recommended)

Online Update

Keeping up with new software as it makes its way through development in a never-ending challenge. Bugs are fixed and new ones appear; last-minute features are unveiled and existing ones dropped. IDG Books Worldwide has always been committed to having its popular Bibles on the shelves of your nearest bookstore on or near the day when the products ships. To help ensure that *Visual InterDev 6 Bible* is as up-to-date and accurate as possible when it is published, we have created a special Online Update site at `http://www.idgbooks.com/extras/interdev6.html`. Please visit us there for a free Visual INterDev online resources we have found valuable.

Feedback, Please!

Your feedback is welcome. Please let us know what you liked and any suggestions you may have for future editions of this book. We would especially like to see the Web applications you create after reading *Visual InterDev Bible*. Please send Debbie Revette an e-mail and let her know the URL. Her e-mail address is `drevette@sprynet.com`.

Acknowledgments

I would like to thank John Osborn for his balanced, thoughtful oversight of this project. I also want to acknowledge the tireless, dedicated, and energetic editing contributed by Denise Santoro. If one of an editor's tasks is to prevent embarrassment, Denise provided ample evidence she was carefully doing her job. In addition, I'd like to thank James P. Sally and Deborah Zelten for their technical review, and D.F. Scott for his contribution.

—Richard Mansfield

First of all, many thanks to everyone at IDG Books who made this book happen. In particular, I thank Denise Santoro, whose positive outlook, attention to detail, and editing expertise contributed greatly to the quality of this book. I'm grateful to my co-author, Richard Mansfield, for the encouragement and advice provided during this, my first book project. Thanks also to Chris Van Buren for getting me involved in this project and to Jay Trimble for being involved at the very beginning. Can you believe it? I'd be remiss if I didn't thank everyone at Microsoft for producing such a great product and letting me get involved with it early on. Most important, I thank my husband and best friend, Greg King, who made many sacrifices to allow me to pursue my dream of writing. Thank you for your patience and understanding.

—Debbie Revette

Contents at a Glance

Contents

● ●

Part VI: Using Databases in a Web   547

Chapter 22: Understanding Data Connections 549

Chapter 23: Working with Data on a Web Page..................................579

Part VII: Managing Web Applications   605

Chapter 24: Site Maintenance and Deployment 607

Chapter 25: Exploring Security Issues 623

Visual InterDev Fundamentals

Visual InterDev: An Overview

If you're working on a data-driven Web application, Visual InterDev 6.0 (VI) is the most powerful and full-featured development environment currently available. Microsoft sells it both separately and as a part of the suite of tools that are bundled together and sold as Visual Studio 6.0.

Microsoft calls VI a *RAD* environment, meaning Rapid Application Development. It could also be called *VAD* because, essentially, it means *visual* application development: if you want a Textbox on your Web page that's connected to your corporate database, you just drag and drop a data command and a Textbox Design-Time Control (DTC) onto the page. Then you connect the Textbox to the data command that retrieves the desired data from the database. The pages of script code necessary to achieve this functionality are automatically written into the Web page, either DHTML or Active Server Pages, your choice. And you're done! That's pretty rapid development, don't you think? You just drag and drop; Visual InterDev writes the script.

In this chapter, we'll first explore how VI fits into the world of Web application development; then we'll take a tour of VI's main features. When you've finished this chapter, you should have a good idea of what VI can do for you. The rest of this book goes into detail about the topics introduced here, providing many hands-on examples and in-depth tutorials.

Visual InterDev in the World of Internet Programming

Each Web application starts as an HTML document, a list of elements, attributes, and content (such as the name of a company, a picture of its products, and so on). As computer languages go, HTML is simple; it's a *page-description* language, meaning that it describes the size and position of text and graphics, and such things as the typeface. For example, if you want a headline in a blue typeface centered at the top of the first page, you could specify a level-1 heading <H1> (the element), the color of that headline (an attribute), and the actual text of the headline:

```
<H1 align=center><FONT color=blue>MegaDyne Corp.</FONT></H1>
```

HTML is simple because (for the most part) it doesn't compute; it doesn't process information in the classic sense that computer languages can. HTML cannot add 1+1.You can, of course, type in HTML source code using something as simple as Notepad. Then why use Visual InterDev if Notepad will work? You use VI to create Web applications for the same reason you might use a car to go shopping — it's easier, faster and, ultimately, more enjoyable than walking and lugging all the bags back home. With VI, you get a huge toolkit of features that make creating a sophisticated Web application far, far easier than it would be by hand-programming in a simple text editor like Notepad. VI gives you everything from design-time code-generating components to dozens of professionally designed templates and themes. What's more, VI works well as a programmer's environment — so you can write script that does compute.

Visual InterDev and Visual Studio

Visual Studio is a huge bundle of languages, utilities, and applications; the Professional Edition of Visual Studio contains the latest versions of Visual Basic, Visual C++, Visual JScript++, and Visual FoxPro. Visual Studio also includes Visual InterDev. You can use the languages to manage data or create objects (components) that you'll want to insert into your Web pages. You use VI to insert those objects. Basically, VI acts as a sophisticated site prototyper, a Web team management utility, a feature-packed page designer, and an Internet programming (scripting) environment. Visual Studio includes Visual InterDev, plus all the latest versions of the languages programmers like to use.

Visual Studio is also sold in a second version called the Enterprise Edition. It includes all the tools in the Professional Edition, plus Visual Database Tools, the Microsoft Visual SourceSafe version control system, the Microsoft Repository, Visual Component Manager, Microsoft Visual Modeler, and development versions of Microsoft SQL Server 6.5, Microsoft Internet Information Server 4.0, Microsoft Transaction Server 2.0, and Microsoft Message Queue Server.

FrontPage versus Visual InterDev

Included with VI is FrontPage 98 (FP), a full-featured designer-oriented application. There isn't a contest between these two excellent Web-page development tools. They are bundled together because they supplement each other, just as the various participants in a Web development team complement each other's talents. There are administrators, webmasters, technicians, database specialists, MIS personnel, programmers, graphic artists, content publishers, marketing and salespeople, and anyone else needed to build and sustain a vibrant, effective site. These people have different kinds of skills; by providing two powerful tools, Microsoft can optimize each application to suit divergent needs. VI is optimized for programmers; FP is optimized for nonprogrammers. Even the user interfaces of their respective IDEs differ. FP resembles Microsoft Office applications; VI resembles Microsoft's Visual Programming (RAD) applications (such as Visual Basic and Visual JScript++). We'll have more to say about FrontPage features shortly.

Visual Basic, Java, VBScript, and JavaScript

VI supports both JavaScript (also known as JScript) and VBScript — both with statement completion features as well as in its debugging tools. In addition, objects created in Visual Basic or Java can be dropped into Web pages within the VI or FP IDEs. There is also support for assisting the programmer in connecting script to objects, so the script can adjust the objects' properties and work with methods and events. Server-side applets or objects are also supported.

VI's Main Features

VI includes a number of powerful tools; here's an overview of the primary features.

Easy database connectivity

Using V1's extensive and efficient database features, not only can you develop your data-driven Web application, but you can also develop your Microsoft SQL Server and Oracle database using the Visual Database Tools. Data View shows you the structure of your database, including tables, columns, stored procedures, and triggers. With the Database Designer, you can create and modify tables, indexes, and relationships in your SQL Server and Oracle database. Query Designer lets you create and execute complex SQL statements in a drag-and-drop environment. In addition, you can create and debug stored procedures and triggers in your SQL Server and Oracle databases. You'll learn about these tools in Chapters 18 through 23.

VI lets you easily connect your site to any ODBC-compliant database with Design-Time ActiveX Controls that utilize ActiveX Data Objects (ADO) technology. VI supports databases through OLE DB and ODBC drivers — including Microsoft SQL Server, Oracle, Sybase, IBM VSAM, IBM DB/2, Informix, Microsoft Access, Paradox, and dBase.

Efficient site prototyping and maintenance

Constructing a coherent, easily navigable, and logical site means organizing the various pages into a sensible structure — and providing the user with an effective navigation bar. VI includes two tools that make site mapping and maintenance a *visual* experience. The Site Designer tool helps you create and maintain the interrelationships between the various pages that, collectively, make up your Web application. Beyond that, these relationships define the links that are constructed for your site based on the data in the site structure file. When you're building a Web application, thoughtful planning and organization can make the difference between a site that visitors find easy to understand and navigate, and one that puzzles nearly everyone (perhaps including you).

A second helpful tool when you're working with the overall organization of a Web application is VI's Link View, shown in Figure 1-1. It's particularly useful when you're maintaining a large, complicated site. A Web application can grow in complexity quickly, and become difficult to manage before you know it. Link View helps you add, replace, or rename your various Web files, and also manage the links between files that can be broken and need to be reestablished. You can easily view dependencies and hyperlinks, and also allow VI to automatically repair broken links for you. Navigation bars are automated too. Often, and with many kinds of tasks, VI allows you to stand back from the messy details and look at the large picture.

The Site Designer and Link View features help by giving you a view from above, then generating the necessary source code to support changes you made by merely dragging and dropping pages around within the site's organization diagram. When you work this way, you're not only far more efficient, you can also keep your primary goals in mind and not get bogged down in the details of writing the source code that supports those goals. You're way beyond Notepad.

Extensive team-based development features

Ample facilities supporting team-based development allow the diverse members of a Web application development team to work comfortably and efficiently on the same site, without stepping on each other's toes. Integrated version control features offered by Microsoft Visual SourceSafe allow you to check files in and out directly from VI. In addition, VI's "Local Mode" lets all team members develop their parts of a Web project in isolation, on their local workstations, running a local Web server. Then, when they're ready, they incorporate their files into the master project on the shared Web server. And, of course, it's no problem if some members of the Web design team want to work in the designer-friendly FP IDE and others prefer the programmer-oriented VI IDE.

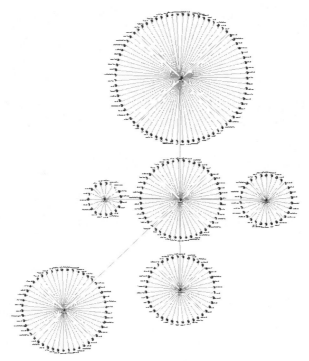

Figure 1-1: Link View quickly reveals the overall structure of even the most elaborate Web applications.

You can easily load a single page, an HTM file, into a Web application you're working on—no matter whether that file was created within FP or VI. In other words, if you create a page in FP, you can add it to a VI project by using the Open File option on VI's File menu. Likewise, a page created in VI can be added to an FP project by choosing the Import option on FP's File menu.

Moving from VI to FP

But what if you've been working on a project in VI for several weeks but decide that it would be far easier to add some tables to the project if you worked in FP? In previous versions of VI, the FP editor was part of the VI Integrated Design Environment (IDE), but now VI and FP are separate, though complementary, applications. It's simple enough to load a VI-created project into FP. Select Open FrontPage Web from the FP Explorer File menu. If you don't see the name of the VI project in the listbox displayed in the Getting Started dialog, click the More Webs button, locate the server, and click the List Webs button. You should see all the VI projects listed for importing into FP. Just save the results as usual when you finish in FP. Any of the VI project's files that you worked on will then be updated.

Disk Paths to Where Projects Are Stored

If you're interested in the disk path to where a project is stored, look for something like this, for FP projects:

```
C:\InetPub\WWWRoot\ProjectName
```

And VI projects will be located in two places: the server (master) copy will be in the same path as the FP, but the primary file will have a .VIP extension (for Visual InterDev Project):

```
C:\InetPub\WWWRoot\ProjectName.VIP
```

On your local (client) computer, you'll find the local copy of a VI project in a path resembling this:

```
C:\My Documents\Visual Studio Projects\ProjectName.VIP
```

You'll learn about all the files that VI creates for a Web project in Chapter 4.

Moving from FP to VI

Importing into VI a project created in FP is also fairly straightforward. Let's assume that you create a project in FP, then work on it for several days but decide you need to involve other people in a team effort to finish building the site. VI is ideal for team projects. You want to import an FP project into VI, then save it as a VI project.

To import an existing FP project into VI, select New Project from the VI File menu. Double-click the New Web Project icon. Connect to the server where the FP project resides. Click Next. Click the option button labeled Connect to an existing Web application on ServerName. Choose the FP filename from the Name drop-down list. Click Finish. You may be asked if you want the VI script library added to this project. This makes design-time controls available to your project, like the PageNavBar described in Chapter 5. Add them if you want them.

FrontPage: excellent page-design tools

FrontPage 98 (FP) is a full-featured, *designer-oriented* application included with VI. FP is a complete IDE (Integrated Design Environment) in its own right, but it serves a different purpose and (generally) is used by a subgroup of a Web design team. FP complements VI's more *programmer-oriented* features. Designed for non-programmers — artists, designers, writers, CEOs — FP includes dozens of useful utilities, shortcuts, Wizards, pre-written solutions, and other aids to accomplishing Web-programming goals quickly. You'll want to know when to use VI and when FP is the better tool.

FP is often a better Web design environment than Visual InterDev. For example, you *can* create a frame or table from scratch by writing the necessary HTML source code. Or, you *can* (much more quickly) *visually* design and drop graphics files, frames, tables, and other complex HTML constructs into existing source code by using FrontPage's efficient tools. VI also supports some of these visual design features (you can, for example, drag a table to resize it in VI's Design View), but FP's capabilities in this area are more extensive and more efficient than those of VI. It's easy to start a site in either FP or VI, then switch to the other application for additional work. Later in this chapter, you'll see how easy it is to shift between VI and FP.

At the time of this writing, there is a serious bug in FrontPage. Most likely, it's been fixed by the time you're reading this (and FrontPage is commercially available). But the bug is so monstrous that we felt you should nevertheless be warned. Make the wrong move and you can wipe out your hard drive. It's luckily not an easy move to make, and so far only one person has reported blasting their drive. But even one's too many. You can use FP to create a disk-based page other than the default location (the default that FP wants to use). This page isn't connected to a server; it's in your specified location. When you specify that you want to store the page on, say, the C: drive, FP asks you whether you want to convert the entire drive to a Web page. Here's the wrong move: *don't click the OK button.* If you do, goodbye C: drive.

A strong debugging suite

VI 6 includes new strong debugging facilities for client-side Web pages, server-side Web pages, and even stored procedures in your Microsoft SQL Server and Oracle databases. You can set breakpoints and step through your source code, even if that causes you to switch to the server, then back to the client, as the script flows between the two locations. In addition, you can debug server-side scripts from a remote PC, if the server is running under IIS 4.0.

Web programming can span more than one computer (part of the code might reside on the user's machine after an HTML page is downloaded, but another part of the code might reside on your Web server). This *distributed* programming offers special challenges to a debugging utility. If you're working on a script, you're most likely on your local machine client-side. Nevertheless, you might have an active server page (ASP) working with the code in the user's browser. No problem. VI can fasten its debugger onto the remote server, enabling you to use all the debugging tools you need in order to check the flow and variations within the script: stepping, breaks, variable watches, the call stack (procedure nesting), and so on. The conditional breakpoints feature is typical of the multifaceted, highly precise control that a programmer has over the debugging process. You can govern such specific conditions as per-thread control and pass counts, along with the more traditional RAD breakpoints such as expression evaluation when a condition is true or changes. The debugger supports VBScript, JScript, and Visual JScript++ 6.0. The major windows in the debugger are shown in Figure 1-2.

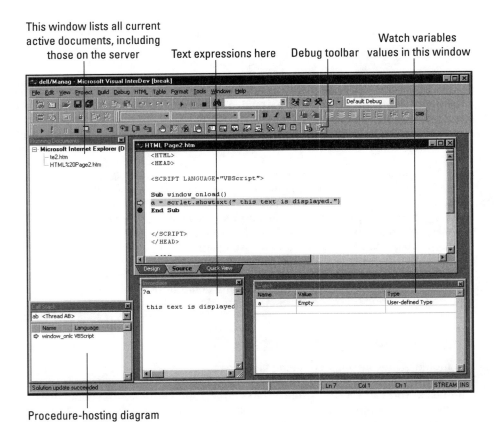

Procedure-hosting diagram

Figure 1-2: Several debugging windows work in concert to help you locate errors in your scripts, even if the script is running on a remote server.

Unrestrained extensibility

As with all of Microsoft's RAD applications, VI and FP are easily customized. Many options are built in. You can display many kinds of information about a project in various optional windows; you can use the templates that Microsoft provides; you can insert objects (Design-time controls, Webbots) that are bundled with VI. But you can also create your own objects, templates, and window arrangements to suit your particular approach to work and to assist you in more effectively reaching the goals of your projects. The VI and FP IDEs offer rich extensibility — you can purchase third-party components, or design your own. You can even work with different editors of your choice if you wish.

Cutting-edge technologies

VI embraces the latest developments in Web programming, including scriptlets, Cascading Style Sheets, ASP, and DHTML. Dynamic HTML conserves Internet bandwidth (avoids slow downloads) because it permits computation on the client-side (in the user's browser) rather than requiring a round trip to the server and back to the user. The result? You can offer users more dramatic, particularly more visually dramatic, Web pages.

DHTML: Active HTML

What is DHTML in practice? The name gives it away. DHTML amplifies HTML by adding a variety of new features. That it's called *dynamic* is an acknowledgment that ordinary classic HTML is, for the most part, static. As nearly everyone agrees, DHTML extends the original DOS-like HTML standard a bit closer toward the ultimate goal: computers that can match, and even exceed, the visual and audio quality of television. DHTML makes possible some of the most dramatic and sophisticated visual effects you'll see on the Internet today. If you want to jazz up your site with subtle, or not-so-subtle, state-of-the-art transitions and animation; give DHTML a try. VI makes working with these effects very efficient: you can script the DHTML in the source window, then see the results instantly by clicking the Quick View tab.

Active Server Pages

VI also includes full support for Active Server Pages. Until recently, the development of pages with which the user could interact and submit information to the server meant programming in Perl, or other cryptic languages. With Active Server Pages, the situation has changed drastically, and everyone who can write a client script with VBScript or JScript can also program the server. Active Server Pages are scripts which are executed on the server, an ingenious idea that is catching on very fast.

Themes, Templates, Layouts, and Cascading Style Sheets

You'll find broad support in VI — and particularly in FP — for the important visual design process. How a Web site looks can be just as important to those restless Web surfers as how the site behaves. Programmers shouldn't look down upon people with visually creative minds — there's room for both kinds of work in the computer world. VI offers several techniques to support the construction of sites with visual coherence and appeal.

First, there are themes. What, technically, is a theme? How is it different from a template, a layout, or a style sheet? On the visible surface, a theme is a collection of visually compatible components: buttons, lines, backgrounds, and other graphics that harmonize because they share complementary colors, textures, shapes, or all of the above. The idea is that a Web site will look more professional if it contains attractive and consistent visuals. What does this mean? It means that within a given theme, you wouldn't be likely to have a color scheme limited to pink and gray because that combination is inherently cheesy. If you aren't sensitive to issues of color and design, you can either use the 54 built-in themes that are supplied by Microsoft's skilled page design artists (or modify them) or you can ask a friend who's graphically talented to help you choose compatible colors, fonts, shapes, and other elements.

Some have found themselves confused about the meaning — in the VI/FP world — of the following terms: *Themes*, *Templates*, *Layouts,* and *Style Sheets*. There are differences:

You're probably familiar with templates if you've worked with word processors. They are simply documents that have been formatted by a professional. In VI, a template works much the same way it does in word processing. A template is merely a pre-designed HTML or ASP page. You can use templates provided by VI, or create your own custom templates for future use, or to provide to your co-workers. In addition to saving time, templates can also help enforce a coherent style within a Web site.

Layouts are the real odd man out; they are quite distinct from the other three concepts. When you choose New Project from the VI File menu, then double-click the New Web Project icon, the New Project Wizard steps you through the job of setting up a new project. One question you're asked is: Do you want to apply a layout? You're given a list of odd-sounding options like Bottom 1 and Right 1. A Layout is rather simple: it's just a description of how you want a navigation, bar or bars positioned on the pages of your project.

A navigations bar is a related set of hyperlinks that allow the user to jump to various locations within your site. Navigations bars are placed within shared borders (a zone in the pages that remains static even when the user moves to a different page — like a running header). VI automatically manages navigations bars for you, updating them as necessary when you change the hierarchical structure of your site, perhaps moving a page that was several levels down to promote it to a position directly under the home page. (By the way, Bottom1 means a pair of Previous and Next buttons (or simple text) hyperlinks will be placed at the bottom of the page. Right 1 means that a list of links to sibling pages — pages that share the same parent as the current page — will appear on the right side of the page.)

All themes are style sheets, but not all style sheets are themes. Technically, a *theme* is a set of Cascading Style Sheets (CSS) that define a coordinated group of elements — fonts, bullets, backgrounds, buttons, and so on — that are colored and contain textures chosen to be graphically compatible and pleasing to the eye. The concept of Cascading Style Sheets is broader: they are lists of definitions for HTML elements. For example, you can redefine the qualities of <H3> (the third-level HTML headline). In other words, you can specify *changes* to the default qualities of an HTML element. Perhaps you want all your third-level headlines to be colored green. Then, whenever you use that element in an HTML document — no matter how often — that element will display those changes, and new qualities you gave it in the Style Sheet. This feature is called *Cascading* Style Sheets; they are available in several kinds, have different levels of impact, and each has its own order of precedence (as well as a distinctive scope within a Web page).

VI makes generating CSSs quite easy. As usual, there's a special tool in VI designed to assist you in rapid development. In this case, it's the CSS Editor, shown in

Figure 1-3. You use this editor to create or modify CSS sheets. If you have a large Web site, you'll appreciate this feature — it can greatly simplify the job of keeping all the buttons, for example, consistent across all 124 pages in your huge site.

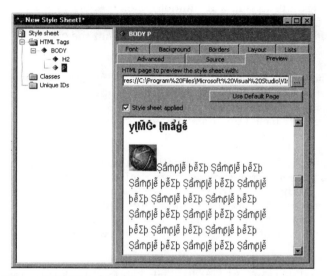

Figure 1-3: Visual InterDev provides many, new Rapid Application Development tools. This is the Cascading Style Sheet Editor.

A template is a Web page you like and want to use as a basis for creating other, similar pages. Any HTML page can be used as a template. Like themes, templates help you avoid repetitive low-level programming while you enforce a consistent look and feel in your site. When you add a page (File | New File) to your project, you'll see two VI templates: HTML Page and ASP Page. These templates are displayed in the right pane of the New File dialog. VI's HTML Page template is a sparse, skeletal framework for creating HTML:

```
<HTML>
<HEAD>
<META NAME="GENERATOR" Content="Microsoft Visual Studio 6.0">
</HEAD>
<BODY>
</BODY>
</HTML>
```

If you develop a page you want to use as a template, copy it to the TEMPLATES subdirectory (under VI's directory). It will then appear in the New File dialog along with the default VI templates.

Scriptlets: A New Kind of Object

You're likely familiar with Java Applets or ActiveX components. Components are objects, with all the benefits that objects offer, including reusability and encapsulation. However, there's now a new kind of object. You can now encapsulate re-usable pieces of raw script using a new technique called *scriptlets*, which rely on DHTML. Recall that the DHTML technology uses facilities built into the browser (IE 4 is the only browser with this capability at this time) to permit the execution of scripts within the user's machine (client-side).

A scriptlet has various advantages over ordinary programming code. To reuse ordinary source code, programmers have had to resort to copying and pasting. This approach has a number of drawbacks, not least of which is the unpredictability of side effects based on duplicated variable names or poorly structured or undocumented source code behaviors.

However, when you write a scriptlet, you can merely call upon it (provide its URL) to execute within a Web page. Like other objects, a scriptlet is encapsulated and exposes an interface (its methods and properties) to allow other developers to make use of it. But it theoretically hides the actual source code from them. Another advantage of scriptlets is that they are built using only HTML and VBScript or JScript — therefore, they download quickly (and are cached for reuse) to the user's machine.

So far, this definition of scriptlets sounds suspiciously like Java Applets or ActiveX components — a reusable, encapsulated object with a public interface. In fact, scriptlets do behave somewhat like components, but scriptlets are created differently: a scriptlet is just a Web page composed of HTML and script. Then the scriptlet is used (by being referenced like any other object) from within a container Web page.

To sum up: Create ActiveX components when you need the heavy-duty language facilities of Visual Basic or other major computer languages. If your job only requires script+HTML, create a scriptlet. Scriptlets appear on the VI Toolbox, along with server objects, ActiveX controls, and Design-Time controls.

VI's Major New Features

So far in this chapter, we've covered what we consider to be the major features of Visual InterDev. If you've been using VI 1.0, you're likely curious to know what Microsoft considers the primary new features in VI 6 (as it's being called). Some of the following features have been mentioned earlier in this chapter, but we thought that current VI users might want a quick summary of the main new elements. Here they are.

WYSIWYG editing

There are now three tabs on the bottom of the VI editor allowing you to view your source code in three ways: Design, Source, and Quick View. Design View is where you can drag and drop objects (such as ActiveX and DTC components); edit text (apply formatting using a toolbar's buttons); add tables and lists; position objects by dragging them around; customize the appearance of objects (using the Properties window); and use the HTML outline window to quickly jump to any element within the page. Design View is an editing window (unlike Quick View), but it also allows you to see what the user will see when the page is loaded into Internet Explorer 4. Source view allows you to edit the HTML source code directly. Because Design View only displays the elements between the BODY tags, you'll have to switch to Source View to edit anything within the <HEAD> tags. Also, script and HTML tags do not appear in Design View. Quick View transforms the editor temporarily into an Internet Explorer 4 window, showing you precisely what your client-side scripted page will look like (and how it will behave) when loaded into the browser. To view any page using server-side script, you'll need to open the page directly in the Web browser.

FP also has three similar editor views that it calls Normal, HTML, and Preview. However, at the time of this writing, FP has an annoying habit of reformatting your source code to suit itself when you switch to Preview, then back to HTML. VI is the programmer's tool.

Debugging features

VI includes a large collection of debugging features for both client-side and server-side script. See the complete description earlier in this chapter.

Drag-and-drop prototyping

Also discussed above is the new Site Designer that allows you to work visually when building the pages that, collectively, make up a Web site. You add, modify, and delete pages by dragging; you create links by physically moving the pages around on-screen. You are, in this process, describing the navigational pathways within your site and, by extension, the overall structure. The Site Designer, and the Link View tool, make it easy to maintain a complex site.

New database access features

New ADO technology makes it extremely easy for you to connect your Web to any database that has an OLE DB or ODBC driver. Once you connect to the database, you build data commands to retrieve a set of data directly from a table or by utilizing a query, stored procedure, or SQL statements. The next thing you do is drop one or more of these data commands on a Web page, either client- or server-script-based. VI automatically creates a Recordset control that manages the data set for the other DTCs on the page. Now you can present the data to the visitor with any of the robust set of Design-Time Controls (DTC), including Checkbox, FormManager, Grid, Label, Listbox, OptionGroup, RecordsetNavBar, and Textbox. After you drop the DTC on the page, just open the powerful Properties Pages dialog box to set the control's properties. It's that simple. Of course, you can always go directly into the source for the page and add all the script code necessary to provide the functionality your application demands.

The CSS Editor

This tool makes creating Cascading Style Sheets quite easy. You select HTML elements you want to modify from drop-down lists, then the Editor creates the source code for you. Also useful: there's a Preview window showing you exactly what your new style will look like to a user.

IntelliSense statement completion

IntelliSense includes several additional kinds of dynamic "help," things that pop out while you're trying to write your script. There's *Quick Type Information* which shows you, in a pop-up window, the complete declaration for any identifier in your source code. Just rest your mouse pointer momentarily on the identifier. There's *Parameter Info*. This one shows you the complete declaration, including the parameter list, for any function to the immediate left of your insertion cursor. What's more, as you type in the function, the next required parameter appears in boldface. There's Code Comments which also pops up a window. It shows you any comments that have been associated with the currently selected member in the members list. Finally, there's the equivalent of Word's AutoCorrect feature. In VI, it's called *Complete Word*; it automatically types in what it thinks you're trying to type in. This happens with both function names and variable names. If it doesn't recognize the word you've typed, it then displays a Members List from which you can insert a member into your source code.

You might find some of these features helpful and efficient; I, personally, don't use them. When I'm programming, I try to keep focused on the goals required by the script or component. I also turn off the auto syntax checking. Luckily, both statement completion and auto syntax checking can be turned off. But, oddly, they are both turned on by default when you first install VI. Perhaps that's to let you know they are there for you if you want them.

To turn off the IntelliSense features, click Options on the VI Tools menu, then click the Text Editor option, and the Per Language option. Likely, the structure of the Options dialog will have changed by the time VI is ready to ship to stores. If you don't find the IntelliSense options located where I've just described, look in Help for their location. Note that you can turn off these options, but selectively; manually invoke them should you want them briefly turned on. Look for them on the Edit menu, which also displays keyboard shortcuts that turn them on.

DHTML

Dynamic HTML (DHTML) transfers the burden of computation from the server (where the Web application resides) to the client (the user's browser). VI fully supports DHTML, including statement completion and the DOM (Document Object Model) in the editor's Source View. You can even shift some database-access burdens to the user's machine by forcing your design-time components to generate client-side data binding script. This important feature is given two chapters in this book (14 and 15) and also appears in other chapters as a side issue.

Local mode development

As mentioned earlier, you can now check out a file or files to work on in your local workstation (your personal computer). This allows you to debug and test your pages before committing them to the master server. There's also a provision that allows you to do the opposite: you can work in *master mode* whereby any changes you've made to a file will be automatically saved to the master server's file (the official version of that file) and also saved locally.

Simplified deployment

You've finished your site. When you're happy with all your efforts and you consider your Web application polished, it's time to let others — on your company's intranet, or out in the world on the Internet — enjoy the fruits of your labors. In other words, it's time to deploy your site to a public server — to move it from your local server. In VI, deployment is accomplished by copying the entire site, support files and all, to the public server. If you want to copy an entire Web application from, say, one production location to another (or from your personal workstation to a master server), VI makes that job easy enough.

This job includes several options, including copying only updated files, creating a second site on the same server with a different name, or creating an entirely new site. If you've got any embedded objects, they must be registered on the server. And all dependencies must be copied to the server as well. VI makes it fairly easy to register any database objects you've included in your project (your site), any Java Applets, and any ActiveX components on the public server that exposes your site to the Internet. VI includes intelligent deployment. There is also a close integration with Microsoft's Transaction Server, permitting the development of strong and scalable Web applications.

Summary

This chapter introduced you to Visual InterDev and all its primary components. You learned about the following major topics:

✦ How VI fits into the overall constellation of Web-design tools. That VI is part of Visual Studio, but is also sold as a standalone Web-development application.

✦ That VI's main features, including FrontPage, are collectively all you'll need to build and maintain even a large, complex Web application. VI includes tools for prototyping, organizing the link structure, managing a Web development team, and writing and debugging script.

✦ How to switch a project between the FrontPage and Visual InterDev IDEs, and how to work on the same page in either environment.

✦ That VI embraces all the latest Web-authoring technologies including DHTML, ASP, Themes, Templates, Layouts, Cascading Style Sheets, and Scriptlets. It not only supports the creation of Web pages using these methods, but it also supports debugging of all the new technologies.

✦ The primary new features in this latest version of VI requested by people using the previous version, VI 1.0. These features include: WYSIWYG Editing; enhanced debugging features (including server-side stepping and breakpoints); drag-and-drop prototyping; expanded database access features; a Cascading Style Sheet editor; IntelliSense pop-out Listboxes, and statement completion; DHTML support; local mode development, and easier site deployment.

✦   ✦   ✦

The Web Development Process

If you're planning to develop a dynamic, database-driven Web application for corporate intranets or the Internet, the *Microsoft Visual InterDev Bible* is just the book for you. Now, let's write some code! Actually, let's not! Not yet anyway. While Microsoft Visual InterDev (VI) is a very powerful tool, it is just that, a tool. In this chapter, you learn how Visual InterDev fits into the process of developing a complex Web application.

Where do you begin? The first step is a fundamental one: *planning*. When done well, planning enables the entire project team to successfully develop and deliver a Web application that meets or exceeds the client's expectations. Tools alone cannot do that. Beginning construction on a Web application without a plan is like building a custom house without talking to an architect and drafting the blueprints based on what you need.

In this chapter, you look at the process of creating software for the Web. Once you've reviewed each phase in the development process, you take a more careful look at what's involved in the first phase, planning a Web project. Then, you look at the composition of a typical project team doing Web application development with VI. The chapter ends with a brief discussion of ongoing project-management activities.

Understanding the Web Development Process

Good Web applications aren't created by chance. It takes a multidisciplined team of knowledgeable professionals, following a formalized process to create a good Web application. Project management is also a critical factor; this is what keeps the team focused and in constant communication with each other.

The Web development process consists of five basic phases:

1. Planning

2. Design

3. Construction and Testing

4. Going Live

5. Production and Ongoing Maintenance

Figure 2-1 shows the Web development process, which is basically a modified waterfall approach. The purpose of the process is for the project team to deliver a high-quality Web application that meets the established goals.

Each phase of the process consists of multiple tasks. In the traditional waterfall approach, the team must complete each task within a phase before they can move ahead to the next phase. The Web development process is more flexible than the traditional waterfall approach. To address the unique needs of each project, the project team chooses which tasks to do within each phase of the process. In addition, the team conducts multiple iterations within the Planning, Design, and Construction phases. For example, the first iteration of the design phase is usually done at a very high level of abstraction followed by a second iteration, which goes into more detail. The third iteration goes into even more detail. This process emphasizes creating live prototypes and HTML mock-ups rather than formal written documents popular with the more traditional waterfall approach. Between each iteration, the team reviews the design with the client to determine if it is accurate. This approach enables the team to incorporate client feedback much earlier in the process, which has a very positive effect on the quality of the finished product.

The team may also segment the application by business function or by any other criterion the project team chooses. Some team members then move ahead to the Construction phase for a given segment while other team members continue in the Design phase. You see this approach represented in Figure 2-2 by the Section 1, 2, and x Construction and Testing boxes. By enabling Construction to begin during the Design phase, you can shorten the schedule and utilize the skills of the team members more fully. (In the traditional waterfall approach, the programmers would not be able to work on the project until the designers were finished with their tasks.)

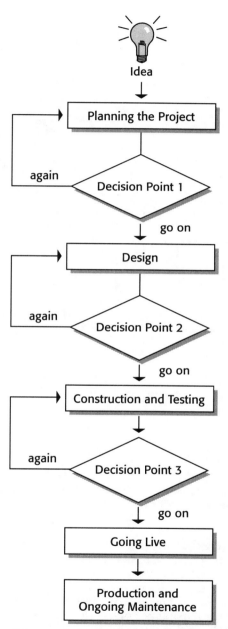

Figure 2-1: The Web development process

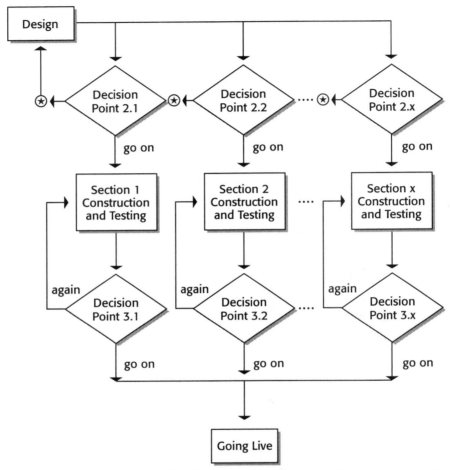

Figure 2-2: Following the Design phase Decision Points, simultaneous Construction and Testing occur on independent sections of the Web application.

Notice the decision points that occur during the transitions between phases. In the schedule, these are also referred to as *milestones,* because they mark a major accomplishment for the project. At these decision points, the project team and client review project assumptions, status, and risks. This group addresses unresolved issues and revises the project plan as needed to ensure they can meet the established project goals. One of the responsibilities of the client is to make a decision on whether to give approval for the project team to move ahead, for example, to start the next iteration or next phase. This approval is often referred to as the client *signing off* on the milestone.

Phase 1. Planning

The first phase in the Web development process is Planning. The goal of this phase is to produce a project plan. One of the key components of the project plan is the schedule. Together, the project team establishes a high-level timeline for the project, broken down by each phase of the process. The project plan also identifies the project goals, the Web application goals, the target audience for the Web application, the development approach, project deliverables, project assumptions, and project risks. Because the project plan is so important to the success of every project, the tasks involved in completing it are described in more detail later in this chapter.

The project team presents the project plan to the client and asks for approval to proceed to the next phase. This is the first decision point and is identified as Decision Point 1 in Figure 2-1. Depending on the client's feedback, the team may need to revise the project plan before the client gives the okay. In the worst-case scenario, the client decides to cancel or postpone the project. It's only the worst case for the team members who may have been looking forward to the revenue or the challenges the project offered. For the company, however, the decision was the right one. After all, the software may be too expensive; the company may need to modify its business process prior to developing an application; or any number of possibilities.

The project plan is often referred to as a *living document* because it is updated several times during the life of the project. The earliest version of the project plan contains very little detail; it may just show the phases and the decision points. As the design activities progress, the plan becomes more specific, including all the tasks and milestones within each phase. Typically, the team agrees to freeze the project plan during one of the decision point meetings. After that point, the focus shifts to following the plan and monitoring progress against the plan as well as managing the risks that might prevent the team from completing the project according to plan.

Phase 2. Design

The second phase in the Web development process is Design. The goals of this phase are to gain client approval of the "look and feel" of the site, the structure of the site, site navigation, the tasks the Web application will perform, and the data that is required. The team uses a number of different tools and techniques to accomplish these goals. The Site Designer in Visual InterDev is a great way to prototype the site structure and navigation.

In addition to business-focused goals for the Design phase, there are a number of technical goals. The team must select, purchase, and install the technology and identify team member qualifications. They must establish guidelines for site design and technology features. During the Design phase, if the project warrants it, the team may begin to section off parts of the Web application. The goal is to identify independent sections of the application on which the team can work without interfering with any other team member's progress.

Once the client agrees that the prototype for a section of the application is on target, the team produces a Project Design Specification that they use in the next phase of the development process, which is Construction and Testing. During the second decision point, which may actually be a series of meetings rather than one big one, the client approves the Project Design Specification for a single section. In Figure 2-2, Decision Points 2.1, 2.2, and 2.x are examples. The client's approval or sign-off signals the start of Construction for that section of the application.

Following is a list of the tasks involved in completing the Design phase:

- ✦ **Functional analysis** — Determine exactly what the user needs to do in the Web application.

- ✦ **Data modeling** — Determine what data is required to be stored for the Web application and design the physical structure of the database.

- ✦ **Information architecture** — Map the structure of the site. This can be done by modeling user navigation through the site and user interaction with the site and with the data.

- ✦ **Technical architecture** — Identify, evaluate, and select project hardware and software based on project goals and requirements. This includes development, testing, and production architectures. Determine if the team will use source control. (See Chapter 4 to learn about using Microsoft Visual SourceSafe for source control.)

- ✦ **Setting up the development and testing environments** — Install the development software on the servers and the local workstations. Set up security. Create construction and testing areas on a nonproduction server.

- ✦ **Establish design goals** — Determine options such as what browser-supported features to use in the Web application and what the maximum acceptable page loading time should be.

- ✦ **Establish stylistic guidelines** — Establish the look of the site, including layout, graphics, font, and site colors.

- ✦ **Establish technical standards** — Identify file- and directory-naming conventions.

- ✦ **Prototyping** — Turn the design ideas into partial reality by creating storyboards and/or Web pages.

- ✦ **Usability testing** — Observe site users working with the prototype and make necessary changes based on whether site/user goals are being met, for example, how the user navigates within a page and through the site.

✦ **Create Project Design Specifications** — Describe each page of the Web application in detail, including graphics, text, and links. Divide the application into sections so the team can work on multiple sections simultaneously.

✦ **Test planning** — Describe detailed software, hardware, and business function test cases and test data.

Phase 3. Construction and Testing

The third phase in the Web development process is Construction and Testing. The goal of this phase is to create a quality Web application that matches the Project Design Specifications. As described in the previous section, some team members will probably start construction on sections of the Web application while other team members continue with the design of other sections. At the decision point following Construction and Testing, the client must give the okay before the entire site or a specific section of the site Goes Live (the fourth phase). This process is identified as Decision Points 3.1, 3.2, and 3.*x* in Figure 2-2.

The following list identifies typical tasks involved in completing the Construction and Testing phase. Chapters 6 through 25 describe how to use VI to accomplish most of the tasks in this phase. Chapter 24 is an exception; it addresses deploying a site, which is key to the Going Live phase.

✦ **Establish development guidelines** — Establish guidelines for working with or without source control, file backup schedules, design-time security, and ways to maximize communication among team members.

✦ **Create skeleton pages** — Create the pages that establish the structure of the site. You can use Site Designer to create the skeleton pages. Once these pages exist, team members can begin working on the functionality specific to each page.

✦ **Test preparation** — Create step-by-step instructions for each test case, and populate the test database with real business data.

✦ **Produce content** — Create graphic, text, sound, and video files for the Web application based on the Design Specification.

✦ **Technical design** — Create low-level technical designs from the information in the Project Design Specification.

✦ **Programming** — Create HTML pages, scripts, components, ActiveX controls, and databases. Unit-test the work in local mode before propagating it to the master Web site.

✦ **Integration** — Integrate HTML pages, scripts, components, ActiveX controls, and databases on the development site. Conduct integration testing to ensure the site is working properly.

✦ **Alpha testing**—Deploy a mirror image of the development site to the testing area when the project team determines the site has reached an acceptable level of functionality. Team members stress-test the site and user acceptance testing begins.

✦ **Beta testing**—Replace the alpha testing site with a mirror image of the development site when the project team determines the alpha version of the site has reached an acceptable level of functionality. Team members and users execute their formal test plans using the test site. Users look for wording problems, missing activities, bugs, design flaws, and areas that are unclear or difficult to use. These may lead to minor or major changes to the Web application as well as future enhancements.

✦ **Defect (bug) fixes**—Record, evaluate, prioritize, and fix the defects (bugs) reported during alpha and beta testing. Production staff participates in the testing and tracking activities as part of their training on the application. (*Defect* is a QA term for bugs in software before it goes into production.)

Phase 4. Going Live

The fourth phase in the Web development process is Going Live. The goal of this phase is to deploy the fully tested beta Web application to the live production server. Visual InterDev commands make this task easy, as you will see in Chapter 24. If a database is involved, the administrator must be especially careful to ensure live data is not damaged or lost. Once the files are in place, the team quickly, tests the live site to confirm all components are functioning as expected.

Once the Web application goes live, the project team's job is basically done. Before disbanding, the team has a postmortem meeting to review what went well and what did not. They use this information to improve the process for the next project. In addition, they make backup copies of the entire development environment, source files, development tools, and documentation. For maximum security, they store a copy of these materials off-site.

Phase 5. Production and Ongoing Maintenance

The final phase in the Web development process is Production and Ongoing Maintenance. The goals of this phase are to keep the site content up to date and to keep the site functioning smoothly.

The Web administrator monitors Web-site-usage reports to ensure the site is delivering the appropriate level of performance. On many of today's Web sites, one or more people in production manually change the content of the HTML pages to keep the site current, which is a very slow, laborious process. Now with VI, you can create a Web application that dynamically updates its content from a database maintained by the business experts. In this way, the company focuses more of its limited resources on the business content and less on the presentation of the site content — a good goal for any Web application.

Planning the Project

Now that you understand how the whole Web development process works, you're ready to take a closer look at the project's Planning phase. Planning is probably the most important phase in the entire Web development process. In this phase, you identify the hows, whats, and whens of the project, such as how much the project will cost, what will be delivered, what the priorities are, and when the project will be completed.

Custom software-development projects on a large scale typically start with a very lengthy formal document, often called a *Request for Proposal* (RFP), describing everything about the project. Often a project starts as someone's good idea, which we'll refer to as Application X. The application might be for a new service, a new product, or a way to reduce costs by automating a manual task. With some initial funding in hand, the person with the idea contacts you, an internal or external technical consultant, to find out what it will cost and how long it will take to build Application X. They typically use this information to build a business case and get the project funded.

Before you can answer any of the person's questions, you'll need to learn a few things from your new client. If you are working from an RFP, you should be able to find this information in the RFP document. What you need to know is identified in the following list, the tasks typically involved in completing the Planning phase:

✦ **Determine the purpose of the project** — Identify what the project must achieve to be successful.

✦ **Determine the purpose of the Web application** — Identify the purpose/goals of the Web application.

✦ **Identify your target audience** — Identify who will use the Web application or an individual section of the Web application.

✦ **Scope the project** — Determine the size of the project.

✦ **Establish client priorities** — Determine the driving factor for the project.

✦ **Agree on approach** — Determine the best approach to meet the goals of the site based on the scope of the project.

✦ **Create a project plan** — Prepare the first version of the project plan, including a schedule, goals, risks, and budget.

Determining the purpose of the project

One of the first things you need to learn is the purpose or goals of the project. What do you need to accomplish and how will you know you have done it? This sounds easy, but quite often it is not. You may interview one or more business people in your efforts to answer this question and each one of them will probably have a different answer. Actually that's okay, because this helps you find the decision maker — the person who is ultimately responsible for the success of the project.

Here's an example of a project idea or business problem for Application X. See if you can identify the project goals. Note that these are not the goals of the Web application; they are the goals of the project. A large company has one site to which many divisions contribute. As the site evolves, each division's section takes on its own look and feel, creating confusion for site visitors. Now the site consists of a large number of pages and the divisions are finding it difficult to keep their HTML pages up-to-date. In addition, the pages often have broken links. The product managers want to be able to update the site pages without authoring HTML pages or having someone else do it for them.

After several meetings with the client, here is a sample list of the project goals on which you agreed. Keep in mind that there is nothing perfect about this list of goals. What's important is that you and your client understand these goals and agree that if these are achieved by the project team, the client will be happy :

- ✦ Replace the existing Web sites with one site that has a common look and feel.
- ✦ Simplify the process of authoring and maintaining site content so business experts can do it quickly and easily while maintaining the common look and feel.
- ✦ Go live with the site in one month.

How will you know you've achieved these goals? A common look and feel is easy to see, but if you use VI's site themes and layouts, you know that new pages automatically look the same. How can you tell if site authoring and maintenance is quicker and easier? You'll have to define what's difficult about the existing system and let the business experts tell you if it's easier. If you measure how long it takes to do a specific task, you'll not only be able to measure how much faster the new process is, you'll also collect a few user acceptance test cases. If the site is not in production in one month, you'll know that pretty soon, too.

Determining the purpose of the Web application

You also need to understand the purpose or goals of the Web application itself. Be sure to consider this question from multiple perspectives. Consider the needs of the business, the Information Technology (IT) department, the target audience, and the technology. In addition, determine how you will know you've achieved these goals.

Ask your client the following questions:

✦ What are the business goals for the Web application? For example,

  • Creating corporate awareness within the market segment

  • Promoting a product or service in a new channel

  • Providing a product or service over the Internet

  • Generating revenue by selling products over the Internet

✦ What must the Web application accomplish in order to be successful?

✦ Does your IT department have standards or guidelines that need to be followed?

✦ Why does the application need to be on the Internet? (This question is especially important because everyone wants to be on the Internet these days.)

Identifying your target audience

Along with defining the purpose of your project and Web application, you want to identify the intended user(s) of the Web application and what each type of user should be able to accomplish on the site.

To do this, ask your client the following questions:

✦ Describe a typical person who will use this Web application.

✦ In general terms, what would this person need to accomplish on this site?

✦ Where is your target audience located? Are they in the same building, complex, city, state, or country?

✦ How often will the average person use the site?

✦ How many people do you plan to have using the site?

✦ Which browser will your target audience use?

✦ What hardware will your target audience use?

You will use this information to prepare the project plan. The information influences what features are needed, the level of security needed, how scalable the solution is, what technology to use in the construction of the site, and how extensive the testing must be, among other things.

Determining the scope of the project

Once you understand what your client is trying to achieve with this Web application and who will use the site, you want to determine the scope of the project. "Scoping out" the project is a highly technical term; it means you need to determine the relative size of the project. Here's a simple example: Suppose you're an architect and your client asks you to construct a building. After making this request, he or she asks, "What do you think it will cost and when will it be ready?" Obviously, you can't answer these questions until you know more about what the client has in mind. At this stage, you don't even know enough to give a ballpark estimate. The wise thing to do is to express interest in the project and ask your client questions. Start out with very general questions and get more specific as you learn more about what the client wants. Here are a few sample questions:

✦ Can you describe what kind of building you want?

✦ What will you use the building for?

✦ How big does the building need to be?

✦ Do you have a picture of a building similar to what you have in mind?

Your goal is to get a feel for how big the building will be. That information will help you generate a ballpark estimate and enable you to compare this project to others you've worked on or are familiar with.

To scope out Application X, you need to go through a similar process. Because this is software, you'll do some basic analysis to determine the functions and features of the Web application. Once you understand more about what these are, you can determine the size and relative complexity of the site. Because your client could want a simple Web site, a complex application that accesses legacy data sources, or anything in between, it's important to establish the scope of the Web application. This information is essential for estimating the time, cost, and resources needed to produce Application X.

Follow these steps to scope out your project:

1. Determine the functions and features of the Web application.

2. Select a Web site model.

3. Select the browser.

4. Review the content.

5. Establish client priorities.

6. Agree on approach.

Determining functions and features of the Web application

In order to scope out your project, you need to find out exactly what functions and features your client needs. Your client probably already wants the site to be like a few other Web sites he or she has seen. In addition, your client may have to surpass a competitor. Because a picture is worth a thousand words, you should sit down with your client and take a look at those sites, as well as a few others. During this surfing meeting, each of you should point out possible features and techniques for Application X. Create a list as you go, identifying the URL for each feature or technique. Here are some example functions and features:

✦ **Credit card transactions** — Application X can collect money via credit card by using secure transactions.

✦ **Restricted access** — Application X can limit access to the site to authorized personnel by prompting for a user ID and password that it verifies against a database of authorized users.

✦ **Customized pages based on prior visits** — Application X can provide these for repeat customers by maintaining a database of individual visitor activities and preferences.

Based on the functions and features you identify, you'll begin to identify Web site model(s) that potentially fit the needs of Application X. In this context, a Web site model is a type of site that implies the presence of specific features by virtue of the type. For example, if your client wants password protection, he or she might want a subscription model, which requires paying users to log on to the site before receiving the services offered on the site. An implied feature is that passwords expire, so additional processing is needed to support that capability. Once you identify the model for the site, if there is one, you will have made significant progress in determining the scope of the project.

Selecting a Web site model

This section surveys some of the most popular Internet and intranet Web application models to help you decide on a model. The list of URLs is limited to corporate Internet sites because you won't have access to company intranet sites during your surfing meeting. Because the main focus is on corporate business clients, entertainment sites are not included.

After the description of each model, you'll find a list of company sites that exemplify the model. If the site uses advanced Web application features such as Active Server Pages (ASP) and database access — features you can build into your application easily with VI — there is a Yes in the column labeled Dynamic. If the filename in the URL ends with .asp, the page is an Active Server Page. While these tables do not contain an exhaustive list of sites, feel free to use them as the foundation for your own custom lists.

Information publication model

Some Internet sites publish information. After all, that's what HTML was designed to do. For these companies, the Web is a strategic marketing tool enabling these companies to promote their products and services. They also use the Web to distribute information about their companies and to post job openings. In many cases, the company simply takes existing printed sales brochures or its annual report and repurposes this material for display on the Web. In Table 2-1, the Autodesk and Microsoft pages exemplify this approach. On the AT&T site, press releases are pulled from a database maintained by business staff.

Table 2-1 Web Site Publication Model		
Site	**URL**	**Dynamic**
AT&T's press releases	http://www.att.com/news/	Yes
Autodesk's annual report	http://www.autodesk.com/compinfo/annrept/1997/index.htm	No
Microsoft's products	http://www.microsoft.com/products/default.htm	No

As discussed earlier, we can't provide an actual example of an intranet information publication model because access to these sites is restricted to company employees. Intranets, however, accomplish the same goals within a company. For instance, many sites are putting up internal company documents, such as employee handbooks, employee benefits manuals, and company phone books.

When these applications are static, someone maintains and formats each page of the document. Because this is a time-consuming and tedious task, it often gets done less frequently than needed. When that begins to happen, the information on the Web site is not up to date. Because this defeats the purpose of having the information on the Web, these companies may want to update their sites to be more dynamic and require less manual maintenance. With the database-driven Active Server Pages capabilities of VI, you can build an application that dynamically updates these publications with less effort by the business staff. (You can learn more about this subject in Chapter 23.)

Corporate infrastructure model

Web intranet applications for corporate infrastructures are becoming increasingly popular. Tools such as VI make it easier for people to build these kinds of sites. Common examples of corporate infrastructure applications are sales force automation, inventory, budgeting, time and expense reporting, customer and contact management, discussion areas, calendars, and scheduling. UPS, for example, changed its package tracking application from an internal application to an external application on the Internet, where anyone can locate a package without human intervention at UPS—a strategic corporate advantage. See Table 2-2 for the UPS URL.

Product support model

Companies often use the Web for product support. By accessing lists of frequently asked questions and known problems or by downloading software patches/corrections/updates, users resolve problems quickly and easily without human interaction, which can save the company money and increase customer satisfaction. In a simple implementation of this model, visitors simply download a copy of a product, as they do on the PKWARE site. In a more sophisticated implementation of the model, visitors must respond to a series of questions before they can download the software, as on the Microsoft site. This information is stored in a database and used for marketing analysis. Table 2-2 lists a few URLs that exemplify the product support model. Take a look at Microsoft's site for an excellent example. Also note that this model isn't only useful for software companies. UPS's site, for instance, provides product tracking for customers.

Table 2-2 Product Support Model		
Site	**URL**	**Dynamic**
Microsoft's online technical support area	`http://support.microsoft.com/support/c.asp?FR=0`	Yes
PKWARE's PKZIP software download	`http://www.pkware.com`	No
UPS package tracking	`http://www.ups.com/tracking/tracking.html`	Yes

Electronic commerce model

Catalog and shopping-cart sites are becoming increasingly popular as users discover the convenience of shopping online and feel safe doing it. Here's how this type of site works: Typically, visitors search through catalog pages or a database of products to locate items they wish to buy. When the person selects an item, it goes into a virtual shopping cart so he or she can make other selections. When finished shopping, the person virtually checks out by reviewing the content of the "shopping cart" and then providing shipping and credit card information. If the visitor placed an order on a prior visit, the site already knows the shipping and credit card information, which speeds the transaction and increases the level of customer satisfaction. In this Web site model, a database of customer information, transaction processing, and secure transactions are all implied features.

Take a look at the J. Peterman Company site listed in Table 2-3. It uses cookies and focused marketing techniques to personalize the shopping experience for each visitor. Peterman tracks the items a visitor looks at during a session. When the shopper returns to the site, Peterman might offer a special deal on the item the person looked at last time but did not buy. Also, if the shopper puts an item in the shopping cart, the site automatically suggests other merchandise that goes with that item.

Table 2-3 Electronic Commerce Model		
Site	*URL*	*Dynamic*
Amazon Books	`http://www.amazon.com`	Yes
HotHotHot	`http://www.hothothot.com/`	Yes
The J. Peterman Company	`http://www.jpeterman.com/`	Yes
Sears Craftsman	`http://www.sears.com/craftsman/`	Yes

Products and services model

The last model is the Web products and services model. In this case, the company conducts business directly on the Internet by immediately delivering a product or service. Visitors to these sites can read current news, look up phone numbers via a directory service, place classified ads, and more. Table 2-4 lists some URLS that use this model.

Because information is the product in this model, a visitor may be required to subscribe to the service to receive the product on a regular basis rather than receive it free. You may want to consider push technology, which was originally introduced by Pointcast, and is currently referred to as Webcasting by Microsoft. This technology literally pushes the information to the user rather than requiring the user to visit the site. For more information on Webcasting, visit `http://www.microsoft.com/ie/press/techinfo-f.htm?/ie/press/whitepaper/pushwp.htm`.

Table 2-4 Products and Services Model		
Site	*URL*	*Dynamic*
AT&T's toll-free directory service	`http://www.tollfree.att.net/`	Yes
The Wall Street Journal Online	`http://www.wsj.com/`	Yes

Web applications developed using Visual InterDev

Table 2-5 lists sites that use Active Server Pages or a database. All sites in this list were developed using Visual InterDev. While Table 2-5 is not an exhaustive list, feel free to use it as the foundation for your own custom list of Visual InterDev applications.

Table 2-5
Web Applications Developed Using Visual InterDev

Site	URL
Microsoft	http://www.microsoft.com/
RCA	http://www.rca-electronics.com/
Hallmark	http://www.hallmark.com/
Jenn-Air	http://www.jennair.com/
Barnes and Noble	http://www.baarns.com/publish/catalog.asp
MSNBC	http://www.msnbc.com/news/default.asp
MSN	http://www.msn.com/default.asp

Selecting the browser(s)

While you're identifying the target audience and the features to implement in the Web application, you need to determine which browsers the visitors will use. Once you know the browser, you will be able to make a number of decisions about the software technology available. If the browser does not support client-side scripting, for instance, you could develop the application using server-side scripting and ASP technology. If the browser supports DHTML and scripting, you could develop the application using those technologies. Finally, if the application is a corporate intranet and the company has adopted Internet Explorer 4.0 as its standard browser, you can use any features in your Web application, such as ActiveX and DHTML.

Reviewing content

Web applications typically involve a great deal of content, which can be anything from a published annual report that needs to go on the site to an Excel spreadsheet that needs to be loaded into SQL Server. Consequently, you need to assess the level of effort it will take to prepare this content for inclusion in the Web application. Make a list of all the content and identify the current and future form this content will take.

Establishing client priorities

Before you can plan your approach to developing this Web application, you need to understand your client's priorities. Ask your client to select his or her top priority from this list:

✦ Time

✦ Cost

✦ Features

✦ Risk

✦ Visibility

The client's top priority will drive the project, because by definition, the most important thing will get the most attention. The other areas may even be compromised or traded off to achieve the top priority. When you know the top priority, you can plan how to handle the other areas. For example, if the project is time driven (time is the top priority), the amount of available time impacts the number and scope of features the team can implement. As a result, the features may need to change to fit in the available time. The same can be said of cost. Following is a list with a few other examples:

✦ **Time** — If the Going Live date is the top priority, costs may go up to meet that date. Features and quality may drop off. In addition, you would need to minimize risk.

✦ **Cost** — If cost minimization is the top priority, you need to minimize risk, prepare a precise project plan, and rigorously manage the project.

✦ **Feature** — If features are the top priority, you need to prioritize the features and expect that costs, risks, and time will be on the high side. Quality may suffer.

✦ **Risk** — Projects that use new technology with an untrained staff (often no one has experience with new technology) have high risk. The plan must allow time and budget for training and multiple prototypes as the project team learns the technology. A focused set of features would be appropriate.

✦ **Visibility** — For projects where visibility is top priority, much effort is devoted to creating presentation-quality versions of the application to use in selling other members of the organization. This takes time away from the actual project work, so the budget will be higher and it will take more time than projects with lower visibility.

Note Some organizations are willing to compromise quality in order to meet the schedule. Treat quality like any other feature of the application: If you want more of it, you might get less of another feature. However, don't forget to recognize the tremendous impact that poor quality will have on your visitors. If the site does not function on certain browser-platform combinations because the team didn't have time to test it, be prepared to lose that whole segment of your audience.

Agreeing on approach

The next task in the Planning phase is to determine the best way to get Application X built and deployed in a reasonable amount of time. Assuming the organization is new to the Web application, or new to VI application technology, we recommend the crawl-before-you-run approach to ensure success for the project and the client. Plan to build the site in phases, starting with an area that has substance yet is manageable. Then, build on your success. You introduce new content and new features as you and the client understand more about what is working and not working on the site.

An alternative approach is to try to build the entire site at one time. This all-or-nothing approach is extremely risky and not recommended due to the low likelihood of success.

Creating a project plan

The project plan is one of the key documents for a project. The project manager is responsible for creating the document, which is used by all team members, technical as well as business. Consequently, the document should be written for the business users to understand. The project plan consists of a number of sections. At minimum, the following four sections must appear in every plan:

✦ **Goals** — This section summarizes the goals that were identified in "Determining the purpose of the project" and "Determining the purpose of the Web application," earlier in the chapter. This section also identifies the key deliverables in business terminology.

✦ **Risks and Assumptions** — In this section, the project manager lists all the assumptions he or she made in creating the schedule. For each risk, the project manager should assess the likelihood of it happening and have a plan for eliminating the risk or minimizing the impact of the risk on the project should it occur.

✦ **Schedule** — In this section, list detailed tasks by phase and milestones with a resource duration, and completion date for each. The project manager creates the schedule by working with the team members to identify tasks based on project scope and estimating how long it will take to design, code, integrate, and test each. The project manager also considers the client's priorities and approach in determining the schedule. To create an optimum schedule, the project manager will depend on a tool like Microsoft Project.

✦ **Budget** — This section is based on the estimates used to set the schedule and the number of resources assigned to the project.

Project Team Composition

Successful VI application teams consist of a variety of professionals, including Web-technology programmers, Web-savvy nonprogrammers, and business-knowledgeable clients.

Project team roles and Microsoft tools

Table 2-6 lists typical project team roles for Web application development using Visual InterDev. For a small Web project, there are fewer people on the team than for a larger project. Team member selection is extremely important to the success of the project. You want to fill each of the roles with a person who possesses the necessary skills and who can work well with the other team members. The necessary skills for each role appear in column 2 of Table 2-6.

Each team member uses tools tailored to his or her specific needs. Visual InterDev is a unique tool because it is specifically designed to enable interdisciplinary teams using specialized tools to work simultaneously on the same Web application. The Microsoft and third-party tools each team member might use appear in column 3 of Table 2-6.

	Table 2-6 Project Team Roles and Tools	
Role	*Necessary Skills*	*Typical Development Tools*
Content designers/Developers	Technical writing Copy editing Graphics Sound Animation	HTML Microsoft FrontPage Adobe Photoshop/Illustrator
Content Webmaster	Manage links Manage files Site usage statistics	Microsoft NT Server Microsoft Internet Information Server
Database designer/Administrator	SQL Data modeling	Microsoft Visual InterDev Microsoft SQL Server Microsoft Access Oracle Informix IBM DB2 Sybase SQL Server

Role	Necessary Skills	Typical Development Tools
Graphic designer/Artist	Digital images Graphics	Microsoft FrontPage Adobe Photoshop/Illustrator Macromedia Director
Project manager	Planning Scheduling Communicating	Microsoft Visual InterDev Microsoft Office Microsoft Project
Software Quality Assurance (SQA) analysts and testers	HTML Browser SQL	Microsoft Internet Explorer Other browsers Microsoft Visual InterDev
System administrator	Operating system (OS) Networking Connectivity Web server	Microsoft NT Server Microsoft Internet Information Server Microsoft Proxy Server Microsoft Transaction Server Microsoft Visual SourceSafe
Technical Webmaster	OS Web server	Microsoft NT Microsoft Internet Information Server Microsoft Proxy Server Microsoft Transaction Server Microsoft Visual SourceSafe
Web programmer	HTML, DHTML, XML CGI, Perl Active X controls VBScript, JScript SQL Visual Basic C++ Java Shockwave	Microsoft Visual InterDev Microsoft Visual Studio Visual C++ Visual J++ Visual Basic Visual Fox Pro

Understanding client roles on a project team

When developing custom software for a client, there are many questions that only the client can answer. The following are a few examples:

✦ What does the Web application need to do?

✦ If the site did this, would it meet your business needs?

✦ Who will make the final decision?

To ensure the team is building what the client needs, the client must actively participate on the project team. Following is a list of roles the client should plan to fill on the project team:

✦ **Decision maker** — This person is ultimately responsible for making the final decision; for example, he or she needs to decide if the Web application meets the business needs. This person usually controls the purse strings, so it is important to get his or her buy-in at the decision points.

✦ **Business sponsor** — This person is typically a business manager who is available to the project team on an as-needed basis to resolve issues for the project team. If the business sponsor can't answer a question, he or she would know who could and make that person available to the team. The business sponsor also has the authority and knowledge to make decisions about the project. This person may be a liaison between the team and a number of people within the client organization, especially if this is a high-visibility project.

✦ **Subject-matter expert** — This person knows the business process better than anyone else. The person may create business content for the site and answer the detailed questions the project team has. In addition, the expert must establish and conduct user acceptance testing. Depending on the nature of the project, there may be one or more subject matter experts.

✦ **Support personnel** — These people will provide ongoing support for the site once the project ends. They learn the site through on-the-job training as they assist with testing and problem resolution.

Ongoing Project Management

Once the client approves the project plan, the project manager can assemble the project team and the Design phase can start. As the project progresses, additional team members join the project to provide their expertise, then leave the project once their tasks are complete. One person, the project manager, stays with the project from start to finish. Throughout the life of the project, the project manager's role is vital to the success of the project. He or she must continuously use the following fundamental skills:

✦ Planning

✦ Estimating and scheduling

✦ Tracking

✦ Communicating

Planning

Once the initial plan is in place, the planning activities are not over. Typically, the project manager's first plan is done at a very high level. As the team progresses through the development process, the project manager continuously adds more detail to the plan. For example, the project manager doesn't know the specifics of the construction phase until the design is completed. In addition, the project manager monitors the risks identified in the project plan, anticipates problems, and has a number of contingency plans ready.

Estimating and scheduling

Estimating and scheduling are truly art forms that are only developed and refined through experience. For each task on the project schedule, the project manager must provide an estimate of the amount of time it will take to complete that task. Typically, the project manager will ask the person who will be doing the actual work to provide the estimate. To be good at estimating, you must understand the tools and techniques you will be using and the design specification for the work being done. Once the project manager gets the estimate (for example, 10 hours), he or she typically revises the figure, in accordance with a number of factors. If the person is new to the team, for example, the project manager may add 50% to the time to allow for the unexpected.

Scheduling is a constant balancing act among the people, resources, features of the application, technology being used, and development process. Rather than change the schedule continuously, the project manager may do it once a week or following a decision point where a decision was made that will impact the schedule. For example, the client may have seen an early prototype and noticed that a field was missing from an input screen. The project manager may have to increase the time originally planned for that programmer to work on that task. A tool such as Microsoft Project is essential for creating and maintaining project schedules.

Tracking

Once work begins, the project manager tracks the actual costs of the team against the estimate in the plan. The project manager must find ways to measure progress, productivity, and quality. In addition to tracking progress, the project manager tracks the features to avoid what's fondly referred to as *feature creep*. Feature creep is the slow, and often unnoticed until it's too late, increase in the feature content of the project. It occurs throughout the life of the project. For example, as you design one feature, you might design it on the robust side versus the simple side. While this may be okay for one feature, it is definitely not okay for 100 features. Feature creep also happens when you encounter unanticipated tasks. So be sure to allow for this in the project plan.

As the project manager notices or anticipates discrepancies, he or she must take action. This involves using other skills. When a problem occurs, the project manager communicates with the team to prevent the same problems from reoccurring. When the project manager discovers feature creep, he or she address the feature creep with the client and negotiates a resolution. When the agreement between the team and the client changes, the project manager updates the plan to reflect the new agreement and communicates the changes to the project team.

Communicating

Communication is extremely important to the success of a project. Team members who are dependent on each other's progress must be able to communicate among themselves to resolve technical and quality issues rapidly. Also, the project team must have a more formal way of communicating with the client to negotiate trade-offs and discuss progress and options.

Without constant written and oral communication, a project team is doomed to failure. E-mail, newsgroups, groupware, status meetings, status reports, and conference calls are all ways to facilitate team communications.

Summary

The Web development process brings about the success of a VI project. In this chapter, you learned the following:

✦ The Web development process consists of five phases: Planning, Design, Construction and Testing, Going Live, and Production and Ongoing Maintenance.

✦ Visual InterDev is a powerful tool that supports design prototyping, code writing, debugging, database development, and site deployment.

✦ Planning is one of the most important activities the project team undertakes. For the project to be successful, the team must understand the purpose for the site, the target audience, and the client's priorities in addition to the features of the site.

✦ The project plan is a very important document that contains information on how much the project will cost, what will be delivered, what the priorities are, and when the project will be completed.

✦ The project team should work closely with the business experts to ensure the project addresses the client's needs.

✦   ✦   ✦

Visual InterDev Architectures

In this chapter, you learn about the four basic architectural
components of Visual InterDev (VI). This chapter also
covers VI's project architecture, consisting of two working
modes, and how the VI architectural components interact in
each working mode. After reading this chapter, you'll
understand the many different ways you and your team can
work with VI's components to design, code, test, and
implement a Web application. You'll also know how to set the
working mode as you progress from development, through
testing and into production.

Visual InterDev's Component Architecture

Visual InterDev offers programmers a robust and flexible
environment for rapidly developing dynamic, database-driven
Web applications. As a programmer, you can install and run
the four basic components of the Visual InterDev architecture
on a standalone workstation or in a more complex client-
server environment, depending on your needs. Following is a
list of VI's four architectural components, also shown in Figure
3-1. A description of each component follows.

✦ Web browser client

✦ Visual InterDev client

✦ Web server

✦ Database server

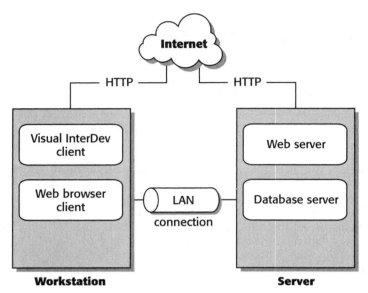

Figure 3-1: A simple configuration of VI's four architectural components, with the Web server and database server on one machine, the VI client and Web browser client on another

Web browser client

A Web browser is an application running on a client workstation. When it is connected to the World Wide Web (also called *the Web*), the Web browser sends requests over HyperText Transfer Protocol (HTTP) to the Web server for a Universal Resource Locator (URL). It receives the resource along with all associated files. The browser formats the HyperText Markup Language (HTML) and displays the page. In addition, the browser executes code contained in the HTML page, for example, client-side scripts and components. With support for features such as frame sets, Cascading Style Sheets, Dynamic HTML (DHTML), and client-side scripts, browsers have become sophisticated. In fact, browsers can be classified as a client application — a Web browser client.

The two major Web browser clients, Netscape Navigator and Microsoft Internet Explorer (IE), can handle most Web applications developed in VI. Each continues to leapfrog the other by introducing the newest state-of-the-art features, such as Cascading Style Sheets and Dynamic HTML. As a result, it is a continuous challenge for a developer to keep current with the different features each browser supports and to learn how each browser supports the same feature differently. While this is not a VI issue per se, it impacts the code a developer writes in VI, the testing a developer conducts, and the performance of the resulting application.

Note Because Netscape and Microsoft frequently release updates to their Web browsers, a detailed analysis of the differences between the two products is beyond the scope of this book. Readers who are interested in learning the latest information on this topic should check this c|net site, which compares the two browsers:

```
http://www.cnet.com/Content/Reviews/Compare/Browsers4/index.html.
```

Visual InterDev client

Visual InterDev runs on a developer workstation running Microsoft Windows NT Workstation, Windows 95, or Windows 98. When the workstation is a node on a local area network and the developer begins working with a Web file, VI requests a copy of the file from the appropriate Web server over HTTP. Because Visual InterDev communicates with the Web server via HTTP, you can develop a Web application with direct access to the Web server or by going through a proxy server. When the developer saves the file, VI sends a copy back to the appropriate Web server for storage. These files can be HTML pages, Active Server Pages, image files, sound files, as well as many others. Using the Visual Database Tools, the developer can also work directly with a database server on his or her workstation or over the LAN connection.

Web server

The Web server is an application that runs on either a server machine or a local workstation. The Web server receives requests for a URL from a Web browser, then locates and returns the page along with all files used on the page. Before returning the page, the Web server runs any server-side scripts it finds in the page. In addition, it sends and receives requests for data to the database server.

In the VI architecture, the developer typically works with two primary Web servers: the master Web server and the local Web server. The master Web server is where the primary copy of the Web application files are stored. All project team members, and possibly even the end-users, have access to the master Web server, which resides on the development server. The local Web server resides on a developer workstation. The developer keeps a local copy of all or a portion of the Web site as he or she makes changes to the site. By using a local Web server to test the local changes to the site, the developer is able to isolate his or her work from the rest of the team's work. This improves team productivity by reducing the chance of a single developer introducing a bug into the Web site and having a negative impact on the other team members.

To take full advantage of the powerful server-side features of VI, the master Web server must support both Active Server Pages (ASP) and FrontPage Server Extensions (FPSE). Because Microsoft's Internet Information Server (IIS 4.0) supports both ASP and FPSE, it is the Web server we use throughout this book. You can also use VI with non-Microsoft Web servers. The non-Microsoft servers supporting FPSE are Apache and Netscape's Enterprise server. The non-Microsoft NT 4.0 servers supporting ASP by using Chili!ASP (an application written by Chili!Soft) are Netscape Enterprise 2.01, 3.0, 3.51, Netscape FastTrack 2.01, 3.01, IBM ICSS 4.2, Lotus Go Webserver 4.6, and Lotus Domino 4.6.1.

When the developer workstation is running Windows NT Workstation, you can use IIS with FPSE for the local Web server. When the machine is running Windows 95 or 98, you can use Personal Web Server (PWS) with FPSE for the local Web server. Because PWS is designed for low-volume usage, it is a great way to share Web pages with other members of your team from your own computer. While PWS supports key IIS features such as ASP, script debugging, Internet Service Manager, and Transaction Server, due to volume considerations, PWS does not support Microsoft Site Server Express, Index Server, and Certificate Server. PWS is included with the NT 4.0 Options Pack.

Database server

For an Internet site, the database server and Web server are typically running on separate machines with the Web server managing access to the database. In this scenario, when the database server receives a request for data from the Web server, it processes the request and returns the retrieved set of data records. The Web server may only use a subset of the retrieved data records, which it formats into HTML text and places on the HTML page. The Web server sends the page to the Web browser, including a record locator. When the browser requests the next page from the Web server, it returns that record locator. The Web server sends the same query to the database server, which returns the retrieved set of data records. The Web server uses the record locator to extract the data from the set of records. It formats the page and sends it with the record locator to the browser, repeating the cycle.

By running the Web server and database server on separate machines, the server administrators can tune each server to maximize responsiveness. In addition, because much of the work is being done on the server, the Web application can run on any browser. Unfortunately, visitors may experience poor responsiveness when they are dealing with a large volume of data or as the load on the two servers increases.

The database is the only optional component in the VI architecture. VI can access any database supported by ActiveX Data Objects (ADO), provided the drivers are available. VI works with all Open Database Connectivity (ODBC)-compliant databases, including Microsoft SQL Server, Oracle, Informix, IBM DB|2, Sybase, dBase, Microsoft Access, Paradox, and Microsoft Visual FoxPro. (You'll learn all about working with databases in VI in Parts 5 and 6 of this book.)

With the introduction of Dynamic HTML (DHTML) in Microsoft Internet Explorer 4.0, the Web browser client can manage access to the database, rather than the Web server. In this scenario, the database server receives a request directly from the Web browser. The server processes the request and returns the retrieved set of data records. The Web browser uses a subset of the data to build a page. When the visitor asks to see more data or to change the way he or she sees the current set of data, the Web browser handles it. This approach improves performance for the visitor and minimizes the load on the servers, and it is a good solution for an intranet application when all visitors can use IE 4.0 and the operations staff can install the necessary database drivers.

While Netscape Communicator 4.0 also supports DHTML, it is not the same DHTML that IE 4.0 supports. In fact, there is no standard for DHTML, which is actually a combination of HTML, Cascading Style Sheets (CSS), and script. In the first half of 1998, the World Wide Web Consortium (W3C), which establishes standards for HTML, released a recommended standard for CSS. At present, it is working on a Document Object Model (DOM) standard. DOM will enable scripts to access and update the elements of an HTML page, such as the size of a line of text. Because these two browsers were released before the W3C standards, each vendor has implemented DHTML differently. In Chapter 23, you learn how to use Visual InterDev to take advantage of IE 4.0's flavor of DHTML.

The focus of this chapter is primarily the developer workstation and the Web server component. As a result, we do not address the database server component in the rest of this chapter. You learn about the database component and the various ways you can configure it in Chapter 22.

Visual InterDev's Project Architecture

A very simple approach to constructing and maintaining a Web site is to work directly with the master set of files, which is how the first version of VI worked. Whenever a developer worked on a Web site, he or she worked directly with the files on the master Web server. As you might know from experience, this approach is very dangerous because without isolating your work from the rest of the team or from the production area, you can very easily introduce a bug that impacts a number of other people. Microsoft recognized the need for a team of developers to produce portions of a Web site in isolation from each other and addressed it very nicely in VI 6.0. In addition to enabling developers to work directly with a master Web application, VI also enables developers to work with a local copy of that Web, called a local Web application. To control which of the two Web applications to work with, the developer must specify a working mode, either master or local. In addition, if a developer is working on a laptop and wishes to take a local Web application to a meeting where there is no connection to the Web server, he or she can work offline.

In order to isolate the development activities on a Web site from the production area, VI tools make deploying a site easy. In this book, we assume that Web application development projects have one Web server for use during construction, another server for use during testing, and a third server for production.

Master and local Web applications

During construction, the master Web application, which is located on the development server along with the master Web server, is the primary repository for all the Web site files, such as HTML (.htm), ASP (.asp), Cascading Style Sheets (.css), and GIF (.gif) files. The developer stores a copy of these files in a local Web application on his or her own workstation, then makes changes and tests the site using the local Web server. Once the developer is confident the local files are functioning properly, he or she saves the files on the master Web server in the master Web application, where the rest of the team can access them.

From VI, a team member creates and/or accesses the master Web application on the master Web server through a Web project. In addition, VI creates an area on the developer workstation for the local Web application. A Web project consists of a set of files (for example, .sln, .vip) that VI uses to maintain information about the master Web application and the local Web application. VI stores the Web project files on the developer workstation with the local Web application files. It does not store any Web project information with the master Web application files on the master Web server (see Figure 3-2).

Note   While a Web project actually consists of a set of files, in the figures in this chapter, we show a Web project as a single box. By representing a Web project this way, we believe it makes the figures less complicated. In fact, it mirrors the way Visual InterDev represents a Web project in Project Explorer.

In addition to keeping track of the folders and files that make up the master and local Web applications, VI uses the Web project to keep track of the data environment, the status of each file, and the status of the project. With VI's Project Explorer, you graphically view a list of the folders and files in the Web application. You can tell which files are in the master and which are in the local Web application, as shown in Figure 3-3. In Chapter 4, you learn what each graphical icon in the Project Explorer represents.

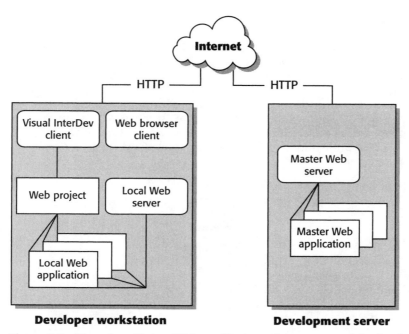

Developer workstation   **Development server**

Figure 3-2: VI works with two Web applications: the master and the local.

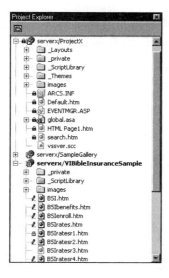

Figure 3-3: The Project Explorer graphically displays your Web project folders and files.

Master mode

When a Web project is in master mode, you work directly with the master Web
application files. To modify a Web site file, you get a local working copy from the
master site and make your changes to it. When you are ready to test your changes,
you click the Quick view tab in VI's WYSIWYG editor. If you are using Active Server
Pages, you must save the file and preview it in the browser. Whenever you save a
file in master mode, VI automatically saves a copy to the local working copy and to
the master Web application, replacing the existing file, as shown in Figure 3-4. When
you browse a Web project in master mode, you are viewing the master Web
application and using the master Web server.

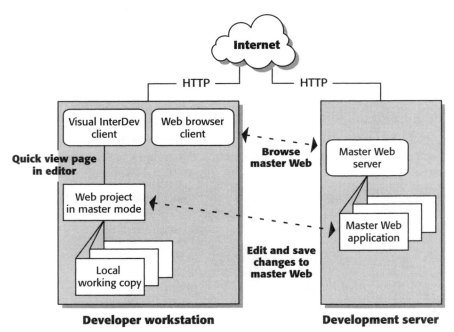

Figure 3-4: Master mode saves changes to the master Web application automatically.

Local mode

When a Web project is in local mode, your work is isolated from the master Web
application. To modify a Web site file, as you did in master mode, you must first get
a local working copy from the master Web application, which VI stores in the local
Web application area. Then, you make your changes, save them, and browse them.
When you save the file, VI only saves it to the local Web application. VI does not

save the file to the master Web application until you specifically tell it to do so. In this way, you can be certain that your changes are not introduced into the master Web application until you are ready (see Figure 3-5). When you browse a Web project in local mode and you have a local Web server, VI automatically creates a virtual root. When the browser loads the pages from the local Web application, the local Web server processes the ASPs and server scripts. If you do not have a local Web server, you can view the local Web application, but you will not be able to process the ASPs and server scripts.

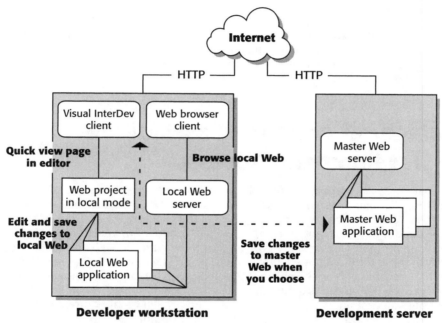

Figure 3-5: Local mode lets you isolate your work from the master copy, until you are ready to update the master.

When you and your team are working on the Web site simultaneously, one of you may add a file to the site or change a file that someone else is working with. If you want to get a list of all the files currently in the master Web application, refresh your copy of the structure of the master Web application shown in Project Explorer. Then, if you want to get a copy of any of the new files, you can get a working copy or get the latest version of your existing read-only copy. You could also do a line-by-line comparison of your local copy and the master. If there are a large number of new files, you can synchronize your local copy of the Web application with the master. If two team members modify the same file, VI assists the last person to save the file in merging the files together, line by line. If this is a frequent activity, the team may want to use Visual SourceSafe to control the source code.

Offline mode

Have you ever needed to take a copy of your Web site to a customer meeting where you didn't have access to the Web server? Not to worry, VI enables you to work offline. Working offline is like local mode but without access to the master Web application. Before going offline, you need to get a local copy of all the files with which you'll be working. Once you're working offline, you can browse the local Web application. If you're running a local Web server, you can even browse the ASP pages. While you can't modify the structure of the site, you can make changes to the existing files and save those changes in the local Web application. When you go back online, if the working mode is master, VI prompts you to save all changes to the master Web area.

Architectures and the Phases of the Web Development Process

In Chapter 2, you learned the five phases of the Web development process: Planning, Design, Construction and Testing, Going Live, and Production and Ongoing Maintenance. During each phase of the process, the Web application is either under development, being tested, or in production. In fact, team members with different job functions are typically involved with the Web application during each of these different states. Developers typically handle development and unit testing activities. When the entire Web application is ready for testing or is in production, SQA analysts simulating site visitors access the Web application. In this section, you examine how VI's component and project architecture interact during each of the following three unique Web application phases:

✦ Development

✦ Testing

✦ Production

Development

While building a Web application, the developer typically works with a Web project in either local or master mode. For team-based development, working in local mode is the preferred approach because each developer can isolate his or her changes from the other developers until they are ready to share them. Master mode lends itself to a single developer, who is not concerned about impacting other developers who might also be working on the site.

A developer can use the Visual Database Tools to access a database server during development. To do this, the developer must either have a database server on their workstation or have an active LAN connection to the database server. Unfortunately, a developer cannot use these tools to access a database via HTTP or through a proxy server. You'll learn about the database architecture in Chapter 22.

Local mode

When working with a Web project in local mode, the developer uses the VI client on the developer workstation and the master Web server on the development server. To edit a file, the developer must first get a working copy from the master Web application on the development server. VI received the file from the master Web server via HTTP and stores the file in the local Web application on the developer workstation. While the developer is working in isolation from the rest of the team, he or she makes changes to the file and saves it locally. When the developer is satisfied with the changes, he or she saves the file to the master Web application on the development server. This copy replaces the file that was already in the master Web application. If another developer modified one of the same files, VI prompts the last person to save the file through a merge process. In Figure 3-6, you see how the components interact during development in local mode.

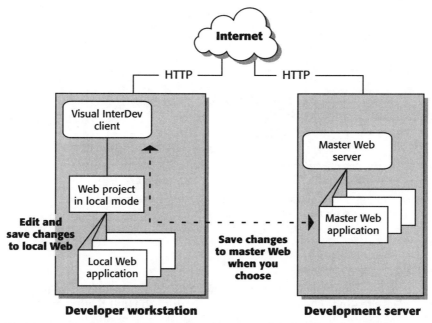

Figure 3-6: During development, developers work in local mode to isolate their changes from the master Web application.

Master mode

In master mode, the developer only uses the VI client on the developer workstation and the master Web server on the development server. The developer works directly with the master Web application on the development server. To edit a file, the developer opens the file. VI receives a copy from the master Web server via HTTP and saves a local working copy on the developer workstation. The developer changes the file and saves it directly to the master Web application, replacing the copy that was already there. If another developer modified one of the same files, VI prompts the last person to save the file through a merge process. In Figure 3-7, you see how the components interact during development in master mode.

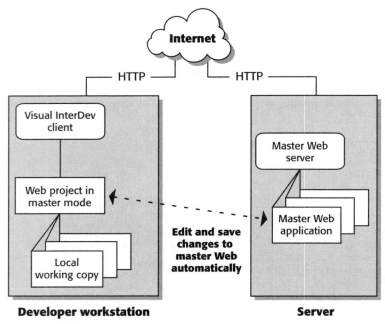

Figure 3-7: During development in master mode, the developer changes the master Web application.

Testing

As with any development effort, Web testing takes two forms: unit testing and integrated site testing. The developer normally does the unit testing on the developer workstation, while an SQA analyst normally does site testing on the development or testing server. Web unit testing involves viewing the modified page(s) in the browser. Because the developer cycles between unit testing and editing, the Web project stays in the same working mode during both steps. If the developer does development in local mode, he or she also does unit testing in local mode.

When the developer finishes unit testing, he or she saves the changes to the master Web application on the development server. At this point, the developer should switch modes from local to master and test the newly integrated changes on the master Web application to ensure the site functions properly.

When enough of the site is functioning, the Web administrator deploys a copy of the master Web application that is on the development server to the testing server. This essentially freezes a copy for testing. When this step is complete, the SQA analysts and user acceptance testers can begin testing. Because they are actually simulating the production environment, they configure their VI components to match the production activities. You learn more about this process later in this chapter.

Local mode

During unit testing, the developer works with the Web browser client, VI client, and the local Web server components on the developer workstation. Using the Quick view tab in the VI WYSIWYG editor, the developer can test simple Web pages. If the page contains server script, Quick view cannot process it. For these features, the developer uses the Web browser client and the local Web server to view the pages saved in the local Web application. In Figure 3-8, you see how VI components interact while unit testing in local mode.

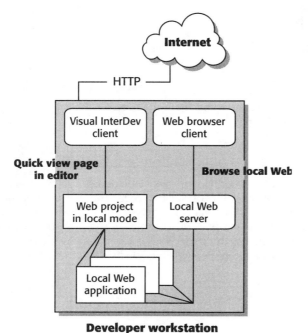

Figure 3-8: During unit testing, the developer working in local mode browses the local Web application.

Master mode

To test changes made in master mode, the developer uses the Web browser and VI client components on his or her workstation and the master Web server on the development server. The developer can use the Quick view tab in the VI WYSIWYG editor to view changes, but it will not handle server script. For these features, the developer uses the Web browser and the master Web server to view the changes saved directly to the master Web application. In Figure 3-9, you see how VI's components interact while testing in master mode.

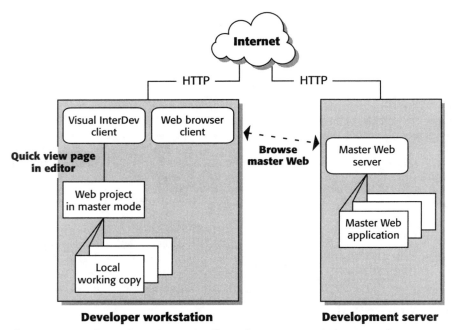

Figure 3-9: During unit testing, a developer in master mode browses the master Web application on the development server.

Production

In production, the mode of the Web project is irrelevant because there is no Visual InterDev client. The site visitor uses a Web browser to access the Web server via HTTP from any client workstation. The Web server receives the request for a URL, then locates and processes any server script prior to sending the page to the local Web browser. The Web browser receives the page, formats it, runs any client script and client components, and displays the page. Figure 3-10 shows the components during production.

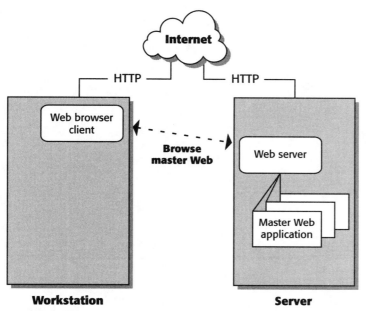

Figure 3-10: During production, the VI client drops out of the picture while the Web browser and Web server do all the work.

Summary

In this chapter, you learned about each of the architectural components of VI and how development teams use them during a typical development project. The following is a summary of the key points:

✦ The four basic architectural components of Visual InterDev (VI) are the Web browser client, the VI client, the Web server, and the database server.

✦ VI project architecture enables a developer to work in either master or local mode. In master mode, the developer works directly with the master copy of the Web application files located on the development server. In local mode, the developer works with a local copy of the Web application stored on the developer's workstation.

✦ A developer isolates his or her work from the other team members in local mode by using the local Web server component and storing changes locally.

✦ Because you may need to share the latest changes to a Web application with other people who may not have access to the Web server, VI also enables you to work offline.

✦   ✦   ✦

Working with VI Web Projects

After reading about the Web development process in Chapter 2, you should have a good understanding of the steps involved in developing a Web application and how Visual InterDev (VI) fits into that process. In this chapter, you build on your knowledge of VI's project architecture, including working in master and local mode as well as working offline. If you are not comfortable with these topics, review the material on VI architecture in Chapter 3.

This chapter starts with an overview of building a Web application. After creating two Web projects, you explore the files and folders VI creates. Then you learn how to work with Web projects and solutions. Because VI is a team-based tool, you then learn how to use Visual SourceSafe for source control.

Building a Web Application

As described in Chapter 2, a Web application development team typically consists of one or more people in the following roles: Web administrator, Web architect, Web developer, HTML author, graphic designer, database administrator, database developer, programmer, SQA analyst, and project manager. Before the team can begin using VI, the Web administrator (admin) sets up a number of Web servers. Typically, the Web admin creates one for development, one for testing, and one for production, depending on the needs of the project.

Each of these areas comes into play as the construction of the Web application progresses through these key milestones:

1. The first step in the construction of a Web application using VI is to create the master Web application, the area

on the Web server where all the files for the Web site are located and shared among the development team members. After installing Visual InterDev and Visual SourceSafe (optional) on the development Web server, the admin creates the master Web application using VI.

2. Once the master Web application directories and initial files are in place on the development Web server, the team begins prototyping the structure of the Web application using Site Designer, as described in Chapter 5. In addition, the team can begin site construction.

   Besides site prototyping during the Design phase, the design team, headed by the Web architect, identifies all the files that need to be created for the Web application. The project manager divides these files among the team members based on skills. Using a tool such as Microsoft Project, the project manager assigns the tasks to each team member and sequences the tasks to ensure the project gets done as quickly as possible. Consequently, all team members are working on various parts of the Web application simultaneously. To ensure all changes are preserved, the team relies on the source control capabilities of Visual SourceSafe.

3. Once the Web site reaches a point were formal testing can begin, the Web admin uses Visual InterDev to deploy a copy of the site from the development server to the testing server. (You learn how to do this in Chapter 24.)

4. Once testing is complete and the client approves the site, the Web admin deploys the site from the testing server to the production server.

Creating a New Web Project

Now that you understand the basic tasks involved in Web application construction and the basic architecture of VI, you're ready to create a Web project along with the master Web application on the development server, which is the physical foundation for the team's construction efforts. Again, if you are not familiar with these terms, please review Chapter 3. Visual InterDev groups related files into projects. In addition, VI groups projects into a solution. A solution can also contain projects from Visual J++. In VI, you can create two types of projects: a Web project or a database project. This chapter focuses on Web projects. To learn about database projects, read Chapter 22.

When it's time to create a new master Web application, the Web admin uses the Web Project Wizard. When VI creates a master Web application, it creates the directory structure on the Web server and places files there. It also creates a directory structure on the local workstation.

Once the master Web application is in place on the Web server, individual team members use the Web Project Wizard to create a Web project on their local workstations. However, rather than create a new master Web on the server, they simply connect to the existing Web application, which the Web admin created. In this case, VI doesn't create anything new on the Web server. It locates the existing

Web application and creates the necessary directory structure on the local workstation.

Creating a master Web application on the Web server

The Web admin, with the necessary permissions on the Web server, is the only team member who creates a new Web application: the master Web application. The Web admin informs the team when the master Web application is in place.

Follow these steps to create a new Web application using the Web Project Wizard:

1. In the File menu, click New Project. The New Project dialog box appears with the New tab selected.

2. Click Visual InterDev Projects in the tree list on the left and the New Web Project icon on the right.

3. In the Name box, enter the name for this Web project. For this example, enter **ProjectX**, as shown in Figure 4-1.

   VI uses this name to create a directory on the local workstation for the solution. Therefore, the name should be unique across all solutions managed by Visual InterDev on the local workstation.

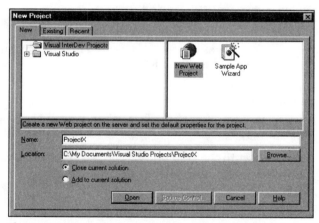

Figure 4-1: Specify the name of your new Web project in the Name box.

4. To change the location for the project files, enter the location or select it using the Browse button to the right of the Location box.

5. If you had previously opened a project in VI, which is known as the current solution, the dialog box includes two radio buttons below Location. If you do not see the radio buttons, skip to Step 7.

To create a new solution, click Close current solution. To add this project to the current solution, click that option. For this example, click Close current solution. You learn about solutions later in this chapter.

6. Click Open. The Web Project Wizard — Step 1 of 4 dialog box appears, as shown in Figure 4-2.

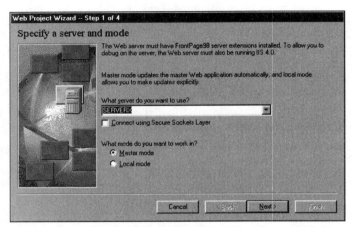

Figure 4-2: In Step 1 of the Web Project Wizard, you designate the server and mode for your new Web application.

7. Enter the name of the Web server or select it from the drop-down list. In this example, the name of my server is SERVERX.

8. If your Web server uses Secure Sockets Layer (SSL), check Connect using Secure Sockets Layer. You learn about SSL in Chapter 25.

9. Click the mode in which you want to work, either master or local. For this example, select Master mode.

10. Click Next for VI to connect to the Web server. The Web Project Wizard—Step 2 of 4 dialog box appears (see Figure 4-3).

11. Select Create a new Web application.

12. Enter a name for the Web. For this example, use the default value.

VI uses this name to create a directory on the Web server, so the name must follow URL naming conventions. In addition, the name must be unique across all Web applications on the Web server.

By default, this name is the same as the project name you entered in Step 3. If you entered a name with spaces in it, VI removes them here. VI uses this name for the Web project.

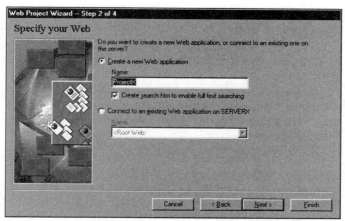

Figure 4-3: In Step 2 of the Web Project Wizard, you enter the name for your new Web application.

13. To enable full text searching in this Web, be sure to check this option.

14. Click Next. The Web Project Wizard — Step 3 of 4 dialog box appears.

15. Select a layout for your Web. (You learn to work with layouts in Chapter 5.) If you do not wish to use a layout, select <none>, as shown in Figure 4-4.

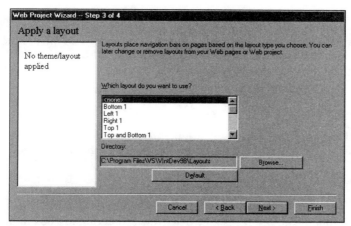

Figure 4-4: In Step 3 of the Web Project Wizard, you select a layout for your new Web application.

16. Click Next. The Web Project Wizard — Step 4 of 4 dialog box appears.

17. Select a theme for your Web. (You learn to work with themes in Chapter 10.) If you do not wish to use a theme, select <none>, as shown in Figure 4-5.

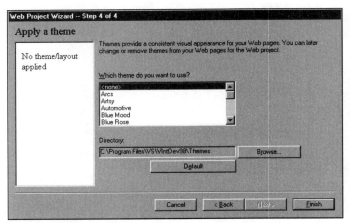

Figure 4-5: Step 4 of the Web Project Wizard, enables you to select a theme for your Web application.

18. Click Finish. VI creates the solution and Web project and opens them in Project Explorer.

    VI creates the `ProjectX` directory and files in the virtual root of the Web server. In addition, VI creates the `ProjectX` directory and files in the working directory on the local workstation. You learn more about the files VI creates in these directories later in this chapter.

Connecting to an existing Web application

Once the admin creates the Web application and the application is in place on the Web server, each team member can create a Web project that connects to that Web.

Follow these steps to create a new Web project that connects to an existing Web application:

1. In the File menu, click New Project. The New Project dialog box appears with the New tab selected.

2. Click Visual InterDev Projects in the tree list on the left and the New Web Project icon on the right.

3. In the Name box, enter the name for this Web project. For this example, enter **MultipleProjects**.

   VI uses this name to create a directory on the local workstation for the solution.

4. To change the location for the local files, enter the location or select it using the Browse button to the right of the Location box.

5. Select Close current solution, which means you want to create a new solution.

6. Click Open. The Web Project Wizard — Step 1 of 4 dialog box appears.

   VI gives the new solution the same name as the project name you entered in Step 3. If you had previously opened a solution and made changes to it, VI prompts you to save the changes.

7. Enter the name of the Web server or select it from the drop-down list. In this example, the name of my server is SERVERX.

8. Click Next. VI connects to the server and the Web Project Wizard — Step 2 of 4 dialog box appears.

9. Select Connect to an existing Web application on *server name,* where *server name* is the name of the server you selected in Step 7. Notice that VI changes the name of the dialog box from Step 2 of 4 to Step 2 of 2.

10. Select the Web Name ProjectX from the drop-down list as shown in Figure 4-6. In this example, ProjectX is the master Web application the Web admin created on the Web server.

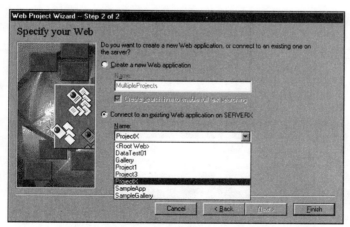

Figure 4-6: In Step 2 of the Web Project Wizard, you connect to an existing Web application.

11. Click Finish. VI creates the solution and Web project and opens them in the Project Explorer.

By default, VI creates a directory and files called `MultipleProjects` in the working directory on the local workstation. You learn about the files VI creates in this directory later in this chapter.

Using the Sample App Wizard

To help with the examples in this chapter, we've provided a sample application on the companion CD-ROM. You'll use the Sample App Wizard to copy this small Web to your workstation. Note that you could use this technique to distribute copies of one of your own Web projects. You must have permission to create a Web application on the Web server in order to complete the following example.

Follow these steps to create a Web project using the Sample App Wizard:

1. Place the *Visual InterDev 6 Bible* companion CD-ROM in your CD-ROM drive.

2. In the File menu, click New Project. The New Project dialog box appears with the New tab selected.

3. Click Visual InterDev Projects in the tree list on the left and the Sample App Wizard icon on the right.

4. In the Name box, enter the name for this Web project. For this example, enter **VIBibleInsuranceSample**, as shown in Figure 4-7.

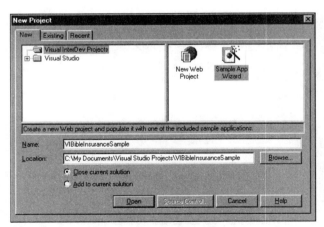

Figure 4-7: Name your new Web project (a sample application) using the New Project dialog box.

5. To change the location for the project files, enter the location or select it using the Browse button to the right of the Location box.

6. Select Close current solution.

7. Click Open. The Sample Application Wizard — Step 1 of 5 dialog box appears.

8. Select a Web application from another source, and then click the Browse button and select the file `SourceCode\Ch04\VIBibleInsurance.INF` from the CD-ROM.

9. Click Next. The Sample Application Wizard — Step 2 of 5 dialog box appears.

10. Enter the name of your Web server or select it from the drop-down list.

11. Click Next. The Sample Application Wizard — Step 5 of 5 dialog box appears.

12. Click Finish.

Understanding Solutions

Solutions are fundamental to the way Visual InterDev works. Visual InterDev shares this logic with Visual J++ because they both share the same IDE. Up to this point, you have only seen how to create a single Web project in a solution because having one project in a solution is the simplest way to organize your work. However, with this type of organization, you may not be able to do everything you need to do.

A solution can contain one or more projects: Web projects and other types of projects. In Visual InterDev, you can only have one solution open at a time. While the files for a master Web application exist on the Web server, you can only access them through a Web project in a solution. In fact, you can access the same Web project from multiple solutions. Why would you want to do this? Because Visual InterDev only lets you copy and move files between projects that are in the same solution. So if you want to copy parts of one Web site to another Web site, you need to put both Web projects in the same solution.

Creating a solution

As you saw when you created the two Web projects, `MultipleProjects` and `VIBibleInsuranceSample`, earlier in this chapter, VI automatically creates a solution. The Web project called `ProjectX` is located in the solution `MultipleProjects` and the Web project `VIBibleInsuranceSample` is in a solution called `VIBibleInsuranceSample`.

If you want to use some of the HTML pages in `VIBibleInsuranceSample` when you build `ProjectX`, you can copy them from `VIBibleInsuranceSample` to

ProjectX, as long as these two Webs are in the same solution. You can accomplish this any of these three ways:

✦ Add the VIBibleInsuranceSample Web project to the MultipleProjects solution.

✦ Add the ProjectX project to the VIBibleInsuranceSample solution.

✦ Create a new Web project connecting to one of the existing Webs, either ProjectX or VIBibleInsuranceSample, and add the other Web project to that solution.

Because Visual InterDev enables you to do any of these, you can organize your work any way you want. In the next section, you learn how to add a second Web project to a solution that contains one Web project. By applying the techniques you learn, you'll be able to create any combination of projects and solutions.

Adding a project to the current solution

Because you can only have one solution open at a time in VI, when you need to work with more than one project, you must add these projects to the same solution. Because Visual InterDev shares solutions with Visual J++, a solution can contain projects from either Visual Studio product installed on your machine. For example, you can add a VI Web project, a VI database project, and a Visual J++ project to a single solution.

Because you can add multiple projects to one solution, project names must be unique across all projects accessed by VI and VJ++. In addition, the projects in a solution can be located in different directories and on different drives.

Now continue the "Connecting to an existing Web application" exercise you started earlier in this chapter. Follow these steps to add an existing Web project to the current solution:

1. If MultipleProjects is the current solution, go to Step 2.

   In the File menu, click Open Project. The Open Project dialog box appears with the Existing tab selected. Select MultipleProjects.sln (see Figure 4-8) and then click Open.

2. In the File menu, click New Project. The New Project dialog box appears with the New tab selected.

3. Select VIBibleInsuranceSample.

4. Click Add to current solution and then click Open.

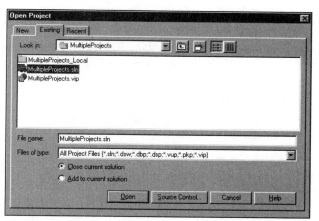

Figure 4-8: To open an existing Web project, select this item.

In Figure 4-9, you see the `MultipleProjects` solution, which contains two projects, `ProjectX` on serverx and `VIBibleInsuranceSample`, also on serverx. Remember that in these examples, the name of my server is serverx. The name of your server will appear wherever you see serverx. Note that `ProjectX` is also in the `ProjectX` solution and `VIBibleInsuranceSample` is also in the `VIBibleInsuranceSample` solution.

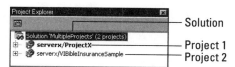

Figure 4-9: Project Explorer showing a solution with two Web projects

Exploring Project Structure: Folders and Files

Up to this point, you've worked with VI to create Web projects. Now you'll use Windows Explorer to see exactly what directories and files VI created on the Web server and the local workstation. You'll also learn about the solution files on the local workstation.

When you create a new Web project, VI does the following:

✦ Creates the folder and subfolders for the Web site on the Web server and adds project files and FrontPage site management files to that directory.

✦ Creates the folder and subfolders for the Web project in the working directory on the local workstation and adds project files to that directory.

✦ If you chose Close current solution, VI creates the solution files in the same directory with the project files on the local workstation.

✦ If you chose Add to current solution, VI updates the information in the solution files in their existing location.

Folders and files on the Web server

In Figure 4-10, you see `ProjectX` in Project Explorer. The first line in Project Explorer always shows the name of the solution and the number of projects in the solution. Because you chose to create a new solution when you created `ProjectX`, VI named the solution `ProjectX` as well.

Figure 4-10: In Project Explorer, you see the folders and files in ProjectX.

The second line shows the VI project, `serverx/ProjectX`, `stationx/ProjectX`, where `serverx` is the name of the Web server and `ProjectX` is the name of the Web application. As you will see in a moment, when you look at this Web from Windows Explorer, the virtual root of the Web server is not the same as the physical directory on the Web server. The virtual root is the location relative to the directory where the Web server is defined. By using the virtual root, VI makes it much easier for you to reference the Web, because the virtual root is the beginning of the URL for your Web. For example, to browse the file `search.htm`, use the URL `http://serverx/ProjectX/search.htm`.

When you click the plus sign (+) to the left of the project, you see that VI automatically created three folders and two files in this Web.

In Figure 4-11, you see `ProjectX` on the Web server in Windows Explorer. The physical directory for the `ProjectX` Web site is `\\serverx\InetPub\wwwroot\ProjectX`, where `serverx` is the Web server, `\InetPub\wwwroot` is the default root directory for the Web used by IIS, and `ProjectX` is the master Web application folder. The files for the Web site are stored in this directory. For a Web site of any size, you typically create subfolders and store the files there. Table 4-1 lists the items VI created on the Web server with a brief description of each.

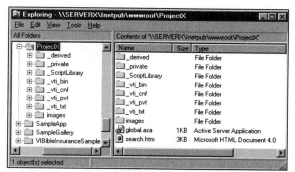

Figure 4-11: In Windows Explorer, you see the folders and files that make up ProjectX on the Web server.

Table 4-1
Folders and Files VI Creates for a New Web Project Called *ProjectX*

Name	Description	Local Workstation	Web Server
`_derived`	VI stores information about this Web site in these folders.	√	√
`_private`		√	√
`_vti_bin`			√
`_vti_cnf`		√	√
`_vti_log`		√	√
`_vti_pvt`		√	
`_vti_txt`			√

(continued)

Table 4-1 *(Continued)*

Name	Description	Local Workstation	Web Server
_ScriptLibrary	VI creates this folder and all the files in the folder, which are tied to the design-time controls in the Toolbox.	√	√
images	VI creates this folder to help you organize your image files.	√	√
global.asa	IIS uses this file to maintain information about the status of your Web site. You learn about global.asa later in this chapter.	√	√
search.htm	When you create ProjectX and choose Create search.htm to enable full text searching, VI creates this file.	√	√
ProjectX.vic	VI stores information on the Visual InterDev project in this file.	√	
ProjectX.vip	VI stores information on the Visual InterDev project in this file.	√	
SolutionName.sln	VI stores information on the Visual Studio solution in this file.	√	
SolutionName.suo	VI stores information on the Visual Studio solution in this file.	√	

Folders and files on the local workstation

In Figure 4-12, you see the Windows Explorer view of ProjectX on the local workstation running Windows 95. The physical directory for the Visual InterDev solution and/or project is drive\My Documents\Visual Studio Projects\ ProjectX, where drive\My Documents\Visual Studio Projects is the default working directory for Visual Studio, and ProjectX is the name of the solution and/or the name of the Web project. VI automatically creates a subfolder with the name ProjectX_Local. If ProjectX is the solution name and not a project name, then VI uses this subfolder to maintain information on the solution. If ProjectX is the name of a Web project, this subfolder is the virtual root for the application on the local workstation and contains all local copies of the Web site files.

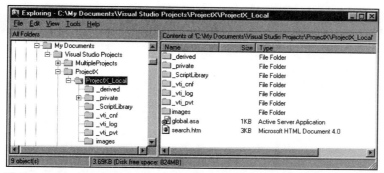

Figure 4-12: In Windows Explorer, you see the folders and files that make up *ProjectX* on the local workstation.

Global.asa

When you create a new Web application, VI creates the `global.asa` file. While you are not required to use this file, if you are developing a sophisticated IIS Web application, you will definitely want to. You might use the `global.asa` file to perform application initialization and shutdown tasks and to store variables used across the Web application. Because this file enables you to manage the current status of an executing Web site, it is not displayed to the users.

When VI creates the initial `global.asa` file, it looks like Listing 4-1:

Listing 4-1: The Initial global.asa File

```
<SCRIPT LANGUAGE="VBScript" RUNAT="Server">

'You can add special event handlers in this file that will
get run automatically when special Active Server Pages
events occur. To create these handlers, just create a
subroutine with a name from the list below that corresponds
to the event you want to use. For example, to create an
event handler for Session_OnStart, you would put the
following code into this file (without the comments):
'Sub Session_OnStart
'**Put your code here **
'End Sub

'EventName               Description
'Session_OnStart         Runs the first time a user runs
                         any page in your application
'Session_OnEnd           Runs when a user's session times
                         out or quits your application
```

(continued)

Listing 4-1 *(Continued)*

```
'Application_OnStart      Runs once when the first page of
                         your application is run for the
                         first time by any user
'Application_OnEnd        Runs once when the web server
                         shuts down

</SCRIPT>
```

The `global.asa` file contains the four event procedures listed in Table 4-2. You add script to these events to control what happens when your application starts or ends and when a session starts or ends. (You work with these event procedures in Chapter 16.)

If you have a data connection in your Web project, VI automatically adds script to `Session_OnStart`. This script contains the connection information in session variables. The Visual Database Tools and the design-time ActiveX controls use this information to connect to the database at runtime. For more information on database connections, see Chapter 22.

<table>
<tr><td colspan="2" align="center">Table 4-2
Event Procedures in global.asa</td></tr>
<tr><td>***Event Procedure***</td><td>***Description***</td></tr>
<tr><td>Application_OnStart</td><td>Runs one time, the first time any user requests any page of your application</td></tr>
<tr><td>Application_OnEnd</td><td>Runs one time, when the Web server shuts down</td></tr>
<tr><td>Session_OnStart</td><td>Runs each time a new user requests his or her first page, any page, in your application</td></tr>
<tr><td>Session_OnEnd</td><td>Runs when that same user's session times out or the user quits your application</td></tr>
</table>

Project Explorer Fundamentals

When you open a project, the Project Explorer window appears, as shown in Figure 4-13. VI organizes the information about the open solution in hierarchical lists in the Project Explorer and Data View windows. The Data View window displays information about the data environment for the project, if there is one. It's easy to move files in

Project Explorer. You simply click the file you wish to move and drag it to the new folder or project. You learn more about the data environment in Chapter 22.

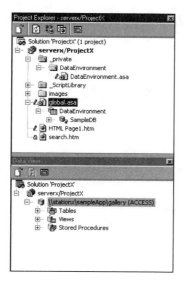

Figure 4-13: The current project in the Project Explorer and Data View windows

Visual Studio enables you to control if a window is shown or hidden. It also enables you to control if these windows are docked or floating. You learn how to work with docking windows and customizing the Integrated Development Environment (IDE) in Chapter 6.

Viewing and hiding Project Explorer and Data View

To view the Project Explorer window, choose one of these three methods:

✦ In the View menu, click Project Explorer.

✦ Enter Ctrl+Alt+J.

✦ In the Window menu, click Project Explorer.

Note You can only use this last method when the Project Explorer window is floating but hidden from view. If Project Explorer does not appear on the Window menu, use one of the other two methods to view the Project Explorer window.

To hide the Project Explorer window, use one of these two methods:

✦ Click the Hide button in the upper-right corner of the window.

✦ Click the Project Explorer window and then click Hide in the Window menu.

Identifying the icons in Project Explorer

Your Web application consists of many files organized in a Web project. Table 4-3 lists the types of files you typically find in a Web project along with the icon you see in Project Explorer.

Table 4-3	
Web Project Icons in Project Explorer	
Icon	**Type of File**
	Active Server Page
	Cascading Style Sheet
	Data environment
	Database connection
	Folder
	GLOBAL.ASA
	HTML page
	Image and other multimedia files (such as .gif or .jpg)
	Project in local mode
	Project in master mode
	Project in offline mode
	Site diagram
	Solution
	Text file
	Working copy (read-only) copy of a file
	Working copy (write-enabled) copy of a file

Managing Solutions

Solutions are a collection of one or more projects. While a given project can only exist once in a solution, that same project can exist in any number of other solutions. It's therefore important that you learn how to manage solutions. Most of the commands that deal with solutions are in the File menu, as shown in Figure 4-14, or the View menu, as shown in Figure 4-15.

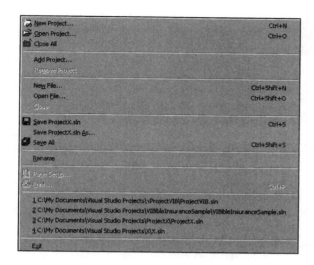

Figure 4-14: The File menu has entries for creating, opening, closing, and saving a solution.

Figure 4-15: The View menu has an entry for solution property pages.

A number of these are also found in the shortcut menu that appears when you right-click the solution name in Project Explorer, as shown in Figure 4-16. Many of these menu items are context-sensitive. Before you can select one of them, you must first select the name of the solution or the name of the project in the Project Explorer.

The menu entries you'll explore in the File menu are New Project, Open Project, Close All, Save *solution name,* Save *solution name* As, Save All, and Rename. The menu entry you'll explore from the View menu is Property Pages. Here's an explanation of each command you can use to manage a solution with the associated menu item and shortcut keys. Table 4-4 shows each function and the associated default shortcut key and icon. An in-depth explanation of each function follows.

Figure 4-16: Right-click the solution name in Project Explorer to see this shortcut menu.

Tip

You can change the shortcut keys from the Options dialog box, in the Tools menu in the Keyboard tab of Environment.

Table 4-4
Commands to Manage a Solution

Command	Shortcut Keys	Icon
Close the solution		🖿
Create a new solution and project	Ctrl+N	🖿
Open an existing solution and project	Ctrl+O	📂
Rename the solution		
Save *name,* where *name* is the solution or project selected in Project Explorer	Ctrl+S	💾
Save *name* As, where *name* is the solution or project selected in Project Explorer	Ctrl+Shift+S	
Save all files		🗇
View property page for the current solution (Visual J++ command)	Shift+F4	🖽

✦ **Close the solution** — Visual InterDev enables you to work with one solution at a time. Whenever you open a solution, Visual InterDev automatically closes the current solution and prompts you to save any changes. To close a solution without opening another solution, click Close All in the File menu. There is no default shortcut key for this action.

✦ **Create a new solution and project** — As you saw earlier in this chapter in "Creating a New Web Project," you don't directly create a new solution in Visual InterDev. During the process of creating a new project in the New Project dialog box, you select the Close the current solution option and thereby create a new solution. The New Project dialog box appears when you select New Project from the File menu. The default shortcut command is Ctrl+N.

Tip

To show the New Project dialog box each time Visual InterDev launches, select that option in the Environment tab of the Options dialog box, in the Tools menu.

✦ **Open a solution and project** — Visual InterDev offers you many ways to open a solution, which is also how you open a project. Because any single project can exist in many solutions, to open the correct project, you must know the solution name. The most direct method of opening a solution is to use the Open Project menu item in the File menu. When the Open Project dialog box appears, select the solution name on the Existing tab and then click Open. You can also select the *solution name*.sln file from the Recent tab in this dialog box.

The New Project dialog box is essentially the same dialog box as Open Project, so you can open a solution using either dialog box. When you open a solution using the Open Project or New Project dialog box, you have the option to Close the current solution or Add to the current solution. A quick way to open a solution you used recently is to click the name of the solution at the bottom of the File menu. The default shortcut key for Open Project is Ctrl+O; for New Project, press Ctrl+N.

Tip

To specify the number of most recently used (MRU) solution names that appear at the bottom of the File menu, select the Environment tab of the Options dialog box, from the Tools menu. Enter the new number of items in *MRU list contains <number of items> items* in the Global section.

✦ **Rename a solution** — To change the name of a solution, select the solution name in Project Explorer and then click File and Rename. As in Windows Explorer, you enter the new name directly in the Project Explorer window. There is no default shortcut key for Rename.

✦ **Save a solution** — To save the current solution without closing it, select the solution name in Project Explorer and then click File and Save *solution name*. The default shortcut key is Ctrl+S.

✦ **Save a solution As** — To save a copy of the current solution without closing it, select the solution name in Project Explorer and then click File and Save *solution name* As. In the Save File As dialog box, enter the location and new name for the solution. There is no default shortcut key for Save As.

✦ **Save All** — This menu item enables you to save all files in a solution without closing the solution. It doesn't check whether changes exist; it simply saves everything. You find Save All in the File menu and the shortcut menu in Project Explorer. The default shortcut key is Ctrl+Shift+S.

✦ **View Property Page** — This is a Visual J++ command. A VI solution has no properties you can set.

Managing Projects

Projects are a collection of Web files, the data environment, and custom software associated with your Web. The master copy of your Web application resides on the Web server and a local copy resides on your workstation. Your working mode determines which set of files you work with at any given time. Most of the menu items that deal with projects are in the File menu, as shown in Figure 4-17, or the Project menu, as shown in Figure 4-18.

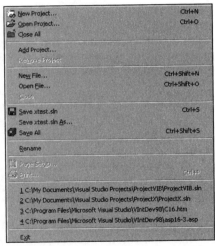

Figure 4-17: The File menu has entries for creating a new project and removing a project from a solution.

A number of these are also found in the shortcut menu that appears when you right-click the project name in Project Explorer, as shown in Figure 4-19. Many of these menu items are context-sensitive. Before you can select one of them, you must first select the name of the project in Project Explorer.

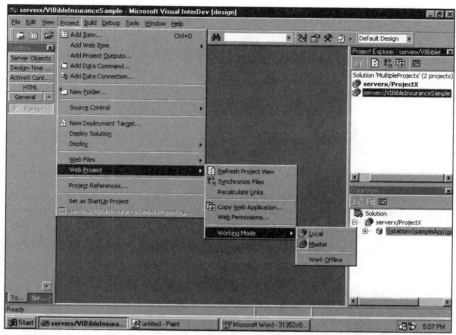

Figure 4-18: The Project menu has an entry for Web project tasks (the highlighted option shown sets the working mode).

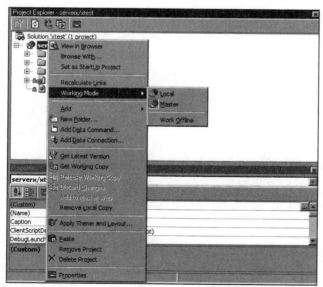

Figure 4-19: Right-click the project name in Project Explorer to see this shortcut menu.

In the File menu, you will explore New Project, Open Project, Add Project, and Remove Project. In the Project menu, you will learn about Add Project Outputs, Web Files, Web Project, Project References, and Set as StartUp Project. You also learn about Property Pages in the View menu. Here's an explanation of the commands you can use to manage a project, including the menu item and shortcut keys. As a quick reference, the associated default shortcut keys and toolbar icon for each function are in Table 4-5. An in-depth explanation of each function follows.

Table 4-5
Commands to Manage a Project

Command	Shortcut Keys	Icon
Add a project to the current solution		
Add outputs to the project (Visual J++ command)		
Create a new project	Ctrl+N	🖥
Delete a project from the current solution		✕
Discard changes made to local copies		🖩
Get a working copy of the project		📇
Get the latest version of the project		📇
Open an existing project	Ctrl+O	📂
Refresh the project view		🔄
Release all working copies in the project		📇
Remove local copies of project files		
Select project references (Visual J++ command)		
Set the project to be the startup project (Visual J++ command)		
Set the working mode		
Local mode		📄
Master mode		📄
Synchronize the local project files with the master project files		📇
View property page for the current project	Shift+F4	🖼

✦ **Add a project to the current solution** — To add an existing project to the current solution, select Add Project in the File menu. You saw an example of this in "Adding a Project to the Current Solution," earlier in this chapter. Another way to add a project to the current solution is to open a project and select the option Add to current solution in the Open Project dialog box. The default shortcut key is Ctrl+O.

✦ **Add outputs to the project** — This is a Visual J++ command.

✦ **Create a new project** — In the "Creating a New Web Project" section of this chapter, you explored the process of creating a new master Web application on the Web server and creating a Web project that connects to an existing master Web application. During the process of creating a new project in the New Project dialog box, you also created a new solution or added the project to the current solution. The New Project dialog box appears when you select New Project in the File menu. The default shortcut key is Ctrl+N.

Tip

To show the New Project dialog box each time Visual InterDev launches, select that option in the Environment tab of the Options dialog box, from the Tools menu.

✦ **Delete a project from the current solution** — Because a Web project can exist in more than one solution on more than one local workstation, Visual InterDev enables you to remove a Web project from the current solution and leave the files on the Web server. It also enables you to remove a Web project from the current solution and then delete the Web project files from the Web server. To delete a Web project, select the project name in Project Explorer and then select Delete from the Edit menu. The Delete Project dialog box appears, confirming the name of the project, and asks you to choose one of these three options:

- Delete the local Web project and all associated files
- Delete the master Web project and all associated files
- Delete both

There is no default shortcut key for this command.

✦ **Discard changes made to local copies** — A normal part of the development process is to implement a functionality two different ways, then see which does the job the best. Once you select the code you plan to use, you must discard the other set of code without introducing it to the master Web application. You can accomplish this by selecting the file or files or the project in Project Explorer and then selecting the Project menu, pointing to Web Files, and clicking Discard Changes. VI replaces the local files with the current version of the master Web application files. It does not save the changes. There is no default shortcut key for this command.

✦ **Get a working copy of the project** — To work on the master Web application with a team of individuals, you need to get a copy of the entire project or specific files that you can either modify or use for testing. In Project Explorer, select the name of the project, a file, or multiple files. Then, in the Project menu, point to Web Files and click Get Working Copy. VI places a write-enabled copy of the selected files on your local workstation. Refer to the section "Using Visual SourceSafe" for additional information on this command.

✦ **Get the latest version of the project** — When a team of people work on the same Web project and one person changes the structure of the Web by adding, deleting, or renaming a file or folder, the other team members will not see these changes automatically. You can synchronize your view of the structure of the Web application with what is currently on the Web server by refreshing your project. To refresh your project, select the project in Project Explorer and in the View menu, click Refresh.

✦ **Open an existing project** — Because projects are always located within one or more solutions, you don't actually open a project, you open a solution. Refer to "Managing Solutions," earlier in this chapter, for a detailed explanation of this topic.

✦ **Refresh the project view** — While you are working on your section of the Web application, other team members may make changes to the master Web. If you want to get a list of all the newly added files, click Refresh Project View under Web Project on the Project menu. There is no default shortcut key for this command.

✦ **Release all working copies in the project** — As you develop your section of the Web application, you create, modify, and save the local working copies of the application files. When you complete construction and testing and are ready to propagate your new files to the master Web application, you use the Release Working Copy menu item under Web Files in the Project menu. If you are not using Visual SourceSafe, VI determines if another team member made any changes to the master copy. If VI detects changes, it prompts you to resolve the differences between the files. Check "Using Visual SourceSafe" for additional information on this command. There is no default shortcut key for this command.

✦ **Remove local copies of project files** — You can delete the local copy of all files associated with a Web project and not save any of the file changes. To do this, select Remove Local Copy from the Project menu under Web Files. VI prompts you to confirm that you wish to discard all changes. There is no default shortcut key for this command.

✦ **Select project references** — This is a Visual J++ command.

✦ **Set the project to be the startup project** — This is a Visual J++ command.

✦ **Set the working mode** — As you remember from Chapter 3, there are three working modes you can use while developing and testing a Web project. The working modes are local, master, and offline. To change the working mode, in the Project menu, select Web Project, select Working Mode, and then click one of the three modes. The icon to the left of the project name in Project Explorer reflects the working mode of the project, as shown in Figure 4-20. There is no default shortcut key for this command.

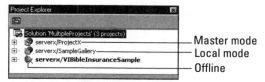

Figure 4-20: Three projects in Project Explorer, each in a different mode

✦ **Synchronize project files** — Because other members of your development team can add files to the master Web application or modify some of the files, you need to be able to get these changes. VI enables you to get a copy of the latest versions of the files you already have on your local workstation, which is known as synchronizing your local workstation with the master Web application. You do this by selecting the Project menu, selecting Web Project, and clicking Synchronize Files. To get the new files, you must Refresh Project View before you Synchronize Files. There is no default shortcut key for this command. Refer to "Using Visual SourceSafe" for additional information on this command.

Whenever you synchronize the project files with the master Web, you can have VI automatically create a read-only copy of all newly added files on the local workstation. To do this, in the Tools menu, select Options, and then select the Web Projects tab under Projects in the tree on the left of the Options dialog box. Under the Project options section, select Get new files when synchronizing with the master Web.

✦ **View the properties page for the current project** — The properties page for a project gives you a great deal of information about the project, such as the local workstation URL and directory and the master URL and directory. In addition, you can set project launch information, the DTC scripting platform, and the default script language on the client and server sides, as well as the project theme, layouts, and Navigation bar labels. The Dependencies page of this dialog box only applies to Visual J++ projects. There is no default shortcut key for this command.

Using Visual SourceSafe

When a team of people work on the same Web application, the integrity of the files is assured if the team uses Microsoft Visual SourceSafe (VSS) to handle their source control needs. VSS is a robust tool that is integrated with Visual InterDev. VSS enables one or more team members to check out the same file directly from VI. It also handles merging the file changes when each team member checks the file back in. VSS also keeps a history of the changes made to each file.

Once the admin installs and configures VSS on the Web server, one team member enables source control for a Web project. With the Web project under source control, the team members can begin checking out files. One user can check out a file at a time (exclusive check out), which is the default, or more than one person can check out the same file at the same time (multiple check outs). When you create a new file and add it to the Web project, it is automatically added to source control. After you are satisfied with the changes you made to a file, you check it in. If multiple people modified the file, VSS detects the differences and automatically prompts you to resolve the conflicts.

Enabling source control for a Web application

Only one team member needs to enable source control for a Web application. You can use any Web project that connects to that Web application, or you can enable source control at the same time you create the new master Web application. Once you put the Web application under source control, any team member currently working with that Web must refresh the project view or close and open the project for source control to take effect.

To enable source control for a Web application, follow these steps:

1. Open a Web project connected to the Web application you wish to put under source control. In this example, use `VIBibleInsuranceSample`.

2. Select the name of the project in Project Explorer.

3. In the Project menu, point to Source Control and select Add to Source Control. The Initial Solution Add dialog box appears.

4. Click Solution to add the entire solution to source control. Click Selection to add the selected project. The Enable Source Control dialog box appears.

5. Verify that the Web project name is correct, and then specify the VSS source control project name. The default is $/*project name*.

6. Click OK. VSS creates the source control project.

In Figure 4-21, you see the `VIBibleInsuranceSample` project in Project Explorer. Notice the new icons. A lock appears to the left of the project name when the project is under source control. A lock appears to the left of a filename when the file is under source control. A check mark appears to the left of a filename when you have checked out a copy of the file.

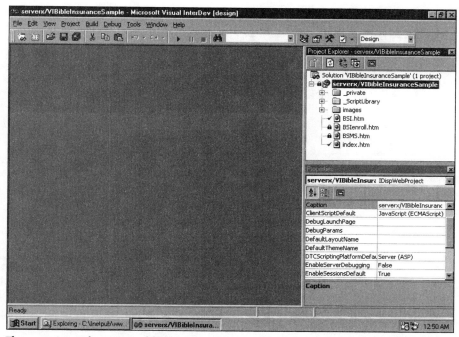

Figure 4-21: When you add a Web project to source control, this is what it looks like.

Checking out project files

When exclusive check out is enabled and you check out a file, you get a write-enabled copy if no one else has a copy. If someone else already has the file, you can get a read-only copy of the file. Once you check out a write-enabled copy of a file, no one else on the team can check out a write-enabled copy.

Follow these steps to check out a file:

1. Select the file in Project Explorer.

2. In the Project menu, point to Source Control and select Check Out *filename*. The Check out item(s) dialog box in Figure 4-22 appears.

3. If you do not wish to check out one of the files in the Items box, clear the check from the box in front of the name.

4. If you do not want to see this dialog box each time you check out a file, select Don't show any more checkout dialogs.

5. Click OK. VI checks the file out of SourceSafe and changes the icon to the left of the name in Project Explorer from a lock to a check.

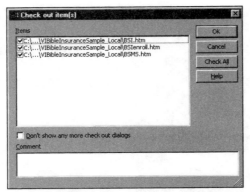

Figure 4-22: The Check out item(s) dialog box shows you the names of the files you are checking out.

If you want to get the latest copy of a file and you are not planning to make any changes to it (for example, you need it for testing), you can get a read-only copy without checking the file out. Select the file in Project Explorer. In the Project menu, point to Source Control and select Get Latest Version.

Checking in project files

When you are finished making changes to a file, you need to check it back into VSS. This new version of the file becomes the current version in the VSS project and is available to be checked out by other team members. To check in a file, select the file in Project Explorer. In the Project menu, point to Source Control and select Check In *filename*.

The Check In command is not the same as the Save command. Save updates the local or master Web application; it does not update the VSS project.

After you work with a checked-out, write-enabled file, and you do not wish to save your changes, you can discard the changes and release the file. This will enable another team member to check out a write-enabled copy of the file. To discard changes for a checked out file, select the file in Project Explorer. In the Project menu, point to Source Control and select Undo Check Out.

Source Control options

To set the source control options in VI, in the Tools menu, click Options and then click Source Control under Environment. The Options dialog box in Figure 4-23 appears. A detailed explanation of each option follows:

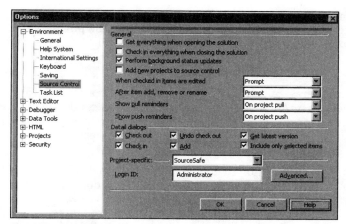

Figure 4-23: VI provides many options for source control.

✦ **Get everything when opening the solution** — Use this option if you want VI to get every file automatically each time you open a solution.

✦ **Check in everything when closing the solution** — Use this option if you want VI to check in every file in a solution automatically each time you close a solution.

✦ **Perform background status updates** — If you are using a product other than Microsoft Visual SourceSafe, this option tells VI to request information from the source control product each time you update a file.

✦ **Add new projects to source control** — Use this option if you want VI to add new projects and new files to source control automatically.

✦ **When checked in items are edited** — After you check a file in, a read-only copy of the file remains on your local system. If you change a read-only file, this option handles the situation in one of three ways:

- **Check Out** — VI automatically checks out a write-enabled copy of the file when you start to edit the file. (VI beeps when it does this.)

- **Prompt** — VI prompts you to check out the file.

- **Do Nothing** — VI lets you change your local copy of the file.

✦ **After item add, remove or rename** — Use this option to have VI Prompt now, Remind later, or do nothing each time you create a new file, remove a file from a project, or rename a file.

✦ **Show pull reminders** — A pull is one of the following source control commands: Get Latest, Check Out, or Undo Check Out. The pull puts the latest version of the file under source control on the local machine. Use this option to control when VI shows you the reminder dialog boxes (every time, only on project pulls, or never).

✦ **Show push reminders** — A push is one of the following source control commands: Check In or Add to Source Control. The push sends the version of the file on the local machine to the source control server. Use this option to control when VI shows you the reminder dialog boxes (every time, only on project pushs, or never).

✦ **Detail dialogs** — Use this option to enable or disable the display of one of the following dialog boxes: Check out, Check in, Undo check out, Add, or Get latest version. If you disable the display of a dialog box from within the dialog box, as shown in Figure 4-23, you can enable its display from here. Use Include only selected items to only include selected items in the dialog box.

✦ **Project-specific** — Enter a Login ID and Advanced options specific to your source control product. When you first access source control, VI uses this information in the login dialog box.

Summary

In this chapter, you examined the fundamentals of Web projects and solutions in Visual InterDev and learned the following:

✦ How the Web admin creates a new master Web application on the Web server

✦ How team members work on the Web application from their local workstations by creating a Web project that is connected to the master Web on the Web server

✦ How to propagate your local changes to the master Web application with the Release Working Copy option

✦ How to refresh your Web project to be sure you're looking at the most current site structure

✦ How to get the changes your teammates have made to the master Web application by synchronizing your files with the master

✦ How to add both Web projects to the same solution when you need to copy files from one Web to another

✦ How Visual SourceSafe enables teammates working on the same Web site to work exclusively on a file or to share files, modify them independently and then merge them together

✦   ✦   ✦

Prototyping a Web Site with Site Designer

As you saw in Chapter 4, VI makes the job of setting up a Web project fairly straightforward. In this chapter, we focus on an alternative way to design and manage a Web site: employing the Site Builder utility that comes with VI. You can create a simpler Web site from scratch. The following example shows you, step by step, how to use site diagrams — a very helpful tool.

The Basics of Site Designer

When you're building a Web site, thoughtful preplanning and organization can make the difference between a site that visitors find easy to understand and navigate, or one that puzzles nearly everyone, perhaps even you. Hyperlinks encourage users to bounce around within your site in a nonlinear fashion. A user expects to traverse your site the way he or she chooses. Users are annoyed when they are forced to follow a predefined path. For example, you shouldn't force a visitor to read your company's annual report before they are allowed to order merchandise.

We cover the important issues surrounding site design in several locations in this book. For example, Chapter 24 goes into link diagramming in depth. In this chapter, we explore a similar tool, the Site Designer. With Site Designer, you view and manipulate a *site diagram,* which makes it easy to prototype, or restructure, a Web site.

The Site Designer's job is to help you create or maintain the interrelationships between the various pages that, collectively, make up your Web site. Beyond that, these relationships define the links that are constructed for your site based on the data in the site structure file.

To learn how to use the Site Designer and associated tools such as Navigation bars, you will prototype a relatively simple site. In the process, you'll discover how useful the Site Designer tool can be.

Creating a site design

From the VI File menu, select New Project, and then choose New Web Project. Name it *Site* and click Next, choosing no layout and no theme. Now in the Project menu, choose Add Item, and then double-click the site diagram icon to create a new site diagram. Note in Project Explorer that a new file has been added to your project, with a default filename *Site diagram1.wdm*. All site diagrams end with a .wdm extension.

At this point, there is only one HTML page, Default.Htm, and it wasn't created by you; the site designer created it and called it your home page. Also, the Site Diagram toolbar popped up, as you can see in Figure 5-1.

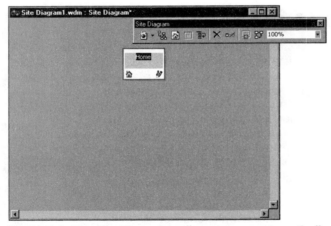

Figure 5-1: The Site Diagram toolbar appears automatically when you work with the Site Designer.

Click the New HTML Page button on the far left of the Site Designer toolbar and a page is automatically added to your site, directly under the home page, and connected to it by a line (see Figure 5-2).

Figure 5-2: When you add a new page, it becomes the child page of the current page you have selected.

Tip

You can also add a new HTML page to a site diagram merely by pressing the Ins key. The new page is added as a child to the page that is currently highlighted. If no page is highlighted, the new page appears by itself, unattached, on the diagram. Similarly, you can remove the selected page from the site diagram by pressing the Delete key. A dialog box pops up asking whether you want the page removed merely from the diagram, or deleted entirely from the project.

Adding automatic child pages

As you can see in Figure 5-2, Page1 automatically became a child page of the home page. Whenever you add a new page to a site diagram, it becomes a child of the currently selected page. The selected page has a red line around it; other pages are framed in blue (these are the default colors).

Now add a child page to Page1 (it will be called Page2 by default). Right-click Page1 and choose New HTML Page, as shown in Figure 5-3. (Right-clicking is an alternative to using the Site Diagram toolbar for many functions.)

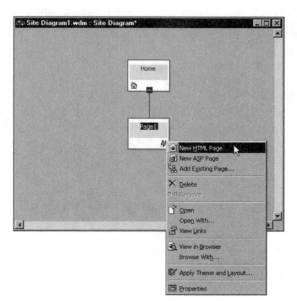

Figure 5-3: Use the right-click menu for many of the same functions located on the Site Designer toolbar.

You should now have a site diagram that looks like Figure 5-3. Notice that none of these added files have yet appeared within your Project Explorer. Click Save All in the File menu and they are added to your Project Explorer list. At this point, you want to create a second page on the same level as Page1, a *sibling page*. Both siblings share the same parent. Right-click the Home page to select it simultaneously, and pop out the menu. Choose New HTML Page and you see the sibling Page3 created next to Page1, as shown in Figure 5-4.

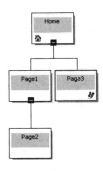

Figure 5-4: Pages on the same level in a tree, with the same parent, are called sibling pages (pages 1 and 3 in this example).

Adding meaningful page names

As this site builds, you want to give each page a more meaningful name than the default names. You can rename a page very easily in Site view, the same way you can rename files in Windows Explorer. Simply click the existing name and type a new one. Rename Page1 to Services and Page3 to Customers. Change Page2 to Sales and add two siblings under Services named Inventory and Personnel. Now your diagram should look like Figure 5-5.

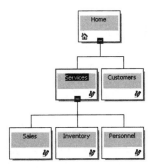

Figure 5-5: To rename a page, just highlight a name and type a new name.

Choose Save All from the File menu and notice that the newly created files show up in Project Explorer under the names you gave them (Personnel.htm, for example), but the older, renamed files remain Page1.htm and Page2.htm. Currently, the only way to rename an existing (already saved) file is to highlight it in the Project Explorer and choose Save As from the File menu. You then have the original and a new copy with the new, Saved As, name. To complete the renaming process, delete the original .htm files (right-click them in Project Explorer). This leaves the new, renamed copied files in the project.

Switching to a horizontal tree

Now try some different views in the site diagram. Click the Rotate button on the far right in the Site Diagram toolbar; this creates a horizontal tree diagram. Then choose *to fit* on the 100% drop-down zoom list; this centers the horizontal diagram, as shown in Figure 5-6.

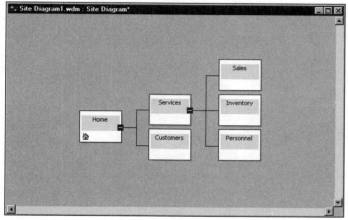

Figure 5-6: The toolbar's Rotate button enables you to rotate the diagram so it becomes a horizontal tree structure.

If the site becomes too large to view in the site diagram easily, you can always collapse some of the child pages. Select the parent whose children you want to hide and click Collapse/Expand, the second button from the right in the Site Designer toolbar. You can always click it again to reveal (expand) any hidden child pages.

Managing by Dragging Pages

It's quite easy to manage and reorganize a site once you have a site diagram. You can simply drag pages around and drop them in new locations. Suppose you want to add a page containing records about your customers and another page containing payments due. You're not yet sure where you want to put these pages, so you add them to the diagram but not to the tree. Right-click the site diagram background to deselect all pages in the diagram simultaneously, and also to pop out a menu. Choose New HTML Page and name it Records. Repeat this step, creating a second page named Payments. At this point, these are orphans (also called independent pages) with no place in the diagram — they merely exist on the background, as shown in Figure 5-7.

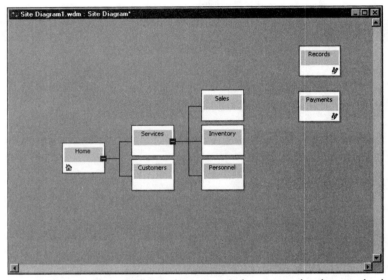

Figure 5-7: Orphans (independent pages) do not need to be attached to other pages to the diagram.

 Tip   You can drag a file from Project Explorer and drop it into a site diagram.

Dropping a child

Try dragging the Payments page until a dotted line appears between it and the customer's page, indicating that it will become a child of Customers when dropped. You might have to collapse the children under Services (or zoom to make the diagram much larger) before you can drop Payments as a new child of Customers. See Figure 5-8 for an example of dragging to create a child.

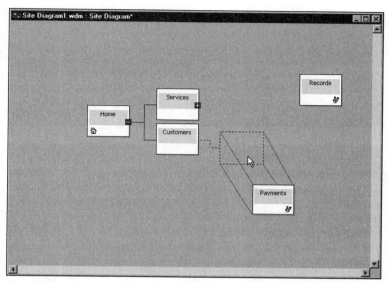

Figure 5-8: Here we drag the Payments page to make it a child, when dropped, of the Customers page.

> **Tip** You can collapse or expand children by clicking the blue – or + symbol where the children attach to their parent.

Add the Records page as a child of the Customer page as well. At any time, you can restructure your site diagram by adding or removing pages, or reorganizing them by dragging them around.

> **Tip** A Web application can include more than one project (see the Add Project option in the File menu). However, each project is allowed only a single Web site file (.wdm). Therefore, you can break up the entire Web application (site) into several projects and several site diagrams (one per project), or you can create a site diagram that contains the entire Web site.

Working with multiple trees

As you can see in Figure 5-9, we right-clicked the background of the site diagram three times, adding a new HTML page each time. We then dragged these independent pages into a tree structure of their own in the upper-left corner. This demonstrates that a single site diagram can contain as many trees as you wish.

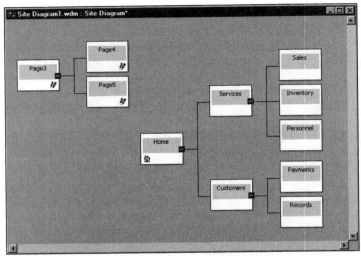

Figure 5-9: A single site diagram can contain as many tree structures as you wish.

You can also easily attach or detach one tree, or segment of a tree, onto a different tree. This is a handy way to experiment with the overall structure of your site. Note that you can drag an entire tree by dragging the home or primary (top-most parent) page. In Figure 5-9, the trees are dragged by dragging Page3 or Home.

The Navigation Bar

In some ways, all the previous discussion of the site diagram in this chapter has been leading up to the PageNavBar design-time control. Of course, site diagrams are useful for visualizing and organizing a site; however, once you have a site diagram, you can, if you wish, add a PageNavBar to further assist you in presenting a coherent, easily navigable site.

A design-time control (DTC) is a component that can be inserted into a page, automatically generating the HTML necessary to accomplish a job. (See Chapter 23 for more information on working with data in a Web page.) DTCs are most often used for attaching a database to a Web page, but there are a few that work toward other purposes.

Creating a Navigation bar

The PageNavBar control displays a set of hyperlinks — as text or buttons — by which a visitor can easily navigate your Web site. What's particularly interesting and helpful about the PageNavBar is it automatically keeps track of changes you make to the site diagram, then updates its output so the hyperlinks remain accurate . . . well, semiautomatically anyway. The FrontPage server extensions are required if you want to use the PageNavBar.

Follow these steps to add a PageNavBar to the example site you've been building:

1. Double-click the home page to open it in the editor.
2. Click the Source tab on the editor.
3. Click in the `<BODY>` section of the HTML to place the insertion point.
4. Click the Design Time Controls tab in the VI Toolbox.
5. Drag a PageNavBar onto the page.
6. Right-click the PageNavBar icon in the editor, and then select Properties to display the Property Pages dialog box, as shown in Figure 5-10.

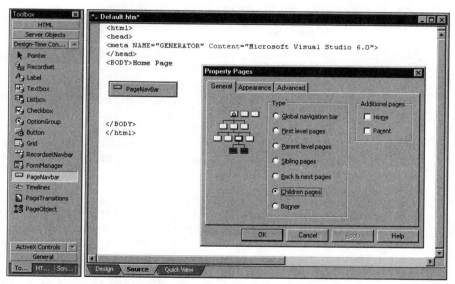

Figure 5-10: Structure your PageNavBar in its property pages.

As you can see in Figure 5-10, the PageNavBar can be configured to display links to various kinds of page relations.

Understanding the Property Pages dialog box

By default, the Property Pages dialog box displays child links. You can also specify that in addition to the category of links displayed (children and parents, for example), the home page or the parent page also be displayed within the list of hyperlinks the user sees on the page where the PageNavBar resides. The different types of links are listed in Table 5-1.

Table 5-1	
Types of Navigator Bar Links	
Link Type	**Description**
Global	Displays the entire site
First level	Displays links to the home page and any other page(s) on its level
Parent level	Displays links to all pages that are siblings of the parent page (the parent of the page holding the PageNavBar, the *active* page)
Sibling	Shows links to any page(s) on the same level as the active page
Back and Next	Links to *adjacent* siblings
Children	Shows any hyperlinks to pages beneath the active page in the tree hierarchy
Banner	Link did not work at the time of this writing.

Click the Appearance tab of the Property Pages dialog box and you can choose between buttons, text, and HTML (this is raw code, `<a href=#URL#>#LABEL#</a>`, that you can customize). You can also choose to have the links displayed across the top of the page or down the left side vertically. The buttons option is also semi-automatic; buttons and graphics will not be displayed unless you also apply a theme to your project.

To apply a theme, right-click the project's name (such as dell//Site) in Project Explorer. Then choose Apply Theme and Layout. Click the Apply Theme option and select a theme from the list. VI adds approximately 12,000 .gif image files to your project, one of which will be used as the buttons in your PageNavBar. Don't be alarmed. Choose Save All in the File menu, and then choose View In Browser in the View menu. If you don't like the buttons or the theme's look, return to VI and right-click the project's name again, choose Apply Theme and Layout, and choose a different theme. Your previous theme will still be part of your site, though, so to delete it, right-click it under the Themes listing in the Project Explorer and choose Delete.

The Advanced tab has a single option: a text box labeled Alternate Page, where you can specify an optional .htm file containing a navigational structure for your page.

For instance, if you have a primary menu page that displays all the main pages in your site, you could type in that primary menu page's URL as the alternate page. If you do, the primary menu page's navigational structure is applied to the PageNavBar links on the current page. Notice that you leave off the / (backslash) when typing in a URL (in other words, the supplied URL must be project-relative). For example, if the page you want to use is named PrimaryMenuPage.asp, you would type **PrimaryMenuPage.asp**, not */PrimaryMenuPage.asp*.

Adding links

You may have noticed that when you first added the site diagram to your project, a new menu item appeared: Diagram. This menu is the tool you use to add page link references to a PageNavBar. Don't try to view the navigational links in Quick View — they never show up there. You have to choose the View In Browser option from the View menu to see the results of the PageNavBar's efforts. But even if you try that, you'll see nothing until you actually add some pages to the PageNavBar. To do this, follow these steps:

1. Click the site diagram to restore focus to it and you should see the home page, with the Services and Customer pages underneath it as its children.

2. Click the Services page so it is highlighted (selected).

3. Choose Add to Global Navigation Bar from the Diagram menu. (There is also a button on the Site Diagram toolbar for this same operation.)

4. Click OK when you're warned that adding the page to the Navigation bar will detach it from its parent in the diagram. Nobody knows why this happens, but you can reattach it later.

5. Now click the Customers page and repeat, adding it to the Navigation bar as well. At this point, your child pages and their children are detached from the home page, as shown in Figure 5-11.

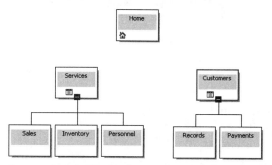

Figure 5-11: Adding pages to the Navigation bar has the peculiar effect of detaching them from their parent page in the site diagram.

6. Now drag the Customers and Services pages back up so they reattach to the home page in the site diagram.

7. Choose Save All from the File menu to update the files.

8. Click the home page in the site diagram to select it, and then choose View In Browser from the View menu. You see the hyperlinks to your two child pages when the home page loads into the browser, as shown in Figure 5-12. (The words *Home Page* are not a hyperlink. We just typed them into the HTML source code of the home page to identify it.)

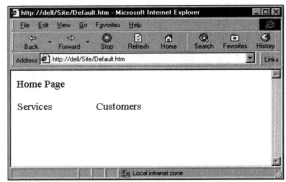

Figure 5-12: Here is the set of two hyperlinks created by the PageNavBar design-time control.

Note that a design-time control generates HTML code during runtime (when a page is displayed in a browser). If you look at the source code underneath the page displayed in Figure 5-12, you'll see something like Listing 5-1.

Listing 5-1: **Automatically Generated Source Code**

```
<html>
<head>
<meta NAME="GENERATOR" Content="Microsoft Visual Studio 6.0">
</head>
<body>Home Page
<br>
<!--METADATA TYPE="DesignerControl" startspan
<OBJECT classid="clsid:705396F5-3471
-11D1-B693-006097C9A884" id=NavBarDTC1
 style="LEFT: 0px; TOP: 0px">
<PARAM NAME="Type" VALUE="5">
<PARAM NAME="IncludeHome" VALUE="0">
```

```
<PARAM NAME="IncludeParent" VALUE="0">
<PARAM NAME="Appearance" VALUE="0">
<PARAM NAME="Orientation" VALUE="0">
<PARAM NAME="UseTable" VALUE="1">
<PARAM NAME="UseTheme" VALUE="1">
<PARAM NAME="HTMLFragment" VALUE="">
<PARAM NAME="CurrentHTMLFragment" VALUE="">
<PARAM NAME="UseObjectSyntax" VALUE="0">
<PARAM NAME="ScriptLanguage" VALUE="0">
<PARAM NAME="FrameTarget" VALUE="">
<PARAM NAME="AlternatePage" VALUE=""></OBJECT>
-->
<!--METADATA TYPE="NavBar" endspan-->
<!--webbot bot="vinavbar" tag="table"
 s-type="children" b-include-home="false"
 b-include-up="false" s-orientation="horizontal"
 s-rendering="graphics" b-use-table="true"
 b-use-theme="true" s-script-lang="VBScript"
 b-use-object-syntax="false" u-page s-target
 s-html-fragment s-selected-html-fragment startspan -->
<table cols="2" cellpadding="0" cellspacing="1">
<tr>
<td class="mstheme-horiz-navtxt-g"
 width="140" height="60"
 onclick="location.href='Page1.htm'" style="cursor: hand">
<a style="text-decoration: none"
 href=Page1.htm>Services</a>
</td>
<td class="mstheme-horiz-navtxt-g"
 width="140" height="60"
 onclick="location.href='Customers.htm'"
 style="cursor: hand">
<a style="text-decoration: none"
 href=Customers.htm>Customers</a>
</td>
</tr>
</table>
<!--webbot bot="vinavbar" endspan i-checksum="63968" -->
<!--METADATA TYPE="NavBar" startspan-->
<!--METADATA TYPE="DesignerControl" endspan-->

</body>
</html>
```

As you can see, the DTC created a table with, in this case, two cells.

There are four tiny icons that are added to special pages within a site diagram. They appear in the lower-left corner, as shown in Figure 5-13.

Figure 5-13: These tiny icons identify a site diagram page as (from left to right) a home page, a modified page, an external page, or a global navigational page.

The Diagram Menu

A Diagram menu mysteriously appears whenever you work with a site diagram. Well, it's not that mysterious; it's supposed to be there to duplicate some of the features you can access by right-clicking a site diagram editor window and duplicate some of the features on the Site Diagram toolbar. Nonetheless, there are three items on the Site Diagram toolbar that are not available by clicking the diagram or clicking a button on the toolbar: Detach From Parent, View Page Breaks, and Recalculate Page Breaks.

Detaching from parent

The Detach From Parent option merely removes the currently selected page in the site diagram (the active page, the one with the focus, the one with a red frame, the one you last clicked) from its parent. Any child pages under the selected page likewise move with it away from the parent. In other words, this command accomplishes what you can do by dragging a page away from its parent in the site diagram. Therefore, having this command on a menu is fairly meaningless — it's easier to drag a page away, and you can move it far enough away by dragging to make it clearly independent of the parent. The menu option merely removes the link lines without moving the child away from underneath the parent.

Viewing page breaks

You can print a site diagram, or any other page in a VI project, by choosing Print from the File menu. The View Page Breaks feature shows you a preview of where, if your site diagram is sent to the printer, page breaks will occur. It adds blue lines within the site diagram where the diagram will end and then begins again on the next piece of paper. This feature is the equivalent of the dotted line in a word processor document that shows you where each page ends.

Recalculating page breaks

Should you add or remove pages to your site diagram after printing the diagram, the page breaks might be wrong when you next print the diagram. The discrepancy is caused because VI doesn't automatically recalculate breaks when you add or subtract pages from a diagram. To solve this staggeringly infinitesimal problem, the Recalculate Page Breaks option is available in the Diagram menu. When you click this option, the page breaks are, as you guessed, recalculated. Then you can rest assured that your printout of the diagram will be the same as the breaks shown via the View Page Breaks option.

Summary

The Site Designer assists you in organizing a site so its internal links create sensible, understandable pathways for users to follow. You want to make it easy for site visitors to get where they want to go, and also to travel back to the home page, or across to sibling pages, without needing to study your site's structure. You might understand what your Web Site looks like, but what about people who come upon your site for the first time? Will it be easy for them to navigate?

In this chapter, you learned the following:

✦ How to make use of the Site Designer utility

✦ How to create a site design from scratch

✦ How to reorganize a site by dragging and dropping pages

✦ How to work with more than one tree, and how to attach or detach trees

✦ How a Navigation bar (the PageNavBar design-time control) assists you in presenting a coherent, easily navigable site

✦ How to add new pages to a Navigation bar

✦ How to use the Diagram menu

✦ How to recalculate and manage page breaks

✦   ✦   ✦

Creating
Web Pages

✦ ✦ ✦ ✦

In This Part

✦ ✦ ✦ ✦

The VI Integrated Development Environment

If you've read the first five chapters, you should feel confident that you can use VI to create and coordinate the development of a Web application. This chapter offers you an overview of all the tools, features, windows, menu options, and utilities that collectively make up the new Visual InterDev Integrated Design Environment (IDE). Our goal in this chapter is to introduce you to the IDE's many facets — so you know what's available if you ever need one of the tools. All too often we buy a sophisticated, multifaceted piece of software, but never learn all the things it can do. For example, I used Outlook Express for years before noticing its powerful archived e-mail text search feature (Ctrl+Shift+F). You can use it to search the complete contents quickly (not just the headers) of your entire archive of messages. How many times did I search by sender, looking through dozens of messages to find the one I wanted? We don't want that to happen to you, so this chapter covers all the bases of Visual InterDev's many features.

We assume you have a basic familiarity with computer concepts. Therefore, we don't spend time in this chapter covering *every* menu item (we don't explain Open or Save As, for example). However, we cover all the menu items that aren't flagrantly obvious. We also look at all the windows you can open on your data or site. Some of them are described only briefly, however, because they're explored in depth in other chapters. We begin by showing you how to create a simple Web site using the IDE's fundamental tools.

Creating a Home Page Using the Source Code Editor

VI has a new editor. It provides you with various views of a Web page, and you can easily switch between these views using the tabs at the bottom of the editor, as shown in Figure 6-1.

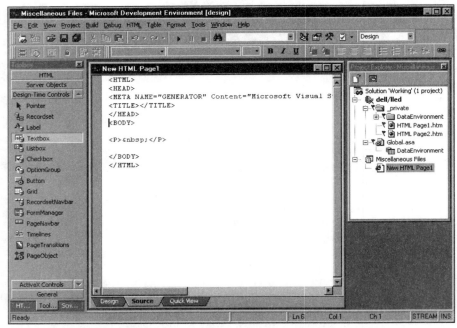

Figure 6-1: This is a typical arrangement of windows within the VI IDE.

Launch VI and choose New Web Project from the New Project dialog box. This dialog box appears by default when you launch VI (or you can click New Project from the File menu). Go through the various steps required by the New Project Wizard, clicking the Next button repeatedly until you can click Finish. (See Chapter 4 for a detailed description of beginning a new project.) Choose a name, but respond No when asked if you want to add a layout or theme. When finished, click New File and the New HTML Page from the File menu. Because we want to start from the same point, organize your VI IDE so it looks like the one in Figure 6-1.

Close any windows that aren't shown in Figure 6-1, and use the VI View menu to open the Toolbox and Project Explorer windows. Also, right-click the toolbar to select the Design, Standard, and HTML toolbars. Turn off any other toolbars that might be showing. Notice that on the far right of the Standard toolbar are buttons that toggle on and off the frequently used Project Explorer, Properties Window, and Toolbox. You can, as you'll see later, rearrange, delete, or add new buttons to any toolbar.

When you first start a new HTML file, VI inserts a small *template* of default HTML source code. Note that this is the meaning of template in VI — a shell of basic HTML source code. See Chapter 10 for a detailed discussion of the differences in VI between templates, themes, style sheets, and layouts. VI comes with three default templates: HTML Page, ASP Page, and Style Sheet. The Style Sheet option isn't a typical template; instead, it opens the CSS Editor. You can also add your own templates. (See Chapter 10 for much more on this, the CSS Editor, and related topics.)

To create a new HTML file, choose New File from the File menu and double-click HTML File (be sure that the Visual InterDev tab is selected in the New File dialog box). You see the following default source template if you click the Source tab at the bottom of the editor window:

```
<HTML>
<HEAD>
<META NAME="GENERATOR"
 Content="Microsoft Visual Studio 6.0">
</HEAD>
<BODY>
</BODY>
</HTML>
```

Your job is to add to this skeleton of source code, inserting whatever HTML code, components, scriptlets, graphics, or other objects you want.

The Main Editor Window

When you double-click a file in the Project Explorer window, the file is loaded into an editing window. As you can see in Figure 6-1, the VI editor is a considerable improvement over VI version 1.0's editor. Consider the editing window's three views (selected by the three tabs on the bottom of each editing window):

✦ **Design view** is where you can add objects, edit text, add tables and lists, position and resize objects, customize the appearance of objects, and use the Document Outline window. (See the following section for more information.)

Design view is an editing window (like Source view, but unlike Quick View), yet Design view also enables you to see what the user will see when the page is loaded into Internet Explorer 4.

✦ **Source view** enables you to edit the HTML source code directly. Because Design view only displays the elements between the <BODY> tags, you'll have to switch to Source view to edit anything within the <HEAD> tags. Also, script and HTML tags do not appear in Design view.

✦ **Quick View** transforms the editor temporarily into an Internet Explorer 4 window, showing you precisely what your page will look like (and how it will behave) when loaded into the browser of a person who visits your Web site.

Now you get instant feedback on your work.

Note   FrontPage also has three similar editor views: Normal, HTML, and Preview. However, FP currently has an annoying habit of reformatting your source code when you switch to Preview, then back to HTML. VI is the programmer's tool.

Design view

Design view is an editor that permits you to:

✦ Add objects (ActiveX components or Java applets)

✦ Edit text (apply formatting using a toolbar's buttons)

✦ Add tables and lists

✦ Position and resize objects by dragging them around

✦ Customize the appearance of objects (using the Properties window)

✦ Use the Document Outline window (View ➪ Other Windows ➪ Document Outline) to jump to any element within the page quickly

When you click the Design tab in VI, you see an editor similar to the drag-and-drop windows found in such Microsoft RAD (Rapid Application Development) tools, such as Visual Basic, Visual C++, Visual J++, and Visual FoxPro. For example, when you want to move, resize, or add components to a VB form, you work in the Form editor. However, when you want to work with the source code "underneath" the user-visible form, you double-click the form or a component on it to get to "code view." Similarly, if you double-click a component that's been added to the Design view, the VI editor takes you down to the Source view. Try it: Click the HTML tab in the Toolbox, and then double-click Textbox to put a standard HTML text box on your page. Note that in Design view, you can drag the outline around the text box to enlarge it. Now double-click the Textbox component in the Design window and you'll cause the Source view to appear. The following HTML was automatically added to your code:

```
<INPUT id=text1 name=text1>
```

If you stretched the text box in Design view, HTML also specifies the new size:

```
<INPUT id=text1 name=text1
  style="HEIGHT: 78px; WIDTH: 200px">
```

Source view

Click the Source tab to edit the source code. Notice that on the bottom of the Toolbox are HTML Outline and Script Outline tabs. The HTML Outline view shows you many, but not all, major HTML element tags — so you can get a general, more abstract view of your document. It won't display common <P> tags but will display an <INPUT> component. You can easily locate a particular area in your page by clicking one of the main components. Also, selecting an element in the HTML Outline simultaneously selects it in the editor window. HTML Outline can be displayed in either Design or Source view. Only elements between the <BODY> tags will be displayed.

The Script Outline tab is similar to the Scripting Wizard in other Microsoft applications. It shows you the components (objects) in your page with an ID or NAME attribute, and it also displays any scripts. Aside from helping you move to any element or script in your page quickly, you can also use the script outline as a helpful reference. Expand the tree view (by clicking the + symbol next to any component) and you see a list of events (triggers) that can be attached to that particular component, as shown in Figure 6-2.

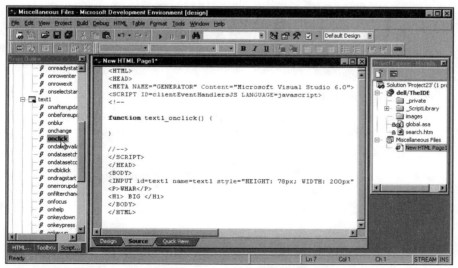

Figure 6-2: Double-clicking the OnClick event in Script Outline inserts an OnClick event handler procedure (Function) template in the HTML source code.

Here's the HTML source code scripting that VI adds when you double-click Text1's `OnClick` event:

```
<SCRIPT ID=clientEventHandlersJS LANGUAGE=javascript>
<!--
function text1_onclick() {
}
//-->
</SCRIPT>
```

For tutorials on scripting, see Chapters 11 through 17.

The editor's Source view features a color-coding scheme to help you distinguish between the various kinds of source code at a glance. By default, HTML commands (tags, such as `<TITLE>` or `<BODY>`) are brown, and tag arguments (attributes, such as *LEFTMARGIN* in the phrase `<BODY LEFTMARGIN = 0>`) are red. The actual particular parameters (the 0 in `<BODY LEFTMARGIN = 0>`) are blue, as are all the `<` `</` and `>` symbols. HTML comments (such as `<!-- Insert HTML here -->`) are gray. This color scheme enables you to visually identify all the primary elements of your HTML source code quickly.

Changing the Color Scheme

VI's default editor color scheme isn't hard-wired. If you prefer a different set of colors, you can design your own. Follow these steps to change the default colors:

1. Choose Options from the VI Tools menu.

2. Double-click Text Editor in the list box on the left of the dialog box to drop down the subfolders.

3. Click Font and Colors.

4. In the Display Items list, select the HTML element you want to adjust.

5. Use the two drop-down list boxes to the right to change to one of 16 background colors (highlight) or one of 16 foreground (text) colors, or change both.

6. Click OK when you're satisfied.

Note that the Reset All button will restore the factory default colors and Courier 10pt as the default font.

Quick View

The final VI editor view is Quick View, which is, in effect, a look at your code as it will appear in Internet Explorer 4. Even components and most kinds of scripting are activated within Quick View. But as you'll notice in several chapters in this book, you sometimes have to switch to a real Internet Explorer browser, then load in your .htm file, before some effects work. DHTML works fine in Quick View, but some server-side behaviors require real Internet Explorer. Note that Active Server Pages (see Chapters 16 and 17) will not correctly execute in Quick View. You must use the View In Browser option on VI's View menu (or use the Open option in Internet Explorer's File menu) to look at the page in Internet Explorer itself.

The Toolbox

Now that you've taken a look at a newly created home page and its main editor window, it's time to examine the IDE's primary tools. The Toolbox is a repository of components, predesigned controls, and other objects, such as the new scriptlets objects described in Chapter 13. As you see in Figure 6-3, the VI Toolbox contains six "pages" — Scriptlets, Server Objects, ActiveX Controls, Design-Time Controls, HTML, and General. Server objects are similar to client-side objects, but they're intended to execute using IIS (Internet Information Server) in server-side script. ActiveX controls are Microsoft's answer to Java applets, and they include all the usual components found on a user-interface (text boxes, list boxes, command buttons, check boxes, progress bars, and more). Design-time controls are specialized programmer-assisting components that, when added to a page, either display a database or generate code facilitating database/HTML programming (see Chapter 23). HTML components include the usual input/output HTML devices, such as radio buttons, submit buttons, and a text area.

Figure 6-3: The VI Toolbox is filled with items (objects) that you can drag and drop onto your Web pages.

You can add these various elements from the Toolbox to your source code in either Source or Design view. Either double-click a Toolbox item or drag it onto the editor. Note that once embedded in your source code, an ActiveX and other types of components might appear as a graphical representation rather than source code — even though you're in Source view. If you would prefer to see items as source code, select (click) one of the graphic controls in the editor window, and then choose View All Controls As Text in the View menu. You can switch back by selecting the View All Controls Graphically option in that same menu. (Also, right-clicking an object in Source view pops out a context menu with a Text or Graphical View option you can click.)

To use any of the Toolbox components, drag them from the Toolbox onto your page at the location you want them to appear. Most controls and objects are displayed graphically in the HTML editor in both Design view and Source view. In Source view, you can specify that you want to see the text version of an object.

The Project Explorer Window

The Project Explorer window is your overall tree view of the folders and files that, collectively, compose the Web site on which you're working, as you can see in Figure 6-4. (See Chapter 4 for an explanation of all the icons in the tree structure.)

Figure 6-4: In the Project Explorer window, you can move between the various files (pages) in your Web site.

By right-clicking a file or folder, you can use the context menu to do a variety of essentially global jobs (most of which are also available on menus). You can change which page or project is the startup (the one executed first when the site is loaded into a browser), recalculate links or apply themes and layouts, manage the versions (local versus master), and accomplish other tasks.

Note that there are five buttons at the top of the Project Explorer. They are, from left to right:

✦ **Open** — Opens an editor window on the currently highlighted file

✦ **Refresh** — Updates the Project Explorer in case files have been added, deleted, or reorganized

✦ **Synchronize** — Files between the local and master versions

✦ **Copy** — Copies the entire Web site to another location (usually done only after you're finished and want to place it on a public server and deploy it to the Internet or intranet)

✦ **Properties** — Displays a tabbed dialog box describing various qualities of the selected file, project, or solution

VI is extraordinarily expansive and customizable. For example, there are shortcut keys for most things you want to do with the IDE. Shift+Esc closes the currently active window. However, you can change the keyboard shortcuts to suit yourself, and even create new sets of keyboard maps for different uses, as you can see in Figure 6-5. To do this, choose Options from the Tools menu, and then select Environment ➪ Keyboard.

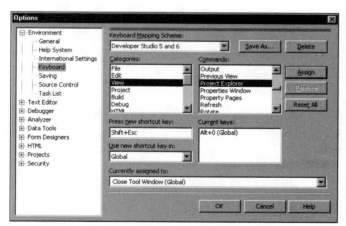

Figure 6-5: Keyboard mapping is one of many kinds of customization offered by VI.

The Properties Window

The Properties window is the fourth and last basic IDE window, joining the Toolbox, the editor, and Project Explorer as the big four that are usually left displayed all the time. Other windows, such as debugging, are usually turned off until needed to free up screen real estate. But the Properties window is used so often that it's left visible

by most programmers. The Properties Window is also frequently attached to
Project Explorer, as you can see in Figure 6-6.

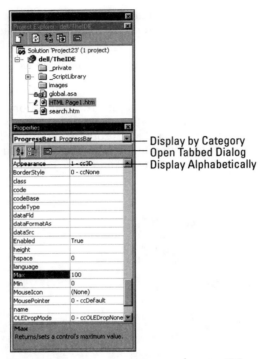

— Display by Category
— Open Tabbed Dialog
— Display Alphabetically

Figure 6-6: To save some space in your IDE,
drag the Properties window up under Project
Explorer to attach them together.

The Properties window displays the properties of the currently selected object. (In
Figure 6-6, it's a progress bar that we added to our page from ActiveX Controls on
the Toolbox). In the Properties window you view, or edit, the various qualities of a
component, such as its size. A progress bar, for instance, has Max and Min
properties, defining how many units of measurement they're divided into (how fine
the resolution of the progress display is).

The properties in the Properties window are design-time properties, meaning you
can change them while designing your page (as opposed to properties that can only
be changed dynamically from within script while a page is loaded in a browser).
Note the three icons at the top of the Properties window. The first two switch
between an alphabetical list of the properties and a categorized list — though the
categories are often misleading. For example, the Appearance category includes

border style, the Attributes category includes height, and the Style category includes the border width. Wouldn't you agree that all three of these properties could be more accurately grouped together under Appearance? The final button is Properties Pages, which displays a tabbed dialog box.

Note   At present, many components don't fully support this way of adjusting their properties. Tabbed dialog boxes are the wave of the future for customization in Microsoft's products, but currently some of them are not working, or not working completely.

The IDE's Various Menus

Now that we've covered the four main windows in the IDE, we turn our attention to the various menus. Recall that we're only going to survey menu items whose meaning and purpose is not painfully obvious. Items you should already be familiar with, such as the Print option in the File menu, will not be discussed. In the process of surveying the menus, we also explain the purpose of the various other IDE windows.

Always remember that when you're dealing with menus, the content of the menus depends on which view you're currently in. Click the Design tab, and then look at the Tools menu. You see Absolute Mode and Snap to Grid options, features that were not on the Tools menu when you were in Source view. Likewise, notice that some menu items are disabled: their text is light gray and when you click them, nothing happens. This, too, is a function of the view you're currently in. It can be context-sensitive in other ways. Some items are only enabled during break mode; some only during debugging; some items are only enabled during debugging when your insert cursor is within a <SCRIPT> zone in the source code. Other items are only enabled when the cursor is located on text or a graphic, or when a project is highlighted (selected) in Project Explorer. In other words, if you can't get something to work, you're probably in the wrong context — try switching views, selecting a project, and so on.

The File menu

The first (and only) item of any obscurity on the File menu is Add Project, shown in Figure 6-7. You might have thought that the project was the entire Web site and you could no more add a new project to your current project than you could add a fireplace to an existing fireplace. Wrong. No soup for you! Several terms swirl around — application, project, Web application, site, Web, and solution. Which encloses which? The outermost container in VI's organization of a Web site is the solution. (Confusingly, the solution is also sometimes described as the Web application.) Take a look at the tree diagram in Project Explorer: the highest level is the solution and underneath it can be as many projects as you want to add to the solution. Lower still is the set of files (Web pages) within each project. For more on the librarian features and VI's organizational nomenclature, see Chapters 2 through 4.

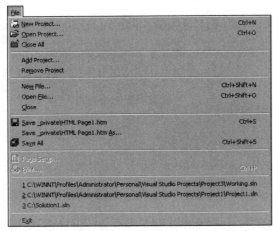

Figure 6-7: The Add Project option in the File menu

The Edit menu, shown in Figure 6-8, contains several obscure entries. To see these options, click the Source tab in the editor window. Also, the Auto list members and Parameter information checkboxes must be checked; access them via Tools ⇨ Options ⇨ Text Editor ⇨ Per Language ⇨ HTML.

Figure 6-8: The Edit menu options

The lesser-known Edit menu options are as follows:

✦ The **List Members** option is designed to display a list box of all the properties and methods available for the currently selected object. You must be working with <SCRIPT> tags for this option to work.

✦ The **Parameter Info** option only works in the <BODY> section on such entries as these:

```
<BODY onload=startTiming() onunload=stopTimer()>
```

Click one of these function names, and you'll see a list of any parameters they require. This can come in handy if you're ready to call a procedure but can't recall what it wants passed to it.

✦ The **Complete Word** feature fills out a script command for you, changing, for example, ms to MsgBox. However, if you're going to use this time-saver (similar to the Autocorrect feature in Word), you'll probably prefer to trigger it with its keyboard shortcut: Ctrl+Space.

✦ The **Advanced** options in the Edit menu are somewhat of a misnomer. There's nothing advanced about adding tabs, promoting a selection into uppercase letters, or displaying dots instead of spaces between words in the editor.

✦ The **Bookmarks** feature enables you to put little placeholders within your source code so you can more easily locate particular lines later. A small, cyan, rounded rectangle icon appears next to any bookmarked line of code. (You add a bookmark using the HTML menu.) I prefer to add comment lines to sections of code I might want to locate later, then search for them using the Find utility in the Edit menu.

One final note about the Edit menu: There's a Go To option that some might find useful during debugging. A debugger often tosses up error messages specifying a particular line of code as the culprit. Go To takes you to a line number within your source code. (You can also look for the current line number in the status bar at the bottom of the VI IDE.)

The View menu

Next is the View menu, shown in Figure 6-9, which enables you to control which windows and toolbars are displayed in the IDE, and offers a few other miscellaneous features.

Figure 6-9: The View menu options

The following are some View menu options you may not be aware of:

✦ The **Open With Browser** option was discussed earlier in this chapter, but note also the Browse With option that enables you to select something other than Internet Explorer as your default, or at least temporary, browser. Note that many of VI's advanced DHTML and scripting features will not work in anything other than Internet Explorer 4.0.

✦ The **View Links option** brings up the Link View window. (Chapter 25 discusses this site management tool.) Sync Script Outline displays the Script Outline window on the Toolbox, discussed in "Source view" earlier in this chapter. We discuss the Debug Windows option later in the chapter.

✦ The **Other Windows** option displays a set of miscellaneous windows you can activate. The Task List window is a to-do organizer wherein you can group, prioritize, and otherwise manage the jobs facing you or your team when creating the current Web site. It can also display warnings or error messages while you're creating script or compiling your page.

✦ The **Visual Component Manager** is a utility (technically, it's an add-in) designed to help you organize and deploy objects such as scriptlets, ActiveX components, design-time controls, and other kinds of components associated with your Web site. The Component Manager includes a Publish Wizard that assists you in "publishing" a component so it can be reused later by you or other developers. When you're working in a world of objects, there are so many components from so many diverse sources and so many versions of those individual components, you need help organizing them. The Component Manager enables you to locate or publish components in an organized way (as opposed to simply dragging and dropping components off your Toolbox and onto your editor window).

Note

At present, the Component Manager is more a goal than a working part of VI. It was designed to work with the various other tools in Visual Studio, such as Visual Basic and Visual J++ (these tools can design components, hence the publishing wizard). VI's only component design capability is scriptlets.

✦ The **Deployment Explorer** is a crude tool at this time, merely offering you the option of copying the Web site to a URL. (See Chapter 25 for more useful tools when you're ready to deploy.)

✦ The **Object Browser**, like the Visual Component Manager, is another of those multi-application tools that works with Visual Basic, Office applications, Java, and so on. The Object Browser is designed to reveal the members of an object to you — a kind of quick reference help window showing you a component's properties, methods, events, and constants. Objects must be "registered" with your project by using the Project References option in the Project menu.

Note

At this time, the Object Browser isn't working properly in VI. And, alas, the usual inconsistency of shortcut keys that plagues so many Microsoft applications is alive and well with the Object Browser. Visual Basic displays it when you press F2; VI uses F12. Visual Basic starts single-stepping with F8; VI uses F11. Some applications launch a search with F3; others require Ctrl+F. We could go on . . .

✦ The **Document Outline window** option in View ➪ Other Windows is merely the HTML Outline window on the Toolbox described previously in "Source view." It's the companion to the Script Outline window.

✦ The **Output** window is used to display the results of SQL PRINT statements. If a SELECT statement returns more than a single variable value (which you can view in the Locals window), you can see it in the Output window.

✦ The **Data View** window displays a visual tree structure that enables you to edit and create database objects residing on a remote database server. You can use it to manage various objects such as tables, triggers, diagrams, stored procedures, and views in Microsoft SQL Server databases, or Oracle 7.0+ databases.

✦ The **Show Tasks** option works with the Tasks window. We deal with the toolbars in a separate section later in this chapter.

✦ The **Define Window Layout** selection brings up a useful dialog box where you can type in a new name, then save your current IDE setup for later recall. There is also a set of default layouts you can select from as well. This makes it possible for you to quickly rearrange the appearance and functionality of the entire IDE. For example, when you're programming script, you likely have the windows open, as shown in Figure 6-1, or some variation of that setup. But your favorite child window organization for debugging is going to be quite different. With this Define Window Layout utility, you can quickly switch between optimal setups. You don't have to go through the tiresome process of opening, positioning, and resizing the necessary windows.

One drawback, though, to this otherwise excellent idea: there is no shortcut key enabling you to switch views quickly. The good news is you can at least define your own shortcut key to the Define Window Layout dialog box by choosing Options from the Tools menu and selecting Environment | Keyboard. Select View in the Categories list, and then locate Define Window Layout in the Commands list. Now you can define something such as Alt+S to open the Define Window Layout dialog box. VI doesn't feature full macro capability yet, but keyboard shortcuts are better than nothing.

✦ The **Full Screen** option eliminates all toolbars and windows, leaving only the menus and the editor window. Why? Perhaps to give you a greater viewing area in Design or Quick View. It is a good way to get a clean, uncluttered workspace fast.

✦ The **Refresh** item does the same thing as pressing F5: it reloads the Quick View and otherwise updates any window whose contents might have changed as a result of editing.

The Project menu

The Project menu, shown in Figure 6-10, covers the global issues involving the current project, particularly issues involving project management. Note that a number of the selections in the Project menu will not work unless you first select a project in the Project Explorer window.

Figure 6-10: The Project menu options

The following Project menu items are worth noting:

✦ The **Add Project Outputs** option displays a dialog box (if a project is selected — highlighted — in the Project Explorer window). You can create projects whose output will be automatically added to one of your projects when you build that project. Among other things, this creates a dependency, a file or files that contribute to your final product and must, therefore, be included when you deploy your site. You can see the dependencies by clicking the Dependencies tab when you choose Properties, after right-clicking a project.

✦ The **Add Data Command** selection is your way to connect to a data source that has file DSNs. The Add Data Connection item does precisely the same thing.

✦ The **New Deployment Target** option enables you to specify a URL where your entire Web site will be deployed (see Chapter 24).

✦ The **Mark As Scriptlet** option in the Web Files submenu creates an object out of the currently selected (in Project Explorer) Web page. Among other interesting results of this action, that .htm file is added to the list of available scriptlets on the Toolbox's Scriptlets list. You can now add this object to any HTML source code just as if it was a more traditional object, such as a text box. Scriptlets can also have members publicly exposed. For more on this interesting and potentially valuable way to encapsulate and reuse your code, see Chapter 13.

✦ The **Project References** option pops up a dialog box with the same name. This is essentially a list of objects (available in object libraries, other applications, .DLLs) that you might want to use in your Web pages. To make these objects available for insertion into your source code, you have to create a reference to the outside application's object library. If you check one of the listed applications, its objects will then be listed in the Object Browser (press F12). Project References is another of those shared utilities you'll also find in Visual Basic, Visual C++, and other Microsoft RAD environments.

After you've set a project reference, you'll likely want to put some of the objects into your Toolbox for easy placement on your Web pages. To see how to do this, refer to the Customize Toolbox option in the "Tools menu" section, later in this chapter.

Note

At present, Project References is not working correctly in VI. Note that setting references does retard the compilation of your Web pages, so only check those code libraries that you actually use. What's more, borrowing objects from other applications' code libraries makes those libraries' dependencies for your Web site — DLLs or other files that must be copied along with your site's files when you deploy (copy entirely to a server) your site. (See Chapter 24 for more information.)

✦ The **Set as StartUp Project** option defines which project — if you have more than one project in your site "solution" — will be first parsed and executed when the site is loaded into a browser. This is similar to the Set as Start Page option for the individual .htm files. A browser, or debugger, must know where you intend your Web site to "begin;" you can't expect a browser to choose among your many pages and decide which one is primary.

The Debug menu

When it's time to track down errors in a program, VI comes to your aid in a variety of ways. And because script is an interpreted language, you can even adjust the source code and immediately test the effects of your changes by switching from the Source view to the Quick View. In the Debug menu, shown in Figure 6-11, you'll find many tools that can assist you in tracking down errors in your scripts.

Figure 6-11: The Debug menu options

The previous version of VI was rather lightweight in its debugging features and every effort was made to correct that weakness in the new VI. As you can see by looking at the Debug menu, there is a substantial suite of tools to help you clean up your source code. Some of the most important debugging windows are shown in Figure 6-12.

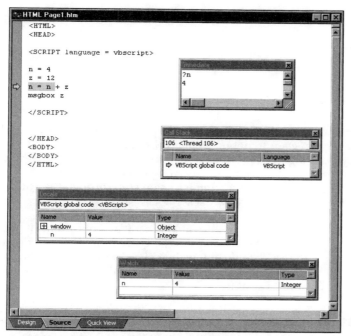

Figure 6-12: VI's various debugging tools in action. Here we're single-stepping through a script.

Note

You might see a Build menu between the Project Menu and the Debug menu. The VI IDE is supposed to share a common shell with other Microsoft RAD (Rapid Application Development) tools, such as Visual J++ and Visual FoxPro. Because there is a possibility that you'll have Java applets in your projects or you'll be using FoxPro, some menu items (and the entire Build menu) appear in the VI IDE. You would expect that if you don't have FoxPro installed on your machine, or don't use Java applets, the Build menu and other menu items would not appear, or would at least be gray (disabled). This is not the case. But the Build menu does not concern you here; instead, consider the Debug menu, which, if you're a programmer, concerns you greatly.

To try VI's primary debugging tools, add a new HTML page to a project, and then type this source code:

```
<HTML>
<HEAD>
<SCRIPT language = vbscript>
n = 4
z = 12
```

```
n = n + z
msgbox z
</SCRIPT>

</HEAD>
<BODY>
</BODY>
</HTML>
```

Now right-click this .htm file in Project Explorer and choose Set as Start Page. (You must do this whenever you want to debug a page.) Now start single-stepping through the code by pressing F11. Notice several debug windows automatically appear, as shown in Figure 6-12. Also, a yellow arrow is displayed in the edit window showing where your current location is as you step through the code. And the current line is displayed with a yellow back-color.

The Locals window is a relatively new feature in Microsoft's applications. If you want to watch the contents of *all* the variables in the current procedure, you don't have to add each of them to the Watch window. Just click View ⇨ Debug Windows ⇨ Locals and press F11 to step through your programming while the Locals window displays the state of every local variable.

Break on expression

VI includes numerous debugging facilities, and one of the most important to any debugging job is generally called *break on expression*. Most debuggers have a way you can specify, for example, the break on whatever line causes the variable z to go below zero (if $Z < 0$). The VI debugger handles this a bit differently but provides all the functionality you'll need. In most debuggers, you can have the debugger keep an eye on one or more variables, and break to display a line where something anomalous took place. Assume that, for reasons you can't figure out, the total employees' figure for your company (held in variable *empl*) goes negative while your program is running. This is an impossibility, yet there it is onscreen: you have minus 12 employees. This kind of error is harder to track down in VI because you cannot set an intelligent breakpoint. We would want to set an expression such as this: *empl < 0*. Then, when the value in the variable *empl* falls below zero, VI could halt the program and display the offending line where this impossible condition becomes true.

To use VI's break on expression facility, select Breakpoints in the Debug menu, and then click the Add button in the Breakpoints dialog box. The New Script Breakpoint dialog box appears and you can describe various kinds of conditional breaks. The Name field is unusual in debuggers: it refers to the function or sub's name.

Several kinds of stepping

VI offers several kinds of stepping, in addition to pressing F11 to single-step through the program. You can Step Over (F10), which is like single-stepping, but it will skip over a procedure (if you're about to step into one). This way you can avoid stepping through a procedure that's been tested and is known good.

You'll find a Step Out (Shift+F11) feature, which is quite new to debugging suites. It speeds through any remaining lines of programming in the current procedure, then stops on the next line in your program outside the current procedure. If you're within a procedure that you're confident isn't causing the bug, Step Out and then resume single-stepping once you're past the current procedure.

Also relatively new is the Run To Cursor (Ctrl+F10) feature. You can click in the programming code somewhere other than your current location. This moves the *insertion cursor*, the blinking vertical line. Press Ctrl+F10 and VI will rapidly execute all the lines between your current location in the code and the location where you placed the cursor. The yellow arrow and yellow back-color will also move to catch up with the location of the cursor.

Toggle breakpoints

If there's a location within the programming code where you want VB to stop during execution, press F9 or click in the left margin of the code window. Either action inserts a breakpoint and displays a red dot. VB will halt execution at this location. You can insert as many breakpoints as you wish. Pressing F9 a second time, or clicking the red dot in the margin, toggles the breakpoint off. VI has a new feature unseen in other debuggers: Disable or Enable Breakpoint (Ctrl+F9). This doesn't delete the breakpoint but merely disables it temporarily. It's also a toggle so you can switch back and forth between enabling and disabling a breakpoint.

You can clear all the breakpoints in your entire program by pressing Ctrl+Shift+F9 (or selecting Clear All Breakpoints in the Debug menu). Pressing Ctrl+B brings up a dialog box with a complete list of all breakpoints in the entire Web application.

Similarly, clicking the Processes item brings up a Processes dialog box that enables you to attach (or detach) the debugger to a running process. You'll see a list of all currently running processes. You can also use this dialog box to halt execution of a process. The Machines list in this window includes all machines to which you're currently connected. The Process, Language, and Debugger pane shows all currently running processes on the machine you selected in the Machines list. Note that the Debug menu also includes a Detach All Processes option that accomplishes mass detaching in one fell swoop.

The Set Next Statement option enables you to skip over some source code while stepping. Assume that you don't want some lines executed, but you want to see what happens when you step through the code following those lines. Just click in the code to place the insertion cursor where you want to resume execution (or stepping). Then press Ctrl+Shift+F10 to make this line the next line to be executed when you resume running or stepping. This would be useful if there was a large For...Next loop, for example, that you want to skip over rather than try to single-step through.

The Show Next Statement item merely displays which statement will be the next one executed. Use this if you forgot where you *Set Next Statement*.

One debugging window you might wonder about (available in the View menu) is the Auto window. It's designed to show you the values of all variables within the scope of currently executing code. The Locals window displays the variables for a single thread, but the Auto window displays *all* threads simultaneously (as long as the variable is in scope).

The HTML menu

The items on the HTML menu, shown in Figure 6-13, are relatively simple and merely offer some shortcuts when you're typing HTML source code.

Figure 6-13: The HTML menu options

✦ If you choose the **Link** option, a small dialog box pops up asking you to fill in the URL for the hyperlink. Then, when you click OK (assuming you typed **www.microsoft.com)**, VI adds the necessary HTML source code to define this as a hyperlink:

```
<A HREF="http://www.microsoft.com"></A>
```

✦ The **Image** option is a rather simple dialog box, enabling you to insert a graphic into your page (for this kind of work, you're better off using FrontPage).

The Table menu

The Table menu, shown in Figure 6-14, is also comparatively straightforward. It assists you in creating and structuring a table. For this task, however, you'll likely find FrontPage's tools more accommodating and efficient.

Figure 6-14: The Table menu options

The Format menu

Although you can format text and manage some simple object (component) formatting (positioning) easily enough in VI, you're generally better off working with visual content in FrontPage. Nonetheless, here are the main points of the Format menu, shown in Figure 6-15.

Figure 6-15: The Format menu options

✦ The **Absolute Positioning** feature enables you to move components around a page to locate them in specified (rather than relative) positions. To use this feature, click the Design view tab, and then drag an option button or some other component onto the editor. With that component selected, choose Absolute Positioning. You'll now be able to drag the component around on the page to move it to a particular location. VI will add the necessary HTML source code to ensure that your component appears where you want it. Here's an example:

```
<INPUT id=radio1 name=radio1
style="LEFT: 198px; POSITION: absolute; TOP: 118px;
 Z-INDEX: 100"
type=radio>
```

✦ Click the **Lock** option to prevent further movement of this control. The selection frame around your component changes (the small, square drag handles disappear). You can toggle locking on and off.

✦ **Z Order** is the third dimension (in addition to *x*, horizontal, and *y*, vertical) when specifying the position of an object. On a two-dimensional plane such as the computer monitor, Z Order specifies which object will appear on top when two objects overlap.

The Tools menu

The Tools menu, shown in Figure 6-16, is traditionally where Microsoft places features that don't fit comfortably in other categories (such as the Format menu).

Figure 6-16: The Tools menu options

✦ The **Publish Component** option brings up the Visual Component Manager Publish Wizard, which helps you register a component so it can be used by other applications. The wizard helps you specify how the component should be stored, how it can be searched for, and how it interacts with IDEs. You can add descriptions of your component, optional source code, optional dependency files, your name, and other peripheral data.

✦ The **View Links on WWW** option brings up a small dialog box enabling you to view a link diagram of any Web page on the Internet. For a cheap thrill, try looking at a massive site like Microsoft's home page. For details on Link view, see Chapter 24.

✦ If you're in Design view, the **Absolute Mode** option appears in the Tools menu. With this enabled, you can freely drag objects around on the page. (It's the same effect as choosing Absolute Positioning from the Format menu, only this option is global to all components.)

Note

Absolute Mode is theoretical at this time; the feature isn't yet working. Likewise, the Snap to Grid option theoretically forces components to line up with an invisible grid, making it easier for you to create good-looking pages (things aren't "just a little off" when you try to align controls, such as a vertical column of buttons). You can specify the granularity of this grid by editing the Horizontal and Vertical Spacing boxes in the HTML Editor section of Tools|Options.

✦ The **Customize Toolbox** option brings up the dialog box, shown in Figure 6-17.

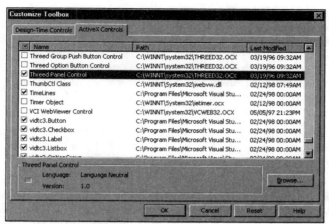

Figure 6-17: Use the Customize Toolbox to add DTCs or ActiveX components.

Do you recall the Project References dialog box discussed earlier in "The Project menu?" When you attach a library of objects to your project, you can then place those objects into your Web pages. However, to simplify the process of adding the objects to your source code (to have VI generate the necessary complicated OBJECT code), you'll want to add objects to your Toolbox. Then, you can just drag objects onto a page and all the rest of the work is done for you. It's here, in the Customize Toolbox dialog box, that you can select which objects to put onto the Toolbox.

Add-ins are one way that RAD IDEs are extensible, enabling you to attach wizards or other utilities to the IDE. These can either be wizards and utilities you've written yourself, or some you've bought from third-party developers. In any case, once an add-in has been properly registered on your system, you can then attach it to your IDE.

Note

At present, no add-ins are available for the VI IDE. This feature is therefore only theo-retical. However, add-ins have been a feature of other RAD applications for several years. The Component Manager (see "The View menu" earlier in this chapter) is an add-in, though in VI, it's a default utility that's part of the menu system from the get go.

✦ The **Options** window reveals a huge collection of customizable features. This is probably the most important feature on most Microsoft Tools menus; it enables you to customize the application. Take a look at those options whose purpose isn't obvious.

- First, under the Environment | General category in Options is the **SDI Environment** feature. By default, VI offers the MDI (Multiple Document Interface), which means VI's main window contains all other child windows — like the editor, the Toolbox, Project Explorer — within it. Move the main window and all the others move with it. By contrast, you can choose the SDI (Single Document Interface) whereby all the child windows are not contained within the main VI window; rather, they reside on the desktop as independent windows.

- We discussed the highly useful **Keyboard** options earlier in this chapter. This feature enables you to associate shortcut key combinations with most of VI's features.

- **Clickwait** (see Text Editor ➪ General in the Options dialog box) is a specification you can edit that permits you to click in a different window (to give it the focus), but the insertion point does not go to this new window. In other words, if you set the Clickwait to 1000 milliseconds, and you press the mouse button before 1 second elapses, the insertion point will not move.

✦ **Drag-and-Drop Editing** means you can select some text in the source code and then drag it and drop it to a new location in the editor window.

✦ On the Debugger ➪ General page, you see an option entitled **Just-in-time debugging**. With this option turned on, the debugger starts immediately if remote procedures execute, or whenever an error is detected in an executing script.

Use the Data Tools ➪ Database Projects page to tell VI which SQL commands to include in the scripts it creates when you use the Copy Script command from the shortcut menu in Data view. VI selects all these options by default. While you can remove these commands from the script file, these options will save you time.

✦ In the **Script details** section, select **Include drop script** if you want VI to include DROP SQL commands in the script. Select **Include permission script** if you want VI to include the permission SQL commands such as GRANT.

✦ In the **Table script details** section, select **Include table indexes** if you want VI to include SQL commands that create table indexes in the script. Select **Include triggers** if you want VI to include SQL commands that define table triggers in the script. Select **Include keys/DRI** if you want VI to include SQL commands that define table keys and declarative referential integrity in the script.

✦ The **HTML Editor page** includes Horizontal and Vertical Spacing boxes where you can define the resolution of the grid used with the Snap to Grid feature (discussed earlier in this chapter).

✦ The **Sign Cabinet option** on the Security|Authentication page of the Options window adds a digital signature to a .cab file in your project. This process — embedding a signature — tells people who download your project into their browsers that it can be traced back to you. In other words, you're stamping the name of your company on the project and presumably guaranteeing to the recipient that there are no viruses in any code or embedded objects (such as ActiveX components) in your code. If a signed Web page component does harm, somebody can be held responsible. A third-party company authorizes you (the control's creator) to "sign" your control. This third party maintains your name and address so if anything goes wrong, everyone knows where to pin the blame: on you. I'm not sure that this level of security offers much true security. Bad people can get digital signatures.

The Windows menu

The only obscure item on the Windows menu, shown in Figure 6-18, is the Dockable option (a toggle). When selected (the default), the child windows (such as Toolbox, editor, and all the other windows within the main VI window) attach themselves to the inner frame of the main window, or even to each other, forming compound windows. This effect bothers some people; it's as if the child windows all become magnetic, rather forcefully magnetic. Move them too close and whammo, they attach themselves. It's easier to experience this effect than learn about it from reading a description. Try turning Dockable off and drag the inner VI windows around to reposition them. Then turn Dockable on and drag them around again, noticing that they don't always stay put where you drop them. Also see how this effect interacts with the SDI and MDI toggle described earlier in this chapter.

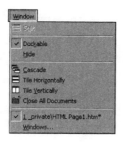

Figure 6-18: The Window menu options

Customizing the Toolbars

The toolbars offer convenient shortcuts, containing icons that trigger most of the items found on most of the menus. As with most recent Microsoft applications, you can rearrange the toolbars to suit yourself — just drag them by the "handles" on their left side (or top side, if you've attached one to either side of the IDE). If a toolbar is not attached to one of the side frames of the IDE, it's just another child window and can be positioned by dragging its title bar.

Beyond positioning, you can further customize the toolbars by right-clicking any toolbar and choosing Customize in the context menu. In the Customize Toolbars dialog box, click the Toolbars tab, and then click the New button to create a totally customized toolbar of your own. The Reset button on that page restores the currently selected toolbar to the factory default set of icons, eliminating any editing you might have done to the toolbar.

While the Customize Toolbars dialog box is visible, you can drag icons to rearrange them within a toolbar, or drag an icon off the toolbar to remove it. To add an icon to a toolbar, drag it from the Commands window in the Commands tab page onto the toolbar and drop it where you want it to appear. As you can see in Figure 6-19, there are many other ways you can customize toolbars, including changing the description that pops up when you hover your mouse cursor over an icon (change the Name item). If you choose the Edit Button Image option, a little graphic utility pops up with the button's icon loaded in it. You can do whatever you want to redesign that icon. Note the Image and Text option. Select this if you have trouble remembering what an icon does; a text description will be added to the graphic. The Begin a Group option adds one of those subtle vertical lines that cluster sets of related icons, visually segregating them from other icons on the toolbar. I find it useful to create one custom toolbar that includes all my most frequently used VI features — then they're only a click away.

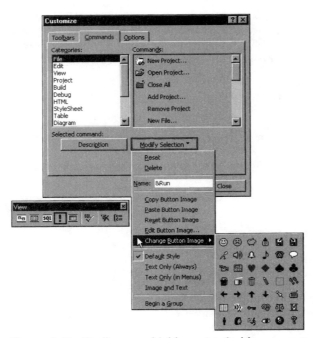

Figure 6-19: Toolbars are highly customizable; you can even create your own icons from scratch using the Edit Button Image feature.

Summary

The goal in this chapter was to make sure you're familiar with all the utilities, features, and capabilities of Visual InterDev's powerful IDE. You many never use some of them. You may never use many of them, but after finishing this chapter, you've got an overview of what the IDE offers and you've discovered the tools that apply to the kind of work you'll be doing with VI. In this chapter, you learned:

✦ How to create a home page using the Source Editor

✦ How to switch between the three views of the main editor with a click

- The *Design view* is where you position, resize, and drag and drop components into a Web page. It is semi-WYSIWYG, but not everything behaves as it will when loaded into a browser (although it may look similar).

- The *Source view* is a full-featured programming editor where you work on HTML and script source code.

- The *Quick view* is a full-WYSIWYG window where you can test the behaviors of objects in your Web page as well as see how things look. You can't do any editing in this window, however.

✦ How the Toolbox works, with a repository of components, predesigned controls, and other objects, such as the new scriptlets objects

✦ How to use the Project Explorer window; it's your overall tree view of the folders and files that collectively make up the Web site on which you're working

✦ How the Properties window enables you to view, or edit, the various qualities of a component

✦ How to employ different menu features in the File, Edit, View, Project, Debug, HTML, Table, Format, Tools, and Windows menus

✦ How to customize Visual InterDev with the Options dialog box

✦ How to manage and personalize your toolbars

✦   ✦   ✦

Using FrontPage 98

Sometimes the shortest distance between two points is FrontPage. Designed for nonprogrammers — artists, designers, writers, CEOs — FrontPage (FP) includes dozens of useful utilities, shortcuts, prewritten solutions, and other aids to accomplish Web-programming goals quickly. As you'll see, a familiarity with FrontPage can often save you considerable time.

In many ways FP is superior to Visual InterDev as a Web design environment. For example, you can create a frame or table from scratch by writing the necessary HTML source code. Or, you can more quickly *visually* design and drop graphics files, frames, tables, and other complex HTML constructs into existing source code by using FrontPage's efficient tools. VI also supports some of these visual design features (you can, for example, drag a table to resize it in VI's Design view). However, many of FP's capabilities are clearly superior — much more extensive and more efficient — than VI's.

Note

At present, the FP source code editor (HTML view) is quite annoying if you're trying to type in code by hand then test it in Preview mode. FP has the nasty habit of imposing its own ideas about source code formatting. If you switch to Preview view, then back to HTML view, you might be surprised at what's been done to "improve" your formatting. Even if this unpleasant reformatting is eliminated by the time the product ships, FP will still remain inferior for hand-programming. The VI editor is superior for writing script and HTML: the VI editor is more of a programmer's environment than the FP editor.

In this chapter, you find out which aspects of Web creation are best accomplished using FP. First you see how to use the FP Corporate Presence Web Wizard to rapidly build a Web site that helps sell a company's products. You discover how easy it is to create a table, insert content, and then format and modify the table. There are times you'll want to write low-level

HTML and create your own script or components. But building the visual interface for an entire, coherent Web isn't one of those times.

This chapter also demonstrates how easy it is to create framesets in FP and accomplish other sophisticated tasks much more quickly than trying to hand-code them from scratch in Visual InterDev. Many kinds of Web programming are best accomplished with VI (writing and testing script, and managing team site development, for example), but in many other situations FP is the tool that proves simpler, more efficient, and more pleasant — or all three.

Note   When menus or toolbars are mentioned in this chapter, it is the FP editor (and its Normal view) that you're intended to use. In those rare cases where the FP Explorer is required (notably to create a Web-wide shared border), you are explicitly told to switch to the Explorer.

Exploring Web Wizards

There are several design-time tools you can use with VI and FP, either built-in or available for adding onto the two editors. These tools have various names — design-time controls, wizards, and templates — and each tool performs slightly differently, though they all endeavor to make life easier for programmers and developers.

Note   For a discussion of the Form Page Wizard, see Chapter 8. That wizard is useful if you want to construct a custom form that accepts input from visitors to your site.

Design-time controls (DTC) are ActiveX components that usually have no user interface but can be dropped into an HTML page. Like a wizard (when the wizard is part of a programming editor), a DTC usually generates source code (HTML or script). The programmer typically makes changes to a DTC's Properties dialog box and those changes are then automatically generated (or adjusted) within the source code.

Wizards, by contrast, step you through a series of dialog boxes to create their source code. Therefore, if you want to make change later, you would directly edit the source code deposited by a wizard, or re-run the wizard. However, to make changes to the code generated by a DTC, you right-click it and make your changes in its properties pages. For now, try using one of the Web-design wizards built into FP.

Note   A *template* produces results similar to a Web-design wizard, but a template is a completed Web that you can adjust to suit your needs by editing the source code. By contrast, a Web-design wizard steps you through a series of dialog boxes, then generates more or less complete source code for you after you've finished going through the dialog box. The code generated by a wizard typically requires little, if any, editing.

Assume you've been given the job of creating a corporate Web site for Ajax Instruments and you must build in a table. Follow these steps to invoke the Corporate Presence Web Wizard in FrontPage:

1. Launch FrontPage Explorer, and then click OK, as shown in Figure 7-1.

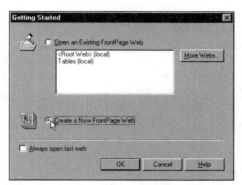

Figure 7-1: This startup dialog box always appears when you first run FrontPage, unless you select the Always open last web option.

Tip

You can toggle the startup dialog box by choosing Options from the FrontPage Explorer Tools menu. In the General tab, choose Show Getting Started Dialog.

If the startup dialog box does not appear, you can go to File | New | Create a New FrontPage Web.

2. Choose Corporate Presence Wizard, name the project **Ajax**, and click OK, as shown in Figure 7-2.

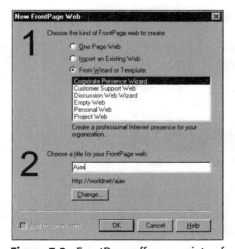

Figure 7-2: FrontPage offers a variety of prebuilt sites and wizards.

3. You see a list of optional pages for your sites. For this example, leave only Products/Services selected, as shown in Figure 7-3. Click Next.

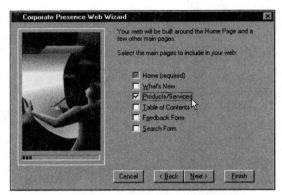

Figure 7-3: Many common site management tasks are automated in FrontPage. For this example, we're limiting ourselves to the Home page and Products/Services frameworks.

4. Leave Mission Statement and Contact Information selected, as shown in Figure 7-4. Click Next.

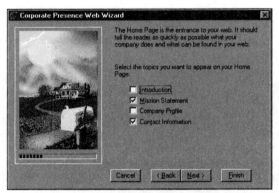

Figure 7-4: The home page designer features four options.

5. The next dialog box asks you how many products and services pages you want to create. Choose zero products and zero services. Click Next.

6. For the running title at the top of each of your pages, leave the defaults as shown in Figure 7-5. Click Next.

7. Choose not to use the Under Construction icon. Click Next.

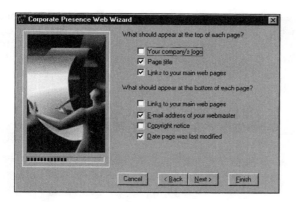

Figure 7-5: In this dialog box, you can specify the running title for each page.

8. Fill in the name and address of your company. Click Next and fill in the phone, fax, and e-mail addresses. Click Next again.

9. Choose the theme for your Web site. Microsoft provides a generous set of professionally designed "looks" from which you can select what best suits your needs. Elements of the page — buttons, check boxes, lines, backgrounds, fonts, and font colors — are all designed to coordinate and provide visual appeal. For Ajax, choose the Automotive theme, as shown in Figure 7-6.

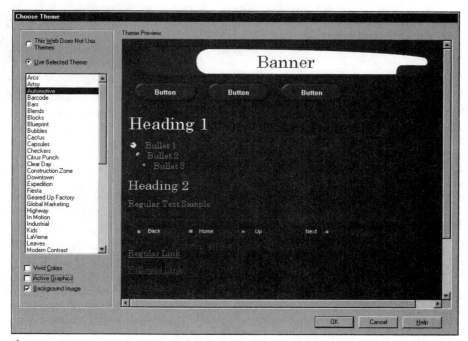

Figure 7-6: FrontPage comes with a large set of predesigned themes that add visual appeal to your Web sites. This is the Automotive theme.

Don't neglect the Active Graphics option in the Theme dialog box. It changes the themes in various ways (usually additional detail, more color variety, 3D effects, and gradients). Clicking the Active Graphics check box transforms the Automotive theme, shown in Figure 7-6, into the more detailed and dynamic version, shown in Figure 7-7. If you compare these two figures, you see Figure 7-6 shows the Automotive theme but without Active Graphics.

Figure 7-7: The Active Graphics option should usually be left selected; it adds value to the design.

10. Click OK to close the Themes dialog box and click Next. Agree to see the Tasks view (displaying the wizard's suggested edits to your site) and click Finish. The wizard suggests that you replace its generic text with something more specific to Ajax. (You probably would have thought of that yourself.)

Now go see the results of your labors. In FrontPage Explorer, select Folder view and double-click Default.htm. You should see something like the preview shown in Figure 7-8. (Click the Preview tab at the bottom of the FrontPage editor.)

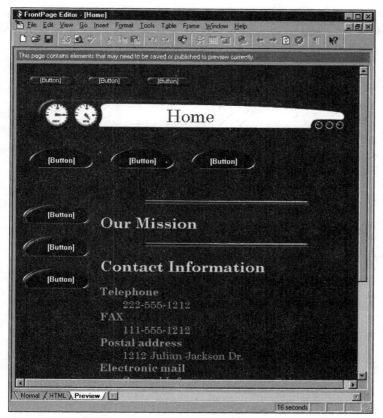

Figure 7-8: With FrontPage, it only takes a few minutes to create the main elements of a complex, attractive Web site.

Now you need to customize the generic text and add the table that the people at Ajax want, a table comparing the three automobiles they offer for sale.

Listing 7-1 shows the HTML that FrontPage's wizard created for you.

Listing 7-1: **FrontPage's Suggested HTML Source Code**

```html
<html>

<head>
<title>Home</title>
```

(continued)

Listing 7-1 *(continued)*

```
<meta name="Microsoft Theme" content="auto 011, default">
<meta name="Microsoft Border" content="tlb, default">
</head>

<body>

<p><!--Webbot bot="PurpleText"
preview="Write an introductory paragraph for your home page
here. This is like the front door to your home on the Internet.
Invite visitors to step in and have a look around. "
--></p>

<hr align="center">

<h2>Our Mission</h2>

<p><!--Webbot bot="PurpleText"
preview="Write one or two short sentences that describe your
company's philosophy and ambitions. Something like, 'To become
the leading provider of ...'."
--> </p>

<hr align="center">

<h2>Contact Information</h2>

<p><!--Webbot bot="PurpleText"
preview="Tell readers how to get in touch with you.
Remember that people can connect to your Web from
anywhere in the world; so provide international versions
of telephone and fax numbers. It's also customary to
provide e-mail addresses for key contact points, such as
sales and customer support. "
--></p>

<dl>
  <dt><strong>Telephone</strong> </dt>
  <dd><!--Webbot bot="Substitution" s-variable="CompanyPhone"
--></dd>
  <dt><strong>FAX</strong> </dt>
  <dd><!--Webbot bot="Substitution" s-variable="CompanyFAX"
</dd --> </dd>
  <dt><strong>Postal address</strong> </dt>
  <dd><!--Webbot bot="Substitution" s-variable="CompanyAddress"
--></dd>
  <dt><strong>Electronic mail</strong> </dt>
```

```
    <dd>General Information: <a
href="mailto:someone@ajax.com">someone@ajax.com</a><br>
    Sales: <br>
    Customer Support: <br>
    Webmaster: <a
href="mailto:someone@ajax.com">someone@ajax.com</a></dd>
</dl>
 </body>
</html>
```

There are three sections within this source code described as "PurpleText;" they are the areas you should replace with your own text. Each of these sections is a comment and is colored green (the FrontPage editor's default color scheme for comments). When you replace the text, you must remove the HTML comment tags (`<!--` and `-->`) surrounding your new text. A browser ignores (does not display) any text falling between the `<!` and `-->` symbols, because those symbols enclose a comment, a note that the HTML programmer wrote to himself or herself as a reminder.

Creating a table

Ajax wants a comparison table that provides the names, weights, MPG, and cost of each of the three car kits it sells. Figure 7-9 shows how easy it is to create a table in FP.

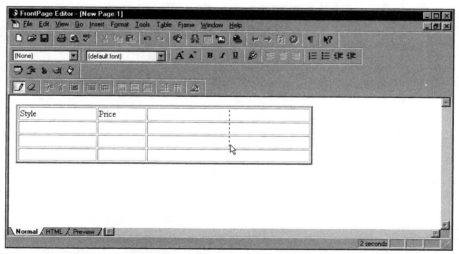

Figure 7-9: It's easy to draw the rows and columns of your table.

One way to go about creating the table is to hand-program an HTML page, like the one shown in Listing 7-2, but that would be a tedious process.

Listing 7-2: Ajax's Comparison Table HTML

```
<html>

<head>
<title>Model</title>
<meta name="GENERATOR" content="Microsoft FrontPage 3.0">
</head>

<body>

<table border="4" width="100%" background="RIBBED.jpg"
height="100">
  <tr>
    <td width="24%" height="19">Model</td>
    <td width="26%" height="19">Price</td>
    <td width="25%" height="19">MPG</td>
    <td width="25%" height="19">Weight</td>
  </tr>
  <tr>
    <td width="24%" height="19">Borgonzoala</td>
    <td width="26%" height="19">$44,500</td>
    <td width="25%" height="19">14</td>
    <td width="25%" height="19">12,000</td>
  </tr>
  <tr>
    <td width="24%" height="19">Tostastas</td>
    <td width="26%" height="19">$88,900</td>
    <td width="25%" height="19">12</td>
    <td width="25%" height="19">16,880</td>
  </tr>
  <tr>
    <td width="24%" height="19">Bandiaria</td>
    <td width="26%" height="19">$156,000</td>
    <td width="25%" height="19">10</td>
    <td width="25%" height="19">14,000</td>
  </tr>
</table>
</body>
</html>
```

Designing the table

Or you can design the table graphically, which is much, much easier. Follow these steps to design and modify a table:

1. Start a new page in the FrontPage editor. From the View menu, select the following toolbars: Standard, Format, and Table. Click the Normal tab to put yourself in the editor's design mode.

2. Click the blank page icon at the top left of the Standard toolbar to start a new page.

3. From the Table menu, choose Insert Table (or, if you want to just drag a pencil icon to create the table, choose Draw Table).

4. An Insert Table dialog box appears. Choose 4 rows and 2 columns. Click OK.

5. Your new table should look like the one in Figure 7-10.

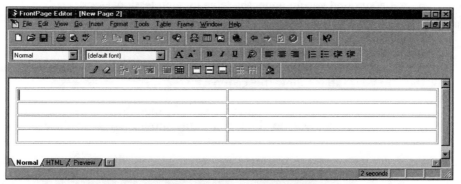

Figure 7-10: You can design a table easily using FP's Table menu.

To add a background texture under the table, follow these steps:

1. Right-click the table and choose Table Properties from the pop-up menu.

> **Tip**
>
> To add a texture (or color) as the background for *individual cells* in a table, put your cursor in the cell you want to change and then right-click and choose Cell Properties from the pop-up menu.

2. Select Use Background Image and locate a .gif or .jpg graphic that you want to insert as the background, as shown in Figure 7-11.

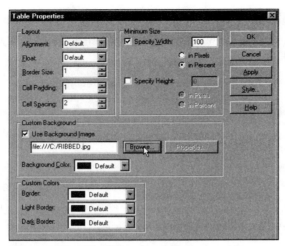

Figure 7-11: This dialog box helps you add a background texture under the table for a professional look.

Formatting

Ajax would like the table to have a frame and additional columns and text. To add them to your table, follow these steps:

1. To provide a frame around the table, change the Border Size option to 4. Click OK to close the dialog box. Your table should now look like Figure 7-12.

Figure 7-12: We've added texture and a wide border to the table.

2. It's time to add two more columns. Click the Draw Table icon on the Table toolbar (see Figure 7-13). Your cursor turns into a pencil and you can draw two vertical lines, thereby creating four columns in the table (refer to Figure 7-9).

Figure 7-13: The Table toolbar enables you to design a table as easily as you would sketch one with pencil and paper.

3. Right-click the blank background in the editor to change the pencil cursor back to the default I-beam cursor (indicating text-insertion mode). (You can alternatively click the pencil Draw Table icon to toggle it off.) Now you can type the text into the cells of the table.

4. Click the upper-left cell and type **Model**, press Tab to move to the next cell and type **Price**. Continue this typing and tabbing until you get the result shown in Figure 7-14.

Model	Price	MPG	Weight
Borgonzoala	$44,500	14	12,000
Tostastas	$88,900	12	16,880
Bandiaria	$156,000	10	14,000

Figure 7-14: At this point, all the text has been inserted into the table.

Further adjustments

The table looks good, but you may want to adjust the font, font size, and spacing of the columns. To do so, follow these steps:

1. Drag your mouse so you highlight just the first row: the headings Model, Price and so on.

2. In the Format toolbar, drop down the Fonts list and change the font to Arial Black or some other font that distinguishes it from the font used in the body of the table.

3. Highlight all the rest of the cells in the body of the table and click the large A icon next to the Fonts list box (in the Format toolbar) if you want to increase the text size.

4. Finally, move your cursor onto one of the vertical lines that separates the columns. The cursor changes to a double-tipped horizontal arrow. Drag the column lines, if you wish, to eliminate most of the wasted blank space in the table. The final result of our fiddling is shown in Figure 7-15.

Model	Price	MPG	Weight
Borgonzoala	$44,500	14	12,000
Tostastas	$88,900	12	16,880
Bandiaria	$156,000	10	14,000

Figure 7-15: After you readjusted the table, it now looks balanced and tightly zoned.

Using the Frames Wizard

Another useful feature in FP is the Frames Wizard. It simplifies creating multi-pane pages. In FrontPage 98, you can manipulate WYSIWYG frames *graphically.* You can either modify existing FP templates or work with your own, original grid. In either case, FP, as usual, does all the HTML source code programming for you. This next example illustrates a variety of useful FP tools, including ways to modify existing Web sites (how to change home pages and adjust internal links), how to add and modify Active Elements (a hover button), as well as various techniques involving frames.

Tip

When you're working with frames in FP, two additional tabs appear at the bottom of the editor. With the No Frames view, you can see how your page will appear to users who have browsers without frame capability.

Now, suppose you want to create a home page for the Ajax Instruments Web site and this page should present general information on a large, right pane while displaying various navigational links in a narrow, left pane. HTML frames are frequently employed in this fashion to divide a page into two zones: links and contents. Frames enable you to subdivide a Web page into child pages, much the same way you can organize (tile) several documents for simultaneous viewing within a word processor editing window. This technique — windows within windows — is sometimes referred to as a *Multiple Document Interface (MDI).*

Adding a frame to a page

FP has no toolbar dedicated to frames, but there is a menu. Follow these steps to add a frame to a page:

1. Start in Normal view in the FP editor and select New Frame Page from the Frames menu.

2. Choose the Contents template, as shown in Figure 7-16. This brings up the template, as displayed in Figure 7-17.

3. It's been decided that the existing home page (created earlier in this chapter for Ajax Instruments) is to be the home page in the right frame. Click Set Initial Page within the larger frame.

Tip

When using frames, avoid using shared borders or a Navigation bar. These latter two techniques are alternative ways a user can navigate a site. Frames serve the same purpose.

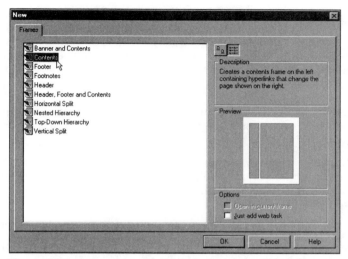

Figure 7-16: FP comes with this set of popular frame layouts.

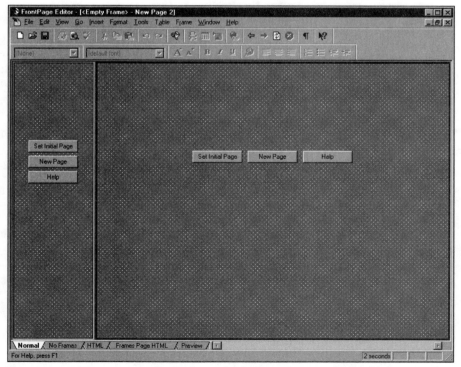

Figure 7-17: FP automatically displays a basic frame layout, along with buttons that enable you to insert an existing or new page into the frames.

Editing frames

While in Ajax's home page, notice that it already contains several buttons the user can click to navigate the site. When you're working in the Normal view of the FP editor, you can edit frames just as you would edit ordinary Web pages. To do so, follow these steps:

1. Select the buttons on the left of the home page (and also those at the top — Home, Feedback, and so on). In other words, remove all buttons from the home page.

2. In the left pane, you now want to create some links to the locations that used to be targeted by the buttons you just removed. Click the New button in the left pane. You get a blank page, but it conforms to the style that governs your entire Ajax site.

3. Select Hover Button from the Active Elements option in the Insert menu.

4. For Button Text, type **News**. Then click the Browse button and double-click the News.htm file to insert it as the Link-to item in the Hover Button dialog box. Adjust the button color, effect, and other qualities of your new button to suit your tastes. You can even add sounds or insert your own choice of graphics on the button by clicking the Custom button in the dialog box.

5. Add additional buttons for Home, Products, and Services. An easy way to do this is to select, then copy and paste, the existing News button. Click the HTML tab and edit each `<param name="text" value="News">` line to change the `value=` to **Home, Products, or Services**. This way you don't have to repeatedly select the qualities of each new button to make them match the original hover button's colors, effect, and so on.

6. Adjust each new button's target as well (`<param name="url" value="http://rtm/myWeb/news.htm" valuetype="ref">` by changing `news.htm` to the appropriate target.htm file. (Home is Default.htm, Services is Services.htm, and so on.).

Tip

An easy way to see the relationships and filenames of your site's pages is to select Navigation view in the FP Explorer, as shown in Figure 7-18.

From the File menu, choose Save, then save the large pane as NewHome and the smaller left pane as NewPane.

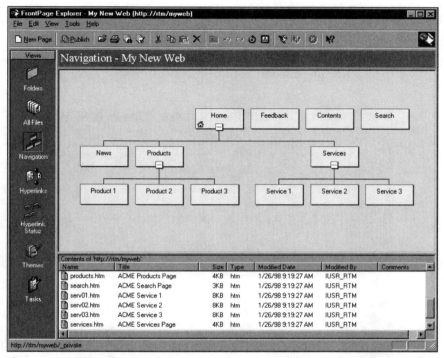

Figure 7-18: In Navigation view, you can get a complete overview of your Web site and also find out the filenames of your pages so you can create links to them easily.

Changing the home page

At this point, you want to make the right pane (NewHome.htm) the home page of this Website. Follow these steps to make a different page into your home page, in this case, a frame:

1. Select All Files view in the FP Explorer. Right-click the current home page (Default.htm), select Rename from the pop-up menu, and then type a different name (**OldHome.htm**).

2. You are notified that hyperlinks are involved. Select No (you don't want them recalculated).

3. Right-click NewHome.htm, choose Rename, and type **Default.htm** to make it the new home page. Agree to let the hyperlinks be recalculated to this page.

4. Select Explorer's Hyperlinks view, right-click, and choose Delete to remove the OldHome and, if it exists, also remove the Table of Contents files from this site.

5. Click the small + symbol in the NewPane icon to expand its links. You should see a schematic similar to the one shown in Figure 7-19.

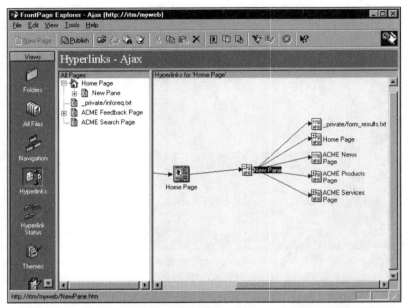

Figure 7-19: This diagram illustrates that your new home page is linked to the NewPane (the left frame) and shows that NewPane has five links.

Using Forms

Forms are HTML's way for a user to send information to your Web site. You can put various input components (text boxes, check boxes, and so on) and also graphics and most other classic Web page elements onto a form.

The HTML code necessary to construct a form and its various fields can be tedious to write from scratch but, as is so often the case, FP makes the job easy, enabling you to construct forms and their various fields by merely choosing from a menu, rather than by writing all the low-level source code.

It's traditional to display two buttons to the user on a form: Reset and Submit. Any user input is erased if the person clicks Reset. The input is sent to your Web site if the user clicks Submit. In the past, the user data was added to a database or a text file on the Web site server, requiring that the database or file be regularly checked for new submissions. However, it is often preferable to have user data sent as e-mail — that way you always know immediately and conveniently that someone has submitted information. FP has a provision to make e-mail the target of a form's handler. (A *handler* is triggered when the user clicks Submit. It takes care of sending the data back to the Web site.) FP also enables you to choose from a variety of different form handlers to suit your needs.

Follow these steps to add a form and some fields to a Web site in FP:

1. In FP's File menu, choose New, and then choose Normal Page.

2. Place your insertion cursor on the page where you want the form to be located (click there with the mouse).

3. Choose Form Field, One-line TextBox from the Insert menu. By adding a Form *Field* (a field is a component like a radio button or text box), you cause FP to build a new form. Notice, too, that FP creates Submit and Reset buttons on the form by default. It always does this unless the form field you select is a "push button."

Note

Unfortunately, the growth of computer languages is not overseen by any governing body that could enforce reasonable consistency. For example, you'll have to memorize the odd usage of *field* when referring to an object like a check box placed onto a form. In other contexts, these objects are called *controls* or *components,* which makes much more sense.

After you complete the three steps described previously, you'll find this rather interesting HTML that FP created underneath the visible surface of the page:

```
<form method="POST" action="--WEBBOT-SELF--">
  <!--Webbot bot="SaveResults" U-
File="http://rtm/myWeb/_private/form_results.txt"
  S-Format="TEXT/CSV" S-Label-Fields="TRUE" --><p><input
type="text" name="T1" size="20"><input
  type="submit" value="Submit" name="B1"><input type="reset"
value="Reset" name="B2"></p>
</form>
```

FP inserted a *WebBot* (now called a *FrontPage component*). This is an object that performs a service — a small utility encapsulated and sealed off from the rest of the application it serves. WebBots are similar to an ActiveX or Java component. Note as well that the default location where the user's data will be sent is a file named form_results.txt that is located in a subdirectory named _private in your Web site.

The following list provides methods for adding functionality to your forms:

✦ **Submitting user input to e-mail** — If you would prefer that user input be submitted to your e-mail address instead of a text file, right-click the form and choose Form Properties from the pop-up menu. Then erase the file path and fill in your e-mail address instead. Also notice the other tabs in the Options for

Saving Results of a Form dialog box. On the Email Results tab, you can choose various formats (HTML, plain text, and several kinds of database-formatted text with different delimiters). You can also specify such options as the e-mail's subject and reply-to lines.

✦ **Replying to the user** — Sometimes you want to send a message back to the user, either confirming or reporting an error in the user's submission. This job, too, is easy with FP's Options for Saving Results of a Form dialog box. Just click the Confirmation Page tab and fill in the URLs of the files you want to send back to the user. Finally, on the Saved Fields tab, you can specify which of the form's fields should be returned to you and also whether you want additional information saved about the user (time, date, browser, and so on). Click OK to close the Saving Results dialog box.

✦ **Creating and editing hidden fields** — Once you're back in the main Form Properties dialog box, click the Advanced button. You can now create or edit hidden fields. In these fields you can add comments — the user will never see these fields but hidden fields will submit data back to you when the user sends in his or her data. You can, for example, describe which particular form is being returned to your server if you have several forms out there. Each hidden field can have a name/value, just like a computer variable has both a name and usually some contents in the variable.

After changing your target from a server disk file to e-mail, FP automatically updates the HTML so it looks something like this:

```
<!--Webbot bot="SaveResults" S-Email-Format="TEXT/PRE"
  S-Email-Address="ert@worldnet.att.net"
  B-Email-Label-Fields="TRUE"
  B-Email-Subject-From-Field="FALSE"
  S-Email-Subject="MyForm" S-Builtin-Fields -->
```

Note

FP includes a Forms toolbar you can activate from the View menu. However, at this time, the Insert menu offers two additional fields (Image and Label) that are currently unavailable on the toolbar.

✦ **Validating user input** — Frequently you'll want to validate the user's input. FP includes facilities for easily checking this input. Right-click the text box you added earlier to the form in the FP editor, and then choose Form Field Validation. In the Validation dialog box, you can insist that the user return text, integer, number, or enforce no constraints. You can also specify data length, punctuation of numeric input, and other requirements.

After you've entered your specifications, once again FP constructs the necessary underlying HTML

```
<!--Webbot
  bot="Validation" S-Data-Type="Integer"
  S-Number-Separators="x" B-Value-Required="TRUE"
  I-Minimum-Length="1" --><input type="text"

name="T1" size="20">
```

Tip   There is a second way to create forms in FP efficiently: the Forms Wizard. To activate it, choose New from the FP File menu and in the list of layouts, double-click Form Page Wizard. You are stepped through a series of dialog boxes asking you what kinds of input you want from the user, in what format, what associated text and components should be used, and how you want the results submitted (to a text file, to a Web page, or via a custom script, for example).

Graphics in FrontPage

One of the strongest features of FP's IDE is its emphasis on managing graphics. There are dozens of tools available to you when you want to design or adjust the *look* of a Web site. For instance, there is clip art — images you can add to buttons to make them look like vivid lights, images to add life to your backgrounds, and much more. FP ships with over 1,000 clip art graphics in its Clip Art Gallery feature (the same utility that comes with Microsoft Office). Many more clip art graphics are available from Microsoft's Clip Gallery Live on the Internet.

Managing clip art

To add clip art (or surf the online gallery), click your HTML page in FP's Normal view where you want the item inserted, and then choose Clip Art from FP's Insert menu. The Clip Gallery appears, as shown in Figure 7-20. If this feature isn't available in FP, you probably decided not to include it during FP's setup. Rerun FP setup (from the Add/Remove Programs feature in Start Button | Settings | Control Panel). This time, select Clip Art to have it added to your FP installation.

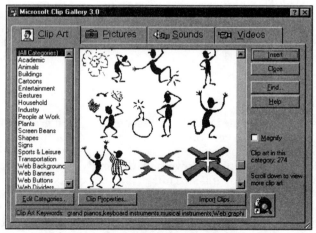

Figure 7-20: This Clip Gallery utility makes it easy to add art, video, sound, and animation to your Web pages.

The FP Clip Gallery also enables you to preview and add more than just clip art graphics to your Web pages; you'll also find sound, video, and animations.

To preview and (optionally) add clip art to your personal gallery, just click the IE icon in the lower-right of the Clip Gallery dialog box shown in Figure 7-20. You'll then be connected to a large collection of elements available over the Internet.

Once you've inserted a graphic into your page, you can easily reposition or resize it; just click it to reveal the drag frame, and then either resize by dragging one of the tabs on the frame, or drag the entire graphic somewhere else on the page.

When you add an image to a page in FP's Normal view, then click that image to select it; a graphics-editing toolbar appears at the bottom of the FP edit window, as shown in Figure 7-21.

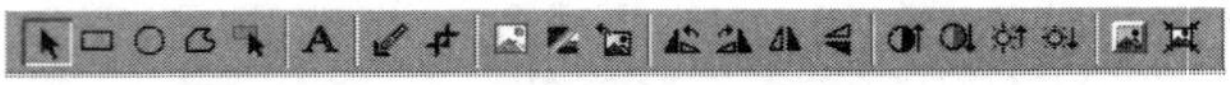

Figure 7-21: This set of graphics-editing tools appears whenever you select an image in FP's Normal view.

These graphics-editing tools are actually quite useful. They include bevel (useful for transforming an ordinary image into a 3D button), crop, flip, rotate, resample (helps to clean up debris in a graphic after you've resized it), and adjust contrast. One helpful feature is the Make Transparent tool (located next to the A text icon). Click this tool, and then click any color within your graphic where you want the background to show through. Also, if you want to add text to a graphic, select the A icon and type whatever you want. This text overlay feature enables you to annotate graphics or create self-descriptive buttons.

If you're adding a text overlay to a graphic, you can adjust the style (boldface, for example), size, or typeface using the usual FP Format toolbar (available from the View menu).

Using thumbnails

You'll sometimes see a gallery of graphics on a Web page, except each graphic is a tiny representation of the real, full-size version. A small version of a graphic is called a *thumbnail*. Thumbnails save space on a page and don't require that the user wait a long time while full-size graphics download. Generally, each thumbnail represents a hyperlink that will open the full-size image if a user clicks its thumbnail.

To create a thumbnail gallery, first choose Options from the FP Tools menu, and then select the Auto Thumbnail tab. You see the dialog box displayed in Figure 7-22.

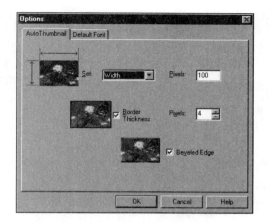

Figure 7-22: You can specify the size of the thumbnail images, along with the size and type of frame around each one.

If you set the Width to 100 pixels, the height is automatically sized to prevent the picture from being distorted (all thumbnails are then 100 pixels wide but will vary in height). Or you can specify the height in pixels and allow the width to vary. Alternatively, you can choose the Shortest Side option and FP will make either the width or the height 100 pixels (or whatever you specify) but will still preserve the aspect ratio to prevent distortion.

Once you've set the resizing method and the frame specifications, you can try out the Auto Thumbnail feature. Add some clip art or graphic images to a page (choose Image from the Insert menu). You might have a collection of graphics of various sizes, like those shown in Figure 7-23.

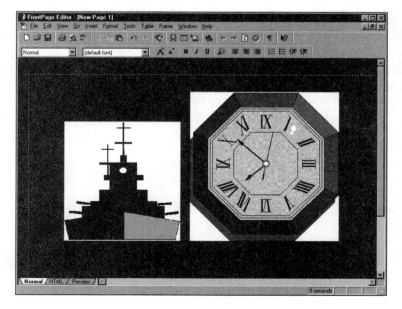

Figure 7-23: Before — This page contains large images and, therefore, takes awhile to load into a browser.

Select each image in turn, by clicking it, and then choose Auto Thumbnail in the Tools menu. The selected graphic will be shrunk and a frame will be added, as shown in Figure 7-24.

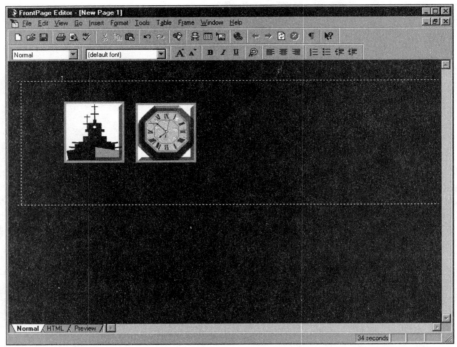

Figure 7-24: After — Now you've got a set of thumbnails that the user can expand individually as desired.

FP has automatically created the following HTML to specify the locations of the original image (href), the small version it created and stored on disk (src), and a text description for those who have graphics turned off in their browsers (alt).

```
<a href="file:///D:/Program%20Files/Micro
soft%20FrontPage/temp/clock.wmf">
<img src="file:///D:/Program%20Files/Mic
rosoft%20FrontPage/temp/clock_small.wmf"
alt="clock.wmf (10550 bytes)" border="4"
 width="100" height="102">
</a>
```

Creating banner ads

Another feature seen in many Web pages is the banner ad. FP includes a WebBot component and an associated Customize dialog box that make creating these animations quite simple. A *banner ad* is a graphic that is replaced by another graphic (or a series of them) every few seconds (the default is five). This animation attracts the user's attention. The user can click the graphic to link to another URL. To build a banner ad, follow these steps:

1. Choose Active Elements from the FP Insert menu, and then click Banner Ad Manager.

2. Click the Add button to select your series of images. (They are saved as graphics .gif files on your site.)

3. Choose among the three possible transition effects. The default dissolve is best. The venetian blind and exploding/imploding box effects are too rapid and jerky. None of these transitions is of TV quality, though these "scene change" visual clues derive from movies and TV.

4. Depending on how your system behaves, you may not be able to preview the effect from within FP. If that's the case, you must save the page, and then from the FP File menu, choose Preview in Browser (or open the file in your browser). Remember that if you ever have problems seeing an effect with FP's Preview view, try saving the page and looking at it in Internet Explorer.

5. If you want the user to be able to click the graphic as a hyperlink, fill in the Link to text box.

If you want to edit a banner ad, right-click the banner ad in FP's Normal view, and then choose Java Applet Properties.

Working with shared borders

The shared borders feature is like a very simple version of Frames. However, instead of fully separate pages sharing the same window, a shared border merely acts like a running header or footer. No matter which page in your Web the user goes to, the same border appears. These static borders can be horizontal or vertical.

To create the shared border(s) for an entire Web, you must open FP's Explorer (you can't do it from the FP editor). Select Shared Borders from the FP Explorer's Tools menu. At this point, you can switch to the FP editor and type your copyright notice, or insert whatever elements you want to appear on each Web page in this shared border. When you finish editing your border(s), select any other pages (.htm files) that are in this Web site (look for them in the FP editor's File menu). When you switch to the pages, you see that all pages now contain the same elements within the border(s) you created and filled with text or some other content. But what if you don't want one of your pages to display the Web-wide shared border, or to display a different border?

Tip   Many of the FP templates and wizards include shared borders (such as the Corporate Presence Wizard you worked with at the start of this chapter). You can override them globally (Web-wide) by modifying them within the FP Explorer as described previously, or you can change individual pages as described shortly.

Tip   You can edit the contents of your shared border anytime. Just click the border to select it, and then make any changes you want. After you save that page, all other pages sharing that border are automatically updated. (FP keeps separate .htm files for each border, naming them TOP.HTM, LEFT.HTM, and so on.)

To specify the border for a particular page, right-click a page and choose Shared Borders. A dialog box pops up and you can choose from among the four possible borders (or include as many of them as you wish). You can also either use the Web default shared borders, or override that setting with a border that appears on the current (active) page only.

Television transitions

A person sitting in front of a TV is described as a *viewer*, but a person working a computer or surfing the Web is described as a *user*—someone more active, more involved in the process. However, television and movies have had nearly a century to develop a sophisticated visual language. This language includes ways to cue the viewer or user that a major transition is taking place. Dissolves, revolving bars, wipes, checkerboards, fade out/fade in—if you visit the control room of a TV studio, you'll see there are hundreds of ways of moving from one scene to another. The idea is to cue the viewer that some important transition is taking place. To do that, you can't just use an abrupt jump cut. Jump cuts are useful *within* a scene, but a major change (moving to a different location, going indoors, moving forward or backward in time) requires a more elaborate transition than a simple cut.

As the bandwidth of Internet/intranets becomes capable of faster and faster page display, the need for visual page transitions increases. At this time, because pages generally arrive on the user's screen so slowly, page transitions are rarely used. However, FP has provisions for them.

To add a page transition to the current page, select Page Transitions from the FP Format menu (you must be in Normal view). You see a choice of 26 effects—splits, strips, bars, wipes, circles, boxes, and blends (most featuring various directional options such as the circle moving inward versus outward). You can also specify the duration of the effect (5 to 10 seconds is good) and when the effect is displayed: page enter or exit, or site enter or exit. To see the effect you've chosen, change to Preview view and switch back and forth between two linked pages. (Make sure they have different backgrounds or different background colors to see the full effect.) Figure 7-25 illustrates the Circle In effect when switching from a plain green background to a page that has a wallpaper background.

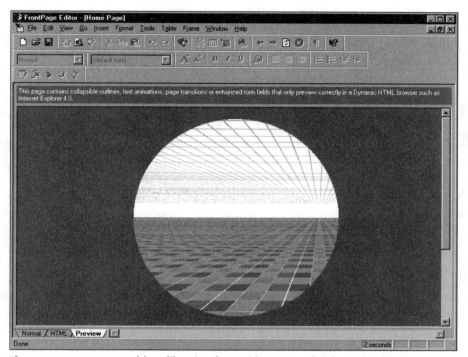

Figure 7-25: You can add TV-like visual transitions to make the move into (or out of) your pages less visually abrupt.

Page transitions are one of the many features in Microsoft's Dynamic HTML proposal. DHTML is discussed later in this chapter, and Chapters 14 and 15 are devoted entirely to this topic.

Other FP graphics techniques

FrontPage 98 supports various additional graphic features. For example, Cascading Style Sheets (CSS) can be added to any project. Just use Notepad or some other plain-text editor and define the styles in which you're interested. Then save the file with the extension .css (for example, NStyle.css) and import that file into your Web (use the Import command in the FP Explorer's File menu). Then type something like the following in between the <HEAD> and </HEAD> tags in the pages you want to conform to the style sheet:

```
<link REL="stylesheet" HREF="Nstyle.CSS" TYPE="text/css">
```

In the .css file you can create various looks for any pages linked to that style. For example, you can define how the H1 headline will look, in this way within the .css file:

```
H1 { font-size: x-large; color: blue }
```

And within the HTML of your Web page, you can merely indicate an H1 headline, knowing that it will be extra large and blue because the style sheet says so:

```
<h1>This large headline is blue. </H1>
```

Tip   FP includes over 50 themes from which you can choose (themes are style sheets that have been designed by professionals to have a coherent, pleasing visual appeal). To add a theme to your project, move to Normal view in FP and choose Theme from the Format menu. For more information on employing themes and using and creating style sheets, see Chapter 10.

Whereas themes and style sheets describe how individual elements should look (the size of buttons, the color of hyperlinks), layouts (also called *templates*) provide you with a professionally designed page. In other words, a layout is a preconstructed page that you edit, adding your custom text and graphics. When you choose New from the FP File menu, a dialog box appears displaying a set of layouts from which you can choose a page design that appeals to you. Among the options: Centered Body, Confirmation Form, Table of Contents, Search Page, and Two-column Body with Two Sidebars. One of the layouts is actually a wizard, the Form Page Wizard, which is interactive: it asks you questions while customizing the page. You can see previews of the various page layouts as well, as shown in Figure 7-26.

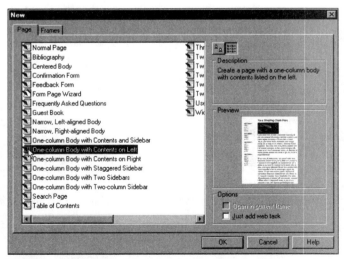

Figure 7-26: FP includes a set of templates (page layouts) offering everything from FAQ to Feedback Form designs. Note the preview of the selected page layout in the right panel.

The term *WebBot* appears to be sinking into that bog reserved for coined computer terms that have fallen out of favor. Now Microsoft seems to be encouraging us to use the generic term *component* for small utilities or applets.

In any case, the only distinction between a FP component (WebBot) and an ActiveX or Java component is that the FP component comes with FP. You insert a WebBot into your HTML by choosing FrontPage Component from the Insert menu. Then choose from among those listed: Comment, Confirmation Field, Hit Counter, Include Page, Insert HTML, Page Banner, Scheduled Image, Scheduled Include Page, or Substitution.

A Property dialog box pops up and you can adjust the style of the component, its contents, or whatever is permitted. You can also right-click at any time on the component while in Normal view and choose Properties to adjust the component.

Also in the Insert menu is a collection of components known as *Active Elements*. These are also built-in components, but unlike the WebBots, the Active Elements *move*. They're animations.

The Wide View: The FrontPage Explorer

While the FP editor gives you various views of a single page, the FP Explorer pulls you back to offer various views of the Web site as a whole: the various pages, files, links, and relationships among those pages.

Hyperlinking: tying the Web together

Working with hyperlinks in FP is simplicity itself. It's easy to add a graphic hyperlink or text hyperlink (to other pages in your site, to locations on your intranet, to locations on the Internet). It's equally easy to see the relationships between your pages in the FP Explorer.

FP makes working with hyperlinks simple. You don't need to fiddle with URLs; just browse (your disk, intranet, or the Internet) to select your target, and FP creates the necessary URL path — either relative or absolute, as necessary. It also generates the text to display to the user and simplifies creating hotspots on graphic-style hyperlinks.

To see how to work with hyperlinks in FP, create several pages in a Web site using the FP editor (select New from the File menu). Now, to create a hyperlink to another page in this Web, choose Hyperlink from the Insert menu (or press Ctrl+K). You see a dialog box including a list of all the pages in your current site. Click one of the listed pages to select it, and then click OK. When the Insert Hyperlink dialog box closes, click the HTML View tab on the bottom of the editor and you see that FP has inserted the URL of your target page as both a text display and an actual URL address, something like this:

```
<p><a href="file:///D:/search.htm">
file:///D:/search.htm</a></p>
```

Also in the Insert Hyperlink dialog box you'll find a drop-down list box where you can choose pages in your Web (or type a different URL). Next to that box is a series of buttons that can also be used to generate the URL for the hyperlink from one of the following:

✦ An Internet page located within your browser

✦ A file on your computer (perhaps a sound .wav file or some such special target)

✦ A hyperlink that sends e-mail (the user is prompted to type a message) or a new Web page (that is simultaneously created and linked)

If you target a page that includes frames, there is a separate dialog box that enables you to specify which frame (or the entire page, a new window, or a parent frame). To see this dialog box, click the pencil icon in the lower-right of the Insert Hyperlink dialog box. Finally, you can also choose a bookmark (if any exist on the selected page) as the target of your hyperlink. A bookmark is a zone *within* a page defined using the HTML A element. Bookmarks enable users to navigate to locations within Web pages, and you can insert bookmarks in the FP editor by selecting some text choosing Bookmark in the Edit menu.

Using graphic hyperlinks

A hyperlink need not be text. Some of the most professional-looking hyperlinks are images. In some situations, the best solution is a graphic that enables the user to click various hotspots within the picture to move to different places. For instance, if your company is selling vacations, you might allow the users to specify their chosen destination by displaying a graphic containing maps of England, Italy, and China. The user can click the country, and the location of that click (and, therefore, which hyperlink should be activated) is reported based on the hotspots.

To create an image-style hyperlink with hotspots, follow these steps:

1. Insert an image into a page (choose Image or Clipart from the Insert menu).

2. Click the image, causing the image toolbar to appear.

3. Click one of the hotspot drawing tools at the left side of the image toolbar, and then draw a hotspot, as shown in Figure 7-27.

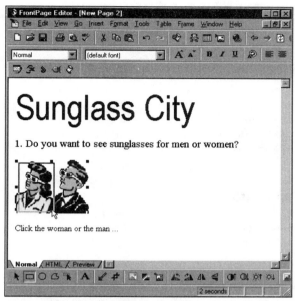

Figure 7-27: Creating clickable hyperlink zones within an image couldn't be easier.

4. After you've drawn your hotspot, the Create Hyperlink dialog box opens.

5. Choose, as the target of this hyperlink, a location within your Web site (a bookmark or page), a disk file, or a location on an intranet or the Internet.

6. You can now test your link. Switch to Preview view, and then click within the hotspot and your browser loads the correct page or file.

Tip If you don't find what you need in the clip art collection that ships with FP, there are thousands more graphics you can access. Just choose ClipArt from the FP editor's Insert menu, and then click the world icon in the lower-right of the Clip Gallery dialog box. You are taken to Microsoft's Clip Gallery Live where you're likely to find just the image you're looking for.

The Navigation bar

An alternative to traditional hyperlinks is the Navigation bar, a WebBot. A Navigation bar requires a shared border, as described earlier in this chapter. If you have a Web page that has a shared border, in the FP editor you can select Navigation bar from the Insert menu. A Navigation bar is a group of hyperlinks to the other pages in a FrontPage Web. FP automatically updates a Navigation bar if you delete, move, or add pages to the Web's structure. For an in-depth explanation of how to add Navigation bars to your site, see Chapter 5.

Push: the Channel Definition Wizard

If you're interested in permitting users to subscribe to your site as a channel or desktop component, you can easily add this *push* capability, as it's called, with FP's Channel Definition Wizard. This technique permits automatic updating of your content on the user's desktop (if the user chooses this option and uses a browser supporting channels), offline viewing, and notification sent to the user when your site is modified.

Specifying channel-wide properties

To specify channel-wide properties, load a Web site into the FP Explorer and from the Explorer's Tools menu, choose Define Channel. The wizard launches. In the first dialog box, you're asked to provide the following general information about your site:

✦ **Title** — The text that identifies your site in the user's browser

✦ **Abstract** — Supposedly a brief definition of your channel that appears when the user's mouse pointer hovers over your site's title. Not currently working.

✦ **Introduction Page** — By default, your home page (Default.htm), but you can enter a different page that will first appear when your site is visited.

✦ **Logo Image** — You should supply two logo graphics. This first graphic is an 80×32 pixel .gif image. If you don't specify one, the browser displays a default channel logo.

✦ **Icon Image** — Identifies each page in your site; this icon should be a 16×16 pixel .gif file.

✦ **Last Modified** — Tells you when you most recently modified the CDF (Channel Definition Format) file

Defining channel page properties

After you've filled in the fields listed previously, click Next. The next dialog box enables you to define the folder where the pages of your site reside. Click Next again and you see the pages in that Web application. In this dialog box, you can exclude some of the pages from your channel if you wish. The next dialog box enables you to set specifications for the individual page. You can adjust the Abstract (similar to the second bulleted item but for individual pages rather than the entire channel). You can also define how each page should be cached (cache based on the user's browser settings, don't cache on user's machine, or cache to permit offline browsing).

The Specify Usage field enables you to select various (or several) behaviors for each page. The page can be part of the channel; e-mail can be sent to all subscribers when the page is updated; the page can be made into a screen saver on users' machines; the page can be a desktop component (a small window that displays push updates, such as a news ticker, on the user's desktop); the page can be hidden from view during the user's online session but available (via hyperlink in your other pages) for viewing offline.

Note

If you choose to make a page available as a desktop component, you must specify its height and width, in pixels. A typical size is 150 × 150.

The next dialog box enables you to stipulate how often the user's browser should contact your site's server to see if any content has been updated. You can specify a start and end date; the defaults are now and forever. Then you define the interval (every two days, every two minutes, whatever seems appropriate). Then you can delay updates until off-peak hours, such as the early morning, to reduce the load on your server.

Finally, you can target a URL of a custom form handler (located in the Web you're defining as a channel). This form handler will accumulate information about the user contact to your channel and obtain updates — the form handler will contain information about the frequency and time of hits. (This feature is optional.)

The wizard concludes by asking that you specify the location of the .cdf file (that you and the wizard have just created) and if you want a button added to the Navigation bar of your home page that will subscribe users to your channel.

If you select this check box, the Channel Definition Wizard adds a child node labeled Subscribe to your navigational structure in the FrontPage Explorer's Navigation view. If you prefer, you can avoid this approach and allow users to subscribe merely by adding a hyperlink (in any of your Web's pages) that points to this .cdf file. When the user clicks that hyperlink, subscription is initiated.

The Prepare for Publishing To option enables you to specify the URL of a remote Web server (intranet or Internet). Leave this option unchecked if you first want to test the channel on your local setup before formally publishing it.

Tip

If you want to customize the text on the Subscribe button, go to Explorer's Navigation view, choose the Subscribe node, and use the Rename command in the shortcut menu.

Summary

FrontPage isn't a poor relation of Visual InterDev. Rather, FP is a powerful Web design tool in its own right, excelling in the efficient generation of the user interface — the surface of a Web site. In this chapter, you learned the following highlights of FP:

✦ FP is superior to VI for most visually oriented Web design jobs. However, although there is some overlap between the two development environments, each has particular strengths.

✦ VI is generally best for managing people working on a Web site as a team, for many advanced programming chores, and other sophisticated, low-level coding work.

✦ FP is usually preferable when you're working on general content. This program features a variety of useful wizards, prebuilt components, templates, and other tools intended to help you efficiently add user interface elements to your site: forms, frames, channels, tables, clip art, other graphics, thumbnails, banner ads, visual transitions, and hyperlinks.

✦   ✦   ✦

Interacting with the User

The Internet is a two-way street: You not only want to display information to your user, you often want to get information back from the user. In this chapter, you learn several techniques to transfer information from the user to your Web site.

Using the Form Page Wizard

You can use forms to gather information from users. A form is a zone on a Web site that contains some input controls (for example, TextBoxes or CheckBoxes) and a button the user clicks when the information has been filled in and is ready to be sent. When the user clicks this submit button, a form handler (a program running on the server) extracts this information, optionally analyzes it, and stores it on a disk. One quick way to create an interactive form is to use the FrontPage (FP) Form Page Wizard.

As you've seen in several chapters in this book, VI is an excellent programming environment with helpful debugging facilities and a well-thought-out editor. However, at this time it lacks macro facilities, wizards, add-ins, and other assistants that can make a big difference in how long it takes to create, for example, an HTML page that accepts information from a user. We can expect VI-specific wizards and other tools to appear in the future — there are provisions for them on VI's menus. For now, however, you'll find FrontPage is often a more efficient tool when you're adding various kinds of graphics, structures, or other content. VI has the superior script-writing editor (FrontPage doesn't yet color-code VBScript keywords, for instance), but you'll want to create a user-input form with FrontPage.

Follow these steps to create a simple form with FrontPage that sends you a user's name and address (so you can e-mail the user your company's catalog, for example):

1. From the FrontPage File menu, select New and choose Form Page Wizard.

2. Click OK, and then click Next in the wizard's first dialog box.

3. Name the page **Catalog** and name the file **Catalog.htm**. Click Next.

4. Click the Add button and when asked to select the type of input you want, choose Contact Information.

5. Click Next, and then choose Name, Postal address, and E-mail address, as shown in Figure 8-1.

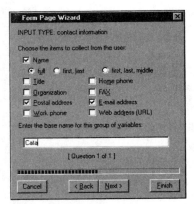

Figure 8-1: When asking users to send their name, address, and e-mail address, this wizard builds the necessary form.

6. Make the base name for these variables **Cata**, and then click Next. Note that whatever name you provide as a base name will be appended to the variable, like this:

```
<td><input TYPE="TEXT" NAME="Cata_FullName" SIZE="35"> </td>
```

7. Click Next twice to get to the Presentation Options dialog box. Choose Numbered List, no table of contents, and request that tables be used. Click Next.

8. Choose to save the results to a text file and provide the name Cata so the wizard will save the results in Cata.txt. Click Finish. These options, enabling you to save the results in various locations, are described in a later section, "Customizing with the Form Properties dialog box."

The wizard generates the HTML in Listing 8-1 for you.

Listing 8-1: The Wizard's HTML Source Code for a Form

```html
<html>

<head>
<meta HTTP-EQUIV="Content-Type"
 CONTENT="text/html; iso-8859-1">
<meta name="GENERATOR"
 content="Microsoft FrontPage 3.0">
<title>Catalog</title>
</head>

<body>

<h1>Catalog</h1>

<hr>

<p>This is an explanation of the purpose of the form ...</p>

<form METHOD="POST" ACTION="--WEBBOT-SELF--">
 <!--WebBot bot="SaveResults" startspan
 U-File="cata.txt" S-Format="TEXT/TSV"
 B-Label-Fields="TRUE" -->
<!--WebBot bot="SaveResults" endspan --><ol>
  <li>Please provide the following contact information:<table>
    <tr>
     <td ALIGN="right"><em>Name</em></td>
     <td><input TYPE="TEXT"
NAME="Cata_FullName" SIZE="35"> </td>
    </tr>
    <tr>
     <td ALIGN="right"><em>Street address</em></td>
     <td><input TYPE="TEXT"
NAME="Cata_StreetAddress" SIZE="35"> </td>
    </tr>
    <tr>
     <td ALIGN="right"><em>Address (cont.)</em></td>
     <td><input TYPE="TEXT"
NAME="Cata_Address2" SIZE="35"> </td>
    </tr>
    <tr>
     <td ALIGN="right"><em>City</em></td>
     <td><input TYPE="TEXT" NAME="Cata_City" SIZE="35"> </td>
    </tr>
    <tr>
```

(continued)

Listing 8-1 *(continued)*

```
        <td ALIGN="right"><em>State/Province</em></td>
        <td><input TYPE="TEXT" NAME="Cata_State" SIZE="35"> </td>
      </tr>
      <tr>
        <td ALIGN="right"><em>Zip/Postal code</em></td>
        <td><input TYPE="TEXT"
NAME="Cata_ZipCode" SIZE="12" MAXLENGTH="12"> </td>
      </tr>
      <tr>
        <td ALIGN="right"><em>Country</em></td>
        <td><input TYPE="TEXT" NAME="Cata_Country" SIZE="25">
</td>
      </tr>
      <tr>
        <td ALIGN="right"><em>E-mail</em></td>
        <td><input TYPE="TEXT" NAME="Cata_Email" SIZE="25"> </td>
      </tr>
    </table>
  </li>
 </ol>
 <p><input TYPE="SUBMIT" VALUE="Submit Form">
<input TYPE="RESET" VALUE="Reset Form"> </p>
</form>

<hr>

<h5>Copyright information goes here.<br>
Last revised: <!--WebBot bot="TimeStamp"
 S-Type="EDITED" S-Format="%B %d, %Y" --></h5>
</body>
</html>
```

You are expected to modify parts of the wizard-created form's text (*Copyright information goes here* and so on). We discuss the Form Page Wizard more at the end of this chapter.

Providing Immediate Response

For now, take a look at how to create a client-side script. This technique provides immediate response and is useful, for example, if you want to simplify the process of validating the user's input prior to its submission back to your server. The script is embedded right in the HTML that goes into the user's browser. Here's an example that provides feedback, reassuring the user that something has, in fact, happened when he or she clicked the Submit button.

Change the Submit button definition to this:

```
<input TYPE="SUBMIT" VALUE="Submit Form" NAME="btnsubmit">
```

Now that you've given this button a name, you can reference it from within VBScript, by using the `OnClick` event, like this:

```
<SCRIPT LANGUAGE="VBScript">
<!--
' when they submit their information, we'll thank them.
Sub BtnSubmit_OnClick
MsgBox "Thank you for sending in your information. Your
catalog will arrive soon!", 0, "Alert"
End Sub
-->
</SCRIPT>
```

Putting script in the head

It doesn't matter where you place the script within the body of the HTML of your page; it can be at the start or at the end or in the middle. The browser will parse it and be ready to react with a message when the user clicks the Submit button. However, it is common practice to put script (JScript or VBScript) within the `<HEAD>` `</HEAD>` tags up at the top of an HTML source code page.

Switching Between FP and VI

Whether you're writing script or HTML, you'll usually find yourself making a change, then switching to see the results (by clicking the Preview button in FP or the Quick View button in VI — why, why do they use two different terms for the same thing?).

Sometimes you have to save the source code to disk, then load it into Internet Explorer rather that use the Preview/Quick View feature. Some types of HTML or script cannot be activated within VI or FP. In particular, some WebBots and other components require that the HTML document containing them be saved to disk or published, then loaded into IE, before they will work properly.

Moving between FP (or VI) and IE during this modify-test cycle is simplified if you use a couple of toolbar buttons. For example, when you've modified the HTML source code, click FrontPage's Save File button (the floppy disk icon on the Standard toolbar) to replace the existing .HTM file of that source code with your updated version. Then press Alt+Tab to switch to Internet Explorer. Click Explorer's Refresh icon (or press F5) to reload the page and see how it works in the browser.

Using the Forms toolbar

If you want to modify your form by adding additional buttons or input controls, select Forms Toolbar from FrontPage's View menu. Make sure you click the tab on the bottom of the FP editor labeled Normal view. You see the toolbar shown in Figure 8-2.

Figure 8-2: To add these controls to a form, simply click an icon and the control appears at your cursor's current location. (You must be in Normal view in FrontPage's editor.)

Customizing with the Form Properties dialog box

When you defined your form with the Form Page Wizard, the final dialog box asked you where you wanted the user's input saved after the user clicked the Submit button. The following are your choices:

✦ A file in your active FrontPage Web

✦ The root Web

✦ Elsewhere on the hard drive

✦ An e-mail address

✦ A FrontPage form handler

✦ A custom handler (ISAPI, NSAPI, CGI, or ASP)

If you want to send the results to the current Web or the root, use a relative URL. In other words, use the default name provided by the dialog box, or provide a name of your own. A relative URL means that part of the address is understood (the server's URL on the Internet, for example, is known and isn't provided in the URL, which is *relative* to the known portion of the complete URL). In other words, if you want the results stored in a file named ANSWER.TXT, located in the root Web, you are required to use the folder named _vti_log. Therefore, you don't provide the entire URL of your server. You provide only the relative portion, like this: /_vti_log/ANSWER.TXT.

If you want the results stored elsewhere on your hard drive, provide the complete path, like this: C:\STORAGE\CATALOG\ANSWER.TXT. To send to an e-mail address, simply supply the ordinary e-mail address, such as MYNAME@WORLDNET.ATT.NET.

After you've specified where you want the results saved, the wizard (or other dialog box if you've right-clicked a form and chosen Form Properties) generates the WebBot HTML source code. It will look something like this:

```
<form action="--WEBBOT-SELF--" method="POST" name="myresult">
<!--WebBot bot="SaveResults" U-File="myresult.txt"
 S-Format="TEXT/PRE" S-Label-Fields="TRUE"
 B-Reverse-Chronology="FALSE" S-Email-Format="TEXT/PRE"
 S-Email-Address="earth@worldnet.att.net"
 B-Email-Label-Fields="TRUE"
 B-Email-Subject-From-Field="FALSE"
 S-Email-Subject="aaaaaaa" S-Builtin-Fields -->
```

Recall that WebBots are objects that, like design-time controls, are run when you save the page in which they reside. (Some WebBots execute when the user loads the page into his or her browser.) You see FP's collection of WebBots when you select Active Elements from the Insert menu. WebBots usually insert HTML into your page, as the previous source code illustrates. The primary drawback to WebBots is that they currently only work within FP. By contrast, the design-time controls used in VI are an ActiveX technology and are, thus, usable in many environments, including FP. (See Chapter 7 for more on WebBots.)

Using Data Validation

Often you'll want to check that the user has entered correct information, and alert the user if changes are required before the information is submitted. FrontPage makes it easy to validate the data entered into a form. Just right-click any input control (such as a text box), and then choose Form Field Validation. (Or double-click an input control and then click Validate.) You *must* be in FP's Normal view for this to work. Click the Normal tab on the bottom of the FP editor window.

For an example, suppose you want to ensure that the user has entered a zip code into the catalog request form. To do this, right-click the Zip/Postal code field (text box) and choose Form Field Validation from the pop-out menu. The Text Box Validation dialog box, shown in Figure 8-3, enables you to enforce a variety of requirements. The user can be requested to enter numbers or text characters in a particular format. You can require a particular type of data (text, integer, or numeric) or the format of the text (limited to characters, digits, whitespace, or another format). When formatting text, you can choose whitespace if you want to permit blank spaces or tabs, carriage returns (pressing the Enter key), and line feeds. If you select Other, you can type additional special characters (such as commas or hyphens) if you want to permit the user to enter these characters.

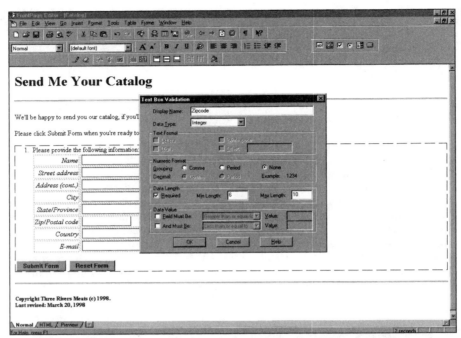

Figure 8-3: To impose restraints on the user, specify the type and qualities of user-entered data in this Validation dialog box.

Filter it your way

You can also insist on a particular punctuation of numeric data (commas, decimals, or periods), define a minimum and/or maximum length (in characters) that the data must be, or define the value of the data. For value, you can choose that the data be equal, less than, more than, or not equal to the value you specify. If the data is text, the comparison will be alphabetical. (You can specify less than *S* and the data the user enters will have to be lower than *S* in the alphabet.) If the data is numeric, the comparison is numeric. (For instance, you could be asking users for their age; you could require that this numeric data be greater than 1 and less than 120.)

For the ZIP or postal code, we're imposing three requirements:

1. The Data Type must be an Integer (no fractions, commas, or periods within the digits the user enters).

2. The Data Length must be a minimum of six digits.

3. The Data Length must be a maximum of eleven digits.

Type an easily understood name in the Display Name field in the Validation dialog box. (We've typed *Zipcode* as the display name.) If you don't enter a plain-English display name, the user will be startled by seeing your HTML variable name (in this case, *Cata-ZipCode*) if a validation error message appears because the user entered invalid data. Users generally won't understand the meaning of a programmer's variable-naming scheme.

If you want to allow for the hyphen in an extended zip code (for example, 23334-2211), choose Text as the Data Type, and then choose Other in the Text Format field of the dialog box and type a **hyphen**.

The Validation WebBot

After closing the Validation dialog box, you can switch to HTML view and see the WebBot that FrontPage has created to check the quality of the user's data in the Zip/Postal code entry box:

```
<td ALIGN="right"><em>Zip/Postal code</em></td>
<td><!--WebBot bot="Validation" S-Display-Name="Zipcode"
 S-Data-type="Integer" S-Number-Separators="x"
 B-Value-Required="TRUE" I-Minimum-Length="6"
 I-Maximum-Length="11" --><input NAME="Cata_ZipCode"
 SIZE="12" MAXLENGTH="10"> </td>
```

You can specify validation criteria for text boxes, drop-down menus, and Option buttons (radio buttons).

Creating a Registration Page

Another common requirement on the Internet is providing users with a way of registering—signing in once and for all—to your Web site. Fortunately, FP has a registration WebBot that accepts a user's name, password, and e-mail address.

To create a registration page, choose New from FrontPage's File menu and select User Registration. The HTML will be created; if you click the Preview button, you see the results shown in Figure 8-4.

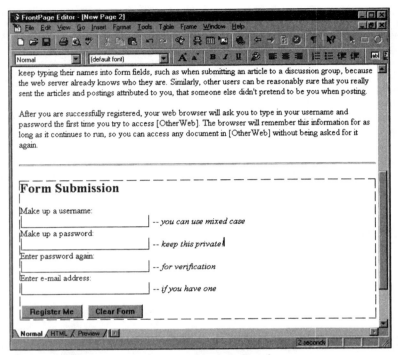

Figure 8-4: FrontPage makes creating a registration page easy.

Note the Register Me button; it's just a typical Submit button with the caption *Register Me* set by the VALUE= attribute. When the user clicks this button, the form handler is activated. You can specify the properties of the form handler by right-clicking anywhere within the form (while in Normal view) and selecting Form Properties. The Form Properties dialog box is shown in Figure 8-5.

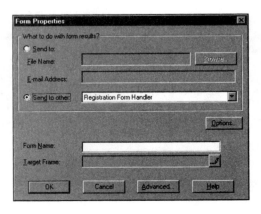

Figure 8-5: In this dialog box, you can tell the form handler where you want the user's name, password, and e-mail address sent.

Click the Options button and you can rename the user-entry fields and specify the Web name. You should leave the Require Secure Password box checked: this forces the user to supply a password that isn't partially a match to the user's real name, and also requires that the password be more than five characters long.

In this dialog box, you can also specify a page that is displayed to the user if the registration doesn't go through — perhaps the password is already used by someone else, for example. Likewise, you can optionally provide the URL of a page to be displayed if the registration succeeds. (For more information on the useful e-mail registration option, see "Submit to E-mail" in Chapter 7.)

Using Other Prebuilt Pages

FP also offers a variety of other user-interaction pages that have already been constructed for you. *Site wizards,* which step you through the process of creating an entire site, are discussed in Chapter 7. The remaining FP page templates and wizards are as follows:

✦ **Confirmation page** — To react when the user submits information such as registration data, you can use the confirmation form, as shown in Figure 8-6.

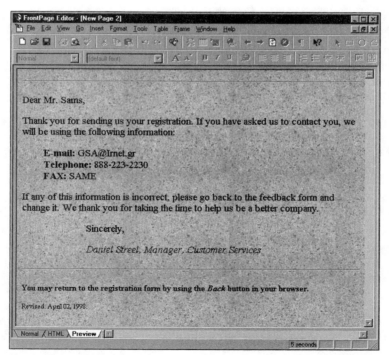

Figure 8-6: Display a confirmation form to the user, after registration or other information has been submitted.

To create a confirmation page, choose New from the FP File menu, and then select Confirmation Form. Notice in the HTML source code how many WebBots are waiting there to process the information that the user submitted in the registration form.

✦ **General feedback page**—If you're interested in general feedback or suggestions, use the feedback form shown in Figure 8-7.

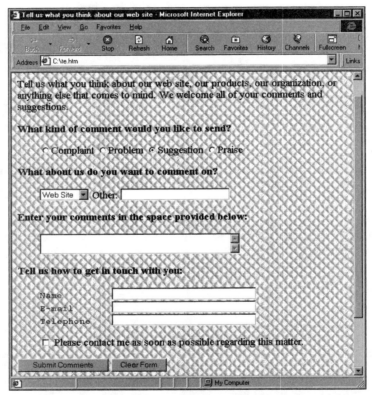

Figure 8-7: This prebuilt form, slightly modified here, is useful for getting general user response or input about your company or site.

✦ **Guest book**—A generic guest book feedback page enables users to simply fill in a text box, then submit those comments, as shown in Figure 8-8.

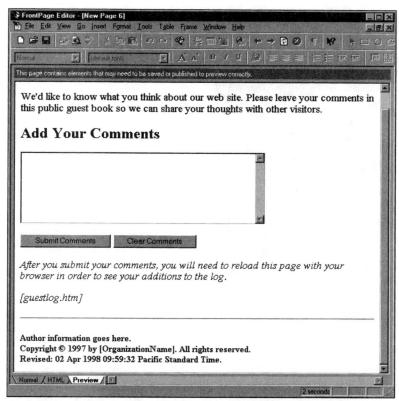

Figure 8-8: The Guest Book template contains a simple feedback text box but no personal information fields.

Building a Custom Form

For many purposes, the most useful of all FP's user-feedback templates is the Form Page Wizard, discussed in the beginning of this chapter. This wizard steps you through the job of building a custom form and includes the following set of 14 form templates: contact information, account information, product information, ordering information, personal information, one of several options, any of several options, boolean, date, time, range, number, string, and paragraph forms.

To try out the Form Page Wizard, from FP's File menu, follow these steps:

   1. Select New and then Form Page Wizard.

2. Click Next twice, click Add, and choose Contact Information.

3. Select ordering information and click Next. You see the custom dialog box appropriate to ordering merchandise, as shown in Figure 8-9.

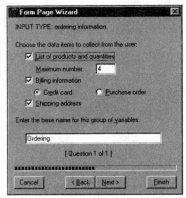

Figure 8-9: If you need to accept a merchandise order from a customer, this template creates the necessary form fields.

4. Click Next and then Add.

5. This time select Personal Information and click Next.

6. Customize the Personal Information dialog box as you wish, and then click Next twice.

7. At this point, you're asked how you want the queries and fields formatted. Choose Bulleted List, and then click Next and adjust the output options as desired.

8. Click Finish and you see that the wizard has typed a great deal of HTML code to define the necessary tables and associated WebBots to generate the input form you requested. The final result is shown in Figure 8-10.

Additional user-interaction techniques are described elsewhere in this book, particularly in the chapters on Active Server Pages. We conclude our survey of FP's features in the next chapter, when we show you how to liven up Web pages with graphics and sound.

✦ How to work with the Form Page Wizard

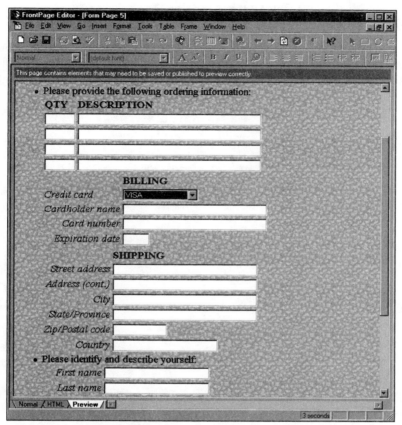

Figure 8-10: A wizard enters the necessary HTML source code to create this complex input form.

✦ How client-side scripting provides immediate response to the user

✦ How to validate data entered in a form

✦ How to create a registration page

✦ How to access the collection of useful prebuilt pages in FP

✦ How to design your own custom feedback mechanisms with the Form Page Wizard

Summary

FrontPage enables you to create an interactive user-input form with the Form Page Wizard. When it comes to generating and manipulating the content of Web pages, FP is a capable tool and should often be your first choice. In this chapter, you learned the following:

✦   ✦   ✦

Adding Graphics and Sound

Graphics are tricky for the Web site designer. You want some graphics, because an all-text page is amateurish and boring. But you don't want those fickle, itchy-fingered Web surfers clicking themselves off your site because it's taking too long for your graphics to load and display. This chapter walks you through the best ways to add graphics and sound to your site.

Limiting Bandwidth

Today's Internet has too little bandwidth, as we all know, to display large photo-realistic graphics effectively, not to mention full-motion video. In fact, even high-quality sound — which requires far less bandwidth than video—is problematic. What to do?

There are three basic solutions to this problem:

✦ Turn off image loading in your browser.

✦ Limit high-resolution photos.

✦ Program local animations into your Web pages.

Turn off image loading

A user can turn image loading off in the browser. This way, the person can see what you have to say but avoid having to wait for your graphics to load. This option is rather hidden in Internet Explorer (IE). To access it, click the View menu, and then choose Internet Options. Click the Advanced tab and scroll down until you see the Show pictures check box in the Multimedia section, as shown in Figure 9-1.

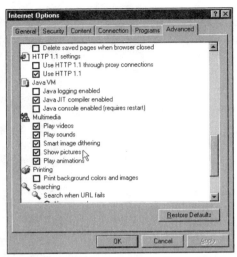

Figure 9-1: A user can turn off graphics by deselecting the Show pictures check box in Internet Explorer.

Even if the user has blocked image loading, he or she can still choose to see an individual graphic by right-clicking the icon that appears and then choosing the Show Picture option from the context menu.

Limit high-resolution photos

Another solution is to avoid photograph-quality visuals and limit yourself to cartoon-quality drawings (often referred to as clip art). It's a matter of file size: A high-resolution photographic image can be 2-4MB, or larger, and that amount of data takes awhile to flow over the wires of the World Wide Web. Sure, there are graphics file formats — JPEG, .JPG, is one — that automatically compress themselves when saved, then uncompress themselves when displayed. But the only improvement such solutions offer is to boost what was a terribly slow transfer to a slow transfer. Ultimately, the solution will have to be much more generous bandwidth on the Internet. When that happens in the next few years, we'll finally be able to watch quality video and listen to quality music on the Internet. But until that happy day, we Web site designers have to wrestle with the beautiful-site-versus-impatient-users trade off.

Text Descriptions

If a user is visually impaired, or has the image loading option turned off, it's a courtesy to provide a text description of your graphic. To do this, you use the ALT attribute, like this:

```
<img src="file:///C:/WINNT/Help/common/onestep.gif"
ALT="onestep.gif (76 bytes)">
```

Also, when a user's mouse pointer is paused on top of a graphic with an ALT attribute, a small pop-up help window appears containing the ALT text.

Program local animations into your Web pages

Yet another way to conserve bandwidth is to program local animations into your pages — animations designed to be processed on the user's computer. You can achieve these effects using the various scripting techniques available with DHTML (see Chapters 14 and 15).

The Basics of Web Graphics

Before we get to advanced graphics and sound techniques, we'll first cover the basics: techniques you can use when you decide to display images on a Web page. When you're working with graphics and sound, FrontPage is your development environment of choice. Recall that VI excels in managing group Web projects, as a programming/debugging environment and as a tool that generally best supports the technical aspects of creating and maintaining a Web site. FP, by contrast, is the superior tool when you're working with content, particularly visual or multimedia content. Therefore, in this chapter, we use FP to enliven Web pages with images and sound.

Using IMG, SRC, and DYNSRC

An image is embedded into a Web page with the IMG tag. Many ancient browsers display a static single image when you use the IMG command. However, Internet Explorer 2.0 and later can show a movie in addition to the static image, as shown in Figure 9-2. Just provide the URL address of an .AVI (Audio Video Interleave) movie for the DYNSRC command:

```
<IMG DYNSRC="d:\clouds.avi">
```

Figure 9-2: You can display a motion video in your pages, like this time-elapse film of clouds racing by.

More often, though, you won't be able to afford the bandwidth of a video, and you'll stick to sending static .GIF or .JPG images to the user, like this:

```
<html>
<head>
<title>New Page 1</title>
<meta name="GENERATOR" content="Microsoft FrontPage 3.0">
</head>
<body>
<p><img SRC="c:\crane.jpg"> </p>
</body>
</html>
```

You can also specify HEIGHT and WIDTH attributes, but unless they match the actual dimensions of the image, you'll distort the image. The crane graphic, shown in Figure 9-3, is, in reality, 95 × 114 pixels, but we stretched it by exaggerating the WIDTH attribute, resulting in the distortion of the image. The following line of code creates this distortion:

```
<img SRC="c:\crane.jpg" HEIGHT="95px" WIDTH="200px">
```

Figure 9-3: Provide the wrong dimension attribute and you'll distort an image in Internet Explorer.

Be cautioned: Stretching dynamically is not considered good HTML programming practice and may not be supported by all browsers. Therefore, if you want to distort an image in this way, do it first in a graphics program such as Paint or Photoshop, and then send the graphic without using the HEIGHT or WIDTH attributes. The image will already be distorted before you send it and all viewers, no matter what browser they use, will see the effect you intend.

Using the Align tag

If you don't specify otherwise, images are aligned with the bottom of the text by Internet Explorer, as shown in Figure 9-4.

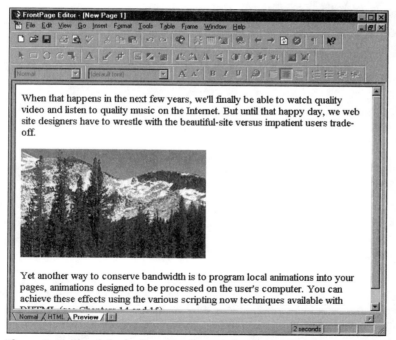

Figure 9-4: The default alignment for text is to surround, but not appear to the right of, the graphic.

If you use `ALIGN=TOP`, a single line of text wraps around the graphic, as shown in Figure 9-5.

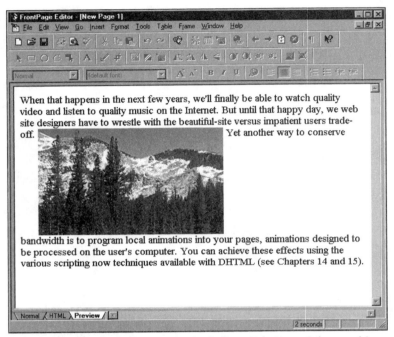

Figure 9-5: ALIGN=TOP inserts a single line at the top of the graphic.

If you use `ALIGN=CENTER`, a single line of text wraps at the middle of the graphic, as shown in Figure 9-6.

FP offers several additional alignment parameters, including `baseline`, `texttop`, and `absmiddle`. They have little practical effect, but you can access them by right-clicking the graphic in FP's Normal (design) mode and then choosing Image Properties from the context menu and clicking the Appearance tab.

However, you're not likely to actually program HTML when FP makes aligning an image easier. For example, you can position an image on the left, center, or right of the page easily in Normal view. Just select the image, and then click the Center button on the Format toolbar. FP makes this adjustment to the HTML code:

```
<p align="center"><img SRC="d:\trees.jpg"></p>
```

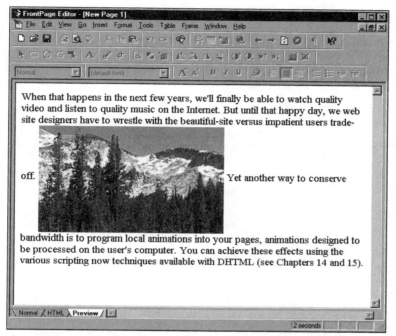

Figure 9-6: ALIGN=CENTER inserts a single line at the middle of the graphic, which looks bizarre.

Also, to add borders and specify margins around an image, switch to Normal view and then right-click the graphic, choose Image Properties, and click the Appearance tab. The Border Thickness option specifies how thick, in pixels, you want to make a black frame around the image. The Horizontal and Vertical Spacing options provide a margin (a blank frame) around the graphic — pushing any surrounding text or other images away from the image.

Tip

When you look at FP's Insert menu, you're given a choice between clip art and images. Images are .JPG or .GIF graphics (usually photos, as distinct from clip art's cartoon drawings). Precisely how FP inserts your chosen image depends on where your insert cursor is within the HTML document (the insert cursor is the blinking vertical line). If your insert cursor is on a blank line between paragraphs of text (surrounded by <p> and </p> tags), the image is placed in a paragraph of its own with its own <p> tags. However, if the insert cursor is within the text, no <p> tags are added to the IMG element, so your image is dropped into the text directly, and the text wraps around the image.

Using wraparound

In most situations, *wraparound,* where the text embraces the graphic, looks best. This is the way newspapers, magazines, and books do it, and there's a reason: Who needs big pools of white space on a page, interrupting the text, just because an image is inserted into the page? Listing 9-1 shows the HTML you use to make text wrap around an image.

Listing 9-1: Wrapping Text Around an Image

```html
<html>
<head>
<title>New Page 1</title>
<meta name="GENERATOR" content="Microsoft FrontPage 3.0">
</head>
<body>
<p>The Horizontal and Vertical Spacing options
 provide a margin (a blank frame) around the
 graphic—pushing any surrounding text or other
 images away from the image. <img ALIGN="LEFT"
 HSPACE="6" VSPACE="6" SRC="d:\brick.jpg">
 Also, to add borders and specify margins
 around an image, switch to Normal View,
 then right-click the <i>graphic</i>, choose
 Image Properties and click the appearance tab.
 The Border Thickness option specifies how
 thick, in pixels, you want to make a black
 frame around the image. Also, to add borders
 and specify margins around an image, switch
 to Normal View, then right-click
 the <i>graphic</i>, choose Image Properties
 and click the appearance tab. The Border
 Thickness option specifies how thick, in
 pixels, you want to make a black frame
 around the image.</p>
</body>
</html>
```

Note that you *must* insert ALIGN="LEFT" or ALIGN="RIGHT" for the word wrap to work, but you *must not use* ALIGN="CENTER". And, you can describe the margin between the graphic and the surrounding text using the HSPACE and VSPACE attributes; give these attributes six to eight pixels for the best look on most monitors.

Figure 9-7 shows the results of Listing 9-1.

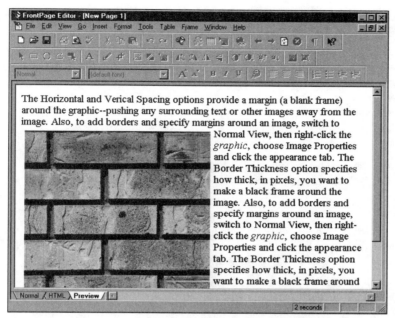

Figure 9-7: Wraparound creates an attractive and effective relationship between text and graphics.

Note

To separate an image from surrounding text, you can use the margins (HSPACE and VSPACE) or use the <p> tags.

Using Backgrounds

The simplest background for a Web site is a color. By default, IE's background color is the Windows default color scheme for the desktop and text. If the user hasn't changed the default, the background is black text on a light battleship-gray background. However, you can change the background color for your site's Web pages like this:

```
<BODY BGCOLOR="#000080" TEXT="#FFFFFF" LINK="#DD90CC">
```

Plain-text color definitions

The BGCOLOR tag defines a blue background with black text and hyperlinks in green. Unfortunately, some browsers don't understand plain-English color commands. If you're working on an intranet using IE, you can avoid the unpleasantness of hexadecimal color identification and simply use one of the 100+ color names that IE understands, as in the following:

```
<BODY BGCOLOR="mediumblue" TEXT="black" LINK="lawngreen">
```

However, FP makes choosing colors easy. Right-click the FP editor while it's in Normal view, and then choose Page Properties and click the Background tab (or choose Background from FP's Format menu). Alas, you're limited to only 16 colors in FP's Page Properties dialog box, as shown in Figure 9-8.

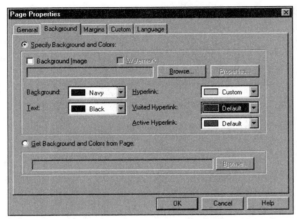

Figure 9-8: You can use this FP dialog box to specify background, text, and hyperlink colors.

Textures

More attractive than a plain-color background is textured wallpaper. You can find textures — marble, wood, sand, and thousands of others — on the Internet or included with software photo collections or graphics applications such as Micrografx's Picture Publisher. You can use the Page Properties dialog box (refer to Figure 9-8) to insert a textured background. Also, most textures are rather small graphics files and are designed to be tiled (repeated many times) across the screen without showing seams. Be aware of the contrast and how dark your backgrounds are, as text can be difficult to read on screen.

Of course, you can also tile your company's logo, or any other image. You should, however, avoid using a huge photographic image or you'll slow down the loading of your page intolerably.

The HTML for a background graphic is included in the BODY element:

```
<body background="file:///C:/screen.jpg">
```

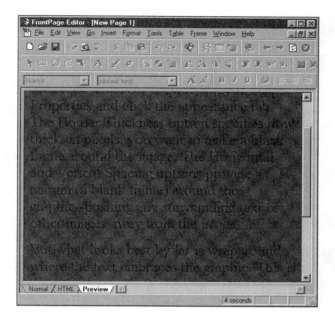

Figure 9-9: BEFORE: Avoid high-contrast or dark backgrounds (or background colors). This dusky texture makes it very hard to read the text.

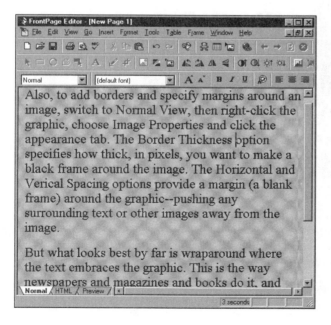

Figure 9-10: AFTER: The same texture as in Figure 9-9, but the contrast has been reduced and the overall image has been brightened in a graphics application.

Graphic Hyperlinks

Any graphic can be used as a hyperlink. The user clicks the graphic and the browser jumps to the target. If you use the A element to define an HREF (a URL target of the link), a blue frame will surround the graphic (see Figure 9-11), alerting the reader that this is a hyperlink. Also, when the user's mouse pointer is held briefly on top of a hyperlinked graphic, the pointer turns into a hand and the ALT text appears as a small pop-up help window. (The hand symbol, though, can also mean that when clicked, a graphic will be enlarged. See "Thumbnails" at the end of this chapter.) Consider the following code:

```
<a HREF="treasure.htm"><img src="file:///D:/treasure.jpg"
ALT="Door to our Treasure Page" width="47" height="53"></a>
```

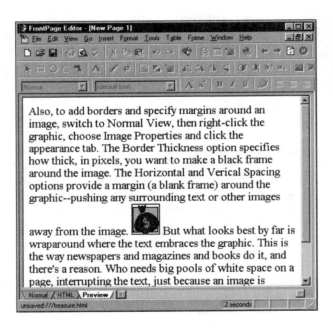

Figure 9-11: When a graphic is a hyperlink, it is surrounded by a blue line (analogous to the default blue underline that designates a text hyperlink).

It's advantageous to make it clear that a graphic is a hyperlink. Underneath it you can display "Click this money bag to go to our treasure pages!" Also, you might not want the default blue frame around your hyperlink graphic. You can get rid of it by using a null BORDER tag, like this:

```
<a HREF="treasure.htm"><img src="file:///D:/treasure.jpg"
BORDER="0"
ALT="Door to our Treasure Page" width="47" height="53"></a>
```

Tip

Recall that you can also create graphic hyperlinks using the Navigation bar component. The PageNavBar control displays a set of hyperlinks — as text or buttons — by which a visitor can easily navigate your Web site, or travel to links outside the site. (For details about this technique, see Chapter 5.)

Inserting hotspot links

You can also subdivide a graphic into a series of internal links — so the user can click various places within an individual graphic to go to various link targets. FP makes the process of subdividing a graphic into link zones quite easy. Follow these steps to create hotspots within a graphic:

1. In FP's Normal view, insert a graphic into your HTML page (from FP's Insert menu, choose Image or Clipart).

2. Select the graphic by clicking it (so the stretch tabbed frame appears around it, as you can see in Figure 9-12).

   The Image toolbar appears, or becomes activated. (It's a very large toolbar, with a black arrow icon on the far left and a resample icon on the far right.) You're interested in the three icons right next to the black arrow: rectangle, circle, and polygon. For our stoplight graphic we want two circular hotspots — one each on the red and green lights.

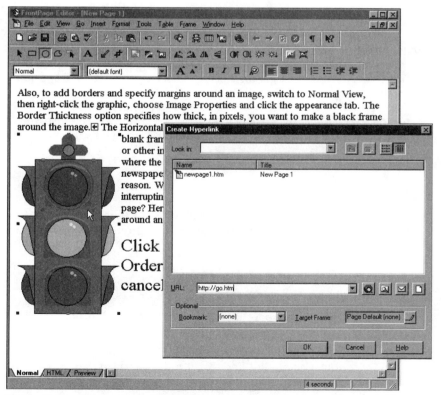

Figure 9-12: It's easy to define hotspots using FP's Image toolbar and this Create Hyperlink dialog box.

3. Click the circle hotspot icon in the Image toolbar, and then, starting in the very center of the green light, drag your mouse to create a circular hotspot. When you release the mouse button, you see the hotspot illustrated in blue and surrounded by its own stretch tabs.

   When a hotspot is, thus, selected (the stretch tabs are visible), you can delete it by pressing the Del key, move it by dragging it, or resize it by dragging one of the stretch tabs.

4. When the Create Hyperlink dialog box appears, provide the target of your link by typing it into the URL box, or by using one of the other tools in this dialog box.

   Note the four icons to the right of the URL box. You can create a URL four ways: use the Web browser to find the target, look for a file on your computer, create a hyperlink that sends you e-mail, or create a new Web page to which this hotspot points.

5. Click OK to close the dialog box.

6. Repeat Steps 3–5 to create a second hotspot over the red stoplight.

Now when a user moves the mouse over the red or green lights, shown in Figure 9-12, the mouse pointer turns into a pointing hand and a click transfers the browser to the target of your hyperlink.

Tip   Don't worry if you don't get the hotspots precisely the size or shape you want. You should usually make them a little larger than the visual target, to make life easy on the user. And, after a hotspot is created, you can always click to select it, then drag it to a new position, or drag one of its stretch tabs to resize it. Likewise, you can always bring up the Edit Hyperlink dialog box by right-clicking a hotspot and selecting Image Hotspot Properties.

Transparency

You can also use the Image toolbar to make a color (only one) invisible in a graphic. This enables you to blend an image into the background color or texture on a page. To do this, follow these steps:

1. Switch to Normal mode in FP's editor.

2. Click the image to select it.

3. Click the Make Transparent button; it's the seventh from the left on the Image toolbar.

4. In the image, click the color you want to make transparent. If you are using a .JPG graphic, you are notified that it must be translated into a .GIF format because .JPG doesn't support transparency.

Sound and Video

As you may have noticed, the Microsoft Clip Gallery dialog box offers sound and video objects in addition to clip art and .JPG/.GIF images. However, you can also directly insert video (.AVI) files and sound files into your pages. To insert a video, start in Normal view, choose Active Elements from the Insert menu, and then click Video. Locate an AVI, RAM, or RA video, clip file, and then click OK. The following HTML code is inserted into your page:

```
<img
dynsrc="file:///C:/Program%20Files/
Microsoft%20Visual%20Studio/VIntDev98/
Samples/Content/Mmedia/Earthsml.avi"
start="fileopen" width="178" height="152"
alt="Earthsml.avi (440228 bytes)"
 align="left">
```

Alignment

As always, if you want the text to wrap around the video (and you almost always do), insert the ALIGN="left" or ="right" attribute. By default, FP inserts objects with no ALIGN specified, and the object therefore drops into the text in the center, leaving huge unattractive wells of white space on either side.

Each time the user loads or refreshes the page displayed in Figure 9-13, the AVI video starts up and plays once. If you want to specify the number of times the video should repeat, or that it run continuously, use the LOOP attribute, like this:

```
<IMG DYNSRC="MYVIDEO.avi"
 LOOP=INFINITE> This will play
 continuously
<IMG DYNSRC="MYVIDEO.avi" LOOP=4>
 This will play four times.
```

The user can stop a video in its tracks by clicking the browser's Stop button.

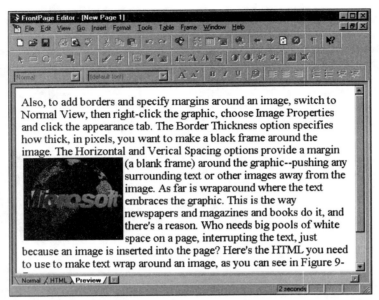

Figure 9-13: You can directly insert a video into your pages, like this .AVI file from the VI Samples folder.

Delays and user-triggers

There is also an optional LOOPDELAY attribute that specifies how long, in milliseconds, the browser should pause between "showings" of the movie. If you've set LOOP to display the video more than once, LOOPDELAY=1500 would cause a 1.5-second delay between when the video ends and restarts.

There is also a START attribute for video objects. Use START to control whether a video automatically starts (as soon as the page has been loaded or refreshed) or whether the user must move the mouse cursor over the image to start the show. START determines what triggers the video, what makes it start (or, if you're displaying a static image, too, when the movie replaces that image). The default is: start="fileopen", which starts the movie as soon as the page loads or refreshes. Or use MOUSEOVER to hold the video until the user moves the mouse cursor over the image. Here the video remains static until the user moves the mouse over it, whereupon it's replaced by the *doggie.avi* video:

```
<IMG DYNSRC="doggie.avi" START="MOUSEOVER">
```

This doggie movie will play once (we've not used the LOOP command to increase the number of plays). Thereafter, it will restart if the user again moves the mouse over the graphic.

Background Music

You can include music in your pages, too. Right-click the page and choose Page Properties. Select the General tab. Type the path or URL to a .WAV or .MID file (or you can specify various other sound file types). Or click the Browse button to locate a sound file. As you can see in Figure 9-14, you can choose the number of times the sound file should repeat, or leave the default: the check box named Forever.

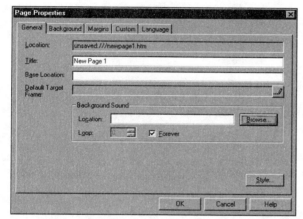

Figure 9-14: Use the Page Properties dialog box to insert background music (what would foreground music be?).

As with the video, the user can restart the music by refreshing or reloading the page, and the browser's Stop button halts the noise. Here's what the HTML looks like for a sound file:

```
<bgsound src="file:///D:/Midi/MOZART/mozart30.mid" loop="-1">
```

A LOOP of –1 is infinite. You can also use the LOOPDELAY attribute.

Tip Remember you can also insert sound and video using the Clip Gallery. Choose Clipart from the Insert menu (you must be in FP's Normal view), and then click the Sounds or Videos tab in the dialog box.

Thumbnails

You've seen images in Web pages that are relatively small so they load quickly and don't take up too much screen space. These are known as *thumbnails,* as shown in Figure 9-15.

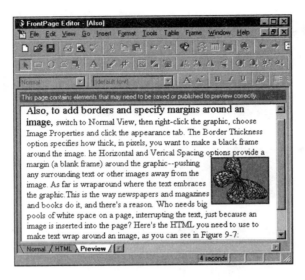

Figure 9-15: A thumbnail is a small preview of a larger graphic.

If the user is interested in seeing a larger version of the graphic, clicking the small thumbnail expands it, as shown in Figure 9-16.

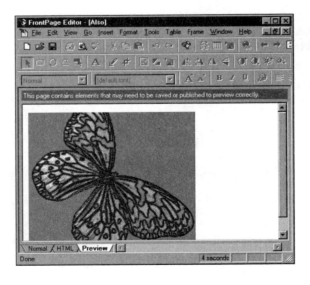

Figure 9-16: Clicking the thumbnail shown in Figure 9-15 displays the graphic full size, by itself, in the browser.

You can create these thumbnails using FP's Auto-Thumbnail feature. Click the graphic you want to make into a thumbnail to select it (you must be in Normal view). Then from FP's Tools menu, choose Options. AutoThumbnail is the only option. You can specify the width, height, and various borders, as shown in Figure 9-17.

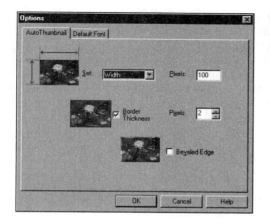

Figure 9-17: The Options dialog box enables you to specify the size and framing of your thumbnail.

The HTML for a thumbnail graphic looks like this:

```
<a href="BUTTER1.jpg"><small><img
src="BUTTER1_small.jpg"
alt="BUTTER1.jpg (20801 bytes)"
 align="right" border="2" width="100" height="83"></small></a>
```

Inserting Scheduled Images

Clicking the FrontPage Component option in the Insert menu (while in Normal view) enables you to insert a *scheduled* graphic complement of an FP WebBot. A *WebBot* is FrontPage's name for a design-time component; it's really like a wizard that inserts source code for you, but it can also include run time behaviors as well. Think of it as another name for *component.* The dialog box in Figure 9-18 shows your options when scheduling image properties.

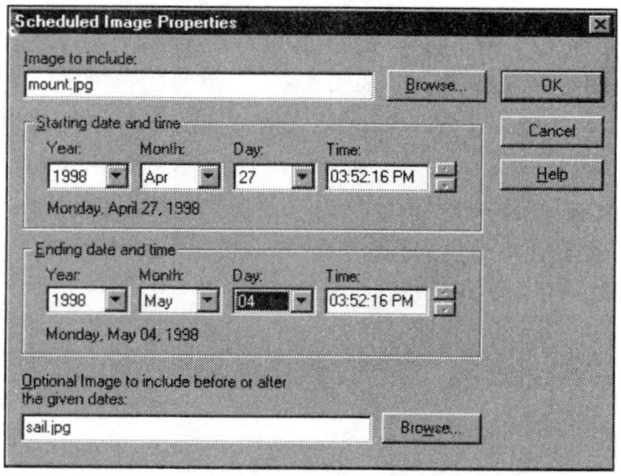

Figure 9-18: This WebBot schedules your images for you.

Choose the options you want in the Scheduled Image Properties dialog box. The starting and ending dates specify the period during which the image will be displayed on the current page. The Optional image at the bottom will be displayed any time outside the starting and ending dates of the scheduled image's display period. Notice that the scheduled display doesn't happen if the user is looking at the page; it is triggered when the page is loaded or refreshed. Also, we suggest you should make changes to the Web (such as incrementing a variable) every day to guarantee the correct timing of the scheduled graphic inclusion.

Summary

Few Web sites are text-only, just as few contemporary computers use DOS, and for many of the same reasons. Pictures may not always be worth a thousand words (it depends on the words), but there's no arguing that pictures and *multimedia* — sound and motion pictures — can enrich communication considerably. Focusing on FrontPage as the tool more capable than Visual InterDev when working with graphics and multimedia, in this chapter you learned some useful concepts and techniques:

✦ Some common-sense rules to remember when making decisions about using graphics in the bandwidth-constricted environment of the Internet

✦ The basic issues surrounding Web graphics

✦ How to blend graphics into text, and the visual importance of wraparound

✦ All about using plain-color backgrounds

✦ How to work with textures

✦ Several ways to add hyperlinks

✦ The features in FP that assist you in creating hotspots

✦ Ways to insert video and sound into your Web pages

✦ Techniques to insert background music

✦ How to schedule images so they appear and disappear at preprogrammed times

✦   ✦   ✦

Working with Themes and Style Sheets

Themes were first introduced in Chapter 7, but what, technically, is a theme? And how is it different from a template, a layout, or a style sheet? (Hint: A Style Sheet is a file containing redefinitions of HTML elements, for whatever purpose. A Theme is one particular kind of Style Sheet whose purpose is to enforce the quality and unity of the visual effects in a Web site.) On the visible surface, a theme is a collection of visually compatible components: buttons, lines, backgrounds, and other graphics that harmonize. The idea is that a Web site will look more professional if it contains attractive and consistent visuals — which means (for example) that within a given theme, you wouldn't be likely to have both orange and green buttons because orange and green are almost always ugly together — a color combination fit only for Halloween.

If you aren't unduly sensitive to issues of color and design, you can either use the 54 built-in themes supplied by Microsoft (or modify them, as this chapter will illustrate), or you can ask a friend who's graphically talented to help you choose compatible colors, fonts, and shapes and other elements.

Tip

If you chose the Custom option during the VI setup process, you might have chosen no themes, or the basic set of 18 themes. If you want to have the choice of all 54 themes (they are generally very well done), run VI's setup.exe program again from the VI CDs.

Layouts and Templates

Some have found themselves confused about the meaning — in the VI/FP world — of the following terms: Themes, Templates, Layouts, and Style Sheets. The following sections discuss the differences between these terms.

Understanding Layouts

Layouts, for example, are quite distinct from the other three concepts. When you choose New Project from the VI File menu, then double-click the New Web Project icon, the New Project Wizard steps you through the job of setting up a new project.

While going through this process, you'll be asked: Do you want to apply a layout? And you're given a list of odd-sounding options like Bottom 1 and Right 1. To answer this question, you'll need to know that a Layout is a description of how you want a *navigation bar or bars* positioned on the pages of your project.

Note

A *navigation bar* is a related set of hyperlinks that allow the user to jump to various locations within your site. Navigation bars are placed within shared borders (a zone in the pages that remain static even when the user moves to a different page). Navigation bars are automatically updated if you change the hierarchical structure of your site, perhaps moving a page that was several levels down so it is promoted to a position directly under the home page, for example. To learn how to create, edit, delete, and otherwise manage navigation bars, see Chapter 5.

By the way, *Bottom1* means a pair of Previous and Next buttons (or simple text) hyperlinks will be placed at the bottom of the page. *Right 1* means that a list of links to sibling pages (pages that share the same parent as the current page) will appear on the right side of the page.

Using Templates

You're probably familiar with templates if you've worked with word processors. They are simply documents that have been formatted by a professional. Perhaps you are looking for a job and have to provide a resume. Rather than beginning from scratch, you can load in a resume template and just replace the existing text with your own data. This way, the appearance of your resume is clean and professional.

In VI, a template works much the same way it does in word processing. A *template* is merely a pre-designed HTML or ASP page. You can use templates provided by VI, or create your own custom templates for future use, or to provide to your co-workers. In addition to saving time, templates can also help enforce a coherent style within a Web site.

When you choose Add Item from the VI Project menu, you'll see the available VI templates in the right pane of the dialog that pops up. At the time of this writing, the templates are: HTML page, ASP page, Style Sheet, and Site Diagram. We explain HTML pages throughout this book. The HTML page template provides this source code:

```
<HTML>
<HEAD>
<META NAME="GENERATOR" Content="Microsoft Visual Studio 6.0">
</HEAD>
<BODY>

<P> </P>

</BODY>
</HTML>
```

Even so, we suspect that the `<P> </P>` will be eliminated by the time the final version of VI ships to stores.

Tip   After you've studied style sheets in this chapter, you may want to connect what you've learned with two other key topics: the *ASP template* (explored in Chapters 16 and 17) and *site diagrams* (explained in Chapter 5).

Themes and Cascading Style Sheets

You may recall from the first paragraph in this chapter that all themes are style sheets, but not all style sheets are themes. Technically, a *theme* is a set of Cascading Style Sheets (CSS) that define a coordinated group of elements — fonts, bullets, backgrounds, buttons, and so on — that are colored and contain textures chosen to be graphically compatible and pleasing to the eye. Cascading Style Sheets are in a broader category: they are lists of definitions for HTML elements. For example, you can redefine the qualities of <H1> (the first-level HTML headline). In other words, you can specify *changes* to the default qualities of an HTML element. Perhaps you want all your first-level headlines to be colored blue. Then, whenever you use that element in an HTML document — no matter how often — that element will display those changes, those new qualities you gave it in the Style Sheet.

They are called *Cascading* Style Sheets because several kinds of style sheets exist (along with several levels of impact); each has its own order of precedence, a different scope within a Web page. A CSS can be used for purposes other than the uniformity of visual design that a theme provides.

Built-in Themes

When developing VI projects, you can use built-in themes from either VI or FP. VI and FrontPage both ship with 54 Themes from which you can choose. They range from the playful messages like "Tilt," (shown in Figure 10-1) to sophisticated designs like "Global Marketing" (shown in Figure 10-2).

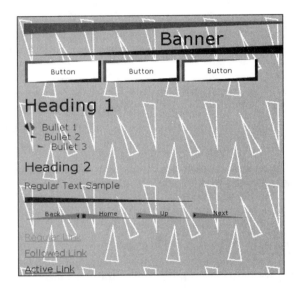

Figure 10-1: 54 Themes ship with VI, including this retro '50s "futuristic" look.

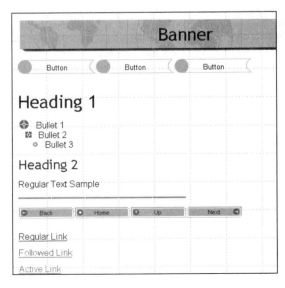

Figure 10-2: Some Themes are sober, like this one, and suitable for serious business Web sites.

When you take a closer look at the existing, built-in Themes, you'll find that each resides in its own directory, and that directory's name is the name of the theme. You're likely to find the Themes in one of these two paths on your hard drive: C :\Program Files\Common Files\Microsoft Shared\MS Themes or C :\Program Files\Microsoft FrontPage\Themes. If you look at the Global Marketing Theme's directory, you'll find a group of images (.GIF files) and a few Cascading Style Sheets (.CSS files). There are also a couple of brief information files (.INF and .UTF8) that describe the Theme version, type (read-only), and title of the Theme.

Themes in VI

You can use a built-in theme in Visual InterDev by selecting New Project from the File menu, then choosing New Web Project (double-click on its icon). This launches the Web Project Wizard. Answer the Wizard's questions and keep clicking the Next button until you get to the Instructions for selecting a theme, as shown in Figure 10-3.

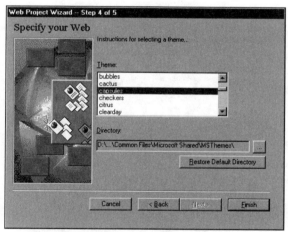

Figure 10-3: In Visual InterDev, you can choose a Theme within this New Web Project Wizard.

You can apply a theme (or layout) at any time to an existing VI project. Right-click the project's name in Project Explorer (a project's name is in boldface), then select Apply Theme and layout from the menu that pops out. Source code similar to the following will be inserted into your project:

```
<LINK REL="stylesheet" TYPE="text/css"
HREF="_Themes/arcs/THEME.CSS" VI6.0THEME="Arcs">
```

```
<LINK REL="stylesheet" TYPE="text/css"
 HREF="_Themes/arcs/GRAPH0.CSS" VI6.0THEME="Arcs">
<LINK REL="stylesheet" TYPE="text/css"
 HREF="_Themes/arcs/COLOR0.CSS" VI6.0THEME="Arcs">
<LINK REL="stylesheet" TYPE="text/css"
 HREF="_Themes/arcs/CUSTOM.CSS" VI6.0THEME="Arcs">
```

Themes in FrontPage

Recall from Chapter 7 that if you're using FrontPage98, you can select a Theme by activating FrontPage Explorer, then clicking the Themes icon in the Views window (or select Theme from the View menu). FrontPage shows better samples of Themes than does VisualInterDev, revealing FP's greater emphasis on the content of a Web page (versus VI's emphasis on programming and coordinating group programming). You can then preview the list of built-in themes, as shown in Figure 10-4.

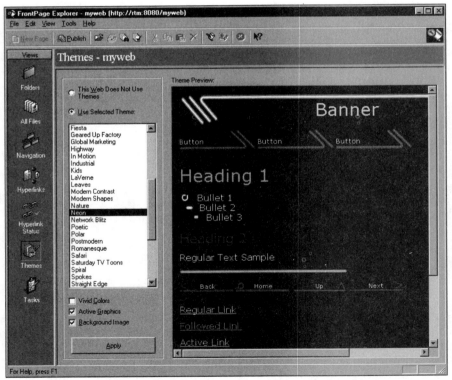

Figure 10-4: Use FrontPage's Explorer to add a theme to an FP project.

Tip

When you apply a Theme to an entire existing web, the fonts, colors, bullets, lines, and other elements will be changed throughout all the pages of the web. These changes cannot be undone.

After you've chosen a theme in FP, you'll see a line similar to the following inserted into the HTML of your document:

```
<meta name="Microsoft Theme" content="neon 011, default">
```

Modification by subtraction

One way to modify an existing Theme is to delete elements within that Theme's directory. VI98 and FrontPage will ignore elements not included in the directory. So, if you want to eliminate, for example, the large bullet in the Global Marketing Theme, just delete or move the file named GLOBUL1A.GIF. (You can usually figure out the meaning of the filenames — Global Bullet 1A, in this case. If using Windows NT, the NT Explorer makes life easy for you by displaying the actual graphic whenever you select one (as you can see in Figure 10-5).

Figure 10-5: NT displays any selected graphic file. The bullet graphic element in the left pane displays the contents of the selected Globul1a.gif file.

Modifying by substitution

You can also modify existing elements by replacing existing graphics files with your own (just use the same filename as the original). For example, if you want to change the look of the large bullet in the Global Marketing Theme, just delete or move the GLOBUL1A.GIF file, and save your new, substituted graphic with that same filename, GLOBUL1A.GIF, in the Global subdirectory.

Figure 10-6 shows a modification of the original large bullet for the Global Marketing Theme, alongside the original:

  Figure 10-6: A comparison of the original (right) bullet and the modified large bullet for the Global Theme (left). Both are shown in their original size, and in expanded versions.

 Note There can be many similar filenames for the elements within a Theme. For instance, the Global Theme includes several bullet files: GLOBUL1A.GIF and GLOBUL1D.GIF. The first one is the large bullet shown in Figure 10-5; the second file is the same bullet, but with a simpler design. The second file is used if you deselect the Active Graphics option when adding a Theme using the FrontPage Explorer or the VI98 Theme dialog.

To see the results of a deleted or substituted element, press F5 to refresh your browser (or editor).

 Caution Avoid editing a theme's .CSS files because you can destroy them that way. The results can become unpredictable or you can simply break the Theme entirely.

Cascading Style Sheets

A Cascading Style Sheet is very similar to a Theme. A style sheet allows you to step back from a document and control its appearance in an abstract way, just as does a Theme. Recall that both work much the same way as templates do in word processors, and offer several advantages over plain HTML. For example, you could define the size, color, and typeface of your secondary headline (H2). Once defined, this specification (the size, color, and typeface) will always remain consistent throughout any document linked to the style sheet. Aside from helping to enforce consistency of design, the style sheet also makes it much simpler to modify a design. If you want to change the typeface, for instance, of your second-level headline, you could merely redefine the H2 style in the style sheet, rather than having to go through an entire Web site and individually redefine each secondary head.

Gaining finer control with CSS

Another benefit of style sheets is that they give you finer control over certain elements than do the plain HTML commands. HTML is usually relativistic (for instance, HTML defines type size as *big, bigger, biggest* rather than 10pt, 14pt, 24pt, which are absolute sizes of type). Using plain HTML, you cannot specify leading (the space between lines of text), point size, and several other elements of the appearance of your pages. Style sheets also allow you to eliminate a number of HTML tags. For example, when you want to create margins in your text, HTML only offers clumsy solutions like the BLOCKQUOTE tag. Using a style sheet, you can specify exactly the margins you're after.

```
<P STYLE="margin-left: 0.5in; margin-right 0.5.in">
This line is governed by a style that will force it to be
 indented within a browser.
</P>
This line is not governed by a style that will force it to be
 indented within a browser.
```

Kerning

A particularly blatant example of accomplishing something using a style that's quite beyond plain HTML is narrowing (or expanding) the spacing between individual letters. Frequently large typesizes look much better when you decrease the space between the letters (this is called *kerning*). To accomplish this, use a variation on the following style, providing a negative letter-spacing to tighten up the characters (see Figure 10-7):

```
<head>
<title>Linking Styles</title>
<style>H1 { font-size: 32pt;letter-spacing: -2pt }</style>
</head>
<BODY>
<H1>THIS IS A NORMAL HEADLINE</H1>
```

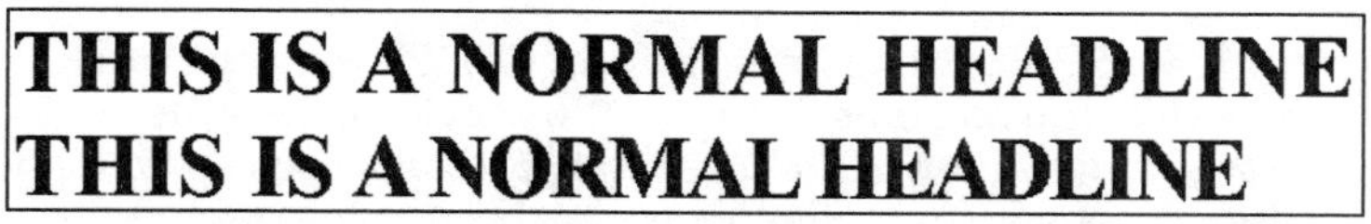

THIS IS A NORMAL HEADLINE
THIS IS A NORMAL HEADLINE

Figure 10-7: Large headlines are generally easier to read and more attractive when you decrease the space between the letters. This effect, shown in the lower headline, could never be achieved with simple HTML commands.

In the previous source code example you can see that multiple arguments can be provided for an individual element, as long as they are separated by semi-colons.

Linking Styles

You can attach styles to your documents in various ways, but the simplest is to use the HTML STYLE command. You can affect an entire page by placing the STYLE within the HEAD section, like this example that defines the main headline style:

```
<HEAD>
<TITLE>Linking Styles</TITLE>
 <STYLE> H1 { font-size: 22pt; color: blue }</STYLE>
 </HEAD>
<BODY>
<H1>THIS IS A MAIN (LEVEL 1) HEADLINE</H1>
```

Now, every time you use the H1 tag in your page, you'll see it displayed in 22pt. blue text.

You can find a complete reference to all the specifications for Cascading Style Sheets at http://www.htmlhelp.com/reference/css.

There are three main ways to use style sheets:

✦ Link a page to an external style sheet.

✦ Create an embedded style sheet on a page.

✦ Use small ("inline") styles for particular elements within a page.

Understanding external sheet files

External sheets provide large-scale (FrontPage Web-wide) consistency. All the documents or pages within a Web will follow the same style rules. External style sheets are named with a .CSS file extension (GLOBAL.CSS, for example). An embedded style sheet (like the one illustrated for the previous H1) is useful only when you are interested in limiting your style to the particular page in which the style is embedded. However, an embedded (or even a brief inline) style will override any specifications in an external style sheet.

"Cascading" means precedence

The idea that there is an order of precedence (one kind of style can override a competing style) is where the term *cascading* comes from. It means that the order of precedence cascades, according to the following rules:

✦ Document author style definitions override user definitions. People can apply their style sheets to your Web site — customizing the look of your pages to suit their own tastes *unless* your style definitions conflict with theirs. In that case, your definitions override theirs. If you want to try applying a personal style sheet to Internet Explorer, right-click on its icon (or filename) and choose Properties to display its property sheets. In the General tab, click the button labeled Accessibility. At the bottom of the Accessibility dialog, you can select the CheckBox named Format Documents Using My Style Sheet, and then type in or browse for the .CSS file that you want to use for your custom style.

✦ User style sheets take precedence over standard browser default definitions (like the default specifications of the standard main headline H1).

✦ Inline styles override embedded style sheets.

✦ Embedded style sheets (and inline styles) override linked (external) style sheets.

Using SPAN commands for larger sections

If you want to use the inline approach, but have a style nevertheless affect an entire block or large region of your document (not just a <P> paragraph), use the SPAN command.

Listing 10-1 shows how to use the SPAN command.

Listing 10-1: **Using the SPAN command**

```
<html>

<head>
<title>Styles</title>
</head>

<body>
<font SIZE="+1" FACE="Arial"><span STYLE="
 font-weight: bold; color: red "><big>
```

```
<p>Conveniently</big> <i>in one location,
you can specify a variety of formatting and
page-design attributes:</i> alignment, background
colors, colors, graphic images, grouped
font specifications, indentation, leading (spacing
between lines of text), margins, point
size, special effects, style (such as italic), typeface,
weight (such as boldface). </span>
<br>
<br>
External sheets provide large-scale (FrontPage
Web-wide) consistency. All the documents or
pages within a Web will follow the same style rules.
External style sheets are named with
a .css file extension (GLOBAL.CSS, for example). <br>
<br>
</p>
</font>
</body>
</html>
```

In this example, the font size and typeface are specified in the traditional HTML fashion. However, a separate style is defined to span a portion of this document, ending with the </SPAN> tag. The style changes the text color to red and the weight to boldface.

Note that you can interrupt a SPAN with a different style, if you wish (employing the override, or cascading effect). Change the example just given: Insert a new line that overrides the red style with a temporary blue style. Only the line between <P> and </P> will be red. That's because you're redefining the meaning of the <P> tag, if only briefly. (You could just as well redefine other tags.) Here's an override style.

```
<SPAN STYLE="font-weight: bold; color: blue">
<BIG>Conveniently</BIG>
<P STYLE="color:red"> We want this red, not blue.</P>
<I>in one location, you can specify a variety
 of formatting and page-design attributes:</I>
```

Embedded Style Blocks

Inline style adjustments are fine for a line or two, but if you find yourself using many of them, you have more or less eliminated a primary advantage of styles: their global efficiency. Remember that it's not difficult to put a style sheet into a document. Just enclose it between <STYLE> and </STYLE> tags. The style block is supposed to appear at the beginning of a document, prior to the <BODY> tag. Any style specifications you list within the style block will affect the entire document.

Defining a new style

To define a new style, start with an HTML tag (like LI, H1, P) or *any other HTML tag* that you want to redefine. Then, enclosed in braces {}, type in a property:specification (such as font:11pt). Remember that you can include as many of these property:specification pairs as you want, separating them by semicolons (as in `font: 48pt "Arial"; font-weight: bold; color: blue`).

Using an embedded style block

Listing 10-2 is an example of an embedded style block, where you define three typefaces. The default BODY will be 11 point Courier, any <P> paragraphs will be 14 point Arial and rendered in red. Any <H1> headlines will be bold, blue, and 48 points large.

Listing 10-2: **An Embedded Style Block Defining Three Typefaces**

```
<HTML>
<HEAD>
<TITLE>Styles</TITLE>
</HEAD>

<STYLE TYPE="text/css">
<!--
 BODY {font: 11pt "Courier"};
 P {font: 14pt "Arial"; color: red}
 H1 {font: 48pt "Arial";
         font-weight: bold;
         color: blue}
 -->
</STYLE>

<BODY>
This is ordinary
<P> This is paragraph style </P>
and this is a
<H1>HEADLINE</H>

</BODY>
</HTML>
```

Style syntax

Note the punctuation for each style definition: *HTML tag, left brace, general parameter, colon, specification, semicolon, any additional parameters, right brace.*

```
P {font: 14pt "Arial"; color: red}
```

Linked Style Sheets

Recall from the "Understanding External Sheet Files" section that if you don't want to embed a style sheet within each of your documents, you can put the style sheet on the hard drive of your server, and merely insert its URL into your documents. When a user's browser comes upon this link, it will open your style file and take appropriate action — just as if you'd embedded the style sheet in the documents' source code.

To do this, create a style sheet (as described earlier under "Embedded Style Blocks"). But, instead of putting it into a document, save it as a file to disk instead. Give it a file extension .CSS.

Let's try it. Here's a simple style sheet:

```
BODY {font: 11pt "Courier"};
P {font: 14pt "Arial"; color: red}
H1 {font: 48pt "Arial";
        font-weight: bold;
        color: blue}
```

Save this in an ordinary text file (you could use Windows's Notepad) as STY.CSS in *the same directory as your documents* for testing purposes. That way, you don't have to provide a complete URL and path, just the filename will do.

Using Classes for Variations

If you want to create several different styles for, say, the P (paragraph) or H (headline) or some other HTML tag, you can create *classes*.

Assume that you want three different paragraph styles: one that's red, one green, and one blue. Define them this way, using whatever .class name you want. In this example, we'll use .red, .green, and .blue, but you can use whatever identifier you choose.

```
<HEAD>
<TITLE>Style Sheets</TITLE>
<STYLE TYPE="text/css">
<!--
P.red {font: 14; color: red}
P.green {font: 14; color: green}
P.blue {font: 14; color: blue}
-->
</STYLE>

</HEAD>
<BODY>
```

This is ordinary body text:

```
<P CLASS=red> This is our red paragraph style </P>
<P CLASS=green> This is our red paragraph style </P>
<P CLASS=blue> This is our red paragraph style </P>

</BODY>
</HTML>
```

Each paragraph in this text now displays the characteristics of the pre-defined paragraph classes. The CLASS attribute defines how the P element will be interpreted by the browser.

Referencing a Linked Style Sheet

There are two ways to reference a linked style sheet (or a linked graphic or linked document, for that matter):

1. To link to another site entirely, provide its complete URL address:

```
"http://altavista.digital.com"
```

2. To link to another document file in the same directory (or on the same hard drive) as the document itself, just provide the filename (or the path on that hard drive):

```
"MYPICT.HTM"
```

OR, for a style sheet, a filename like this:

```
"STY.CSS"
```

So, assuming that you've saved your STY.CSS file in the same directory as your source code (your .HTM file), here's how to provide a link to that style sheet to the .HTM document. As with an embedded style sheet, you put a link to a style sheet *within the <HEAD> … </HEAD> area of your document* (before the <BODY> tag):

```
<HEAD>
<TITLE>Style Sheets</TITLE>
<LINK REL=STYLESHEET HREF="STY.CSS" TYPE="text/css">
</HEAD>
<BODY>
This is ordinary
<P> This is paragraph style </P>
and this is a
<H1>HEADLINE</H>

</BODY>
</HTML>
```

Using VI's CSS Editor

The VI CSS Editor can simplify creating your own style sheets. Select your project's name in the VI Project Explorer (this enables VI's Add Item feature). A project name is always boldface, to distinguish it from the files *within* that project. Then, from the Project menu, choose Add Item and double-click the Style Sheet icon, as shown in Figure 10-8.

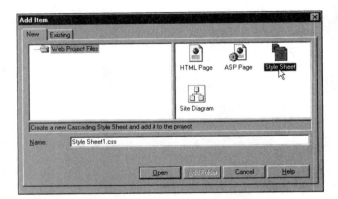

Figure 10-8: Click this icon to use the Cascading Style Sheet Editor.

Creating a style sheet independently

Alternatively, you can create a style sheet even if you're not currently working on a Web project in VI. Select New File from the File menu, then click Visual InterDev in the left pane and choose Style Sheet in the right pane. Once you've activated the CSS Editor, you'll see the properties dialog shown in Figure 10-9.

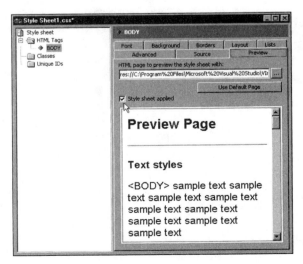

Figure 10-9: The Preview tab shows you the results of your handiwork in the Style Sheet Editor.

Redefining HTML elements

The CSS editor allows you to redefine any HTML element recognized by Internet Explorer 4. When you fire up the CSS editor, by default it starts with the BODY tag selected. Following is an example of defining a style for <BODY>.

1. Click the Font tab. Double-click Arial in the Installed Fonts list, thereby transferring it to the Selected Fonts list.

2. Now double-click Lucida Sans. The Selected Fonts list specifies which fonts you want displayed, in your order of preference. Given that the user's computer might not have the same fonts installed as your computer has, the user's browser will search down your Selected Fonts list trying to find a match. In our example, if the user's browser cannot find Arial, your first choice, it will next try to find Lucida Sans. You can also specify color, size, and various font styles such as italic. The Weight option defines how dark, how boldface, the characters should be. The Size and Weight options can be absolute (you name the precise size you want, such as 24 pt., a medium headline size) or relative. Relative means relative to the element's container. For example, if you're defining an <H1> headline and specify Relative and Larger, all H1 heads will have a font size larger than the <BODY> font size (or whatever other container the H1 is in, such as a <DIV>).

3. Choose a Medium absolute font size and Mediumblue color.

4. Now click the Borders tab in the CSS Editor.

5. Choose Double as the Style and pick a color.

6. Under Width, select General, then Thick, as shown in Figure 10-10.

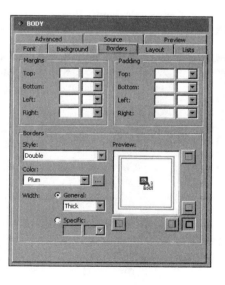

Figure 10-10: In this dialog, you can design borders around your elements, as well as specify margins and padding (the distance between the interior border and an element's contents, such as text).

7. Now click the Preview tab in the CSS dialog and you'll see your border and text styles in effect within the sample page (as shown in Figure 10-9 earlier).

Toggle between plain and styled HTML

Try clicking the Style Sheet Applied check box on the Preview tab; you can toggle back and forth between a plain HTML element and your redefinition of it — a nice touch. Also notice that you can specify that one of your own Web pages be the preview page. Just click the Browse button in the Preview tab to locate the .HTM file you want to see.

Click the Source tab to see the source code STYLE definition you've created. In this example, you'll see something like this:

```
<STYLE>
BODY
{
  BORDER-BOTTOM: plum double thick;
  BORDER-LEFT: plum double thick;
  BORDER-RIGHT: plum double thick;
  BORDER-TOP: plum double thick;
  COLOR: mediumblue;
  FONT-FAMILY: Arial, 'Lucida Sans';
  FONT-SIZE: medium
}
</STYLE>
```

Adding other elements

Now that you've defined the body, you might want to also define additional HTML elements using the CSS editor. Right-click the word BODY on the left side (the tree structure) of the CSS. You'll see the context menu shown in Figure 10-11.

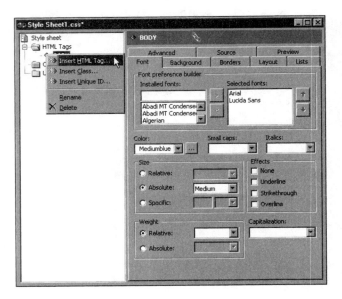

Figure 10-11: Right-click on an element to define additional elements.

As you can see, you simply need to select the Insert HTML Tag option to redefine any other HTML element, such as P or H1.

Modifying HTML tags

To modify HTML tags, choose Insert New HTML Tag from the context menu described earlier, then type in H1, or select H1 from within the drop down list (in the Insert New HTML Tag dialog that appears when you choose Insert HTML Tag from the context menu). Then click OK. Note that H1 has now been inserted into the tree diagram, as a subsidiary element under BODY. You can now proceed to define the qualities you want to give to an H1 headline. Make it a different color and font than the <BODY>.

Creating new classes

If you want to have several specifications for a single HTML element, you can create classes by selecting the Insert New Class option when you right-click on an element in the tree. Recall that classes redefine a single element by using the . (period) to separate the element name from a class name, such as: P.red {font: 14; color: red} P.green {font: 14; color: green} P.blue {font: 14; color: blue}. Classes can also allow a definition of a style shared among two or more elements.

Inserting unique IDs

The final option on the context menu that appears when you right-click an element allows you to Insert a Unique ID. Unique ID styles are indicated by a # (pound) sign inserted into the name of the style: #BlueHead or H1#BlueHead. The Unique ID styles are used to identify DHTML elements within scripts. Here's an example showing you how to use the identifier *#locat* within a style definition to specify a DIV with an ID named *locat*. The qualities that your style defines for the DIV are specified between braces {}, as shown in the following code:

```
<HTML>
<HEAD>

<STYLE TYPE="text/css">
#locat {POSITION: relative; VISIBILITY: visible;
 TOP 100; LEFT: 20}
</STYLE>

</HEAD>

<BODY>

<DIV ID="locat">
Base this Div on a style.
</DIV>
```

```
</BODY>
</HTML>
```

Linking to a Web Page

Now that you've defined a style sheet, let's link it to a Web page to see the effects in the real world. Select Add Item from the Project menu, then choose HTML page. Click the Source tab in the editor, then type the following between the HEAD elements in your new HTML page:

```
<HEAD>
<LINK REL=STYLESHEET HREF="Style Sheet1.CSS" TYPE="text/css">
</HEAD>
```

By default, VI names the first style sheet created by the CSS editor Style Sheet1.CSS, so if you've renamed your style sheet, change this HREF= to reflect the new name. Here is the complete test HTML page source code:

```
<HTML>
<HEAD>
<LINK REL=STYLESHEET HREF="Style Sheet1.CSS" TYPE="text/css">
</HEAD>
<BODY>

<H1>HERE IS OUR NEW HEAD</H1>
<P>Styles are defined for this page by a CSS.</P>

</BODY>
</HTML>
```

Click Quick View to see the results of your efforts, as shown in Figure 10-12.

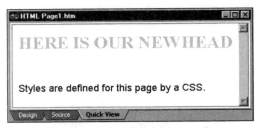

Figure 10-12: You can link any page in your project to the .CSS file, thereby applying the custom styles to that page.

You can bring up the CSS Editor at any time while you're working on a project that contains a CSS file. Just double-click on the CSS file in the Project Explorer.

Summary

Several important Web page design topics were covered in this chapter, where you learned

- ✦ Distinguishing between layouts, themes, style sheets, and templates.
- ✦ How to use an existing template to enforce consistency within a Web site and to simplify the development of a site.
- ✦ How to create new templates of your own.
- ✦ About Cascading Style Sheets which are, after all, the basis of themes.
- ✦ How to master the CSS Editor, a utility that assists you in creating style sheets of your own.

✦   ✦   ✦

Working on the Client Side

Introduction to Client-Side Components

If you need to create more dynamic Web applications, you've probably considered using ActiveX and/or Java components. If you're a developer familiar with Object Linking and Embedding (OLE) controls, you'll get up to speed on ActiveX controls very quickly. After all, they are the third generation of OLE controls (OCX). Because Java is much newer, you may not be as familiar with it as you are with ActiveX. In either case, this chapter gives you an overview of both Web component technologies along with a comparison of their strengths and weaknesses. You learn the syntax for adding an ActiveX control and a Java applet to an HTML page.The chapter closes by showing you how to use the VI HTML Editor to add an ActiveX control to a Web page and set the properties.

Survey of Web Components

Would you like to create dynamic, highly interactive Web pages quickly and easily? Then you want to use active Web components such as ActiveX controls and Java applets. Components are getting a lot of attention these days because they are reusable pieces of software that you can assemble into an application with minimal effort. While component technology is a much-anticipated goal for the entire software industry, the Web technology is immature and changing constantly. Nonetheless, whether you are an experienced Web page designer or new to HTML, this chapter shows you how simple it is to incorporate existing Web components into your Web applications.

The most common Web components are ActiveX and Java. Client-side ActiveX components are called ActiveX controls, and server-side ActiveX components are called Active Server Components. Client-side Java components are called Java applets and server-side Java components are called Java Servlets. A JavaBean is similar to an ActiveX component and as such is used to build Java applets and Servlets. The introduction of Dynamic HTML (DHTML) permits you to create a control from an HTML page called a scriptlet.

Although client-side Web components typically have a user interface, they might only perform a business calculation and return a value. Server components never have a user interface. They perform services to build HTML pages on the Web server. This chapter focuses on ActiveX controls and Java applets. You work with scriptlets and server-side components later in this book.

ActiveX controls

ActiveX technology has been around for a number of years. Microsoft originally called it Object Linking and Embedding (OLE), a technology for creating compound documents. In OLE 2, Microsoft added conventions and libraries to allow different software modules to interact in an object-oriented manner and called it Component Object Model (COM). To address the specific needs of the Internet, Microsoft created a streamlined version of COM called ActiveX. This framework allows ActiveX components written in different programming languages to communicate with each other. In addition, if the platforms support ActiveX, these components can be on different machines and different operating systems. This is called a *Distributed Component Object Model* (DCOM).

ActiveX controls are COM components used to build Web pages and applications. As the demand for more sophisticated Web capabilities increases, programmers already familiar with ActiveX and COM technology are developing Web sites that take advantage of the power of ActiveX controls.

 Note   It is important to distinguish between the terms *ActiveX* and *ActiveX controls*. ActiveX refers to a large group of related technologies including COM and DCOM, which enable interactive content in Web applications. An ActiveX control is a reusable software component that was written utilizing these technologies.

ActiveX controls come in a variety of familiar Windows objects, such as drop-down menus, radio buttons, and list boxes. Examples of the more sophisticated controls built specifically for the Web are the Microsoft NetShow and ActiveMovie controls. More than a thousand ActiveX controls are available for purchase.

Strengths and weaknesses

It is controversial whether to use ActiveX controls in Web applications. This section discusses how this object model works, along with the strengths and weaknesses of using ActiveX controls in Web applications. Armed with this knowledge, you can make an informed decision about whether to use ActiveX controls in your Web application.

Note For information on the latest developments in ActiveX technology, visit the Microsoft ActiveX Web site at http://www.microsoft.com/activex.

Platform support

ActiveX controls are multiplatform, which means they are compiled into the native code of the target system (machine and operating system). These platforms are currently supported: Windows 95, 98, and NT, and the Mac. UNIX, IBM, HP, and Digital platform support is currently under development.

The advantage of the multiplatform approach is fast execution on the target platform. In addition, as the developer you have the ability to tune the control for optimum performance on each platform as well as to take advantage of the specific capabilities of each platform. Unfortunately, if the control uses the Windows Application Programming Interface (API), the control needs to be ported to each target platform. Unless you are developing an intranet application, where you have total control over the target platforms of your users, you'll invest additional time and money creating and supporting platform-specific versions of a custom control. Rather than develop a custom control, you could purchase one from a third-party developer.

Download

ActiveX control files are actually Dynamic Link Libraries (DLLs), which contain the code for the specific features being implemented, along with library routines. In addition to what's in the DLL file, the control may require additional software to run. In this case, the developer packages the set of files in a cabinet (.cab) file for download. Once the file is on the user machine, it is uncompressed and registered. Because the file size is relatively large and because it takes time to uncompress and register a control, the delay experienced the first time an ActiveX control loads can be long.

Typically, once a control is registered on a user machine, the browser uses it rather than downloading another copy. To be sure the user always runs the most current version of the control, however, the Web page developer can specify a version number for a control in the Web page. When the browser encounters the <OBJECT> tag, it checks to see if the correct version of the control exists locally. If not, the browser downloads it. Consequently, this control will always load slowly.

Performance

Because Active X controls are compiled into the native code of the target system, they execute fast. Developers can achieve optimum performance on each platform by creating a unique version of the control specifically tuned for each platform. This is a very complex and costly endeavor that only a few organizations are willing and able to undertake.

Security

Because ActiveX controls are in native code, they have access to all of the capabilities of the end user's machine. That means that these controls can read and write files, allocate memory, and print. Consequently, an unscrupulous person can easily create a malicious ActiveX control that can damage the end user's machine. Fortunately, control developers can use Microsoft's Authenticode system to sign their ActiveX control. What this does is tell the end user who the control's developer was and whom to hold accountable if the control causes problems. Organizations such as VeriSign Commercial Software Publishers CA issue digital certificates. When a control developer wishes to have a control digitally signed, they must pay the certification authority and submit an application stating they meet certain qualifications. The certification authority verifies the application information and manages the certificates.

When the browser downloads a control, the dialog box shown in Figure 11-1 appears. The dialog box shows the control that the browser is downloading along with the control developer and the certification authority. The user has the option of allowing — or not allowing — the browser to download and register the ActiveX control.

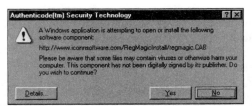

Figure 11-1: The Authenticode™ Security Technology dialog box appears when the browser downloads a control.

Availability

Thanks to the great popularity of Visual Basic and Visual C++, many developers have the knowledge and experience that is needed to create ActiveX controls. In addition, developers can use other products such as Microsoft Visual J++, Borland's Delphi 3.0, and Powersoft's PowerBuilder 5.0 to create ActiveX controls. Even with this large source of experienced developers, if your company is not capable of undertaking a custom development effort, there is a booming market for controls produced by third parties. You can locate ActiveX controls that are for sale on the Internet at `http://browserwatch.internet.com/activex.html` and at `http://www.microsoft.com/msdn/thirdparty/`.

Browser support

Web browsers execute Web pages. Because these same Web pages contain ActiveX controls, for the browser to run a page that contains an ActiveX control, the browser must be capable of handling ActiveX controls. This type of browser is called an ActiveX container because an ActiveX control can only execute in an ActiveX container.

Unfortunately, not all browsers support ActiveX controls. Naturally, Microsoft's Internet Explorer 4.0 does, so if your users are using Windows, they are likely to be running this browser. If some of your users have a Netscape browser, you can purchase ScriptActive, a plug-in made by nCompass to support ActiveX on Netscape Navigator 3.*x* and Netscape Communicator 4.*x*.

Java applets and JavaBeans

Java is an object-oriented programming language developed by Sun Microsystems. Although it was modeled after C++, it was designed to be portable. You may be familiar with the Java slogan, "write once, run anywhere." This refers to the fundamental principle that underlies the Java language — you only need to write a Java application one time. This is possible because it can run on any system on which a Java virtual machine (JVM) is installed, and JVMs are available for most popular operating systems.

This "write once, run anywhere" capability has made Java very popular among Web developers, where it is crucial for an HTML page to run on any system. A special type of Java application called an applet runs in a Java-enabled browser; that is, one that has a JVM.

With the tremendous popularity of the Java language came the JavaBean specification. Like COM, this specification allows Java developers to create modular, reusable components, so that they can build applications more quickly. In addition, these components can communicate with each other, which lets developers build more robust applications.

Java applets

Created specifically for the Internet, the Java applet is a self-contained module that may or may not have a user interface. Typically, a dynamic and interactive Java applet displays an image, runs animations, or displays text in the HTML page.

Unlike ActiveX components that only run on the target platform, Java applets run on any platform. Here's how that works. After writing a Java applet, the software developer compiles it with the Java compiler, which creates a file of bytecode. The developer inserts the Java applet into an HTML page using the ⟨APPLET⟩ tag pair. You learn how to add a Java applet to an HTML page later in this chapter. When the client browser encounters the ⟨APPLET⟩ tag, it downloads the Java bytecode file and passes it to the JVM. The JVM, which is embedded in the browser, reads the bytecode and translates it into native code, which it runs. Although it looks as if the browser is running the applet, the JVM is actually running it.

Note   If you are working with a browser that supports the HTML 4.0 standard, instead of using the ⟨APPLET⟩ element to insert a Java applet, you can use the ⟨OBJECT⟩ element. For more information on the HTML 4.0 standard, see Appendix B.

It is this fundamental design principle of the Java language, that only the JVM processes the bytecode, which allows Java to run anywhere there is a JVM. To implement this design principle, a JVM must be written for every target machine and operating system. And as is typical of any evolving technology, as the Java language grows and changes, the JVMs must be upgraded to support the newest capabilities. End users must upgrade as well. Unfortunately, during the transition, end users with older JVMs cannot take advantage of the newest features. To be realistic, this problem is inherent everywhere in the Web because the Web is evolving at such a rapid pace. You may have experienced this in the browser wars between Microsoft and Netscape as HTML evolves. As a developer of Web applications, be aware of this situation and take appropriate steps to handle it.

JavaBeans

With the simple component model in the original Java language, components could not interact with each other. Voilà! JavaBeans component architecture comes to the rescue. This architecture defines components, modular reusable code, and how they will communicate with other Java components. As a direct consequence of this specification, developers can create Java-based components in new ways not previously possible.

A further development of this component concept is the JavaBean, a reusable software component similar to an ActiveX control. In this context, JavaBeans refers to a component rather than to the architecture. This unfortunate double meaning for JavaBeans can be confusing though no more confusing than the double meaning for ActiveX technology and controls. Unlike ActiveX components, which can interoperate with any COM components, JavaBeans components only interoperate with other Java components. The main advantage of this limitation is how simple it is for a Java programmer to create a Java application. This is not to say that JavaBeans can only communicate with JavaBeans. They can interoperate with ActiveX components via bridges.

To use JavaBeans in your Web pages, you first include them in a Java applet, then add the applet to your page. As with ActiveX controls, you can use all kinds of JavaBeans in your Web pages. For instance, you can use a Bean for spell checking and a Bean to add font capabilities to your text. There are also database Beans for connecting your page to a database. Remember that Beans can interact with other Beans and like ActiveX controls, JavaBeans are reusable.

Strengths and weaknesses

With all the current excitement surrounding Java, it's easy to think you're missing something if you're not using Java in your Web application. This section discusses the strengths and weaknesses of using Java on the Web so that you can make your own decision.

> For information on the latest developments in Java technology, visit the Java Technology Home Page at http://java.sun.com/.

Platform support

By design, the Java language is cross-platform, which means it runs on any platform where there is a Java Virtual Machine, which is most of the popular platforms. When used on the Web, the JVM in the browser runs the Java software component in the form of bytecode.

The advantage of being portable across all platforms is that you write the code once. This saves a great deal of time and maintenance effort. The disadvantage of this approach is that execution is slower. Although this is a major issue for many people, many other people are working to speed Java programs. Microsoft's approach, which was implemented in Internet Explorer (IE) 4.0, is a just-in-time (JIT) compiler that translates Java bytecode into native machine code while the bytecode is running.

Another clear disadvantage of portability is the lack of access to native functions, which limits the capabilities, including the user interface, of the Java applet. The Security section discusses a recent development that is intended to circumvent this limitation.

Download

The bytecode file that the browser downloads for a Java applet is exactly the same file for every machine and operating system. Because the unique libraries required for each platform are stored locally with the JVM rather than downloaded with the bytecode, the size of the file downloaded for a Java applet is smaller than for the comparable ActiveX control. Thus, relatively speaking, a Java applet downloads faster than an ActiveX control. In addition, a Java applet does not have to be registered with the operating system (OS), which saves more time.

Performance

Because the JVM translates the bytecode into the native code of the local platform, Java by its very nature executes more slowly than native applications. One of the newest approaches to improving performance is to include a just-in-time compiler with the JVM as Microsoft does in Internet Explorer 4.0. A number of companies are also working on other techniques for speeding Java performance.

Security

As more forms of businesses become dependent on the Internet for their very existence, Internet security is central to the adoption of the technology. By design, the Java environment is secure. The language handles unintentional errors such as accessing illegal memory and passing in the wrong number of parameters. To protect the user system from malicious programs, Java applets are not permitted to access native functions such as file input/output (I/O) and memory allocation. This approach is called a "sandbox" because the application can't do anything bad within this well-confined space.

Unfortunately, Web developers are finding the sandbox too restrictive. To develop more sophisticated applications, these developers are demanding access to native functions. While the sandbox is not being eliminated, Java is allowing digitally signed applets, a security model similar to what ActiveX uses. Trusted applets can now be stamped with a digital certificate that identifies the author. Untrusted applets are restricted to the sandbox, whereas trusted applets are allowed to leave it. If the trusted applet damages a system, the end user can hold the applet's author responsible. With these two changes, use of native functions and the capability to leave the sandbox, Java applets are competing in the same arena with ActiveX.

Availability

Because Java and JavaBeans are relatively new, the lack of development tools and code libraries has made it very difficult for software developers to become productive in Java. The strong interest in the language fueled by the "write once, run anywhere" slogan, as well as the anti-Microsoft sentiment, is sure to keep the Java fire burning for many years to come. In fact, every day you see more and more JavaBeans available through third-party developers.

Browser support

Because it is a hot new programming language, Java technologies are evolving rapidly. As a result, when the Java platform is upgraded, the JVMs must also be upgraded. It is not unusual to find an older browser in the field that does not support the current version of the Java platform. This problem is not unique to Java. In fact, HTML and ActiveX share the same issue, which means Web page developers must deal with this situation in their code.

ActiveX control versus Java applet

In the last two sections, we discussed the strengths and weaknesses of ActiveX controls and Java applets. In Table 11-1, you see a comparison of the two. In general, ActiveX controls are a good fit if you plan to develop an intranet application that is limited to Windows users. On the other hand, if your priority is cross-platform support and native capabilities are not an issue, Java applets are a good fit. When the requirements are not this clear cut, the decision is much more difficult.

Caution   The information in this comparison provides an introduction to ActiveX and Java. Before making a decision on which technology your organization will adopt, we advise you to conduct a more in-depth technical evaluation, which is beyond the scope of this book.

Table 11-1
Comparison of ActiveX Controls and Java Applets

Product Features and Functions	ActiveX Control	Java Applet/JavaBeans
Platform support	Windows 95, 98, and NT, Macintosh, and Unix on Intel, Apple, HP 9000 series, and Sun SPARC and Ultra	Windows 95, 98, and NT, Macintosh, Unix on Intel, Apple, Digital Alpha, HP 700 series and 9000 series, Sun SPARC and Ultra, IBM RS/6000, and more
Performance	fast on Windows	generally slower than native apps
Access to native capabilities	yes	can leave sandbox when trusted
Security	less	more
Browser support	Microsoft Internet Explorer and Netscape Navigator with a plug-in	Microsoft Internet Explorer and Netscape Navigator plus others
Length of download	longer	shorter
Availability of experienced developers and developer productivity tools	many	fewer, but increasing
Availability of third-party components	more than a thousand	more than a thousand
Ease of development	complex	simple
Maturity of technology	in later stages	in early stages

Working with Client-Side Components

VI provides two ways for you to insert a component into a Web page. In VI's HTML Editor, you can drag the component from the toolbox and drop it on the page or you can type in the appropriate HTML tag. For an ActiveX control, you use the `<OBJECT>` tag and for a Java applet, you use the `<APPLET>` tag. After dropping the ActiveX control, you can customize the way it looks and acts by setting or changing the properties of the control in the Properties dialog. The properties of a Java applet have to be manually set because the VI interface does not support it.

To control the location of the component on your HTML page, use any of the positioning techniques currently available, such as tables, layouts, and Cascading Style Sheets. If you are using DHTML, you can position the control absolutely. Finally, to incorporate the control into the logic of your application, you link the control's methods to events by writing the appropriate script. Scripting is discussed in Chapters 12 and 13. DHTML is discussed in Chapter 14.

<Object> element

The `<OBJECT>` tag identifies the ActiveX control, the location of the control, and how to display the control on the HTML page. Here is a simple example of the HTML text for the TextBox ActiveX control.

```
<OBJECT
CLASSID="clsid:8BD21D10-EC42-11CE-9E0D-00AA006002F3"
id=TextBox1 width=250>
<PARAM NAME="FontName" VALUE="MS Sans Serif">
</OBJECT>
```

The statements for the TextBox control are located between the `<OBJECT>` tag pair. You can type in these statements, but why do that when VI will generate them for you. All you need to do is drop the control on the page, and then visually set the property values. You learn how to do this later in this chapter.

In this example, the first attribute of the TextBox control is `CLASSID= clsid:8BD21D10-EC42-11CE-9E0D-00AA006002F3`, which tells the browser where to find the control in the Windows Registry. The next attribute is `id= TextBox1`, which is the name you use to refer to this instance of the TextBox control when you set the properties in VI, or reference it in script. In this example, VI automatically named the control `TextBox1`, but you can change the id. The attribute `width=250` tells the browser to display the control in an area 250 pixels wide. The final attribute shown in this example is `PARAM NAME="FontName" VALUE="MS Sans Serif"` — which tells the browser to use the MS Sans Serif font to display the text inside the text box.

Listing 11-1 is a more complex example that uses the TextBox control. When you use VI's integrated development environment (IDE) to set a property, it automatically generates statements for all of the control's parameters.

Listing 11-1: **Example of TextBox Control**

```
<OBJECT classid="clsid:8BD21D10-EC42-11CE-9E0D-00AA006002F3"
height=28
id=TextBox1
style="HEIGHT: 45px; LEFT: 0px; TOP: 0px; WIDTH: 242px"
width=17>
<PARAM NAME="VariousPropertyBits" VALUE="746604571">
<PARAM NAME="BackColor" VALUE="2147483653">
<PARAM NAME="ForeColor" VALUE="2147483656">
<PARAM NAME="MaxLength" VALUE="0">
<PARAM NAME="BorderStyle" VALUE="0">
<PARAM NAME="ScrollBars" VALUE="2">
<PARAM NAME="DisplayStyle" VALUE="1">
<PARAM NAME="MousePointer" VALUE="0">
<PARAM NAME="Size" VALUE="6403;1191">
<PARAM NAME="PasswordChar" VALUE="0">
<PARAM NAME="ListWidth" VALUE="0">
<PARAM NAME="BoundColumn" VALUE="1">
<PARAM NAME="TextColumn" VALUE="65535">
<PARAM NAME="ColumnCount" VALUE="1">
<PARAM NAME="ListRows" VALUE="8">
<PARAM NAME="cColumnInfo" VALUE="0">
<PARAM NAME="MatchEntry" VALUE="2">
<PARAM NAME="ListStyle" VALUE="0">
<PARAM NAME="ShowDropButtonWhen" VALUE="0">
<PARAM NAME="ShowListWhen" VALUE="1">
<PARAM NAME="DropButtonStyle" VALUE="1">
<PARAM NAME="MultiSelect" VALUE="0">
<PARAM NAME="Value" VALUE="">
<PARAM NAME="Caption" VALUE="">
<PARAM NAME="PicturePosition" VALUE="458753">
<PARAM NAME="BorderColor" VALUE="2147483654">
<PARAM NAME="SpecialEffect" VALUE="2">
<PARAM NAME="Accelerator" VALUE="0">
<PARAM NAME="GroupName" VALUE="">
<PARAM NAME="FontName" VALUE="MS Sans Serif">
<PARAM NAME="FontEffects" VALUE="1073741824">
<PARAM NAME="FontHeight" VALUE="240">
<PARAM NAME="FontOffset" VALUE="0">
<PARAM NAME="FontCharSet" VALUE="0">
<PARAM NAME="FontPitchAndFamily" VALUE="2">
<PARAM NAME="ParagraphAlign" VALUE="1">
<PARAM NAME="FontWeight" VALUE="400">
Your browser is not able to display ActiveX controls.
</OBJECT>
```

For browsers that do not support the <OBJECT> element or if ActiveX controls are disabled, you can include special HTML text between the <OBJECT> tag pair. If it is possible, these HTML statements can provide the visitor with an alternative way to accomplish the same task. When the browser encounters the <OBJECT> element that it cannot render, it processes the HTML text. In the previous example, rather than display a text box, the browser displays the text "Your browser is not able to display ActiveX controls."

The most commonly used attributes of the <OBJECT> element are CLASSID, CODEBASE, HEIGHT, ID, PARAM, STYLE, and WIDTH.

CLASSID

The CLASSID, or class identifier, tells the browser where to locate the component. For an ActiveX control, the CLASSID typically looks similar to this: classid=clsid:8BD21D10-EC42-11CE-9E0D-00AA006002F3.

When an ActiveX control is installed on the user's machine, the CLASSID is added to the Windows Registry. If the browser is not able to find the control in the Registry, it uses the CODEBASE attribute to locate and download a copy of the control.

CODEBASE

The CODEBASE tells the browser where on the Internet to locate the component, if the browser was not able to find it using the CLASSID. For an ActiveX control, the CODEBASE is a Uniform Resource Locator (URL).

An ActiveX control is packaged in one of these three ways:

1. **Portable Executable** — a single executable file such as .exe, .dll, or .ocx.

2. **Cabinet File** — a single compressed file with the extension .cab that contains one or more executables and an INF file.

3. **INF File** — a single file with the extension .inf that contains information on what files to download and how to install them.

Caution

Microsoft does not recommend using an INF file in CODEBASE. This file presents a security risk because you cannot sign an INF file.

You can also specify a version number for an ActiveX control to ensure the user works with the correct version of the control. The format of the version number is X,X,X,X.

Information in the Windows Registry

If you'd like to see what information is stored in the Windows Registry, follow these steps:

1. Run Regedit.

2. Open the HKEY_CLASSES_ROOT **branch.**

3. Open the CLSID **branch.**

4. Press Ctrl-F and enter the CLASSID **or the name of the control.**

HEIGHT

HEIGHT is the height of the control on the HTML page. You can enter the HEIGHT in number of pixels (for example, 450) or as a percentage of the page height (for example, 50%).

ID

The ID is the name you assign to this instance of this ActiveX control. You use the ID when you refer to this instance of this control in script.

The rules for IDs are:

1. Maximum length = 200 characters (letters, numbers, and/or underscores)
2. Begin with a letter
3. Case-sensitive
4. Unique among all objects

PARAM

PARAM tells the browser to pass the name of the parameter and the value of the parameter to the component. You use PARAM to set the properties of the component. Use the documentation for the ActiveX control to get a list of all the possible properties and values.

STYLE

STYLE tells the browser how to display the control within the Cascading Style Sheet. The four arguments to the STYLE attribute, HEIGHT, LEFT, TOP, and WIDTH, are each followed by a colon (:), a number, and the letters px. For example: style="HEIGHT: 45px; LEFT: 0px; TOP: 0px; WIDTH: 242px", **where**

✦ HEIGHT is the height of the control in pixels,

✦ LEFT is the number of blank pixels the browser displays to the left of the control,

✦ TOP is the number of blank pixels the browser displays above the control, and

✦ WIDTH is the width of the control in pixels.

WIDTH

WIDTH is the width of the control on the HTML page. You can enter the WIDTH in number of pixels (for example, 450) or as a percentage of the page width (for example, 50%).

\<Applet\> element

This is an example of the HTML code for a Java applet — the Search applet. The Java applet is located on the CD-ROM. It is called /SourceCode/Ch11/ search.class and was written by Rick Leinecker whose Web site is http://www.infinitevision.net.

```
<APPLET CODE="Search.class" height=50 width=250>
<PARAM NAME= "searchItems" VALUE=3>
<PARAM NAME= "search1" VALUE="Microsoft">
<PARAM NAME= "url1" VALUE="http://www.microsoft.com">
<PARAM NAME= "search2" VALUE="Netscape">
<PARAM NAME= "url2" VALUE="http://www.netscape.com">
<PARAM NAME= "search3" VALUE="Sun">
<PARAM NAME= "url3" VALUE="http://www.sun.com">
</APPLET>
```

The statements for the Search applet are located between the \<APPLET\> tag pair. Because VI does not support Java applets in the IDE, you need to type in all of the statements. In this example, the first attribute of the Search applet CODE="Search.class" tells the browser to find the applet by the name of search.class in the same location where it found the current HTML page. The next two attributes, height=50 and width=250, tell the browser to display the applet in an area 50 pixels high and 250 pixels wide. The final attribute is PARAM, which the browser passes to the applet, and which the applet uses to set its initial properties values. The most frequently used attributes of the \<APPLET\> element are CODE, CODEBASE, HEIGHT, NAME or ID, PARAM, and WIDTH.

CODE

CODE is the name of the applet file. If CODEBASE does not exist, the browser looks for the applet in the same directory that it used to load the HTML page.

CODEBASE

CODEBASE tells the browser the path to use to locate the applet on the Internet. It must be combined with the name of the CODE to form the URL for the applet, for example, CODEBASE=http://serverx/projectx/. When combined with the filename CODE="search.class", the URL is http://serverx/projectx/search.class.

HEIGHT

HEIGHT is the height of the control on the HTML page. You can enter the HEIGHT in number of pixels (for example, 450) or as a percentage of the page height (for example, 50%).

NAME or ID

You assign the NAME to this instance of this applet. You use the NAME when you refer to this instance of this applet in script.

The rules for NAME are:

1. Maximum length = 200 characters (letters, numbers, and/or underscores)

2. Begin with a letter

3. Case-sensitive

4. Unique among all objects

PARAM

PARAM tells the browser to pass the name of the parameter and the value of the parameter to the component. You use PARAM to set the properties of the component. Use the documentation for the Java applet to get a list of all the possible properties and values.

WIDTH

WIDTH is the width of the control on the HTML page. You can enter the WIDTH in number of pixels (for example, 450) or as a percentage of the page width (for example, 50%).

Properties

A component has a unique set of properties, which the component uses to control the way it looks and acts, such as size, color, font, and text. The specific properties available for any given component depend on the type of component. For example, an image control may have PictureSizeMode and SpecialEffects, whereas a control that handles text might have ForeColor and Value properties.

When you set properties at design time with the PARAM attribute, you provide the component with the initial values to use when the browser first displays the page. For an ActiveX control, you can either enter PARAM statements for each of the properties you wish to set or use VI's IDE. We discuss how to do this later in this chapter. For Java applets, you must enter a PARAM statement for each property.

The following lines of code, which appear within the <OBJECT> tag pair, set the values for two of the properties of the TextBox control:

```
<PARAM NAME="ScrollBars" VALUE="2">
<PARAM NAME="FontName" VALUE="MS Sans Serif">
```

The ScrollBars property is set to a value of 2, which shows a vertical scroll bar. The FontName property is set to MS Sans Serif, which is the font the control will use for the text it displays.

You can also set the value of a property at runtime with this syntax:

```
ComponentName.PropertyName = NewValue
```

ComponentName is the ID of the control and PropertyName is the name of the property. For example, to turn on the AutoSize property of the TextBox1 control, use this line of Javascript code:

```
TextBox1.AutoSize=True
```

You'll learn more about working with script in Chapters 12 and 13.

Methods

A method is an action you can ask the component to perform. To invoke a method, use this syntax in your Javascript code:

```
ComponentName.MethodName(argument);
```

ComponentName is the ID or NAME of the component and MethodName is the name of the method you are invoking. The method name is followed by parenthesis ( ) and a semicolon (;). You pass parameters to the method by placing them between the parenthesis. The component's documentation provides a list of all the methods and valid arguments. For example, if the Search1 Java applet supported the alert method to display text, the Javascript statement that invokes this method would look similar to this:

```
Search1.alert("Please enter another company name.");
```

Events

An event is an action that occurs in the Web browser, such as the visitor entering text in a text box. While the event originates in one component, any component on the page can handle it through an event procedure written in script. Not only do a large number of ActiveX controls recognize many of the same properties, but they also recognize many of the same events such as the onclick, ondblclick, onmousedown, and onmouseup events, to name just a few. For example, if your page contained a text box called Textbox1 and a button called Button1, you could create the Button1_onclick event handler to handle the onclick event.

```
<SCRIPT LANGUAGE="VBScript">
Function Button1_onclick()
  If Textbox1.value = "" then
    alert("You must enter a value!")
  End if
End Function
</SCRIPT>
```

When the visitor clicks the button, this event handler checks to see whether the value for Textbox1 is blank. If it is, the message "You must enter a value!" appears.

Using the VI HTML Editor

This section provides step-by-step instructions on working with an ActiveX control in the HTML Editor. You'll drag an ActiveX control from the Toolbox and drop it on an HTML page. In addition, you'll set the properties of the control using the Properties window.

Adding ActiveX controls to the Toolbox

Before you can add an ActiveX control to an HTML page, you need to be sure it appears in your Toolbox. By default, VI only shows a subset of the controls available on your machine. If you do not see the ActiveX control in your Toolbox, follow these steps to add it:

1. Right-click anywhere in the body of the Toolbox and select Customize Toolbox from the shortcut menu. The Customize Toolbox dialog appears.

2. Click the ActiveX Controls tab, which is shown in Figure 11-2. This list contains all of the controls registered on your system.

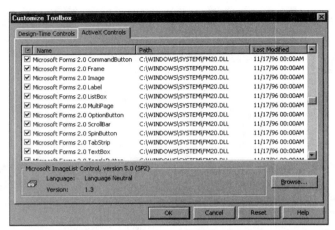

Figure 11-2: The ActiveX controls tab in the Customize Toolbox dialog shows you all the controls that are registered on your system.

3. Place a check to the left of each of the ActiveX controls in the list that you want to see in the Toolbox. If you want to remove a control from the Toolbox, make sure there is no check to the left of the control. For this example, check all of the Microsoft Forms 2.0 controls.

4. Click OK.

The ActiveX Controls tab of the Toolbox contains the controls you checked (Figure 11-3). You may need to scroll through the list of controls to see them all. For this example, the Microsoft Forms 2.0 controls you checked appear with only their short name, such as Textbox, rather than Microsoft Forms 2.0 Textbox.

Figure 11-3: You can drag any of the controls that appear on the ActiveX Controls tab of the Toolbox to your HTML page.

Tip If the items in the Toolbox are gray, you can't work with them. You can only work with the Toolbox when you have an HTML or ASP file open in the Editor.

Inserting a control

In the HTML Editor, an ActiveX control is inserted by typing the HTML statements or by dragging the control from the Toolbox. After dropping the control where you want it on the page, the <OBJECT> statements that VI generates can be customized.

Follow these steps to insert an ActiveX control directly on an HTML page:

1. Create a new HTML page and call it **ActiveXSam.htm**.

2. Click the Source tab and replace the line of text

   ```
   <P> </P>
   ```

   with

   ```
   <P> Comment: </P>
   ```

3. On the Toolbox, click the ActiveX Controls tab and locate the TextBox control.

4. Drag the TextBox control and drop it on a blank line following the line you entered in Step 2. A graphical representation of the control appears, as shown in Figure 11-4.

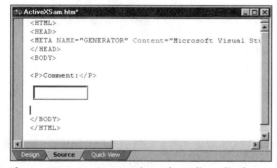

Figure 11-4: In Source view, the Editor displays controls graphically.

Tip Visual InterDev does not allow an ActiveX control to be inserted between an <OBJECT> tag pair. To replace an ActiveX control with another control, select the control and delete it before you insert the new control.

5. To view the actual <OBJECT> statements, on the View menu, click View All Controls As Text. The graphical image of the control changes to these HTML statements:

```
<OBJECT
CLASSID="clsid:8BD21D10-EC42-11CE-9E0D-00AA006002F3"
id=TextBox1>
</OBJECT>
```

Notice that VI assigned a default ID to the control, which is the name of the control followed by a sequential number. You can change this if you want the control to have a more meaningful name.

6. Save the HTML file and click the Quick View tab to preview it in the browser. Test the control by entering a large amount of text. Notice that the text scrolls out of sight as you enter more than the control can display, as shown in Figure 11-5. The properties of the control are customized later in this chapter.

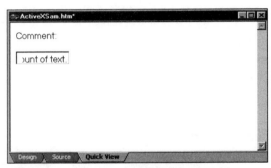

Figure 11-5: Here's what the default Textbox control looks like in Quick View.

Editing a control

You can edit an ActiveX control from the HTML Editor by either modifying the HTML code in Source view, or by dragging and dropping the edges of the control in Design view.

Now continue the "Inserting a control" exercise you started earlier by following these steps to change the width and height of the control:

1. Open ActiveXSam.htm in the HTML Editor and switch to Design view by clicking the Design tab.

2. Select the Textbox control by either clicking the control in Design view or by clicking the name of the control in the HTML Outline window, as shown in Figure 11-6.

Figure 11-6: Click the name of the control in HTML Outline to select the control in Design view.

3. In Design view, drag and drop the edges of the control to increase the width and height of the control. The next section describes a more precise way to set the width and height.

4. Save the HTML file and click the Quick View tab to preview it. Test the control by entering a large amount of text. Notice that when you enter more text than the control can display, it scrolls out of sight.

Setting control properties

To set the properties for a control, you can either type the code directly in the HTML Editor or you can use the Properties dialog that VI provides. The Properties window for a Textbox control is shown in Figure 11-7.

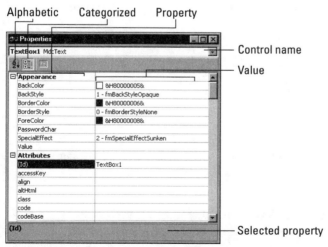

Figure 11-7: The Properties window can be used to set a control's properties.

The Properties window is quite easy to use, once you know how. The following is a list of the elements of the Properties dialog shown in Figure 11-7 and how to use each:

✦ **Control name** — This drop-down box shows the name of the currently selected control. The other items displayed in the Properties window apply to this control.

✦ **Alphabetic button** — Use this button to sort the list of properties in alphabetical order.

✦ **Categorized button** — Use this button to group the list of properties into these categories: Appearance, Attributes, Behavior, Data, Font, Misc, Scrolling, and Style. The properties are in alphabetical order within each category.

✦ **Property column** — The first column in the table contains all of the properties for this control.

✦ **Value column** — The second column in this table contains the current value for each of the properties in the first column.

✦ **Selected property** — The name of the currently selected property appears at the bottom of the window.

You can continue to edit your control. Follow these steps to change the property settings for the Textbox control:

1. Open ActiveXsam.htm in the HTML Editor, click the Design tab, and select the Textbox control.

2. In the Properties window, set these properties to the listed values:

.height	100px
width	250px
MultiLine	True
ScrollBars	2-fmScrollBarsVertical
WordWrap	True

3. Save the HTML file and click the Quick View tab to preview it. Test the control by entering a large amount of text. Notice that the scroll bars appear when you fill the control, as shown in Figure 11-8.

Figure 11-8: Here's what the TextBox control looks like with scroll bars.

The code you just generated is shown in Listing 11-2. Don't be concerned if you get different values for some of the parameters as long as height, width, VariousPropertyBits, and ScrollBars match.

Listing 11-2: **Example of TextBox Control**

```
<OBJECT
classid=clsid:8BD21D10-EC42-11CE-9E0D-00AA006002F3
height=100
id=TextBox1
style="HEIGHT: 100px; WIDTH: 250px" width=250>
<PARAM NAME="VariousPropertyBits" VALUE="2894088219">
<PARAM NAME="BackColor" VALUE="2147483653">
<PARAM NAME="ForeColor" VALUE="2147483656">
<PARAM NAME="MaxLength" VALUE="0">
<PARAM NAME="BorderStyle" VALUE="0">
<PARAM NAME="ScrollBars" VALUE="2">
<PARAM NAME="DisplayStyle" VALUE="1">
<PARAM NAME="MousePointer" VALUE="0">
<PARAM NAME="Size" VALUE="6615;1376">
<PARAM NAME="PasswordChar" VALUE="0">
<PARAM NAME="ListWidth" VALUE="0">
<PARAM NAME="BoundColumn" VALUE="1">
<PARAM NAME="TextColumn" VALUE="65535">
<PARAM NAME="ColumnCount" VALUE="1">
<PARAM NAME="ListRows" VALUE="8">
<PARAM NAME="cColumnInfo" VALUE="0">
<PARAM NAME="MatchEntry" VALUE="2">
<PARAM NAME="ListStyle" VALUE="0">
<PARAM NAME="ShowDropButtonWhen" VALUE="0">
<PARAM NAME="ShowListWhen" VALUE="1">
<PARAM NAME="DropButtonStyle" VALUE="1">
<PARAM NAME="MultiSelect" VALUE="0">
<PARAM NAME="Value" VALUE="">
<PARAM NAME="Caption" VALUE="">
<PARAM NAME="PicturePosition" VALUE="458753">
<PARAM NAME="BorderColor" VALUE="2147483654">
<PARAM NAME="SpecialEffect" VALUE="2">
<PARAM NAME="Accelerator" VALUE="0">
<PARAM NAME="GroupName" VALUE="">
<PARAM NAME="FontName" VALUE="MS Sans Serif">
<PARAM NAME="FontEffects" VALUE="1073741824">
<PARAM NAME="FontHeight" VALUE="240">
<PARAM NAME="FontOffset" VALUE="0">
<PARAM NAME="FontCharSet" VALUE="0">
<PARAM NAME="FontPitchAndFamily" VALUE="2">
<PARAM NAME="ParagraphAlign" VALUE="1">
<PARAM NAME="FontWeight" VALUE="400">
</OBJECT>
```

Summary

In this chapter, you learned these essential points:

✦ How component software in the form of ActiveX controls and Java applets provide you with powerful self-contained modules of code that you can use to quickly add specialized functionality to your Web application.

✦ How client-side ActiveX controls are a good fit if you are planning an intranet application limited to Windows users.

✦ How client-side Java applets are a good fit if your priority is cross-platform support and native capabilities are not an issue.

✦ VI's Toolbox can be customized to include any ActiveX control on your machine.

✦ ActiveX controls can be dragged from the Toolbox to a Web page and the control's properties can be set quickly and easily in the Properties window.

✦ How the <OBJECT> element can be used to insert an ActiveX control and the <APPLET> element for a Java applet.

✦   ✦   ✦

Scripting

VBScript is Microsoft's answer to JavaScript. You can use either scripting language to create executable code in Web pages. Programming code (scripts) used for computing in an intranet or Internet is more sophisticated than the page-description language HTML, yet scripts are less sophisticated than full programming languages such as Visual Basic or Java (scripts have tools, for example, that can access a hard drive).

In this chapter and others that cover scripting in this book, we include examples of both VBScript and JScript (or JavaScript, essentially the same thing as JScript except JScript also supports the Internet Explorer 4 object model).

VBScript and JScript: A Rosetta Stone

The beginning of this chapter is an overview of the different ways VBScript or JScript accomplish the same job — generally a matter of slight variations in syntax. It isn't possible to actually *teach* JScript or VBScript within the scope of this book, but if you know either language, the following side-by-side comparison of the main differences should enable you to translate between the languages. It's quite easy to convert source code from one script to the other. Perhaps *Rosetta Stone* is too strong a term for what follows, but for those who need this information, the comparison is useful.

The following few pages should be particularly useful to those who know JScript and would like to know VBScript, or vice versa. After this brief tutorial, we move on to explore scripting itself — programming for the Web. We provide examples in both VBScript and JScript in this chapter, and elsewhere in this book. Translating between the two is a matter of learning a relatively few basic rules.

Using variables

In JScript, you define variables in the same way you do in VBScript except you can use the optional JScript `var` command. `Var` is optional in the first instance because it is a global variable. A global variable (in both languages) is one that is defined outside of any procedure (a sub or function). When declared globally, the variable is usable by all the script within the page. However, in the following example, we've declared the variable `thisvar` twice, once globally and once locally (within a procedure). You *must* use the `var` command if you're using the same variable name both globally and locally, as we did in this example. JScript allows this and considers these to be two different variables entirely, as seen in Listing 12-1.

Listing 12-1: **A Sample JScript**

```
<HTML>
<HEAD>

<SCRIPT LANGUAGE=javascript>
<!--

thisvar = 44

function varshow () {
var thisvar = 12;
z = alert ("In the function thisvar = " + thisvar)
}

//-->
</SCRIPT>

</HEAD>
<BODY>

<input type=button name=clickthis value=clickthis
onclick="varshow()">

</BODY>
</HTML>
```

To run the previous example, click the Quick View tab in Visual InterDev after copying the previous source code into the VI editor with the Source tab selected. You'll notice that the message box (the `alert` — there is no `msgbox` command in JScript) displays 12, indicating that the local version of this variable is active within the function. If you remove the line: `var thisvar = 12;` the message box displays 44.

Commenting Out Code

You can temporarily "remove" a line of code by commenting it out by using two slashes, like this:

```
// var thisvar = 12;
```

The ' (single quote) symbol comments out a line of VBScript:

```
' var thisvar = 12;
```

Listing 12-2 shows a translation of the previous JScript into VBScript.

Listing 12-2: **The Sample JScript Translated to VBScript**

```
<SCRIPT LANGUAGE=VBScript>
<!--

thisvar = 44

function varshow ()
thisvar = 12
z = alert ("In the function thisvar = " & thisvar)
end function

//-->
</SCRIPT>
```

Note that VBScript has a dim command that is used much the same as the JScript var command; however, the use of dim is usually optional. Also, you cannot use dim at all if you're assigning a value to the variable. (This is illegal VBScript code: dim thisvar = 12.)

Other differences between VBScript and JScript are equally minor. JScript uses { } symbols to enclose the function, with } indicating the end of the function. VBScript ends the function with the end function command. Both languages use the HTML comment symbols <!--//--> to enclose their entire script. This prevents the source code from puzzling a user. Without those comment symbols, if the user's browser cannot handle the script, the source code is displayed as text. With the comment symbols, nothing is displayed.

VBScript makes a distinction between the + operator (which is used mathematically to add numbers) and the & operator, which concatenates pieces of text (strings). JScript uses + for both operations; it does not recognize & (used to connect strings).

Both languages have no facility for explicitly declaring a variable's type. (There is no Dim Z As String, for example.) Instead, both languages interpret the type of variable based on whatever you assign to it. If you assign something within quotation marks, for example, the variable is *typed* as a string (text) variable.

In JScript, a semicolon is used to indicate the end of a complete statement (a complete action, such as n + n or thisvar = 44). Most often, a statement is placed on a line of its own in source code. You would press Enter each time you wanted to write the next statement. However, if you put two statements on the same line, a semicolon is required, to show JScript where the first statement ends and the second one begins. Following is an example:

```
N = 12; Z = 18
```

The semicolon is optional for statements that are each on their own, separate line. Even so, it is considered good programming practice to end each statement with a semicolon, even if, as usually happens, each statement *is* on a line by itself. VBScript uses the colon (:)to separate statements that are on the same line.

```
N = 12: Z = 18
```

However, VBScript never uses the colon when a statement is on a line of its own.

Caution VBScript isn't case-sensitive (ThisVar, Thisvar, and thisvar are considered the same variable name). JScript *is* case-sensitive, so those three names would be considered three distinct variables! Case-sensitivity in JScript also applies to function names, parameters passed to functions, and so on. For this reason, many programmers protect themselves by always using lowercase when programming in JScript.

Creating arrays

Arrays are variables that are clustered together so they can share a single variable name but be distinguished by having different index numbers (thearrayname[0] as opposed to thearrayname[1]). In JScript, you create an array using the new Array command, as shown in Listing 12-3 (the word *Array* must have an initial capital *A*).

Listing 12-3: Creating a New Array with the New Array Command

```
<HTML>
<HEAD>
<SCRIPT LANGUAGE=javascript>
<!--

thearray = new Array(2);

thearray[0] = "First Name ";
thearray[1] = "Second Name ";
thearray[2] = "Third Name ";

alert (thearray[0] + thearray[1] + thearray[2]);

//-->
</SCRIPT>
</HEAD>
<BODY>

</BODY>
</HTML>
```

As you can see in the previous example, an array named thearray is created with three elements (three separate locations to hold information, equivalent to three different variable names: thearray[0], thearray[1], and thearray[2]). Notice that, like VBScript, an array defined as having an upper index number of 2 actually has three elements because the first, lowest element is the "zeroth" element. Then we assign values to each of the three "containers" and display them in an alert box.

VBScript creates arrays using the dim command. (Dim is optional when creating a variable but required when creating an array.) Listing 12-4 shows the VBScript translation:

Listing 12-4: The Array Translated to VBScript

```
<SCRIPT LANGUAGE=VBScript>
<!--

Dim thearray(2)
```

(continued)

Listing 12-4 *(continued)*

```
thearray(0) = "First Name "
thearray(1) = "Second Name "
thearray(2) = "Third Name "

alert (thearray(0) & thearray(1) & thearray(2))

//-->
</SCRIPT>
```

As you see, JScript *defines* the size of an array by enclosing the number of elements within parentheses (2). So does VBScript. However, when reading or assigning values to the elements of an array, JScript switches to brackets — `thearray[0]` — while VBScript sticks with parentheses in all references to an array — `thearray(0)`.

JScript advantages

JScript has three features that make its array scripting superior to VBScript's. First, you can define a dynamic array in JScript by leaving out a specified number of elements when you create the array.

```
thearray = new Array();
```

In VBScript, you must use the `ReDim` command to create a dynamic array, and the VBScript solution is less elegant. A dynamic array is one that grows or shrinks in size automatically, as you add or subtract elements by assigning values to the elements within the array. In other words, you need not specify the array's size ahead of time.

The second advantage of JScript arrays is that they can be implicitly created, just like ordinary variables, by merely assigning values:

```
thearray = new Array("First Name ","Second Name ","Third Name ");
alert (thearray[0] + thearray[1] + thearray[2]);
```

VBScript doesn't permit instantiation of an array like this, by implication. VBScript arrays must be explicitly defined before you can assign values to them.

Finally, and most impressively, JScript arrays can have named (text) indices.

```
<SCRIPT LANGUAGE=javascript>
<!--
```

```
thearray = new Array("one","two","three");
thearray["one"] = "This is the zeroth element."
alert (thearray["one"]);

//-->
</SCRIPT>
```

As you can see, the named elements use a text index. This comes in handy when you are working with, for example, a set of named buttons and want to reference elements within an array by words rather than index numbers, as shown in Listing 12-5.

Listing 12-5: **Using Named Elements**

```
<HTML>
<HEAD>
<SCRIPT LANGUAGE=javascript>
<!--

thearray = new Array("one","two","three");
thearray["one"] = "This is the zeroth element!"


function arrayshow(whatspassed) {

alert(thearray[whatspassed]);

}

//-->
</SCRIPT>
</HEAD>
<BODY>
<input type=button name=one value=clickthis
onclick="arrayshow(this.name)">
</BODY>
</HTML>
```

JScript also has a couple of additional array features, a prototype property, and a description property. These, combined with the features described previously, make JScript the clearly superior language when it comes to handling arrays.

Procedures

VBScript permits two kinds of procedures: subs (also known as subroutines) and functions. JScript has only functions.

A procedure is a self-contained, small set of statements that perform a particular job. If you have five buttons on your Web page and you want to display an alert each time a button is clicked, you *could* write separate script code for each button. Or, more efficiently, you could write a single procedure that is triggered by every button.

In VBScript, a sub and a function are essentially identical, except a function can return information to the calling button or whatever else called the function, as you can see in Listing 12-6.

Listing 12-6: A Function Can Return a Value

```
<SCRIPT LANGUAGE="VBScript">
<!--

n = varshow
alert (n)


function varshow ()
thisvar = 12
varshow = thisvar
end function

//-->
</SCRIPT>
```

If you created a sub varshow () above, you couldn't assign a value to n in the previous example. Instead, you can only trigger (call) a sub, but not receive a return value from the sub, as shown in the following code snippet:

```
varshow

sub varshow ()
thisvar = 12
alert (thisvar)
end sub
```

One way to make a sub perform like a function is to create a global variable (any variable defined outside a procedure). Then, because such a variable can be accessed from anywhere in the page, your sub can assign a value to it that can then be accessed in the area of the script that called the sub. A function, though, can directly return a value to the caller, as illustrated by the previous example: `n = varshow`. The name of the function becomes a kind of variable that gets passed back, as illustrated in the previous example: `(varshow = thisvar)`.

Here's another way to explain this distinction between a sub and function: A function is usually called within a complete statement: `n = varshow` or `alert(varshow)`. A sub, though, cannot be used within a larger statement — a sub is a complete statement in itself.

Operators

Before finishing this comparison of JScript and VBScript by discussing program flow, we should first compare some of the operators used in these languages.

Arithmetic

The arithmetic symbols are the same +, -, *, and / for addition, subtraction, multiplication, and division.

Increment/Decrement

JScript increments a number with a ++ symbol that isn't used in VBScript:

JScript: i++

VBScript: i = i + 1

In either case, the value of i is raised by 1. Similarly, JScript uses -- to decrement and VBScript uses i = i - 1.

Comparisons and If Then

Variables are compared using all the same symbols (*n* > *b* means *n* is greater than *b*, *n* <= *b* means *n* is less than or equal to *b*, and so on). The only difference is JScript tests for equality using ==, whereas VBScript tests equality using = as you can see in Listing 12-7.

Listing 12-7: **JScript Uses = = to Test for Equality**

```
<SCRIPT LANGUAGE="JScript">
<!--

z = "once"

if (z == "once")
alert ("It's once.");
else
alert ("It's not.");

//-->
</SCRIPT>

</HEAD>
<BODY>
</BODY>
</HTML>
```

Note   Note that when you *assign* a value, you use the single =, but when you test a value for equality, you use the double = =. In VBScript, the single = is used in both activities.

Should your if response (or else response) require more than a single line of source code, you must enclose the lines in braces.

```
z = "once"

if (z == "once") {
alert ("It's once.");
alert ("It's once again.");
}
else {
alert ("It's not.");
alert ("It's not again.");
}
```

Both VBScript's elseif and JScript's else if commands enable you to insert additional tests and responses within the overall if structure.

```
z = "once"

if (z == "once")
alert ("It's once.");
else if (z == "twice")
alert ("It's twice.");
else
alert ("It's not anything.");
```

Overcoming Loose Variable Typing Ambiguities

It's nice that we can allow the programming language to figure out what type of variable is being used (is it the number 12 or the text characters 1 and 2?). However, sometimes this "loose variable typing" can create ambiguities. What happens if you attempt to add the number 2 to the character 3?

```
x = "2"
y = 3
z = x + y

alert (z)
```

Will z be the number 5 or the concatenated string 23? (VBScript attempts to get around this problem by using + for addition and & for concatenation of strings.) The answer to the JScript in the example turns out to be 5, favoring the numeric variable type in this situation.

But what about when you compare two different kinds of variables in a test for equality?

```
<SCRIPT LANGUAGE="JScript">
<!--

x = 3;

if (x == "3")
alert ("it's the text 3");
else
alert ("it's NOT the text 3");

//-->
</SCRIPT>
```

This results in Internet Explorer 4's browser claim that x is the text 3, returning "true" in the comparison.

VBScript's if structure is similar, but it requires the additional commands then and end if and doesn't enclose the test condition within parentheses, nor does it use braces:

```
<SCRIPT LANGUAGE="VBScript">
<!--

z = "once"

if z = "once" then
alert ("It's once.")
else
```

```
alert ("It's not.")
end if

//-->
</SCRIPT>

</HEAD>
<BODY>
</BODY>
</HTML>
```

One final difference: VBScript uses <> and JScript uses != to test for inequality as follows:

```
if (z != "once")
```

versus

```
if z <> "once" then
```

Looping

Repeating something is a common requirement in programming. To repeat something, both VBScript and JScript include several loop structures that do something repeatedly a specific number of times, or until a condition is satisfied.

For

The easiest looping technique to understand is the for...next structure in VBScript, and the comparable for structure in JScript. Listing 12-8 shows how VBScript deals with this..

Listing 12-8: **The Easiest Loop**

```
<HTML>
<HEAD>

<SCRIPT LANGUAGE="VBScript">
<!--

for i = 1 to 3
a = a & i & " "
next

alert(a)

//-->
</SCRIPT>
```

```
</HEAD>
<BODY>

</BODY>
</HTML>
```

In this example, we tell VBScript that we want to loop three times, and each time we want to add the value of the loop counter (the variable *i*) to the variable *a*. The result is displayed: 1 2 3.

The JScript version requires that you first define *a* as a variable, as shown in Listing 12-9.

Listing 12-9: **You Must Define the Variable**

```
<SCRIPT LANGUAGE="JScript">
<!--

var a = ""

for (i=1; i < 4; i++){
a += i + " ";
}

alert(a)

//-->
</SCRIPT>
```

In the JScript version, the `for` command is followed by three parameters enclosed in parentheses and separated by semicolons:

```
for (the initial value of the counter; the condition that ends
the looping; the increment of the counter)
```

In Listing 12-9, we state that the counter *i* begins with a value of 1 and the looping will continue as long as *i* remains lower than 4. Then we increment *i* (raise it by 1).

While

Both languages have a `while` structure similar to an `if` structure, but a `while` structure continues to loop while an expression, such as n<4, remains true:

```
<SCRIPT LANGUAGE="VBScript">
<!--

n = 2

while n < 4
    n = n + 1
    alert(n)
wend

//-->
</SCRIPT>
```

The equivalent in JScript appears as follows:

```
<SCRIPT LANGUAGE="JScript">
<!--

n = 2

while (n < 4){
    n ++
    alert(n)
}

//-->
</SCRIPT
```

Do

Both languages (JScript starting with Netscape 4) now have a `do` loop structure. It is similar to the `while` structure but is more powerful and more easily understood.

In JScript, the exit condition appears at the very end of the structure, within a `while` test, as follows:

```
<SCRIPT LANGUAGE="JScript">
<!--

n = 2

do {
    alert(n)
    n ++
```

```
}while (n < 4)

//-->
</SCRIPT>
```

JScript, as you can see, merely inverts the `while` structure, positioning the test at the end, rather than the beginning, of the loop. VBScript is similar:

```
<SCRIPT LANGUAGE="VBScript">
<!--

n = 2

do
    alert(n)
    n = n + 1

loop while n < 4

//-->
</SCRIPT>
```

An alternative VBScript approach uses the `until` command:

```
n = 2

do
    alert(n)
    n = n + 1

loop until n = 4
```

The difference between `while` and `until` is functionally the same as the difference between *rake while there are leaves on the lawn* and *rake until there are no leaves on the lawn*. However, using one or the other of these structures can make the meaning of the code clearer in various situations.

Also, remember that in VBScript, you can use the following structure with both the `until` and `while` commands:

```
Do Until n = 4
    N = n + 1
Loop
```

Decision-making

The if...then...elseif...else structure, described previously, is one way of looking at a situation and making a decision about what to do next. There is a structure, called switch in JScript and select case in VBScript, that does precisely what if... does, but some people consider it more readable, as you can see in Listing 12-10.

Listing 12-10: VBScript's Select Case Structure

```
<SCRIPT LANGUAGE="VBScript">
<!--

n = 2
select case (n)

    case(1)
        alert("It's one.")
    case(2)
        alert("It's two.")
    case else
    alert("It's neither.")

end select

//-->
</SCRIPT>
```

A similar structure, rendered this time in JScript, is shown in Listing 12-11.

Listing 12-11: The JScript Version of VBScript's Select Case

```
<SCRIPT LANGUAGE="JScript">
<!--

n = 2
switch (n) {

    case 1:
        alert("It's one.");
        break;
    case 2:
        alert("It's two.");
        break;
```

```
    default:
        alert("It's neither.")

}

//-->
</SCRIPT>
```

Note that with a switch, JScript oddly doesn't use parentheses, but it does require the braces and the `break` command to indicate that the program should jump out of the structure (past the close brace }).

Of course, this survey doesn't convey the depth of either VBScript or JScript, nor does it cover all the points. However, with this brief Rosetta Stone showing both languages side by side, you should be able to translate an example script from one language to the other. Now we get into the details of how, in real-world Web sites, scripting is used.

Understanding Client and Server Scripts

You can create client scripts or server scripts. If you are using Microsoft Internet Information Server (IIS), you can put both or either of these types of scripts into a file with an .asp extension. These files can contain both client and server scripts in the same page, if you want to write them that way. (For an in-depth discussion of server scripts, see Chapters 16 and 17.)

A client script is executed by the user's browser. It is executed immediately if the script code is placed within the `OnLoad` event, but can also be placed within other events such as the `OnClick` event of a button. In that case, the script will only be carried out if the user clicks that particular button. You can also simply write scripts that are *not enclosed within a procedure* (a function or sub or event, placing the script between, for example, the `Sub PgName_OnLoad` and `End Sub` commands). If you do write some script outside a procedure, it will be executed in the order the browser reads the source code on the page (script higher on the page will be executed first). Such out-of-procedure scripts are called *global* or *inline*.

In any case, the user's browser reads the HTML and displays things and also parses any scripts in the page — responding by carrying out whatever the script requests. Remember that HTML by itself cannot add 1+1; it is designed to display things but has very little facility for what we think of as *computing*.

By contrast, server scripts are not executed (or even sent) to the user's browser. Rather, they are executed by IIS immediately after the page is requested by the user, but before it is sent to the user's browser. When the user gets the page, any server scripting has been executed already by IIS and is not sent to the user as part of the page.

You can see the difference between client and server scripts: client scripts run on the user's machine. So they are useful when you want to, for example, validate that the user has correctly entered a phone number or some other data — before it is submitted back to your Web site. By contrast, a server script would be appropriate if you need to check the user's request for sensitive information in a database at your end (the server end). Is the user on a list of people allowed to see this information? Is the request going to be honored or not?

In this chapter, we focus on client scripts.

Building Scripts in Visual InterDev

VI enables you to create scripts in two ways:

✦ Create it in Source view in the VI editor by just typing in your script.

✦ Use a design-time control that assists you by inserting some script for you and enables you to specify values or properties in the DTC's property dialog box (right-click the DTC in Source view), then creates the appropriate script code for you. To see the design-time controls available in Visual InterDev, make sure the Toolbox is visible (select it from the View menu). Click the   ✦ Design-Time Controls tab on the Toolbox, as shown in Figure 12-1.

Figure 12-1: The list of available design-time controls

To add or remove design-time controls, choose Customize Toolbar from the VI Tools menu. Click the design-time control bar and select or deselect any of the listed controls.

The Limitations of Wizards

All these utilities are generally of limited usefulness (the exception is when you're generating server-side or database-access codes). However, in general, VBScript includes many commands that the wizards don't offer and can't assist you with. Wizards are not substitutes for knowing the VBScript language and being able to write the source code yourself. No wizard can really step in and thoroughly simplify a computer language, just as there is no tool that can transform a clumsy writer with a limited vocabulary into a good writer. Languages are too subtle and powerful to be reduced to dialog boxes and step-throughs.

The Script Wizard and Script Builder are odd tools, really. They are too complicated for novices (they won't know the meaning of many of the commands in the language), yet they are far too restrictive for anyone who actually knows Visual Basic (of which VBScript is merely a subset).

Note

Of course, you can also use other tools to build a script, such as Microsoft's free utility, the ActiveX Control Pad. It includes a wizard similar to the Script Builder in VI (or design-time controls).

Creating a new script in Source view

To write a simple client-side script, follow these steps:

1. From the VI File menu, choose New File, and then choose HTML file.

2. Select the Source view in the edit window.

3. Type **SCRIPT** (in boldface) into the HTML source code that VI has already supplied as a basic template for any HTML page, as you can see in Listing 12-12.

Listing 12-12: **A Simple Script**

```
<HTML>
<HEAD>
<META NAME="GENERATOR" Content="Microsoft Visual Studio">
<META HTTP-EQUIV="Content-Type" content="text/html">
<TITLE>Document Title</TITLE>
```

(continued)

Listing 12-12 *(continued)*

```
<SCRIPT LANGUAGE="VBScript">

alert "This page is loaded!"

</SCRIPT>

</HEAD>
<BODY>


</BODY>
</HTML>
```

Notice that a script is placed between two HTML tags: `<SCRIPT LANGUAGE="VBScript">` and the ending tag, `</SCRIPT>`. This alerts the browser that it must attempt to execute the enclosed programming (as opposed to its usual job of locating, retrieving, and displaying HTML formatting). In the previous example, we're saying that when this current window is loaded, display a message box. The VBScript command `alert` works much the same as the Visual Basic `MsgBox` command. JScript doesn't contain a `MsgBox` function, so you must use `alert`. The only change you must make to the previous VBScript to transform it into JScript is this:

```
<SCRIPT LANGUAGE="JScript">
alert ("This page is loaded!");
```

To test this example, click the Preview button in the VI editor. You'll see the result shown in Figure 12-2.

Figure 12-2: Use the VBScript alert command to communicate via message box with the user.

Notice also that the script is placed in the header of the HTML page rather than the body. There's no particular reason why you can't put script in the body, but by convention, scripts that are not enclosed within a procedure are generally placed between the `<HEAD>` and `</HEAD>` tags. Recall that you need not place a script within a `Sub...End Sub` structure (or in a function) unless you want the script specifically triggered by an event (such as `Button_OnClick`). If you want the script executed once (when a user loads your page), you can simply write the script inline (no procedure is used, no event), as we've done in the previous example. Scripts used within procedures, however, often go within the `<BODY>` section of the HTML.

Writing code for VBScript-incompatible browsers

What happens if the user's browser doesn't have the VBScript engine and cannot, therefore, understand and execute this script? The browser displays the entire script as text, confusing many viewers. Internet Explorer, of course, has VBScript built in, but not all other browsers are capable of handling VBScript. The solution to this dilemma is to make the VBScript optional by surrounding it with HTML comment tags. When you do that, a VBScript-capable browser will execute the code, but other browsers that can't handle VBScript will simply ignore (not display) the script. Here's what it looks like:

```
<SCRIPT LANGUAGE="VBScript">
<!--
alert "Watch out!"
-->
</SCRIPT>
```

There is also a `MsgBox` command in VBScript. It can be used two ways.

✦ **As a Statement** — You can use a message box in its *Statement* mode (you can even omit the parentheses) if you merely want to tell the user something and don't care about the user's reaction:

```
MsgBox ("Please remember to enter your name before requesting
budget information.")
```

✦ **As a Function** — Functions always return some information to your program, so they are always coded in the form of an "equation":

```
X = MsgBox ("Are you sure you want to quit the program?", 4)
```

Use the *Function* style of a message box when you want information back from the user. Here we added the `,4` to the `MsgBox` command, causing it to display Yes and No buttons for the user to click. Without `,4`, the message box would have displayed the single OK button, which is the default.

If the user clicks the Yes Button, X will contain 6, and clicking the No button returns 7 to X. Therefore, your program can use X to decide what to do based on the user's response.

```
If X = 6 Then End
```

If you know Visual Basic, you'll likely notice that VBScript behaves quite similarly to its parent language. Indeed, VBScript is smaller — it's missing disk-access commands, for example. But it can do many of the same things that its bigger parent does. One interesting use of script is you can directly manipulate the current document in the user's browser.

Tip   JScript has no `MsgBox` command; you must use the `alert` command.

Managing a Document

The document object is accessible to your scripting. To give you practice and experience using VBScript on the client side, it's worth spending some time looking at ways you can interact with the user's current document. Put some script into that document and you have considerable control over it, all on the client side.

The document as object

VBScript and JScript see an HTML document as an *object*. This means you can do things with a document or its content from within the script. One common use of the document object is to reference HTML controls that have been used within an HTML form. In this example, there is a form we've named *MyForm*. To refer to it (and the controls on Myform) within VBScript, use the syntax: Document.MyForm. In Listing 12-13, the `Set` command creates an object variable that can later be used to address the Document.MyForm object in the code.

Listing 12-13: Using Set

```
<HTML>
<HEAD>

<SCRIPT LANGUAGE="VBScript">

Sub Submit_OnClick
 Dim F
 Set F = Document.MyForm
    z = F.Text1.Value
    If IsNumeric(z) or z = "" Then
MsgBox "Please type in your name, not your address or phone
number."
    Else
MsgBox "We'll send it in."
' Submit Form to server
 End If
End Sub
```

```
</SCRIPT>

</HEAD>
<BODY>

<FORM NAME="MyForm">
Please type in your name:
<INPUT NAME="Text1" TYPE="TEXT" SIZE="42">
<INPUT NAME="Submit" TYPE="BUTTON" VALUE="Submit">
</FORM>
</BODY>
</HTML>
```

The previous example uses the procedure-style script, enclosing the script within an OnClick procedure and, therefore, executing only when the user clicks the button named Submit. Note that this code checks what the user has entered to see that something *was* entered and that it's not numeric. This validation takes place in the user's computer, not on the server, therefore the response is faster and more efficient. That is the primary advantage of client-side scripting.

Using the SCRIPT FOR Command

There's an alternative way of setting up a script and attaching it to a particular object on the page. In the following example, the SCRIPT FOR command is used rather than the more typical structure (Sub ObjName_OnClick). In this book, we stick with the classic approach, using sub and function structures for procedures rather than the approach illustrated in the following code:

```
<INPUT TYPE="Button" NAME="Button1" VALUE="Click">

<SCRIPT FOR="Button1" EVENT="onClick" LANGUAGE="VBScript">
MsgBox "Button Pressed!"
</SCRIPT>
```

A Warning About JScript

JScript, in an effort to speed up source code interpretation, places some burdens on the programmer that are taken care of for you by the VBScript interpreter. Recall that variables, function names, keywords, and other words used in JScript must be capitalized consistently. JScript is case-sensitive: it considers ThisVar, thisVar, ,and thisvar to be four distinct variable names. Likewise, you must type *while* not *While*. One disadvantage of this case-sensitivity is that HTML is not case-sensitive (nor is VBScript); it's a convention in HTML to use mixed-case for various commands, and events in particular, such as OnClick or OnMouseOver.

In JScript, you must avoid capitalizing — *stick with all lowercase* (use *onclick*, for example). Alas, even this avoid-capitalization-when-using-JScript rule has its exceptions: in IE 3 and 4 ,client-side objects methods and property names are case-insensitive. This means you can use any capitalization you wish when working with client-side objects, such as the document, in IE. But if you intend a JScript to run on Navigator, you must stick with lowercase for these objects! (Variable names and function names *are* case-sensitive in IE JScript.) The bottom line: stick with lowercase letters, write exclusively for Navigator, or switch to VBScript.

Direct text insertion

Another use for the document object is to put some text directly onto an HTML page *from within VBScript*. As you know, you can put text onto an HTML document by merely typing it in between <HTML> and </HTML> in the body of your HTML source code. But what if you want to display different text depending on how the user responds to some queries, or the time of year? How can you dynamically adjust your displayed text? If you want to put some text onto a page from within VBScript, use the Document.Write command:

```
Document.Write "Put this directly on the page."
```

In HTML there's no way to calculate and display the results as plain text on the document. With VBScript, you can, for example, tell the user the date when, 30 days from now, the person's subscription expires. And you can put this right on the page with ordinary text, as shown in Listing 12-14.

Listing 12-14: **Dynamic Calculations**

```
<HTML>
<HEAD>
<SCRIPT LANGUAGE="VBScript">
<!--
```

```
N = DateValue(now)
N = N + 30 'add 30 days

Document.Write "<BIG>SUBSCRIPTION NOTICE</BIG>"

Document.Write "<P>Your sub expires on " & N

-->
</SCRIPT>
</HEAD>

<BODY>

<BIG>Important Notice...<BIG>
<P><P>

</BODY>
</HTML>
```

Notice in the previous example that when you use `Document.Write`, you're not simply printing text. In fact, you're feeding HTML source code to the browser. Therefore, you can include any HTML commands, as we've done previously with `<BIG>` and `<P>`.

JScript's current date/time functions are buggy and difficult to use (for example, you must calculate the number of milliseconds in a month: 1000 * 60 * 60 * 24 * 30, then add it to today's time).

Document properties

Like other objects, the document object has a set of properties. There are several properties that you can manipulate or query to expand the utility of your scripts. It's worth your while to learn what these properties are, and how they can be used in your scripts to query or modify the qualities of the document object.

Anchors

Anchors are a list (an "array") of the hypertext links within the document. See the section "Links."

bgColor, fgColor

`bgColor` and `fgColor` are the background and foreground (text) colors of the document, as seen in Listing 12-15.

Listing 12-15: Colors

```
<BIG>OUR CORPORATE FORECAST</BIG>
<BR><BR><BR>
<INPUT NAME="Button1" TYPE="BUTTON" VALUE="Submit">

<SCRIPT LANGUAGE="VBScript">
<!--
Sub Button1_OnClick
    document.bgColor = "Red"
End Sub
-->
</SCRIPT>

A JScript version:

<SCRIPT FOR="Button1" EVENT="onclick()" LANGUAGE="JScript">
<!--
    document.bgColor = "Red";
-->
</SCRIPT>
```

Cookie

Cookie reports or changes the cookie of a document. A *cookie* is some data that is left on the user's hard drive. It can provide information to your script about the user's previous visit to your site (so you can customize it for him or her). Cookies are also a way to store truly global variables. In fact, there are numerous situations where you might want to leave some information on the client side, then later retrieve it, as you can see in the following source code:

```
<BODY>
<script language="VBScript">

f = "We made this in five hours."
document.cookie = f

C = document.cookie
msgbox C

</script>
</BODY>
</HTML>
```

An Alternative to Naming a JScript Procedure Within the Object's Tags

Placing an event handler — EVENT="onclick()" — within script tags, as illustrated previously, is an alternative to naming a JScript (or VBScript) procedure within the object's tags, like this:

```
<HTML>
<HEAD>
<SCRIPT LANGUAGE="JScript">

function trigger() {
 alert("Function is triggered.")
}
</SCRIPT>

</HEAD>
<BODY>

<INPUT onclick=trigger() TYPE="BUTTON" VALUE="Click">

</BODY>
</HTML>
```

However, the EVENT="onclick()" technique only works in IE, not Navigator.

Tip

Many scripts and most HTML can be easily and quickly tested in VI. All you have to do is click the Preview button and you can see the results of your source code as they would appear in a user's browser. However, some kinds of code will not execute properly in Preview mode. Therefore, if you're not getting the results you expect (usually this means that nothing happens; no error codes are displayed, but what you expect just doesn't occur), you must save the HTML page to a disk file, then load it into Internet Explorer or another browser. Then, in a browser, the code will behave as expected. The previous example of using a cookie is one such case. In Preview mode, you get a blank message box. When you choose Save .HTM from the VI File menu (or press Ctrl+S), then run Internet Explorer and choose Open from its File menu to load in your .HTM file, this message is displayed: "We made this in five hours."

Forms

A list (an "array") of any forms within the document. See the section, "Links."

Specifying Colors

You can define colors with either hexadecimal numbers or, as we've done in these examples, ordinary English words such as *White*. There are 140 English words you can use to specify colors. The following 16 work in most browsers: Aqua, Black, Blue, Fuchsia, Gray, Green, Lime, Maroon, Navy, Olive, Purple, Red, Silver, Teal, White, and Yellow. The following 124 color definitions made their appearance first in Internet Explorer 3.0. You can expect, however, that this list of color definitions will likely become the standard and will, in the future, apply to any color definitions (such as backcolor), not just hyperlinks. Here is the official list:

aliceblue, antiquewhite, aqua, aquamarine, azure, beige, bisque, black, blanchedalmond, blue, blueviolet, brown, burlywood, cadetblue, chartreuse, chocolate, coral, cornflowerblue, cornsilk, crimson, cyan, darkblue, darkcyan, darkgoldenrod, darkgray, darkgreen, darkkahki, darkmagenta, darkolivegreen, darkorange, darkorchid, darkred, darksalmon, darkseagreen, darkslateblue, darkslategray, darkturquoise, darkviolet, deeppink, deepskyblue, dimgray, dodgerblue, floralwhite, forestgreen, fuchsia, gainsboro, ghostwhite, gold, goldenrod, gray, green, greenyellow, honeydew, hotpink, indianred, indigo, ivory, khaki, lavender, lavenderblush, lawngreen, lemonchiffon, lightblue, lightcoral, lightcyan, lightgoldenrodyellow, lightgreen, lightgrey, lightpink, lightsalmon, lightseagreen, lightskyblue, lightslategray, lightsteelblue, lightyellow, lime, limegreen, linen, magenta, maroon, mediumaquamarine, mediumblue, mediumorchid, mediumpurple, mediumseagreen, mediumslateblue, mediumspringgreen, mediumturquoise, mediumvioletred, midnightblue, mintcream, mistyrose, moccasin, navajowhite, navy, oldlace, olive, olivedrab, orange, orangered, orchid, palegoldenrod, palegreen, paleturquoise, palevioletred, papayawhip, peachpuff, peru, pink, plum, powderblue, purple, red, rosybrown, royalblue, saddlebrown, salmon, sandybrown, seagreen, seashell, sienna, silver, skyblue, slateblue, slategray, snow, springgreen, steelblue, tan, teal, thistle, tomato, turquoise, violet, wheat, white, whitesmoke, yellow, yellowgreen.

There are various shades of gray in the previous list, including lightslategray, slategray, gray, darkslategray, darkgray, and lightgrey. Wait a minute. *Lightgrey?* How did this *gray-with-an-e* get into the list? If you spell it *Lightgray* it won't be recognized, so you have to get the misspelling right with Lightgrey. However, all the other shades of gray must be spelled *gray*.

LastModified

Reports the date of the last modification of the document, as follows:

```
<script language="VBScript">
D = document.lastmodified
msgbox D
</script>
```

LinkColor

Changes the color of hypertext links, like this:

```
<BODY>

<A HREF="keypress.htm"> Click here to go to an alternative
page.</A>

<script language="VBScript">
    document.LinkColor = "Green"
</script>

</BODY>
```

You can also read (find out) the current LinkColor:

```
document.LinkColor = "Silver"
X = document.LinkColor
MsgBox X
```

The result will be expressed in hex: #C0C0C0.

Note

> There is a related property, vLinkColor, that sets or reads the color of visited links. (Links change color when those sites on the Internet have been visited by the user.)

Links

A list (an "array") of the hypertext links within the document. These links are themselves *objects*, illustrating that objects can be contained within other objects (Document.Links). You can't "write" an object onto an HTML page. However, you can write the links' HREF, as illustrated in Listing 12-16.

Listing 12-16: **Link Objects**

```
<HTML>
<HEAD>
</HEAD>

<BODY>

<A HREF="keypress.htm">
Click here to go to an alternative page.</A>
<BR>
<A HREF="http://www.microsoft.com">
Click here to go to Microsoft.</A>
<BR>
```

(continued)

Listing 12-16 *(continued)*

```
<A HREF="http://altavista.digital.com">
Click for a Search Engine </A>
<br><br><br>

<SCRIPT language ="VBScript">
x = document.links.length
document.write "There are " & x & " links on this page:" &
"<BR><BR>"

for i=0 to x - 1
document.writeln document.links(i).href
document.write "<BR>"
next

</SCRIPT>

</BODY>
</HTML>
```

Note   Usually, programmers put SCRIPT source code within the HEAD section of the HTML. However, if you expect your script to check something in the HTML source code, you'll want to put the script *after* (lower than) the HTML it's supposed to analyze. All code on a page not encompassed within a sub or function is executed top down by the browser. The key thing to remember is that HTML outside the scope of this "global" code might as well be output using Document.Write.

Notice that the Links.Length code provides the actual number of links (in this example, 3). However, the links' "array" begins counting from zero, so you need to use X – 1 as the upper limit of your loop when querying this array. At the start of this example, we create three links. Then, in our script, we find out how many links there are (X), and, within the For...Next loop, use document.links(i).href to write their names directly onto the document itself.

Referrer (the URL location of the current document)

You'll see VID, for Visual InterDev, along with the version number, if you enter this in Script view, then press the Preview tab.

```
<script language="VBScript">
S = document.location
msgbox S
</script>
```

Document methods

Methods are capabilities, jobs that an object knows how to accomplish. You'll want to familiarize yourself with the tasks a document can do.

The `WriteLn` method provides an automatic carriage return, while the `Write` method does not, as shown in Listing 12-17.

Listing 12-17: **Using WriteLn**

```
<HTML>
<HEAD>
<TITLE>Document Properties</TITLE>
</HEAD>
<BODY>

<PRE>
<SCRIPT LANGUAGE="VBScript">
document.writeLn "This line ends in a carriage return (new
line)."
document.write "These lines go "
document.write "together."
</SCRIPT>

</BODY>
</HTML>
```

In this final example involving the document object, both the ordinary HTML method of displaying text and the VBScript method are illustrated. Notice that with VBScript, information can be displayed that is dynamic, that depends on conditions, as in Listing 12-18.

Listing 12-18: **Display Text Dynamically**

```
<HTML>
<HEAD>
<TITLE>Document Object</TITLE>
</HEAD>
<BODY>
<BR>
<INPUT NAME="Button1" TYPE="Button" VALUE=" Click me for a
Thrill! ">
<BR>
This is ordinary HTML text.
```

(continued)

Listing 12-18 *(continued)*

```
<BR><BR>
<PRE>
<SCRIPT LANGUAGE="VBScript">

Document.WriteLn "This is VBScript text, put upon the page
dynamically"

Sub Button1_OnClick ()
Msgbox Document.Title
End Sub
</SCRIPT>
</BODY>
</HTML>
```

Navigator-Specific Scripting

Internet Explorer isn't, of course, the only browser. IE appears to be gaining on Netscape Navigator in the same fashion the IBM PC gained on the Mac, but if you're programming for the Internet, you might want to take into account that some differences exist between IE and Navigator. For example, to detect whether a user is in Navigator or IE, you can use this script. (Note that at this time Netscape doesn't support VBScript, but future versions probably will.)

```
<SCRIPT language="VBScript">
dim browsr

Sub Window_OnLoad ()
if navigator.appName = "Netscape" then
browsr = "Nets"
end if
End Sub
</SCRIPT>
```

Within your HTML, any time you need to know which browser is hosting your document, you can query the browser variable. As always, the JavaScript version of the previous code requires extra punctuation, shown in the following code snippet:

```
<SCRIPT language="JavaScript">
var browsr="";

function Window_OnLoad(){
if (navigator.appName == "Netscape") {
```

```
var browsr="Nets";
}
</SCRIPT>
```

Or, more simply, whenever you're concerned that you have to write some browser-specific code, you can simply use the Navigator command, as follows:

```
if navigator.appName = "Netscape" then
' put Netscape-specific code here
else
' put IE-specific code here
end if
```

Also be aware that some users turn off their browser's graphics capability to speed up the display. To avoid slighting these users, you might want to provide redundancies. For instance, if you display a graphic with hotspots as a way of allowing the user to choose between hyperlinks, you should duplicate those hyperlinks in a text-only list.

Summary

This chapter introduced you to programming script. In the chapter, you learned the following:

✦ How the same tasks are accomplished in both VBScript and JScript. (Presumably, someone familiar with VBScript will be able to translate the examples in this book written in JScript into VBScript, and vice versa, by looking at this brief but relatively comprehensive tutorial on the language differences.)

✦ How client-side scripting is contrasted with server-side scripting (Active Server Pages, as they're called, are covered in Chapters 16 and 17)

✦ How to manage a document as an object (we include a list of document object properties and methods)

✦ How to tell which browser is currently active

In the next chapter, we go more deeply into scripting, including some advanced techniques and some cutting-edge scripting technology that goes by the deceptively blithe name of *scriptlets*.

✦   ✦   ✦

ActiveX Integration and Advanced Scripting

Chapter 12 discussed the basics of adding script to a Web page. In this chapter, we delve deeper into the uses for and techniques of scripting and show you how to build your own ActiveX controls. We then discuss several ways to connect script to what are now being called components (objects such as CommandButtons and ActiveX controls or Java Applets). When you add a component to a Web page, it's often necessary to also write a script so that the component actually does something when the user clicks it or otherwise interacts with it. Later in the chapter, we discuss how to use the API (the Application Programmer's Interface — the procedures available in an OS) from an ActiveX control. Finally, we introduce a recent programming development: creating script objects that can be encapsulated (sealed off) and easily reused (no more copying, pasting, then debugging source code). These *scriptlets* are related to dynamic HTML (DHTML) and serve as an introduction to that topic, which is the subject of Chapter 14.

Understanding ActiveX Components

Since the release of Visual Basic 5 (VB), it has been relatively easy for everyone to construct their own ActiveX components. What's more, you don't even need VB. You can create objects with the free version of Visual Basic from Microsoft, Visual Basic Control Creation Edition (VBCCE).

Note **VBCCE can be downloaded from** `http://www.microsoft.com/vbasic/ prodinfo/cce/default.htm`

Later we use VBCCE to create a custom Label component that is usable in Visual InterDev or FrontPage and which you can add to your Web pages. This Label will have the capability to center text both horizontally and vertically (the standard Label component can only center horizontally). But before we can create a custom Label component, we must modify an ordinary text box so it acts as a specialized password-entry component.

So far we've looked only at the capabilities of VBScript and JavaScript. Script languages work well enough in Web pages as a means of adding computational power to HypertText Markup Language (HTML). Script languages also provide a way of managing components such as TextBoxes, submit buttons and prebuilt ActiveX- or Java-based controls. But a script language isn't sophisticated enough to create your own components. Enter VBCCE.

Until the 1997 introduction of VB 5 and VBCCE, a Basic programmer could not build an ActiveX control. Visual Basic and other languages could use controls; every version of VB, even VBScript, and most IDEs (integrated design environments) such as Visual InterDev include a Toolbox with a standard set of controls, such as OptionButtons and Labels that you can add to a Web page or Basic program. But until VB 5 and VBCCE, the ActiveX controls themselves had to be written in C or Delphi. Now you can have the best of both worlds: the ease and efficiency of programming in Visual Basic, coupled with the power and sophistication of creating your own .OCX objects (another name for ActiveX controls/components).

Any language, application, or platform that supports ActiveX controls can use the .OCX controls you build. This expanding ActiveX-capable universe includes Visual Basic, Microsoft Office applications such as Word and Access, and Internet Explorer— and, in the future, the Windows desktop (we hope) and even, perhaps, Netscape.

How to Build Your First Control

VBCCE makes it simple for you to design and compile a unique, self-contained ActiveX control. Let's say that you want to create a password-entry box. It will be a small, single-line TextBox-type component, but it will permit the user to type only nine characters. Also, it will display nine asterisks (*********) instead of the characters themselves.

To create your new control, follow these steps:

1. Install VBCCE from the Microsoft Web site and run it.
2. Choose ActiveX control from the dialog box shown in Figure 13-1.

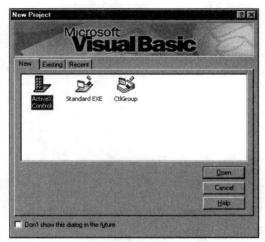

Figure 13-1: The Control Creation Edition of Visual Basic begins with this dialog.

3. You'll then see a blank VB Form and the familiar IDE. It's familiar to anyone who has worked with a Microsoft programming language, or professional tool like VI. The VBCCE IDE is shown in Figure 13-2.
4. Double-click the TextBox icon in the Toolbox to place it on the Form. Then drag it to make it only slightly larger than the text font inside (the "Text1").
5. In the Properties window, change the Name property from Text1 to PWordEntry. If you don't see the Properties Window, press F4 to bring it up.
6. Select Project1 Properties in the Project menu.
7. Change the Project Name to Entry, as shown in Figure 13-3. This will be the filename used for this project.

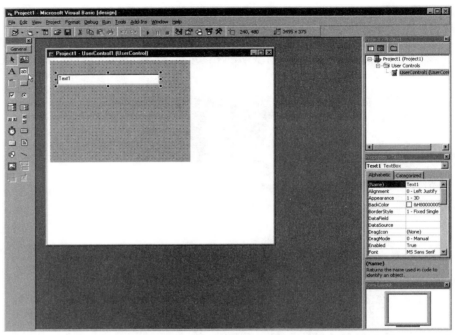

Figure 13-2: Using the VBCCE IDE you can put a TextBox on the empty UserControl (ActiveX Control).

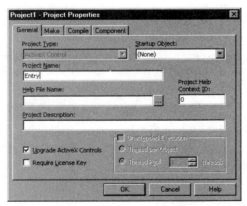

Figure 13-3: The project name (the filename) is changed in the Project Properties General tab.

8. Click the OK button to close the Properties window.

9. Remove the default Text1 caption inside the TextBox. Just double-click the Text property in the Properties window and press the Del key to remove the unwanted Text1.

10. In the Properties Window, change the TextBox's MaxLength property to **9** and the PasswordChar property to *****.

11. Move the TextBox to the upper-left corner of the Form, then reduce the size of the Form so it just embraces the TextBox, as shown in Figure 13-4. This way the user won't see an extraneous bit of framing around the control. Users (yourself, or the developers or programmers to whom you give this control) will want the control to be framed by *their* container — their Form or HTML document. They don't want a gray border around their container. Always eliminate this artifact or your component will look ugly if it is placed on a different color background.

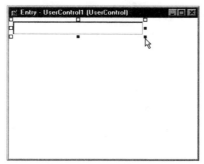

Figure 13-4: Always reduce the size of the host Form so that it just frames an ActiveX control, eliminating the extraneous framing around the control.

12. Close the design window by clicking the small x icon in the upper-right corner of the Form.

Accessing your new control's toolbar button

As soon as you close the design window, take a look at the Toolbox (shown in Figure 13-5). Your new PWordEntry control is in the corner among the other (built-in) ActiveX controls such as the ListBox and Image. With your control on the Toolbox, you can test your new control without leaving the VBCCE IDE.

Figure 13-5: Your new component is added to the VBCCE Toolbox.

Testing your new ActiveX control

Here's how to test the new password-entry control:

1. Start a regular ("standard") VB project (as opposed to an ActiveX .OCX user-control-type project) in VBCCE by clicking Add Project in the File menu. When you choose the Add Project option, you're actually having VBCCE embrace two entire projects (programs) within the single instance of the IDE. This is a novelty in IDE capabilities, but it's necessary to be able to efficiently test a newly created object such as the password-entry control.

2. Double-click Standard EXE.

3. Double-click your PWordEntry control on the Toolbox; it appears on Project1's Form.

4. Press F5 to run Project 1 and test this new control.

5. Type something into your PWordEntry custom TextBox and notice that it only permits you to type nine characters. It also refuses to display any characters other than the asterisk. Just what you wanted!

The test should look similar to the Form displayed in Figure 13-6.

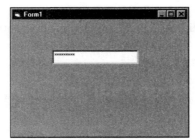

Figure 13-6: The custom PWordEntry control looks like this during the testing phase.

Registration: The Final Step

Once you're satisfied that your new control is well tested and ready for general use, you can compile an official .OCX version. This registers it and adds it to the components available for use with VI, any version of Visual Basic (including VBA, which is built in Microsoft Office applications such as Word, VBCCE, and the commercial versions of VB), and other languages that can use ActiveX controls.

Compiling is simple

To compile your control, double-click `PWordEntry` in the Project Explorer window, so that your user-control design window becomes the active window (and the Entry project becomes the active project, of the two currently embraced by the IDE). Then choose Make Entry.ocx from the File menu (this assumes that you named this project *Entry* as suggested in Step 7 earlier). Click the OK button.

When VBCCE finishes the compilation, the new ActiveX control is registered by Windows and is available for use by any ActiveX-capable language or application. If you give your ActiveX control to other developers or programmers, the registration process is done during setup.

Check the registration

To see that your Entry ActiveX control has been registered, close both Projects currently open in the VBCCE IDE, then open a new, Standard EXE project by selecting New Project in the File menu. Notice that your Entry control has disappeared from the Toolbox. To add it to the Toolbox, press Ctrl+T (or choose Components from the Project menu). Go down the list of controls until you find Entry, then select it and close the Components dialog by clicking OK, as shown in Figure 13-7.

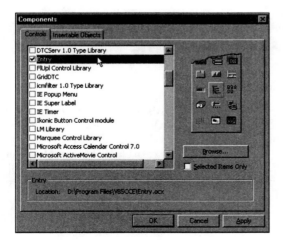

Figure 13-7: Your new component has been registered with your operating system.

Your new component has been compiled and registered with your operating system. Click the OK button and check it out: there's your custom ActiveX password-entry control on the Toolbox, ready to be added to any future Visual Basic applications or Web pages that you design.

If you still don't believe that you've actually created and registered a new ActiveX component, run VI and right-click the Toolbox (if it's not showing, select it on VI's View menu). Choose Customize Toolbox, then click the ActiveX Controls tab in the Customize Toolbox dialog. Locate the Entry.PWordEntry control in the list of available components. Select it and click OK, as shown in Figure 13-8.

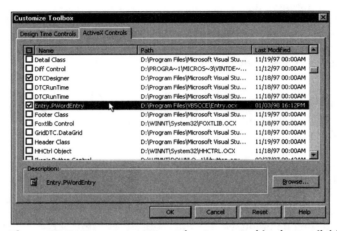

Figure 13-8: Your new password-entry control is also available for use in the VI IDE, as shown here.

You can now double-click the password-entry control to add it to your HTML documents, just like the other ActiveX controls, as shown in Figure 13-9.

Creating a New Component with the ActiveX Control Wizard

Wizards can be quite useful. It's true that some Wizards are daft and seem to have little point — you wonder why people created them when they don't really do much. But other Wizards are highly useful: they can take care of extensive and tedious clerical or housekeeping jobs for you. Our next project is to create a new component with one of the best Wizards we've ever seen — the ActiveX Control Interface Wizard, which comes with VBCCE and is also included in the commercial versions of VB. The Wizard can do much of your work when you're building an

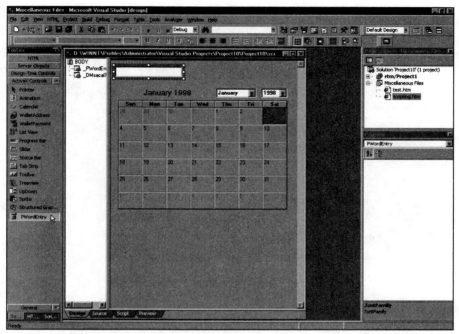

Figure 13-9: Your password-entry control appears on the VI Toolbox and can be added to your Web documents just like other ActiveX Controls.

ActiveX control. The Wizard also makes it easy to create Property Pages for your controls — those "index card" tabbed dialogs that pop up when a developer double-clicks the entry Custom in the Properties window of an IDE. Property pages are an easy way for developers to modify the qualities of a component that they're adding to their project or Web page.

Creating private and public properties

When you create a component, you'll often base it on an existing component — as you did earlier when you used a TextBox to create the PWordEntry component. Your first step is to look at the properties of the original control and determine which of those properties to "expose" because you want to permit a developer to adjust them, and which properties to conceal. For example, if you build a new component out of the standard VB Label control, are you going to allow developers access to the Label's BackColor property? If you do, programmers using your control will be able to specify the background color of your new control. If you don't, programmers will have to accept whatever color you specified for the control when you created it. In other words, decide which properties are to be public (variable) and which are to be private (hardwired).

The best way to understand how to restrict or provide properties to the users of your controls is to use the ActiveX Control Creation Wizard to build a new Label control that will center itself vertically as well as horizontally. When you're modifying an existing control, you get to grant yourself wishes. What, for example, do you want in a Label? One thing that always bothers us about the classic Label control is that its Alignment property centers the Label's text horizontally, but not vertically, within the Label frame, as shown in Figure 13-10. Let's build a Label that centers its text in both directions.

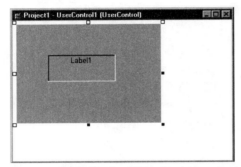

Figure 13-10: The traditional Label control aligns text horizontally, but not vertically, within the Label frame.

To create the NewLabel component, follow these steps:

1. Start VBCCE running or, if it is running, press Ctrl+N to start a new project.

2. Choose ActiveX Control.

3. You want to inherit some of the existing, built-in properties of the classic Label. This is called *mapping*. You decided to map the Font, ForeColor, and BackColor properties. Each property requires a pair of property procedures, and also a PropertyBag (similar to a *cookie*) that holds information about a component's various properties between runtimes. Click the Add-Ins menu and choose ActiveX Control Interface Wizard. If it's not available on the Add-Ins menu, choose Add-Ins Manager and select it.

4. Click Next to get to the Select Interface Members dialog, shown in Figure 13-11, where you decide which properties to map and which to leave hidden.

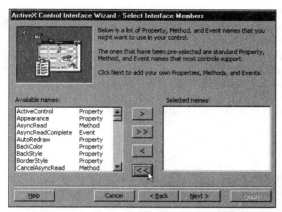

Figure 13-11: You decide which properties to map (inherit) and which to leave hidden from the developer in the Select Interface Members dialog.

5. Move all the members in the right list (Selected Names) to the left list (Available Names) by clicking the lowest button with the << symbol on it (see the mouse arrow in Figure 13-11).

6. Press the Ctrl key while clicking these Available Names: AutoRedraw, BackColor, Font, ForeColor, TextHeight, and TextWidth. TextHeight and TextWidth provide the precise measurement of the current Message in the current FontSize. This information enables you to center the Message within the SuperMsg control.

7. Click Next and then click New. The Add Custom Member dialog box appears, as shown in Figure 13-12. Add a custom member named **Message** in the Name text box and check property under Type. Click OK and then click Next.

Figure 13-12: The Add Custom Member dialog box permits you to add new Properties, Methods, or Events (collectively called the *members* of a component) of your own.

8. Map all the members to UserControl except Message, as shown in Figure 13-13. Click Next. When you map a member, you're borrowing the functionality of the original and copying it to your new CustomControl. In other words, if you choose to map the Font property, your new component will provide a Font property that can be adjusted by a developer using your component.

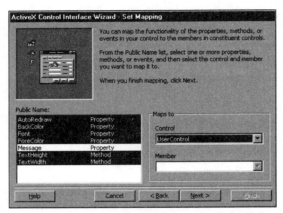

Figure 13-13: Press the Ctrl key and select all the properties listed except Message, which is your custom property.

9. Define the Data Type of the Message property as a String and set the default to "NewLabel" (erase the default 0).

10. Click Next, then click Finish.

You can ignore the report; we discuss the issues it explains now. Your source code should include all the members you mapped, plus a `WriteProperties`/ `ReadProperties` pair that preserves the settings of the properties, and, finally, your custom Message property. If you double-click the UserControl in VBCCE, you should see the source code in Listing 13-1.

Listing 13-1: The VBCCE-Created Source Code

```
'Default Property Values:
Const m_def_Message = "NewLabel"
'Property Variables:
Dim m_Message As String
```

```vb
'WARNING! DO NOT REMOVE OR MODIFY THE FOLLOWING COMMENTED
LINES!
'MappingInfo=UserControl,UserControl,-1,TextWidth
Public Function TextWidth(Str As String) As Single
  TextWidth = UserControl.TextWidth(Str)
End Function
'WARNING! DO NOT REMOVE OR MODIFY THE FOLLOWING COMMENTED
LINES!
'MappingInfo=UserControl,UserControl,-1,TextHeight
Public Function TextHeight(Str As String) As Single
  TextHeight = UserControl.TextHeight(Str)
End Function
'WARNING! DO NOT REMOVE OR MODIFY THE FOLLOWING COMMENTED
LINES!
'MappingInfo=UserControl,UserControl,-1,ForeColor
Public Property Get ForeColor() As OLE_COLOR
  ForeColor = UserControl.ForeColor
End Property
Public Property Let ForeColor(ByVal New_ForeColor As OLE_COLOR)
  UserControl.ForeColor() = New_ForeColor
  PropertyChanged "ForeColor"
End Property
'WARNING! DO NOT REMOVE OR MODIFY THE FOLLOWING COMMENTED
LINES!
'MappingInfo=UserControl,UserControl,-1,Font
Public Property Get Font() As Font
  Set Font = UserControl.Font
End Property
Public Property Set Font(ByVal New_Font As Font)
  Set UserControl.Font = New_Font
  PropertyChanged "Font"
End Property
'WARNING! DO NOT REMOVE OR MODIFY THE FOLLOWING COMMENTED
LINES!
'MappingInfo=UserControl,UserControl,-1,BackColor
Public Property Get BackColor() As OLE_COLOR
  BackColor = UserControl.BackColor
End Property
Public Property Let BackColor(ByVal New_BackColor As OLE_COLOR)
  UserControl.BackColor() = New_BackColor
  PropertyChanged "BackColor"
End Property
'WARNING! DO NOT REMOVE OR MODIFY THE FOLLOWING COMMENTED
LINES!
'MappingInfo=UserControl,UserControl,-1,AutoRedraw
Public Property Get AutoRedraw() As Boolean
  AutoRedraw = UserControl.AutoRedraw
End Property
Public Property Let AutoRedraw(ByVal New_AutoRedraw As Boolean)
  UserControl.AutoRedraw() = New_AutoRedraw
  PropertyChanged "AutoRedraw"
End Property
```

(continued)

Listing 13-1 *(continued)*

```
Public Property Get Message() As String
  Message = m_Message
End Property
Public Property Let Message(ByVal New_Message As String)
  m_Message = New_Message
  PropertyChanged "Message"
End Property
'Initialize Properties for User Control
Private Sub UserControl_InitProperties()
  Set Font = Ambient.Font
  m_Message = m_def_Message
End Sub
'Load property values from storage
Private Sub UserControl_ReadProperties(PropBag As PropertyBag)
  UserControl.ForeColor = PropBag.ReadProperty("ForeColor",
&H80000012)
  Set Font = PropBag.ReadProperty("Font", Ambient.Font)
  UserControl.BackColor = PropBag.ReadProperty("BackColor",
&H8000000F)
  UserControl.AutoRedraw = PropBag.ReadProperty("AutoRedraw",
False)
  m_Message = PropBag.ReadProperty("Message", m_def_Message)
End Sub
'Write property values to storage
Private Sub UserControl_WriteProperties(PropBag As PropertyBag)
Call PropBag.WriteProperty("ForeColor", UserControl.ForeColor,
&H80000012)
  Call PropBag.WriteProperty("Font", Font, Ambient.Font)
  Call PropBag.WriteProperty("BackColor",
UserControl.BackColor, &H8000000F)
  Call PropBag.WriteProperty("AutoRedraw",
UserControl.AutoRedraw, False)
  Call PropBag.WriteProperty("Message", m_Message,
m_def_Message)
End Sub
```

The Wizard's code deserves some explanation. Although to us — the creators, developers, and users — controls seem fairly substantial, they repeatedly flicker in and out of existence. When a project is opened in the IDE (the VI, VBCCE, or other design environment), or when you press F5 to test a program, or when a window is opened or closed by the user — all these and many other situations create or destroy controls. Every time a control is created, the ReadProperties events are triggered, which restore properties that had previously been set in the Properties window during design-time. Each time a control is destroyed, VB uses the

WriteProperty events to store the current status of a control's properties in a file: .FRM or .FRX files for the controls on a Form; .CTL or .CTX files for a UserControl.

Suppressing a Properties window

VB automatically displays to the developer any custom property you create for your UserControl in the Properties window during design-time. If you don't want developers to have access to a property in the Properties window, follow these steps to suppress it:

1. Select Procedure Attributes in the Tools menu. If Procedure Attributes is disabled, double-click UserControl1 in the Project Explorer.

2. In the Name list, choose the member you want to suppress.

3. Click the Advanced button.

4. Select "Hide this member" in the Attributes section.

You can relax about all the seemingly complex code required to add a property and use the ActiveX Control Interface Wizard to assist you in mapping properties. Typing all these procedures (four for each property) is not only tiresome, but the Wizard makes it unnecessary to hand-code this source code. The Wizard does all this housekeeping and clerical coding for you.

Contacting the API

To finish the NewLabel custom control, the following code must be added by your typing it in. No Wizard can substitute entirely for a programmer — so far, anyway.

Double-click the UserControl to get to its code window, move the cursor to the very top of the source code (in the General Declarations section), and type this in:

```
Private Declare Function TextOut Lib "gdi32" Alias "TextOutA"
(ByVal hdc As Long, ByVal x As Long, ByVal y As Long, ByVal
lpString As String, ByVal nCount As Long) As Long
```

Making use of the GDI

The TextOut function used in the preceding code isn't a procedure in our code; it's not a function that you're going to write. Instead, it's a function in the GDI (Graphical Device Interface), which is a vast collection of functions (and a few subroutines) that displays on-screen elements. All Windows programs go through the GDI when they draw or print to the screen, or perform other graphics-related tasks. Programmers, too, can employ the functions in the GDI, as the following example illustrates. All you have to do is declare one of the API procedures as the preceding code shows, then your program can trigger that procedure, as we do here with the following line:

```
z = TextOut(UserControl.hdc, tw, th, message, Len(message))
```

The GDI is one part, albeit a major part, of the entire Windows API. Why, though, use the API at all? Generally speaking, you use the API because there is no way within the programming language that you're using to accomplish something. In this example, we're trying to center text within a label. We can calculate the center using Basic, and we can also use Basic to calculate the starting position for the text once we've calculated the center. But, there is no provision in Basic for printing text at a screen coordinate. The Basic Print command uses logical "lines" and "character spaces" as arguments for the screen location of text it displays; this is too crude a coordinate system to horizontally center the text within the label. This compels us to use the API TextOut routine, which accepts highly precise coordinates.

Tip   You can find out all about the Windows API and how it can be accessed from Visual Basic in *Visual Basic 6 Secrets* by Harold Davis, published by IDG Books Worldwide.

Now, back to our example. The Resize event of your UserControl is where most of the action takes place. Type the code in Listing 13-2 into the Resize event of UserControl1.

Listing 13-2: **The Resize Event**

```
Private Sub UserControl_Resize()
UserControl.Cls
scw = UserControl.ScaleWidth
sch = UserControl.ScaleHeight
'calculate center for message
tw = UserControl.TextWidth(message) / 2
th = UserControl.TextHeight(message) / 2
tw = (scw / 2) - tw
th = (sch / 2) - th
z = TextOut(UserControl.hdc, tw, th, message, Len(message))
End Sub
```

The calculation of the variables *tw* and *th* provides an x,y coordinate that is used by the TextOut function to print the Message property in the center of the SuperMsg control.

Now you want to add a line to the `Let BackColor`, `Let ForeColor`, `Let Message`, and `Set Font` procedures that will trigger the `Resize` event. This way, when the developer changes any of those properties — either during design-time or at run-time — the change will be displayed at once in the SuperMsg control.

At the bottom of those four procedures, just above the `End Property` command, type **UserControl_Resize**, like this:

```
Public Property Set Font(ByVal New_Font As Font)
 Set UserControl.Font = New_Font
 PropertyChanged "Font"
 UserControl_Resize
End Property
```

Finally, set the `ScaleMode` for your UserControl to pixels (the API requires this unit of measurement).

```
Private Sub UserControl_Initialize()
ScaleMode = 3 'set to pixels
End Sub
```

In the `ReadProperties` procedure, the line that reads the Message should be near the top. If it's at the bottom of that procedure, the `Resize` event won't display a Message during run-time (unless it is changed in the source code). Remember that properties set during design-time in the Properties window are saved to a `PropertyBag` and then read back at the start of runtime. If the line that reads the Message is near the bottom of the `ReadProperties` procedure, the `Resize` event will have done its job before the default Message is read, so the Resize event will see an empty Message (""). The `ReadProperties` procedure should look similar to Listing 13-3.

Listing 13-3: **The ReadProperties Procedure**

```
'Load property values from storage
Private Sub UserControl_ReadProperties(PropBag As PropertyBag)
 m_Message = PropBag.ReadProperty("Message", m_def_Message)
 UserControl.ForeColor = PropBag.ReadProperty("ForeColor",
&H80000012)
 Set Font = PropBag.ReadProperty("Font", Ambient.Font)
 UserControl.BackColor = PropBag.ReadProperty("BackColor",
&H8000000F)
 UserControl.AutoRedraw = PropBag.ReadProperty("AutoRedraw",
True)
End Sub
```

In other words, you have to edit the Wizard's source code to move the m_Message line to the top of this procedure; the Wizard, for all its wisdom, places that line at the bottom.

Testing the NewLabel

Test this UserControl the usual way. Select Add Project from the File menu and add a Standard EXE-type project. Close the NewLabel design window so the UserControl icon appears on the ToolBox. Add a NewLabel to Form1 of the Standard EXE project. Try to adjust its properties in the Property window and try to run it. You'll see something similar to Figure 13-14 with the text always centered inside the label, no matter how you resize it.

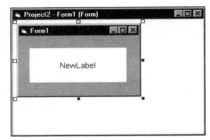

Figure 13-14: Your finished NewLabel component is ready to be compiled (choose Make Project1.OCX on the File menu).

Building Scriptlets

Creating ActiveX components can be both easy and useful. Components are objects, with all the benefits that objects offer, including reusability and encapsulation. But you can also encapsulate reusable pieces of raw script using a different and very new technique called *scriptlets*. Dynamic HTML is a technology that uses facilities that are built in the browser (Internet Explorer (IE) 4.0 is the only browser with this capability at this time) to permit the execution of scripts within the user's machine (client-side). DHTML expands the capabilities of HTML by providing numerous animation, graphics, and interactivity features. Chapters 14 and 15 are devoted entirely to this useful amplification of the hitherto-static HTML language.

The advantages of scriptlets

A scriptlet has several advantages over ordinary programming code. To reuse ordinary source code, programmers have to resort to copying and pasting. This approach has a number of drawbacks, not least of which is the unpredictability of side effects from duplicated variable names or poorly structured (or undocumented) source–code behaviors.

When you write a scriptlet, however, you can merely call on it (provide its URL) to execute it in a Web page. Like other objects, a scriptlet is encapsulated and exposes an interface (its methods and properties) to allow other developers to make use of it. But it theoretically hides the actual source code from them. Another advantage of scriptlets is that they are built using only HTML and VBScript or JavaScript — therefore, they download quickly (and are cached for reuse) to the user's machine.

So far, this definition of scriptlets sounds suspiciously like Java Applets or ActiveX components — a reusable, encapsulated object with a public interface. In fact, scriptlets do behave similarly to components, but they are created differently: a scriptlet is just a Web page composed of HTML and script. Then, as you'll see, it is referenced from within another Web page as an object. Create ActiveX components when you need the heavy-duty language facilities of Visual Basic or other major computer languages. If your job only requires script+HTML, create a scriptlet. Remember that script languages (JavaScript or VBScript) are missing whole sets of commands that are found in the larger parent languages Java, Visual Basic, and C. Script has no system-access commands (it cannot get to the user's hard drive or printer, not to mention the Registry). Some developers believe that stripping script languages of system access offers a degree of protection against virus attacks resulting from downloading scripted pages over the Internet. In other words, some people set up their browsers' security filters to permit embedded script, but to warn them of an embedded component prior to downloading a Web page that contains it. (In IE4, the security filtering is set from the Security tab of the Internet Options item on the View menu.)

Scriptlets versus includes

A scriptlet also differs from a server-side *include*. An include permits automatic adding of script and HTML to documents before they are sent to the user. A scriptlet, however, like an Applet or component object, is cached (only downloaded to the user once) and is also encapsulated. The user can see the source code provided by an include because it's merely inserted into the HTML of the document as pure source code.

Scriptlets can be created in and tested in VI, and are also supported in FrontPage because it supports the standard <OBJECT> tag. Enough of the preliminaries; let's create a simple scriptlet to get an idea what all the fuss is about.

Creating a simple scriptlet

Now let's build an elementary, bare bones scriptlet to get a feel for the techniques involved. Listing 13-4 shows the source code for a simple scriptlet that always shows the words "Our Message Is…" and then adds whatever additional text you want it to display.

Listing 13-4: **A Simple Scriplet**

```
<HTML>
<script language="javscript">
function public_showtext(x) {
place.innerText = x; }
</script>
<body>
<h3>Our Message Is…</h3>
<DIV id="place"></DIV>
</body>
</HTML>
```

Save this from Notepad or the VI editor to your C drive with the filename TE2.HTM. It's an ordinary .HTM file, but we're going to place it in another HTM file as an OBJECT. At the most elementary level, that's what makes it a scriptlet—treating an HTM file as an *object*.

By using the term *public,* we're exposing this function to the outside, to the other HTM file that includes the scriptlet object. showtext is a method of our scriptlet, as opposed to a property. We'll get to the source code distinction between properties and methods shortly. For now, notice that all this method does is display some text below our H3 headline (the H3 headline will always display when this scriptlet is placed in some other HTML file). To display additional text below the *Our Message Is…* headline, the programmer who creates the host HTML page (the *container* page) must use the showtext method of this scriptlet.

We'll use the OBJECT element to embed the scriptlet in a document and use the scriptlet's showtext method to display additional text. For clarity, let's refer to the HTML that has a scriptlet in it as the container HTML or page. First, create a new, separate HTML page in the VI editor and put the following source code in it. Listing 13-5 shows the container page with our *te2* scriptlet inside it as an object.

Listing 13-5: The Container Page with the te2 Scriptlet as an Object

```
<HTML>
<HEAD>
<SCRIPT LANGUAGE="VBScript">
Sub window_onload()
a = scrlet.showtext(" This text is displayed.")
End Sub

</SCRIPT>
</HEAD>
<BODY>
<OBJECT height=300 id=scrlet DATA="c:\te2.htm"
    type=text/x-scriptlet width=300 VIEWASTEXT>
</OBJECT>
</BODY>
</HTML>
```

Note that the DATA attribute points to the URL where the scriptlet file is located and the ID attribute gives the object a name that it can be referred to within this container document. When this document loads (window_onload), we trigger the showtext method. We gave the scriptlet the ID *scrlet* so that's how we refer to it within the script:

```
a = scrlet.showtext(" this text is displayed...")
```

Tip   You can easily insert a scriptlet's OBJECT reference into a container by right-clicking on the scriptlet's filename (TE2.HTM in this example) in the VI Project Explorer and then choosing the Mark As Scriptlet option. A Scriptlets tab is added to the Toolbox. Double-click on the scriptlet's name in the Toolbox (or drag it to an open HTML page in the editor) and it will appear as a box. To see the OBJECT definition of your scriptlet, right-click that box and choose Text View.

If you run the container HTML from within VI, click the Quick View tab and you'll see that the showtext method displays the text we fed to it:

```
Our Message Is...
This text is displayed.
```

If You Have Problems...

We hesitate to describe the IE4/VI/FP support of the new scriptlet technology as fragile. However, all the code in this book has been carefully tested and we are confident that it works, including the scriptlet examples in this chapter. Nonetheless, you might experience problems getting these scriptlets to run in VI, FrontPage, or when you choose View in Browser from the VI View menu or the FrontPage File menu.

There can be a variety of reasons for these problems. Perhaps you have the scriptlet file in a path or with a filename that you're referencing incorrectly in the container. Also, in some situations (FrontPage's IDE, for example), you can mix and match languages. For example, in the previous example, the container uses VBScript but the scriptlet is written in JavaScript. However, if you try that in other contexts—notably the VI IDE—the scriptlet will fail to receive any passed parameters. So, to be on the safe side, stick to a single language for both the container and the scriptlet.

Make these changes to the earlier VBScript in Listing 13.5 to translate the container script into JavaScript:

```
<SCRIPT LANGUAGE="JScript">
function doit(){
a = scrlet.showtext(" this text is displayed...")
}
</SCRIPT>
<BODY onload="doit()">
```

Creating scriptlet properties

There are three ways to create a property in a scriptlet and expose it to outside scripts (in container pages that hold the scriptlet OBJECT). Some programmers prefer to create a *public var*, but if you want to create a read-only property, use the get_ approach (see the following example code). Also, at this time, the public var technique is not working and, in any case, exposing variables within an object (making them public) is considered bad Object-Oriented Programming (OOP) programmer practice. You're supposed to hide your data within an object and manage any changes to that data through public properties.

When you call on one of the scriptlet's member procedures, you drop the Public_Put or Public_get part of the code. You use just the name of the scriptlet in the OBJECT definition attached to the name of the member procedure. The following example assumes that you've defined a member procedure in the scriptlet similar to this one:

```
Sub public_put_textcontents(yourtext)
```

When you want to assign a value to this property, drop `public_put` and replace it with the name you've given the scriptlet object using `ID=` in the container page (for this example, we name it *Norma*), as shown in the following code:

```
<OBJECT id=Norma data=slet.htm type=text/x-Scriptlet></OBJECT>
Norma.textcontents = "This Message"
```

Note   Scriptlets handle properties in a way similar to the way that Visual Basic (version 5 and after) handles the properties of objects, but with one difference. In VB, you create a pair of procedures named `Property Let` and `Property Get` to allow outside entities to assign or query the property. With scriptlets, you create a pair of procedures named `public_put` and `public_get` to accomplish the same things. Also, if you're used to Java, note that VBScript permits two kinds of procedures: Subs—which don't return any value to the caller—and Functions (which do return a value to the caller).

Listing 13-6 is a more complex scriptlet that illustrates how to create both methods and properties. Outlook Express needs two files: one for the scriptlet and the other for the "container" code that references the scriptlet file.

Listing 13-6: **A More Complex Scriptlet**

```
<HTML>
<HEAD>
<TITLE>Scriptlet</TITLE>
<SCRIPT LANGUAGE = VBScript>
Dim howfast
' this property is called by: scriptletname.howfast = 80
Sub public_put_howfast(amount)
howfast = amount
End Sub
' this method is called by:
scriptletname.runitnow(NameOfPicture.Jpg)
Sub public_runitnow(pic)
ourpicture.Src=pic
timr = Window.SetInterval("doit", howfast)
End Sub
'this is a private procedure and isn't
'available to the outside container
Sub doit()
If ourpicture.Style.PixelLeft >= Document.Body.OffsetWidth -
ourpicture.width
Then ourpicture.Style.PixelLeft = 0
Else
ourpicture.Style.PixelLeft = ourpicture.Style.PixelLeft + 10
```

(continued)

Listing 13-6 *(continued)*

```
End If
End Sub
</SCRIPT>
</HEAD>
<BODY>
<IMG ID = ourpicture STYLE="position:relative;top:0;left:0" >
</BODY>
</HTML>
```

Listing 13-7 is the container for Listing 13-6.

Listing 13-7: **The Container file**

```
<HTML>
<HEAD>
<TITLE>Container</Title>
<SCRIPT LANGUAGE = VBScript>
Sub Window_Onload()
scl.howfast = 80
scl.Width = Document.Body.OffsetWidth
'replace "c:\crane.jpg" with the path
'to a .jpg or .gif file on your computer
scl.runitnow("c:\crane.jpg")
End Sub
</SCRIPT>
</HEAD>
<BODY>
<!-- Change data=slet.htm to the path
of your scriptlet's .htm file -->
<OBJECT data=slet.htm height=100
 id=scl style="LEFT: 0px; TOP: 0px"
type=text/x-scriptlet VIEWASTEXT></OBJECT>
</BODY>
</HTML>
```

In the scriptlet just shown, we're offering the outside world the scriptlet's services with a property (named `howfast`) and a method (`runitnow`). As you can see, the only difference between the code that creates a property and the code that creates a method is that the property requires the term `public_put` (or `get_`), whereas the method eliminates the `put_` (or `get_`) and simply uses the term *public_* alone. The syntax that creates a property is:

```
Sub public_put_howfast(amount)
```

This syntax creates a method:

```
Sub public_runitnow(pic)
```

Things are different in the container page that calls a scriptlet. The distinction between property and method in the container page is that you use the = command to assign a value to a property as follows:

```
scriptletname.howfast = 80
```

Use parentheses, however, to pass a value to a method:

```
scriptletname.runitnow(NameOfPicture.Jpg)
```

The scriptlet here uses the DHTML setInterval command to start a timer that will repeatedly trigger the procedure named doit. The idea is that the scriptlet causes a graphic to scoot across the container page. The doit procedure is encapsulated. It's not available to the container page and it's not public. However, the public property howfast is exposed to the container and specifies how often, in milliseconds, the doit procedure should be triggered. The public method, runitnow, receives the URL (or file path) of the graphic the container wants to move, and also starts the whole process running.

Each time doit is fired, it first checks to see if the graphic has reached the right side of the scriptlet object and, if so, resets the Left property of the graphic to 0. If not, the graphic is moved 10 pixels to the right. The image (IMG) named *ourpicture* is contained in the scriptlet. It is given the URL of the graphic after that URL is passed to the scriptlet from the container.

In the container, our first job is to make the scriptlet object as wide as the container (the graphic moves *within the scriptlet*).

```
scl.Width = Document.Body.OffsetWidth
```

It is common practice to describe a scriptlet's dimensions in terms of the container's dimensions. It is also common practice to put this description in the initialization section of the container's script: Sub Window_Onload(). If you don't adjust the scriptlet's dimensions (or position) it will be as big as (and located where) specified in the OBJECT definition.

```
<OBJECT data=slet.htm height=100 id=scl
 style="LEFT: 0px; TOP: 0px"
    type=text/x-scriptlet VIEWASTEXT></OBJECT>
```

In a scriptlet's OBJECT definition, the `data=` parameter points to the scriptlet's URL. The `id=` parameter provides the name that is used within the container to identify the scriptlet. The `type=` parameter defines this object as a scriptlet, and the `VIEWASTEXT` parameter tells the editor to display the scriptlet's HTML OBJECT definition rather than show it as a graphic object. Right-click a graphic representation of a scriptlet to pop up a menu that includes the Text View option, as illustrated in Figure 13-15.

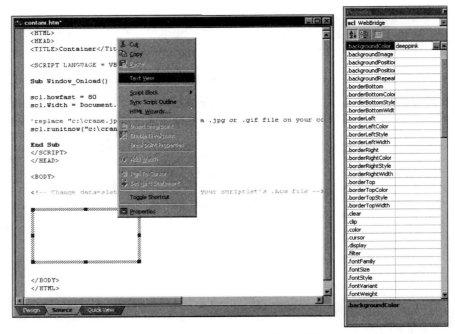

Figure 13-15: Because the scriptlet is selected in the editing window, its properties are displayed in the properties window on the right.

Raising Events in Scriptlets

Like any good object, a scriptlet can have events in addition to its properties and methods. Properties are *qualities* of an object, such as its width. Methods are actions an object can do, such as starting animation (setting a timer, in the example given earlier). Events, however, are things that happen *to* an object (such as being clicked). An event offers the programmer a way to specify a reaction: for example, what should the script do if the object is clicked? Let's see how scriptlets can raise (also known as "triggering" or "firing") an event in a container.

Passing a standard DHTML event

Let's say that you want to alert the container page (raise an event in that page) whenever the user clicks in the scriptlet. You can pass any standard DHTML event from the scriptlet to the container using the following syntax. (DHTML is discussed in detail in Chapters 14 and 15.)

```
Sub Document_OnClick()
Window.external.bubbleEvent()
End Sub
```

This means that whenever the scriptlet is clicked, it will pass that event along (bubble it up) to the container page, where it can be detected and handled like this:

```
Sub scrlet_OnClick()
MsgBox "The scriptlet says it was clicked."
End Sub
```

Note

IE4 also includes a new way to handle events: *bubbling.* Think lava lamps. In other browsers, if an HTML element fired an event, but there was no event handler to react to that event, the event died. With IE4's event bubbling, a fired event bubbles up the object hierarchy, going from child element to parent element on up the object model until it reaches the very top—the document object. It stops bubbling only if it is handled somewhere along its upward movement. This is why when a scriptlet triggers an event within a container, the command is called bubbleEvent().

Assuming that *scrlet* is the ID= parameter you specified as the name of the scriptlet OBJECT within the container, consider the following code snippet:

```
<OBJECT data=slet.htm id=scrlet
type=text/x-Scriptlet VIEWASTEXT></OBJECT>
```

Netscape Navigator 4, like Internet Explorer 4, responds to events. The difference between IE4 and all other browsers is that IE4 allows every HTML element to trigger a rich set of mouse and keyboard events. Other browsers' event handling is restricted to a small group of HTML elements capable of firing events: anchors, applications, form elements, image maps, and objects. The common events that IE4 permits for every HTML element are: onmouseover, onmouseout, onmousedown, onmouseup, onmousemove, onclick, ondblclick, onkeypress, onkeydown, onkeyup. (There are other DHTML events—a total of 39—but not all HTML elements feature all DHTML events.)

Defining custom events

What do you do if there is no standard DHTML event that you can bubble? There is a way to define custom events of your own devising in scriptlets. In the scriptlet, use this syntax to raise an event.

```
window.external.raiseEvent(EventName, Object)
```

EventName is a string to describe what happened (this string will be used the event handler in the container) and Object can be any script object, but ordinarily is Window.Event. You should realize that there is only that *one* custom event-raising syntax within the scriptlet: window.external.raiseEvent(*EventName, Object*). If you want to raise more than one custom event, the container will distinguish them by the EventName (not by having separate procedures for each custom scriptlet event). The container uses the EventName to respond with appropriate code. In the following example, the container asks if this scriptlet event is named "upper," and, if so, it tells the user not to use uppercase.

```
Sub scrlet_OnScriptletEvent(mssg, o)
If mssg = "upper" Then
MsgBox "Please don't use uppercase letters."
End If
End Sub
```

Were there additional custom events raised by the scriptlet, they would all still be handled within this single OnScriptletEvent procedure in the container. They would be distinguished by the EventName (called mssg in the above container procedure).

In the following example, we raise an event in the scriptlet if the user tries to type a capital letter in the scriptlet's TextBox. The scriptlet's TextBox onkeypress event checks whether the keycode the user presses is less than 97, meaning it's not lowercase. If that happens, an event is raised in the container and the term *upper* is passed to let the container know that the user tried to type in the wrong kind of character in the scriptlet's TextBox. We also use the following code to prevent the offending uppercase letter from appearing within the TextBox:

```
Window.Event.ReturnValue = NULL
```

Listing 13-8 lists the scriptlet.

Listing 13-8: **Raising an Event**

```
<HTML>
<HEAD>
<SCRIPT LANGUAGE = VBScript>
```

```
<!--
'property
Function public_get_num()
public_get_num = TBox.Value
End Function
'property
Function public_put_num(n)
TBox.Value = n
End Function
'Raise an event
Sub TBox_OnKeyPress()
'create an object variable
Dim Happening
Set Happening = Window.Event
'if it's uppercase, raise the event, and throw away the
keypress
If Happening.KeyCode < 97 Then
Window.External.RaiseEvent "upper", window.event
    Window.Event.ReturnValue = NULL
End If
End Sub
-->
</SCRIPT>
</HEAD>
<BODY>
This is the Scriptlet<BR>
<Input Type="Text" ID = TBox>
</BODY>
</HTML>
```

Listing 13-9 lists the container.

Listing 13-9: **The Container File**

```
<HEAD>
<TITLE>Container</Title>
<SCRIPT LANGUAGE = VBScript>
<!--
Sub Window_Onload()
scrlet.Width = Document.Body.OffsetWidth
End Sub
'Here's the custom Event
Sub scrlet_OnScriptletEvent(mssg, o)
If mssg = "upper" Then
MsgBox "Please don't use uppercase letters."
End If
End Sub
```

(continued)

Listing 13-9 *(continued)*

```
'read the scriptlet property and make it the button caption
Sub clkbttn_OnClick()
clkbttn.Value = scrlet.num
End Sub
-->
</SCRIPT>
</HEAD>
<BODY>
<OBJECT data=slet.htm id=scrlet
 type=text/x-Scriptlet VIEWASTEXT></OBJECT>
<BR>
<BR>
This is in the container<BR>
<INPUT TYPE = "Button" ID = clkbttn
 VALUE="Click to transfer scriptlet value." >
</BODY>
</HTML>
```

There is, of course, much more that you can do with scriptlets and DHTML. Many DHTML ideas are developed in Chapters 14 and 15, and you're sure to think of ways to use, and reuse, scriptlets yourself. Once the cutting-edge technology of scriptlets settles and becomes, we hope, a standard and stable feature of Internet programming, it will be a boon to programmers and developers.

Summary

The primary focus of this chapter is advanced object-oriented Web programming techniques. This divides into two primary sections: designing and integrating ActiveX components (controls) that you build yourself and the new technology of scriptlets. You learned about the following topics:

✦ How to build a custom component to solve a problem or add features that you need, but that are not available within the classic, prebuilt components.

✦ To add your new component to the standard toolbox along with the classic components like the TextBox.

✦ Ways to use two projects opened simultaneously within the IDE to test your new ActiveX control.

✦ To alert the operating system that your new component exists by registering your component.

✦ All about one of the most serviceable and impressive Wizards we've ever used: the ActiveX Control Creation Wizard.

✦ How to further encapsulate your work by suppressing properties within the properties window of your component, so that developers cannot fiddle with a property you want hidden.

✦ That Windows programmers have long resorted to the huge collection of procedures within the Windows OS itself. You learned how to put these procedures in the API to work for you.

✦ That there is a new OOP tool for Web programmers: scriptlets. You learned how to write them, and how to give them properties, methods, and events (either by mapping standard events or by creating new events of your own). And, finally, you learned how to test and debug scriptlets.

✦　　✦　　✦

Dynamic HTML

The name gives it away. That this addition to traditional HyperText Markup Language (HTML) is called *dynamic* is an acknowledgment that ordinary HTML is, for the most part, static. As nearly everyone agrees, Dynamic HTML (DHTML) moves the original DOS-like HTML standard a bit closer to its ultimate goal: computers that can match, and even exceed, the visual and audio quality of television. When computer multimedia content reaches that level, it will have several advantages over TV's analog storage and transmission. Of course, we're still some distance from the convergence of the Web and High-Definition TV. Nevertheless, motion video compression techniques and other technologies and proposals, such as DHTML, continue to move us in that direction.

DHTML is an exciting, and quite large, topic. In this chapter and the next, we introduce DHTML, show you how to write it and test it in Visual InterDev, and provide examples of some of the best effects and techniques that DHTML makes possible. However, the topic really deserves a book of its own, of which there are many, such as *Dynamic HTML* by Shelley Powers (IDG Books Worldwide).

DHTML Basics

Ordinary HTML is sent to a user's browser with the intent that some data (text or pictures) be displayed. Such a display is basically hard-wired, inert, passive, and still. DHTML, however, improves the HTML page-description language by adding programming features, with all the interactivity, mutability, animation and active, client-side processing that modern, visually rich, computer programming implies.

The DHTML proposal gives developers and programmers a way (through script languages) to move, instantiate (bring into existence), resize, and otherwise modify the elements and attributes of HTML. Internet Explorer (IE) 4.0 is DHTML-capable; indeed, Microsoft has said that DHTML is the most significant feature in Internet Explorer 4.0. The browser contains various components (multimedia controls) that also reside within the user's computer as part of IE4. Both user-side scripting and the user-resident components make sophisticated audio and visual effects far more efficient than if the components (or the results of server-side scripting) had to be sent over the Internet. Even a static still graphic image can take way too long to traverse the narrow bandwidth most of us have to put up with on today's Internet.

The Document Object Model

The basis for Microsoft's DHTML initiative is the Document Object Model (DOM). This is a hierarchical structure that allows a programmer to reference (and manipulate) any object in a Web page (tables, forms, graphics, styles, and so on). IE4 supports the full DOM; every object in a page is made available to the programmer. Netscape is in the process of permitting this full access, but it hasn't happened yet.

DOM allows programmers to use scripting languages to access and exploit all HTML elements (elements are all the major commands, that is, the tags, of HTML, such as A, AREA, BIG, FORM, FRAME, H1, and so on). This means that in theory you can use DHTML to programmatically control all attributes (the qualities of elements, such as ALIGN, BORDER, BGCOLOR, HREF, SIZE, ONCLICK, and so on), all Cascading Style Sheet properties, and all embedded objects, graphics, and text. Everything, in other words, that comprises a Web page. DTHML fractures HTML into pieces, which the programmer can then manipulate in the user's browser (client-side). These manipulations take place at once; the browser does not have to refresh the page. The manipulations can be triggered in many ways: by events (such as the user clicking a graphic or moving the mouse over that graphic), at a predetermined time, repeatedly at a defined interval, or by virtually any other programmatic trigger. Earlier HTML was seriously hampered because it had provisions for only a few events, and those events only worked with a few elements. Now all the elements work with a rich set of events.

The objects in DOM

Following is a list of all of the objects in the DHTML DOM. The items in all-caps are traditional HTML elements.

A	ACRONYM	ADDRESS	all
APPLET	applets	AREAanchors	areas
B	BASE	BASEFONT	BGSOUND
BIG	BLOCKQUOTE	BODY	BR
BUTTON	CAPTION	cells	CENTER
children	CITE	CODE	COL
COLGROUP	COMMENT	DD	DEL
DFN	DIR	DIV	DL
document	DT	elements	EM
EMBED	embeds	event	external
FIELDSET	filters	FONT	FORM
forms	FRAME	frames	FRAMESET
H1	H2	H3	H4
H5	H6	HEAD	history
HR	HTML	I	IFRAME
images	IMG	INPUT	INS
KBD	LABEL	LEGEND	LI
LINK	links	LISTING	location
MAP	MARQUEE	MENU	META
navigator	NEXTID	OBJECT	OL
OPTION	options	P	PLAINTEXT
plugins	PRE	Q	rows
rules	S	SAMP	screen
SCRIPT	scripts	SELECT	selection
SMALL	SPAN	STRIKE	STRONG
STYLE	style	styleSheet	styleSheets
SUB	SUP	TABLE	TBODY
TD	TEXTAREA	TextRange	TFOOT
TH	THEAD	TITLE	TR
TT	U	UL	userProfile
VAR	window	XMP	

Part III ✦ Working on the Client Side

As you see, some of these objects appear to be duplicates such as SCRIPT and scripts. They're not actually duplicates. A SCRIPT (singular) can be manipulated as an object, but so can a group of scripts be manipulated together as a single object called a collection. These two entities can both be considered valid objects in the same way that a stamp album can be thought of as object, as can a single stamp in that album. And you can manipulate the entire collection as an object, or choose, instead, to manipulate only one of the objects within the collection.

Members within an object

Each object has members. Members are collectively the object's properties, methods, and events. Properties are qualities (like TextFont is a property of the H1 object); methods are things that an object can do (the Table object has an InsertCell method that adds a new cell to the table); events are things that can happen to an object, usually as the result of something the user does. For example, the BODY object — and most other objects — have an OnClick event that allows you to specify what behaviors should be carried out if the object is clicked. You specify those behaviors by writing script source code within the OnClick procedure, as is done in the VBScript example in Listing 14-1.

Listing 14-1: **Specifying Behaviors**

```
<SCRIPT language="VBScript">

dim browsr

Sub Window_OnLoad ()
if navigator.appName = "Netscape" then
browsr = "Nets"
else
browsr = "Not Nets"
end if
alert (browsr)

End Sub

</SCRIPT>
```

Listing 14-2 is an example of JavaScript handling the onclick event (JavaScript requires extra script to handle events).

Listing 14-2: **The JavaScript Version**

```
<HTML>
<HEAD>

<SCRIPT LANGUAGE=javascript>
<!--

function document_onclick() {

alert("This document was clicked!");

}

-->
</SCRIPT>


<SCRIPT LANGUAGE=javascript FOR=document EVENT=onclick>
<!--
return document_onclick()
-->
</SCRIPT>

</HEAD>
<BODY>
</BODY>
</HTML>
```

The following are complete lists of the members of all the objects currently in the DHTML DOM. Some of these members are illustrated in this chapter and elsewhere in this book. However, if you're interested in a description of a specific member and its syntax for use in one of your scripts, you should contact Microsoft's DHTML Web site and download the Internet Client SDK (Software Development Kit) from `http://www.microsoft.com/msdn/sdk/inetsdk/help/default.htm`. It contains a complete reference to each object and member in the DHTML DOM.

Object properties

Following is a list of the 327 properties currently available in the DHTML DOM. Many of these properties are specific to just one object; other properties, such as height, can be used with many objects.

AccessKey	action	activeElement
align	aLink	alinkColor
alt	altHTML	altKey
appCodeName	appMinorVersion	appName
appVersion	availHeight	availWidth
background	backgroundAttachment	backgroundColor
backgroundImage	backgroundPosition	backgroundPositionX
backgroundPositionY	backgroundRepeat	balance
behavior	bgColor	bgProperties
border	border	border
borderBottom	borderBottomColor	borderBottomStyle
borderBottomWidth	borderColor	borderColor
borderColorDark	borderColorLight	borderLeft
borderLeftColor	borderLeftStyle	borderLeftWidth
borderRight	borderRightColor	borderRightStyle
borderRightWidth	borderStyle	borderTop
borderTopColor	borderTopStyle	borderTopWidth
borderWidth	bottomMargin	browserLanguage
bufferDepth	button	cancelBubble
caption	cellIndex	cellPadding
cellSpacing	charset	checked
classid	className	clear
clientHeight	clientInformation	clientLeft
clientTop	clientWidth	clientX
clientY	clip	closed
code	codeBase	codeBase
codeType	color	colorDepth
cols	colSpan	compact
complete	connectionSpeed	content
cookie	cookieEnabled	coords
cpuClass	cssText	ctrlKey
cursor	data	dataFld

dataFormatAs	dataPageSize	dataSrc
defaultCharset	defaultChecked	defaultSelected
defaultStatus	defaultValue	defer
dialogArguments	dialogHeight	dialogLeft
dialogTop	dialogWidth	direction
disabled	display	domain
dynsrc	encoding	event
expando	face	fgColor
fileCreatedDate	fileModifiedDate	fileSize
fileUpdatedDate	filter	font
fontFamily	fontSize	fontSmoothingEnabled
fontStyle	fontVariant	fontWeight
form	frame	frameBorder
frameSpacing	fromElement	hash
height	Hidden	host
hostname	href	hspace
htmlFor	htmlFor	htmlText
httpEquiv	id	indeterminate
index	innerHTML	innerText
isMap	isTextEdit	keyCode
lang	language	lastModified
left	leftMargin	length
letterSpacing	lineHeight	link
linkColor	listStyle	listStyleImage
listStylePosition	listStyleType	location
loop	lowsrc	map
margin	marginBottom	marginHeight
marginLeft	marginRight	marginTop
marginWidth	maxLength	media
method	Methods	mimeTypes
multiple	name	noHref
noResize	noShade	noWrap

object	offscreenBuffering	offsetHeight
offsetLeft	offsetParent	offsetTop
offsetWidth	offsetX	offsetY
onLine	opener	outerHTML
outerText	overflow	owningElement
padding	paddingBottom	paddingLeft
paddingRight	paddingTop	pageBreakAfter
pageBreakBefore	palette	parent
parentElement	parentStyleSheet	parentTextEdit
parentWindow	pathname	pixelHeight
pixelLeft	pixelTop	pixelWidth
platform	plugins	pluginspage
port	posHeight	position
posLeft	posTop	posWidth
protocol	readOnly	readOnly
readyState	reason	recordNumber
recordset	referrer	rel
returnValue	returnValue	rev
rightMargin	rowIndex	rows
rowSpan	rules	screenX
screenY	scroll	scrollAmount
scrollDelay	scrollHeight	scrolling
scrollLeft	scrollTop	scrollWidth
search	sectionRowIndex	selected
selectedIndex	self	shape
shiftKey	size	sourceIndex
span	src	srcElement
srcFilter	start	status
style	styleFloat	systemLanguage
tabIndex	tagName	target
text	textAlign	textDecoration
textDecorationBlink	textDecorationLineThrough	textDecorationNone

textDecorationOverline	textDecorationUnderline	textIndent
textTransform	thead	tfoot
title	toElement	top
topMargin	trueSpeed	type
updateInterval	units	URL
url	urn	useMap
userAgent	userLanguage	vAlign
vAlign	value	value
verticalAlign	visibility	vLink
vlinkColor	volume	vspace
width	wrap	x
y	zIndex	

Object methods

This is a list of the 104 methods currently available in the DHTML DOM. Not every object can use every method.

Add	addChannel	addImport
addReadRequest	addRule	alert
assign	back	blur
clear	clear	clearInterval
clearRequest	clearTimeout	click
close	close	collapse
compareEndPoints	confirm	contains
createCaption	createElement	createRange
createStyleSheet	createTextRange	createTHead
createTFoot	deleteCaption	deleteCell
deleteRow	deleteTFoot	deleteTHead
doReadRequest	duplicate	elementFromPoint
empty	execCommand	execScript
expand	findText	focus
forward	getAttribute	getAttribute
getBookmark	go	inRange

insertAdjacentHTML	insertAdjacentText	insertCell
insertRow	isEqual	isSubscribed
item	javaEnabled	move
moveBy	moveEnd	moveStart
moveTo	moveToBookmark	moveToElementText
moveToPoint	navigate	nextPage
open	parentElement	pasteHTML
previousPage	prompt	queryCommandEnabled
queryCommandIndeterm	queryCommandState	queryCommandSupported
queryCommandValue	refresh	reload
remove	removeAttribute	replace
reset	resizeBy	resizeTo
scroll	scrollBy	scrollTo
scrollIntoView	select	select
setAttribute	setEndPoint	setInterval
setTimeout	showHelp	showModalDialog
start	stop	submit
tags	taintEnabled	write
writeln	zOrder	

Object events

This is a list of the 39 events currently available in the DHTML DOM. Not every event can be fired for every object. (The term *fire* has caught on to describe the activation of an event, which is more traditionally known as *triggering* an event.) Chapter 12 includes a list of the document object and window object events, in the section "Event Handlers."

Onabort	onafterupdate	onbeforeunload
onbeforeupdate	onblur	onbounce
onchange	onclick	ondataavailable
ondatasetchanged	ondatasetcomplete	ondblclick
ondragstart	onerror	onerrorupdate
onfilterchange	onfinish	onfocus

onhelp	onkeydown	onkeypress
onkeyup	onload	onmousedown
onmousemove	onmouseout	onmouseover
onmouseup	onreadystatechange	onreset
onresize	onrowenter	onrowexit
onscroll	onselect	onselectstart
onstart	onsubmit	onunload

Understanding hierarchies

You've probably worked with hierarchies in your previous programming. For example: `Form1.Text1.ForeColor = Blue` is a hierarchical reference to objects within objects (the TextBox object within the Form object), ending with a Property of TextBox's (the color of the text). Objects are referenced in order; that is, a parent comes before a child (container comes before contained), separated by periods: for example, `document.title`.

In the DOM, the outermost object (the container) is the *Document*. In Visual Basic, if you wanted to display a message box to the user containing the title of the current Form, you would write this programming:

```
Private Sub Form_Load()
MsgBox Form1.Caption
End Sub
```

To display the title of a document using script and the document object, use this code:

```
<Script = "VBScript">
alert (document.title)
</Script>
```

The Window Object

The Window object is the top-level object. You can use this object to discover the window's Uniform Resource Locator (URL) or construct buttons that mimic the Back and Forward buttons in the browser, which move to different URLs through the history of the user's surfing (you can't find out the actual URLs as text, you can only fire them). You can also use Window to determine whether the current document is simple, or contains a frame set and is thus broken into one or more child windows. Listing 14-3 is an example of the Window object in action.

Listing 14-3: Using the Window Object

```
<html>

<head>
<script LANGUAGE="VBScript">
function Colorit(colr)
   window.event.srcElement.style.color = colr
   window.event.srcElement.style.fontSize = "40"
end function
</script>
</head>

<body>

<h3 ID="Thisone" onmouseover="Colorit('red')"
STYLE="color:black;font-size:18">Make me red</h3>

<h2 ID="Thatone" onmouseover="Colorit('green')"
STYLE="color:black;font-size:10">Make me green! </h2>
</body>
</html>
```

When the user moves the mouse over one of these headlines, the font size is increased and the color is changed. Notice that the srcElement identifies which headline first fired the event. In this case, the event is OnMouseOver, which means that the user simply entered the headline's space with the mouse pointer. Also notice that the desired color is passed to the function. The original STYLEs for these headlines is a small font (10) and black color.

The same effect, in JavaScript, requires only a few adjustments to the SCRIPT section:

```
<script LANGUAGE="JScript">
function Colorit(colr) {
   window.event.srcElement.style.color = colr;
   window.event.srcElement.style.fontSize = "40";
}
</script>
```

Listing 14-4 demonstrates some additional objects that you can manipulate, particularly the Document object, which is the next object down in the hierarchy from Window.

Listing 14-4: **Using the Document Object**

```
<html>

<head>
<title>Moving A Graphic</title>

<script LANGUAGE="JScript">
var r;

function StartMove()
{
  document.all.Pict.style.pixelLeft =
document.body.offsetWidth;
  document.all.Pict.style.visibility = "visible";
  r = window.setInterval("MoveLeft()",40);
}


function MoveLeft()
{
  document.all.Pict.style.pixelLeft -= 10;
  if (document.all.Pict.style.pixelLeft<=0) {
    document.all.Pict.style.pixelLeft=0;
    window.clearInterval(r);
  }
}
</script>

</head>

<body onload="StartMove()">

<h4>Here it comes!</h4>

<p>The picture passes behind the text because
 we set the picture's Z-Index to -1.
<img ID="Pict" STYLE="visibility:hidden;
position:absolute;top:0; left:0;
 z-index:-1" SRC="d:\dog.gif"> </p>
</body>
</html>
```

Listing 14-5 is the VBScript version, so you can see how to use that script language to invoke the built-in setInterval and clearInterval methods of the object model.

Listing 14-5: **The VBScript Version**

```
<html>

<head>
<title>Moving A Graphic</title>
<script LANGUAGE="VBScript">

sub StartMove()
  document.all.Pict.style.pixelLeft = document.body.offsetWidth
  document.all.Pict.style.visibility = "visible"
  r = setInterval("MoveLeft",40)
end sub

sub MoveLeft()
Set rt = window
  document.all.Pict.style.pixelLeft =
document.all.Pict.style.pixelLeft -10
  if document.all.Pict.style.pixelLeft <=0 then
    document.all.Pict.style.pixelLeft=0
    clearInterval()
     end if
end sub
</script>

</head>

<body onload="StartMove()">

<h4>Here it comes!</h4>

<p>The picture passes behind the text
 because we set the picture's Z-Index
 to -1. <imgID="Pict" STYLE="visibility:hidden;
position:absolute;top:0; left:0; z-index:-1"
SRC="d:\dog.gif"> </p>
</body>
</html>
```

The Document Object

Below the Window object is the Document. The Document object is the container for all other objects within a given Web page, and you can use it to access, find out, or change the qualities of any element within the document. Elements are themselves considered objects, but they are contained within the Document object (as in Document.Title). Each element, in turn, contains either other subordinate (nested) element objects or content (text or graphics), along with any attributes that have been specified. (Attributes are the equivalent of Properties. In other words, in most programming languages and some applications, a Property is a quality of an object, such as the color of text.)

Collections

Some of these objects are actually collections (array-like groups) of objects. In general, an object that ends in *s* is a collection. However, the All object is also a collection (of everything on the document). As you might fear, consistency isn't much enforced when you're referencing objects or object strings (several objects separated by periods) such as these:

```
document.frames.ThisFrame.document.
body.style.backgroundColor="blue"
```

Sometimes, you just have to hack away, trying different combinations of objects in the string, until you hit a version that works. To illustrate this inconsistency, consider the following code. There are two buttons. Clicking one button changes the contents of a frame; clicking the other button changes the background color of the frame. You would think that you could reference that same frame with the same object string. But you can't. Listing 14-6 shows the code.

Listing 14-6: **Different References, Same Frame**

```
<HTML>
<HEAD>

<SCRIPT LANGUAGE="VBScript">
Sub NewContent()
  document.all.ThisFrame.src="Next.htm"
End Sub

sub NewColor()

document.frames.ThisFrame.document.
body.style.backgroundColor="blue"
end sub
</SCRIPT>

</HEAD>

<BODY>
  <IFRAME id=ThisFrame src="star.htm">
  </IFRAME>
```

```
 <BUTTON onclick=NewContent()
id=b1>Load new contents...</BUTTON>
 <BUTTON onclick=NewColor()
id=b2>Turn a new color...</BUTTON>
</BODY>
</HTML>
```

Notice that when you change the contents (the .HTM file) of the frame, you use the All collection, but when you change the background color, you must use the Frames collection.

Similarly, every element between the HTML tags in a document is an object; it has a TagName Property. Listing 14-7 shows how you can display all the elements and the children in an HTML page.

Listing 14-7: **Showing All the Elements**

```
<HTML id=ThisPage>
<HEAD>

<SCRIPT LANGUAGE="VBSCRIPT">

sub Collecti()

text1.value = window.ThisPage.all.length

for i = 0 to ThisPage.all.length - 1
     text1.value = text1.value + "   " +
ThisPage.all(i).tagName
next

text2.value = window.ThisPage.children.length


for i = 0 to ThisPage.children.length - 1
text2.value = text2.value + "   " + ThisPage.children(i).tagName
next
end sub

</SCRIPT>

</HEAD>
```

```
<BODY onload=Collecti()>

<DIV>
THE ALL COLLECTION:
<BR>
<INPUT id=text1 LANGUAGE=vbscript
 onhelp="" style="HEIGHT: 32px;
 WIDTH: 546px"> </DIV>
<BR>
THE CHILDREN COLLECTION:
<INPUT id=text2 LANGUAGE=vbscript
onhelp="" style="HEIGHT: 32px;
 WIDTH: 546px"> </DIV>
</BODY>
</HTML>
```

Running this HTML displays the first TextBox fill with `10 HEAD TITLE SCRIPT BODY DIV BR INPUT BR INPUT DIV` and the second TextBox fill with `2 HEAD BODY`.

Instead of the `Window.ThisPage.All`, you could use a different, and more common, diction: `Document.All`, like this:

```
text1.value = document.all.length

for i = 0 to document.all.length - 1
  text1.value = text1.value + "   " + document.all(i).tagName
next
```

As shown in the previous source code, you can reference items in an All collection by index number within the "Array" (All(I)). Objects, however, are often referenced by their ID instead of an index number, as you did with Text1 and Text2:

```
Text1.value = document.all.length
```

You can query the All collection and adjust Properties or use methods with the resulting items. The All collection remains current, so, for example, if an object is deleted dynamically, it disappears from the All collection. Interestingly, every item has its own All collection to represent the entire set of objects within it. If, for example, we had used the NAME attribute instead of ID for the TextBoxes, we could have given both TextBoxes *the same name*. This would have the effect of creating a new All collection of two text boxes, both named, for example, Text1 yields the answer (2):

```
msgbox document.all("Text1").length
```

The ID attribute requires unique identifiers each time it is used within a document (Text1, Text2, and so on). The Name attribute can be used over and over with the same identifier (OurText, OurText, and so on). At this time, however, Netscape doesn't recognize the ID attribute unless it is used within a Cascading Style Sheet. Nothing prevents the use of duplicate ID identifiers, although you're not supposed to. If you do use duplicate ID identifiers, the duplicates automatically become a collection, just like duplicate Name identifiers.

These are all the collections in the DHTML DOM:

all	anchors	applets	areas	cells
children	elements	embeds	filters	forms
frames	images	imports	links	options
plugins	rows	rules	scripts	styleSheets
tbodies				

Manipulating Everything

You can easily change the properties (attributes) of any element in a document, but you can do even more. Once Microsoft's DHTML gurus decided to explode HTML into a million fragments, they went ahead and did a thorough job. In addition to manipulating attributes, you can also dynamically change the HTML itself. In other words, you can change the elements (tags) and any contents within those elements. This feature gives you control over everything. And, as a bonus, the computation required to dazzle a user with DHTML takes place within the user's high-speed RAM rather than at your server or (ever so slowly) over the Internet. This makes startling dissolves and other cool — but computation-intensive — special effects efficient enough on most contemporary computers so as to be visually quite satisfying. You can toy with a variety of these special effects in Chapters 7 and 15.

To change the contents within a pair of container elements (such as `DIV`, `H2`, or `SPAN`), you can exploit the `innerHTML` or `innerText` properties. To change an element itself, including its contents, you use the `outerHTML` property. Here's how it works. Let's assume that you have a bit of text: `<P>This text</P>` that you want to change to `<P>Get off me!</P>` when the user moves the mouse cursor over the text. Try the example in Listing 14-8.

Listing 14-8: Using innerText

```
<html>

<head>

<script language="JavaScript">
function GetOff() {
ThisHead.innerText = "Get Off Me!!";
}
function RestoreIt() {
ThisHead.innerText = "This Text";
}
</script>


</head>

<body>

<h2 id="ThisHead" onmouseover="GetOff();"
onmouseout="RestoreIt();">This Text</h2>
</body>
</html>
```

With this source code, you give a headline an ID of "ThisHead" and specify two functions that are fired depending on what the user does with the mouse cursor. Then, when either of those functions is fired, the innerText property of the <H2> element is changed.

Using text versus HTML

The two properties that end in text — innerText and outerText — provide you with the text contents of your target, minus the tags. The two properties that end in HTML — innerHTML and outerHTML — provide the same contents, but also include all the HTML tags. In practical terms, when you give IE4 a piece of text using the innerHTML or outerHTML commands, the browser parses this as actual HTML. But when you use innerText or outerText, you get mere text and IE4 displays it, but does not parse it. For instance, if you attempt to replace the entire <H1>...</H1> element by using outerText:

```
ThisHead.outerText = "<H1>Get Off Me!!</H1>";
```

the user will see the tags, as in this display:

```
<H1>Get Off Me!!</H1>
```

In other words, the user will see the text, plus the tags, rather than the parsed version (the text only).

To understand the differences between these four properties, look at Table 14-1 and assume you have an element similar to this:

```
<P>Some text with a <STRONG>strong</STRONG> word in it.</P>
```

Table 14-1
The Four Text/HTML Properties

Property	Result
innerText	Some text with a **strong** word in it.
outerText	Some text with a **strong** word in it.
innerHTML	Some text with a < STRONG >**strong**</STRONG > word in it.
outerHTML	<P>Some text with a < STRONG >**strong**</STRONG > word in it.</P>

Both Text versions appear the same, but if you assign new values to these two properties, the results are different. The difference is that outerText replaces both the text *and the element*. If you have a headline:

```
<h1 id="AHead">Change This</H1>
```

and replace it by using:

```
AHead.innerText = "This Text";
```

the result is:

```
<h1 id="AHead">This Text</H1>
```

If you replace it by using outerText, the <H1> tags are also replaced (and disappear):

```
This Text
```

Working with the InsertAdjacent methods

There are two additional ways to manipulate source code dynamically. If you want to preserve the existing elements or text and add new elements or text to the existing code, you can use insertAdjacentHTML or insertAdjacentText. These methods make it easy to insert new items in lists and other kinds of text, or to add tags. Figure 14-1 shows you the locations where the various insertions take place.

Figure 14-1: Use the four InsertAdjacent methods to add text or tags to your code.

Listing 14-9 is an example of how to use these methods.

Listing 14-9: **Using InsertAdjacent**

```
<HTML>
<HEAD>

<SCRIPT LANGUAGE="JScript">
function addSome()
{
document.all.Para1.insertAdjacentHTML
("afterBegin", "<B>This is </B>");

document.all.Para1.insertAdjacentHTML
("beforeEnd", "to this text.");
}
</SCRIPT>
</HEAD>
<BODY onload="addSome()">

<DIV ID="Para1">what to add
</DIV>

</BODY>
</HTML>
```

Avoiding the impossible

Clearly, you cannot use the inner and outer properties to accomplish things that are impossible. For instance, the <P> tags cannot enclose a second <P> pair. Attempt to nest <P>s and you'll fail. You can, of course, replace an entire <P> pair with a new <P> pair, including new contents.

Also, you cannot create self-modifying scripts. You can change content within HTML elements (or the elements plus their contents) but you cannot change the scripts themselves. Other impossible moves include attempting to replace an IMG with text, or vice versa; the contents being replaced must be of the same basic type — text or graphics. You could achieve this kind of replacement indirectly by deleting an entire element of, say, text, then inserting a new graphics element in its place. Finally, when working with tables, you can use the inner properties to replace the contents of a TD element, or replace the entire TABLE element with the outer properties. But you can't manipulate any other table elements.

Using the TextRange Object

It's fine to be able to change things, but sometimes you have to first parse a page — look through it and find out what's there. Now, you might well say, "I wrote the source code so I should know what's there. Why would I have to search the page to find out its contents?" The answer is because DHTML pages are dynamic and they can change in ways you couldn't know about when you wrote the original source code. For example, a user might make changes based on options or choices you gave them, or the user might interrupt a process — and how can you know where in the process that a user will halt things?

The TextRange object contains all the text between <BODY> and </BODY> (or you can limit it to the text in input elements such as Button, TextArea, and Input). A programmer creates a TextRange object by creating an object variable, then filling it with the TextRange the programmer is interested in. A TextRange object that is created for the BODY will exclude any text within a TextArea, Input, or Button zone.

Once you've created a TextRange object, you can manipulate the text. You can search, replace, highlight, change words to italic, and otherwise edit the text. The TextRange object provides a set of methods (commands) that are similar to those found in the Edit menu of a word processor — except that you can use them in your scripts.

Listing 14-10 is an example of a TextRange object that contains all the text within the BODY of the document.

Listing 14-10: **TextRange in the BODY**

```
<HTML>
<HEAD>

<SCRIPT LANGUAGE="JScript">

function seeText()
{
var texrng = document.body.createTextRange();
alert (texrng.text);
}
</SCRIPT>

</HEAD>

<BODY onload=seeText()>

<H1>This is a headline</H1>

This is part of the text.

</BODY>
</HTML>
```

When the code in Listing 14-10 is run, the Alert box shown in Figure 14-2 displays.

Figure 14-2: Each piece of text in the BODY is displayed when the TextRange object is used.

VBScript handles object variables somewhat differently than JavaScript. Listing 14-11 shows the VBScript version of the above code.

Listing 14-11: **The VBScript Version**

```
<HTML>
<HEAD>

<SCRIPT LANGUAGE="VBScript">

sub seeText()
dim texrng
set texrng = document.body.createTextRange()
msgbox (texrng.text)
end sub
</SCRIPT>

</HEAD>

<BODY onload=seeText()>

<H1>This is a headline</H1>

This is part of the text.

</BODY>
</HTML>
```

Using htmlText with TextRange

As you might have guessed, the TextRange object has an htmlText property in addition to its text property. If you want to get the tags in addition to the raw text, use htmlText like this:

```
alert (texrng.htmlText);
```

This is similar to the distinction between innerText and outerHTML. You can both read and write the TextRange object's text property, but the htmlText property is read-only. If you want to change the text and tags using the TextRange object, you must resort to a special pasteHTML method of the TextRange object, as shown in Listing 14-12.

Listing 14-12: **The pasteHTML Method**

```
<HTML>
<HEAD>

<SCRIPT LANGUAGE="JScript">
```

```
function replaceText()
{
var txrg = document.body.createTextRange();

txrg.pasteHTML("<H1>The is the new text</H1>");
}
</SCRIPT>

</HEAD>

<BODY onclick=replaceText()>

<H2>This is the text.</H2>

</BODY>
</HTML>
```

Understanding the many methods of TextRange

The `TextRange` object can perform many tricks on text because it has many methods. For example, you can adjust the range in many ways. If you want to select, then edit, the first word in the `TextRange`, you use the `Collapse` method (it reduces the range to the very start of the text if you provide no alternative argument). Then you can use the `Expand` method to select a character, word, sentence, or the entire range. After your new range is selected, you can adjust the style of the text with the `execCommand` method. Listing 14-13 is an example that changes the first word in the document to italic.

Listing 14-13: **Changing the First Word**

```
<HTML>
<HEAD>

<SCRIPT LANGUAGE="JScript">

function AdjustText()
{
var r = document.body.createTextRange();
r.collapse();
r.expand("word");
r.execCommand("Italic");
}
</SCRIPT>
</HEAD>

<BODY onclick=AdjustText()>
```

(continued)

Listing 14-13 *(continued)*

```
<P>This is the text. This is more.</P>

</BODY>
</HTML>
```

The `FindText` method is similar to the search text commands in other computer languages, such as InStr in Visual Basic. `FindText` requires three parameters: the target string; the number of characters to search through (a positive value indicates a forward search and a negative value searches backward); and whether or not you're looking for a full-word match and if the search is case-sensitive (2 indicates a full-word match is required, 4 means case-sensitive, 6 means case-sensitive and full-word). Only the first (target string) parameter is required. Otherwise, the search defaults to partial word (any characters, no space delimiting required) and case-insensitive. Listing 14-14 is an example that uses the `Select` method to invert the text so the user can see the selection.

Listing 14-14: Inverting Found Text

```
<HTML>
<HEAD>

<SCRIPT LANGUAGE="JScript">
function FindText()
{

var r = document.body.createTextRange();

if (r.findText("eas")==true) {
  r.select();
}}

</SCRIPT>
</HEAD>
<BODY onload=FindText()>

<P>This is the text. This search is easy.</P>

</BODY>
</HTML>
```

Listing 14-15 provides the VBScript Version.

Listing 14-15: The VBScript Version

```
<SCRIPT LANGUAGE="VBScript">
function FindText()
dim r
set r = document.body.createTextRange()

if r.findText("eas") then
  r.select()
end if
end function
</SCRIPT>
```

Searching and replacing

To search through a document for pieces of text, and to then replace those pieces with some other text, you use the text property of the TextRange object, as shown in Listing 14-16.

Listing 14-16: Using the Text Property of the TextRange Object to Search and Replace

```
<HTML>
<HEAD>

<SCRIPT LANGUAGE="JScript">

function ReplaceText()
{
var rg = document.body.createTextRange();
for (i=0; rg.findText("is")!=false; i++) {
  rg.text = "was";
}
alert ("There were " + i + " replacements.");
}
</SCRIPT>
</HEAD>

<BODY onclick=ReplaceText()>

<P>Here is the text. The search is easy.</P>
</BODY>
</HTML>
```

Defining and manipulating a TextRange within a component

The TextRange object isn't limited to the Document.Body object. A TextRange can also be defined and manipulated in a component such as a Button. In Listing 14-17, when the user clicks a Button, it's transformed.

Listing 14-17: Button Transform

```
<HTML>
<HEAD>
<SCRIPT LANGUAGE="JScript">
function ReplaceText()
{
var x = document.all.tags("BUTTON");
if (x!=null) {var t = x[0].createTextRange();
  if (t != null) {
    t.text = "Thanks!";
}}
}
</SCRIPT>
</HEAD>
<BODY onclick=ReplaceText()>
<BUTTON onclick=ReplaceText() style="HEIGHT: 39px; WIDTH:
170px"
type=button>Click Me</BUTTON>
</BODY>
</HTML>
```

In this example, the script first creates a collection of all buttons on the document, then places this collection in the variable *x*. Then a second object variable, *t*, is created to hold the TextRange object for the zero (first) Button in the collection. Finally, the *text* property of that TextRange is used to change the button's caption from *Click Me* to *Thanks*.

Manipulating TextRanges

Should you need to, you can duplicate TextRange objects (create a new TextRange object variable from an existing one); position TextRange objects; discover their relationship to each other (is one contained within the other? Is one a duplicate of the other?); or cause the browser to scroll until the TextRange becomes visible to the user.

In the following code, a `TextRange` object that contains all text within the body of this document is created. Then a second `TextRange` object is created that is a duplicate of the first `TextRange` object. Both are then displayed, followed by the result of a comparison (true, they are equal) and a check to see if one is within the same range as the other (also true). You can't compare the two object variables like this (txr1 == txr2 or in VBScript, txr1 = txr2) because they are separate objects and are not, in the classic sense, equal although their contents are equal. Instead of == or =, you must use the special comparison command `isEqual` (it works the same way in both VBScript and JavaScript), as shown in Listing 14-18.

Listing 14-18: **Using isEqual with TextRange**

```
<HTML>
<HEAD>

<SCRIPT LANGUAGE="JScript">
function adjustText() {

var txr1 = document.body.createTextRange();

var txr2 = txr1.duplicate();

alert (txr1.text);
alert (txr2.text);
alert (txr1.isEqual(txr2));
alert (txr1.inRange(txr2));
}
</SCRIPT>
</HEAD>
<BODY onload=adjustText()>

<H1>This is a headline</H1>
This is the body text.

</BODY>
</HTML>
```

Make the changes in Listing 14-19 to create a VBScript version of the above.

Listing 14-19: **The VBScript Version**

```
<SCRIPT LANGUAGE="VBScript">
sub adjustTextR()
dim txr1
set txr1 = document.body.createTextRange()
dim txr2
set txr2 = txr1.duplicate()

msgbox (txr1.text)
msgbox (txr2.text)
msgbox (txr1.isEqual(txr2))
msgbox (txr1.inRange(txr2))

end sub
</SCRIPT>
```

If you want to force the user's browser to scroll until your TextRange is in view, use the scrollIntoView method. (This method can also be used with most other HTML elements.) Here's an example:

```
var txr = document.body.createTextRange();
txr.scrollIntoView(false);
```

Using the optional parameter *false* causes the TextRange to become visible at the bottom of the user's screen, or as close to the bottom as possible. If you leave out that parameter, or use *true,* the document will be scrolled until the text is positioned at the top of the screen.

Now that you've seen how DHTML works, the next chapter focuses on some of the more glamorous special effects and eye-popping animations that you can insert into your Web sites to make them truly state-of-the-Web-art.

Summary

This chapter introduced you to the powerful DHTML language, an amplification of traditional HTML. You learned about these topics:

✦ The powerful, exciting, new world of DHTML programming.

✦ Why Microsoft introduced Dynamic HTML in Internet Explorer 4.0.

✦ The important underlying framework of DHTML—the Document Object Model.

✦ The various ways you can access the objects within DOM.

✦ How to manipulate objects' members.

✦ How to navigate object hierarchies.

✦ How to manage collections.

✦ That you could actually manipulate everything on a Web page, except script itself.

✦ The many ways to use the `TextRange` object.

✦   ✦   ✦

Cutting-Edge Effects

◆   ◆   ◆   ◆

In This Chapter

Employing timers for animation effects

Working with DIV and SPAN

Handling clipping regions

Expanding and collapsing Outlines

Animation with filters and transitions

◆   ◆   ◆   ◆

Chapter 14 discussed the basics of DHTML. This chapter discusses some of the most dramatic and sophisticated visual effects you'll see on the Internet. This chapter, too, discusses DHTML, but here we look at some of the advanced effects made possible by this technology. If you want to jazz up your site with subtle, or not-so-subtle, state-of-the-art transitions and animation, you're in the right place. And VI makes working with these effects very efficient: you can script the DHTML in the source window, then see the results instantly by clicking the Quick View tab. Let's get started.

Using Timers

Timers are useful for animation because timers can repeatedly trigger the movement of an image or a piece of text in small increments. Timers can also trigger delayed effects to make something happen at a particular time. Timers are also employable as stopwatches, kitchen timers, metronomes, or ordinary clocks.

Because timers are a built-in feature of the Window object, you do not need to specify an object when using one. That's because the Window is the default object; it's understood, and need not be mentioned for the same reason that you need not mention USA when addressing a letter to Florida.

To handle all the different tasks timers can handle, DHTML features two kinds of timers:

◆ `setTimeout` — Fires only once, as if you had set a kitchen timer and it ticked down until the time had passed, then rang its bell just that one time.

◆ `setInterval` — Fires repeatedly (at whatever interval you request) like a metronome.

To have an event occur at a particular time (say 12:25 p.m.), you create a timer using `setInterval` (the metronome) and have it repeatedly fire a function or subroutine that checks whether Now is `<=` to a variable in which you placed Now when the document first loaded (use the `onload` event, as illustrated in the following example code).

Use setTimeout for single-fire actions

Listing 15-1 shows how to use `setTimeout` to make a piece of text disappear four seconds after the document is loaded into the user's browser.

Listing 15-1: Using SetTimeout to Make a Piece of Text Disappear

```
<HTML>
<HEAD>
<SCRIPT LANGUAGE="VBScript">
dim timerhandle
function Disappear()
Head1.style.visibility = "hidden"
end function
function startTiming()
timerhandle = setTimeout("Disappear",4000)
end function
sub stopTimer
  clearTimeout (timerhandle)
end sub
</SCRIPT>
</HEAD>
<BODY onload=startTiming() onunload=stopTimer()>

<H1 ID="Head1">This text is about to go away...</H1>
<BR><BR>

</BODY>
</HTML>
```

We defined a function named `startTiming` that fires when the page is first loaded. The `startTiming` function executes a `SetInterval`-style timer. A timer can have three arguments. First is the script, the thing that's supposed to happen when the timer's countdown is finished. This is usually a function or subroutine. In the previous example, we trigger the Disappear function. The next argument is the time, expressed in milliseconds (4000 milliseconds = 4 seconds); it can be a string or integer. The final argument is optional and specifies the language in which the script (the first argument) is written.

It's good programming practice to destroy all timers that you create. You don't want them floating around after their document is exited. To do that, you can use the clearInterval or clearTimeout functions and present them with an argument that contains the timer's ID (created when you start the timer and saved in a variable for just this purpose).

Visible versus display

We used the visibility property rather than the alternative display property. Both properties can show and hide an element, but display causes the browser to reformat the page so that the space that was occupied by the invisible element is now used by any surrounding content. In other words, display causes the page to close up and use the space occupied by the now-hidden content. The visibility property holds that space vacant and makes it available to the hidden content, should it reappear.

The JavaScript version

Listing 15-2 is the JavaScript version of Listing 15-1, the VBScript example. You must always remember that JavaScript is case-sensitive, so many programmers use only lowercase for JavaScript variables, function names, and so on. However, there are always those lovely exceptions to the rule and they are responsible for countless bugs. In the following example, you must capitalize the *T* in setTimeout. It's a built-in function and has capitalization rules all its own.

Listing 15-2: **The JavaScript Version**

```
<HTML>
<HEAD>
<SCRIPT LANGUAGE=javascript>
var timerhandle;
function disappear(){
Head1.style.visibility = "hidden";
}
function starttiming(){
timerhandle = setTimeout("disappear();",4000);
}
function stoptimer() {
  clearTimeout(timerhandle)
}
</SCRIPT>
</HEAD>
<BODY onload=starttiming() onunload=stoptimer()>

<H1 ID="Head1">This text is about to go away...</H1>
<BR><BR>

</BODY>
</HTML>
```

Use setInterval for repeated actions

The alternative timer style, setInterval, fires repeatedly like a metronome. (The setTimeout style only works with Navigator 4 or Internet Explorer (IE) 4.0; setInterval works with nearly all browsers in use today.) The setInterval timer can easily animate objects, as Listing 15-3 illustrates.

Listing 15-3: Animating Objects with setInterval

```
<HTML>
<HEAD>
<SCRIPT LANGUAGE="VBScript">
dim timerhandle
dim l 'final left location of message
function startMove()
n = document.body.clientwidth / 2 'get center
m = document.all.TextToMove.scrollwidth
l = n-m/2

document.all.TextToMove.style.pixelLeft = -m
'start off left side of page
timerhandle = setInterval("Motion()",40)
end function
function Motion()
document.all.TextToMove.style.pixelLeft =
document.all.TextToMove.style.pixelLeft + 6
  if document.all.TextToMove.style.pixelleft >= l then
    document.all.TextToMove.style.pixelleft = l
    clearInterval(timerhandle)
  end if
End Function
</SCRIPT>
</HEAD>
<BODY onload=startMove()>

<DIV ID="TextToMove" STYLE="position:absolute;top:20;
">The Timer is moving this text.</DIV>
<BR><BR>

</BODY>
</HTML>
```

Recurrent firing of a function

The primary difference between the earlier example using setTimeout (to make text disappear) and this example of animation and is that now we're interested in a repeated firing of the timer. The DIV text is moved a little more to the right each time the Timer is fired, which requires us to use the setInterval command.

We define a variable *l* that will specify the pixel location (left pixel) where our scrolling message should eventually stop so that it's centered in the browser. When you define a variable *outside* a Function or Subroutine, it has greater scope and can be accessed from all procedures — all Functions and Subroutines — within that page. If you define a variable within a procedure, only a script that also resides in that same procedure can access it.

When this page is loaded, the startMove function calculates *l* then positions the DIV text off the left side of the browser at -*m*. Then setInterval creates a timer that repeatedly fires at intervals of 40 milliseconds, which causes the Motion function to repeatedly execute until a final condition is satisfied (the message reaches the center of the browser at *l*).

Display the countdown, then go

Listing 15-4 is a JavaScript example that displays the number of seconds as it counts down to a setTimeout firing, at which point the browser switches automatically to Microsoft's home page. This example also illustrates a direct text writing technique using document.write and innertext, which were explained in Chapters 13 and 14.

Listing 15-4: **Displaying the Countdown**

```
<HTML>
<HEAD>
<SCRIPT LANGUAGE=jscript>
var countdown = 4;
function gotoms() {
if (0 == countdown) // now go to microsoft
      document.location = "http://www.microsoft.com";
else {
 countdown -= 1;
 document.all.showem.innerText = countdown + " ";
setTimeout("gotoms()", 1000);
 // wait yet another second, then trigger gotoms again
   }
}
</SCRIPT>
</HEAD>
<BODY ONLOAD="SetTimeout('gotoms()', 1000)">
We'll be going to Microsoft's home page in
<SPAN ID="showem">
<SCRIPT LANGUAGE=jscript>
      document.write(countdown);
</SCRIPT>
</SPAN>
seconds.
</BODY>
</HTML>
```

We created our dynamic sentence "We'll be going to Microsoft's home page in *n* seconds" using the SPAN element. That way, there are no carriage returns. If you do want a carriage return before and after a block of text or graphics, use the DIV element instead. That's our next topic.

Working with DIV and SPAN

As the previous section on `setTimeout` and `setInterval` illustrated, when we move a piece of text, a block of text (or text plus graphics) can be accessed by enclosing it within a <DIV> </DIV> element pair. There is another, very similar element, SPAN, that can also be used to define a block of content. Both DIV and SPAN are useful when working with DHTML, but there is a difference between them. DIV causes a line break before and after its contents (as if you had put a <BR> at the start and end of the text). SPAN doesn't do that; it's a so-called *inline* element that inserts its contents without any break to separate it from the surrounding contents. Other than that distinction, you can use DIV or SPAN interchangeably and in the following discussion of the uses of DIV you can assume that SPAN behaves the same way.

DIV can enclose text, graphics, or components, including multimedia objects. In other words, DIV cordons off a region within a page, which you then can manipulate as a unit, affecting all the contents simultaneously. This is useful for positioning, animating, and other effects that are to operate on an entire region. You can even put a SPAN within a DIV container, and vice versa.

A DIV can be positioned and, otherwise, affected by specifying various style attributes such as position (relative or absolute), top, left, width, height, z-index, visibility, and so forth. (Z-index is the 3-D depth specification, which is comparable to left and top, but in, practice, z-index describes which objects block or overlap other objects; that is, which objects are "on top" of others.)

You can specify all these attributes in the DIV tag itself so that they take effect when the page is loaded into the browser:

```
<DIV ID="Div1" STYLE="position:absolute;left:80">My Text</DIV>
```

or within a script that fires later, after the page is loaded, based on user-actions, a timer, or some other trigger that executes the script:

```
document.all.Div1.style.left = 45
document.all.Div1.style.backgroundcolor = "yellow"
```

Enlarging Clipping Regions

Another useful animation technique is to enlarge a clipping region, progressively revealing a block of text or a graphic. A clipping region defines a window through which an item shows. Think of the kitchen window as a clipping region. There is a flowerpot sitting on the windowsill that is within the region and the refrigerator behind the window is only half-visible. Therefore, from the outside looking in, you can see the flowerpot, but only part of the refrigerator, so the refrigerator is clipped.

Put another way, if you specify a clipping region that is smaller than an item, part of that item will not be visible. You can manipulate the clipping region in various ways to animate the revelation of a block of text or graphics. In Listing 15-5, the text within the DIV block is slowly revealed, which is a nice visual effect.

Listing 15-5: **The Slow Reveal**

```
<HTML>
<HEAD>
<SCRIPT language="VBSCRIPT">
dim timerhandle
dim m 'length of message
dim c 'amount of clipping (the argument for right position)
Function startMove()
m = document.all.TextToShow.scrollwidth
timerhandle = setInterval("Reveal()",20)
End function
Sub Reveal()
c = c + 3
'top right bottom left
n = cstr(c)
z = "rect (0 " + n + " 20 0)"
document.all.TextToShow.style.clip = z
if c >= m then
clearInterval(timerhandle)
end if
End Sub
</script>
</HEAD>
<BODY>
<BUTTON onClick="StartMove()" id=button1>Reveal the
DIV</BUTTON>
<BR>
<DIV ID="TextToShow" STYLE="position:absolute;top:80;
clip:rect(0 0 0 0);">Display all this text.</DIV>
</BODY>
</HTML>
```

The key to this animation is the repeated adjustment of the argument that specifies the right side of the clipping region. The top, bottom, and left arguments remain the same. The clip property takes a text variable as its argument, with all four specifications included in the single variable, like this: "0 20 20 0" and with the arguments in this order: *top right bottom left*.

To adjust the specification for the right side of the clipping region, we first force the value of the integer *c* to become a string variable: `n = cstr(c)`. Then we combine *n* with the unchanging three other specifications: `z = "rect (0 " + n + " 20 0)"`. Finally, the clip property is incremented: `document.all.TextToShow.style.clip = z`.

You could use this technique to create a variety of visual transitions, replacing one graphic with another, or sliding a window open in several ways, mimicking the *wipes* used on TV.

Displaying Outlines

You've probably seen those space-saving collapsible/expandable lists at various Web sites. Similar to drop-down list boxes or menus, these "outlines" display only a single line of text until the user clicks that line, which causes a hidden list to move into view.

Alternatively, an entire outline is initially displayed, but the user can click main section heads in the outline to collapse those sections that are of no interest. Such tricks are designed to conserve real estate on the user's screen and avoid the necessity of adding scrollbars or forcing the user to page down or otherwise maneuver to locate content that's not visible.

Building outlines with FrontPage

You could create these collapsible/expandable lists by hand, writing all the source code and using `LI`, `event.srcElement.getAttribute`, `CLASS` and other commands. Building outlines, however, is much, much easier if you just let FrontPage do it for you. FrontPage has a built-in outline creator.

Follow these steps to create a collapsible outline in FrontPage:

1. Click the Normal View tab in the FrontPage editor.

2. Type in your first headline (an outermost element that never disappears).

3. Highlight it by dragging your mouse cursor across it.

4. Choose Bullets & Numbering from the Format menu.

5. If you are using a Theme for your document, select Use images from current theme; otherwise, click the Plain Bullets tab and click one of the three visible bullet types.

6. Click the Enable Collapsible Outlines checkbox.

7. Click OK to close the dialog.

8. Deselect your first headline (click anywhere outside it on the document).

9. Press Enter to move to the next line.

10. Click, twice, the Increase Indent button at the far right of the Format Toolbar, as shown in Figure 15-1. If this toolbar isn't visible, select Format Toolbar from the View menu.

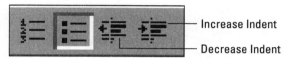
— Increase Indent
— Decrease Indent

Figure 15-1: Click the Increase Indent and Decrease Indent buttons to increase or decrease the indentation in the outline.

11. Type in a subcategory (a topic contained within the first headline).

12. Press Enter and type in the next subcategory. Continue until you are finished with the subtopics under headline one and are ready to type in headline two.

13. To move back to the headline level, press Enter to get to an empty line, then click the Decrease Indent button twice. Now type in your second headline, as shown in Figure 15-2.

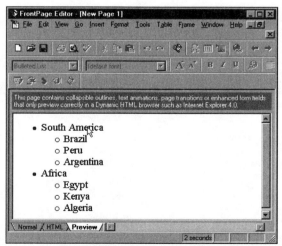

Figure 15-2: In this complete collapsible outline, click on a main headline and the subcategories will disappear or reappear.

Click either headline

Click the Preview tab and you'll see that you can click either main headline to collapse (or expand) the subheads. If you want to make some adjustments to the source code — and you will — you'll have to do a bit of search and replace on the HTML source. Click HTML view and a comment at the top of the source code tells you what must be changed before you can edit the source code in Listing 15-6.

Listing 15-6: **The Headline Source Code**

```
<html>
<head>
<title>New Page 1</title>
<meta name="GENERATOR" content="Microsoft FrontPage 3.0">
<script LANGUAGE="JavaScript" FPTYPE="dynamicoutline">
<!--
// If you want to change this script,
// you must also make the following
 // changes so that FrontPage will not
// overwrite your new script.
 // In the script tag, change
// type="dynamicoutline" to type="mydynamicoutline"
 // In function dynOutlineEnabled, change //"dynamicoutline" to
"mydynamicoutline"
 // Throughout the HTML content,
 //change dynamicoutline to mydynamicoutline
 // Change function dynOutline
 //to function mydynOutline in the script
 // In the body tag, change
 //onclick="dynOutline()" to onclick="mydynOutline()"
 function getControlTag(src)
 {
  TRok = false
  while ("HTML" != src.tagName)
  {
    TRok = true
   if ("LI" == src.tagName)
    return src
   if ("TR" == src.tagName)
   {
     if(TRok)
      return src
     return null
   }
   src = src.parentElement
  }
  return null
 }
 function dynOutlineEnabled(src)
 {
  while ("HTML" != src.tagName)
```

```
    {
      if(null != src.getAttribute("dynamicoutline", false))
        return true
      src = src.parentElement
    }
    return false
  }
  function containedIn(src, dest)
  {
    while ("HTML" != src.tagName)
    {
      if (src == dest)
        return true
      src = src.parentElement
    }
    return false
  }
  function dynOutline()
  {
    var ms = navigator.appVersion.indexOf("MSIE");
    ie4 = (ms>0) &&
(parseInt(navigator.appVersion.substring(ms+5, ms+6)) >= 4);
    if(!ie4)
      return;
    var src = event.srcElement
    src = getControlTag(src)
    if (null == src)
      return
    if (!dynOutlineEnabled(src))
      return
    var idx = src.sourceIndex+1
    while (idx < document.all.length &&
containedIn(document.all[idx].parentElement, src))
    {
      srcTmp = document.all[idx]
      tag = srcTmp.tagName
      if ("UL" == tag || "OL" == tag || "TABLE" == tag)
        srcTmp.style.display = srcTmp.style.display == "none"
? "" : "none"
      idx++;
    }
  }
//-->
</script></head>
<body onclick="dynOutline()">
<ul dynamicoutline>
 <li>South America<ul dynamicoutline>
   <li>Brazil</li>
   <li>Peru</li>
   <li>Argentina</li>
  </ul>
 </li>
```

(continued)

Listing 15-6 *(continued)*

```
<li>Africa<ul dynamicoutline>
  <li>Egypt</li>
  <li>Kenya</li>
  <li>Algeria</li>
 </ul>
</li>
</ul>
</body>
</html>
```

There is at least one edit to make—you want the cursor to change from a pointer to a hand when it passes over each main head. This alerts the user that the main heads can be clicked. To change the cursor, surround the main heads with <SPAN> or <DIV>, like this:

```
<li><span style="cursor: hand">South America</span>
<ul mydynamicoutline>
```

Using Filters

Full-page transitions are often clumsy looking because manipulating a browser full of graphics can't be handled smoothly by many of today's personal computers. You need over 200MHz, and a fast video card. However, if you limit yourself to applying your fades, dissolves, wipes, and other filter and transition effects to individual images or pieces of text, the effect will be both smooth and impressive.

Using blendTrans: the most elegant filter

Listing 15-7 illustrates what we consider to be the most elegant and useful of all the filters: the blendTrans.

Listing 15-7: The blendTrans Filter

```
<html>
<head>
<script language="JavaScript">
function showit() {
    fadeit.filters(0).Apply();
    fadeit.style.visibility = "visible";
    fadeit.filters(0).Play();
}
</script>
</head>
```

```
<BODY TOPMARGIN=22 onload="showit()">
<div id="fadeit" style="width: 100%;
 visibility: hidden; filter:blendTrans(duration=11)">
<CENTER><H1>THIS IS GOING IN...</H1><CENTER>
</div>
</BODY>
</html>
```

Note To change this script to VBScript, just replace JavaScript with VBScript, remove the braces (}) and semicolons, and add End Function just above </script>.

Using specialized filters

Figures 15-3 through 15-8 illustrate the various filters by using variations (different parameters for the filter property) in the following source code. Remember to substitute the path to a .GIF or .JPG file on your hard drive for the "D:\DOG.GIF" used in this example:

```
<html>
<head>
</head>
<DIV STYLE="position: absolute; filter: alpha(opacity=34)">
<CENTER><H1>THE ALPHA <IMG SRC="D:\DOG.GIF"></IMG>EFFECT</H1>
</CENTER>
</DIV>
</BODY>
</html>
```

There are 15 separate filters: Alpha (transparency level), Blur, Chroma (forces a color to become transparent), Drop Shadow, FlipH, FlipV, Glow, Grayscale, Invert, Light, Mask, Shadow (a solid, not gray shadow), Wave, and Xray (emphasizes the edges).

Without any filters applied, D:\DOG.GIF looks like Figure 15-3.

Figure 15-3: This is the original text and graphic without applying a filter.

To set the amount of opacity, apply the Alpha filter, as shown in Figure 15-4. To create a blurred effect, apply the Blur filter, as shown in Figure 15-5.

Figure 15-4: To change the opacity of D:\DOG.GIF, the Alpha filter is applied — filter: alpha(opacity=34).

Figure 15-5: To create a blurred effect to D:\DOG.GIF, the Blur filter is applied — filter:blur(add=1, direction= 130, strength=19).

The Chroma (Color=#000000) filter renders a particular color invisible; in this case, the color black. Any black in the text or graphics disappears.

To create a drop shadow to your graphic, apply the DropShadow filter, as shown in Figure 15-6.

Figure 15-6: To create a drop shadow to D:\DOG.GIF, the DropShadow filter is applied — <DIV style="FILTER: DropShadow(Color=#808080, OffX=3, OffY=4); POSITION: absolute">.

To horizontally flip your graphic, apply the FlipH filter, as shown in Figure 15-7.

Figure 15-7: Applying the FlipH filter horizontally flips D:\DOG.GIF — Flip horizontally: <DIV style="FILTER: FlipH; POSITION: absolute">.

To create a glow effect in your graphic, apply the Glow filter, as shown in Figure 15-8.

Figure 15-8: Applying the Glow filter to D:\DOG.GIF gives the image a glow effect — Glow: <DIV style= "FILTER: Glow(Color=#808080, Strength=7); POSITION: absolute">.

Recall that you can combine as many filter effects as you wish, merely by listing them after the `filter:` command. The order in which you list (and thereby apply) filters to an object affects the result. Here are two examples, with the filter application order switched, to illustrate the precedence issue:

```
<DIV STYLE="position:absolute;height:233;
filter: shadow(color=gray, direction=135)
glow(color=skyblue, strength=144)">
  <h3>Shadow, then Glow.</h3>
</DIV>
```

In Figure 15-9, we apply Glow, then Shadow:
<DIV STYLE="position:absolute;height:233;filter: glow(color=skyblue, strength=144) shadow(color=gray, direction=135)">.

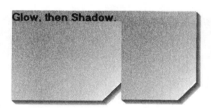

Figure 15-9: This figure illustrates a multiple effect achieved by applying Glow and then Shadow.

In Figure 15-10, we reverse the order that was used in Figure 15-9 and apply Glow, then Shadow: <DIV STYLE="position:absolute;height:233;filter: shadow(color=gray, direction=135) glow(color=skyblue, strength=144)">.

Figure 15-10: This figure illustrates the effect of applying the filters in reverse order (Shadow, then Glow).

Manipulating filters

You can access the filters *collection* for each element in your page. You can, therefore address a filters collection from your script just as you would other kinds of object collections. There are three ways to access a particular filter from within the filters collection. Any of these approaches works fine. Here they are in JavaScript:

```
zone.filters.alpha.opacity = zone.filters.alpha.opacity + 2
zone.filters["alpha"].opacity =
 zone.filters["alpha"].opacity + 2
zone.filters[0].opacity = zone.filters[0].opacity + 2
```

If you're using VBScript, you must use parentheses instead of brackets:

```
zone.filters("alpha").opacity =
zone.filters("alpha").opacity + 2
zone.filters(0).opacity = zone.filters(0).opacity + 2
```

The filters collection

Each element supports a filters collection. Listing 15-8 gracefully fades a graphic into visibility by progressively increasing the opacity setting of the Alpha filter. (Be sure to replace C:\CRANE.JPG in the source code with a path to a .JPG or .GIF graphic file that's on your computer.)

Listing 15-8: **A Graceful Fade**

```
<HTML>
<HEAD>
<SCRIPT LANGUAGE="VBScript">
dim timerhandle
dim l
function startshow()
timerhandle = setInterval("fadein()",40)
end function
function fadein()
l = l + 5
zone.filters.alpha.opacity = zone.filters.alpha.opacity + l
if l > 100 then
        clearInterval(timerhandle)
end if
End Function
</SCRIPT>
</HEAD>
<BODY onload=startshow() TOPMARGIN=22>
<img id=zone src=c:\crane.jpg
 style="filter: alpha(opacity=2)">
</BODY>
</HTML>
```

The particular line to notice in this code is: `zone.filters.alpha.opacity = zone.filters.alpha.opacity + 1`. We are accessing the filters collection within the `img` element (named `zone`). In this way, the opacity property of the Alpha filter can be dynamically adjusted to fade the graphic into view.

Collections with transitions

You can also refer to the filters collection when you're working with revealTrans, or other transitions, as in Listing 15-9.

Listing 15-9: Referring to the Filters Collection when Working with revealTrans

```
<HTML>
<HEAD>
<script language="JavaScript">
function showtime(){
divzone.filters.revealTrans.apply()
divzone.innerText = "WATCH THE WAVE AND BUBBLE REPLACEMENT"
divzone.filters.revealTrans.play()
}
</script>
</HEAD>
<BODY topmargin=40 leftmargin=40 onload=showtime()>
<FONT SIZE=25>
<div id=divzone style="height:350;width:550;
filter:wave(strength=24) revealTrans(transition=3
duration=14)">
SEE THIS REPLACED BY SOMETHING ELSE BEFORE YOUR VERY EYES
</div>
</BODY>
</HTML>
```

Working with filter strings

Interestingly, you can bypass the object model as a way of accessing and changing filters. Instead, you can read or write to a *filter string*. If you want to see the parameters of a filter, ask the style object. However, it's considered best to manipulate filters directly as objects. You can always include a filter within a style (or style sheet) and just set it to Enabled=0, which keeps it turned off until you dynamically turn it on with Enabled=1 within a function or by the user pressing a button. If necessary, you *can* resort to manipulating the *filter string* instead. When would it ever be necessary? Well, perhaps you are accessing a database and can't know in advance which filter will be requested by the data streaming in. In such cases, knowing how to manipulate filter strings is handy.

Reading a filter string

To see how this works, insert the following line in the previous example, in the `showtime( )` function just below `revealTrans.play`.

```
alert(divzone.style.filter);
```

In a VI Quick View of the example page, an alert box tells you:

```
Wave(strength=24) revealTrans(transition=3 duration=14)
```

What's especially useful about the filter string is that it allows you to write to an object. This is another way to progressively change an element's filter.

Writing a filter string

Each of the filters can be added to a filter string, then applied to an object to modify that object's style. This can be another way to change filters over time, to create an animation effect, or to add a new filter on demand, as Listing 15-10 illustrates.

Listing 15-10: **Adding a New Filter**

```
<HTML>
<HEAD>
<SCRIPT LANGUAGE="VBScript">
function startshow()
zone.style.filter = zone.style.filter & " glow()"
End Function
</SCRIPT>
</HEAD>
<BODY onload=startshow() TOPMARGIN=22>
<FONT SIZE=12>
<DIV id=zone style="FILTER:
 DropShadow(Color=#808080, OffX=3,
 OffY=4); POSITION: absolute">
THIS IS IN SHADOW & IT GLOWS TOO
</DIV>
</BODY>
</HTML>
```

In the function, we cause a Glow filter to be applied to the existing DropShadow filter, by just writing to the filter string:

```
zone.style.filter = zone.style.filter & " glow()"
```

Here's the JavaScript version:

```
zone.style.filter = zone.style.filter + " glow()"
```

Using Transitions

Strictly speaking, a transition is a visual move between two images (or text) that takes place over time. A filter, by contrast, is usually just a special effect, like a drop shadow, that appears when the document is first displayed and doesn't ordinarily change over time. Of course, the distinction between filters and transitions isn't firm: you could use timers to apply, remove, or exaggerate filters over time.

IE 4 includes two transitions: blend and reveal. Blend is similar to a dissolve: one image slowly fades into another. There is no morphing — the shapes don't change. The first image gradually disappears as the second appears. You can also use blend on a single image (or text) to fade it in or out in relation to the background (see the earlier section, "Using blendTrans: the most elegant filter").

The reveal transition effect creates various kinds of wipes: horizontal blinds (like opening or closing venetian blinds), checkerboard, and so on (see Table 15-1 to come).

Listing 15-11 demonstrates all 24 reveal transition wipes.

Listing 15-11: **The 24 Reveal Transition Wipes**

```
<HTML>
<HEAD>
<SCRIPT Language="VBScript">
toggle = true
function first()
y = setInterval("transit()", 200)
end function

function transit()
dim obj
set obj = showtime
    if obj.filters.item(0).Transition = 23 then
        obj.filters.item(0).Transition = 1
    else
obj.filters.item(0).Transition = obj.filters.item(0).Transition
+ 1
        obj.filters.item(0).Apply()
    end if
```

(continued)

Listing 15-11 *(continued)*

```
        toggle = not toggle
        if toggle = true then
            obj.style.backgroundColor = "darkorchid"
        else
            obj.style.backgroundColor = "deepskyblue"
        end if

        obj.filters.item(0).Play()
end function

</SCRIPT>
</HEAD>

<BODY onload=first()>
<DIV id="showtime" style="position: absolute;
 top:40; left:40; font-size:85;
 text-align:center;
 background-color:deepskyblue; filter:
revealTrans(Transition=1, Duration=2)"
onfilterchange=transit()>TRANS</DIV>
</BODY>
</HTML>
```

In this example, there are several aspects of creating a transition. First, the filter for the DIV is defined as a revealTrans type. A transitioning object also has an onfilterchange event that fires when the transition is finished. In the example, we merely restart the function we named *transit*. When invoking a transition, you want to first use the Apply command. It begins the transition by stopping all repainting of the text or image, thereby preparing the object for the actual transition effect. After the Apply command, you trigger the transition effect itself with the Play command. Notice, too, that we're referring to a filters collection, which is discussed later.

Use this syntax to define a transitionwipe:

```
filter: revealtrans(duration=duration, transition=transitionwipe)
```

For example:

```
style="position: absolute; filter: revealTrans(Transition=1,
Duration=2)"
```

Duration specifies how rapidly you want the transition to execute. It can be defined using a decimal (floating point) to specify seconds or milliseconds. In this example, 2 means the transition will complete in two seconds.

The *transitionwipe* value can be an integer between 0-23, as shown in Table 15-1.

Table 15-1 The Transitions	
Transitionwipe	*Value*
Box in	0
Box out	1
Circle in	2
Circle out	3
Wipe up	4
Wipe down	5
Wipe right	6
Wipe left	7
Vertical blinds	8
Horizontal blinds	9
Checkerboard across	10
Checkerboard down	11
Random dissolve	12
Split vertical in	13
Split vertical out	14
Split horizontal in	15
Split horizontal out	16
Strips left down	17
Strips left up	18
Strips right down	19
Strips right up	20
Random bars horizontal	21
Random bars vertical	22
Random	23

You can use either the reveal- or the blend-style transitions with these HTML objects: BODY, BUTTON, DIV, IMG, INPUT, MARQUEE, SPAN, TABLE, TD, TEXTAREA, TFOOT, TH, THEAD, and TR.

Summary

This chapter expanded on the basics of DHTML that were discussed in Chapter 14. We gave you a sample (*it was really only a sample*) of some of the dramatic or subtle cutting-edge techniques you can use to bring your Web site alive and make it look truly professional. Among the techniques you learned:

✦ That animation means changing something over time, so using Timers is a natural approach.

✦ That there is an important difference between the two kinds of Timers. `setTimeout` and `setInterval`. `setTimeout` acts like a kitchen timer: it counts down, then goes off only once. `setInterval` acts like a metronome: it keeps ticking at whatever regular interval you specify.

✦ That there is a difference between DIV and SPAN when you're cordoning off a region within a Web page. DIV inserts the equivalent of <BR> before and after its region, whereas SPAN is an "inline" element, which means that it fits its contents within the existing HTML without inserting carriage returns.

✦ That clipping regions are like a video viewfinder — they frame some things and exclude other things. You can use them to progressively hide or reveal objects by changing the size of the clipping region.

✦ How to use expanding or collapsing "outlines" to save screen space

✦ How to animate with filters and transitions

✦ That there are 24 different kinds of wipes you can use

✦ How to dynamically change filters with the filter collection or, if necessary, filter strings.

✦   ✦   ✦

Working with Active Server Pages

Introduction to Active Server Pages

Creating HTML documents and publishing them on the Web are straightforward processes. You can even make your pages dynamic with scripts, Java applets, and ActiveX controls. The matter of how these pages interact with the server has always been somewhat painful to deal with, because CGI scripts are difficult to write. Microsoft introduced several technologies to enable clients and servers to interact with one another, but none of these technologies were simple and flexible at once. The Internet Database Connectivity component, for example, simplifies publishing of live data from databases, but it's not as powerful and flexible as the ISAPI component. The ISAPI component, on the other hand, requires C++ programming and isn't nearly as simple.

The situation changed drastically with the introduction of Active Server Pages (ASPs). ASPs are script-enabled pages that are executed on the server and that generate HTML code on the fly. It is this resulting code that is delivered to the client. You, the Web developer, don't have to worry about such issues as how to read the values of the parameters passed to the server by the client, or how to submit the HTML documents to the client. The Web server takes care of this for you automatically. Because Active Server Pages are executed on the server, they can access any of the components on the server, such as databases, text files, and OLE servers.

Most important, Active Server Pages are HTML pages with script code, and the script interpreter is located on the server. This means that even a Web author can develop Web pages that interact with the server and provide up-to-the-minute information, based on visitor-supplied criteria. VBScript is the simplest scripting language available, and it can now be applied to the server, too. In this and the following chapter, we are going to look at the basics of developing Active Server Pages and the objects exposed by the server to simplify the interaction between clients and the server. These include objects that extend VBScript's power by allowing it to access databases on the server and read the parameters passed by the client.

Understanding Active Server Pages

Active Server Pages (ASPs) are a variation of standard HTML pages that are processed on the Web *server* before being delivered to the Web browser client. ASPs contain standard HTML tags and script (VBScript or JavaScript) statements, as well as references to special objects that reside on the server. When the Web server processes the ASP, it literally produces an HTML page on the fly. This HTML page is then transmitted to the Web browser client, where the client-side scripts are processed along with the HTML page prior to displaying the page. This means that the client never sees the server scripts, because they were executed on the server. In addition, the output of the server scripts must be valid HTML code (text plus optional HTML tags), or the browser will fail when it processes the page on the client.

ASP generates HTML code from the server

Active Server Pages, a feature of the Web server (Internet Information Server and the Personal Web Server), is actually not an extension to HTML. ASP does not require browsers that support special features. On the contrary, it can produce standard HTML code that can be viewed on any browser.

To understand how ASP works and what it can do for your Web site, let's look at a simple example. In the previous chapters, you learned how to write HTML files and how to activate them with VBScript. Listing 16-1 is a simple HTML document that displays the six levels of headers.

Listing 16-1: **HTML Showing Six Levels of Headers**

```
<HTML>
<BODY>
<H1>Level 1 Header</H1>
<H2>Level 2 Header</H2>
<H3>Level 3 Header</H3>
<H4>Level 4 Header</H4>
<H5>Level 5 Header</H5>
```

```
<H6>Level 6 Header</H6>
</BODY>
</HTML>
```

The same output could also be produced with the help of a client script, which uses the Document object's Write method to send HTML tags to the browser's window. Listing 16-2 shows a client-side VBScript that produces the same output as in the HTML code in Listing 16-1.

Listing 16-2: A Client-Side VBScript Showing Six Levels of Headers

```
<HTML>
<SCRIPT LANGUAGE=VBScript>
Document.Clear
Document.Open
For i = 1 to 6
    Document.Write "<H" & i & ">Level " & i & "Header</H" & i &
">"
Next
</SCRIPT>
</HTML>
```

This script uses the Document object (which you learned about in Chapter 12), scripting, and a loop counter to produce the corresponding Header (<H>) tags.

Add an HTML file called VBS1.HTM to your Web project and paste the text in the file \Chapter 16\16-2.txt on the companion CD-ROM, into the body of the HTML page. Save it and then click the Quick View tab in the WYSIWYG editor. The VBS1.HTM page contains a script that is executed in the client browser and accesses the document displayed through the Document object of the IE Scripting Object Model. And this is the essence of the client-side VBScript: to dynamically produce HTML code. You can include additional statements that will make this document unique on each browser, such as the current time on the client. The statement

```
Document.Write "The date is " & Date()
```

will display the current date on the client. The same script will produce different results when executed on different Web browser clients. Figure 16-1 shows how the results of this script appear in Internet Explorer.

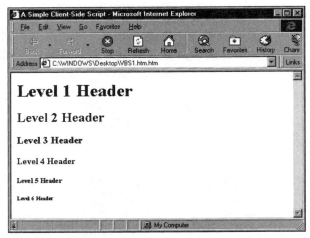

Figure 16-1: The output of a simple client-side script

Distinguishing server from client functionality

Client-side scripts are useful, but there's only so much you can do on the client. Typically, client scripts are used to validate data entered on a form by a visitor. If the visitor hasn't supplied a required value or has entered an invalid value, a small client script can detect this type of error one field at a time and prompt the visitor to correct the error. By validating visitor input on the client, Web pages behave more like applications. However, if the information entered into the form is sent directly to the Web server without any client-side processing, the Web server scans all of the fields in the form and detects all of the errors at one time. The Web server then creates an HTML page that it sends back to the client telling the visitor all of the problems to correct. This approach shifts processing to the server and makes the application more robust. You use both HTML tags and VBScript statements in the same Web page to produce these results on the server, with the help of an Active Server Page.

Structurally, an ASP page is a text file saved with an .ASP extension. Logically, it's an HTML file, which may contain server-side script commands, either VBScript or Java Script. The Web server sends any HTML code to the Web browser client unmodified but processes the script commands. The result of this processing is more HTML code, which is also sent to the client browser, where it is processed by the browser. The browser sees a straight HTML page just as though it had requested the HTML file from the Web server, when, in reality, it has requested an ASP page.

Now let's look at the contents of an ASP file that produces the same output as Listings 16-1 and 16-2, which we presented earlier. The content of the ASP file is shown in Listing 16-3.

Listing 16-3: An ASP Page Showing Six Levels of Headers

```
<%@ Language=VBScript %>
<HTML>
<BODY>
<H1>HTML Headings</H1>
<% For i=1 To 6 %>
    <H<% =i %>> Level <% =i %> Header</H<% =i %>>
<% Next %>
</BODY>
</HTML>
```

The first statement in Listing 16-3 tells the Web server which script language, VBScript or Java Script, this ASP file uses. The six headings will be generated from within the loop, which is implemented with VBScript commands. The VBScript commands in this ASP are the same as in Listing 16-2, which is a client-side script, with one difference: They must be enclosed in a pair of <% and %> tags. These tags tell the Web server that the commands must be processed locally on the server side, and the output they produce should be transmitted to the client, along with the other HTML statements on the page. Here's the loop clause that will display the six headings:

```
<% For i=1 To 6 %>
    <H<% =i %>> Level <% =i %> Header</H<% =i %>>
<% Next %>
```

The first and last lines set up a loop that's executed six times. Notice that the VBScript instructions are enclosed in <% and %>. Again, the client will never see these tags; they'll be executed on the server.

The loop's body is a bit more involved. When the server processes the loop clause, it replaces the <% =i %> text with the value of the variable i maintained by the VBScript interpreter running on the server. Here, variable i is equal to 1 in the first iteration of the loop, 2 in the second iteration, and so on. The characters outside the special tags <% and %> are sent to the client as they appear in the script. The first time the loop is executed, this text line will be transmitted to the client:

```
<H1>Level 1 Header</H1>
```

This is the result of substituting all the instances of the expression `<% =i %>` with the value of the variable i. After the second iteration, this string will be transmitted to the client:

```
<H2>Level 2 Header</H2>
```

The `<%` and `%>` delimiters need not appear on the same line as the VBScript commands between them. Often they are placed on separate lines, especially when they enclose a block of instructions, in order to make the code easier to read. You'll see some examples of this later.

Just save the text from the file for Listing 16-3 with an .ASP extension, and you have created an ASP file, ready to be opened in any browser. The client browser doesn't need to be Internet Explorer. Even the simplest browser that can render straight HTML will display the output of this ASP file, which is shown in Listing 16-4. However, if you open the ASP file locally, rather than have the Web server process it, the ASP page will not work properly. Remember: the client browser cannot process any script between `<% %>` tags. These statements can only be processed by a Web server that supports ASP.

Listing 16-4: **HTML Code Output by the ASP in Listing 16-3**

```
<HTML>
<BODY>
<H1>HTML Headings</H1>
<H1> Level 1 Header</H1>
<H2> Level 2 Header</H2>
<H3> Level 3 Header</H3>
<H4> Level 4 Header</H4>
<H5> Level 5 Header</H5>
<H6> Level 6 Header</H6>
</BODY>
</HTML>
```

Notice that the HTML statements in Listing 16-4 are identical to the statements in Listing 16-1. The difference between the two is that you created the file in Listing 16-1 but the Web server created the file in Listing 16-4. The instructions that the Web server used to create that Web file appear in Listing 16-3.

An ASP file is like a programmable HTML file. In contrast to straight HTML and client-side scripts, Active Server Pages are processed on the server, for two reasons. First, processing the ASP pages containing script and HTML on the server permits client browsers to continue receiving straight HTML code, which they know how to render. Second, when the Web server executes the script, it can access objects and data that are not available to the client browser. As you will see here and in Chapter 23, ASP pages can access databases on the server and provide up-to-the-minute data to the clients. Or they can contact any OLE server application installed on the server to extract or process information and then furnish it to the client browser. For example, a server may perform complicated math operations that cannot easily be packaged as a client-side ActiveX control or document. Besides, not all browsers support ActiveX components. By having computation-intensive operations performed on the server, you can easily incorporate advanced features into plain HTML pages.

Testing Active Server Pages

You can easily test an HTML document from the Visual InterDev WYSIWYG editor by simply clicking the Quick View tab. Documents that contain server-side scripts can only be processed on the Web server. If you are editing the ASP file, save it and in the Project Explorer, right-click the filename and select View in Browse from the shortcut menu.

Mixing Client- and Server-Side Scripts

In this section, I want to give you an idea of what you can do with server-side scripts and how simple it is to program the server. If you have done any CGI programming on the server with Perl or other UNIX languages, you will appreciate the simplicity of Active Server Pages.

Server-side scripts produce HTML output that is rendered directly on the client computer by the Web browser. The HTML output may also contain client-side scripts. It is possible within an ASP page to combine scripts that are executed on the client and other scripts that are executed on the server. Here is a simple example that calls for both types of scripts. Let's say you want to build a page that displays the current date and time on both the server and the client, in essence, to figure out the difference between the time zones on the two computers. Figure 16-2 shows the output of the LTIME.ASP page that does exactly that.

To display the local time on the client, you need a few lines of client-side VBScript code:

```
<SCRIPT LANGUAGE=VBScript>
Document.Write "The local time is " & Time()
Document.Write "<BR>"
Document.Write "and the date is " & Date()
Document.Close
</SCRIPT>
```

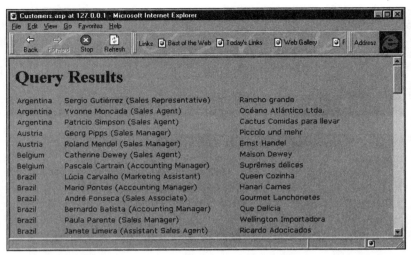

Figure 16-2: The LTIME.ASP page displays the local time on the server and client computers.

The time on the server must be generated by a server-side script on the fly and transmitted to the client as part of the HTML document. The server-side script that displays the server's time and date is shown here:

```
<% ServerTime = Time %>
<% ServerDate = Date %>
The time at the server's location is <% =ServerTime %>
<BR>
and the date is <% =ServerDate %>
```

All you have to do now is combine the two scripts into a single ASP file and insert some HTML code to produce the headers. The complete listing of the Active Server Page that generated the page shown in Figure 16-2 appears in Listing 16-5.

Listing 16-5: The ASP That Generated the Output Shown in Figure 16-2

```
<%@ Language=VBScript %>
<HTML>
<BODY>
<% ServerTime = Time %>
<% ServerDate = Date %>
<FONT FACE="Verdana" Size=3>
<H1>Server's Local Time</H1>
<BR><BR>
The time at the server's location is <% =ServerTime %>
```

```
<BR>
and the date is <% =ServerDate %>
<P>
<HR>
<H1>Client's Local Time</H1>
<SCRIPT LANGUAGE=VBScript>
Document.Write "The local time is " & Time()
Document.Write "<BR>"
Document.Write "and the date is " & Date()
Document.Close
</SCRIPT>
</BODY>
</HTML>
```

In VI, add an Active Server Page to your Web Project and replace the code it automatically generates with this code. Save it and open it in Internet Explorer to see a page similar to the one in Figure 16-2. If you are testing this script on a stand-alone machine or a local area network, the time is the same on both client and server. If you really want to see some difference between the times, ask a friend in another time zone to connect to your Web server and open this page. If you've saved it in the Web server's root folder as LTIME.ASP, your friend should address a URL like `http://194.24.192.203/ltime.asp`. You can find out the IP address of your computer by running the WINIPCFG utility, shown in Figure 16-3. This is your very own, unique address on the Internet, unless you use a dial-up connection, in which case, this address changes everytime you connect to your ISP's computer.

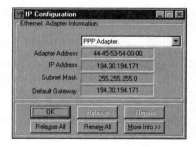

Figure 16-3: The WINIPCFG utility displays your IP address on the Internet.

You can easily figure out whether two computers are on the same or different time zones by comparing the difference between their times and dates. If it's 3 hours and 59 minutes and some seconds, for instance, the actual time difference is three time zones, unless one of them is in Newfoundland, for instance, whose exclusive time zone rests on the half-hour in between Quebec and the Atlantic Ocean. Of course, the calculations must take place as soon as the page is downloaded and stored in a global variable. The HTML page gets the latest times on the client and server machines only when the page is processed by the Web server and the Web browser, an event that happens each time the browser requests a new copy of the page. But how can I subtract a value that's calculated on the server from a value that's calculated on the client? It's an interesting technique you can use in your scripts. You must pass the value calculated on the server as part of a client script. Here's how it's written:

```
Document.Write "The time difference is " & _
        DateDiff("s", "<%= ServerTime %>", Time) & " seconds"
```

These instructions must be inserted into the server-side script. When executed on the server, they will generate a client-side script like this:

```
Document.Write "The time difference is " & _
        DateDiff("s", "11:59:52", Time) & " seconds"
```

The `DateDiff()` function calculates the difference between two date/time values in any interval (seconds, minutes, days, and so on). After the server has substituted the `ServerTime` variable with its actual value, the client receives a fairly straightforward client-side script.

Client/Server Interaction

Active Server Pages were introduced to simplify the interaction between clients and servers. The Internet — specifically, the Web — is a client/server environment. The key characteristic of a client/server environment is that the information resides on the server and the client requests information. The processing of the information takes place on either client or server, or both, wherever it's more convenient. As much processing as possible should be done with client-side scripts, to ease some of the burden on the server.

Conceptualizing the client/server interaction model

A client/server model requires that the two computers be able to exchange information. The client should be able to make requests, and the server should supply the requested information. The interaction model deployed over the Web is quite simple. The document displayed on the browser's window contains hyperlinks that point to specific documents on the server. Each time the user clicks on a hyperlink, the specified document is downloaded and rendered by the browser. To request another document, the viewer must click on another hyperlink. This model is quite simple and works very nicely. At least it worked nicely during the early years of the Web. It gave millions of users access to a vast world of information.

This client/server model is quite limited, however, compared to other client/server environments. For example, suppose the user wishes to request an arbitrary document from the server. Imagine you have stored an entire encyclopedia on the server and the user is allowed to retrieve any entry. Building a Web page listing all the entries in the encyclopedia is clearly out of the question. The user should be able to submit a word, or combination of words, to specify the information he or she wants to view. But the Web interaction model doesn't allow this. The browser must request a specific document for the server to supply.

Note For purposes of this discussion, the server IP address is assumed to be 194.10.193.101. You will need to substitute this address in your own experiments with the IP or DNS address of your own server, or with 127.0.0.1 if you're using Personal Web Server.

The solution to this problem is to allow the browser to pass information to the server in the form of HTTP requests. In other words, fool the browser into thinking that it's requesting another document with a nonstandard URL. For example, if a list of best-selling products already exists on the server as a separate HTML document called BestSellers.htm, a call to http://184.10.193.101/BestBuy.htm will retrieve that document and display it on the client. If the list of best-selling products is determined from a database retrieval, then the client should request another document, one with a nonstandard URL, such as http://184.10.193.101/ Send_me_the_bestsellers_for_this_week, because the browser does not know the exact URL for the page. The browser thinks it's requesting another document, but the server knows that it must execute a program (or script) to determine the requested URL. This program determines the list of best-selling products, formats that list as an HTML document, and sends that page to the Web browser on the client.

Passing parameters to the server

Requesting simple documents from the Web server is no big deal, even if these documents are scripts such as Active Server Pages. For the client/server interaction model to be really flexible, the client should be able to pass information to the server. For example, the client should be able to tell the server "My master wants to see the bestselling titles for the first week of January," or "My master wants to see the customers from Brazil only."

This information can be passed to the server in the form of parameter values. These are placed at the tail end of the URL that points to the application that will process these parameters. Parameters have a name and an associated value, which is expressed in this syntax:

```
parameter=value
```

When you're using a form to collect data from the viewer, *parameter* is the name of a control on the form and *value* is the control's value. Multiple parameters are concatenated with an ampersand character (&), as shown here:

```
LastName=Mansfield&FirstName=Richard
```

You append a parameter string to the URL by placing a question mark (?) after the name of the application that will process it on the server—which is coincidentally the name of the ASP file. If the value (contents) of a control contains a space, given that URLs may not contain spaces, it must be replaced by a plus sign (+), like so:

```
LastName=Mc+Chesney&FirstName=Richard
```

There are many other characters with special meaning in the HTTP protocol that cannot appear in the parameter string. For example, the double quote character (") can't appear at any point following the server script's name. Other illegal characters are the forward slash (/) and the ampersand character itself (&). Any special character — that is, any character that is not a letter or digit — is replaced with the hexadecimal representation of its ASCII value prefixed with the % symbol. The & symbol is encoded as %26, and the % symbol is encoded as %25. The parameter values are encoded by the browser, but you should be aware of this coding scheme if you want to create URLs from within your scripts.

You can use the Server.URLEncode method to apply the URL encoding rules for you. This line of script

```
<%Response.Write(Server.URLEncode _
("LastName=Mc Chesney&FirstName=Richard")) %>
```

produces the output

```
LastName%3DMc+Chesney%26FirstName%3DRichard
```

To see this technique of passing values to the Web server in action, start Internet Explorer and connect to a search engine, such as Infoseek. Then enter this search argument:

```
+"Active Server Pages"+Demo
```

This search will return pages that contain both the string "Active Server Pages" and the word "Demo."

The URL in the browser's Address Box will appear as follows:

```
http://www.infoseek.com/Titles?qt=%2B%22Active+Server+Pages%22+
%2BDemo&col=WW&sv=IS&lk=noframes&nh=10
```

The program that performs the search on the server is called `Titles`. This program it could be a Perl script or an Active Server Page; from the browser's point of view, it doesn't make any difference. The query is the value of the parameter `qt`. Notice how double quotes and spaces are encoded. The parameter string includes additional parameters, such as `nh` (the number of hits to be transmitted to the client each time), and `lk` (which specifies that the page to be returned should contain no frames).

There are basically two methods for building a parameter string. The first method is to provide an HTML `<FORM>` element, where the viewer can enter information, and click a Submit button, which automatically sends the form's contents to the server. The other method is to build the URL from within a script. The following VBScript statements prompt the user for some input and then pass the information entered to the Web server by way of the `Navigate` method:

```
SearchValue = InputBox("Enter one or more items to search for,
separated by commas")
Window.Navigate "/Scripts/Lookup.asp?Search=SearchValue"
```

The `Navigate` method causes the browser to request another HTML document by supplying its URL to the server. In this case, the URL is the name of an Active Server Page followed by a parameter string. Notice that the URL written here is relative to that of the current document, in that it begins with a forward slash (/). This request will be sent to the same Web server from which the current page was read. The parameter passed to the server is `Search`, whose value may contain multiple items, separated by commas. It is the `Lookup` script's responsibility to parse the string and extract the items.

Maintaining State Between Sessions

So far, you've gotten a high-level look at how Web browser clients interact with Web servers. In this section, you'll take a closer look at this interaction by examining the problems the Internet protocol presents to Web developers. Once you understand the problems, you'll learn how you can use the `Application` and `Session` objects to address them.

How should a Web server remember its clients?

The protocol employed by the Internet presents another dilemma developers must deal with: A Web server accepts thousands of requests on a daily basis, and some Web servers may service millions of users. Furthermore, everyday new users connect to the server. It is, therefore, impossible for the server to maintain an active connection with the client browser and use that connection to interact with the user. So everytime a client browser makes a request, a new session is established. This session remains alive only for as long as the server is transmitting the requested document. When the transmission is done, the session is terminated. Because the protocol itself cannot maintain information about the connection between the sessions, it is referred to as *stateless*. When the same client requests another document, a new session is established. You might have noticed that, everytime you click on a hyperlink, the message "Connecting..." appears in the browser's status bar. Even though the requested document resides on the same server, a new session must be established.

The Internet protocol dictated that a very simple interaction model be deployed on the Web. However, programmers have figured out how to overcome this limitation by emulating a true client/server environment. The solution to the problem of maintaining a state between pages viewed by a single client can be implemented either on the client, or on the server. The simpler approach is for each page to communicate with the other pages on the site through tokens left on the client computer. On the server, each session gets an ID and has its own space on the server where it can store information. This information is private to the specific session, and no other sessions (other viewers) can access it.

Before we look at the techniques for passing information among the pages of a Web site, let's look at some case studies that will help you understand the limitations of each method. Many sites allow their viewers to purchase items, which are displayed on different pages. As you browse through the pages of a site, you can purchase items and place them in a "shopping cart." You can actually purchase a few items, jump temporarily to another site, and then continue shopping. The items already purchased will wait in the shopping cart until you return. You can even shop on different sites at the same time and jump from one site to the other. Each site maintains its own shopping basket. These sites use a technique based on tokens, which are called *cookies*. These cookies are stored on the client side and can be read only by a specific Web site. This is how certain sites remember your name and your preferences, and they welcome you each time you connect to these sites. You'll see how cookies are created and handled shortly.

By comparison, some sites require that you register and log in with a user ID and password, either because you must pay some sort of subscription fee, or because they want to collect information about the viewers (for example, Microsoft's Site Builder page). A site that's open only to members or subscribers must maintain a list of registered users, including their user IDs and passwords, personal preferences, optional billing methods, and so on. When a new member registers to the site, that user fills out several forms before being allowed to log in. These sites (Site Builder included) do not use cookies. Instead, they store the information for each registered user in a database, and they consult this database everytime a user attempts to connect.

After this lengthy introduction to the client/server model deployed on the Web, its limitations, and workarounds, we're ready to discuss the ASP object that will enable you to develop interactive Web sites, and even Web applications.

The Application object

The Application object represents an ASP application, which is the collection of all ASP files that belong to a site. This is an interesting name, if you think about it. A Web site that includes ASP files is not just a site, it *is* an application. It's possible for the viewers of the same site to communicate with each other. For example, you can develop a Web site where users can leave messages for other users. When new users connect, you can look up the variables of the Application object and display the appropriate messages to selected users.

The purpose of the Application object is to store values, which can be shared among the users of an application. You can also use the Application object on pages that are posted on the Internet (to display counters, for example). To create a new variable, or change the value of an existing variable in the Application object, use statements like these:

```
<%
Application("WelcomeMessage") = "Happy Valentine's Day!"
Application("MaxScore") = 254000
%>
```

Here, WelcomeMessage is a string variable and MaxScore, a numeric one. Of course, WelcomeMessage must be changed after February 14.

The Application object provides two methods: Lock and Unlock. The Lock method prevents other clients from modifying any of the Application object's properties, and the Unlock method makes the variables of the Application object available to the other scripts again. To make sure that no other client is attempting to set (or read) the same variable at the time the script accesses it, first lock the Application object, then change the variable, and finally unlock the object, as shown here:

```
<%
Application.Lock
Application("WelcomeMessage") = "Happy Valentine's Day!"
Application("MaxScore") = 254000
Application.Unlock
%>
```

You can use the `Application` object to build a simple visitor counter by keeping track of a variable, as in the next example:

```
<%
Application.Lock
Application("Visitors") = Application("Visitors") + 1
Application.Unlock
%>
```

These instructions must be executed in the home page of your site, which is displayed the first time a user connects to your site. You can then display the value of the `Visitors` variable on your Web page with an instruction like this:

```
You are visitor # <% = Application("Visitors") %>
```

Note   To make certain that a variable belonging to the `Application` object maintains its value, you must save it in a local file and retrieve it, update it, and save it again. See the description of the `TextStream` object in the following chapter for a discussion of how to access files on the server through server-side VBScripts. All `Application` object variables must be initialized when the home page of the application is first loaded, an action that is signaled by the `Application_onStart` event. As long as the server is up and running, the application maintains the values of its variables.

To save messages for selected users, use login names as variable names. For example, if a user logs in as "GameMaster," create a variable for her named `GameMaster`, as follows:

```
<%
Application.Lock
Application("GameMaster") = "Welcome, Fighter"
Application.Unlock
%>
```

The `Application` object also recognizes two events:

✦ `Application_onStart` — Triggered when the application starts. Use this event procedure to execute initialization code. For instance, the value of the page hit counter could be read from a text file.

✦ `Application_onEnd` — Triggered when the application ends. Use this event procedure to execute cleanup code. For instance, the page hit counter value could be saved to a text file. (This approach will not work if the server crashes, in which case, the `Application` object won't get a chance to save the page hit counter's value; but more on this later.)

The `Application` object is the most general object of ASP and can be accessed from within any script published on the site. Each site has a single `Application` object, and you should use it to store information to be shared among all viewers and all sessions.

The Session object

Another useful object is the `Session` object, which describes the current session. An instance of the `Session` object is created automatically everytime a user connects to the Web server, and it is terminated when the particular session is abandoned with the `Abandon` method or times out. Each time a new viewer connects to the Web, the `Session_onStart` event is fired to signify the beginning of a new session.

Note

A single user may establish multiple sessions at once. He or she can start another instance of Internet Explorer and connect to the same site. Although there's only one viewer application on the client — albeit with multiple windows — the Web server sees two or more sessions and maintains as many `Session` objects. To share information between the sessions, scripts must go through the `Application` object, as each `Session` object is private and can't be accessed from within another session's scripts.

You can program the `Session_onStart` event to initialize the session. If your Web site requires that users register first, you can display a page that prompts the user for a user ID and password. If the same viewer has connected before, you can display a custom page.

The `Session_onStart` event is also a good place to insert code that implements counters. You have seen how to create `Application` variables (which every page on the site can see), with instructions like these:

```
<%
    Application.Lock
    Application("Hits") = Application("Hits") +1
    Application.Unlock
%>
```

The `Hits` variable is initialized as part of the `Application` object, so that it can be accessed and incremented from within every `Session_onStart` event.

You can also create `Session` variables, which are local to a particular connection and released when the session ends. The following statement, if placed in the `Session_onStart` event in the GLOBAL.ASA file (covered in the next section), remembers when the user connected to the site:

```
<%
    Session("Connected") = Time()
%>
```

You can use the `Connected` variable to maintain statistics about the viewers, such as how long they remain connected to your site; or to display on a page how long any user has been connected. When a session ends, the `Session_onEnd` event is fired. Use this event to clean up any variables allocated to the particular viewer.

A common use of the `Session` object is for storing variables, which are used by your Active Server Pages to personalize the Web pages sent to the user. For example, you may keep track of the viewer's favorite background image or theme, topics he's particularly interested in, the last date he connected to your site, and so on. With this information at hand, you can create highly personalized pages with server-side scripts. But how do we know that a user has been to our site before? If the site requires registration, the user's ID is all the information we need. We can use this ID to search a database on the server and extract the user's preferences. Again, this approach is not very practical for sites to which a small number of viewers will connect. The more practical approach is to store the customization information on the client computer in the form of a cookie, and retrieve it when the client connects to the Web site.

You can retrieve the cookies from the client computer with the help of the `Request` object. For example, assuming that the two cookies named `LastConnection` and `UserName` contain the date of the last connection to your site and the user's name, respectively, the following statements retrieve the values of the corresponding cookies from the client and store them in `Session` variables:

```
<%
    Session("ConnDate") = Request.Cookies("LastConnection")
    Session("UID") = Request.Cookies("UserName")
%>
```

These statements must appear in the `Session_onStart` event, so that the two variables will be available to all the scripts on the server. For example, you can add the following script to your home page, to display how long the user has been missing:

```
<%
    Response.Write "We missed you for "
& Date() - Session("ConnDate") & " days"
%>
```

The `Session` object provides two properties: `SessionID` and `Timeout`. `SessionID` is a unique identifier for the session, and you can read it from within your scripts, but you can't set its value. You should not save this value either, because it's different for each session. The same viewer will be assigned a different `SessionID` the next time he or she connects to the site.

The `Timeout` property defines a time-out period for the session, in minutes. If the viewer doesn't request another page within so many minutes, the session is terminated automatically.

Finally, the `Abandon` method allows you to terminate a session from within a script, with a statement like this one:

```
Session.Abandon
```

The GLOBAL.ASA file

You've read about the `Application` and `Session` variables and events. Where do you enter the handlers for these events? Every Web site may have a file with extension .ASA, which is a global Active Server Page. When your Web server is IIS, this file is called GLOBAL.ASA file and contains the `Application` and `Session` event handlers. In Listing 16-6, you see a typical GLOBAL.ASA file.

Listing 16-6: **GLOBAL.ASA**

```
<SCRIPT LANGUAGE="VBScript" RUNAT="Server">
Sub Application_onStart()
' {Put statements to initialize the Application here}
' {For example, read the page hit counter from a text file}
End Sub

Sub Application_onEnd()
' {Put statements to end the Application here}
' {For example, write the page hit counter to a text file}
End Sub

Sub Session_onStart()
    Application.Lock
    Application("Hits") = Application("Hits") + 1
    Application.Unlock
End Sub
</SCRIPT>
```

This script outlines the steps for maintaining a page hit counter with an `Application` variable, through both `Application`'s and `Session`'s events. As long as the Web server is running, the `Hits` variable maintains its value. If the server is shut down or crashes, however, the `Hits` variable will be reset. That's why it's a good idea to save its value to a disk file from time to time using the `FileSystemObject` object's methods, which are described in the following chapter.

As you can see, the technique suggested here is not perfect. If the server crashes, then the next time it restarts, it will read the `Hits` variable's value from the disk file and it will no longer be up-to-date. You can save the variable's value everytime it's updated, or insert an `If` clause that stores it to the disk file everytime it's been increased by 10 or 100, like this:

```
If Application("Hits") Mod 100 = 0 Then
    {Enter code to save the page hit counter to disk}
End If
```

Summary

In this chapter, you took a look at Active Server Pages and learned:

✦ That Active Server Pages are text files that contain HTML statements, client-side script code, and server-side script code.

✦ That server-side script is just like client-side script but must be surrounded by the `<% %>` tag pair.

✦ How the Web server processes the server-side script in an Active Server Page to create an HTML page, which it sends to the Web browser.

✦ How to send information to the Web server by encoding it in the URL.

✦ How to use the `Application` and `Session` objects to maintain the state between sessions and exchange information among the site's scripts.

✦ That the GLOBAL.ASA file is used by IIS to store the `Application` and `Session` event handlers.

✦ ✦ ✦

Server-Side Scripting and Components

✦ ✦ ✦ ✦

In This Chapter

Understanding the Request object

Understanding the Response object

Understanding the Server object

Using custom ActiveX Server components

✦ ✦ ✦ ✦

In this chapter, we'll continue our discussion of the objects and variables exposed by Active Server Pages for server-side scripting. These objects can't be all covered in a single chapter, so we'll focus on the most important and most useful ones, which we'll explore in depth. The other objects will be mentioned briefly; you should consult the Visual InterDev help files to learn more about their roles in server-side scripting. The objects we are going to discuss in this chapter are these:

✦ Request — When a client contacts the Web server with the URL of an Active Server Page, use this object to retrieve the values of the parameters. You can also use this object to request the values of the cookies stored on the client.

✦ Response — The Response object provides methods for sending output to the client, similar to the Document object's Write method.

✦ Server — The Server object gives you access to the properties and methods of the server. Use this object to contact other applications on the server.

The Request Object

The Request object retrieves the values (parameters) that the client browser passes to the server during an HTTP request. The Request object can be used to retrieve values of these collections:

- ✦ `ClientCertificate`—The values of fields stored in the client certificate that is sent in the HTTP request
- ✦ `Cookies`—The values of cookies sent in the HTTP request
- ✦ `Forms`—The values of form elements in the HTTP request body
- ✦ `QueryString`—The values of variables in the HTTP query string
- ✦ `ServerVariables`—The values of predetermined environment variables

ClientCertificate

An interesting property of the `Request` object is the `ClientCertificate` property, which contains information about the security of the client. The `ClientCertificate` object contains many values, which you can access with this expression:

```
Request.ClientCertificate(key)
```

where *key* can have one of the following values:

- ✦ `Subject`—A string with values that contain information about the subject of the certificate. The values of the Subject field depend on the issuer of the certificate. If Subject is an empty string, then the client doesn't provide a certificate.
- ✦ `Issuer`—Another string that contains information about the issuer of the certificate
- ✦ `ValidFrom, ValidUntil`—Two date values that specify the certificate's validity period. The certificate is valid if the current date falls between these two dates.
- ✦ `SerialNumber`—The certificate's serial number, as ASCII text
- ✦ `Certificate`—This field returns the contents of the certificate in ANSI format. There's very little reason to ever access this field from within your scripts.
- ✦ `Flags`—A set of flags that provide additional client certificate information

Cookies

The `Cookies` property of the `Request` object returns the cookie values stored on the client. To retrieve the value of a cookie named "FavoriteBooks," use the expression

```
Request.Cookies("FavoriteBooks")
```

You'll see how the `Cookies` property of the `Request` object is used in the section "Using Cookies," later in this chapter, along with the `Cookies` property of the `Response` object, which reads the values of the cookies on the client.

Forms

The `Forms` collection contains the values of the controls on the Form and can be accessed using the control's name as index. To access the value of the control named Name on the Form, use the statement

```
Request.Forms("Name")
```

QueryString

The `QueryString` collection retrieves the values of the variables in the HTTP query string, that is, the values encoded after the question mark (?) in the HTTP request. These are the values of the Form's elements passed by the client using the `GET` method. To retrieve the value of a parameter with the `QueryString` collection, use a statement like the following one:

```
ParValue = Request.QueryString(parameter)
```

In this statement, *parameter* is the name of the variable in the HTTP query string to retrieve. For example, if a client calls the TestPage.asp file as

```
http://ASPages/TestPage.asp?Name=Joe+Doe&EMail=JDoe@local.net
```

the query string is

```
Name=Joe+Doe&EMail=JDoe@local.net
```

`Name` and `EMail` are the names of two controls, where the user has entered some information. To retrieve the values of these two parameters, use the following statements:

```
Request.QueryString("Name")
Request.QueryString("EMail")
```

If you retrieve the value of the property `Request.QueryString` without any parameters, it will return the entire query string. The `Cookies` property lets you request the values of specific cookies, already stored on the client, or create new cookies. This property is discussed at length in the section "The Response Object," later in this chapter.

ServerVariables

`ServerVariables` is a property of the `Request` object and is a collection of the server's environment variables. To find out the value of a variable, replace *<variableName>* with its name in this expression:

```
variableValue = Request.ServerVariables(<variableName>)
```

The server provides the environment variables listed in Table 17-1. These values can be read from within your script.

Table 17-1
Variables in the Request.ServerVariables Collection

Variable	Description
AUTH_TYPE	The authentication method used by the server when the client makes an attempt to access a protected script
CONTENT_LENGTH	The length of the query string passed by the client
CONTENT_TYPE	The type of the data passed by the client. This variable is used with requests made with the POST and PUT methods.
GATEWAY_INTERFACE	The version number of the CGI specification supported by the server
LOGON_USER	The Windows NT account that the user has logged in to
PATH_INFO	The script's path name, as passed by the client
PATH_TRANSLATED	The translated version of the PATH_INFO variable, after the substitution of virtual path names with physical path names
QUERY_STRING	The string following the ? after the script's URL
REMOTE_ADDR	The IP address of the host making the request. This information is always known but can't be used to identify a user, because it changes between sessions. On a local area network with fixed IP addresses, you can use this property to identify workstations.
REMOTE_HOST	The name of the host making the request (if known)
REQUEST_METHOD	The method used to make the request. For the HTTP protocol, this variable is GET or POST (the method is specified in the HTML code of the document that makes the request).
SCRIPT_NAME	The virtual path of the script
SERVER_NAME	The server's host name. If the host name is not known, then an IP address or an alias is returned.
SERVER_PORT	The number of the port on the server to which the request was made

Variable	Description
SERVER_PORT_SECURE	This variable is 1 if the request was made from a secure port, 0 otherwise
SERVER_PROTOCOL	The name of the protocol that was used in the request (usually HTTP)
SERVER_SOFTWARE	The name of the Web server software that answered the request
URL	The URL of the site

To create a hyperlink pointing to your server by name, use a statement like this one:

```
<A HREF = "http://
<% = Request.ServerVariables("SERVER_NAME") %>
/Scripts/MyPage.asp">
Click here to return to my home page</A>
```

Example using the Request object

The Request object is one of the most useful objects of the Active Server Pages. Let's see through an example how it's used to retrieve the parameter values from the HTTP request header. The document shown in Figure 17-1 is a straight HTML page with an HTML form. The user fills in three fields and clicks the Submit button to send them to the server.

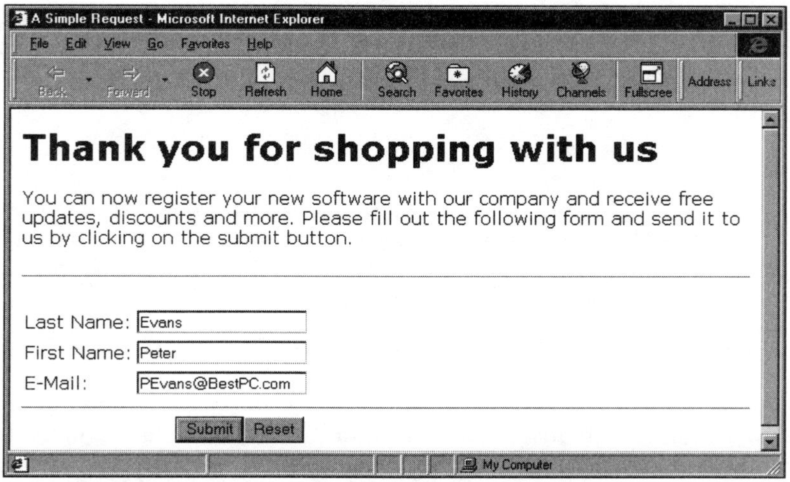

Figure 17-1: A Web page with a simple form

Add an HTML file to your Web project and call it SOFTWARE_REG.HTM. Replace the code in the Source pane of the editor with the code in Listing 17-1, which generated the document shown in Figure 17-1.

Listing 17-1: **SOFTWARE_REG.HTM**

```
<HTML>
<TITLE>A Simple Request</TITLE>
<BODY>
<FONT FACE="Verdana">
<H1>Thank you for shopping with us</H1>
You can now register your new software with our company
and receive free updates, discounts
and more. Please fill out the following form and send it
to us by clicking on the submit button.
<P>
<HR>
<FORM NAME=SoftReg
ACTION="Software_Reg.asp"
METHOD=GET>
<TABLE>
<TR>
<TD>Last Name: <TD><INPUT TYPE=INPUT NAME="LName" LEN=20>
<TR>
<TD>First Name: <TD><INPUT TYPE=INPUT NAME="FName" LEN=20>
<TR>
<TD>E-Mail: <TD><INPUT TYPE=INPUT NAME="EMail" LEN=20>
</TABLE>
<HR>
<INPUT TYPE=SUBMIT VALUE="Submit"><INPUT TYPE=RESET
VALUE="Reset">
</FORM>
</FACE>
</BODY>
</HTML>
```

The Submit button at the bottom of the form requests the document specified with the ACTION attribute of the FORM tag and appends the contents of the controls on the HTML form automatically. For the field values shown in Figure 17-1, this string will be transmitted to the server:

```
http://serverx/Scripts/Software_Reg.asp?LName=Peter&FName=Evans
&EMail=Peter_Evans@BestPC.com
```

Let's develop a script that reads the values submitted by the client, formats them as an HTML table, and returns them to the client browser. This simple example demonstrates how to retrieve the parameter values passed to the server by the client. In Visual InterDev, add an Active Server Page to your Web project and call it SOFTWARE_REG.ASP. Replace all of the code in the Source pane of the editor with the lines in Listing 17-2.

Listing 17-2: SOFTWARE_REG.ASP

```
<%@ Language=VBScript %>
<HTML>
<BODY BGCOLOR=silver>
<FONT FACE="Verdana">
<CENTER>
<H1>Query Parameters</H1>
</CENTER>
The following lines were produced by an Active Server
Page on the server. The SOFTWARE_REG.ASP page retrieves the
query parameters from the URL, with which the ASP file
was called (you can see this URL in your browser's Address
Box).
<BR>
<BR>
<BR>
<SCRIPT LANGUAGE=VBScript RUNAT=Server>
   Response.Write "<FONT FACE=Verdana>"
   Response.Write "<CENTER>"
   Response.Write "<TABLE BORDER RULES=All WIDTH=300>"
   Response.Write "<TR><TH BGCOLOR=lightyellow>Name</TH>
<TH BGCOLOR=lightyellow>Value</TH></TR>"
   Response.Write "<TR><TD><B>" & "Last Name" & "</TD><TD>" &_
         Request.QueryString("LNAME") & "</TD></TR>"
   Response.Write "<TR><TD><B>" & "First Name" & "</TD><TD>" &_
         Request.QueryString("FNAME") & "</TD></TR>"
   Response.Write "<TR><TD><B>" & "E-Mail" & "</TD><TD>" &_
         Request.QueryString("EMAIL") & "</TD></TR>"
   Response.Write "</TABLE>"
   Response.Write "</CENTER>"
</SCRIPT>
</BODY>
</HTML>
```

The SOFTWARE_REG.ASP file is an HTML document with a server-side script, which calls the `Request` object's `QueryString` property to retrieve the values of the parameters. Notice that the names of the parameters are used as indices.

Another item worth noticing on this page is the use of the `RUNAT` attribute of the `SCRIPT` tag. The `RUNAT=Server` parameter tells the Web server that the entire script must be executed on the server. This also explains why we used the

Response object's Write method. You could have written another script, by mixing text, HTML tags, and VBScript statements. The code would have been very difficult to read, because of the intervening <% and %> tags. With the Write method, we pass the entire string to be sent to the client as an argument and enclose the entire script with the tags

```
<SCRIPT LANGUAGE=VBScript RUNAT=Server>
```

and

```
</SCRIPT>
```

View SOFTWARE_REG.HTM in the browser, and then fill in the form and submit it. The server will return a page like the one shown in Figure 17-2 with the values of the parameters you entered.

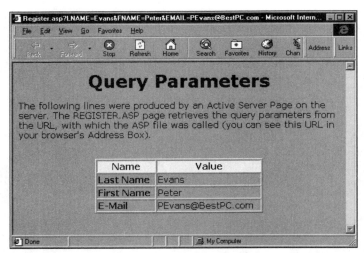

Figure 17-2: This page was created on the fly by SOFTWARE_REG.ASP, based on the values submitted by the SOFTWARE_REG.HTM page shown in the previous figure.

The Response Object

By default, an Active Server Page sends its output to the Web browser on the client. Everything that's not embedded within the server-side script tags (<% and %>) in the .ASP file is assumed to be HTML code and is transmitted as well. Server-side script statements are executed on the server, and their output (if any) is sent to the client. You can also use the Response object to send output to the client. In many ways, the `Response` object is similar to the `Document` object. The `Document` object provides a `Write` method, which is the only `Document`-object method than can be called from within client-side scripts. The `Document` object only provides one method that you can use in an ASP to send output to the client, but the `Response` object provides a number of methods, including

✦ `Write`

✦ `Clear`

✦ `End`

✦ `Flush`

✦ `BinaryWrite`

✦ `Redirect`

The Write method

The `Write` method writes a string to the current HTTP output. Its syntax is

```
<% Response.Write string %>
```

where *string* is the data to write to the current HTTP output. This argument is a variant and can contain text, numeric values, or dates. However, it can't contain the combination "%>." To display the delimiter, use the escape sequence "%\>." The longest string you can pass to the `Response.Write` method with a literal argument can't exceed 1,022 characters (VBScript limits static strings to 1,022 bytes). If the string is stored in a variable, you can specify longer strings.

You can use the `Write` method of the `Response` object to create a client-side script and embed it in the HTML document, as we did in the SOFTWARE_REG.ASP page of the last section:

```
<% Response.Write "<SCRIPT LANGUAGE=VBScript>" %>
<% Response.Write "MsgBox Date" %>
<% Response.Write "</SCRIPT>" %>
```

The advantage of using the `Write` method over mixing HTML tags and VBScript commands is that scripts using the `Write` method don't contain too many delimiters and the resulting server-side script is easier to read.

Other methods

You probably won't have much opportunity to use the other methods of the `Response` object, listed here. Although they are very specialized, you should know about each of them, in case you need to use one:

✦ **The** `Clear` **method** — The `Clear` method erases any buffered HTML output. You can use this method before sending output to the client with the `Write` method, or to handle error cases. The `Clear` method will work only if the `Response.Buffer` property has been set to False. The syntax of the `Clear` method is

```
<% Response.Clear %>
```

✦ **The** `End` **method** — The `End` method causes the Web server to stop processing the script and return the current result. The remaining contents of the file are not processed. The method's syntax is

```
<% Response.End %>
```

✦ **The** `Flush` **method** — The `Flush` method sends all the characters gathered to the HTTP output stream. Use the `Flush` method to display a string like "Processing, please wait..." and then continue with a time-consuming process. The viewer will see the message and will not attempt to reload the page by pressing F5 (which isn't going to help a process that takes long to complete).

✦ **The** `BinaryWrite` **method** — This method allows you to place binary information (the bytes making up an image, for example) to the output stream. This method is not used commonly with ASP files, which are text files.

✦ **The** `Redirect` **method** — This method redirects the browser to another URL. The information passed to the server in the form of parameter values is appended automatically to the new URL, and another browser receives the request.

Properties

The properties of the `Response` object control how the HTML output stream is to be processed. A brief description of each property follows:

✦ **The** `Status` **property** — This property forces the server to send the response value.

✦ **The** `Buffer` **property** — This is a True/False value that indicates whether the output of the script is buffered. If the `Buffer` property is False, then you can't use the `Flush` method.

✦ **The** `ContentType` **property** — This property specifies the HTTP content type for the response and is usually TEXT/HTML.

✦ **The** `Expires` **and** `ExpiresAbsolute` **properties** — Normally, pages are cached on the browser so that they can be displayed instantly (without having to be downloaded from the server) if the user requests them again. The period of time a page remains cached on the client can be specified with the `Expires` property. Set this property to `0` to force the client to reload the page every time it's requested (provided the page contains time-critical information, of course). The `ExpiresAbsolute` property is a date and time value that determines when the page will expire on the client.

The Cookies collection

Another property of the `Response` object is the `Cookies` collection, which lets you store cookies on the client computer. If the specified cookie does not exist, it is created. If it exists, it takes the new value and the old value is discarded. The syntax of the `Cookies` collection of the `Response` object is

```
Response.Cookies(cookie)(key)|.attribute = value
```

where *cookie* is the name of the cookie. To specify a simple cookie and its value, use a statement like this one:

```
Response.Cookies(ServerName)="www.myserver.com"
```

The *key* argument is an optional specification that the cookie is a dictionary, and *key* is set to `value`. The `attribute` argument specifies information about the cookie itself and can have one of these values:

✦ `Expires` — Specifies the date on which the cookie expires.

✦ `Domain` — If specified, the cookie is sent only to requests to this domain.

✦ `Path` — If specified, the cookie is sent only to requests to this path, and not to every page in the virtual folder.

✦ `Secure` — Specifies whether the cookie is secure.

✦ `HasKeys` — Specifies whether the cookie contains keys (in other words, is a dictionary).

All arguments are write-only, except for the `HasKeys` argument, which is read-only. The `value` argument specifies the value to be assigned to the key or an attribute.

To create a cookie with a key, use statements like these:

```
Response.Cookies("Preferences")("ForeColor") = "Blue"
Response.Cookies("Preferences")("BackColor") = "lightyellow"
```

To determine whether a cookie has keys, use this syntax:

```
Response.Cookies("Preferences").HasKeys
```

If `myCookie` is a cookie dictionary (in other words, if it contains keys), the preceding value evaluates to True. Otherwise, it evaluates to False. The following statements will create a cookie on the client and set various attributes:

```
Response.Cookies("Favorites") = "NBA"
Response.Cookies("Favorites").Expires = "December 31, 1999"
Response.Cookies("Favorites").Domain = "myserver.com"
Response.Cookies("Favorites").Path = "/NBAScores"
Response.Cookies("Favorites").Secure = FALSE
```

The first line sets the `Favorites` cookie value. Presumably, the server uses this cookie to display NBA scores on the home page. The remaining lines set the various attributes. The cookie expires at the end of 1998, is not secure, and is sent to the virtual folder NBAScores only. If a page from another virtual folder requests the cookie values, it won't see this cookie.

An example using a Request object

The example in this section demonstrates the `Cookies` collection of the `Request` object and consists of two files: the COOKIE.HTM file shown in Listing 17-3 and COOKIE.ASP. The COOKIE.HTM file saves a few cookie values on the client computer, whereas the COOKIE.ASP file retrieves the values of the cookies and displays them on another page. In a practical situation, you would save information about the visitor in the cookie. Each time that visitor visited your Web site, you'd look for this information and use it to personalize the site. For example, you might show visitors' names on the Web page or direct visitors to their favorite pages of your site.

Listing 17-3: **COOKIE.HTM**

```
<HTML>
<HEAD>
<TITLE>Request.Cookie Object Demo</TITLE>
<SCRIPT LANGUAGE="VBScript">
Sub MakeCookiesBttn_onClick()
    Document.Cookie = "LName=Evans"
    Document.Cookie = "FName=Peter"
    Document.Cookie = "EMail=PEvans@BestPC.com"
    MsgBox "The cookies were saved."
End Sub
Sub ShowCookiesBttn_onClick()
    Window.Navigate "Cookie.asp"
End Sub
</SCRIPT>
</HEAD>
<BODY>
<H1>Request.Cookies Object Demo</H1>
<P>
```

```
Click on the Make Cookies button to create
the following three cookies on the client computer:
<P>
<CODE>
LName=Evans
<BR>
FName=Peter
<BR>
EMail=PEvans@vmedia.com
</CODE>
<P>
Then click on the Show Cookies button to call the COOKIE.ASP
document to display the values of the cookies
with the Request.Cookies collection.
<P>
<INPUT TYPE=BUTTON VALUE="Make Cookies"
NAME=MakeCookiesBttn>
<BR>
<INPUT TYPE=BUTTON VALUE="Show Cookies"
NAME=ShowCookiesBttn>
</BODY>
</HTML>
```

In Visual InterDev, add an HTML file to your Web project and call it COOKIE.HTM. In the Source pane of the editor, paste the code in Listing 17-3 over the automatically generated code. Click the Quick View tab to test the page. The COOKIE.HTM file is shown in IE in Figure 17-3.

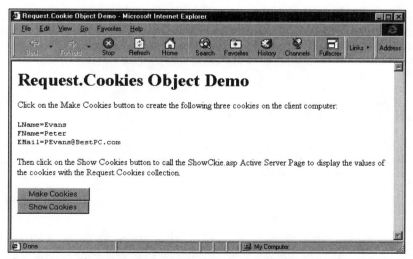

Figure 17-3: The COOKIE.HTM page leaves three cookies on the client computer, which are later read by an ASP page.

Before you run COOKIE.HTM, you need to create the file COOKIE.ASP. In Visual InterDev, add an Active Server Page to your Web project and call it COOKIE.ASP. Replace the code in the Source pane with the code in Listing 17-4. Save the file.

Listing 17-4: **COOKIE.ASP**

```
<%@ Language=VBScript %>
<HTML>
<H1>Request.Cookies Collection</H1>
The following cookies were found on the client
for this server:
<P>
<%
For Each cookie in Request.Cookies
%>
        <%= cookie %> = <%= Request.Cookies(cookie)%>
        <BR>
<%
Next
%>
</HTML>
```

View COOKIE.HTM in the browser and click the Make Cookies button to write the cookie values on the client computer. The script of COOKIE.HTM displays a message box stating that the cookies were saved. Next, click on the Show Cookies button to request the COOKIE.ASP page.

The Web server process the page. The server-side script uses a loop to scan all the items in the Request.Cookies collection and extracts the names and values for each cookie. Normally, the server script should know the names of the cookies so that it can process them directly. It is possible, however, to retrieve not only their values, but their names, too, from the Request.Cookies collection. The loop's counter, *cookie,* is the name of the current cookie, and its value can be retrieved with the property Request.Cookies(*cookie*). Figure 17-4 shows the output of the COOKIE.ASP page for the given cookie values.

The values of the cookies saved by the COOKIE.HTM page are hard-coded into the script. You can create a form in which the user can enter various cookies values, and the script will actually save them on the client computer.

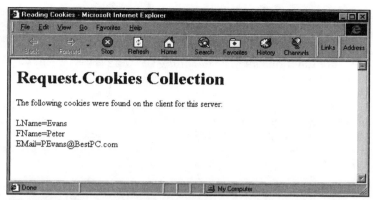

Figure 17-4: The output of the COOKIE.ASP page, which reads the values of the cookies saved by the COOKIE.HTM file shown in Figure 17-3

The COOKIE.HTM page won't save any cookies on the client computer, unless it's opened from a Web server. In other words, Quick View will display COOKIE.HTM in Visual InterDev, but the script won't save any cookie values on the client computer. Cookies are specific to a server, and there are no "local cookies." Moreover, only an Active Server Page from the same server can read the values of these cookies. The browser knows which site has placed the cookies there and will supply them only to the same site.

The cookies that the COOKIE.HTM page will save on the client computer won't last for long. They will expire at the end of the current session, because they don't have the expires attribute. To add an expiration date to a cookie, append the string

```
;expires=date
```

to the cookie value. The date value should be a date expression such as "Tue, 31 Dec 1996 12:00:00 GMT" that specifies an expiration date for the cookie. Cookies without an expires attribute expire at the end of the current session.

The Cookies property of the Response object provides a simpler method to create cookies and specify expiration dates. To leave a cookie value and specify an expiration date, use two statements like these:

```
<%
    Response.Cookies("LName") = "Evans"
    Response.Cookies("LName").Expires = "December 31, 1999"
%>
```

The Server Object

The `Server` object provides access to methods and properties on the server that perform common utility functions such as encoding URL and HTML strings and keeping track of file paths.

The `Server` object has one property, `ScriptTimeOut`, which sets a time limit for a script's execution and several methods. The `ScriptTimeout` property specifies the maximum amount of time a script can run before it is terminated. Its default value is 90 seconds. The timeout will not take effect while a server component is processing (for example, an operation on a database that takes a while to complete won't be timed out).

Use the following methods of the `Server` object to manipulate text, locate files in the virtual directory, and URL-encode a string:

- ✦ `MapPath`
- ✦ `CreateObject`
- ✦ `URLEncode`
- ✦ `HTMLEncode`

The MapPath method

The `MapPath` method maps a specified relative or virtual path to the corresponding physical directory on the server; it must be used when opening files for input or output with the `TextStream` object, discussed later in this chapter. Its syntax is

```
Server.MapPath(path)
```

where *path* is the relative or virtual path to be mapped to a physical directory. If *path* starts with either a backward or forward slash (/ or \), the `MapPath` method assumes that the path argument is a virtual path. If *path* doesn't start with a slash, the `MapPath` method returns a path relative to the directory of the .ASP file being processed.

Normally, your script shouldn't care about the actual value returned by the `MapPath` method, as it's passed as an argument to another method, usually the `CreateTextFile` and `OpenTextFile` methods, which create or open a file, respectively. These methods are discussed in the section "Accessing the Server's File System" later in the chapter.

The CreateObject method

The `CreateObject` method creates an instance of a server component. A *server component* is an OLE Automation server, an application that exists on the server computer. After a server component has been created, you can call its methods and properties from within the Active Server Page.

There are also a few components that are installed along with the Active Server Pages and that can also be accessed through the `CreateObject` method. The server components we are going to explore in this chapter are the ActiveX Data Objects component (ADO), which allows your script to access databases on the server; the FileSystem component, which allows your script to access files on the server; and the Browser Capabilities component, which lets your script know the capabilities of the browser used to view the a page.

An OLE Automation server is a program without a visible user interface. Applications contact this application through a set of properties and methods it exposed (properties and methods are known as *members* and form the server's interface). To access an OLE server, you must first create a variable that references the application with the `CreateObject` method. The syntax of the `CreateObject` method is

```
Server.CreateObject(progID)
```

where `progID` is the type of object to create. The value of the `progID` argument for any given server can be found in the Registry. This method returns an object variable, through which you can access the Server component's methods and properties, just as you do with traditional programming languages such as Visual Basic. One of the objects of the Active Server Pages component is the AdRotator component, which presents multiple advertisements at a specified location on an Active Server Page. We won't discuss this component here, but in order to use it, you must first create an instance of the object in your script with the statement:

```
<% Set AdObject = Server.CreateObject(MSWC.AdRotator) %>
```

After you have added the `AdRotator` object to the page that contains the script, you can use it. The following statement tells the server where to find information about the ads to be displayed on the current page:

```
<% AdObject.GetAdvertisement(adsFile.txt) %>
```

Another interesting control exposed by the `Server` object is the `BrowserType` control, which gives your script information about the capabilities of the browser on which the page is displayed. We'll discuss the `BrowserType` control shortly, but before you can use it in your script, you must first create an instance of the control with a statement like this:

```
<% Set BrowserObject = Server.CreateObject(MSWC.BrowserType) %>
```

This statement instantiates the BrowserType control on the page and returns a reference to it, which is stored in the `BrowserObject` variable. Then you can use this variable's properties to find out whether the browser supports specific features. The `Tables` property, for instance, returns True if the browser can render tables.

```
<% If BrowserObject.Tables = True Then %>
   {output a table to the browser}
<% Else %>
   You need a table-friendly browser to view the page you
requested.
<% End If %>
```

Notice the use of the `<%` and `%>`, which delimit the sections of the script that must be executed on the server. The literal to be displayed on a client that doesn't support tables is not embedded in these two tags (so that the Web server will transmit it directly to the client).

The URLEncode method

The `URLEncode` method applies URL encoding rules to a string. Its syntax is

```
Server.URLEncode(text)
```

where `text` is the string to be URL encoded. Use this method to prepare URLs with parameters. The statement

```
<%= Server.URLEncode("Function name 4-cos(X/3)") %>
```

will pass the client the string

```
Function name 4%2Dcos(X%2F3)
```

All characters that are not letters or numeric digits are replaced with their hexadecimal values, prefixed with the % symbol.

The HTMLEncode method

The `HTMLEncode` method applies HTML encoding to a string. Its syntax is

```
Server.HTMLEncode(text)
```

where `text` is the string to be HTML encoded. Use this method to place HTML listings on the page. The statement

```
<%= Server.HTMLEncode("The <IMG> tag doesn't have a
matching </IMG> tag") %>
```

will send this string to the browser's window:

```
The &lt;IMG&gt; tag doesn't have a matching &lt;/IMG&gt; tag
```

Accessing the Server's File System

Although it's not possible to access the client computer's file system from within your client-side scripts (unless you add a special ActiveX component on your page, which most viewers won't allow to be installed on their system, anyway), VBScript provides two objects that let you do this. These objects can be used only from within server-side scripts.

The two objects are the `FileSystemObject` and `TextStream` objects, which were introduced with VBScript 2.0 and give a script access to text files. The `FileSystemObject` gives your script access to the server computer's file system, and the `TextStream` object lets your script open, read from, and write to text files. These objects can't be used with binary files, because this would make VBScript unsafe even on the server.

The FileSystemObject object

To gain access to a server's file system, you must create a `FileSystemObject` with the `CreateObject` method:

```
Set fs = CreateObject("Scripting.FileSystemObject")
```

Variable `fs` represents the file system. You can access text files on the server computer's disk with the methods of the `FileSystemObject`, which are described next.

CreateTextFile method

The first method of the `FileSystemObject` object creates a text file that returns a `TextStream` object, which in turn can be used to read from or write to the file. The syntax of the `CreateTextFile` method is

```
<% fs.CreateTextFile(filename, overwrite, unicode) %>
```

The `filename` argument specifies the name of the file to be created and is the only required argument. The `overwrite` argument is a Boolean value that indicates whether you can overwrite an existing file (if True) or not (if False). If the `overwrite` argument is omitted, existing files are not overwritten. The last argument, `unicode`, indicates whether the file is created as a Unicode or ASCII file.

If the `unicode` argument is True, the new file will be created as a Unicode file; otherwise, it will be created as an ASCII file. If omitted, an ASCII file is assumed.

To create a new text file, you must first create a `FileSystemObject` object variable and then call its `CreateTextFile` method, as follows:

```
<%
    Set fs = CreateObject("Scripting.FileSystemObject")
    Set TStream = fs.CreateTextFile("c:\testfile.txt", True)
%>
```

The `TStream` variable represents a `TextStream` object, whose methods allow you to write to or read from the specified file.

OpenTextFile method

In addition to creating new text files, you can open an existing file with the `OpenTextFile` method, whose syntax is

```
<% fs.OpenTextFile(filename, iomode, create, format) %>
```

The `OpenTextFile` method opens the specified file and returns a `TextStream` object that can be used to read from or write to the file.

The filename argument is the only required one. The value of the `imode` argument is one of the constants:

✦ `ForReading` —The file is opened for reading data.

✦ `ForAppending` — The file is opened for appending data.

The `create optional` argument is a Boolean value that indicates whether a new file can be created if the specified filename doesn't exist. The last argument, `format`, is also optional and can have one of the following values, which indicate the format of the opened file. If the format argument is True, the file is opened in Unicode mode; if it's False, the file is opened in ASCII mode. If it's omitted, the file is opened using the system default (ASCII).

To open a `TextStream` object for reading, use these statements:

```
<%
    Set fs = CreateObject("Scripting.FileSystemObject")
    Set TStream = fs.OpenTextFile("c:\testfile.txt",
ForReading)
%>
```

After a `TextStream` object has been created, you can use these methods to read from and write to the file.

Read method

The `Read` method reads a specified number of characters from a `TextStream` object. Its syntax is

```
TSream.Read(characters)
```

where `characters` is the number of characters to be read from.

ReadAll method

The `ReadAll` method reads an entire `TextStream` (text file) and returns the resulting string. Its syntax is simply

```
Text = TStream.ReadAll
```

ReadLine method

The `ReadLine` method reads one line of text at a time (up to, but not including, the newline character) from a `TextStream` file and returns the resulting string. Its syntax is

```
NextLine = TStream.ReadLine
```

Skip method

This method skips a specified number of characters when reading a `TextStream` file. Its syntax is

```
TStream.Skip(characters)
```

where `characters` is the number of characters to be skipped.

SkipLine method

The `SkipLine` method skips the next line when reading from a `TextStream`; its syntax is

```
TStream.SkipLine
```

The characters of the skipped lines are discarded, up to and including the next newline character.

Write method

The `Write` method writes the specified string to a `TextStream` file. Its syntax is

```
TStream.Write(string)
```

where `string` is the string (literal or variable) to be written to the file. Strings are written to the file with no intervening spaces or characters between each string. Use the `WriteLine` method to write a newline character or a string that ends with a newline character.

WriteLine method

This method writes the specified string followed by a newline character to the file. Its syntax is

```
TStream.WriteLine(string)
```

where `string` is the text you want to write to the file. If you call the `WriteLine` method without an argument, a newline character is written to the file.

WriteBlankLines method

Writes a specified number of blank lines (newline characters) to the file. Its syntax is

```
TStream.WriteBlankLines(lines)
```

where `lines` is the number of blank lines to be inserted to the file.

The `TextStream` object provides a number of properties that allow your script to know where the pointer is in the current `TextStream`. These properties are described next.

AtEndOfLine property

This is a read-only property that returns True if the file pointer is at the end of a line in the `TextStream` object; otherwise, it returns False. The `AtEndOfLine` property applies to files that are open for reading. You can use this property to read a line of characters, one at a time, with a loop similar to this one:

```
<%
    Do While TSream.AtEndOfLine =False
       newChar = TStream.Read(1)
       {process character}
    Loop
%>
```

AtEndOfStream property

This is another read-only property that returns True if the file pointer is at the end of the `TextStream` object. The `AtEndOfStream` property applies only to `TextStream` files that are open for reading. You can use this property to read an entire file, one line at a time, with a loop like this one:

```
<%
        Do While TStream.AtEndOfStream = False
        newChar = TStream.ReadLine
```

```
        {process line}
    Loop
%>
```

Column property

This is another read-only property; it returns the column number of the current character in a TextStream line. The first character in a line is in column 1. Use this property to read data arranged in columns without tabs or other delimiters between them.

Line property

This is a read-only property that returns the current line number in the TextStream. The Line property of the first line in a TextStream object is 1.

Example using the TextStream object

The TEXTFILE.ASP page demonstrates several of the TextStream object's methods. When this file is called, it creates a text file on the server computer and writes a few lines in it. Then it opens the file, reads its lines, and displays them on an HTML page, which is returned to the client computer. As you will see, it uses the Write method of the Response object to send its output to the client. Let's start with the ASP file's listing, shown in Listing 17-5.

Listing 17-5: TEXTFILE.ASP

```
<%@ Language=VBScript %>
<HTML>
<HEAD>
<TITLE>Working with Text Files</TITLE>
</HEAD>
<BODY BGCOLOR=#E0E0E0>
<CENTER>
<H1>Working with Text Files</H1>
</CENTER>
<%
  Set FileObj =
Server.CreateObject("Scripting.FileSystemObject")
  TestFile = Server.MapPath ("/AXPages\textfile.txt")
  Set OutStream= FileObj.CreateTextFile (TestFile, True, False)
  str1 = "This file was created on " & Now()
  OutStream.WriteLine Str1
  OutStream.WriteLine "This is the second line in the file"
  OutStream.WriteBlankLines(1)
  OutStream.WriteLine "This is the fourth line in the file"
  Set OutStream = Nothing
  Response.Write "The contents of the textfile.txt '" &
TestFile & "':<BR>"
```

(continued)

Listing 17-5 *(continued)*

```
    Response.Write "<HR>"
    Set InStream= FileObj.OpenTextFile (TestFile, 1, False,
False)
%>
    <PRE>
<%
    Response.Write Instream.Readline & "<BR>"
    While InStream.AtEndOfStream = False
        TLine = Instream.ReadLine
        If Trim(TLine) <> "" Then
            Response.Write TLine & "<BR>"
          Else
            Response.Write "<P>"
          End If
    Wend
    Set Instream=Nothing
%>
</PRE>
</BODY>
</HTML>
```

The Server object's `CreateObject` method is used to create a `FileSystemObject`, through which the script can access the server's hard disk. Then it calls the `MapPath` method to map a virtual folder to the actual folder name and specify a full path name. `OutStream` is a `TextStream` object, whose `Write` method we use to write to the file. After the desired lines have been written to the file, we set the `TextStream` object variable to `Nothing` to release the resources it occupied. In Figure 17-5, you see the HTML page created by TEXTFILE.ASP. It shows the lines of text the active server page read from a simple text file on the server.

In the second half of the script, we create another `TextStream` object to read the lines of the same file. The file's lines are read with a `While...Wend` loop, which examines the value of the `TextStream` object's `AtEndOfStream` property to find out how many lines to read from the file:

```
While InStream.AtEndOfStream = False
        TLine = Instream.ReadLine
    {process TLine text line}
Wend
```

The output is formatted with the `CODE` tag and displayed as a listing. Notice how the use of the `Response` object minimizes the need for `<%` and `%>` delimiter tags in the document.

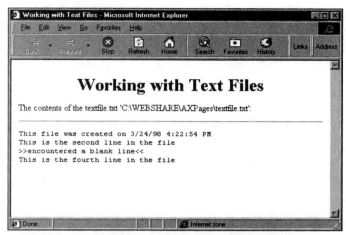

Figure 17-5: The HTML page output by TEXTFILE.ASP

The Active Server provides a few more objects, which we will briefly mention here. To access these additional objects, you must first create an object variable with the `CreateObject` method. The additional Active Server components are these:

✦ Browser

✦ Content Linking

✦ AdRotator

The Browser component

The Browser component allows your script to obtain information about the browser being used for viewing the site. As you recall, Active Server Pages don't require Internet Explorer or any special features on the part of the browser. The output they produce can be viewed on any browser. You, the developer, however, may want to add to your pages features that may not be supported by all browsers. Such features as frames and tables can be taken for granted on nearly all modern browsers, but some browsers may not support certain other features. The Browser component lets you find out from within your code whether a browser supports a specific feature.

To use the Browser component, create an object variable with a statement like this one:

```
Set BrowserFeatures = CreateObject(WSCF.Browser)
```

Then use the properties of the `BrowserFeatures` object variable to find out whether the browser supports features such as tables or frames. To make sure a page with frames will be displayed correctly on the client, use an `If` structure like this one:

```
If BrowserFeatures.Frames = True Then
    {use the IFRAMES tag to display frames}
Else
    {display a version of the page without frames}
End If
```

To find out whether the client supports VBScript or JavaScript, use these properties, respectively:

```
BrowserFeatures.VBScript
BrowserFeatures.JavaScript
```

The Content Linking component

Many Web sites have a standard format: They contain pages that must appear in a specific order. Tutorials, for example, are read in a specific order. The pages of such Web sites contain usually three buttons: the Previous button (which takes the viewer to the previous page), the Next button (which takes the viewer to the next page in the sequence), and a Home, or Table of Contents, button (which takes the viewer to another page in the site). The design of similar sites is straightforward, but it's also an error-prone process. The Content Linking component can automate the process by listing all the pages of the site and their relations in a text file. Using this file, the Content Linking control will automatically place the appropriate buttons at the bottom of each page and will also create the site's table of contents. Not only can this component automate the process for you, it will also maintain the site as you insert and remove pages.

The AdRotator component

A standard feature of any popular site is the ads that are usually displayed at the top or the bottom of each page. To manage a large list of ads, the Active Server provides the `AdRotator` object, which lets you specify a list of ads (HTML documents and/or images) and display them in an either specific or random order. The information needed by the server to insert ads on the pages of the site is stored in a text file, which the `AdRotator` reads to adjust the pages accordingly. Because all ads are displayed in the same area of the page, the design of the page is not affected.

Custom ActiveX Server Components

In this chapter, you saw how to use the Active Server's built-in components. You can also build your own ActiveX Server components, but you can't do that with VBScript. You must use a more traditional language such as Visual Basic or Visual C++. ActiveX components have certain advantages that you should take into consideration. ActiveX Server components are executable files, which run much faster than VBScript code. If you have certain VBScript routines you're using over and over in your projects, it will probably behoove you to implement the same functionality as an ActiveX component. If the same components are used by many Web authors in your organization, you should also consider packaging these components as ActiveX components. Once you have tested an ActiveX component, other developers can't fiddle with its code and there's no way to break an application that works. If you use the same scripts in more than one project, there's always the danger that you may attempt to enhance the control for one project and break another. This can't happen with ActiveX components, because only their developer can touch the source code and enhance it. Developers simply use such an object by calling its properties and methods.

You must develop ActiveX components if you need to add functionality that simply can't be achieved with VBScript. This is what the built-in server components do. They provide functionality that can't be duplicated with VBScript. Even if some routines can be implemented in VBScript, their coding may get quite complicated. VBScript is not a powerful programming language, and it can use as much help as you can give. If your server application has to perform complicated tasks, such as calculating planetary orbits, you should probably use a language that's better suited for scientific calculations.

Developing custom ActiveX Server components is not a terribly complicated process. If you are at all familiar with Visual Basic, you can develop your own custom ActiveX components. Visual Basic, itself, recognizes two project types called ActiveX EXE and ActiveX DLL, which produce ActiveX components. All you have to do is register the executable file with the computer where the Web server is running and then use it from within your scripts. The actual code is very similar to the code you'd write for a standard VB application, and there are wizards that will help you automate much of the process.

You can also use any of the numerous available server applications in your Web applications. Many packages for statistical calculations, for example, expose all of their functionality through a set of properties and members. The same is true of Office applications, too, although there's not much you can do with Word or Excel in the context of a Web application. To create an instance of Excel, for example, use a statement like this one:

```
Set EXL = CreateObject(Excel.Application)
```

After the `EXL` object variable has been created, it exposes all the members of the Excel application. For example, you can call the `Evaluate` method, which calculates a math expression. The following short segment displays the value of a math expression:

```
<%
expression = Cos(0.999)/Log(1.001)
Result = EXL.Evaluate(expression)
%>
The value of <% =expression %> is <% =Result %>
```

Summary

In this chapter, you took a closer look at Active Server Pages features and learned:

✦ How to work with the `Request` object to retrieve the values (parameters) that the client browser passes to the server during an HTTP request. The `Request` object can be used to retrieve values of these collections: `ClientCertificate`, `Cookies`, `Forms`, `QueryString`, and `ServerVariables`.

✦ How to work with the `Response` object to send output to the client, focusing on the `Cookie` collection.

✦ How to work with the `Server` object that perform common utility functions like encoding URL and HTML strings, and keeping track of file paths.

✦ What's involved in working with custom ActiveX Server components.

✦   ✦   ✦

Using the Visual Database Tools

Exploring the Visual Database Tools

With the Visual Database Tools (VDTs), you can create, execute, view, modify, and delete database objects. That includes tables, columns, indexes, constraints, relationships, stored procedures, and triggers for MS SQL Server and Oracle databases. In addition, you can view, insert, and update data, as well as create and modify queries, views, and SQL scripts for any ODBC-compliant database. You do all this from Visual InterDev 6.0 (VI) while you are directly connected to your database. With VDTs, you can develop a database-driven Web application and the associated database from the same environment. Not only are these tools powerful and visual, they're also convenient.

In this chapter, you'll learn the basic features of the Visual Database Tools and how these features relate to different ODBC-compliant databases. Then you'll create a database project and load the sample SQL Server database. Once you've done that, you'll take a quick tour of the four components that make up the Visual Database Tools, namely Data View, Query Designer, Database Designer, and the SQL Editor. You'll then learn more about these components in Chapters 19 through 21.

Visual Database Tools Basics

In this section, you'll learn what VDT features you can use with your database product and which features of VDT are available with the each of the different Microsoft products they bundle it with.

VDT Features by Database

One of Microsoft's goals in producing the Visual Database Tools was to create a single user interface to access every ODBC-compliant database. You'll see as you work with each of these tools that Microsoft has achieved this goal. The company deserves a lot of credit for this accomplishment because each database implements SQL commands differently. They focused their efforts and delivered the features to three groups of databases: SQL Server, Oracle, and all other ODBC-compliant databases. They created an ODBC driver for Oracle that fully utilizes the capabilities of Query Designer. Due to the diversity of these databases, only certain features are available to each of these three database groupings. Table 18-1 shows you the features supported for SQL Server, Oracle, and all other ODBC-compliant databases.

Table 18-1
ODBC-Compliant Database Support for VDT Features

Visual Database Tools Feature	Oracle 7.x	Microsoft SQL Server 6.0	6.5	7.0	All Other ODBC-compliant Databases
Query Designer					
Create, save, and execute queries.	√	√	√	√	√
Browse data.	√	√	√	√	√
Add, modify, and delete data.	√	√	√	√	√
SQL Editor					
Create, modify, and run stored procedures and triggers.	√	√	√	√	
Debug stored procedures.		√	√	√	
Database Designer					
Create and delete tables, columns, relationships, indexes, and constraints.	√		√	√	

VDT Features by Microsoft Product

Microsoft includes the Visual Database Tools with Visual InterDev 6.0, Visual J++ 6.0, Visual C++ 6.0, Visual Basic 6.0, SQL Server 7.0, and Visual Studio 6.0. Considering that Microsoft sells stand-alone, Professional, and Enterprise Editions of each of those products, Table 18-2 shows you which VDT features are included with each Microsoft product.

Table 18-2 VDT Features by Product Packaging		
VDT Feature	**Standalone Products and Professional Edition**	**Enterprise Edition**
View database objects	√	√
Execute database objects	√	√
Create, modify, and delete database objects		√

Preparing to Access Data from a VI Project

Before using the Visual Databse Tools to access a databse, you must create either a Web project or a database project in VI. You can do so here, defining a data connection to tell VI the type of your database, where to find it, and what drivers to use when connecting to it. You'll also learn how to restore the sample SQL Server database on the companion CD-ROM (in the SourceCode\Ch18 file).

VI projects and data connections

You can define a VI project as either a Web project or a database project (see Chapter 4). An overview of each project type follows.

Overview of a Web project

A Web project is what a team uses to develop a single Web application. VI by default, you can't access a database from a Web project without first adding data connections for all your ODBC-compliant databases. When you've done so, the Web project uses a Data View window to display a list of database objects. You can use those objects to create data commands you can drop on a Web page. (To connect that data to an ActiveX control for entry or display, use VI's Design-Time Controls.)

Overview of a database project

A database project allows a developer to connect directly to one or more databases and create database objects, queries, and SQL scripts. Using the Visual Database Tools, the developer can create database objects for MS SQL Server and Oracle databases. All project files, SQL scripts, and queries are stored locally in the default directory.

If you're working with a new database, modifying the database, or creating new queries or stored procedures for this project, you need to work in a database project. You can test the database modifications you make quickly and easily. When you save a database object to the database on the server, anyone with access to that database automatically has access to that database object through Data View.

Whenever you work with the examples in Part V, "Using the Visual Database Tools," you'll use a database project. In Part VI, "Using Databases in a Web," you'll work with a Web project that has a data connection to the database.

Installing the Sample SQL Server Database

The chapters in Part V, "Using the Visual Database Tools," and Part VI, "Using Databases in a Web," use a sample SQL Server database in the examples. The name of the database is Register, which you will find under VIB_SAM.DAT on the companion CD-ROM in the folder called \SourceCode\Ch18. If you are using MS SQL Server 7.0 or an earlier version, and if you can arrange for your SQL Server administrator to restore this database, you'll be able to follow along with each of the exercises in these chapters.

Because the database objects and data already exist in the Register database, if you want to perform the exercises in Chapter 19, you'll need to work with an empty database. Ask your database administrator to create a second database for you called Registration. Do not restore the sample database to this database. In Chapter 19, you'll use the Registration database to create each of the database objects and load data to the tables.

Note

The Microsoft SQL Server 6.5 that I used to create the sample database was running on an Intel machine and was configured to use the default character set and sort order. For you to be able to restore the sample database, your SQL Server 6.5 or newer version must also be running on an Intel machine and be configured to use the default character set and sort order. For you to be able to restore the sample database, your SQL Server 6.5 or newer version must also be running on an Intel machine and be configured to use the default character set and sort order.

If you are not able to install the sample database, you can follow the step-by-step instructions in this chapter to create the database objects. You can then use the techniques in Chapter 20 to add the raw data located in comma delimited text files to each of the tables in the database. The text files, customer.txt, custometo session.txt, formofpayment.txt, session.txt, sessionfocus.txt., and typeofsession.txt are located on the companion CD-ROM in the \SourceCode\Ch19 folder.

To restore the sample SQL Server database, follow these steps:

1. Create an SQL Server database called **Register** with a size of 5MB.

2. From the Tools Menu of SQL Enterprise Manager, click Database Backup/Restore. The Database Backup/Restore dialog box appears.

3. Click the Restore tab.

4. Select the Register Database you created in step 1.

5. Click the From Device button.

6. Click the Add Device button.

7. Enter **Register** in the Name box. In the Location box, browse for the file \SourceCode\Ch18\VIB_Sam.DAT on the companion CD-ROM.

8. Click the Create button. The Restore From Device dialog box appears.

9. Select Register in the list of Devices and Files.

10. Click the Restore Now button. A progress dialog box appears, and SQL Server begins restoring the database.

11. Close the dialog box when it completes the restore.

12. Close the Database Backup/Restore dialog box.

Creating a database project

Follow these steps to create a database project in Visual InterDev:

1. On the File menu, click New Project. The New Project dialog box appears with the New tab selected.

2. Open the Visual Studio branch in the hierarchy on the left and click Database Projects.

3. Select New Database Project on the right.

4. In the Name box, enter the name for this database project. For this example, enter **register_admin**, as shown in Figure 18-1.

5. To use the default location for the project files that appears in the Location box, go to step 6.

   To change the location for the project files, enter the location or select it using the Browse button to the right of the Location box.

6. To create a new solution, click Close current solution. If you need to work with this project and another project at the same time, click Add to current solution. If you do not have a solution already open in VI, you will not see these two options.

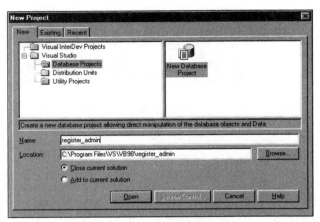

Figure 18-1: Use this dialog box to create a new database project.

7. Click Open. The Select Data Source dialog box appears.

8. On the File Data Source tab, select the data source name (DSN) from the list that points to the database you will use in this project. For this example, select the DSN that accesses the sample SQL Server database called Register. In Figure 18-2, we selected `VIBible_Sample_Register.dsn`, which is the name we gave to this DSN when we created it. (See the next sidebar for more information on DSNs.)

Cross-Reference

If you need to create a DSN, skip ahead to Chapter 22, where you learn how to do this. Once you've created the DSN for the Register database, return here and continue with this exercise.

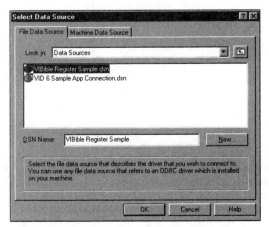

Figure 18-2: Select the File Data Source name for your database.

9. Click OK. The new database project appears in Project Explorer with the database in Data View. Figure 18-3 show these two windows.

Figure 18-3: Here's what a new database project looks like in Project Explorer and Data View.

10. If the DSN is a connection to a database with security, the database engine prompts you with a login dialog box. The default values match the values you entered when you defined the DSN. Enter the Password, if you have one. Click OK. Figure 18-4 shows the SQL Server Login dialog box for the Register database.

Figure 18-4: You'll only have to log in to the database once per work session.

Understanding Data Source Names (DSN)

In order to connect a Visual InterDev project to a specific ODBC-compliant database on a particular database server, you must choose a DSN.

There are two types of DSNs: a file DSN and a machine DSN. A file DSN stores information about a database connection in a file. A machine DSN stores the information in the Windows Registry of the machine where you created the DSN. In order to use this project on another machine, that machine must have the database connection information in the same Registry address. As a result, the machine DSN is less portable than a file DSN.

When you establish the database connection for your database project, the information stored in the file DSN is copied to the global.asa file for the project. As a result, you no longer need the file DSN.

Working with Data Connections

Project Explorer and Data View, which operate like Windows Explorer, make it easy to find each of the database objects in your solution. (See the following sidebar for more information on database objects.) Within a solution, the project sits at the top of the hierarchy. Below the projects, if there is a data connection, a Data View window will appear. Data View lists the databases in each data connection. Below each database, Data View lists the tables and then below that, the columns for each table.

Project Explorer

To access a database from a VI project, you need a data connection. Project Explorer shows the data connection implemented one way for a database project and another way for a Web project. Consider the database project first. For each data connection in a database project, Project Explorer lists the Query and SQL Script files you've created for that connection. The data connection for a Web project appears under the global.asa file under Data Environment. In the Data Environment, you create data commands that define a set of data to work with. You'll work with data commands in Chapter 23.

In Figures 18-5 and 18-6, you see Project Explorer for a solution that contains two projects: one a database project and the other a Web project. Figure 18-5 shows the detail of the database project, and Figure 18-6 shows the Web project expanded. Notice that the Web project has two data connections. In Table 18-3, you'll find a description for each of the data-related icons that appear in Project Explorer. For more information on the other icons in Project Explorer see Chapter 4.

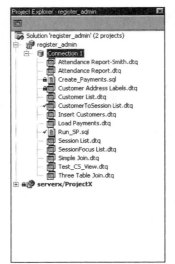

Figure 18-5: Here's what a database project looks like in Project Explorer.

Database Objects

A database is made of these components, called database objects:

✦ **Column** — A column is like a field in a record. A column has properties that define the type and length of data it holds. A primary key column uniquely identifies each row in a table.

✦ **Constraint** — Constraints are rules that Microsoft SQL Server applies to new values for a column. If the value does not pass the rule check, SQL Server does not add it to the database.

✦ **Index** — An index is used to access the rows of a table in a particular order. A single column or group of columns is defined as an index.

✦ **Key** — A key is the combination of columns that uniquely identifies each row in a table. There are two types of keys, primary and foreign.

✦ **Relationship** — A relationship is said to exist between two tables when a primary key column in one table is a column, or foreign key, in another table. It is a way to organize data and save physical storage space by not storing duplicate copies of the same data in both tables.

✦ **Stored procedure** — A stored procedure is the SQL-equivalent of a compiled program. It begins as SQL statements, user-declared variables, and flow-control statements, such as if statements. Then it is compiled and saved to the database as a stored procedure. You run a stored procedure by calling it from an application or from another stored procedure.

✦ **Table** — The data in a database is logically grouped into files of related data. In the relational world, data tables are visualized as grids of columns and rows. A row is like a record in the table, and a column is like a field in the row.

✦ **Trigger** — A trigger is a special type of stored procedure that automatically executes when data in a specific table is deleted, inserted, or updated.

✦ **View** — A view is a virtual database table. By definition, views consist of columns from other tables or from other views in a database. Because a view looks just like a database table, with rows and columns, you use a view just as you use a table. However, because a view is virtual, it does not actually contain data. It just looks as if it does because when you run a select query against the view, data is retrieved from the database.

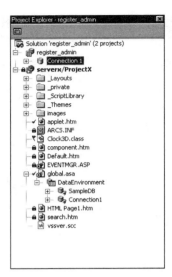

Figure 18-6: Here's what a Web project looks like in Project Explorer.

Table 18-3
Data-Related Icons in Project Explorer

Data View Icon	Name	Description
	Checked Out	This file is registered in the source control library and is checked out.
	Data Connection from a Database Project	This is a collection of information on how to access a specific database from a project. It is the same as a data connection from a Web Project with a different icon.
	Data Connection from a Web Project	This is a collection of information on how to access a specific database from a project. It is the same as a data connection from a database project with a different icon.
	Data Environment	This is used to store data connections for a Web project, which are used in server scripts to access the database.

Data View Icon	Name	Description
	Database Project	This is used to access databases on servers from VI. It consists of data connections, SQL scripts, and queries.
	Global.asa file	This file is used by the Web application and IIS to perform typical application initialization and shutdown tasks. Data Connection information is stored in this file for Web projects.
	Query	These SQL statements select and retrieve, insert, update, or delete data in a database. This file can be copied to other database projects.
	Solution	This is how you access projects from VI. It is the highest level in the hierarchy you see in Project Explorer and Data View.
	SQL Script	This set of SQL statements is similar to a stored procedure, but the file is stored locally and can be executed against multiple databases. This file can be copied to other database projects.
	Under Source Control	This file is under source control but not checked out.
	Web Project in Master Mode	Used to access a Web application from VI, it consists of data connections, as well as Web project files such as HTML, ASP, and GIF.

Data View

Whenever the current solution contains a data connection, the Data View window appears. Figure 18-7 shows the Data View window, which reflects a live connection to the database, for a solution that contains a database project and a Web project.

Figure 18-7: Data View shows you these four folders for a typical SQL Server database.

The four folders under the data connection are Database Diagrams, Tables, Views, and Stored Procedures. If you are working with an Oracle database, two more folders exist: Synonyms and Functions. Check the documentation for VI for additional information on VDT support for Oracle databases.

At the highest level of the hierarchy, Data View lists each of the projects in the solution. As you can see in Figure 18-7, this solution contains two projects. To expand a level in the hierarchy, simply click the + sign. When you expand a project, you see the databases in that project. When you expand a database, you see the categories: Database Diagrams, Tables, Views, and Stored Procedures.

Note   The information you see in Figure 18-7 is stored in the project's information file. When you click the database or any of the four folders, Visual InterDev uses the data connection information to activate the connection to the database. If the connect attempt is unsuccessful, an error message appears.

Table 18-4 shows each of the icons in the Data View tab along with a description of what the icon represents. The icons that do not appear in Figure 18-7 are explained in the next four sections.

Table 18-4
Icons in the Data View Window

Data View Icon	Name	Description
	Column	This subdivides a row in a table or view, like the fields in a record.
	Database	After the icon, you see the name of database followed by the name of the server where the database is located in parenthesis.

Data View Icon	Name	Description
	Database Diagram	This is a graphical representation of the data objects in your database.
	Database Diagrams Folder	This contains all database diagrams defined for the database.
	Database Project	Used to access databases on servers from VI, this consists of database diagrams, tables, views, and stored procedures.
	Parameter	This is a value prompted for when you run a stored procedure.
	Solution	This is how you access projects from VI. It is the highest level in the hierarchy you see in Project Explorer and Data View.
	Stored Procedure	This contains SQL statements and is precompiled and stored in the database on the server. Below a stored procedure you see the columns and parameters the stored procedure uses.
	Stored Procedures Folder	This lists all stored procedures in this database.
	Table	This is conceptually like a spreadsheet with rows and columns of data, where a row is like a record in a file, and a column is like a field in a record. Below a table you see the columns and triggers defined for the table.
	Tables Folder	Lists all tables in this database.
	Trigger	A special type of stored procedure associated with a table. When a predetermined event occurs, the database automatically executes the trigger.
	View	A view is a virtual table created by a query and consisting of columns from one or more tables in the database. Below a view you see the columns used by the view.
	Views Folder	This lists all views in a database.
	Web Project in Data View	Used to access a Web application from VI, this consists of database diagrams, tables, views, and stored procedures.

Database Diagrams

When you expand the Database Diagrams folder, you see the names of the database diagrams defined for this database. Below each diagram, you see a list for the table included in the diagram and below each table, you see the columns. In Figure 18-8, you see one database diagram called Define Tables, which contains ten tables. The last table, called Type_of_Session, shows two columns.

Figure 18-8: From Data View, you can see every table and column included in a database diagram.

Tables

When you expand the Tables folder, you see a list of all the tables in the database. Below each table, you see column names and triggers. Figure 18-9 shows the Customer table, which has 18 columns and one trigger. When you select a column, the Properties window shows you the data type and size of that column.

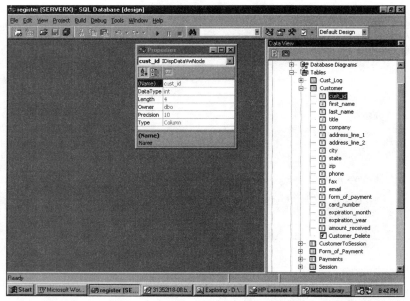

Figure 18-9: While you look at the columns in a table from Data View, you can see the Properties window, too.

Views

When you open the Views folder, it is similar in appearance to the Tables folder. Below each view, you see all the columns in the view. The only difference is that views cannot have triggers. When you select a column, the Properties window shows you the data type and size of that column. In Figure 18-10, you see the Customer Sessions view, which consists of five columns.

Figure 18-10: Data View shows all columns in a View.

Stored Procedures

Under the Stored Procedures folder, you see a list of all the stored procedures created for that database. Below the stored procedure, you see the names of the columns and parameters used in the procedure. When you select a column or parameter, the Properties window shows you the data type and size of that object. In Figure 18-11, you see one stored procedure, CustomerEnrollment, with three columns and two parameters.

Figure 18-11: Data View shows you all columns and parameters in a stored procedure.

Overview of Database Designer

Database Designer is a Visual Database Tool that lets you define, modify, and delete the database objects in a previously defined database from a graphical user interface. Although these features work exclusively with Oracle, Microsoft SQL Server, and Microsoft Access, you can also simply use database diagrams to document the structure of one of these databases. Because a database can be quite large and complex, Database Designer gives you a great deal of control over displaying a diagram. You can zoom the diagram, arrange the objects on one or more pages, add annotations, and control the detail of the information that displays in the tables. See Figure 18-12.

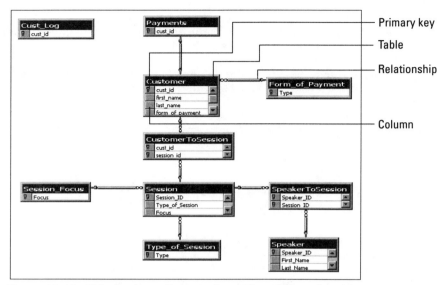

Figure 18-12: This database diagram shows the tables, primary keys, and relationships in the Register database.

If you must have the proper permissions, you can define and delete tables, columns, indexes, constraints, and relationships. In addition, you can make changes to the structure of the database, such as inserting columns in a table and changing column data types. Database Designer generates the SQL change code to match all of the actions you perform in a database diagram. You can use this code to track the changes you make to the database or run it against the database during non–prime shift hours.

In the Database Designer, you have three ways to handle your work. You can save it and update the server immediately. You can save the SQL change script generated while you worked and apply it to the database at another time. Or you can work with different designs and discard them without impacting the database on the server. This option makes it possible for developers to try numerous design alternatives without impacting the database on the server. See Chapter 19, "Creating and Updating a Database," for detailed information on using Database Designer.

Overview of Query Designer

Query Designer lets you create and execute complex SQL statements to retrieve data from your database. You can then browse the live data in your database. If you have the proper permissions, you can even add, change, and delete data while you browse. Specifically, you can create these six types of queries in the Query Designer:

✦ Select

✦ Insert

✦ Insert Value

✦ Update

✦ Delete

✦ Make Table

Query Designer is the most visual of the Visual Database Tool. It is also one of the most versatile tools, because it works with any ODBC-compliant database. Depending on your preference, you can work in one, two, or three different self-synchronizing panes: the Diagram, Grid, and SQL panes. Figure 18-13 shows the four panes that form Query Designer.

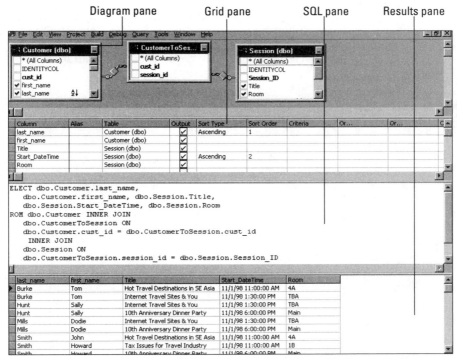

Figure 18-13: See the same query in the top three panes with the results in the bottom pane of Query Designer.

To build a query or a view, follow these simple steps:

1. Drag database objects from Data View and drop them into the Diagram pane, which automatically joins related tables.

2. Select the columns in each table you want to include in the results.

3. Select/Enter sort criteria.

4. Select/Enter filter criteria.

5. Select/Enter group by criteria.

6. Select/Enter expressions.

7. Click the Run button to see the results immediately.

This interactive process allows you to build a complex query in an iterative fashion, by adding complexity a little at a time. If you need to create extremely complex queries, you can enter your own ANSI-standard SQL statements or modify the SQL statements that Query Designer generates for you.

While browsing the results of a query or the entire database following an Open command, if you have the necessary permission, you can modify the data or add rows of new data directly in the Results pane. This is a great way to build the test data you need. And don't forget that you can do this with any ODBC-compliant database. See Chapter 20, Database Queries, for detailed information on Query Designer.

Overview of the SQL Editor

When you're ready to create a stored procedure, trigger, or SQL script, the SQL Source Code Editor is where you'll want to do it. Because it displays keywords in blue, you can visualize the structure of your SQL statements. Figure 18-14 shows the SQL statements for a stored procedure in the SQL Editor and the results in the Output pane. You can also debug stored procedures from the Editor.

You can create and execute stored procedures and triggers only for the latest versions of Microsoft SQL Server and Oracle databases. In Chapter 21, Advanced SQL Features, you learn how to use the Source Code Editor to create stored procedures, triggers, and SQL scripts.

Output pane   SQL Editor pane

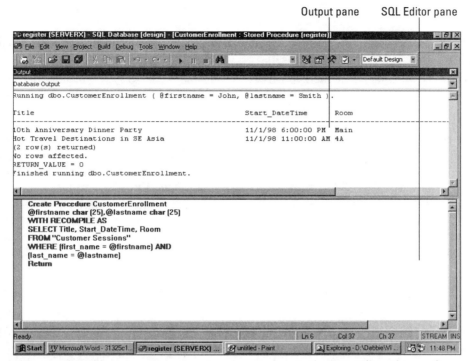

Figure 18-14: When you execute a stored procedure in the SQL Editor, the results appear in the Output pane.

Summary

You've just taken a quick look at the Visual Database Tools and what you can do with each of them. In this chapter, you learned:

✦ The Visual Database Tools are actually four components: Data View, Query Designer, Database Designer, and the SQL Editor.

✦ VDT feature support varies for Oracle, Microsoft SQL Server, and all other ODBC-compliant databases. The full VDT product capabilities are available with the Enterprise Edition of Microsoft Visual Studio products.

✦ Before you can access data from a VI project, you must create either a database project or a Web project and add a data connection to it.

✦ Project Explorer and Data View work like Windows Explorer. They show you the structure and composition of database objects in a project.

✦ With Query Designer, you create, modify, and execute six types of queries against any ODBC-compliant database. You can build a complex query visually or by directly entering the SQL statements. You can also enter and change data in your database while browsing.

✦ Database Designer lets you define tables and relationships in Microsoft SQL Server, Microsoft Access, and Oracle databases. You can apply the changes immediately, save the SQL change script and change the database later, or discard your changes without impacting the database.

✦ SQL Editor allows you to create and modify stored procedures, triggers, and SQL scripts. In addition, you can debug stored procedures directly from your workstation.

✦　　✦　　✦

Creating and Updating a Database

The database development process begins with logical data modeling and then progresses to the design and creation of the physical database. Once you have a model of the database you plan to create, you'll move to the Visual Database Tool called Database Designer. In this chapter, you'll continue working with the sample MS SQL Server database called Register that you installed in Chapter 18. You'll create tables, columns, keys, relationships, indexes, and constraints. You'll learn to prototype changes, as well. Finally, by the end of the chapter, you'll even be prepared to deal with future changes to the design of the database.

Logical Data Modeling

There are basically two approaches you use to model the data for your Web application. First you take a process-driven approach, where you focus on the business processes or activities siteusers perform, and then identify the data elements used during each activity. Next you take a data-driven approach, where you focus on the data or things you want to store data about, and finally you ask the question, "What do we want to know about each of these things?" You test your theory by looking at real business data. The project team will probably use both of these methods summarized here.

+ **Process analysis** — Identify the data needed to support each business process or activity.

+ **Data-driven analysis** — Identify data entities, data attributes, and relationships between data items.

You start with a very rough model of the data and business based on high-level information. As you learn more about one area, you add detail to the models. Then you ask more questions about each area of the business and the data. You continue to revise the model and ask questions. These iterations continue. There is a little problem with this approach, if you haven't guessed it already. When do you stop? There are no absolutes, but to avoid the "paralysis of analysis," you could time-box this phase of the development process by setting a finish date and doing as many iterations as you can fit in that timeframe. Another approach is to set a maximum number of iterations. If you don't find a way to box yourself in and then move on, you may never finish modeling the data.

Note   Although a full exposure to data modeling is beyond the scope of this chapter, we've tried to hit the highlights, which will always be useful to someone new to database design.

Process analysis

Process analysis begins with identifying the visitors to the Web site and the activities they need to undertake. To better understand process analysis, this section will take you through a conference registration example in which a typical visitor to an Internet site is a potential conference attendee who wants to learn as much about the conference as possible and register. A typical visitor to an intranet site for the conference would be a speaker, who wants to know who has signed up for the session. In column 1 of Table 19-1, you see a list of potential visitors, and in column 2, you see activities for each.

Using process analysis, you could consider each activity from the perspective of the visitor and identify the data needed to support that activity. For example, to permit an attendee to register online, you need the attendee's name, contact information, and payment information. You also need to know which sessions he or she wants to attend. The Data column in Table 19-1 is a first cut at creating this list.

Table 19-1 **A Process Analysis of Conference Registration Web Site plus a First Cut at a Data List**		
Visitor (User)	*Activity*	*Data*
Conference Attendee	Learn about the conference. When Where What it's about Who will be exhibiting What special events are planned Who should attend What it will cost	Name of conference Date of conference Location of conference Address, City, State, Zip Map Brief description of conference List of sessions List of exhibitors: Name Logo URL List of special events: Description Date, time Location List of types of people (e.g., travel agent, agency owner, corporate specialty) Benefits to each type Conference cost schedule
Conference Attendee Speakers	Learn how to get assistance (before and during the conference). Get more information. Help/questions answered.	800 number E-mail Fax Address, city, state, zip Register by phone, fax, mail.
Conference Attendee	Register for the conference online. Fill out form online. Submit payment online	Name (first, last) Title Company Address, city, state, zip Phone, fax, e-mail Name on card. Type of credit card (Visa, MC, Amex) Card number Expiration date Amount charged

(continued)

Table 19-1 *(continued)*		
Visitor (User)	**Activity**	**Data**
Conference Attendee	Learn about hotels in the area.	List of hotels Name Location Phone Range of rates Map
Conference Administrative Staff	How much money have we taken in and by what form of payment?	$ by type of credit card Count of people by type of credit card
Conference Administrative Staff	Learn who has registered for the conference and how they learned about the conference.	Name Company State Question on how they learned about conference
Conference Administrative Staff Speaker	Learn who has registered for a specific session.	Session Name Speaker Company
Conference Administrative Staff Speakers	How to contact speakers.	Speaker Company Phone E-mail Specialty

Note   To keep the Conference Registration example simple enough to follow but not too trivial, we limited our focus to people using the Web site prior to the start of the conference. Naturally, the databases created for the Web application would also be used to address on-site conference activities, for example, to produce the attendee, speaker, exhibitor, and staff badges and to produce a schedule for each attendee.

Data-driven analysis

Using basic data modeling principles, you then identify the entities, attributes for each entity, and relationships between the entities. After a few iterations, you'll produce the first cut of the entity-relationship (E-R) diagram shown in Figure 19-1. You will use the E-R diagram later in the chapter when you create the physical database. The E-R diagram is also a powerful communication tool. Because the team has a shared understanding of what needs to be done, the E-R diagram improves communications and the overall quality of the application.

The three basic E-R modeling concepts are:

✦ **Entity** — Something you need to keep information about. Entities are represented as boxes in an E-R diagram and are implemented as tables in a relational database.

✦ **Attributes** — Things you want to know about the entity. Attributes are implemented as columns in a relational table. Although attributes are not usually shown in an E-R diagram, you see them in Figure 19-1 because the model is small enough to allow it.

✦ **Relationships** — Relationships between entities are represented in the E-R diagram by lines. Relationships are implemented as foreign keys.

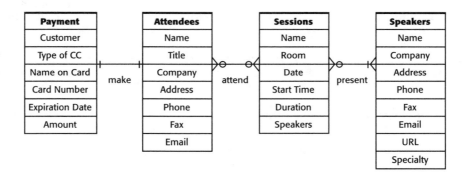

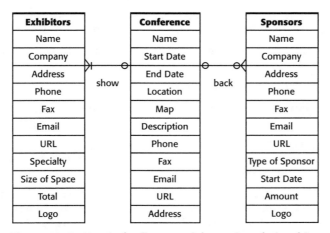

Figure 19-1: Here's the first cut of the entity-relationship diagram for the Conference Registration application.

Entities

To identify the entities, you ask the question, "What do we need to keep information about?" For the conference registration application, you need to keep information about people who register, speakers, exhibitors, payments, sponsors, special events, and registration. Because this process is quite subjective, this simple rule helps you name the entities consistently:

> *Because an entity refers to a single instance (row in the relational table), the name of an entity must be singular.*

Using this rule, you rename the entities. People becomes Customer; Speakers becomes Speaker, and so on. The entity names appear at the top of each box in Figure 19-1.

In addition to the entity name, you need to provide a definition for each entity. The definition must clearly distinguish one instance from another instance of the same entity. It must also distinguish a single instance of one entity from a single instance of another entity. Keep in mind that the effort you put into naming and defining these entities will help clarify not only your thinking but the thinking of the entire team. If the programmers writing queries against the database make incorrect or inconsistent assumptions about what a table contains, the quality of the application will suffer. Here is a revised list of entities in the Register database with a definition of each.

✦ **Customer** —A person who registers to attend the conference is a customer, no matter what form of payment is used.

✦ **CustomerToSession** — Links a customer to each session that person is registered to attend.

✦ **Session** — A session is a meeting that is part of the conference such as a special event, presentation, or a panel discussion lasting one, two, or three hours in a room, with one or more speakers and zero or more customers.

✦ **SpeakerToSession** — Links a speaker to each session that speaker is going to speak at.

✦ **Speaker** — A person who speaks at a session.

✦ **Form_of_Payment** — This covers all the possible ways that a Customer can pay.

✦ **Type_of_Session** — An administrative description of a session, this entity has an impact on the size of the room. It may also influence whether there is a special charge for the session.

✦ **Session_Focus** — A category describing the topic of a session, this entity gives additional information that the title of the session may not convey. Customers can use it to determine if they want to attend a session.

Attributes

Now consider the Speaker entity. Ask the question, "What do we want to know about a Speaker?" The answer: name, contact information, area of specialty, and sessions the speaker will be conducting. What else might you want to know? This is where the business area experts can help a lot. Ask them.

Table 19-2 is an example of real data and "candidate" attributes for Speakers. They are called "candidates" because they need to pass a few tests before they can be declared the real thing.

Table 19-2 Candidate Attributes for the Speaker Entity			
Name	*Session Code*	*Session Title*	*Specialty*
John Smith	B203	Doing Travel Business on the Web	Computer
Buzz Jones	T101	Hottest Travel Spots	South America
John Smith	T101	Hottest Travel Spots	Far East

Here are a few simple rules for identifying attributes:

✦ Each attribute represents only one fact. Speaker name, for example, is actually two attributes: first name and last name.

✦ An attribute cannot contain hidden data. The first session code begins with a "B" because it is a business topic. This is hidden data and needs to be identified separately.

✦ The values of an attribute cannot be duplicated. Each time a session code, like "T101," appears, the title, Hottest Travel Spots, is repeated. Maintenance would be much easier if you had a separate table for Session that included the name of the session.

✦ An attribute must not be derived from other attributes. There isn't an example of this in the Speaker entity, but there is in the Exhibitor entity. The total cost to an exhibitor is the cost per square foot of the exhibit area, times the number of square feet. Because total cost can be derived from the other two pieces of information, you do not need to include it in the model.

✦ Some combination of attributes should be able to uniquely identify each row. This is called the *primary key*. The speaker name is a candidate for the primary key, but as you can see, the values are not unique. How do you tell the two John Smiths apart? To establish a unique primary key for Speaker, you add a Speaker ID attribute.

Tables 19-3 and 19-4 contain the revised list of attributes for the Speaker entity and the new Session entity. Keep in mind that there is no one way to model this data or any data. If you just follow the few basic rules just listed, you'll do fine.

Table 19-3				
The Revised Speaker Entity				
Speaker ID (primary key)	**First Name**	**Last Name**	**Session ID (foreign key)**	**Specialty**
107	John	Smith	203	Computer
134	Buzz	Jones	101	South America
079	John	Smith	101	Far East

Table 19-4		
The Revised Session Entity		
Session ID (primary key)	**Title**	**Focus**
101	Hottest Travel Spots	Travel
203	Doing Travel Business on the Web	Business

Relationships

Now you need to identify the relationships between the entities. Consider any two entities, such as Session and Speaker, and ask the question "What is the relationship between Session and Speaker?" The answer follows:

Each Speaker may conduct one or more Sessions.

and

Each Session must be conducted by one or more Speakers.

These relationship statements are very formal, which is good because it allows everyone on the team, including the business experts, to share the same understanding of the data. Now decompose these two statements.

✦ **Each** — The sentence always begins with the work "Each," so you focus on a single instance of the entity.

✦ **Speaker, Session** — These are the entity names. Now you see why entity names are singular.

✦ **May** — Use "may" when the relationship is optional.

✦ **Must** — Use "must" when the relationship is required.

✦ **Conduct, be conducted by** —The name of the relationship in both directions. The relationship is simple and easy to communicate when you use the same verb in both directions.

✦ **One, one or more** — "One" and "one or more" quantify the relationship and are known as the *type* of relationship.

Relationships are categorized into these three types, as shown in Figures 19-2 through 19-4:

✦ **One-to-one**

> *Each Attendee must make one Payment.*
>
> and
>
> *Each Payment must be made by one Attendee.*

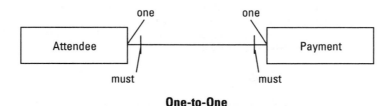

One-to-One

Figure 19-2: An example of a one-to-one relationship

✦ **One-to-many**

> *Each Conference may offer one or more Sessions.*
>
> and
>
> *Each Session must be offered by one Conference.*

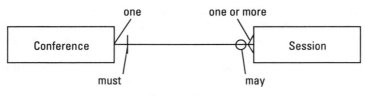

One-to-Many

Figure 19-3: An example of a one-to-many relationship

✦ **Many-to-many**

Each Speaker may conduct one or more Session.

and

Each Session must be conducted by one or more Speakers.

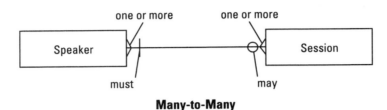

Many-to-Many

Figure 19-4: An example of a many-to-many relationship

Many-to-many relationships occur frequently in data models, as they have in the Conference Registration model. Unfortunately, in the relational database world, you cannot physically create them. As a result, you have to convert the many-to-many relationship into two or more one-to-many relationships with a junction entity, which you can physically create. Here's an example.

Consider this many-to-many relationship:

Each speaker may conduct one or more session.

and

Each session must be conducted by one or more speakers.

In Tables 19-3 and 19-4, you identified a Speaker entity and a Session entity.

Note   Oops! Looks like you didn't include sample data for the case where a speaker conducts multiple sessions. As often happens in modeling, you might not think of a situation until you identify the relationship. Because you're still in the early stages of modeling and it is an iterative process, it's no big deal. You just add it now. If you were in the final testing phases of the application when you discovered this situation, it would be much more difficult to address. That is why it is so important to do a thorough job in the design phase, when it does not cost as much to change.

Table 19-5 shows an example of the speakers conducting multiple sessions.

Table 19-5
Speaker Entity with Speaker Conducting Multiple Sessions

Speaker ID (primary key)	First Name	Last Name	Session 1 ID (foreign key)	Session 2 ID (foreign key)	Session 3 ID (foreign key)	Specialty
107	John	Smith	203	145	089	Computer
134	Buzz	Jones	101	122		South America
079	John	Smith	101			Far East

In this table, a speaker can conduct up to three sessions, but doesn't this violate one of the attribute rules? Session ID is duplicate data. To correct this, you create a junction table and associate speakers to sessions, as shown in Tables 19-6 and 19-7.

Table 19-6
The Revised Speaker Entity

Speaker ID (primary key)	First Name	Last Name	Specialty
107	John	Smith	Computer
134	Buzz	Jones	South America
079	John	Smith	Far East

Table 19-7
Revised Speaker-to-Session Entity (Implemented as a Junction Table)

Speaker ID (primary key) (foreign key)	Session ID (primary key) (foreign key)
107	203
107	145
107	089
134	101
134	122
079	101

Figure 19-5 summarizes many of the refinements covered so far in this chapter.

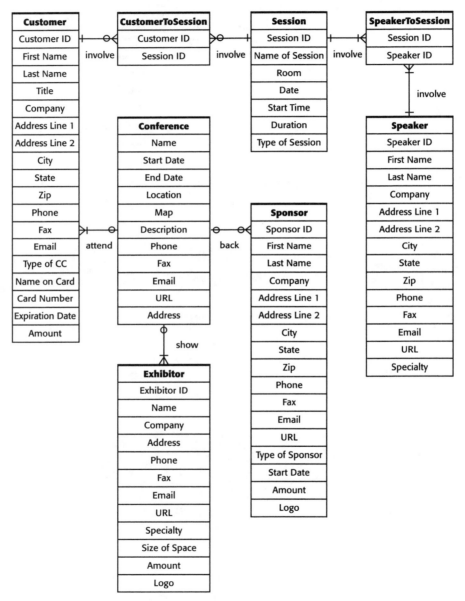

Figure 19-5: Here's the revised entity-relationship diagram for the Conference Registration application.

Designing the Physical Database

Before you physically create the database and database objects in VI, you need to determine the exact physical structure. This is often referred to as creating the physical database design from the logical data model. In order to create the physical database design, you need to understand Microsoft SQL Server 6.5, the database we use in this chapter. This section covers enough of the fundamentals of SQL Server for you to design simple databases. The physical database design for each of the tables in the Register database appear in Appendix A.

Note   For more in-depth information on Microsoft SQL Server 6.5, we recommend a book such as *SQL Server 6.5 Secrets* by David Rensin and Andrew Fedorchek and published by IDG Books Worldwide.

To create the physical database design from the logical data model, follow these simple steps:

1. Identify a table for each entity in the E-R diagram shown in Figure 19-5 that you plan to implement in this version of the application.

2. Identify a column for each attribute in each entity.

3. Identify lookup tables for columns with a limited number of valid values. For more information on this subject, see the section "Lookup Tables" later in this chapter.

4. Identify the characteristics of the database.

This section describes the physical characteristics of a Microsoft SQL Server database, which you need to know in order to define the physical structure of your database. Then you'll use the physical design to actually create the database.

The physical design of a database includes each of these characteristics:

✦ Database properties

✦ Table name

✦ Column properties

✦ Primary and foreign keys

✦ Indexes

✦ Constraints

Database properties

The two database properties you define are the name of the database and the initial space to allocate for the database. The database name follows the rules for identifiers, which are explained in the sidebar that appears in this chapter. Work with the database administrator to estimate the initial space required for the database. The administrator will use these two pieces of information to create the database on the server.

Table name

Table names follow the rules for identifiers. A table name cannot be the same as that of another table, any relationship, or any constraint within a database.

Column properties

Each column in a table has these properties:

- ✦ **Column name** — Column names follow the rules for identifiers. Each column name must be unique within a table. It cannot be the same as any relationship or constraint.

- ✦ **Data type** — Data types describe the characteristics of the data in a column and how it is stored. Data type names are not case-sensitive. The system provides a predefined list of data types, and users can define their own data types. See Table 19-8 for a complete list of system-defined data types.

- ✦ **Length** — The length is the number of bytes of storage space set aside for that column. You may only change the length of `binary`, `char`, `varbinary`, or `varchar` columns. Database Designer provides a default value for columns of the other data types.

- ✦ **Precision** — The precision of a numeric column is the maximum number of digits the column uses. It is automatically set to 0 when you select the data type, unless the data type is decimal or numeric. In those two cases, the precision is set to 18. You may only change the precision of decimal or numeric columns.

- ✦ **Scale** — The scale of a numeric column is the maximum number of digits to the right of the decimal point. It must be less than the value for Precision. It is automatically set to zero when you select the data type, unless the data type is `decimal` or `numeric`. Scale does not apply to floating-point numbers.

- ✦ **Allow NULL** — You have the option to allow or not allow NULL values in a column. If the column is a primary key, Allow NULL must be set to No. A NULL means the value for a column is unknown or has not been provided. It is not the same as zero or blank.

- ✦ **Default value** — You can specify a default value that the system will assign to a column if the user leaves it blank. For text strings, enclose the default value in single quotes. The system automatically surrounds the default value in parenthesis. If you do not assign a default value and you allow NULLs, the system will insert a NULL if the user leaves the column blank.

✦ **Identity, Identity Seed, or Identity Increment** — You can define only one column in a table as an Identity column. This column contains a system-generated sequential value that uniquely identifies each row in the table. The data type must be `decimal`, `int`, `numeric`, `smallint`, or `tinyint`. NULL values are not permitted and neither is a default value. The Identity Seed is the value to assign to the Identity column for a new row in the table. Identity Increment is the amount to add to the Identity Seed to generate the next Identity Seed value.

Table 19-8
Microsoft SQL Server System-Defined Data Types

Type of Data	System-Defined Data Type	Description
Binary	binary	Choose `binary` when all data values will be approximately the same length. The default length, which you can change, is 10 bytes. It can hold up to 255 bytes of fixed-length binary data. Due to the fixed storage length, columns of this type are accessed somewhat faster than `varbinay` columns.
		You can create relationships between `binary` and `varbinary` columns.
	varbinary	Use `varbinary` when you expect variable-length binary data with a maximum length of 255 characters or nulls, which you can set. The default length is 50.
		You can create relationships between `binary` and `varbinary` columns.
Character	char	Choose `char` when all data values will be approximately the same length. The default length, which you can change, is 10 bytes. It can hold up to 255 bytes of fixed-length character data. Due to the fixed storage length, columns of this type are accessed somewhat faster than `varchar` columns.
		You can create relationships between `char` and `varchar` columns.
	varchar	Use `varchar` when you expect variable-length character data with a maximum length of 255 characters or nulls, which you set. The default length is 50. Trailing blanks are ignored.
		You can create relationships between `char` and `varchar` columns.

(continued)

Table 19-8 *(continued)*

Type of Data	*System-Defined Data Type*	*Description*
Date and Time	datetime	The length is 8 bytes. Although you enter a date or time in standard format, the system stores them in an internal format. Data values range from January 1, 1753, to December 31, 9999. You can omit either value, but if both are omitted, the system sets the value to January 1, 1900, at 12:00 a.m.
	smalldatetime	Use smalldatetime for dates from January 1, 1990, to June 6, 2079. The length is 4 bytes.
Exact Numeric	decimal	Choose decimal for exact numeric data. The precision property specifies the maximum number of digits to store. The scale property specifies the maximum number of digits to the right of the decimal place.
	numeric	Numeric is identical to decimal and is provided for ANSI compatibility. We recommend you do not create numeric data types in a new database.
		Use either numeric data types or decimal data types throughout your database to avoid having the system convert between decimal and numeric. You will not be able to establish a relationship between a decimal column and a numeric column.
Approximate Numeric	float	Choose float for positive and negative floating-point numbers. The storage size is 8 bytes.
	real	Use real when you need less precision than float. The length is 4 bytes.
Integer	int	Choose int to hold whole number data with values between −2,147,483,648 and +2,147,483,647 bytes. The length is 8 bytes.
	smallint	Use smallint for data values between −32,768 and 32,767. The length is 2 bytes.
	tinyint	Use tinyint for whole numbers between 0 and 255. The length is 1 byte.

Type of Data	System-Defined Data Type	Description
Monetary	money	Choose `money` for monetary values between −922,337,203,685,477.5808 and +922,337,203,685,477.5807. These values are stored in 8 bytes as double-precision integers.
	smallmoney	Use `smallmoney` for monetary values between −214,748.3648 and +214,748.3647. The system displays these values with 2 digits of precision. The length is 4 bytes.
Special	bit	Choose `bit` when all data values are either 1 or 0. Although the system accepts data values other than 1 and 0, it converts them to 1. The default length is 1 byte, but 7-bit columns can be combined into a single byte.
	sysname	Use `sysname` for a column that references the name of a database object in the Microsoft SQL Server system table. The length is the same as a 19-character `varchar` column.
	timestamp	Use this in only one column of a table to automatically track when a row in a table is inserted or updated.
Text and Image	image	Choose `image` to hold variable-length binary data that may be as large as 2,147,483,647 bytes. The default length is 16 bytes. You cannot use this data type for variables or parameters in stored procedures.
	text	Use `text` for variable-length data with a maximum of 2,147,438,647 characters. The default length is 16 bytes.

Primary and foreign keys

The *primary key* is a column or group of columns that uniquely identify a single row in the table. The primary key cannot have a NULL value.

The *foreign key* is a column or group of columns in a table that are actually a primary key in another table. The values of the foreign key do not need to be unique and may contain NULLs.

Indexes

You define an index for a single column or group of columns. The name of the index follows the rules for identifiers and must be unique among all indexes in a database. In addition, it cannot be the same as any table, column, constraint, or relationship.

You use the index to access the rows in a table in a particular order. It's important to note that you do not physically reorder the rows in the table to get it in a certain order; rather, you use an index. For example, to get a list of the customers sorted in order by their last name, you use an index on the last name column. You do not sort the actual rows in the table. We'll create indexes for the Register database later in this chapter and use them when we query the database in Chapter 20.

Before you create indexes, you need to decide which columns to index and which type of index to use.

Which columns should you index?

Although indexes allow you to access your data in a particular sequence, you should not create a large number of indexes for a single table. Indexes take up room on the disk and slow down the processes of adding, changing, and deleting rows. So if your application updates the table often, you may want to limit the number of indexes for the table.

We recommend creating indexes for columns you query a lot. Until you create your queries, you may not know which columns you query a lot. Don't worry! You can create indexes at any time and experiment with how they impact performance. If you find you do not need an index, you can delete it.

What types of indexes can you define?

In addition to a normal old index, you can create three special types of indexes in the Database Designer.

- ✦ **Cluster index** — Use a cluster index when you need extremely fast access to the data. In this case, the data in the table is physically stored in the order of the index values. You can only define one cluster index per table. Consider using a cluster index if you use queries with range checks like <, >,<=, and >=.

- ✦ **Primary key index** — A primary key index is a special type of unique index. When you identify a column or multiple columns as the primary key for a table, Database Designer automatically creates a primary key index.

- ✦ **Unique index** — Use a unique index when no row has the same index value as another row. For example, you would apply a unique index to the Social Security number column in an employee database because no two employees in the table can have the same Social Security number. Database Designer considers NULLs in multiple rows as duplicate data, so be sure the Allow Null column property is off.

Constraints

Constraints are rules that Microsoft SQL Server applies to new values for a column. If the value does not pass the rule check, SQL Server does not add it to the database. We'll create constraints for the Register database later in this chapter. You can create these five different constraints in the Database Designer.

- ✦ **Check** — Use a check constraint when you want the system to verify that new values meet certain criteria before accepting them. For example, the value for month must be between 1 and 12.

- ✦ **Default** — Use a default constraint when you want the system to automatically provide a value when the user does not. You define the default constraint as a column property, specifically, the default value.

- ✦ **Foreign key** — The Database Designer automatically puts a foreign key constraint on columns you define as foreign keys. As a result, the system will not allow a value in the foreign key column unless it exists in the table where it is the primary key. This feature is useful for lookup tables, such as Type_of_Session.

- ✦ **Primary key** — The primary key constraint is identical to the primary key index. It makes sure that each value in a column is unique and not NULL.

- ✦ **Unique** — Use a unique constraint when you want the system to ensure that all values for a column or group of columns are unique, even if you allow NULLs. You cannot define a unique constraint on the primary key columns. You can define more than one unique constraint on a table.

Rules for Microsoft SQL Server 6.5 Identifiers

The following rules apply to identifiers, which are server names, database names, and database object names.

- ✦ Identifiers can be from 1 to 30 characters long and consist of letters, numbers, and symbols.

- ✦ The first character of an identifier must be a letter or the symbols _ , @, or #.

- ✦ If an identifier begins with @, it is a local variable.

- ✦ If an identifier begins with #, it is a temporary object.

- ✦ The rest of the characters of an identifier must consist of letters, numbers, and the symbols _ , $, and #.

- ✦ Identifiers cannot contain spaces, unless they are quoted identifiers. Quoted identifiers are beyond the scope of this book. In addition, if you use spaces in object names, you will have problems referring to the objects in script.

Lookup tables

A *lookup table* is a a small table that contains all possible data values for a column in another table. Typically it consists of two columns: an id and a description. Have you ever filled in an address form on an HTML page and, rather than enter the State, selected the value from a scrolling list? The 50 values in the list could have come from a lookup table. Tables 19-9, 19-10, and 19-11 show the values for the three lookup tables: Form_of_Payment, Type_of_Session, and Type_of_Session_Focus. In Chapter 20, "Database Queries," you learn how to load this data into the three tables.

Table 19-9
Values for the Form_of_Payment Table in the Register Database

Column 1	Column 2
Type	Description
1	Cash
2	Check
3	Visa
4	Master Card
5	American Express
6	Press Pass
7	Complimentary Admission

Table 19-10
Values for the Type_of_Session Table in the Register Database

Column 1	Column 2
Type	Description
1	Special Event
2	Session

Table 19-11
Values for the Type_of_Session_Focus Table
in the Register Database

Column 1	Column 2
Focus	Description
1	Travel
2	Business
3	Computer
4	New Age

Understanding Database Designer

Once the database administrator creates the database on the development server, you can use the Database Designer to create, modify, or delete database objects for that database. Remember: from Visual InterDev you can only manage a database in a database project, which you learned how to create in Chapter 18. In this section, you'll learn that the Database Designer lets you do these things:

✦ Create views of the database using database diagrams.

✦ Add, change, and delete database objects using database diagrams.

✦ Save or discard changes.

Database diagram content

Database diagrams give you a graphical view of the structure of your database, a view you can customize quickly and easily. Their structural elements, or *database objects*, you see in database diagrams like the one in Figure 19-6.

✦ **Tables** — The data in a database is logically grouped into files of related data. The name of a table typically identifies the type of data stored in the table. For example, if the table name is Customer, you can assume that the data in that table is for a customer.

✦ **Columns** — In the relational world, data tables are visualized as grids of columns and rows. A row is like a record in the table, and a column is like a field in the row. A column has properties that define the type of data it holds. A primary key column uniquely identifies each row in a table. An example of a primary key column in the Customer table is cust_id.

✦ **Relationships** — A relationship is said to exist between two tables when a primary key column in one table is a column in another table. It is a way to organize data and save physical storage space by not storing duplicate copies of the same data.

Primary key column　　　　　Tables

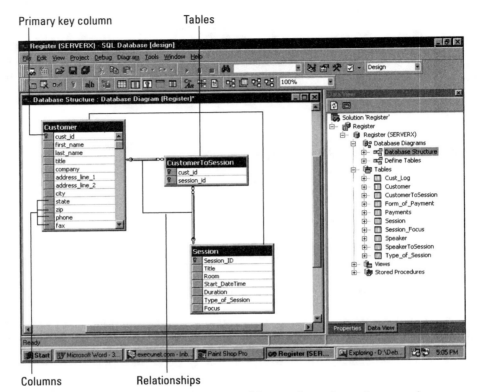

Columns　　　　　Relationships

Figure 19-6: A Database diagram shows tables, a primary key column, and relationship database objects.

Working with database objects

When you open a database diagram, you are directly connected to the database on the server. In the database diagram, you can create, modify, and delete these database objects:

- ✦ Tables
- ✦ Columns
- ✦ Relationships
- ✦ Indexes
- ✦ Constraints

You'll learn to do each of these things later in this chapter.

Saving changes

Although you have a database diagram open in Database Designer, you control how and when the changes you make impact the master copy of the database, by doing one of these things:

✦ Save the table or database diagram you changed, which immediately modifies the database on the server

✦ Discard your changes

✦ Save the Transact-SQL code to a script file. Database Designer automatically generates this code as you change the database diagram. You can modify the saved script file, if necessary, and use it to modify the database at another time. If your workplace allows only a database administrator to update databases, you can pass the script file on to that person.

With Database Designer, you can experiment with different database structures to see which physical structure is best for your application and your environment. You have not permanently changed the database on the server until you save the database diagram.

Working with a Database Diagram

You can create new database objects in a database diagram, modify existing objects, or use the diagram to review the current definitions of a database. In this section, you'll learn how to work with a database diagram. The first thing you must do is create a database diagram. Then you'll add a table. With one table in your diagram, you'll learn many different ways to customize the display of your diagram to meet your needs.

Creating a database diagram

Follow these steps to create a database diagram in a database project:

1. Open or create a Database project for the sample Register database. Remember to use the Registration database if you plan to do the example in this chapter.

2. On the Project menu, point to Add Database Item and click Diagram. A blank diagram pane appears with the Database Diagram toolbar. For a list of what each of the Database Diagram toolbar button does, see Table 19-12.

3. To save the database diagram, on the File menu, click Save DatabaseDiagramX, where X is the sequential number VI assigns to each diagram as you create it. In the Save dialog box, enter the name of the database diagram and then click OK. For this example, use **DefineTables**.

Table 19-12
Buttons on Database Diagram Toolbar

Button	Name	Description
	New Table	Click to create a new table.
	Remove Table from Database	Select the table you wish to delete from the database and click this button. A dialog box appears asking you to confirm the delete.
	Remove Table from Diagram	Select the table you wish to remove from the current Database Diagram and click this button. VI does not delete the table from the database.
	Set Primary Key	Select the column or columns in a table that you wish to make the primary key for that table and click this button. A small key appears in the row selector area for that row or those rows.
	New Text Annotation	Click to add a text field to the database diagram that you can use for annotation. You can position the text box anywhere on the diagram by dragging an edge.
	Save Change Script	Click to save the Transact-SQL statements for the changes you just made. A dialog box appears showing you the statements.
	Show Column Properties	Click to change the view to show all properties in columns.
	Show Column Names	Click to change the view to show only the table and column names.
	Show Key Columns	Click to change the view to show the table and key column. Columns that are part of a relationship link remain.
	Show Table Names	Click to change the view to show only the table names.
	Show Custom View	Click to change the view to the currently defined custom view.
	Show Relationship Label	Click to toggle display of description for each relationship in the database diagram.
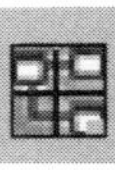	View Page Break	Click to toggle display of page break lines.
	Recalculate Page Breaks	Click to automatically recalculate and redisplay the page break lines.
	Add Related Tables	Select a table in the diagram and click this button to add all tables linked to it.

Button	Name	Description
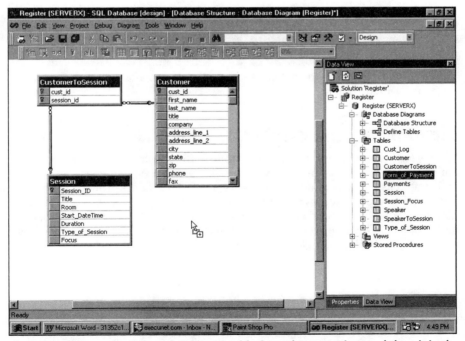	Autosize Selected Tables	Select a table and click this button to automatically display all rows and columns based on the current view.
	Arrange Selection	Click to automatically arrange the selected tables in the diagram to optimally display the relationships.
	Arrange Tables	Click to automatically arrange all tables in the diagram to optimally display all relationships.
`100%`	Zoom	Click to change the value in the Zoom box to increase or decrease the magnification of the Database Diagram pane.

Adding tables to the database diagram

It's easy to add tables to the open database diagram. Position the Data View window and the Database Diagram pane side by side, as you see in Figure 19-7. Click and drag the table name in Data View and drop it on the diagram.

Figure 19-7: Drag the Form_of_Payment table from the Data View and drop it in the database diagram to add it.

VI automatically displays the table in the database diagram, and the relationships that it has with the other tables in the diagram, as shown in Figure 19-8.

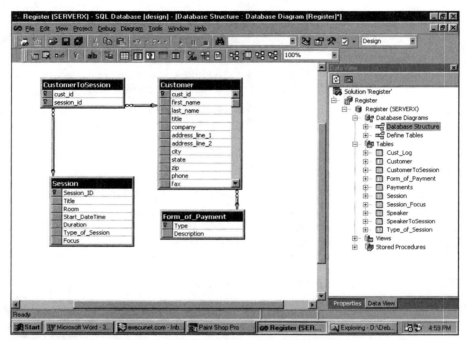

Figure 19-8: Here's what the database diagram looks like after you drop the Form_of_Payment table.

Customizing the display of a database diagram

VI gives you many different ways to customize the display of information in a database diagram. You can display from as little as the table names and relationships to as much as every column and property in all of the tables. You can also arrange the diagram to print across multiple pages with descriptive text. The database diagram display commands are located on the toolbar, the shortcut menu, the View menu, and the Diagram menu. For a complete list of the commands on the View menu, see Table 19-13, and for the Diagram menus, see Table 19-14.

Table 19-13
The View Menu for Database Diagrams

Menu Item	Description
Column Properties	Changes the view to show all properties in columns of the selected table(s).
Column Names	Changes the view to show only the table and column names for the selected tables(s).
Keys	Changes the view to show the table and key column as well as all columns that are part of a relationship link.
Names Only	Changes the view to show only the table names.
Custom	Changes the view to the currently defined custom view.

Table 19-14
The Diagram Menu for Database Diagrams

Menu Item	Description
New Text Annotation	Adds a text field to the database diagram that you can use for annotation. You can position the text box anywhere on the diagram by dragging an edge.
Add Related Tables	Adds all tables linked to the selected table.
Modify Custom View	Opens the column selection dialog box in Figure 19-9. Use this to select the property columns to display in the diagram. When you select Custom on the View menu, the diagram changes, as shown in Figure 19-10.
Show Relationship Labels	Toggles the display of the description for each relationship on and off.
View Page Breaks	Toggles the display of page break lines on and off.
Recalculate Page Breaks	Automatically recalculates and redisplays the page break lines.
Autosize Selected Table	Automatically displays all rows and columns based on the current view. Use this when you manually resize a table.
Arrange Selection	Automatically arranges the selected tables to optimally display the relationships.
Arrange Tables	Automatically arranges all tables in the diagram to optimally display all relationships.

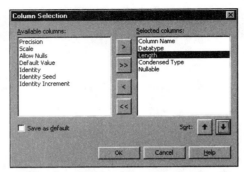

Figure 19-9: Select the property columns to create a custom table view.

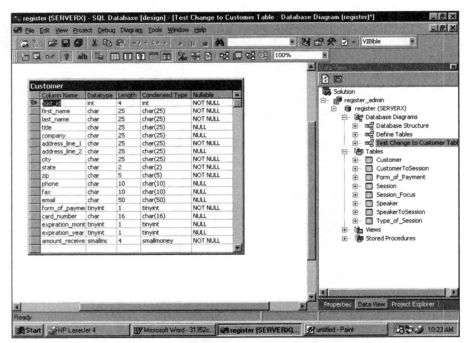

Figure 19-10: Here's the custom view that matches the definition in Figure 19-8.

Creating Database Objects

Now that you have a database and a database diagram, you are ready to create your first table. The process of creating a table consists of these five steps:

1. Create a new table.
2. Define a primary key.
3. Create a relationship between two tables.
4. Create an index.
5. Define a constraint.

Creating a new table

Now continue the "Creating a Database Diagram" exercise you started earlier in this chapter. You'll use the information in Appendix A to create the Customer table in the sample Register database. Follow these steps to create a table in the current database diagram:

1. In the open database diagram pane, right-click a blank area outside a Table and click New Table on the shortcut menu. The Choose Name dialog box appears.

2. Enter the name of the table, and then click OK. For this example, enter **Customer**. A blank Column Properties view, like the one you see in Figure 19-11, appears.

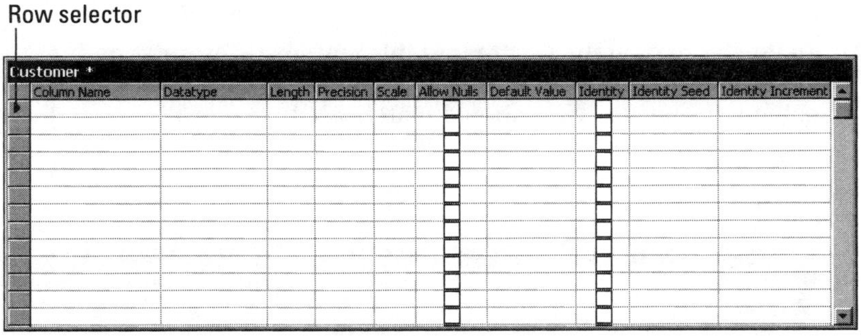

Row selector

Figure 19-11: Here's the blank Column Properties view you use to define a new table.

3. In the first row of the Column Name column, enter the name of the first column in the table. For this example, enter **cust_id**, which is the first column in the Customer table. Press the Tab key to move to the next column, Datatype. Database Designer automatically enters char in the Datatypes column and 10 in the length column.

4. In the Datatype column, enter **int**, the data type of the cust_id column, or select int from the drop-down list. Press the Tab key to move to the next column, Length.

5. In the Length column, enter **4**, and then press the Tab key.

Tip   Before you can save a new table, at a minimum, you must enter values for the column name, data type, and length column properties for all rows.

6. In the Precision column, enter **0**. The default value is 10. Press the Tab key.

7. In the Scale column, the default value is 0. Press the Tab key.

8. In the Allow Nulls column, click the check box to remove the check. When the check box is clear, NULLs are not allowed. When the check box is checked, NULLs are allowed. Press the Tab key.

9. In the Default column, press the Tab key. When you enter a default value that is a text string, enclose the value in single quotes; 'TBA' is an example.

10. In the Identity column, make sure there's a check in the box. Database Designer automatically assigns the value of 1 to the Identity Seed and Identity Increment columns.

    We are finished entering the column properties for the first column of this table, cust_id. You are not able to enter the primary key, foreign key, index, or constraint information in this series of steps because they are not column properties. You'll find out how to define them later in this chapter.

11. To finish creating the Customer table, enter the information for each of the other columns in the Custom table in Appendix A. When you finish, the column properties view should match what you see in Figure 19-12.

Primary key indicator

Column Name	Datatype	Length	Precision	Scale	Allow Nulls	Default Value	Identity	Identity Seed	Identity Increment
cust_id	int	4	10	0			✓	1	1
first_name	char	25	0	0					
last_name	char	25	0	0					
title	char	25	0	0	✓				
company	char	25	0	0	✓				
address_line_1	char	25	0	0					
address_line_2	char	25	0	0	✓				
city	char	25	0	0					
state	char	2	0	0					
zip	char	5	0	0					
phone	char	10	0	0	✓				
fax	char	10	0	0	✓				
email	char	50	0	0	✓				
form_of_payment	tinyint	1	3	0					
card_number	char	16	0	0	✓				
expiration_month	tinyint	1	3	0	✓				
expiration_year	tinyint	1	3	0	✓				
amount_received	smallmoney	4	10	4					

Figure 19-12: Enter all of these column properties to define the Customer table.

Because you're probably getting concerned about saving your work, here's a tip. Before you click Save on the File menu, skip ahead to the section called "Saving Your Changes." This section explains the options Database Designer offers you for handling database changes. When you're ready, return to Step 12 and create the remaining database tables.

12. Repeat steps 1 through 11 for the CustomerToSession, Session, SpeakerToSession, Speaker, Form_of_Payment, Type_of_Payment, and Session_Focus tables. Don't forget to save your work.

Save time when you need to define one or more columns that are the same as columns you previously defined. Select the row with the column properties you plan to copy. On the Edit menu, click Copy. Select the row in the new table where you want to place these column properties. On the Edit menu, click Paste. It's important to note that you copied only the column properties. You did not copy data in the database.

Defining a primary key

Continue the "Creating a Table" exercise you started in the last section. To define a primary key for a table in your database diagram, follow these steps:

1. Select the row or rows you want to define as the primary key. To continue defining the Customer table, select the cust_id row.

2. On the Edit menu, select Set Primary Key. A small key, as shown in Figure 19-12, appears at the beginning of the row to indicate the columns that are part of the primary key for a table. In addition, Database Designer automatically creates a primary key index.

3. Repeat these steps for each table in the database. Remember to save your work.

Creating a relationship

After you define the primary keys for all the tables in this database diagram, you can create relationships between the tables. To do this, you relate the primary key column in the first table to a matching column in the second table. In this example, the value in the Foreign Key column in the tables in Appendix A is the table name where the column is a primary key. Use this information to define the relationships in the Register database.

Now continue with the exercise started in the "Creating a Primary Key" section. To create a relationship between two tables in your database diagram, follow these steps:

1. Position the two tables in the database diagram pane so that you can see the primary key columns in the first table and the title bar and a few columns in the second table. In the Register database, do this with the Customer table and the CustomerToSession table.

2. Select the primary key column(s) in the first table. In the example, select the `cust_id` column in the Customer table.

3. With the mouse pointer over the row selector for the primary key in the first table, drag the pointer to the second table. For this example, drag the row selector of the `cust_id` column in the Customer table and drop it on the title bar of the CustomerToSession table. The Create Relationship dialog box appears.

4. In the Create Relationship dialog box, VI automatically assigns the Relationship name. You can change it if you want. Check that the column and Table names in the Primary key table are correct. Also check that the table name in the Foreign key table column is correct. Finally, select the column name for the Foreign key table from the drop-down list. Click OK to create the relationship. A line connecting the two tables appears in the database diagram, as shown in Figure 19-13. A small key icon appears on the primary key side of the relationship. An infinity symbol appears on the foreign key side of a one-to-many relationship.

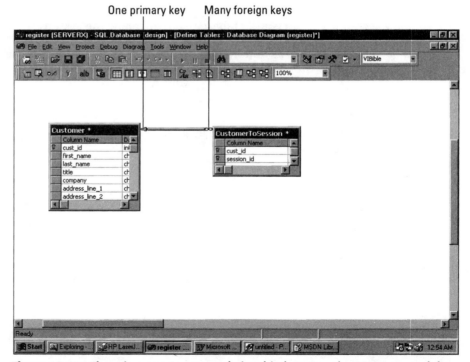

Figure 19-13: There is a one-to-many relationship between the Customer and the CustomerToSession tables.

5. Repeat these steps for each foreign key in the physical database tables shown in Appendix A. Don't forget to save your work.

Creating an index

You've already seen how to create a primary key, the most typical type of index. To define another type of index in a table, continue with the exercise in "Creating Relationships" by following these steps:

1. Select the table you want to index. In this example, select the Customer table.

2. Right-click the table and select Properties from the shortcut menu. The Property Pages dialog box appears.

3. Click the Indexes/Keys tab. Although you have not used this dialog box before, there is an index, PK_Customer, in the list. Database Designer automatically creates an index whenever you define a primary key. The name begins with "PK_" — which stands for primary key — and ends with the table name.

4. Click the New button. Database Designer automatically assigns a name to the new index. This name begins with "IX_" — which stands for index — and ends with the table name. You can change the Index name to something more meaningful, if you like.

5. Under Column name, enter or select first_name and last_name, the names of the columns you want to index.

6. To create a unique index, select the Create UNIQUE check box and the Index option, as shown in Figure 19-14. If you want to allow duplicate values during an update or when adding new data, select the Ignore duplicate keys option.

7. To create a clustered index, select the Create as CLUSTERED check box. Select one of the options to handle ordering the data in the database and one of the options for handling duplicate rows.

8. Close the Properties dialog box. The index is not saved until you save your changes to the database diagram or table.

9. Repeat these steps for each index identified in the physical database tables shown in Appendix A.

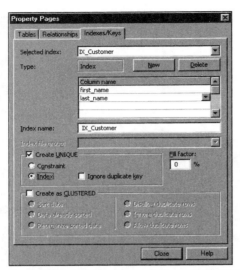

Figure 19-14: It's easy to define a UNIQUE index for a table using the Property Pages.

Defining a constraint

Constraints are a way to have SQL Server check data before adding it to the database. When you want to check a rule before adding data, you can use a check constraint. If all data in a column must be unique, then you can use a unique constraint.

Defining a check constraint

Now continue with the exercise you used in the "Creating an index" section. To define a check constraint for a column in your database diagram, follow these steps:

1. Select the table where you want to define a check constraint. In this example, select the Customer table.

2. Right-click the table and select Properties from the shortcut menu. The Property Pages dialog box appears.

3. Click the Tables tab.

4. Click New button in the CHECK constraint for table and columns section. Database Designer automatically assigns a name to the new check constraint. This name, CK_Customer, begins with CK_ (representing a check constraint)

followed by the table name, and it ends with _x, where x is a sequential number beginning with the number 1, which is assigned to the second check constraint you define. You can change the constraint name to something more meaningful, if you like, as long as it is unique.

5. In the Constraint expression box, enter the Transact-SQL expressions for the check constraints.

   In this example, enter this statement to ensure that expiration_month is a value between 1 and 12:

   ```
   expiration_month >= 1 AND expiration_month <= 12
   ```

6. Click New and in the Constraint expression box, enter this statement to ensure that expiration_year is a value between 0 and 99, as shown in Figure 19-15:

   ```
   expiration_year >= 0 AND expiration_year <= 99
   ```

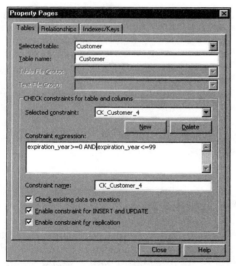

Figure 19-15: You can define a CHECK constraint for a table using the Property Pages.

7. Close the Property Pages dialog box. The check constraints are not saved until you save your changes to the database diagram or table.

8. Repeat these steps for each check constraint identified in the physical database tables shown in Appendix A.

Defining a unique constraint

To define a unique constraint for a column in your database diagram, follow these steps:

Note

We have no example for a unique constraint because the Register database does not have one.

1. Select the table where you want to define a unique constraint.

2. Right-click the table and select Properties from the shortcut menu. The Property Pages dialog box appears.

3. Click the Index/Keys tab.

4. Click the New button. Database Designer automatically assigns a name to the new index. This name begins with "IX_" and ends with the table name. You can change the name to something more meaningful, if you like, as long as it is unique.

5. Under Column name, enter or select the names of the columns where you want to define the unique constraint.

6. Click the Create UNIQUE check box.

7. Select the Constant option.

8. Close the Property Pages dialog box. The index is saved when you save your changes to the database diagram or table.

Tip

If you want to control the sort order of the data values and how to handle duplicate keys, use a unique index rather than a unique constraint.

Modifying Database Objects

During and after a development effort, you may have to add additional features to the application and/or make changes to the features already implemented. These changes may result in changes to the structure of the database. For example, you could add a column to a table or delete an existing table.

Although this section addresses how to make these types of changes to the structure of the database and database objects, you will also need to ensure that these changes are also made to the data in the database as a separate step. Database Designer generates the SQL script to handle all of the changes you make in a database diagram. When a database contains a large volume of data, executing the change script may take a long time. Consequently, you'll need to test your changes to the data structure rather than gather the SQL change script and run it at a time convenient to the users of the database and production.

Inserting a column

Follow these steps to insert a column in a table:

1. Select the table in the database diagram. Set the view to show the column names and properties.

2. Select the row containing the column name where you want to insert a new column.

3. Right-click the row and select Insert Column from the shortcut menu. VI adds a blank row above the row you selected.

4. Now enter values for the properties of that new column.

Deleting a column

Follow these steps to delete a column from a table:

1. Select the table in the database diagram. Set the view to show the column names.

2. Select the row containing the column name you want to delete.

This command takes effect immediately. There is no dialog box to confirm the action. You cannot undo a delete column from the Edit menu.

3. Right-click the row and select Delete Column from the shortcut menu. VI deletes the column.

Removing a table from a database diagram

Follow these steps to remove a table from a database diagram:

1. Select the table in the database diagram.

2. Right-click the table and select Remove Table from Diagram from the shortcut menu. If you have made changes to the table, VI prompts you to save the changes.

Deleting a table from a database

Follow these steps to delete a table from a database:

1. Select the table in the database diagram.
2. Right-click the table and select Delete Table from Database from the shortcut menu. A confirmation dialog box appears.
3. Click Yes to permanently delete the table from the database.

Deleting a relationship

Follow these steps to delete a relationship from a database:

1. Select the relationship line in the database diagram.
2. On the Edit menu, click Delete Relationship from Database. A confirmation dialog box appears.
3. Click Yes to permanently delete the relationship from the database.

Modifying and/or deleting a table property

The properties of a table consist of the definitions for the primary key, indexes, and constraints. You can modify the definitions of each of these types of items from the dialog box. To delete these items, simply clear the contents of the fields used to define them. You cannot delete a relationship within the Property dialog box.

Saving Your Changes

Perhaps you need to experiment with the physical design of the database. In some cases, you'll want to keep the changes you made. But you may find a change undesirable and want to discard it without impacting the database on the server. Perhaps you don't have permission to modify the structure of the database or you can only make the changes during off-production hours. We explain how Database Designer allows you to do all of these things.

Recognizing when you have not saved changes

If a database diagram contains unsaved changes, an asterisk (*) appears in the title bar after the name of the diagram. When you save the diagram, the asterisk disappears. When you change a database object in a table or a database diagram, an asterisk (*) appears in the title bar of the table after the name (see Figure 19-16). When you save the table or the diagram, the asterisk disappears.

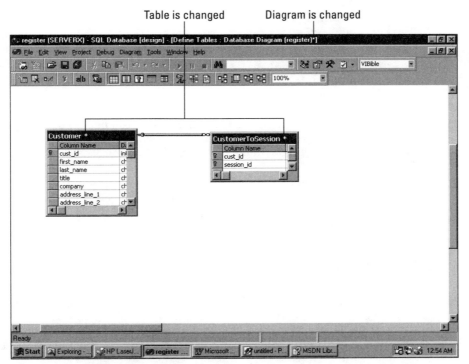

Figure 19-16: You can tell if a diagram or table has change by the * after the name.

Saving diagram changes

If you want to save all the changes you made and permanently update the database on the server, follow these steps:

1. Select the database diagram and then on the File menu, click Save *<database diagram name>*.

2. If this is the first time you've saved the database diagram, the Save As dialog box appears. Enter the name for the database diagram and click OK.

3. If any of the tables in the database diagram had unsaved changes, the Save dialog box appears. Review the list of tables to save to the database. To save a copy of the list of tables to a file, click Save Text File. A message box shows you the name of the text file. Click OK.

4. Click Yes to update the tables on the database server.

Saving table changes

If you want to save the changes to one or more tables and permanently update the database on the server, follow these steps:

1. Select the tables you want to save.

2. On the File menu, click Save Selection.

3. In the Save dialog box, review the list of tables that will be saved to the database. To save a copy of the list of tables to a file, click Save Text File. A message box shows you the name of the text file. Click OK.

Note

Database Designer saves these text files in the working directory for this project, with the default filename DbDgm*x*.txt, where *x* is a sequential number.

4. Click Yes to update the tables on the database server.

Deciding not to save changes

If you decide not to save your changes to the database diagram, you can get rid of your changes without impacting the database on the server. If you have more than one database diagram open and you wish to save the changes in any of them, follow the instructions for saving changes in this section. Close the database diagrams you save. If you wish to get rid of changes you made without impacting the database on the server, follow these steps:

1. Display the database diagram with the changes you wish to discard in the right pane.

2. On the File menu, click Close.

3. A dialog box appears, asking if you want to save changes to the diagram. Click No.

4. If your changes affected other tables, the Unsaved Changes Exit dialog box appears. Click No.

5. Even though you closed the database diagram, changes you made remain in memory. To ensure these changes in memory do not affect other database diagrams, return to step 1 and repeat these steps for each open database diagram.

Saving SQL change scripts

With Database Designer, you visually make changes to the database in memory. Rather than save the changes to the database on the server, you may want to save a SQL change script so that you or another person can edit and run it at a later time using isql, the MS SQL Server command-line utility. You may want to save a SQL change script first and then save the database diagram updating the database on the server. In this case, you could use the SQL change script as a permanent record of the changes you made or use it later to create an identical database. Whatever your specific needs, follow these steps to create an SQL change script:

1. On the File menu, click Save Change Script.

2. In the Save Change Script dialog box, click Yes, as shown in Figure 19-17.

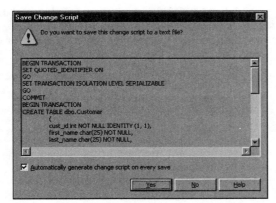

Figure 19-17: Choose Save Change Script to keep a permanent record of changes to the database.

3. A message box shows you the name of the Save Change Script file. Click OK.

4. A message box shows you the name of the file. Click OK.

Other Database Issues

Now that you have created the structure for a database, you should create a backup copy. Typically, during the construction and testing phases, you'll identify changes you want to make to the structure of the database. Be sure you have made a backup copy of the database before you change the structure. If something happens to the database, if, for instance, you save some major changes when you meant to discard them, you can restore the database using your backup copy. At some point in the development process, the database structure will stabilize. If it doesn't, we recommend you consider freezing the structure for the current version of the application, or you risk missing your scheduled completion date. Negotiating a compromise between feature content, resources, and the schedule are normal challenges for software development projects.

Summary

So was that great, or what! You really covered a lot of material in this chapter. In this chapter, you learned:

✦ How to create a logical data model based on a functional analysis of the conference registration sample application. You identified entities, attributes, and relationships. You learned basic data modeling rules, which you used to revise the logical database model.

✦ How to produce a physical database design using the logical model and the reference material in Microsoft SQL Server 6.5. In the design, you identified each table in the database with column names and the attributes for each column.

✦ How to use the Database Designer, one of the Visual Database Tools, to create a database diagram and all the tables in the database.

✦ The three options for handling the changes you can make to a database.

✦ How to save your work and immediately update the database on the server.

✦ How to discard your work and not affect the database on the server.

✦ How to save the SQL Change Script generated by your changes and apply them to the database at a later time.

✦ How to create a primary key for each table, relationships between the tables, table indexes, and constraints.

✦   ✦   ✦

Database Queries

The Visual Database Tool you work with in this chapter is Query Designer. With this tool you can create and run queries that retrieve data from any Open Database Connectivity (ODBC)-compliant database. In addition to querying a database, if you have the right permissions, you can insert, update, and delete the data in the database.

First you will learn the basics of Query Designer and create a simple query. Then you'll create more advanced queries that include expressions, table joins, sorting the results, aggregating data, grouping the results, and parameterized queries. Because queries don't work well without data in the database, you'll learn how to add test data to your databases by working with the sample Registration database that you created in Chapter 18. As often happens, you'll make mistakes and learn how to correct them. Finally, you'll work with the other types of queries, such as insert, make table, update, and delete to load data.

Understanding Query Designer

Query Designer is a very powerful tool that lets you create a wide variety of Structured Query Language (SQL) queries quickly and easily. Before creating your first query, you need to understand how to work with Query Designer. This section discusses these topics:

- ✦ Query Designer windows
- ✦ Toolbar buttons
- ✦ Query window basics
- ✦ Query execution
- ✦ Working with Save queries

Query Designer windows

The Query Designer user interface consists of the four panes shown in Figure 20-1:

✦ **Diagram** — The diagram pane shows the input sources, either tables or views, you use in the query. Each input source appears in its own window along with the name of the input source, the names of the columns, and an icon indicating how the column is used in the query. Joins appear as lines connecting the input source windows.

✦ **Grid** — In the grid pane, you specify the options for the query, including which columns, the sort order for each column, how to group the results, and any selection criteria.

✦ **SQL** — The SQL for the current query appears in the SQL pane. You can edit these SQL statements or enter your own.

✦ **Results** — The results of the most recently executed query appear in the Results pane. You can edit the data in the cells, add new rows, and delete rows.

Diagram pane   Grid pane

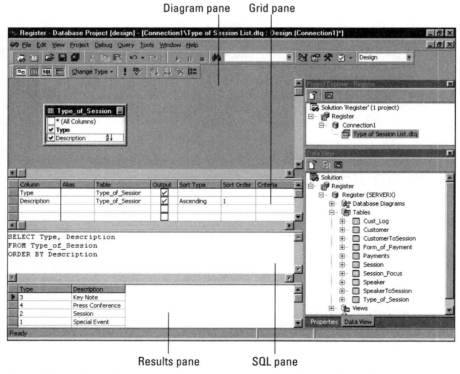

Results pane   SQL pane

Figure 20-1: Query Designer's user interface consists of these four windowpanes.

Toolbar buttons

Table 20-1 explains how to use each button on the Query Designer toolbar.

<table>
<tr><th colspan="3">Table 20-1
Query Designer Toolbar Buttons</th></tr>
<tr><th>Button</th><th>Name</th><th>Click to</th></tr>
<tr><td></td><td>Show Diagram Pane</td><td>Toggle between showing and hiding the Diagram pane.</td></tr>
<tr><td></td><td>Show Grid Pane</td><td>Toggle between showing and hiding the Grid pane.</td></tr>
<tr><td>SQL</td><td>Show SQL Pane</td><td>Toggle between showing and hiding the SQL pane.</td></tr>
<tr><td></td><td>Show Results Pane</td><td>Toggle between showing and hiding the Results pane.</td></tr>
<tr><td>Change Type ▾</td><td>Change Type</td><td>Convert the current query to a one of these types of queries, while keeping as much of the current query as possible:
Select
Insert
Insert Value
Update
Delete
Make Table</td></tr>
<tr><td>!</td><td>Run Query</td><td>Execute the current query or stored procedure.</td></tr>
<tr><td>SQL ✓</td><td>Verify SQL Syntax</td><td>Determine if the syntax of the SQL statement is correct for the database. A message appears if there is a syntax error.</td></tr>
<tr><td>A↓Z</td><td>Sort Ascending</td><td>Add the selected column(s) to the Grid pane with Ascending in the Sort By column.</td></tr>
<tr><td>Z↓A</td><td>Sort Descending</td><td>Add the selected column(s) to the Grid pane with Descending in the Sort By column.</td></tr>
<tr><td></td><td>Remove Filter</td><td>Remove the search conditions defined for the selected column(s) in the input source pane.</td></tr>
<tr><td></td><td>Group by</td><td>Toggle between showing and not showing the Group By column in the Grid pane.</td></tr>
</table>

Tip

To move from one pane to another, simply click anywhere in the pane you want to use, press F6, or press Shift+F6.

Query window basics

Whether you prefer to point and click or type, Query Designer has something for you. You create a query by working in one, two, or three of the four panes (Diagram, Grid, SQL, and Results). Because these panes are synchronized, when you make changes in one pane, Query Designer automatically updates the other two panes with the same changes. Once you make a change to the query, Query Designer dims the Result pane to indicate that it is not synchronized with the three query panes.

When you work in the Diagram and Grid panes, you can create select, insert, update, and delete queries automatically. In the SQL pane, you have the full power of the SQL language at your fingertips. The SQL pane, which is a SQL editor, formats your SQL statements as you enter them. If you change focus to another pane, Query Designer parses your SQL statements and attempts to update the Diagram and Grid panes. If you enter a SQL statement that Query Designer can't represent graphically in the Diagram and Grid panes, Query Designer dims those panes to indicate that they are not synchronized with the SQL pane.

Note

We do not teach you SQL in this book. If you would like more detailed information on writing SQL statements for your database, we recommend reading *SQL for Dummies*, author published by IDG Books Worldwide.

Although one or more of the panes is dimmed, in most cases, you can still work in that pane. You can scroll and modify the query or results. If a change you make creates a query that Query Designer can represent graphically, those panes are no longer dimmed.

You can use Query Designer in full-screen mode to get access to the most screen space possible. To get into full-screen mode, click Full Screen on the View menu. Query Designer appears along with the menu bar. A toolbar containing the Full Screen button and the Data View window float above the Query Designer panes. To get out of full-screen mode, click the Full Screen button on the toolbar or click Full Screen on the View menu.

Query execution

Once you create your query, you can run it in Query Designer. As long as it returns results, you will see the results in the Results pane. Even if your query retrieves a large number of rows, you'll start seeing your results right away because Query Designer runs the query incrementally. If your query does a Delete, Insert, or Update, you won't see data in the Result pane, but you will receive a message stating how many rows your query affected.

Working with a saved query

The two basic ways to work with a saved query are by working on the design of the query or by running the query.

Working on the design

To modify the SQL statements behind a query, open the query in Design mode by right-clicking the name of the query in Project Explorer and selecting Design on the shortcut menu. The Query Designer panes appear exactly as they were when you last saved the query.

Running the query

If you just want to see the results of the query, open the query by double-clicking the name of the query in Project Explorer or right-clicking it and selecting Open on the shortcut menu. The Results pane appears and the results set displays row by row as VI runs the query.

Creating Simple Select Queries

In this section, you create a simple select query using Query Designer. To do this, you need to add a new query to a database project or to a Web project that has a data connection. You then add an input source to the select query and select the data columns in the input sources to include in the results set. Then, you save and run the query, and view the results. The following sections take you through this process.

Getting started

A query can be created in a database project or in a Web project that has a data connection. Although you can add a query to any existing database project, in the following exercises, you use a new database project.

For these exercises, you work with the sample Register database provided on the companion CD-ROM. If you haven't already done so, install the sample Register database before continuing. Instructions for installing it are found in Chapter 18.

After installing the sample Register database, follow these steps to create a query:

1. Open a database project or a Web project with a data connection.

2. In Project Explorer, select the data connection.

3. Right-click the data connection and click Add Query on the shortcut menu. The Add Item dialog appears.

4. Enter the name of the query. For this example, enter **Type of Session List**, as shown in Figure 20-2.

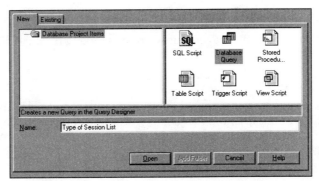

Figure 20-2: To create a new database query, click Add Query and enter the name of the new query.

5. Click Open. Query Designer appears with four blank panes and the Type of Session List query appears in Project Explorer below the connection.

Selecting the input sources

An input source for a query is a table or a view. Before you can work with the data in the input source, you must first place it in the Diagram pane. In this section, you continue with the exercise begun in "Getting started."

In Data View, select one or more of the tables and drag them to the open Diagram pane. For this example, drag the Type_of_Session table to the Diagram pane of the `Type of Session List` query. A window appears in the Diagram pane for the Type_of_Session table and a shell set of SQL select statements appears in the SQL pane, as shown in Figure 20-3. By default, the type of query is a select query. We discuss how to create the other types of queries later in this chapter.

Selecting data columns

After you add a table to the Diagram pane, you must add individual columns from the table to the query. You can display column in the query results, sort by it, select by it, or summarize it. Wherever you can use a column, you can also use an expression. You'll learn more about expressions later in this chapter. Query Designer lets you add individual columns or all of the columns to a query.

Shell SQL select statements

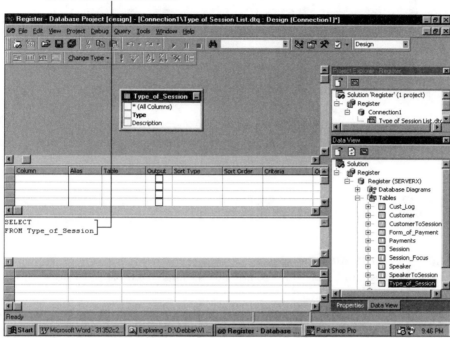

Figure 20-3: If you add a table to the Diagram pane, Query Designer creates these SQL statements.

Adding individual columns

Working with the exercise from the section "Selecting the Input Sources," use one of these three methods to add the `Type` column to the query:

Method 1	In the Diagram pane, click the checkbox to the left of the data column you want to include in the query.
Method 2	In the Diagram pane, select one or more data columns and drag them to the Column column in the Grid pane.
Method 3	In the Grid pane, click in the first empty cell in the Column column and select a data column from the drop-down box.

Figure 20-4 shows how Query Designer looks after you add one data column to a query, no matter which of the three methods you use. Remember that Query Designer keeps the panes synchronized. In the Diagram pane, a check appears to the left of the data column you added to the query. In the Grid pane, a row appears in the grid for the data column you added. In the SQL pane, the select statement includes the data column you added.

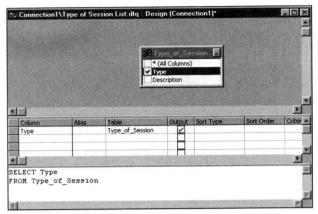

Figure 20-4: This is how Query Designer looks after one data column has been added to a query.

Adding all columns in a table

Use one of these three methods to add all columns in a table to a query:

Method 1 In the Diagram pane, click the check box to the left of * (All Columns).

Method 2 In the Diagram pane, select * (All Columns) and drag it to the Column column in the Grid pane.

Method 3 In the SQL pane, enter `table_name.*` in the Select statement, where *table_name* is the name of your table. For example, to include all columns in the Type_of_Session table in the output, enter this SQL statement:

```
SELECT Type_of_Session.*
FROM Type_of_Session
```

Figure 20-5 shows how Query Designer looks after you add all data columns to a query, no matter which method is used to add all data columns. Remember that Query Designer keeps the panes synchronized. In the Diagram pane, a check appears to the left of the data column you added to the query. In the Grid pane, a row appears in the grid for the data column you added. In the SQL pane, the select statement includes the data column you added.

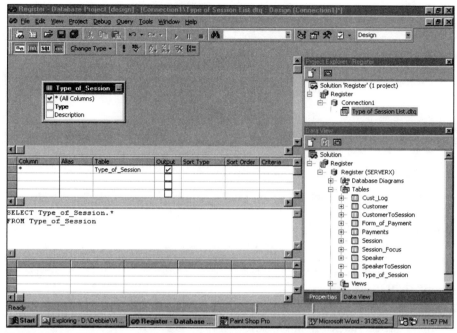

Figure 20-5: This is how Query Designer looks after all data columns have been added to a query.

Saving a query

To save the query, click Save *<query name>* on the File menu or click the Save button on the VI toolbar.

Enter the name and location of the file the query is stored in. It is not stored in the database. This query file contains the layout of the Query Designer panes in addition to the SQL statement. The name of the query appears under the database connection node for the project in Project Explorer.

Verifying, running, and stopping a query

When you are finished creating your query, you can run it to retrieve data from the database. If you entered the SQL statements in the SQL pane and would like to check the syntax of your SQL statements, you can verify the query. If your query is running for a long time, or if you would like to stop it for any reason, you can stop the query.

Verifying a query

Use one of these two methods to verify the SQL statements in the SQL pane:

Method 1	On the Query menu, click Verify SQL Syntax.
Method 2	Click the Verify SQL Query button on the Query Designer toolbar.

Running a query

Use one of these two methods to run your query:

Method 1	On the Query menu, click Run.
Method 2	Click the Run button on the Query Designer toolbar.

When you run a query, the results appear in the Results pane. To learn about working in the Results pane, go to the "Getting the Results" section. Even if the query returns a large number of rows, you don't have to wait until all of the data is retrieved to begin seeing the results. Query Designer begins showing you the results right away.

If you ran a Delete, Insert, or Update query, a message box appears and displays the number of rows that were impacted by your query.

Query Options

To display the Options dialog, click Options on the Tools menu. On the Data View tab under Data Tools, you can set these three query options:

✦ Maximum number of rows to return for any query run in Design View. The range of possible values is from 1 to 9999 rows. The default is 500 rows.

✦ Number of seconds a SQL query runs before it is canceled. The range of possible values is from 1 to 65,535 seconds (18.2 hours). The default is 30 seconds.

✦ Number of seconds VI attempts to login to the database before it is canceled. The range of possible values is from 1 to 65,535 seconds (18.2 hours). The default is 15 seconds.

Stopping a query

Because the query starts displaying results right away, you may notice the results are not what you expected. To stop the query, use one of these two methods:

Method 1	Right-click the Results pane and click Clear Results on the shortcut menu.

Method 2	Run a new query.

Getting the results

Once you run a select query, you can view and print the results. If the results are not correct, you can clear the Result pane and run another query.

Clearing results

When you enter a new query, Query Designer dims the Result pane to indicate the contents do not match the current query. To clear the content of the Result pane, right-click the Result pane and click Clear Results from the shortcut menu.

Viewing results

Use one or more of these four methods to view the data in the Results pane:

Method 1	Use the vertical and horizontal scroll bars.
Method 2	Use the mouse to move to a specific cell or press the navigation keys such as Tab, PgUp, PgDn, Home, End, right arrow, left arrow, up arrow, down arrow, etc.
Method 3	Right-click the Result pane and on the shortcut menu, click First, Last, Next, Previous, or Row to display a specific row.
Method 4	Click the Edit menu, then point to Go to Row and click First, Last, Next, Previous, or Row to display a specific row.

Printing results

The content of the Results pane can be copied to the clipboard and pasted in another Windows program where you can format and print it. The Query Designer separates the columns with Tab characters and the rows with the carriage return and linefeed characters.

Follow these steps to print the results of a query:

1. In the Results pane, select the data values you wish to print.
2. Copy these values to the clipboard by using Ctrl+C or by clicking Copy on the Edit menu.
3. Switch to the Windows program you intend to use for printing.
4. Paste these values in the other Windows program by using Ctrl+V or by clicking Paste on the Edit menu.
5. In the Windows program being used for printing, format and print the results.

More Advanced Select Queries

Although you may occasionally create a simple select query to display all the columns in a table, it is more likely that you'll create more complex queries that use expressions and joined tables, as well as that sort, aggregate, filter, and group the rows of data. This section discusses how to use Query Designer to include each of these SQL features in your select queries.

Deriving data using expressions

A basic data-modeling rule is to not include derived data in a model. As a result, you may also not include that derived data in the physical database. To view derived data, you use an expression. You can use an expression in a query in all the same ways you use a column. You can display the data values resulting from an expression, sort by the values of an expression, and search using an expression.

Text concatenation, the math operators +, -, *, and /, and functions are used to build an expression. A name can be assigned to the expression by using the Alias column in the Grid pane.

The following is an example of a text concatenation expression with an alias. The Customer Table has First_Name and Last_Name columns, rather than a Full_Name column that contains both the first and last name. When you need to view the full name in a query, you simply create an expression that combines the two columns with a space between the column aliases. Here's the SQL query:

```
SELECT (first_name + ' ' + last_name) AS Name
FROM Customer
```

Note   For text concatenation, enter a + in the Grid pane. Query Designer converts it to the specific concatenation operator your database recognizes. When you enter an expression directly in the SQL pane, use the specific concatenation operator your database recognizes. For functions, refer to your database's documentation to determine which functions it supports.

Joining tables

To include data from more than one table in a query, you must join the tables. A virtual table is the result of joining two tables and contains data from both tables. When you join three tables, a virtual table results from the first two tables, and that virtual table combines with the third table to form the final virtual table. You designate columns from all joined tables to include in the result set. This section describes the different types of joins and how Query Designer displays them, and then you create a query using a join.

Classifying the types of joins

The type of join establishes the data that appears in the results set. Joins come in these two basic flavors:

✦ **Inner Join** — This is the default join in the Query Designer. This type of join displays rows of data that have matches in both tables being joined. For example, joining the Customer table with the Type of Payment table displays only the rows from the customer table with a value in the type of payment column and only the rows from the Type of Payment table with values in the Customer table. You create a join using this example later in this section.

✦ **Outer Join** — This type of join displays rows of data even if there is no match between the tables used in the join. In an outer join, the first table is called the left table and the second table is called the right table. These are the three types of outer joins:

- **Left Outer Join** — All rows in the left table are included in the results set, even if there is no match in the second table. If a row in the second table does not have a match in the first table, it is not included.

- **Right Outer Join** — All rows in the right table are included in the results set, even if there is no match in the first table. If a row in the first table does not have a match in the second table, it is not included.

- **Full Outer Join** — All rows in both tables are included in the results set.

Understanding how Query Designer automatically joins

In Chapter 19, Database Designer was used to define a relationship between two tables by linking a column in one table to the primary key of another table. When you add more than one table to a query, Query Designer tries to determine if the tables are related by checking these three conditions:

✦ Do both tables contain a column with the same name, the same data type, and is one column the primary key in one of the tables

✦ Does the database contain information that indicates that the tables are related

✦ Can you create a search condition that looks for the same value in a column with the same name in both tables

If one of these conditions is satisfied, Query Designer automatically joins the two tables. If the join created by Query Designer is not what you need for the query, you may change it or delete it.

Displaying a join

Figure 20-6 shows Session and Session_Focus in the Diagram pane of a query. The line connecting these two tables indicates that these two tables are joined. The primary key for Session_Focus is the Focus column, which is identical to the Focus column, also known as a foreign key, in the Session table.

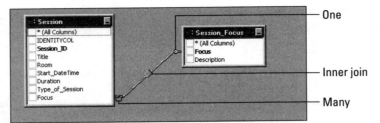

Figure 20-6: The Design pane shows that the Session and Session_Focus tables are joined.

The ends of the join line connect the columns involved in the join definition. If one of the columns is not included in the query, the join line connects to the title bar of the table. Query Designer displays a join line for each relationship between two tables. A key symbol represents the one side of a one-to-one or one-to-many relationship. An infinity symbol represents the many side of a one-to-many relationship. No symbol appears on the end of a join line when Query Designer is not able to determine the type of join.

Figure 20-7 shows the data in the Session table.

Session_ID	Title	Focus
2	10th Anniversary Dinner Party	<NULL>
3	Hot Travel Destinations in SE Asia	1
4	Tax Issues for Travel Industry	2
5	Internet Travel Sites & You	2
6	Press Conference	<NULL>

Figure 20-7: Session table data

Figure 20-8 shows the data in the Session_Focus table.

Focus	Description
1	Travel
2	Business
3	Computer
4	New Age

Figure 20-8: Session_Focus table data

Figure 20-9 shows the results of the query from the two tables joined. The sessions with no focus do not appear in the join query and the focus with no matching session also does not appear in the join query.

Figure 20-9: The query result from an inner join only includes matching data from the Session table and the Session_Focus table.

Title	Description
Hot Travel Destinations in SE Asia	Travel
Tax Issues for Travel Industry	Business
Internet Travel Sites & You	Business

Creating a query with a join

In this section, you create a select query based on the data in three tables. You work with the Register database to list each customer and the sessions they registered to attend. Because this involves the Customer and Session tables, you also need to use the CustomerToSession table, which joins them.

Follow these steps to create a select query using more than one table:

1. Create a new query in the database project for the Register database and call it **Three Table Join**.

2. Add the Customer, Session, and CustomerToSession tables to the Diagram pane.

3. In the Diagram pane, select the first_name and last_name columns in the Customer table. Select the title, start_time, and room columns in the Session table. Query Designer adds these columns to the Grid pane.

Tip

If you selected the room column before you selected the start_datetime column, the columns will display in the Result pane out of sequence. To move the start_datetime column before the room column, select the room row in the Grid pane, drag it above the start_datetime row, and drop it.

4. Click the Run button on the Query Designer toolbar. Figure 20-10 shows all four panes for this query.

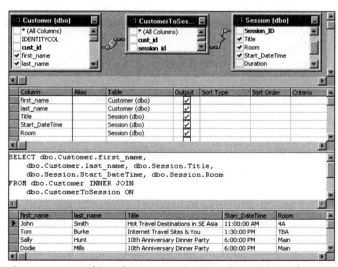

Figure 20-10: This select query shows columns from three tables using Inner Join.

5. Save the query.

Sorting the results

By default, the rows in the result set appear in database order. As a result, the rows need to be sorted in a more meaningful order. In this section, you continue with the example that was started in the previous section and sort the results by the customer's last name. This provides a list of customers and sessions in alphabetical order by last name.

Continue working with the Three Table Join query and follow these steps to sort the rows:

1. In the Grid pane, select the last_name row.

2. Click the cell in the Sort Type column and select the sort sequence, either Ascending or Descending, from the drop-down list box. For this example, select Ascending.

   If you are sorting by more than one column, be sure to specify the sort order for each column.

3. Click the Run button on the Query Designer toolbar. Figure 20-11 shows the select query and the results. The Sort Ascending symbol to the right of last_name in the diagram pane indicates that the data in this column will be sorted in ascending order in the results set.

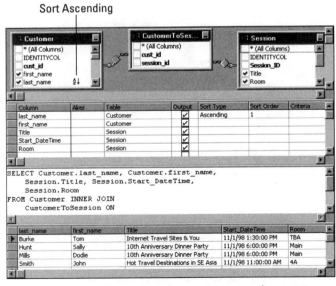

Figure 20-11: Sorting a query is easy—just set the sort type for the columns you want to sort by.

4. Save the query.

Aggregating the results

In the last example, you saw a list of all the customers who registered for the conference. What if this list contained several hundred or more than a thousand customers? You'd probably want to know things such as "How many people are registered?" and "How much money have you received?". You can create a query that aggregates information from more than one row. To do this, you apply one of the functions in Table 20-2 to a column in a query.

	Table 20-2 Aggregation Functions	
Function	**Description**
AVG(exp)	Calculates the average of the values in the column. It ignores NULL in the count.
COUNT(exp), COUNT(*)	Counts the number of non-NULL values in the column. When you want to group the results set, use *, which included NULL values in the count.
MAX	Displays the largest numeric or alphabetic value in the column. It ignores NULL.
MIN	Displays the smallest numeric or alphabetic value in the column. It ignores NULL.
SUM	Calculates the total of the values in the column.

Follow these steps to count the number of non-NULL rows in a table:

1. Create a new query in the database project for the Register database and call it **Attendance Report**.

2. Add the Customer table to the Diagram pane.

3. In the Diagram pane, select the last_name column. Query Designer adds the last_name column to the Grid pane.

4. In the Grid pane, right-click last_name and select Group By from the shortcut menu. A column called Group By appears to the right of the Sort Order column in the Grid pane.

5. In the Group By column, select Count from the drop-down list.

6. Enter a meaningful Alias. For this example, enter **Attendance**.

7. Click the Run button on the Query Designer toolbar. Figure 20-12 shows the select query and the results. Notice the Aggregation symbol to the right of last_name in the Diagram pane. This indicates that an aggregation function is applied to that column.

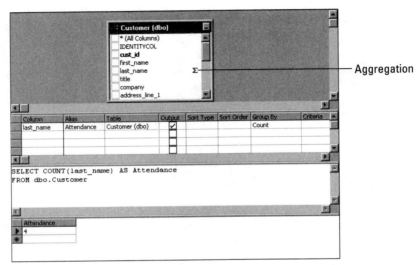

Figure 20-12: This query uses a function in the Group By column of the Grid pane to count all the rows.

8. Save the query.

Grouping the results

The last section showed you how to get Totals, Averages, and Counts for the entire query. This section shows you how to get the same information grouped by the unique values within a column. This is called grouping the results and appears as a GROUP BY clause in an appropriate SQL statement. For example, you could get a list of the States where the customers are located and an attendance count for each State.

Continue using the Attendance Report you created in the "Aggregating the Results" section. Follow these steps to group the attendance by State:

1. Select the State column in the Diagram pane. In the Group By column of the Grid pane, the value Group By is automatically entered for State.

2. In the Grid pane, drag the State column above the last_name column.

3. Click the Run button on the Query Designer toolbar. Figure 20-13 shows the select query and the results. The Group By symbol to the right of State in the Diagram pane indicates that values in this column will be grouped in the results set.

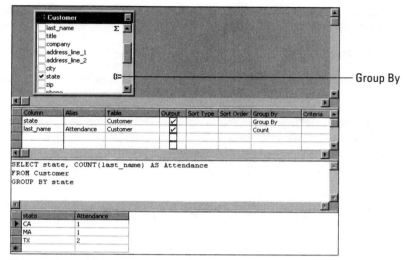

Figure 20-13: This query counts the rows grouped by state.

4. Save the query.

Using filters

To focus on less than all the data in the database, you use a filter, which is also referred to as a search condition. Filters appear as a WHERE clause in a SQL statement. When you run a query containing a filter, the database engine compares each row in the database to the filter and includes only the rows that match the criteria in the results set.

A simple filter consists of these three items:

✦ **filter_expression** — usually the name of the column to filter

✦ **operator** — the math operators are +,-,*, and /, and functions

✦ **filter_value** — the value to search for

Here are a few examples of filters:

✦ To search the customer table for all customers with the last name of Smith, use this:

```
WHERE last_name = 'Smith'
```

✦ To search the Session table for all sessions without a Description, use this:

```
WHERE Description IS NULL
```

✦ To search the customer table for all customers who have not paid their registration fee, use this:

```
WHERE amount_received = 0
```

Follow these steps to apply a filter to the Attendance Report query you began earlier in this chapter:

1. In the Diagram pane, select the last_name column. A row appears in the Grid pane for last_name with the value Group By in the Group By column. Query Designer adds the last_name to the query results.

2. In the Grid pane, drag this row to the top of the Grid pane, making it the first column in the query results.

3. In the first blank row at the bottom of the Grid pane, select last_name in the Column column. Make sure the Output column is not selected. Select Where in the Group By column. Enter = 'Smith' in the Criteria column. This is the filter for the query. It does not appear in the query results.

4. Click the Run button on the Query Designer toolbar. Figure 20-14 shows the select query and the results. Notice the Filter symbol to the right of last_name in the diagram pane. This indicates that values in this column will be filtered in the results set.

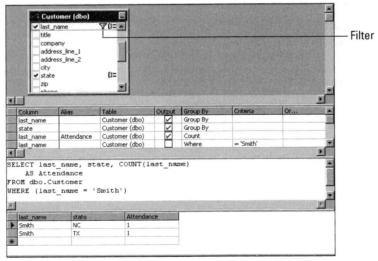

— Filter

Figure 20-14: When you need results for specific data values, use a filter.

5. Save the query as **Attendance Report-Smith**.

Creating a parameter query

The last section showed how to add a filter, or search criteria, to a query when you want to look for data that meets a specific condition. If you want to search for all the customers named Smith, you'd create a query similar to this:

```
WHERE last_name = 'Smith'
```

If you want to search for all the customers named Jones, you'd create another query like this:

```
WHERE last_name = 'Jones'
```

At this rate, you'd need a separate query for each name. Rather than do that, create a query with a parameter of "?" instead of using a specific filter_value. The clause looks like this:

```
WHERE last_name = ?
```

When you run a query with a parameter in Query Designer, the Define Query Parameters dialog box appears prompting you for the value. If you have more than one parameter in the same query, you can use named parameters to distinguish one from the other.

Use the Attendance Report-Smith query you created earlier and follow these steps to add an unnamed parameter to the query:

1. In the Grid pane, in the last_name row with the value of = 'Smith' in the Criteria column, change the value of the Criteria column to = ?.

2. Click the Run button on the Query Designer toolbar. The Define Query Parameters dialog appears.

   Notice the question mark (?) under Parameter Name. This is the unnamed parameter.

3. In the first row of the Parameter Value column, enter **Smith**, as shown in Figure 20-15.

Figure 20-15: Enter any value as the Parameter Value for a Parameter query.

4. Click OK. Figure 20-16 shows the select query and the results.

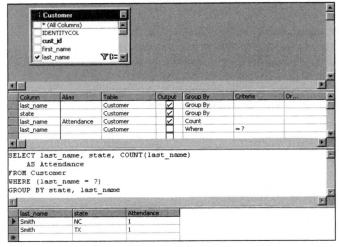

Figure 20-16: A parameter query lets you use one query to return many different results.

5. Save the query as **Attendance Report-Ask**.

Loading Data

Once you create a database, you need to test it to confirm that you defined it correctly. Typically, when it's a new database and your database tool supports it, you might enter a small amount of test data by hand. In this section, you use Query Designer to visually add, change, and delete data from the database.

Once you're sure you've defined the database properly, you can run SQL Insert queries to insert a much larger volume of data. Once that data is in place, the rest of the team can start building and testing Web pages that access the database. In addition to the Insert Query, this section discusses Insert Values Query, Make Table Query, Update Query, and Delete Query.

Results pane

One of the quickest ways to add a small amount of test data is to create a simple select query that includes all columns. After you run the query, you can add the test data directly in the Results pane. In fact, you can add, modify, and delete any data in the database in the Results Pane. Although Query Manager may not be capable of determining whether you have permission to add, create, or modify the data, the database engine can make that determination. If you do not have the proper permission, the database engine displays a message and does not update the database.

Working with the data in a table

You can add and change data in a single table by entering the new data values in the desired cells in the Results pane and saving your changes to the database. Table 20-3 contains a list of Query Designer edit operations and the actions you take to perform each operation.

Table 20-3
Query Designer Edit Operations

Edit Operation	Action
Cancel Changes to a Cell	To cancel your changes to the current cell, press Esc from the cell you changed.
Cancel Changes to a Row	To cancel your changes to the current row, press Esc from a cell on the row you have not changed.
Enter a NULL	Press Ctrl+zero.
Enter currency	When you enter a number, use the format specified in the Regional Settings in the Control Panel.
Enter a date	When you enter a number, use the short form for dates specified in the Regional Settings in the Control Panel.
Enter a number	When you enter a number, use the format specified in the Regional Settings in the Control Panel.
Enter a time	When you enter a number, use the format specified in the Regional Settings in the Control Panel.
Save Changes to a Row	To save changes to a row of data, move to another row in the grid. If you switch panes, Query Designer does not automatically save your changes to the database.

If another person on your team is updating or deleting rows from the database, the row will be locked and you will not be able to edit it.

You cannot edit these types of columns:

✦ binary

✦ BLOB

✦ identity

✦ memo

✦ timestamp

Validating data changes

Query Designer can do some data checking, but it may not stop you from entering invalid data. In any case, when you save a row, the database does check data values before adding them to the database. If data is invalid, the database issues a message and does not add the data to the database. Unfortunately, these error messages are often difficult to understand.

If you are sharing a table with other users, you and the other users could make changes to the same data at the same time. When you save a row in the table, Query Designer compares the version of that row to the same row in the database. If the two versions are different, Query Designer displays a message and offers these alternatives:

1. Save your changes by replacing the row in the database. This basically discards the changes the other user made.

2. Discard the changes you made to the row.

3. Cancel the save and remain on the row with the changes you made. You can create a new query, view the "new" data, compare it to your changes, and decide how to proceed.

Adding test data

Follow these steps to enter the test data in the Form_of_Payment table in the Registration database:

1. Create a new query.

2. Add the Form_of_Payment table to the Diagram pane.

3. Click *(All Columns) in the Form_of_Payment window. Query Designer adds the columns you selected to the Grid pane.

4. Click the Run button on the Query Designer toolbar.

5. In the first row of the grid in the Results pane, enter **1** in the Type column and **Cash** in the Description column. Notice the pencil icon at the beginning of the row you are editing. Press Tab to save this row to the database and add a blank row in the Results pane.

6. In the second row, enter **2** in the Type column and **Check** in the Description column. Press Tab to save this row to the database and add a blank row in the Results pane.

7. Continue entering data values until the Form_of_Payment table contains all the data shown in Figure 20-17. Press Tab on the last row to save the data for that row to the database.

Pencil icon

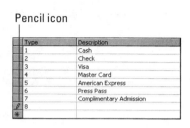

Figure 20-17: You can add rows in the Results pane of a simple select queries.

Changing data

When you identified the specific values for the Form_of_Payment lookup table, you wanted them to be as easy to understand as possible. Consequently, you did not use abbreviations for any of the descriptions. Unfortunately, several of the values are so long that they make the column very wide, too wide for most reports. Now you want to shorten the descriptions from those in Figure 20-17 to those shown in Figure 20-18. The new descriptions are no more than five characters wide.

Type	Description
1	Cash
2	Check
3	Visa
4	MC
5	AmEx
6	Press
7	Comp

Figure 20-18: The shortened descriptions in Form_of_Payment are no more than five characters.

To change the existing values in a table, follow these steps:

1. Create a new query.

2. Add the Form_of_Payment table to the Diagram pane.

3. Click *(All Columns) in the Form_of_Payment window. Query Designer adds the columns you selected to the Grid pane.

4. Click the Run button on the Query Designer toolbar.

5. In the Result Pane, select each cell with the long description and change each to the shorter description, one by one. See Figure 20-18.

6. After you change the value for the last row, click a cell in another row to save the changes to the database.

7. Close the query without saving it.

Deleting data

You can either delete the value in any column, in a row, or you can delete the entire row. To delete the value in a column, press Ctrl+0(zero) to replace the value with a NULL, if the column allows it. If the column does not allow NULL, then you need to determine if there is another way to accomplish your objective. You may need to enter the default value for the column or delete the entire row.

Tip

If a column holds text values and you enter spaces to remove the existing text from view, you are not actually removing the data from the cell. You are just replacing it with space characters. Replace it with NULL (Ctrl+0) instead.

To delete a row of data in a table, follow these steps:

1. Create a new query.

2. Add the table to the Diagram pane.

3. Click *(All Columns) in the table window.

4. Click the Run button on the Query Designer toolbar.

5. In the Result pane, select the row or rows to delete.

6. Press Delete or click Delete on the Edit menu. A message box appears asking you to confirm the delete.

7. Click Yes to delete the selected row(s).

8. Close the query without saving it.

Insert Query

Use an Insert Query to copy data from one table to another. You can also copy data to the same table. An Insert Query uses the INSERT INTO SQL syntax.

You continue working with the Registration database in this section. During the development effort, the team noticed that it needed to move the payment information out of the Customer table. The database administrator created a new table called Payments and you must write the Insert Query to copy the data from the Customer table to the Payments table.

An Insert Query is defined by specifying the source table(s) and the destination table, as well as the source and destination columns in each table. You can also sort, filter, and group the data.

Follow these steps to create an Insert Query:

1. Create a new query and call it **Load Payments**.

2. On the Query Designer Toolbar, select Insert from Change Type. The Insert Into Table dialog appears.

3. Select the destination table from the list of all tables in the data connection. For this example, select Payments, as shown in Figure 20-19. Click OK.

Figure 20-19: When you create an Insert Query, you must select a destination table.

4. Add the source table to the Diagram pane. In this example, add the Customer table to the Diagram pane.

5. Select the columns in the source window. Query Designer adds the columns you select to the Grid pane. For this example, select cust_id, form_of_payment, card_number, expiration_month, expiration_year, amount_received.

6. In the Append column of the Grid pane, select a column in the destination table for each column you selected from the source table. In this example, Query Designer automatically selected the columns because the names of the columns are the same in both tables.

7. Using the same method that you used for the Select Query, specify any sort, filter, and/or Group By information.

8. Click the Run button on the Query Designer toolbar. A message box appears stating how many rows were affected by the Insert Query. (See Figure 20-20.) If an error occurred, a message box appears.

9. Click OK.

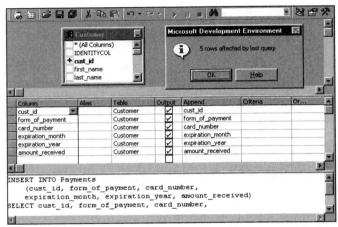

Figure 20-20: When the Insert Query works, you see this message box.

Insert Values Query

With the Insert Values Query, you can add rows to a table. An Insert Values Query uses the INSERT INTO SQL syntax. An Insert Values Query is defined by specifying the table, the columns, and the values to insert.

Follow these steps to create an Insert Values Query:

1. Create a new query.

2. On the Query Designer Toolbar, select Insert Values from Change Type.

3. Add one table to the Diagram pane.

4. Select the columns in the Diagram pane. Query Designer adds the columns to the Grid pane.

5. In the Grid pane, enter the values for each column in the New Value column. Query Designer provides no assistance in formatting the new values so be sure you know what values are valid for each column.

6. Click the Run button on the Query Designer toolbar. A message box appears stating how many rows were affected by the Insert Values Query. If an error occurred, a message box appears.

7. Click OK.

Make Table Query

Make Table Query does exactly what an Insert Query does, but it also creates the destination table. A Make Table Query uses the SELECT...INTO SQL syntax. Unfortunately, not all databases support this syntax.

Make Table Query is defined by specifying the name of the new table and the source table(s), as well as the columns in the source table. You can also sort, filter, and group the data.

Follow these steps to create a Make Table Query:

1. Create a new query.
2. On the Query Designer Toolbar, select Make Table from Change Type. The Make Table dialog appears.
3. Enter the name of the destination table. If the table is not in the current database, enter the fully qualified table name, including the database, owner, and table. Click OK.
4. Add the source table(s) to the Diagram pane.
5. Select the columns in the source window. Query Designer adds the columns you select to the Grid pane.
6. Using the same method that you learned for the Select Query, specify any sort, filter, and/or Group By information.
7. Click the Run button on the Query Designer toolbar. A message box appears stating how many rows were affected by the Make Table Query. If an error occurred, a message box appears.
8. Click OK.

Update Query

Update Query is used to change data in one or more rows. Update Query uses the UPDATE SQL syntax. Update Query is defined by specifying the table, the columns, and the new value or expression to use to update the data. You can also use filter criteria to select the rows to update.

Follow these steps to create an Update Query:

1. Create a new query.
2. On the Query Designer Toolbar, select Update from Change Type.
3. Add one table to update to the Diagram pane.
4. Select the columns in the Diagram pane. Query Designer adds them to the Grid pane.

5. In the New Value column of the Grid pane, enter the new value for the column. You can enter an expression such as `column * .50` to reduce the column value for the selected rows by 50 percent. Query Designer provides no assistance in formatting the new values, so be sure you know what values are valid for each column.

6. Using the same method that you learned for the Select Query, specify any filter criteria.

7. Click the Run button on the Query Designer toolbar. A message box appears stating how many rows were affected by the Update Query. If an error occurred, a message box appears.

8. Click OK.

Delete Query

Delete Query allows you to delete one or more rows from a table. A Delete Query is defined by specifying the table and the filter criteria to select the rows of data to delete from the table.

Follow these steps to create a Delete Query:

1. Create a new query.

2. On the Query Designer Toolbar, select Delete from Change Type.

3. Add one table to the Diagram pane.

4. If you do not wish to delete all rows, enter the filter criteria to select the rows to delete. You can select the column for the filter directly in the Grid pane or drag the column from the Diagram pane to the Grid pane.

5. Click the Run button on the Query Designer toolbar. A message box appears stating how many rows were affected by the Delete Query. If an error occurred, a message box appears.

6. Click OK.

Summary

In this chapter, you took a quick look at Query Designer and learned:

✦ The basic concepts of querying a database using Query Designer. You created and ran queries using single and multiple tables. You sorted, filtered, grouped, and aggregated the data.

✦ That Query Designer consists of four synchronized windows — Diagram, Grid, SQL, and Results — so that when you change one window, VI changes the others to match.

✦ To add input sources to a query by dragging a table name from Data View to the Diagram pane.

✦ To select single and multiple data columns for the query by using either the Diagram pane or the Grid pane.

✦ How to verify SQL statements that you entered in the SQL pane.

✦ How to derive data by using expressions in the query.

✦ How to join tables in the Diagram pane and how to create queries using joined tables.

✦ To sort the results of a query.

✦ To aggregate the results of a query as well as use functions to average, count, and summarize the data.

✦ To group the data results by the unique values in a column.

✦ How to filter out unwanted data and to display just the desired values by using expressions, operators, and filter values.

✦ How to create a parameter query that prompts for one or more values and that filters the results based on your input.

✦ How to manually add new rows of data to a table and how to change values for individual columns as well as delete entire rows. In addition, you learned how to create update, insert, and delete queries to handle larger volumes of data.

✦   ✦   ✦

Advanced SQL Features

This chapter discusses four of SQL's fundamental features: views, stored procedures, triggers, and Structured Query Language (SQL) scripts. These features are so common that you will probably use most of them in every database project you work on. In this chapter, not only will you learn to work with these features in Visual InterDev, but you'll also find out when you need them and why to use them. If you're like most developers, you'll be especially interested in finding out how to debug MS SQL Server's stored procedures and triggers from your own workstation, which is running the Enterprise edition of Visual Studio, because most databases don't support this feature. You'll continue working with the sample Microsoft SQL Server database called Register, which you learned how to install from the companion CD-ROM in Chapter 18. (You can also use the Registration database from Chapters 19 and 20.)

Views

Views are virtual database tables — with rows and columns — that you can use in the same ways you use database tables. For example, you can query a view, see the results set, and even change the data in the database from the results set. However, unlike the database tables, because a view is virtual, it does not physically contain any data. It just looks like it contains data because, when you run a select query against the view, you see data in the Results pane. The data for a view actually resides in a query results set on the server that the database updates whenever you use the view.

Most Open Database Connectivity (ODBC)-compliant databases support views. You create a view with a query, which is then precompiled and stored in the database on the server. As a result, anyone using the database can have access to the views you create and vice versa. Your database may not allow certain clauses, such as ORDER BY, in the SQL statements you use to create a view. Check your database system's documentation to determine what clauses are allowed.

When to use a view

During the detailed design phase of the Web application development effort, you may notice patterns in your report queries. These patterns may be indicators that you should be employing a view instead of a report query. Here are a few situations where you might consider switching:

✦ If you find several queries that join the same tables and select many of the same columns, consider defining one or more standard views for them. In some cases, a view may execute more slowly than if you were to access the tables directly. For high performance production environments, benchmark the two techniques.

✦ If several developers write similar queries that join the same tables each time, you can create those queries faster using views.

✦ If you find yourself needing to limit access by a group of users to certain columns of a database, you can create a view containing just the columns this class of user may access.

Working with View Designer

In this section, View Designer is used to create, save, change, open, and delete views. View Designer is one of the Visual Database Tools and is very similar to Query Designer, which was discussed in Chapter 20. It has the same four panes: Diagram, Grid, SQL, and Results. Table 21-1 describes what each button on the View Designer toolbar does. Because a View is a select query, there is no need to change the type of query in Query Designer.

	Table 21-1	
	Query Designer Toolbar Buttons	
Button	**Name**	**Click to**
	Show Diagram Pane	Toggle between showing and hiding the Diagram pane.
	Show Grid Pane	Toggle between showing and hiding the Grid pane.
	Show SQL Pane	Toggle between showing and hiding the SQL pane.
	Show Results Pane	Toggle between showing and hiding the Results pane.
	Run Query	Execute the current view.
	Verify SQL Syntax	Determine if the syntax of the SQL statement is correct for the database. A message appears if there is a syntax error.

Button	Name	Click to
	Remove Filter	Remove the search conditions defined for the selected column(s) in the input source pane.
	Group By	Toggle between showing and not showing the Group By column in the Grid pane.

Creating views using View Designer

Follow these steps to create a new view:

1. Right-click the Views folder in Data View, and select New View from the shortcut menu, as shown in Figure 21-1. The four panes of View Designer appear.

Figure 21-1: You create a new view from Data View by selecting New View from the shortcut menu.

2. Create a select query just as you would in Query Designer or enter the SQL statements directly in the SQL pane. You can use filter criteria and Group By, but you cannot sort the results in the definition of a view.

   For this example, drag the Customer, Session, and CustomerToSession tables into the Diagram pane. Select last_name and first_name in the Customer window and select title, start_datetime, and room in the Session window.

3. Click the Run button on the View Designer toolbar. The results appear in the Results pane.

4. On the File menu, click Save *<view name>*. When you create a new view, VI automatically gives it the temporary name View*X*, where *X* is a sequential number. The Save New View dialog appears.

5. Enter the view name. For this example, enter **CustSessions**.

Note

Because the view is stored in the database, the name you choose for it must be unique among all database objects. If the name is already used, an error message appears prompting you to use another name.

6. Click OK. The view appears in Data View below the View folder. Open the View to show a list of the columns included in the view, as shown in Figure 21-2.

Figure 21-2: In Data View, you see all the columns that are included in a view.

Testing a view

You can test the view by creating a query that uses the view or by opening the view. In this exercise, you create a query to test the new `CustSessions` view. How to open the view is discussed a bit later. Follow these steps to test a view from a query:

1. Create a new query. For this example, create a query called **Test_CS_View**.

2. Drag the view to the Diagram pane. For this example, drag CustSessions.

3. Select the columns to include in the query. For this example, rather than select *(All Columns), select each column one at a time. Assign an Ascending sort to last_name and then to first_name.

4. Click the Run button on the Query Designer toolbar. Figure 21-3 shows the select query and the results.

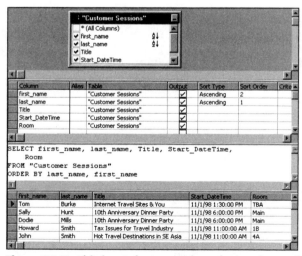

Figure 21-3: This is a select query based on a view rather than on a database table.

5. Close the query without saving it.

Working with views

You can use the Data View window to copy, delete, design, open, and refresh views. You cannot rename a view, but you can copy it to a new name and delete the original view. If you are using Microsoft SQL Server, you can encrypt your views, which is explained in the sidebar. In Data View, right-click the name of the view, then click one of these commands on the shortcut menu:

✦ **Copy** — The SQL statements for the view are copied to the Windows clipboard.

✦ **Delete** — A dialog box asks you to confirm the delete. Click Yes to delete the view.

✦ **Design** — The four View Designer panes appear displaying the definition of the view.

✦ **New View** — The four View Designer panes appear. You will find instructions for creating a View in "Creating Views using View Designer" earlier in this chapter.

✦ **Open** — The view runs and the results appear in the Results pane.

✦ **Refresh** — Occasionally you will need to refresh your list of views, because other members of the development team may add views to the database while you are working. After refreshing, the View folder lists all the views on the database server.

Encrypting a View

If you are using Microsoft SQL Server, you can encrypt your views, which prevents other users from editing or viewing them. When you encrypt a SQL Server view and save it, you will not be able to change the view, so be sure you've made all the changes you want to make before you save the encrypted view.

Follow these steps to encrypt a Microsoft SQL Server view:

1. Open the Design of the view.

2. Right-click in the Grid, SQL, or Results pane and select Properties from the shortcut menu.

3. Select Encrypt view in the Options section.

4. Click Close.

5. Save the view.

Stored Procedures

A stored procedure, a database object, is the SQL equivalent of a compiled program or subroutine. You can use Visual Database Tools to create stored procedures for SQL Server 6.x and higher and Oracle 7.x and higher. You create a file of SQL statements, user-declared variables, and flow-control statements, such as IF statements. Then you compile the file and save it to the database as a stored procedure. Finally, you run it by calling the stored procedure from an application or another stored procedure.

Understanding when to use stored procedures

Because each Web application has unique needs, you must understand the tradeoffs when faced with the decision whether or not to use stored procedures. Table 21-2 lists the advantages and disadvantages of using stored procedures.

Table 21-2	
Advantages and Disadvantages of Using Stored Procedures	
Advantages	*Disadvantages*
Faster SQL execution	Inability to balance load on database server
Reduce network traffic	Loss of portability
Reuse SQL logic	
Produce consistent results	

An SQL statement executes faster as part of a stored procedure because the statement is precompiled, and because most databases optimize the execution of stored procedures to ensure that they run faster. Because the SQL statements in a stored procedure are already on the server, they don't have to be transferred from the client to the server to be run there. This saves time in transferring the file and reduces network traffic.

When an application executes the same SQL statements in a number of places, creating a stored procedure allows multiple areas within the application to share those statements. For example, a good candidate for a stored procedure is a set of business rules for calculating sales commissions. Once the stored procedure is working properly, that code never needs to be written again, resulting in lower maintenance costs. Application quality is higher because the stored procedure always reports the data consistently, no matter which application calls it.

Unfortunately, load balancing, which is what the server administrators do when they move executables to different servers, by reducing the volume of work on one machine and increasing it on another, can become an issue for the database server if a large number of applications run stored procedures. Separating the business logic from the database by using a *three-tier architecture* (see sidebar) is a popular alternative.

Another disadvantage of stored procedures is the loss of portability that occurs when the developer creates a stored procedure that takes advantage of capabilities unique to the database management system (DBMS). Performance improvements and quicker development time are common reasons to incorporate DBMS-specific features in stored procedures.

Three-Tier Architecture

The three-tier architecture evolved from the original two-tier Client/Server (C/S) architecture. As two-tier applications became more sophisticated — for example, utilizing stored procedures to centralize business rules processing on the server — the load on the database server increased. With no way to balance the load on the database server across other servers, architects came up with a third tier. As you can see in Figure 21-4, the three components of this architecture are the client, the transaction or Web server running the business and application logic, and the database server.

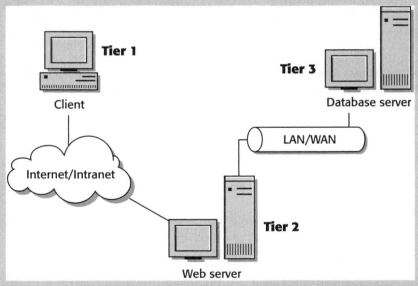

Figure 21-4: The three components of three-tier architecture are the client, the Web server, and the database server.

(continued)

(continued)

By isolating the business and application logic from the database logic, the load on the server is segmented and has the potential for distribution across multiple servers.

In Chapter 3, you were introduced to Visual InterDev's own architecture. If you review it, you'll find that it is a three-tier architecture. As a developer, it is up to you to design and construct your application to take advantage of the benefits of this architecture, and Visual InterDev makes your job easier.

Currently, Web applications face another problem: too much network traffic sending files back and forth between the client and the Web server. Developers are beginning to shift some of the load from the two servers back to the client system, by using Java applets, ActiveX controls, and Dynamic HyperText Markup Language (DHTML).

Creating a stored procedure

In this exercise, you create a stored procedure with the SQL Editor. You continue working with the sample Register database to produce a list of the sessions a specific customer is registered for, along with when and where each session will be held. This example uses the CustSessions View you created earlier in "Creating Views Using View Designer." Because you want to be able to use this stored procedure for any customer, rather than hard-code the name of the customer in the stored procedure, you use parameters to specify the name at runtime.

1. In Data View, right-click the Stored Procedures folder and click New Stored Procedure on the shortcut menu. The following SQL statements automatically appear in the SQL Editor pane:

```
Create Procedure StoredProcedure1
/*
    (
        @parameter1 datatype = default value,
        @parameter2 datatype OUTPUT
    )
*/
As
    return
```

2. Replace all of those lines with these SQL statements:

```
Create Procedure CustomerEnrollment
@firstname char(25),lastname char(25)
WITH RECOMPILE AS
SELECT Title, Start_DateTime, Room
FROM "CustSessions"
WHERE (first_name = @firstname) AND
(last_name = lastname)
Return
```

In this example, the name of the stored procedure is CustomerEnrollment. Because stored procedures are database objects, each must have a unique name.

3. On the File menu, click Save StoredProcedure*X*, where *X* is an automatically assigned sequential number. VI automatically recognizes the name of the stored procedure, CustomerEnrollment, from the first line of the code. The name appears under the Stored Procedure folder in Data View.

Note

If there is a syntax error in the stored procedure code, you will not be able to save it. A dialog will appear describing the error. Click OK to close the dialog box and to correct the error. When the syntax of the SQL statements is correct, save the stored procedure.

4. In Data View, click the plus (+) sign to the left of the stored procedure name to open the branch. A list of the columns and parameters in the stored procedure is displayed, as shown in Figure 21-5.

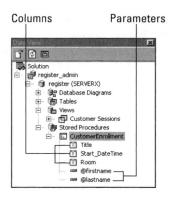

Columns   Parameters

Figure 21-5: All stored procedures are found in the Stored Procedures folder in Data View.

Testing and debugging stored procedures

Now that you've created the stored procedure, you need to make sure that the logic is correct and that you can integrate it into your Web application. There are several ways to test a stored procedure. This section discusses three test methods.

✦ Creating an SQL script to execute a stored procedure

✦ Running the stored procedure from Data View

✦ Debugging the stored procedure

When you execute a stored procedure from a SQL script, you are calling it from within another SQL procedure. You may do this because this stored procedure performs one step within a series of steps. For example, if you are producing a report on sales commissions due this quarter, the calling routine might execute a Select statement to get the appropriate record set, then call the stored procedure to calculate the sales commission.

You can run the stored procedure directly from Data View to simulate the situation where you directly execute the stored procedure from your Web page (which we discuss in Chapter 23). Finally, you can use the debugger to run the stored procedure and isolate logic errors. Once you locate them, you can correct the errors and begin testing again.

Creating a specific SQL script to execute a stored procedure

Follow these steps to create a specific SQL script to test a stored procedure with parameters:

1. In the Project Explorer, right-click the data connection and select Add SQL Script on the shortcut menu. The Add Item dialog appears.

2. In the Name box, enter a name for the script and click Open. The SQL Editor window opens.

3. In the SQL Editor window, enter this SQL statement:

```
EXECUTE CustomerEnrollment 'John', 'Smith'
```

4. Save the SQL script by pressing Ctrl+S.

5. Right-click in the SQL Editor pane and select Execute. The SQL script runs the stored procedure. Figure 21-6 shows the Output pane.

Note   In the last section of this chapter, you learn how to create a specific SQL script to grant execute permission for this stored procedure. If you are unable to execute this query, skip ahead to that section now.

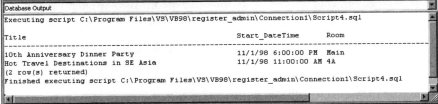

Figure 21-6: When you run a stored procedure, you see what it does in the Output window.

Running a stored procedure in Data View

Follow these steps to run a stored procedure with parameters in Data View:

1. In Data View, right-click the name of the stored procedure. In this example, select CustomerEnrollment.

2. Click Execute on the shortcut menu. The Execute dialog box appears.

3. The dialog has one row for each parameter for which you must provide a value. The first column displays the type of values you must enter in the Value column. For this example, enter **John** in the first row and **Smith** in the second row, as shown in Figure 21-7.

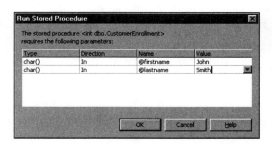

Figure 21-7: When you run a stored procedure with named parameters from Data View, you enter the values in this dialog box.

4. Click OK. The results appear as text in the Output pane, as shown in Figure 21-8.

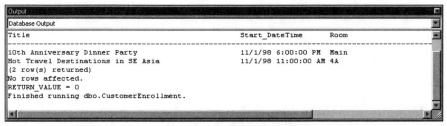

Figure 21-8: When you run a stored procedure from Data View, the results appear in the Output pane.

Debugging a stored procedure

In MS SQL Server, you can use the SQL debugger to debug stored procedures and triggers. You work with the SQL debugger much like you do with the other Visual Studio debuggers and the VI debugger for scripts. However, rather than debug SQL statements while they are running, you debug them from the SQL editor.

Note   If the debugger is not available, check to see that the server and client components were installed and configured to support SQL debugging. You will need to run SQL Server under a user account and not under the System Account which has too high a level of security to communicate with SQL Debugger.

You begin debugging a stored procedure when it is open in the SQL Editor. You can set breakpoints by clicking in the column to the left of the SQL statement, as shown in Figure 21-9. Right-click the SQL Editor pane and select Execute to start running the stored procedure. When a breakpoint occurs, you can step through the code, checking values and states as you go.

Breakpoint

```
Create Procedure CustomerEnrollment
@firstname char (25),@lastname char (25)
WITH RECOMPILE AS
SELECT Title, Start_DateTime, Room
FROM "Customer Sessions"
WHERE (first_name = @firstname) AND
(last_name = @lastname)
Return
```

Figure 21-9: This stored procedure has a breakpoint set, which allows you to step through the code to check values and states.

Debug the code by using the commands on the Debug menu. You cannot use the `Set Next Statement` command to change the order in which your instructions are executed. Also, you cannot use the Auto and Immediate windows in the SQL debugger. To view values returned by a Select statement, look in the Local window if the result is a single value, or look in the Output window if it is a set of values.

Working with stored procedures

In addition to creating a stored procedure, running it, and debugging it from Data View, you can copy, delete, open, and rename stored procedures. You can also refresh the list of stored procedures you see in Data View. Once you create a stored procedure, to ensure other users can execute it, you can grant execute permission. In Data View, right-click the name of the stored procedure then click one of these commands on the shortcut menu:

✦ **Copy** — The SQL statements for the stored procedure are copied to the Windows clipboard.

✦ **Debug** — See "Debugging a Stored Procedure" earlier in this chapter for information on debugging a stored procedure.

✦ **Delete** — A dialog box appears asking you to confirm the delete. Click Yes to delete the stored procedure.

✦ **Execute** — The stored procedure runs.

✦ **New Stored Procedure** — Enter a name for the stored procedure and a blank SQL Editor window appears. See "Creating a Stored Procedure" earlier in this chapter for information on this topic.

✦ **Open** — The SQL statements for the stored procedure appear in the SQL Editor.

✦ **Refresh** — Because another member of the development team may add a stored procedure to the database while you are working, occasionally you will need to refresh your list of stored procedures.

✦ **Rename** — Enter the new name in Data View as you would when renaming a file in Windows Explorer. VI automatically changes the name of the stored procedure on the first line of the file.

Granting execute permissions

If you create a stored procedure in Microsoft SQL Server, you can grant execute permission to all other users, individual users, or to groups of users. In Oracle Database Server, if you do not own the database, you must grant execute permission to all users.

Follow these steps to grant execute permission for your stored procedure to other users:

1. Create a new SQL script file by right-clicking the data connection in the Project Explorer and selecting Add SQL Script from the shortcut menu. The Add Item dialog appears.

2. In the Name box, enter a name for the script and click Open. The SQL Editor window opens.

3. Enter the following SQL statement in the script file, replacing <stored procedure name> with the name of your stored procedure and <name> with either Public, to grant permission to every user, or the name of the user or the group:

```
Grant Execute On <stored procedure name> To <name>
```

For example, to grant execute permission for the stored procedure called CustomerEnrollment to every user, enter this SQL statement:

```
Grant Execute On CustomerEnrollment To Public
```

4. Save the SQL script by pressing Ctrl+S.

5. Right-click in the SQL Editor pane and select Execute. The SQL script runs the Grant Execute statement.

Triggers

A trigger is a special type of stored procedure that automatically executes when data in a specific table is deleted, inserted, or updated. You create a trigger just as you create a stored procedure. You create a file of SQL statements, user-declared variables, and flow-control statements such as IF statements. Then you compile the file and save it to the database as a trigger. Finally, you run it by performing the action that the trigger is defined to handle.

Understanding when to use triggers

The two primary reasons to use a trigger are to enforce the following:

✦ **Business rules** consist of logic that is specific to the use of the application. For example, the Web application that visitors use to register for a conference might only allow a customer to register under a press pass when that customer is a member of the press, which is confirmed by a table lookup.

✦ **Referential integrity** ensures that if a row is deleted from a primary key table, all associated rows in the foreign key table are deleted first. Using the Register database example, when a customer is deleted, referential integrity ensures the rows in the CustomerToSessions table for that customer are deleted as well. While many DBMSs automatically maintain the referential integrity of the tables in a database, they may not handle cross-database conditions, but a SQL Server trigger can.

Each application has unique needs, so you must understand the tradeoffs when you face having to make a decision whether to use triggers. Table 21-3 lists the advantages and disadvantage of using a trigger.

Table 21-3	
Advantages and Disadvantages of Using Triggers	
Advantages	*Disadvantages*
Execute automatically and immediately.	Can slow an insert or update operation when complex or cascading triggers execute.
Can cause triggers in other tables to execute. This phenomenon is cascading triggers.	
Can execute more complex logic than possible with check constraints, including cross-table and cross-database checking.	

Creating a trigger

Creating a trigger includes defining the table it applies to, indicating the action that must occur to initiate the trigger, e.g., UPDATE, INSERT, DELETE, and specifying the SQL commands the trigger will perform.

Follow these steps to create a trigger:

1. In Data View, right-click the name of the table where you are creating the trigger, then click New Trigger on the shortcut menu. These SQL statements automatically appear in the SQL Editor pane:

```
Create Trigger Customer_Trigger1
On dbo.Customer
For /* Insert, Update, Delete */
As
    /* If Update (column_name) ...*/
```

2. Replace Customer_Trigger1 in the first line with the name you wish to give the trigger.

3. Remove the transactions /*Insert, Update, Delete*/ from the list, as they will not activate the trigger. Replace them with the action that will.

4. Replace *IfUpdate (column_name) with the SQL statements that comprise the body of the trigger.

5. On the File menu, click Save. The name of the trigger appears in the Tables folder under the trigger table, as shown in Figure 21-10.

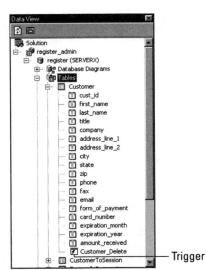

Figure 21-10: When you save a trigger, it appears under the Tables folder in Data View.

— Trigger

Let's continue here with the earlier example of the SQL code for a trigger on the Customer table. Whenever a customer is deleted from the Customer table, the trigger is executed and adds a row to the Cust_Log table. Each row in Cust_Log consists of these columns:

✦ **cust_id** — identifier for deleted customer from Customer table

✦ **last_name** — surname of deleted customer from Customer table

✦ **first_name** — given name of deleted customer from Customer table

✦ **action** — type of transaction that occurred, which is a Delete

✦ **time_stamp** — date and time the deletion occurred

Listing 21-1 shows the complete source code for the trigger procedure.

Listing 21-1: Trigger to Create an entry in Cust_Log Whenever a Customer is Deleted

```
Create Trigger Customer_Delete
on Customer
For Delete
As
Declare @ID int, @now datetime,
@last char(25), @first char(25)
Select @ID=deleted.cust_id,
@last=deleted.last_name,
@first=deleted.first_name,
@now=getdate()
From deleted
Insert into Cust_Log
(cust_id, last_name, first_name, action, time_stamp)
values (@ID, @last, @first, 'Delete', @now)
```

Testing triggers

To test the trigger, you must simulate the actual event the trigger is written to handle. To test the trigger shown in Listing 21-1, you must delete a customer from the Customer table and then query the Cust_Log table to confirm that a row was added for the customer you just deleted. You can use the Visual Database Tools to quickly do each of these steps. In Data View, double-click the Customer table name under the Tables heading. The Results pane appears, showing the rows of data in the Customer table. In the Results pane, select the row for the customer you wish to delete and press the Delete key. A dialog appears asking you to confirm the delete. Click Yes. The row of data disappears. Now, in Data View, double-click the Cust_Log table name under the Tables heading. (If you don't see this table, create it as discussed in Chapter 19.) The Results pane appears, showing the rows of data in the Cust_Log table. You should see a row for the customer you just deleted from the Customer table.

Working with triggers

Triggers can be created, edited, and deleted in Data View. Like stored procedures and views, triggers are database objects stored on the database server. In Data View, right-click the name of the trigger, then click one of these commands on the shortcut menu:

✦ **Delete** — A dialog box appears asking you to confirm the delete. Click Yes to delete the trigger.

✦ **Open** — The SQL statements for the trigger appear in the SQL Editor.

SQL Scripts

A SQL script is a text file that contains SQL statements that you run against a database. A SQL script resides on the client machine in a VI database project rather than on the database server. You create these files in SQL Editor or by saving the SQL Change script created by Database Designer, as discussed in Chapter 19. SQL script files have an extension of .sql. When you create them in VI, the default directory is the data connection directory for the project. VI provides a number of templates that you can use to create SQL scripts for commonly performed tasks such as querying the database, or creating a table, view, stored procedure, or trigger.

Understanding when to use SQL scripts

A SQL script is used to execute an SQL statement against a database from Visual InterDev. In earlier sections, you created one SQL script to execute a stored procedure and another to grant execute permission for that stored procedure. A SQL script can also be used to create or change a database object in multiple databases, such as the development, testing, training, and production databases for your Web application.

Creating a SQL script

If you can write SQL commands, then you can create a SQL script. In this section, you learn to create SQL scripts using these methods:

✦ SQL Editor
✦ Template
✦ SQL Change Script

Using SQL editor

Follow these steps to create a SQL script using the SQL Editor:

1. In the Project Explorer, right-click the data connection and select Add SQL Script from the shortcut menu. The Add Item dialog appears.

2. Enter a name for the script, and click Open. For this example, enter **Run_SP**. The SQL Editor window opens and the SQL script appears in the Project Explorer under the data connection, as shown in Figure 21-11.

SQL Script icon   Query icon

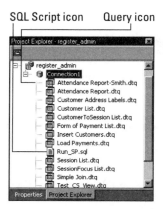

Figure 21-11: When you save a SQL script, it appears in the Project Explorer under the data connection.

Note

If Source control is active for your database project, when you click Open, the Push Add to Server dialog shown in Figure 21-12 appears asking you when to add the file to Visual SourceSafe. You can add it now, later, or do nothing. If you add it now, VI automatically checks the file out for you. If you decide to add the file later, refer to the steps in the "Working with Source Control from a Database Project" sidebar for step-by-step instructions.

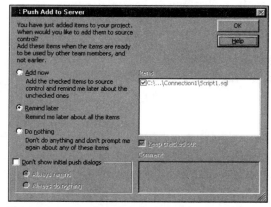

Figure 21-12: All these choices for source control are presented when you create a new file.

3. Enter your SQL statements in the SQL Editor window. For this example, enter this line of SQL:

```
EXECUTE CustomerEnrollment 'John', 'Smith'
```

4. Save the SQL script by pressing Ctrl+S.

Using a template

Visual Database Tools provides the five templates listed in Table 21-4. These templates will help you create SQL scripts to handle the common tasks described in the table. You must know how to write SQL commands and be familiar with the specific SQL statements supported by your database.

Table 21-4
SQL Script Templates

Template	Description
Database Query	Brings up Query Designer, which you can use to create a new query.
Stored Procedu...	Brings up a template for a stored procedure that you can customize. The template includes SQL statements that let you drop, create, and set permissions on the stored procedure.
Table Script	Brings up a template for a table that you can customize. The template includes SQL statements that let you drop, create, and grant permissions on the table.
Trigger Script	Brings up a template for a trigger that you can customize. The template includes SQL statements that let you drop, create, and grant permissions on the trigger.
View Script	Brings up a template for a view that you can customize. The template includes SQL statements that let you drop, create, and grant permissions on the view.

Follow these steps to create an appropriate SQL script based on the Table Script template:

1. In the Project Explorer, right-click the data connection and select Add SQL Script from the shortcut menu. The Add Item dialog appears.

2. In the right pane of the dialog, select Table Script.

3. Enter the name of the SQL script and click Open. For this example, enter **Customer_TMP**, as shown in Figure 21-13. The SQL Editor window opens and the SQL statements in Listing 21-2 appear.

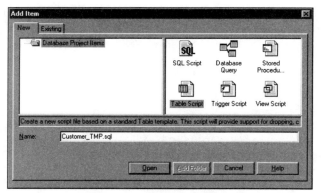

Figure 21-13: The Table Script template will help you create a new table quickly.

4. In the SQL editor pane, replace `Table_Name` with the name of your table.

5. Enter the Column definitions between the parentheses ( ) following the `CREATE TABLE` command. Add any other statement necessary to create keys, indexes, and constraints.

6. Customize the `GRANT SELECT ON` statement to the level of permission you wish to allow.

7. Save the SQL script.

Listing 21-2: **SQL Template for Table Script**

```
IF EXISTS (SELECT * FROM sysobjects
WHERE type = 'U' AND name = 'Table_Name')
  BEGIN
    PRINT 'Dropping Table Table_Name'
    DROP  Table Table_Name
  END
GO

/********************************************************
** File:
** Name: Table_Name
** Desc:
**          This template can be customized and is found in:
**
**
** Auth:
** Date:
*********************************************************
**          Change History
*********************************************************
```

```
** Date:      Author:    Description:
** ----       ----       ----------------
**
********************************************************/

PRINT 'Creating Table Table_Name'
GO
CREATE TABLE Table_Name
(


)
GO

GRANT SELECT ON Table_Name TO PUBLIC

GO
```

Tip

These templates include a GRANT statement, which applies to views, stored procedures, and tables. An easy way to GRANT permissions is to create and execute a SQL script that contains the GRANT statement. Here's one that lets anyone execute the stored procedure called CustomerEnrollment:

```
GRANT EXECUTE ON CustomerEnrollment TO PUBLIC
```

Using SQL change scripts

When you work in a database diagram, you can save the SQL change scripts that it generates and add it to a database project. Chapter 19 discusses how to work in database diagrams and what a SQL change script is.

To save an existing SQL change script to a database project, follow these steps:

1. In the Project Explorer, right-click the data connection and select Add SQL script from the shortcut menu. The Add Item dialog appears.
2. Click the Existing tab.
3. Select the Change Script.
4. Click Open. The Change Script appears in the Project Explorer under the data connection. If you wish to give the file a more meaningful name, use the Rename command.

Testing SQL scripts

Follow these steps to execute a SQL script:

1. In the Project Explorer, right-click the name of the SQL script and select Execute from the shortcut menu. The Output window appears.

2. The results of the SQL script appear in the Output pane. Review the messages to determine if the SQL script executed successfully. Close the window when you are finished.

Working with SQL scripts

In addition to creating and executing an SQL script, from the Project Explorer, you can copy, delete, and open a script in SQL Editor, open a script in another editor, rename a script, and add a script to Source Control. In the Project Explorer, right-click the name of the SQL script, then click one of these commands on the shortcut menu. Refer to the sidebar for information on working with Source Control.

✦ **Copy** — The SQL statements that are in the SQL script file are placed on the Windows clipboard.

✦ **Delete** — The file is immediately deleted. A confirmation dialog appears. Click Yes to permanently delete the file.

✦ **Execute** — The file runs and the Output pane displays the status.

✦ **Open** — The file appears in the SQL Editor.

✦ **Open With** — The Open With dialog appears. Select the name of the editor or click the Add button to add another editor program to the list. Click Open. The selected SQL file appears in a separate window for the editor program.

✦ **Rename** — Enter the new name in the Project Explorer as you would when renaming a file in Windows Explorer.

Tip

If you want an editor other than SQL Editor to be the default editor, click the Set As Default button. The next time you use Open or Add SQL Script, the editor will appear as the default editor.

Working with Source Control from a Database Project

When you use source control with a database project, you can track the changes you make to SQL script files. By saving SQL change scripts in SQL script files, you can also track all of the changes you make to the database. This can be very useful information if you ever need to recreate the database or track down a problem.

Before you can add a file to source control, the database project must be enabled for source control. You do this in the Project Explorer by right-clicking the database project name, and selecting Add to source control in the shortcut menu. VI will prompt you to add all existing files to source code at this time. If you choose not to do it then, you can do it later by following the instructions given next.

If you are using Microsoft Visual SourceSafe (VSS) for source control, the VSS administrator must create the VSS database that you will use for the database project and the Login ID and password that you will use.

To add a SQL script to source control, in the Project Explorer, right-click the SQL script and select Add <script name> to source control on the shortcut menu. The Add to Source Control dialog appears. Click OK. VI adds the file to SourceSafe and checks it out for you.

Before you can edit a file that is under source control, you must check it out for edit. If you have not done this and attempt to change the file in SQL Editor, VI prompts you to check out a copy of the file. When you are finished making changes, you must check in the modified copy of the file. You do this by right-clicking the name of the SQL script in the Project Explorer and on the shortcut menu, clicking Check In <file name>, where <file name> is the name of the SQL script file.

Summary

In this chapter, we discussed the advanced SQL features of the Visual Database Tools and learned about these topics:

✦ The advanced SQL features are views, stored procedures, triggers, and SQL scripts.

✦ How to create a view in a database by creating a select query in View Designer.

✦ How to test a view by creating a query that uses the view.

✦ How to create stored procedures for common business rules processing on the server and how to grant execute permission.

✦ How to test and debug stored procedures.

✦ How to create and test a trigger to enforce business rules and referential integrity.

✦ How to build a SQL script and store it locally for use against multiple databases.

✦ How to add source control to a database project and check SQL script files in and out.

✦   ✦   ✦

Using Databases
in a Web

Understanding Data Connections

This chapter introduces all the fundamental concepts necessary to connect a data source to your Web application. It covers Microsoft's Windows Distributed InterNet Applications Architecture (DNA), a three-tier architecture, and Universal Data Access (UDA) architectures, which is Microsoft's strategy for providing access to all data in the enterprise, as well as VI's data architecture. The fundamental concepts discussed include data connection, data environment, data commands, recordsets, and design-time controls.

In this chapter, you continue working with the sample Microsoft SQL Server database Register. Instructions for installing it from the companion CD-ROM are found in Chapter 18.

After you've learned all these new concepts, you create a file and a machine Data Source Name, then use one of them when you add a data connection to your Web project.

Microsoft's Vision

Microsoft wants to make it easy for developers to build robust, data-driven Internet applications because the faster they can build them, the more of them the corporate world will demand. To foster this vision, Microsoft has promoted the Windows Distributed InterNet Applications Architecture (DNA), which describes a three-tier architecture supported by tools and distributed operating environments. Universal Data Access is a key component of this architecture because it accesses relational and nonrelational data in place. This capability is of tremendous interest to corporations that have zillions of bytes of data disbursed throughout their organizations, in legacy systems, e-mail, and Excel spreadsheets to name just a few places. Visual InterDev is one of the first Microsoft tools to deliver the capabilities envisioned by DNA. This section discusses Microsoft's vision and its associated architectural components.

In addition, you'll discover three different ways to add a database server into your Web application's development and runtime environments. Finally, you'll learn the advantages and disadvantages of controlling access to data from the server side and from the client side of a Web application.

Microsoft Windows DNA

Microsoft has always championed the use of the PC platform in the business environment. Microsoft has often pushed the hardware envelope by delivering operating system capabilities, such as Windows 95 and Office 97, which taxed the capabilities of the then-current PC hardware. The early 1990s saw the rapid increase in popularity of the Internet in the business community as a global information network. At that time, browsers designed to function identically on all hardware platforms primarily handled access to the Internet. What this meant was that many of the unique features of the PC platform lay dormant when the user was connected to the Internet from a PC. Microsoft recognized the need to concurrently utilize the capabilities of the PC platform and the Internet from the same application space. Thus, Windows DNA was presented.

This architecture, which is shown in Figure 22-1, defines a standard set of Windows-based services that developers use to create distributed business applications that take full advantage of both the PC environment and the Internet. The core of DNA is a three-tier architecture consisting of the User Interface, Business Processes, and Data Storage. On the left side are the Component Object Model (COM)-based tools that support the construction of the central three tiers. Visual Studio 6, including Visual InterDev 6, fit in this area. The Distributed Operating Environment, on the right side of Figure 22-1, consists of the platforms on which these Microsoft products run: Internet Explorer (IE) 4.0, Internet Information Server (IIS), SQL Server, Open Database Connectivity (ODBC)-compliant databases, as well as many others.

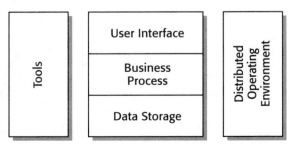

Figure 22-1: Microsoft's DNA is a three-tier architecture comprised of the User Interface, Business Process, and Data Storage.

The next section focuses on the third tier of the DNA architecture: Data Storage. You can find more information about DNA at the Microsoft Web site at http://www.microsoft.com/dna.

Universal data access

Universal Data Access (UDA) is Microsoft's strategy to provide access to all data in the enterprise — relational as well as nonrelational. Rather than requiring a business to move its data to a common corporate database, UDA allows the business to access this data where it currently resides, across the entire enterprise. The design philosophy for UDA (see Figure 22-2) includes:

✦ Providing access to all data stores–for example, ODBC-compliant, spreadsheets, e-mail, text, video, mainframe data, and more.

✦ Making the unique requirements of each data store transparent to the developer working with a standard programming interface.

✦ Sharing retrieved data with multiple processes by storing it in memory, rather than retrieving it multiple times for different users.

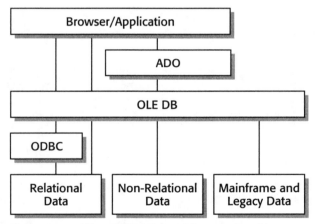

Figure 22-2: Microsoft's UDA architecture provides access to all data in an enterprise without requiring the data to be located in one place.

Microsoft Data Access Components (MDAC) implement the Universal Data Access vision. MDAC 2.0, currently shipping with Visual InterDev 6.0, consists of these component architectures:

✦ Object Linking and Embedding Database (OLE DB)

✦ Open Database Connectivity (ODBC)

✦ ActiveX Data Objects (ADO)

✦ Remote Data Services (RDS, formerly known as Advanced Database Connector (ADC))

Check Microsoft's Web site at `http://www.microsoft.com/data` for more information on UDA.

OLE DB

OLE DB is a set of COM-based Application Programming Interfaces (APIs) that provide high-performance access to all data stores in the UDA. It's based on the highly successful ODBC interface, but extends the interface to handle all data sources. As Figure 22-3 shows, there are three types of OLE DB applications:

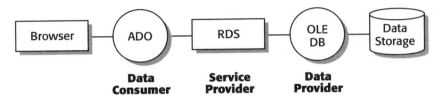

Figure 22-3: A typical OLE DB application consists of a data provider and a consumer serviced by RDS.

✦ **Data Providers** interface directly with the actual data storage mechanism and expose the data. For example, the OLE DB provider for SQL Server exposes SQL Server. Microsoft's first OLE DB provider was for ODBC. Consequently, all ODBC data sources are supported under UDA. Visual InterDev 6.0 supports connections to OLE DB providers.

✦ **Data Consumers** use the data exposed by the data provider. ADO is the quintessential data consumer.

✦ **Service Providers** offer a service between the data consumer and the provider. RDS is a service provider.

ODBC

Because ODBC supports only relational data structures and because it is not COM-based, it would not, by itself, address the goals of DNA. To build on ODBC's widespread support in the marketplace, Microsoft created a wrapper for ODBC so it could continue to work in the context of OLE DB. This allows existing systems to continue functioning. All new applications should plan to use OLE DB.

ADO

ActiveX Data Objects are client-side application components that use the data exposed by an OLE DB provider. ADO is a new and rapidly evolving architecture based on Remote Data Objects (RDO) and Data Access Objects (DAO), which ADO will eventually replace. Examples of ADO objects are asynchronous data connections, data commands, recordsets, collections, fields, and parameters. These objects are discussed later in this chapter and in Chapter 23.

RDS

Remote Data Services (RDS, formerly known as Advanced Database Connector (ADC)) interfaces with ADO and provides services between it and the OLE DB provider across the Internet. Examples of services include conveying a query from the client to the Web server and then packaging the retrieved data as an ADO recordset and conveying it to the client. The ADO recordset is cached on the client machine and disconnected from the server.

Data-Driven Web Application Configurations

When you build a data-driven Web application with Visual InterDev, there are three basic ways to configure your database and Web server. In this section, we discuss the strengths and weaknesses of each. Next, we discuss what's involved in managing access to data from the server-side and from the client-side. With this information, you'll be able to make informed decisions about these issues as you design and construct your Web application.

Configuration options

Visual InterDev supports any ODBC or OLE DB data source, including products from Microsoft, Oracle, Informix, and Sybase. In Chapter 3, you learned that the four components of the VI architecture are the Web browser, Visual InterDev client, Web server, and database server. The focus in Chapter 3 was on nondatabase-related configurations, but this section focuses on the different ways you can configure a database server within your Web application development environment.

While the Web server and the database server are both servers, they each have unique capabilities and each place unique demands on the hardware and system services. As a result, you need to understand why you might configure your development, test, and/or production environments in one of these three ways:

✦ A single server machine running both Web server and database server

✦ Separate machines for the Web server and database server

✦ A single machine for the Web server running the database server on a client workstation machine

Single-server machine

Figure 22-4 shows the hardware configuration that runs both the Web server and database server on the same machine. Developer workstations must be connected to the database server via a LAN connection during the construction phase of the project.

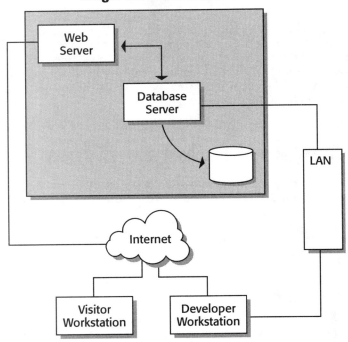

Single-Server Machine

Figure 22-4: You can run the Web server and the database server on the same machine.

This is a typical configuration during the construction phase of a development project, when your project resources are limited and the demand on the two servers is low. Unfortunately, the response time for developers can be very slow if the resources of this one server machine begin to be taxed by a large volume of users or by extremely resource-intensive processing. It is also a less reliable configuration because if the machine is out, you have neither Web nor database services.

Unique server machines

Figure 22-5 shows the hardware configuration with the Web server and database server on separate machines. The Web server and developer workstations are connected to the database server via the LAN.

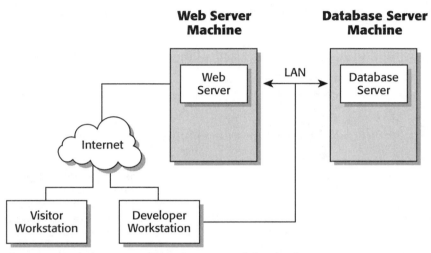

Figure 22-5: You can run the Web server and the database server on separate machines.

This configuration provides the opportunity for the best performance. As the number of users increases, the system administrator has the most flexibility for optimizing server performance. In addition, this configuration makes it possible to upgrade hardware separately for each server. With each server on a separate machine, this configuration can also provide more reliability because if one machine goes down, the other one continues to function. This is an expensive alternative when you consider operational costs alone. However, if this were an e-commerce site where company revenue was dependent on delivering a reliable, high-performance service, this configuration would be money well spent.

Database server on workstation

Figure 22-6 shows the hardware configuration that runs a Web server with the database server running on a developer workstation. The Web server and other developer workstations are connected to the database server via a LAN connection during the construction phase of the project.

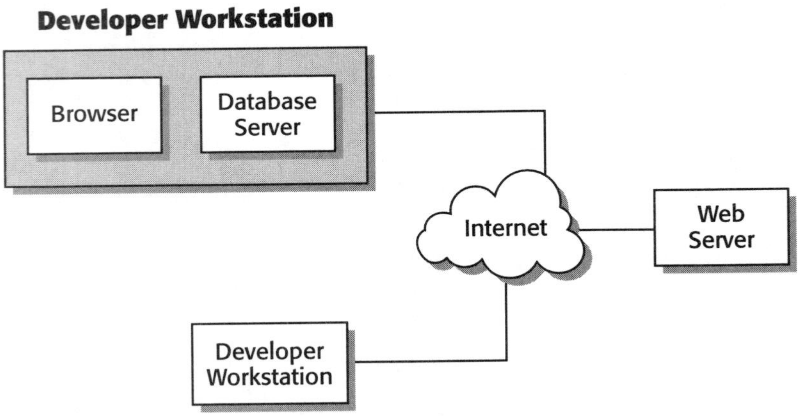

Developer Workstation

Figure 22-6: You can run the database server on a developer workstation.

This is a typical configuration during the testing phase of a development project because the demand on the two servers is low. Unfortunately, the response time for this configuration is slower than the other two configurations because the typical workstation is not as powerful as the typical server machine. Also, the developer workstation is running additional processes initiated by the developer.

Server-side vs. client-side script control of data

Microsoft currently provides two ways to control the data for a Web page, either from server-side or client-side script commands. While each of these types of pages involves many complex steps, Visual InterDev makes it easy for you to create either by using Design-Time Controls (DTC) and VI's Scripting Object Model. You don't even have to be aware of the underlying processing that is occurring.

When a server script manages access to the data

For an Internet site, the database server and Web server are typically running on separate machines with the Web server managing access to the database. In this scenario, this is what happens when the Web server manages access to the data:

1. The visitor decides to view a page of data. The browser sends a request for a Uniform Resource Locator (URL) to the Web server.

2. The Web server locates and processes the URL, which is an Active Server Page (ASP). This page contains a request for a set of records from a database. The Web server executes a script to connect to the database, and then sends the request for data to the database server.

3. The database server processes the request and returns the retrieved set of data records to the Web server. At this point, the database server knows nothing about that set of data records.

4. The Web server continues executing the ASP script, which establishes the current record in the set of data records. The Web server places the fields from the current record on the HyperText Markup Language (HTML) page as text. It then sends the page to the browser along with a current record indicator. At this point, the Web server discards the data records.

5. The visitor views the page and then clicks the Next button.

6. The browser sends a request for the next page to the Web server, along with the current record indicator.

7. The Web server determines that the browser wants to move to the next record in the data set. It sends the original query to the database server, which returns the retrieved set of data records.

8. The Web server uses the current record locator to move to the next record. It extracts the data from the current record. It formats the page and sends it along with the new current record identifier to the browser.

   The process continues at step 5.

Table 22-1 lists the advantages and disadvantages of server scripts managing access to the data.

Table 22-1	
Advantages and Disadvantages of Server Scripts Managing Access to the Data	
Advantages	*Disadvantages*
Application runs on any browser	Pages load slowly as browser waits for Web server to build the page.
	Increased database server processing as the same set of data records is retrieved multiple times.
	Increased network traffic between browser and Web server as visitor moves through set of data records.
	High processing overhead on Web server to return to where it was when it created the previous data page so it can move to the next record.
	Browser unable to work with the data in the page because it is HTML text and can't be distinguished as data fields.

When client script manages access to the data

After seeing how complicated server-managed access is, you will be pleasantly surprised at how relatively simple client-managed access is. This is what happens when script on the browser manages access to the data:

1. The visitor decides to view a page of data. The browser sends a request for a URL to the Web server.

2. The Web server locates the URL, which is a Dynamic HTML (DHTML) page.

3. The Web server sends the page to the browser.

4. When the browser receives the page, an RDS control in the page sends the request for data to the database.

5. The database server processes the request and returns the retrieved set of data records to the browser. At this point, the database server knows nothing about that set of data records.

6. The browser receives the set of data records and binds the data to the controls on the page.

7. The browser displays the page and caches the set of data records and the current record indicator.

8. The visitor views the page and then clicks the Next button.

9. The browser processes the script behind the Next button, which navigates to the next data record.

    The process continues at step 7.

With Internet Explorer 4.0, Microsoft introduced DHTML and the data-binding capabilities supported by RDS that allow client-side scripts to manage access to data. No other browser currently supports this capability (see sidebar on Extensible Markup Language (XML), which is a way to describe the data on an HTML page). If a company has adopted IE4 as its default browser, that company becomes a perfect candidate for an intranet application that utilizes client-side scripting to manage data. This technique does require that the latest version of data access software be installed on the database server machine.

Table 22-2 lists the advantages and disadvantages of client scripts managing access to the data.

Table 22-2
Advantages and Disadvantage of Client Scripts Managing Access to the Data

Advantages	Disadvantages
Data is retrieved from the database once, thereby reducing the load on the database server and network traffic back and forth between the browser and the Web server.	Application only runs on the IE4 browser.
Because the browser moves to the next record and redisplays the page, system response is much faster than when the server does it.	Client system may not handle the volume of data very well; for example, the performance of the system may be slow.
Data is displayed faster because the data records are transferred from the database server to the browser asynchronously. This means the browser can start displaying the first data record before it receives all of the data.	
Additional capabilities are possible on the client side, such as sorting the data, without going to the database server to sort it.	

XML

Extensible Markup Language (XML) and HTML are both markup languages based on the Standard Generalized Markup Language (SGML). However, HTML is used to markup text and XML is used to markup data. HTML's primary goal is to format text by centering it or making it bold. Typical tags include `<P>` to start a new paragraph, and `<FONT size=4>` to control the size of the text characters. XML's primary goal is to describe the data on the page. There are no typical tags in XML; they are all unique to the data being described. For instance, if the data is about customers, `<CUSTOMER>` might be a tag. Here's an example of an XML document that describes broadcast TV and cable TV programs:

```
<Programs>
  <TV>
    <show date="05/14/98" network="NBC">Seinfeld</show>
    <show date="05/07/98" network="NBC">Seinfeld</show>
    <show date="05/10/98" network="FOX">The X-Files</show>
  </TV>
  <Cable>
    <show date="05/27/98" network="TNT">Babylon 5</show>
```

(continued)

(continued)

```
    </Cable>
  </Programs>
```

Although HTML allows you to control the way a page appears, taking into account the data on the page, it does not allow you to do anything with the data, such as add to it, search it, or sort it. To allow data to be shared as easily as HTML files, the World Wide Web Consortium (W3C) has defined a standard for XML. Microsoft saw the potential of XML and added support for it in Internet Explorer 4.0.

Now both HTML documents and XML documents can be distributed and shared across machines, companies, and countries. Unfortunately, there is no standard that specifies how to visually present the data.

Because XML is such a new standard, very few XML tools exist for developers or Web page authors. Although you can enter XML code directly in VI's source editor, VI 6.0 does not have any built-in support for XML. For the latest information on the XML standard, check the W3C web site at `http://www.w3c.org`.

VI's Data Architecture

When you're ready to put your database and your Web application together in Visual InterDev, you need to make these preparations:

1. Add a data connection.
2. Create data commands.
3. Display the data using Design-Time Controls (DTC).

When you add a data connection to a Web project, the project knows what database to access, where it is located, and how to communicate with the database. Once the connection is in place, you can create data commands. These command files are data-environment objects connected to a database object — whether a table, view, stored procedure, or SQL statement. Rather than include SQL statements in multiple files within the Web application, data command files can be referenced, like a subroutine that is shared by the entire team of developers. VI makes it easy to access and display data. All you need to do is drag the data command and data elements to a page and VI automatically inserts data-bound Design-Time Controls and generates the script to connect it all together. Finally, you can customize these controls through property pages.

In the rest of this section, we discuss VI's data architecture as you explore data connections, data commands, and DTCs. The rest of this chapter focuses on data connections. Chapter 23 discusses data commands and using DTCs to display data on a Web page.

Adding a data connection

To access data from a Web project, you must first add a data connection to the project. VI makes the setup process easier by letting you use a data source name (DSN) to specify the database name, type, and location. Then, if your database requires it, you can define a login ID and password. Once that's done, VI adds a data environment node to your Web project under GLOBAL.ASA, as shown in Figure 22-7. Below the data environment is the data connection to the database.

Figure 22-7: When you add a data connection to a Web project, VI adds the data environment node.

Here is a more detailed description of each VI term associated with a data connection:

✦ **Data Connection** — A data connection consists of all the information necessary to connect a Web project or database project to a particular database. For a SQL Server database, this includes the name of the database, the type of database, the location of the database, and database login information during construction and during production. The first time you use anything in the database, VI tries to establish the data connection. When this happens, the database may prompt you for your login password.

✦ **Data Source Name** — The first step in adding a data connection is to select the data source name (DSN), which is information about what driver to use to connect to a specific database. You can create a DSN when you're adding a connection and then you can reuse the DSN with other VI database and Web projects.

✦ **Data Environment (DE)** — A data environment exists whenever a VI Web project is connected to a database. It holds the data connections and data commands. These commands are similar to components because you can reuse them throughout the Web project. In order for these data connections and commands to be used anywhere in the Web application, the information in the data environment is stored in the GLOBAL.ASA file.

✦ **GLOBAL.ASA** — Internet Information Server uses this file to maintain information about the execution status of your Web application. You add scripts to the event procedures in the GLOBAL.ASA file to handle typical application initialization and shutdown tasks. The event procedures are `Application_OnStart`, `Application_OnEnd`, `Session_OnStart`, and `Session_OnEnd`. Because IIS maintains the GLOBAL.ASA file on the server, any page in the Web application has access to these events and variables through server scripts.

If the Web project has a data connection, VI automatically adds script that contains the connection information in session variables to the `Application_OnStart` procedure. Visual Database Tools and the DTCs use this information to connect to the database at runtime. An exercise later in this chapter steps you through the creation of this data connection.

Creating data commands

Data View shows you the databases to which the project has connections. In the nodes below each database are the database objects available to you. You can use these database objects to create data commands. VI shows these commands in the Project Explorer under the branch for the database. Each of these data commands selects records from the database using a table, a view, a stored procedure, or SQL statements. Each record retrieved by a data command consists of one or more individual fields, which are like the columns in a relational table. The field names appear below each data command in the Project Explorer.

The Data View window in Figure 22-8 shows you that ProjectX is a Web project that contains two data connections: one to an Access database called Gallery, and the other to a SQL Server database called Register. The one visible view is CustSessions. In the Project Explorer, you see the global.asa branch with a node called DataEnvironment and two database connections, Gallery and Register. Within the Register database are five data commands: `Customers`, `CustSchedule`, `SessionList`, `CustSchedSQL`, and `CustSchedView`. Under the `CustSchedSQL` command are the columns of the Register database that this command retrieves: Title, Start_DateTime, and Room.

Figure 22-8: The data environment shows you the databases and data commands in your project.

A data command—also called a *DE command*—is a data environment object that is connected to a database object. The four types of data commands are based on which database object they use to retrieve data: a table, a view, a stored procedure, or SQL statement. Table 22-3 shows the icons that appear to the left of each data command in Project Explorer.

Table 22-3 Project Explorer Data Command Icons	
Icon	**Description**
	Data command based on a table or a view
	Data command based on a stored procedure
	Data command based on SQL statement
	Field available in the recordset retrieved by the data command

Data commands are similar to components because you can reuse them in a Web project. Because there is only one copy of a DE command per project, whenever you change a command, all of the pages in the Web project that use it immediately see the change. Unfortunately, you are not able to put data commands under Source Control in this version of VI, which can create problems. For example, if the Web application uses a data command based on SQL statements and one member of the team inadvertently modifies the SQL statements, any page in the entire Web that uses that data command is immediately affected. With Source Control, the data command could easily be restored to the version prior to the change. Without Source Control, you'd have to find a backup copy of the data command file and use it to restore the original SQL statements.

Displaying the data

Visual InterDev provides you with two ways to create Web pages that access and display data. One way is to use InterDev's Design-Time Controls, which handle low-level scripting automatically. A second way is to write all the low-level scripts yourself. Fortunately, there is a third option: to let the DTCs do most of the work and then customize the page with scripts as needed.

Note   Rather than teach you to write scripts to build your own custom data-driven Web pages, in this chapter and the next, we focus on showing you how to use the many robust design-time tools included with Visual InterDev. You can learn a great deal about this type of scripting by studying the source of the pages you create using DTCs.

For a Web page to access data in your database, simply drag a data command from the data environment and drop it on the page above any other data-bound controls.

If you want to manage access to the data from the client side, use an HTML file. To manage access to the data from the server side, use an ASP file. VI automatically generates the correct script based on the type of file you are using. In response to the drag-and-drop, VI places a Recordset DTC on the page. This is a special control that manages the set of records returned by the data command. It must be included in any page that accesses data. This control does not appear on the page when you bring it up in the browser.

To display individual data fields retrieved by the data command, you simply drag a field from the data environment in the Project Explorer, then drop it on the page where you want it to appear. Be sure you drop it below the Recordset object. If the field is textual or numeric, VI automatically places a data-bound text box control on the page. If the field is Boolean, VI places a data-bound check box control on the page. Finally, you bind or connect these controls to the Recordset object, which passes the appropriate data to each control. You go through this process in detail in Chapter 23.

Design-time controls

DTCs allow you to generate data-driven Web pages quickly and easily. DTCs are powerful tools that serve these purposes:

✦ **Displaying Data** — While some of these controls are connected to data and have no user interface, the purpose of most of these controls is to display data.

✦ **Generating Scripts** — Whenever you set a property of a DTC, you are indirectly generating the script for the control to behave a certain way. In other words, the DTC generates code so you don't have to.

These DTCs are included with VI: `Recordset`, `RecordsetNavBar`, `Textbox`, `Option`, `Listbox`, `Checkbox`, `FormManager`, and `Grid`. You control how each of these controls looks and acts though the controls' Properties dialog.

Scripting Object Model

Visual InterDev's Scripting Object Model (SOM) makes it easier for you to create Web applications by creating an object-oriented programming model similar to what Microsoft Visual Basic already uses. You work with a variety of objects that are the same whether you are working on server-based or client-based pages. Before you can work with this model, you must activate it. Because DTCs use SOM, when you add one to a page, unless the model is already enabled, VI automatically prompts you to enable it.

The Recordset control

The Recordset control is a DTC that creates a Recordset object. The control consists of a data connection and a data command. When the page executes, the Recordset control connects to the database, submits the retrieval command, and creates the Recordset object when it receives the set of records returned from the database. The data-bound DTCs on the page get their data from the Recordset control, which manages the data for the page. More than one Recordset control can reside on a page, allowing access to multiple sets of data from a single page.

Think of the Recordset *object* as a table of data formatted into rows and columns. However, the terminology is different. Rather than rows, there are *records*. Rather than columns, there is a *fields collection*. A Recordset object consists of one or more records, and a record consists of one or more fields. The object also maintains a pointer to the current record in the set.

Using the Recordset object's properties, you can preset certain aspects of the Web database application, such as where the script that accesses the data is run — client or server. Using the Recordset object's methods, you can issue directives, such as to move the current pointer to another record, open and close the recordset, or update and add records.

Multiple projects in a solution

You can have multiple projects in a single VI solution that accesses data. If you are creating a database specifically for this Web application, you may want to have a database project that you use to create and maintain database objects and a Web project in which you use the database, in the same solution. That way you can have multiple windows open while you develop a stored procedure in one window and use it in a Web page in another window.

Data Source Names

When you add a data connection to a Web project or create a new database project, Visual InterDev asks you to select the name of the data source to use, either a file DSN or a machine DSN. The DSN contains information about a data source, such as the type of database, the name of the database, and the location of the database. It is similar to a component in the sense that you can reuse it whenever you create a data connection to a specific database. VI uses the information to connect you to the database while you're developing the Web application. It is also used by the DTC at runtime to connect the application to the database.

In this section, we discuss both types of DSN, *file* and *machine*, and when to use each type. We also walk through the steps involved in creating a DSN of each type in VI. A new DSN can also be defined in the ODBC Data Source Administrator in the Control Panel.

File data source

A file data source name is a file with a .DSN extension that contains information about connecting to a database. The file is located in /Program Files/Common Files/ODBC/Data Sources/.

Why use a file DSN?

When you add a data connection to a project in Visual InterDev, the information in the .DSN file is copied to the GLOBAL.ASA file. Consequently, you no longer need the .DSN file. This type of connection is referred to as a *DSN-less connection*. This means that the Web application will run on any system because it has all the information it needs to connect to the database. File DSNs are the best choice for Web applications.

Creating a file DSN for the SQL Server database

To add a data connection to a project, open the project, right-click the project name in the Project Explorer, and select Add Data Connection from the shortcut menu. The Select Data Source dialog shown in Figure 22-9 appears. Follow these steps to add a new file DSN:

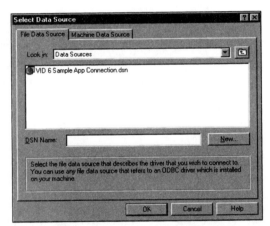

Figure 22-9: If you don't see the file DSN you want to use in the list, click New to create one.

1. In the Select Data Source dialog, click the File Data Source tab.

2. Click New. The Create New Data Source dialog appears.

3. Select the driver for the database. For this example, we selected SQL Server (see Figure 22-10).

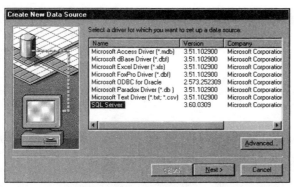

Figure 22-10: The SQL Server driver was selected for the database.

4. Click Next>. The Create New Data Source dialog appears.

5. Enter the filename and location of the DSN file, or click Browse and select the location, as shown in Figure 22-11. In the DSN Name box, enter the name you wish to use for the file DSN. In this example, we entered C:/Program Files/ Common Files/ODBC/Data Sources/VIB Register Sample (see Figure 22-11) because this DSN will connect to the sample Register database. When you are finished defining the DSN, this filename will appear in the Select Data Source dialog shown in Figure 22-9, so be sure to give it a meaningful name.

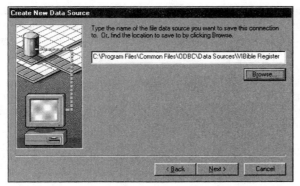

Figure 22-11: Enter the location and filename to use for this DSN in the Create New Data Source dialog box.

6. Click Next>. A dialog appears asking you to confirm the information you've entered so far. If you notice an error, click <Back and correct it. If the information looks correct, click Finish. The next dialog that appears depends on the type of database this DSN is connecting to. Because this example shows you how to connect to a SQL Server database, the Create a New Data Source to SQL Server dialog appears.

7. In the Description box, enter a meaningful description for this file DSN.

8. In Server, enter the name of the SQL Server for this database, as shown in Figure 22-12.

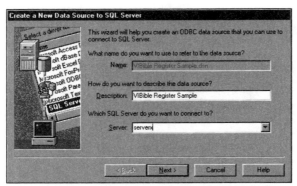

Figure 22-12: Enter a description and the name of the SQL Server to use for this DSN in the Create a New Data Source to SQL Server dialog box.

9. Click Next>. The Create a New Data Source to SQL Server dialog appears.

10. Select whether you want SQL Server to verify the authenticity of the login ID with NT authentication or SQL Server authentication.

Note

NT authentication uses a secure connection to SQL Server. SQL Server uses integrated login security but not a secure connection. Rather than prompt for an ID and password, it uses your NT ID as your SQL Server ID. SQL Server uses standard login security and prompts you for an ID and password.

11. If you selected With SQL Server authentication using a login ID and password entered by the user, you must enter a SQL login ID and password. See Figure 22-13. When you click Next>, this information is used to determine the default SQL Server settings.

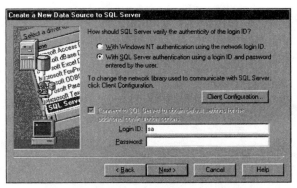

Figure 22-13: Select either the NT authentication or the SQL Server authentication level of login security to use for this DSN.

12. Click Next>. The Create a New Data Source to SQL Server dialog appears.

13. Change the default database or let the system default to the database assigned to the login ID.

14. Select the check boxes for the options that your database administrator advises you to use. Figure 22-14 shows the selections we made for this example.

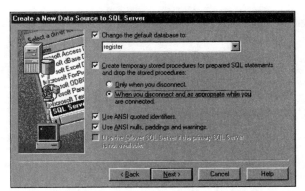

Figure 22-14: Ask your database administrator which settings to select in this dialog.

15. Click Next>. The Create a New Data Source to SQL Server dialog appears.

16. Choose the character set translation method to use, and whether to use Regional settings for displaying currency, numbers, dates, and times, as shown in Figure 22-15.

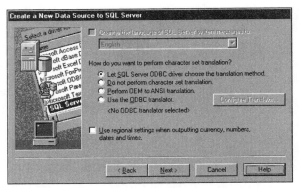

Figure 22-15: You need to determine how you want to handle character translation and currency, number, date, and time displays in this dialog box.

17. Click Next>.

18. If you want to **Save long running queries to the log file**, check the appropriately named box and enter the name of the file and the maximum length of a query. If you want to **Log ODBC driver statistics to the log file**, check that equally well named box. See Figure 22-16.

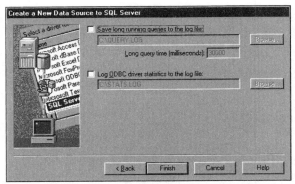

Figure 22-16: You should select these boxes if you want to log long queries and driver statistics.

19. Click Finish. The ODBC Microsoft SQL Server Setup dialog shown in Figure 22-17 appears.

Figure 22-17: Review the content of this dialog box then, if all is correct, click OK to create the file DSN.

20. Review the contents of the dialog. If you notice an error, click Cancel, then click <Back to correct the error. If the information is correct, click OK. The Select Data Source dialog appears. The list of file DSNs includes the one you just created, as shown in Figure 22-18. Now you can continue adding a data connection to your project.

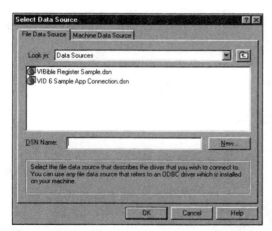

Figure 22-18: After you create a new file DSN, it is added to this list.

Machine data source

Unlike the file DSN, which stores the information about the database connection in a file, the machine DSN stores the information in the Windows Registry of the machine on which the DSN is created.

There are two types of machine DSNs: *system* and *user*. Create a system DSN when you want all the users on a machine or system to use the same connection. Create a user DSN when only one user on the machine can use the data connection.

Why use a machine DSN?

When you add a data connection that uses a machine DSN to a Web project or a database project, VI adds to the GLOBAL.ASA file a pointer to the entry for the machine DSN in the Windows Registry files. To use this same data connection on other machines, every machine — including the Web server, plus all developers, testers, and visitor workstations — must have the same entry at the same address in their Registry files. Obviously, this option does not allow for much portability.

A machine DSN is useful when you're developing a Web application, because you can easily switch to a different database by changing the entry in the Windows Registry. Otherwise, if you needed to change the database when you used a file DSN, you'd have to edit the GLOBAL.ASA file for every project in which it was used.

Creating a machine DSN

To add a data connection to a project, open the project, right-click the project name in the Project Explorer, and select Add Data Connection from the shortcut menu. The Select Data Source dialog appears. Then follow these steps to add a new machine DSN:

1. In the Select Data Source dialog, click the Machine Data Source tab, as shown in Figure 22-19.

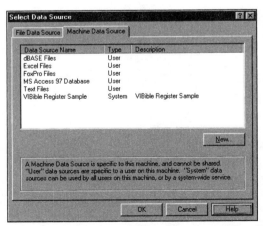

Figure 22-19: If you don't see the machine DSN you want to use in the list, click New to create one.

2. Click New. The Create New Data Source dialog appears

3. Select the associated option to create either a User or System DSN. In this example, we chose to create the System Data Source option, as shown in Figure 22-20.

Figure 22-20: Your options are to create either a user or a system machine DSN.

4. Click Next>. From this point forward, the process of defining a machine DSN is identical to the process of creating a file DSN beginning at Step 3.

How to determine the kind of DSN your project is using

If you don't remember what type of DSN you used when you added the data connection to your project, here's an easy way to find out: double-click the GLOBAL.ASA file in the Project Explorer. The file opens in the source editor. Read through the next two sections on identifying a file DSN and a machine DSN, then examine your GLOBAL.ASA file for a match.

What a file DSN adds to the GLOBAL.ASA file

Listing 22-1 shows you the script code added to the GLOBAL.ASA file for the sample Web project, Project*X*, which has a data connection to a SQL Server Register database located on server*x*, based on a file DSN.

Listing 22-1: GLOBAL.ASA File's Application_OnStart Procedure Using a File DSN

```
<SCRIPT LANGUAGE=VBScript RUNAT=Server>
Sub Application_OnStart
    '==Visual InterDev Generated - startspan==
    '--Project Data Connection
        Application("Register_ConnectionString") =
        "DRIVER=SQL Server;SERVER=serverx;
        User Id=sa;APP=Developement Environment;
        WSID=STATIONX;DATABASE=register;
        UseProcForPrepare=2"
        Application("Register_ConnectionTimeout") = 15
        Application("Register_CommandTimeout") = 30
        Application("Register_CursorLocation") = 3
        Application("Register_RuntimeUserName") = "sa"
        Application("Register_RuntimePassword") = ""
    '-- Project Data Environment
        Set DE =
Server.CreateObject("DERuntime.DERuntime")
        Application("DE") =
        DE.Load(Server.MapPath("Global.ASA"),
        "_private/DataEnvironment/DataEnvironment.asa")
    '==Visual InterDev Generated - endspan==
End Sub
</SCRIPT>
```

What a machine DSN adds to the GLOBAL.ASA file

Listing 22-2 presents the code added to the GLOBAL.ASA file when a data connection that uses a machine DSN is added to the project. This is the same SQL server Register database that is used in the previous file DSN example.

If the value of the connection string begins with "DSN," then the data source is based on a machine DSN. In this case, when the application runs, the connection string looks in the Windows Registry for the DSN.

Listing 22-2: GLOBAL.ASA File's Application_OnStart Procedure Using a Machine DSN

```
<SCRIPT LANGUAGE=VBScript RUNAT=Server>
Sub Application_OnStart
    '==Visual InterDev Generated - startspan==
    '--Project Data Connection
        Application("Connection1_ConnectionString") =
        "DSN=VIBible Register Sample;User Id=sa;
        PASSWORD=;Description=VIBible Register Sample;
        SERVER=serverx;APP=Development Environment;
        WSID=STATIONX;DATABASE=register;UseProcForPrepare=2"
        Application("Connection1_ConnectionTimeout") = 15
        Application("Connection1_CommandTimeout") = 30
        Application("Connection1_CursorLocation") = 3
        Application("Connection1_RuntimeUserName") = "sa"
        Application("Connection1_RuntimePassword") = ""
    '-- Project Data Environment
        'Set DE = Server.CreateObject("DERuntime.DERuntime")
        'Application("DE") =
        DE.Load(Server.MapPath("Global.ASA"),
        "_private/DataEnvironment/DataEnvironment.asa")
    '==Visual InterDev Generated - endspan==
End Sub
</SCRIPT>
```

Adding a Data Connection to a Web Project

When you are ready to access a database from your Web application, follow these steps to add a data connection to a Web project:

1. In the Project Explorer, right-click the name of the project.

2. Select Add Data Connection from the shortcut menu. The Select Data Source dialog appears.

3. Click the tab for the type of data source you want to use, either file DSN or machine DSN.

4. Select the name of the DSN from the list. If the name does not appear in the dialog, follow the procedure for creating a new DSN outlined earlier in the section "Data Source Names."

5. Click OK. The database may prompt you for a login ID and password. Enter this information and click OK. VI adds a DataEnvironment node below the GLOBAL.ASA file in the Project Explorer. It also adds script to the GLOBAL.ASA file. The Connection Properties dialog appears. Whenever you change a connection property, the new value is written to the GLOBAL.ASA file.

6. On the General tab, the default name for the connection shown in the Connection Name box is Connection*X*, where *X* is a sequential number assigned by VI. Enter a more meaningful name for the connection if you like.

   Select the appropriate option for the Source of the Connection, either ODBC data source name, a Data Link file, or a connection string (the default), as shown in Figure 22-21.

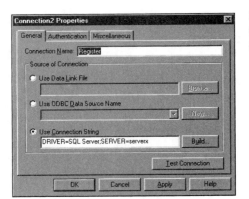

Figure 22-21: Set the General properties for the data connection on this tab.

7. On the Authentication tab, enter the default login IDs and passwords to use during design-time and runtime for the Web application that uses this connection. In the Prompt Behavior box, select when to prompt for logon information during design-time, as shown in Figure 22-22. If you do not want to prompt your site visitors for a database ID and password, make sure you set Prompt Behavior in the Run-time section to Never.

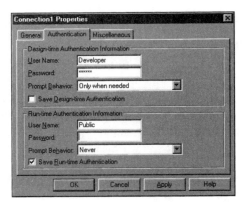

Figure 22-22: Enter the default login IDs and passwords in the Authentication properties for the data connection.

8. On the Miscellaneous tab, enter the timeout values, select the location of the cursor library, and add any additional parameters for the connection string. See Figure 22-23.

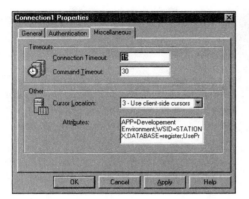

Figure 22-23: On the Miscellaneous tab, set the values for the data connection's timeout, cursor location, and other properties.

9. Click OK to save the new property settings to the GLOBAL.ASA file.

Summary

In this chapter, we examined data connections in Visual InterDev. Here's a summary of what you learned:

✦ Microsoft's DNA and UDA help developers create distributed Internet applications that take full advantage of the PC while accessing any type of corporate data.

✦ A database server can be added to a VI Web application environment on the same machine as the Web server, on a separate machine, or on a developer workstation. There are pros and cons to each of these configurations.

✦ VI's data architecture consists of a data connection, data environment, data commands, recordsets, and Design-Time Controls.

✦ Data Source Name comes in two flavors: *file* and *machine*. Each has its own advantages.

✦ When you add a data connection to your Web project, VI provides you with a robust Properties dialog that lets you easily specify every aspect of the connection.

✦   ✦   ✦

Working with Data on a Web Page

In Part V, you learned how to work with the Visual Database Tools (VDTs) to create a database – as well as how to create queries, views, stored procedures, and SQL script. In Chapter 22, you learned how to create a data connection, which tells a Web project everything it needs to know to locate and access a database and add it to a Web project. In this chapter, you work with data on a Web page. This chapter teaches you how to create data commands and add them to a Web page and how to use Visual InterDev's Design-Time Controls (DTC), which are special ActiveX controls that display the data on the page.

The chapter ends with a number of examples. In these examples, you continue working with the sample SQL Server Register database. Instructions for installing a copy of Register, which is located on the companion CD-ROM, are found in Chapter 18.

Understanding Data Commands

A data command, or Data Environment (DE) command, consists of a data connection and a set of data retrieval instructions. When used on a Web page, the data command provides the information needed to connect the Web page to the database and to retrieve a set of records from the database. The data source for a data command is a database table, a view, a stored procedure, or a set of SQL statements.

After you place a data command on a Web page, VI automatically connects the Web page to the data command's database by using a Recordset DTC. When you define a data command, you are encapsulating the data connection and the data retrieval commands. Data commands are very convenient when you need to change the retrieval commands. When you use a data command on multiple Web pages, you change the data command file and the entire Web project is updated. If you do not use data commands, and instead enter the data connection and retrieval information directly on each Web page, making changes becomes a very time consuming and error-prone endeavor.

In this section, you create one of each of the four different types of data commands. In the next section, you add a data command to a Web page and learn how to work with the Recordset DTC. Before you can add a data command to a Web project, you must first add a data connection for the database. For complete instructions on how to add a data connection, refer to Chapter 22. If you wish to follow along with the example in this chapter, you will need a data connection to the sample Register database.

Data commands based on a table or a view

When you want to retrieve all rows in the table or view, create a data command with a data source that is a database table or a view. If you base the command on the table, all columns will be returned. If you base it on a view, only the columns in the view will be returned. If you do not plan to display all of the fields in the table or view on the Web page, you should consider using either a stored procedure or a set of SQL statements. The extra unused fields add unnecessary load to the network.

Follow these steps to create a data command with a table as the data source to a Web project:

1. In the Project Explorer, open the GLOBAL.ASA branch and the Data Environment node, and then right-click the data connection for the database to which this data command will apply. Select Add Data Command from the shortcut menu. The Command*X* Properties dialog appears, where *X* is a sequential number VI assigns to new data commands. In this example, use the data connection for the Register database.

2. On the General tab:

   a. Enter a descriptive name for this data command in the Command Name box. For this example, enter **CustPayments**.

   b. Next to Connection, select the data connection from the list. If there is only one data connection in the project, this value is set automatically.

   c. In the Source Data section, click Data Object and then select Table or View from the drop-down list. For this example, select Table.

   d. Select the name of the database object in Object Name. For this example, select dbo.Customer as shown in Figure 23-1.

When you select the Object Name box, you activate the data connection to the database. A login dialog may appear with the default Login ID that you provided when you defined the data connection. Enter the password and click OK.

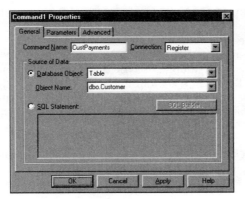

Figure 23-1: The properties of a new data command based on a Table are defined on the General tab.

3. Click OK. VI adds the new data command, CustPayments, below the data connection in the Project Explorer, as shown in Figure 23-2. Below the data command, is the list of fields that will be retrieved when the data command is executed.

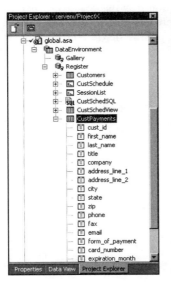

Figure 23-2: The Project Explorer displays all the fields in the CustPayments data command.

Data commands based on a stored procedure

You may want to create a data command with a stored procedure as the data source because it allows you to precisely control the data retrieved, and also because it runs faster than data commands based on tables, views, or SQL statements.

Create a data command based on a stored procedure by following these steps:

1. In the Project Explorer, open the GLOBAL.ASA branch and the Data Environment node, and then right-click the data connection for the database for this data command. For this example, use the data connection for the sample Register database. Select Add Data Command from the shortcut menu. The CommandX Properties dialog appears, where X is a sequential number VI assigns to new data commands.

2. On the General tab:

    a. Enter a descriptive name for this data command in the Command Name box. For this example, enter CustScheduleSP.

    b. Next to Connection, select the data connection from the list. If there is only one data connection in the project, this value is set automatically.

    c. In the Source Data section, click Data Object and then select Stored Procedure from the drop-down list.

    d. Select the name of the stored procedure in Object Name. For this example, select dbo.CustScheduleSP.

3. On the Parameters tab, each of the parameters used by the stored procedure appears in the Parameters list on the left. Select a parameter from this list and the properties of that parameter appear in the fields on the right, as shown in Figure 23-3. You can hard-code a specific value to use for a parameter each time this data command executes by entering it in the value box.

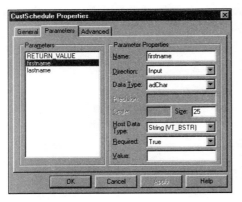

Figure 23-3: The Command Properties dialog box tells you what parameters the stored procedure needs.

4. Click OK. VI adds the new data command CustScheduleSP below the data connection in the Project Explorer. Below the data command is the list of fields that will be retrieved when the data command is executed.

Data commands based on SQL statements

You may want to use specific SQL statements as the data source for a data command, because the SQL statements allow you to precisely control the data retrieved.

To create a data command based on SQL statements, following these steps:

1. In the Project Explorer, open the GLOBAL.ASA branch and the Data Environment node, and then right-click the data connection for the database for this data command. For this example, use the data connection for the sample Register database. Select Add Data Command from the shortcut menu. The Command*X* Properties dialog appears, where *X* is a sequential number VI assigns to new data commands.

2. On the General tab:
   a. Enter a descriptive name for this data command in the Command Name box. For this example, enter CustSchedSQL.

   b. Next to Connection, select the data connection from the list. If there is only one data connection in the project, this value is set automatically.

   c. In the Source Data section, click SQL Statement and then either enter the SQL statements in the box or click SQL Builder to use Visual Database Tool's Query Builder to help you create the SQL statements visually. Chapter 20 teaches you to use Query Builder. For this example, enter the SQL statements shown in Listing 23-1, which prompts for a customer name and then retrieves a list of the sessions for which a customer is registered.

Listing 23-1: **List of Sessions for Prompted Customer**

```
SELECT Session.Title, Session.Start_DateTime, Session.Room
FROM Customer, CustomerToSession, Session
    WHERE Customer.cust_id = CustomerToSession.cust_id
    AND CustomerToSession.session_id = Session.Session_ID
    AND (first_name = ?)
    AND (last_name = ?)
```

3. Each of the parameters used by the SQL Statements appears in the Parameters list at the left of the Parameters tab. Select a parameter from this list and the properties of that parameter appear in the fields on the right. Adjust these parameters as follows:
   a. In the Name field, assign each parameter a meaningful name. In this example, assign First Name to Param1 and Last Name to Param2.

b. In the Value box, enter a default value to use when this data command executes. Use this technique when you first introduce a data command io a Web page to ensure the page functions properly. For this example assign John to Param1 and Smith to Param 2 (see Figure 23-4).

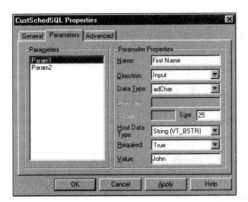

Figure 23-4: Default values for a parameter are set in the Command Properties dialog.

4. Click OK. VI adds the new data command, `CustSchedSQL`, below the data connection in Project Explorer. Below the data command is the list of fields that will be retrieved when the data command is executed.

Data-Bound DTCs Included with VI

Data-bound DTCs allow you to connect your Web page to data, retrieve that data, and display it. Most DTCs consist of an ActiveX control, but not all of them have a visual component. All of them, however, do generate the script code that makes DTC work.

Table 23-1 shows a list of the data-bound DTCs that appear in the Design-Time Controls tab of the Toolbox, along with a brief description of each DTC. You work with many of these controls in the examples featured in the rest of this chapter.

Tip

To activate the Toolbox, open a Web page in the Source Editor. If in your Toolbox you don't see one of the DTCs listed in Table 23-1, right-click anywhere in the Toolbox and select Customize Toolbox. In the dialog that appears, select the name of the DTC you are looking for and click OK.

Table 23-1
Data-Bound DTCs in the Toolbox

Icon	Name	Description
Insert 1	Checkbox	Displays a box that is either checked or unchecked.
Insert 2	FormManager	Creates an event-driven form.
Insert 3	Grid	Displays data from a Recordset in rows and columns.
Insert 4	Label	Displays text.
Insert 5	Listbox	Provides a single box with a down arrow that displays a list of values
Insert 6	OptionGroup	Displays a radio button next to an item belonging to a set of choices. The visitor may only choose one item in the set.
Insert 7	Recordset	Manages the set of records retrieved by the data command.
Insert 8	RecordsetNavBar	Displays navigation buttons that allow the visitor to move forward and backward though the recordset.
Insert 9	Textbox	Displays values and accepts input from the visitor.

Working with the Recordset DTC

Of all the data-bound DTC controls, Recordset is the most important. Without it a Web page could not access or display data. Consider the case of a Web page with three DTCs on it: a Recordset DTC to get and manage the data and two text boxes to display data values. The Recordset DTC consists of a data connection and a data command. When the Web page is executed, the Recordset control connects to the database, submits the retrieval command, and creates the Recordset object when it receives the set of records returned from the database. The other data-bound DTCs on the page get data fields from the Recordset control, which manages all the data in the recordset object. Figure 23-5 shows how these components interact.

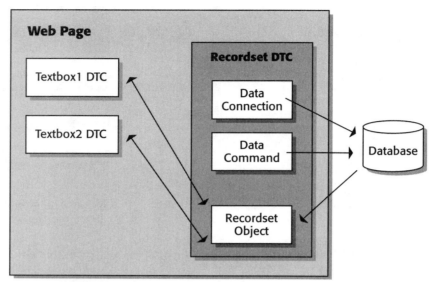

Figure 23-5: Here's how the DTCs Recordset object, data command, and data connection interact on a Web page.

Properties

As with any ActiveX control, you determine how the control functions by assigning values to its properties. VI has made it very easy for you to set the properties of the Recordset DTC through a Properties Pages dialog. The control uses the values displayed in this dialog to create lines of script to connect to the database, retrieve data, and manage the results set for the other controls on the page. If you drag a data command from Project Explorer to the Web page to automatically create the Recordset control, the Properties values are supplied automatically. You learn how to do this later in this chapter.

Properties is organized into these four tabs:

✦ **General** – Use this tab, shown in Figure 23-6, to assign a meaningful name to the control. The default name is Recordset$X$, where X is a sequential number assigned to each Recordset control on the page. The name you assign must be unique for the page. You use it in script when you refer to this control. The other information on the page is derived from the properties of the data source used to create the control: table, view, stored procedure, or DE command.

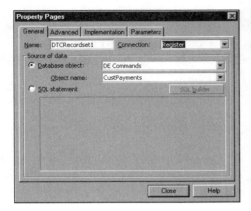

Figure 23-6: Use the General tab of the Recordset Properties Pages to set the name and data source for the control.

✦ **Advanced** – This tab contains information used to control how the data connection is handled, for example the maximum number of records to return and how long to let the retrieval run before timing out. If the data source for the control is a DE command, these values are inherited from the DE command and cannot be modified here.

✦ **Implementation** – The properties on this page control the scripting platform and how the recordset is handled. The two most important properties on the page are Scripting Platform and Automatically Open the Recordset.

✦ **Scripting Platform** – The default value is Inherit from Page, which tells the Recordset control and all DTCs that use it what type of script to generate – either client or server scripts. Set this value to Client (IE 4.0 DHTML) when you want the controls to generate client scripts. When you bind a DTC to this Recordset, the DTC inherits the value of this setting. To set the scripting platform for the page, click on the page and, in the Properties window, select DOCUMENT in the list box at the top of the window. Select DTCScriptingPlatform in the list of properties, and then select Client or Server. (In Chapter 22, we discussed the advantages and disadvantages of controlling access to the data from the client and server.)

✦ **Automatically Open the Recordset** – Check this box when you want the Recordset control to automatically pass data to the other DTCs on the page as soon as it creates the Recordset object.

✦ **Parameters** – This tab, shown in Figure 23-7, displays settings for all the parameters used by the control's data source. When the data source is a DE command, these values can be set in the DE command's properties dialog and inherited by the Recordset, or set here for the Recordset. When you set them at the data command, everyone on the team that uses the data command gets the same results. In this example, everyone gets John Smith as the customer. When you set them in the Recordset, you can test different data values, such as Jane Doe.

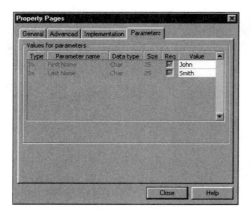

Figure 23-7: On the Parameters tab you can set the values for any parameters needed by the data source used by the Recordset control.

Adding Data to a Web Page

Before the data command can work with data on a Web page, you must first place the command on the page. This creates the Recordset control and binds it to the data source. Then you must place individual data fields on the page for display. These fields are retrieved by the data command and reside in the results set.

Adding a data command to a page

To add a data command to a Web page, first open either an Active Server Page or an HTML page. Then, in the Project Explorer, drag the data command to the page. A Recordset control appears, as shown in Figure 23-8.

Figure 23-8: When you drop a data command on a page, VI creates a Recordset control.

Right-click the Recordset control and select Properties. The Properties page dialog appears. On the General tab, the Values for Connection, Database object, and Object name are automatically set to match the data command that you dropped on the page.

Listing 23-2 shows the code automatically generated when you drop the CustPayment data command on a new HTML page.

Tip

To view the source code behind a DTC, click the Source tab in the editor window and then on the View menu, click View All Controls as Text.

Listing 23-2: VI Automatically Generates Code When You Drop a Data Command on an HTML Page

```
<!--METADATA TYPE="DesignerControl" startspan
<OBJECT classid="clsid:9CF5D7C2-EC10-11D0-9862-0000F8027CA0"
 id=DTCRecordset1 style="LEFT: 0px; TOP: 0px">
  <PARAM NAME="ExtentX" VALUE="12197">
  <PARAM NAME="ExtentY" VALUE="2064">
  <PARAM NAME="State"
VALUE="(TCConn=\qRegister\q,TCDBObject=\qDE\sCommands\q,
TCDBObjectName=\qCustPayments\q,TCControlID_Unmatched=
\qDTCRecordset1\q,TCPPConn=\qRegister\q,RCDBObject=
\qRCDBObject\q,TCPPDBObject=\qDE\sCommands\q,
TCPPDBObjectName=\qCustPayments\q,TCCursorType=\q3\s-
\sStatic\q,TCCursorLocation=\q2\s-\sUse\sserver-
side\scursors\q,TCLockType=\q3\s-\sOptimistic\q,
TCCacheSize_Unmatched=\q100\q,TCCommTimeout_Unmatched=
\q30\q,CCPrepared=0,CCAllRecords=1,TCNRecords_Unmatched=
\q10\q,TCODBCSyntax_Unmatched=\q\q,TCHTargetPlatform=
\q\q,TCHTargetBrowser_Unmatched=\qClient\s(IE\s4.0\sDHTML)
\q,TCTargetPlatform=\qInherit\sfrom\spage\q,RCCache=
\qRCBookPage\q,CCOpen=1,GCParameters=(Rows=0))"></OBJECT>
-->
<script language="JavaScript"
src="_ScriptLibrary/EventMgr.HTM"></script>
<script language="JavaScript"
src="_ScriptLibrary/Recordset.HTM"></script>
<script language="JavaScript">
function _initDTCRecordset1()
{   DTCRecordset1.setRecordSource('DRIVER=SQL Server;
SERVER=serverx;User Id=sa;PASSWORD=;
APP=Developement Environment;WSID=STATIONX;
DATABASE=register;
UseProcForPrepare=2', 'select * from dbo.Customer');
  DTCRecordset1.open();
}
CreateRecordset('DTCRecordset1', _initDTCRecordset1);
</script>

<!--METADATA TYPE="DesignerControl" endspan-->
```

Adding a field to a page

Now continue with the "Adding a Data Command to a Page" exercise you started earlier. Follow these steps to add a field to the Web page:

1. Open either an Active Server Page or an HTML page that contains a Recordset control.

2. In the Project Explorer, open the branch for the data command you used to create the Recordset control. The fields in the data command appear.

3. In Project Explorer, drag a field to the page. If the field is text or numeric, a Textbox DTC appears. If the field is Boolean, a Checkbox DTC appears. Figure 23-9 shows the Design view of the HTML page in the WYSIWYG (What You See Is What You Get) editor after dropping the first_name field on the page.

Figure 23-9: When you drop a text or numeric field from the data command on the page, VI creates a data-bound Textbox DTC.

Listing 23-3 shows the code VI automatically generates when you drop the first_name field on the page shown in Listing 23-2.

Listing 23-3: **VI Automatically Generates Code When You Drop a Text Field from the Data Command on an HTML Page**

```
<P>
first_name
<!--METADATA TYPE="DesignerControl" startspan
<OBJECT classid="clsid:B5F0E469-DC5F-11D0-9846-0000F8027CA0"
 height=19 id=Textbox1
style="HEIGHT: 19px; WIDTH: 120px" width=120>
<PARAM NAME="_ExtentX" VALUE="3175">
<PARAM NAME="_ExtentY" VALUE="503">
<PARAM NAME="id" VALUE="Textbox1">
<PARAM NAME="ControlType" VALUE="0">
```

```
<PARAM NAME="Lines" VALUE="3">
<PARAM NAME="DataSource" VALUE="DTCRecordset1">
<PARAM NAME="DataField" VALUE="first_name">
<PARAM NAME="Enabled" VALUE="-1">
<PARAM NAME="Visible" VALUE="-1">
<PARAM NAME="MaxChars" VALUE="20">
<PARAM NAME="DisplayWidth" VALUE="20">
<PARAM NAME="Platform" VALUE="1">
<PARAM NAME="LocalPath" VALUE="">
 </OBJECT>
-->
<script language="JavaScript"
src="_ScriptLibrary/TextBox.HTM"></script>
<script language="JavaScript">
function _initTextbox1()
{
    Textbox1.setDataSource(DTCRecordset1);
    Textbox1.setDataField('first_name');
    Textbox1.setMaxLength(20);
    Textbox1.setColumnCount(20);
}
CreateTextbox('Textbox1', _initTextbox1);</script>

<!--METADATA TYPE="DesignerControl" endspan-->
</P>
```

DTC Scripting Platform

The scripting platform determines where script on a page is run - either on the client workstation in the browser or on the server by the Web server. A Design-Time Control inherits the setting for its scripting platform from the Recordset to which it's bound. The value of the Recordset's scripting platform property, which is set on the Implementation tab of the Recordset Property Pages, determines whether the Recordset inherits the scripting platform from the page, or whether it is on the client or on the server. The DTC scripting platform of the page or document is set when VI creates the page. The default value of the DTCScriptPlatform property for an Active Server Page is Server (ASP). The default value for an HTML page is Client (IE 4.0 DHTML). You can change this default value by changing the value of the DTCScriptPlatform property in the Property window for the DOCUMENT. Figure 23-10 shows from where the Recordset and the other DTCs on the page inherit the value of their DTC scripting platform property.

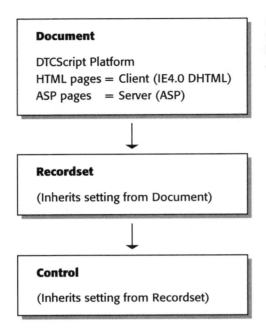

Figure 23-10: The DTC scripting platform is set at the document level and inherited by the Recordset and all DTCs.

DTC Examples

In this section, you create four Web pages that use different controls to provide access to the data in the sample Register database. In "Example 1: browsing data — single record per page," you use the Recordset, Textbox, and RecordsetNavBar controls. In "Example 2: browsing data — multiple records per page," you use Recordset, Grid, and RecordsetNavBar controls. In "Example 3: browsing data — hard-coded parameter values," you use the Recordset, Textbox, and RecordsetNavBar controls again, but this time the data command requires two parameters. Finally, in "Example 4: event — driven form," you use the Recordset, Textbox, RecordsetNavBar, and FormManager DTCs to browse, edit, and add data to a table.

Example 1: browsing data — single record per page

This example uses the Textbox and RecordsetNavBar DTCs. The data command is based on the Customer Table in the Register database. To see the finished page, view the file `\Chapter 23\Example23-1.asp` on the companion CD-ROM. Figure 23-11 shows the finished page in IE 4.

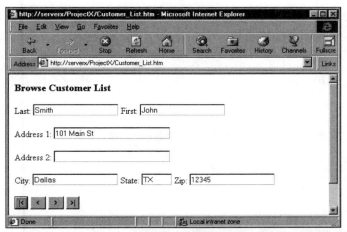

Figure 23-11: You can use the RecordsetNavBar and Textbox to browse through data one record at a time.

Follow these steps to create a Web page that you can use to browse one database record at a time:

1. Create a data command based on the Customer Table, and call it Customers.

2. Create a new Active Server page, and call it Customer_List.asp. Click the Design tab in the editor.

3. Drag the data command `Customers` from the Project Explorer to the page. A Recordset DTC appears and a dialog prompts you to enable the Scripting Object Model for this page. Click Yes.

4. In the Project Explorer, under the data command `Customers`, one by one, drag the fields last_name, first_name, address_line_1, address_line_2, city, state, and zip, and drop them on the page below the Recordset DTC. Format the page as it appears in Figure 23-11.

5. Drag a RecordsetNavBar from the Design-Time Control tab of the Toolbox to the page, below the City text box.

6. Right-click the RecordsetNavBar on the page and select Properties from the shortcut menu.

7. In the Data section on the General tab, select the name of the Recordset from the drop-down list. Click OK.

8. Save the page.

9. View the page in the IE 4 browser.

Example 2: browsing data – multiple records per page

This example uses the Grid DTC. The data command is based on the CustSessions view in the Register database. This view joins three tables: Customer, CustomerToSession, and Session. To see the finished page, view the file \Chapter 23\Example23-2.htm on the companion CD-ROM. Figure 23-12 shows the finished page in IE 4.0.

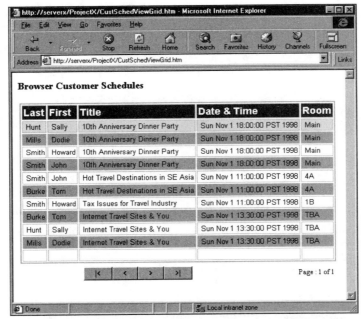

Figure 23-12: You can use the RecordsetNavBar and Grid to browse through data multiple records at a time.

Follow these steps to create a Web page that you can use to browse multiple records on a page:

1. Create a data command based on the CustSessions view that you created in Chapter 21 and call it **CustSessions**.

2. Create a new HTML page and call it **CustSessions.asp**. Click the Design tab in the editor.

3. Drag the data command CustSessions from the Project Explorer to the top of the page. A Recordset DTC appears and a dialog prompts you to enable the Scripting Object Model for this page. Click Yes.

4. Drag a Grid from the Design-Time Control tab of the Toolbox to the page and drop it below the Recordset DTC. The Grid DTC appears.

5. Right-click the edge of the Grid and select Properties from the shortcut menu. The Grid's Properties dialog appears.

6. On the Data tab, in the Recordset box, select the name of the Recordset from the list. The names of the fields in the recordset appear in the Available fields box.

7. Select the fields in the Available fields box that you want to appear in the Grid. For this example, select all of the fields. The fields appear in the Grid columns box in the order in which you select them.

8. To change the text that appears above the columns in the Grid, select the row containing the name of the column in the Grid columns box. In the Edit columns section, enter the new column heading in the Header box.

9. Click Update to save each new value, which appears in the Header column in the Grid columns box. Change all the headers to match the values you see in Figure 23-12.

10. On the General tab, make sure Display header row is checked.

11. On the Format tab, make sure Fixed column width is checked, and set the value of Alignment to Left.

12. On the Advanced tab, change the value for <TABLE to align=left.

13. On the Navigation tab in the Page navigation section, make sure Enable paging is checked. This will display navigation buttons below the grid on the Web page.

14. Enter **5** in the Records/page box. This box controls the number of rows displayed in the grid, which you can't do by sizing the grid in the editor.

15. Click OK to save the Property settings.

16. Format the page so that it appears similar to Figure 23-13, and then save the page. In the Grid, you can adjust the column by dragging the line between the two column headers to the left or right.

17. View the page in the IE 4 browser.

Note

One of the cool new features of DHTML is the capability to manipulate the Recordset object on the client. For example, you could offer the visitor the ability to sort the data displayed in the grid by last name or by title. DHTML lets you do this in the Web browser client without going back to the server to retrieve the data sorted in a different order. To learn more about the Recordset object, read the article "What's New in **Remote Data Service 1.5**" located at http://www.microsoft.com/data/ado/adords15/docs/adcwtnu.htm.

Example 3: browsing data–hard-coded parameter values

This example uses the Textbox and RecordsetNavBar DTCs. It also uses the data command `CustSchedSQL` that you created earlier in "Data Commands Based on SQL." The example is based on SQL statements that require two parameters: last_name and first_name. To see the finished page, view the file `\Chapter 23\Example23-3.asp` on the companion CD-ROM. Figure 23-13 shows the finished page in IE 4.

Figure 23-13: The CustSchedSQL data command uses two parameters to filter the data.

Follow these steps to create a Web page that you can use to browse one database record at a time using a data command that requires two parameters:

1. Create a new ASP page and call it **CustSchedSQL.asp**. Click the Design tab in the editor.

2. Drag the data command `CustSchedSQL` from Project Explorer to the page. A Recordset DTC appears, and a dialog prompts you to enable the Scripting Object Model for this page. Click Yes.

3. Right-click the Recordset control and select Properties from the shortcut menu. The Properties Page appears.

4. On the Parameters tab, enter **John** under the Value column for first_name and enter **Smith** for last_name, as shown in Figure 23-14.

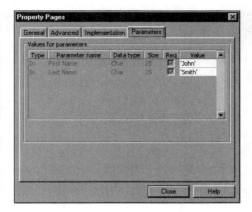

Figure 23-14: The values for parameters in the Recordset control are set on the Parameters tab.

5. Click Close.

6. In the Project Explorer, under the data command `CustSchedSQL` drag all of the fields to the page. Format the page as it appears in Figure 23-13 above.

5. Drag a RecordsetNavBar from the Design-Time Control tab of the Toolbox to the page.

6. Right-click the RecordsetNavBar on the page and select Properties from the shortcut menu.

7. In the Data section, select the name of the Recordset from the drop-down list.

8. Save the page.

9. View the page in the IE 4 browser.

Example 4: event-driven form

This example uses the Button, Textbox, RecordsetNavBar, and FormManager DTCs. `SessionList` is the data command and it is based on the Sessions table in the Register database. The goals of this page are to allow the visitor to browse the contents of the Session table, to make any changes or corrections to the data, and to add new sessions to the table. Figure 23-15 shows the finished page in IE 4.

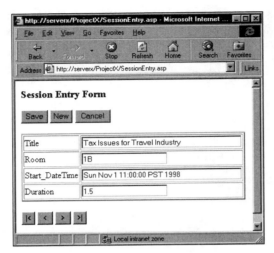

Figure 23-15: FormManager is used to create an event-driven form that can be browsed, updated, and added to by a Web page visitor.

Before starting this example, you need to do a little design work. When creating an event-driven form, you must decide what modes to support and the events that trigger changing from one mode to another. In addition, you need to determine in advance what other actions should occur when the mode changes.

This form will have two modes: Update and Add. In Update mode, the visitor sees all values in the database and can change any value. In Add mode, the visitor can only add new records to the table. These modes are mutually exclusive. The user cannot add data in Update mode and cannot modify existing data in Add mode. However, all of the fields are write-enabled in both modes.

Table 23-2 shows the modes and buttons that are active in each mode, and whether they trigger a mode change. Here's an example of how to read the table by examining the first row. In Add mode, when the visitor clicks the Clear button, the values that appear in the four data fields are cleared out so the visitor can enter the values again.

In Add mode, when the user clicks the Add button, the `UpdateRecord` method saves the values on the Web page to the database. The `MoveFirst` method shows the first record in the Recordset on the page. The mode switches to Update.

Note   While developing this example using VI Release Candidate 1 software, we found that unless the `MoveFirst` method was included, we could not use the RecordsetNavBar to move between the records once a record was added.

In Add mode, when the visitor clicks the Cancel button, the `MoveFirst` method discards any values entered in the four text boxes on the page by redisplaying the first record and switching to Update mode.

In Update mode, when the visitor clicks the New button, the `AddRecord` method adds one record and the `MoveLast` method lets the user enter values into the new record. The four text box controls are cleared out before switching to Add mode.

In Update mode, when the user clicks the Save button, the `UpdateRecord` method saves the values on the page to the database. The page remains on the same record and the mode stays in Update.

In Update mode, when the user clicks Cancel, `MoveNext` followed by the `MovePrevious` methods discard any changes made in the four text boxes and redisplay the values in the database. The mode stays in Update.

	Table 23-2 List of Modes and Transition Events		
Mode	**Button**	**Actions**	**Mode After Action**
Add	Clear	Session Value <NULL>	
		Room Value <NULL>	
		StartDT Value <NULL>	
		Duration Value <NULL>	Add
Add	Add	Recordset.UpdateRecord()	
		Recordset.MoveFirst()	Update
Add	Cancel	Recordset.MoveFirst()	Update
Update	New	Recordset.AddRecord()	
		Recordset.MoveLast()	
		Session Value <NULL>	
		Room Value <NULL>	
		StartDT Value <NULL>	
		Duration Value <NULL>	Add
Update	Save	Recordset.UpdateRecord()	Update
Update	Cancel	Recordset.MoveNext()	
		Recordset.MovePrevious()	Update

Table 23-3 shows the status of every button and display control when each mode is active. The two modes, Update and Add, appear in the columns and there is one row for each button and control on the page. The buttons are Save, New, Add, Clear, and Cancel. The four design-time Textbox controls are Session, Room, StartDateTime (StartDT), and Duration.

Here's an example of how to read the table by examining the first row. In Update mode, the Save button is active and visible. In Add mode, the Save button is inactive (not active) and hidden (not visible). This means that in Update mode you can click the Save button, but you don't see it in Add mode.

Table 23-3 Status of Each Button in Each Mode				
Button & Display Control	Update Mode Status	Update Mode Visibility	Add Mode Status	Add Mode Visibility
Save	Active	Visible	Inactive	Hidden
New	Active	Visible	Inactive	Hidden
Add	Inactive	Hidden	Active	Visible
Clear	Inactive	Hidden	Active	Visible
Cancel	Active	Visible	Active	Visible
Session	Active	Visible	Active	Visible
Room	Active	Visible	Active	Visible
StartDT	Active	Visible	Active	Visible
Duration	Active	Visible	Active	Visible

To construct an event-driven Web page, follow these basic steps:

1. Create the data command called `SessionList`, which is based on the Session table. To be able to add records to the database, the cursor type for the data command must be set to either Keyset or Dynamic. Use the Advanced tab of the data command's Properties dialog to set this value.

2. Create an Active Server page and call it **SessionBandE.asp**.

3. On the Design tab of the editor, drop the data command at the top of the page. The Recordset DTC appears, and a dialog prompts you to enable the Scripting Object Model for this page. Click Yes.

4. Place all the desired fields and the RecordsetNavBar DTC on the page. In this example, we added a table and placed the fields on different rows in the table. Be sure to place the RecordsetNavBar DTC below the fields.

5. Place five button DTCs on the page immediately below the Recordset control and change the Captions to Save, New, Add, Clear, and Cancel.

6. Drag the FormManager DTC from the toolbox to the bottom of the page below the RecordsetNavBar DTC. Figure 23-16 shows the page in the Design tab of VI's source editor.

Buttons   Recordset Navbar   Textbox Controls

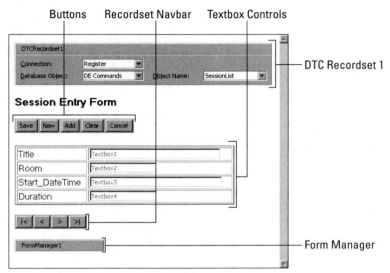

Figure 23-16: This is a data-bound form displayed in the Design tab.

7. To add the modes to the FormManager control, right-click FormManager and select Properties from the shortcut menu. The FormManager Properties dialog appears.

8. On the Form Mode tab, enter the names of the two modes, Update and Add, in the New Mode box, and click the right arrow to add the mode to the list on the right. Make sure Update is the default mode.

9. Use the information in Table 23-3 to set the properties and modes for each display control and button.

    ✦ To make a control or button active, set the disabled property to false.

    ✦ To make a control or button inactive, set the disabled property to true.

    ✦ To make a button visible, use the show() method.

    ✦ To make a button hidden, use the hide() method.

Note

Based on our experience with VI Release Candidate 1, we recommend that you set the visibility last because once you've hidden the control, you cannot be certain that any other property settings that you make actually take effect.

In the Form Mode list, select one of the modes you entered in step 6 above. In the Actions Performed For Mode grid, select the Object name for each button and control in column 1 of Table 23-3. Then select the property and enter the value or select the method. For example, To make the Save button active in Update mode, select Update in the Form Mode box, and in the first row of the Actions Performed For Mode box, select the Save button object name from the drop-down list. On the same row, move to the Member column and select the `disabled` method. Finally, in the last column, enter false. Figure 23-17 shows Add mode, where Textbox2 is Room and the Member value disabled is false, which means the Textbox control for Room is Active.

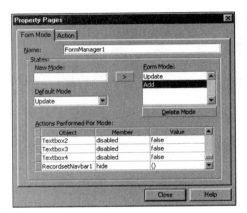

Figure 23-17: Modes are entered in the FormManager's Property pages.

10. In the Action Tab, use Table 23-2 to help you enter the values in the Form Mode Transitions grid. If another action must occur prior to the transition from one mode to another, select a row in the Form Mode Transitions grid and enter the values for the action in the Actions Performed Before Transition grid. Figure 23-18 shows you the actions performed on text boxes 1, 2, 3, and 4-in Update mode when the `onclick` event for the New button occurs. The action replaces the value of the four text boxes with "". This action occurs before the transition from Update mode to Add mode and ties back to the fourth row of Table 23-2.

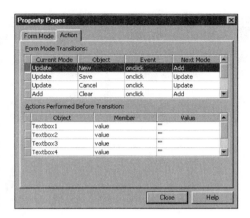

Figure 23-18: In the Form Manager's Property pages, enter the transitions first and then the actions performed prior to the transitions.

11. Save the page.

12. View and test the page in the IE 4 browser.

Summary

In this chapter, you worked with data on a Web page and learned the following material:

✦ Data commands are reusable modules that combine a data connection with a set of data retrieval instructions. You created data commands based on a table, a stored procedure, and a set of SQL statements.

✦ Data-bound Design-Time Controls are ActiveX controls that connect a Web page to a database, retrieve a set of data records, and display that data. You learned about the nine DTCs that are included in Visual InterDev.

✦ Recordsets are the most important of all the data-bound DTCs. The Recordset DTC consists of a data connection and a data command. When the Web page is executed, the Recordset control connects to the database, submits the retrieval command, and creates the Recordset object. The other data-bound DTCs on the page get fields from the Recordset control, which manages all the data in the Recordset object.

✦ How to work with Data Commands, the Recordset DTC, fields, Textbox DTCs, the RecordsetNavBar DTC, Grid DTCs, button controls, and the FormManager DTC to build data-driven DHTML and Active Server Pages.

✦   ✦   ✦

Managing Web Applications

Site Maintenance and Deployment

A Web site can grow in complexity quickly and become difficult to manage before you know it. Throughout this book, you've learned tactics and techniques to help control the several members of a team during the process of building a Web site. However, once a site is built, it still has to be managed. Files might need to be added, replaced, or renamed; and links between these files can be broken and need to be reestablished. In this chapter, we focus on managing an existing Web site and pay particular attention to the various tools provided by Visual InterDev to accomplish this job.

Reorganizing a Web Project

To understand the fundamentals of reorganizing a Web project, we create a simple, one-page site. Then we add new pages, add links among the pages, move and rename files, and see how to recalculate or repair broken links. This way, you get a good feel for Link View, a VI tool that can assist you in maintaining a complex site.

Start VI and choose New Project from the File menu. Double-click New Web Project in the right pane of the New Project dialog. Click Next to attach to your server. (If you don't know the name of your server, open the Network icon in Control Panel, then look at the Identification tab and see the name under Computer Name.)

In the Specify Your Web dialog page, name this new project **Linkings**. Click Next, and choose Top1 as your Layout, then click Next and click Finish. You don't need a Theme for this exercise. Choose Add Item from the Project menu and double-click the HTML Page icon. Repeat that, so that there are two HTML pages in your project, PAGE1.HTM and PAGE2.HTM.

Click Page1 to select it. Make sure you're in the Editor's Source View and that the HTML toolbar is visible. It has a link icon on the far right, as shown in Figure 24-1.

 Figure 24-1: Make sure the HTML toolbar is visible, with this link icon on its far right.

If you don't see the HTML toolbar, select Toolbars from the View menu and click HTML to add it to your other toolbars.

We want to link Page1 to Page 2, so click somewhere within the `<BODY>` of Page1 to establish the insertion point for your link and click the link icon. In the Hyperlink dialog, click the Browse button and click the + symbol in the Projects list next to your Linkings project to expand the list. In the right pane, double-click Page2.htm and click OK to close the dialog. The link-to page is now inserted in Page1, so add this text description to the link:

```
<A HREF="http://dell/Linkings/HTML Page2.htm">Click to go to
Page 2</A>
```

Now select Page2 and insert this in its `<BODY>` (replacing the word dell with the name of your server):

```
<P><A href="http://dell/Linkings/HTML Page1.htm">Click to go to
page 1</A></P>
```

You now have two pages linked to each other. To see how this organization looks in a graphic diagram, right-click Page1.htm in the Project Explorer. (If the Project Explorer isn't visible, select it in the View menu.) Click the View Links option in the pop-up menu, and you'll see the relationship illustrated in Figure 24-2:

Figure 24-2: The relationship between the pages and elements in your site as seen from Link View.

Figure 24-2 contains two arrows with a ball (nub) on one end and a tip on the other. The ball end indicates a hyperlink, and the tip end indicates the target of that link. Therefore, Page2 has a link to Page1 and Page1, in turn, has a link to Page2. Page1 is in the center of the diagram and is the largest icon because it's the page we initially selected when requesting View Links from the right-click pop-up menu. (You can alternatively select View Links from the View menu.)

Notice also the small + symbol in the upper-left of the Page2 icons. This tells you that Page2 has an additional link that's not currently being illustrated for that icon. The Page2 on the left isn't displaying an arrow from Page1 going *in*. And the Page2 on the right isn't displaying an arrow to Page1 going *out*. The + symbol means that there is more to see — other link(s) — and you can click on the + symbol to reveal those additional links.

Condensing, expanding, and zooming

If you do expand a page symbol by clicking on its + symbol, the + changes to a - symbol indicating that you can collapse the additional link(s) for a more convenient, larger scale view of the overall structure. In this way, you can expand or collapse a complicated Web site's link view to see as much or as little as you wish. As you might imagine, a large site could contain hundreds of links, so there has to be a facility for simplifying the structure. A second way of simplifying a link diagram is to zoom out (making the page icons and arrows smaller) so you can see more.

You probably noticed the Link View toolbar depicted in Figure 24-3 that pops out (usually) when you request a link view. (If you don't see it, choose Toolbars on the View menu and select Link View.)

Figure 24-3: You can maneuver through a link diagram with the tools on this Link View toolbar.

Sometimes pulling back by selecting a smaller zoom factor can give you a more abstract view of your overall site design; if you look at a complex site, an abstraction can be helpful. As an example, select View Links on WWW from the Tools menu. Then type in the Uniform Resource Locator (URL) of a complex, large site such as www.microsoft.com shown in Figure 24-4.

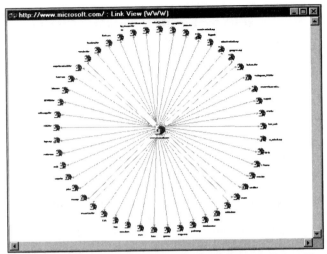

Figure 24-4: Site diagrams, such as this one of Microsoft's Web site, can be quite complex. You must zoom out to see the actual structure. This view is 37 percent of the normal view.

Right-click on five of the page icons shown in the pinwheel in Figure 24-5 and choose Expand Links to see the link relationships in that page. You'll create a diagram similar to the one shown in Figure 24-5.

Close the Web link view of Microsoft's massive site diagram, and return to our little two-page site view. Try clicking the Change Diagram Layout button — the third button from the left on the Link View toolbar. In this view, items surround the selected page on either side like two fans, no matter how many of them there are. This view, shown in Figure 24-5, is called *horizontal layout*, as distinct from the *radial layout* illustrated in Figure 24-6. The alternate diagram style fans all links out along the sides of the main page, in semicircles. The incoming links are shown on the left side, the outgoing links on the right side.

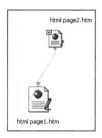

Figure 24-5: Horizontal layout

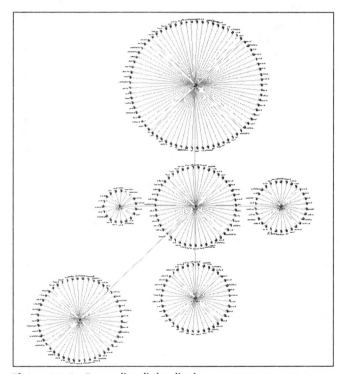

Figure 24-6: Expanding links displays even more structures in a large Web site.

The radial view shows *either* incoming or outgoing links, but not both at the same time. Click the Change Diagram button to switch to radial view, then try clicking the three buttons to the right of the Change Diagram button: Show In Links, Show Out Links, Show In and Out Links.

Now it's time for an experiment: What happens if you rename Page2? Click Page2 in the editor to select it, then choose Save HTML Page2.htm File As... and name it **Page2a.htm**. If you look at the link diagram, it is now incorrect (Page2 is still listed). Right-click on the diagram and choose Refresh. Now you'll see the diagram shown in Figure 24-7.

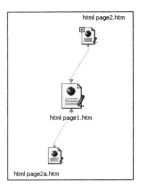

Figure 24-7: Renaming a file from Page2 to Page2a and then refreshing the diagram produces a diagram that looks like this.

What gives? You haven't really renamed Page2; you've merely created a new file identical to Page2 that is named Page2a. Right-click Page2 in the Project Explorer and choose Delete. Then refresh the Link diagram. Now, in the editor, remove the entire link in Page2a that targets Page1: `<A HREF="http://dell/Linkings/HTML Page1.htm">Click to go to page 1</A>`.

With that line removed, you no longer have a link in the code to Page1, but refreshing the Link Diagram does not cause VI to detect this. The diagram still shows a link arrow from Page2a to Page1. In this case, the problem is that you have not yet saved Page2a. With Page2a highlighted (selected) in the Project Explorer, press Ctrl+S to save it to disk, then refresh the diagram. It will now be correct.

Repairing broken links

A broken link occurs because the target of a link has been deleted (as we deleted Page2), or if the target has been moved or renamed. Broken links can also be caused by typographical errors in the URL specification in the source code. However they occur, you want to see and repair them. Click the Show Out Links button in the Link View toolbar (the fifth icon over from the left). You should see

Page1 linking to the (nonexistent) Page2. That's because deleting or renaming Page2 does not change Page1's source code, thereby creating the no-longer-valid link. This code still resides in Page1:

```
<A HREF="http://dell/Linkings/HTML Page2.htm">Click to go to
page 2</A>
```

Hold your mouse pointer on a broken link icon and a tooltip will pop out, telling you the reason for the broken link. This tooltip is shown at the top of Figure 24-8.

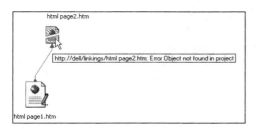

Figure 24-8: A broken link is illustrated by the broken-icon symbol.

Note that the tooltip in Figure 24-9 says that the object (Page2) was not found in the project. A second way to identify broken links is to select the root of the project (in this case, it's dell/Linkings, the second line in Project Explorer) and choose Broken Links Report from the View menu. In our example, this message appears in the Output window:

```
Unused files in project:
   html page1.htm
   html page2a.htm
   search.htm
Broken links in project:
   html page2.htm: broken link from html page1.htm
Broken external links:
Broken links report complete. All items have been added to the
task list.
```

We now know that Page1 contains an incorrect reference, so edit the link in Page1's source code so that it points to Page2a instead of Page2. Now *save Page1 to disk,* refresh the link diagram, and all will be well.

Automatic repairs

Making repairs to links by hand is fine with small projects where only one person is developing a simple site. But with a group working together on a large site, things can quickly get out of hand. Select Options on VI's Tools menu, and click Projects. The dialog shown in Figure 24-9 is displayed. You can allow VI to automatically repair broken links, on both the local and master server, with the "Repair links in referring files" option selected.

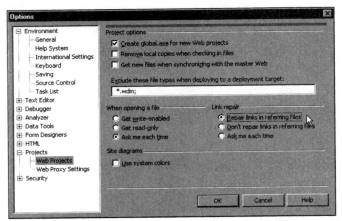

Figure 24-9: Visual InterDev's options for Web projects include automatic repairing of links.

Tip   You can also select or deselect link repair by right-clicking the root name (*server-name*/Linkings) in the Project Explorer, then choosing Properties and the General tab. The specifications for link repair in the Options dialog will apply (notification or automatic).

Link symbols and scope

There are a handful of symbols in Link View — in addition to the vivid broken-page icon — which help you visualize the types of pages and the relationships between them. For example, there are four document icons, which display the status of files on your local server or the master server. These icons also show whether a page is checked out under source control.

Modes of operation

You can work in VI in either local or master mode. If you are working within a development team, it is suggested that you work in local mode to avoid clashes and version problems between files you change and changes made to those same files by others on the team. However, if you are working alone (the master server isn't your personal production server), you can work in master mode safely. You switch between these modes by selecting the project in Project Explorer, then choosing Web Project from the Project menu and clicking Working Mode. Both local and master modes assume you are working online. The third possibility — working *offline* — means that you're not connected to a Web server at all.

Whether or not you're working offline has an effect on the scope of a link diagram. When working online, your link diagram will display the links for files located in your local Web project, the master Web application, and also any other URLs associated with your application's pages. When working offline, the scope of links displayed is reduced to only those files located on your local Web project.

Figure 24-10 shows the icons indicating the various states of files, as displayed in a link diagram.

Figure 24-10: The icons in a link diagram represent several file states.

The kinds of files that might be displayed in a link diagram are:

✦ A **Working File** is a copy of the master file that is accessible on the local Web server, which you can both view and edit. Usually the file will have been "checked out" under Source Control and will, therefore, display a red check mark.

✦ A **Local File,** like a working file, is a copy of the master file, but it can only be viewed - it cannot be edited. If the file is under Source Control, a blue padlock symbol is added.

✦ A **Personal File** doesn't exist yet (and may never exist) in the master Web application. Instead, it exists only locally, and must later be submitted to the master application if you so decide. The link diagram indicates a personal file with a blue flag.

✦ A **Master File**, symbolized by a grayed (disabled) document icon, is the one primary copy of the file located on the master Web server, that is accessible to everyone working on the Web site. If this file is under Source Control, a blue padlock symbol is added.

Content icons

Another set of link diagram icons symbolizes the type of document involved in a link: generally .ASP, .HTM., .GIF., or .AVI. To our example Linkings project, you could add links to an .ASP file, to the GLOBAL.ASA file, or to a video .AVI, as well as to a couple of images, by way of source code similar to the following that appears in Page1.HTM. Be sure to replace the SRC= attribute with paths to files on your system.

```
<A HREF="http://dell/Linkings/HTML Page2.htm">Click to go
to page 2</A>
<A HREF="http://dell/Linkings/ASP Page1.asp"></A>
<A HREF="http://dell/Linkings/global.asa"></A>
<img src="file:///C:/Sunflowr.jpg" width="187"
height="283"
alt="Sunflowr.jpg (11693 bytes)">
<img dynsrc="file:///C:/WINNT/clock.avi" start="fileopen"
width="321" height="321"
alt="clock.avi (82944 bytes)">
```

```
<p><img src="file:///C:/WINNT/Help/common/bestwith.gif"
width="88" height="31"
alt="bestwith.gif (9132 bytes)">
```

Save Page1.HTM to disk, right-click the icon for Page1 in the link diagram, and choose Refresh. The result of adding the five links will appear in your link diagram, as shown in Figure 24-11:

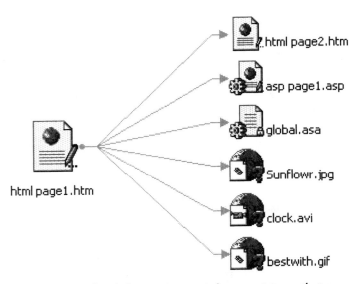

Figure 24-11: The six icons represent document types that are now linked to Page1.

Some of the icons displayed in Figure 24-12 may alter in appearance. For example, the three multimedia icons, currently symbolized by a globe, may change to particularized icons, such as a large video camera symbol.

Note the **?** symbol (it's red) attached to the multimedia files' icons in Figure 24-11. This symbol indicates that VI cannot determine the status, or *link state*, of these files — in other words, VI can't determine whether or not the link remains valid or is broken. To get rid of the red **?**, just right-click on the icon in the link view and choose Verify, or click the Verify button on the Link View toolbar. The icon will either appear broken in half or, if the link is valid, the **?** will disappear.

Link view toolbar filters

The Link View toolbar includes several buttons we've not yet covered. On the far left, the Expand Links button is enabled only if you select an object in the link diagram that contains a + or - in the upper-left corner of its icon. The + or - indicates that you can hide or reveal links to or from that object. Clicking the Expanded Links button toggles the visible state of these additional links in the diagram. Next to that button is the Verify button, which is enabled only when you select an icon with a red **?** in it, as shown in Figure 24-11.

Show repeated links

The seventh button from the left on the Link View toolbar is a toggle button named Show Repeated Links. With this button depressed, *every* link in a page with multiple links is displayed. For example, assume you have a table of contents in your home page with five links to different locations in *a single page* where definitions of your various products are displayed in five paragraphs. With the Show Repeated Links button depressed, there would be *five* arrows from the home page to the definitions page. There would also be five separate icons for the definitions page. If you leave the Show Repeated Links button deselected (its default state), then multiple links from a single page to another single page are displayed as a single arrow to a single target icon. This obviously simplifies the link diagram.

The eighth button from the left in the Link View toolbar is a toggle button named Show Links Inside Pages. When depressed, the link diagram displays an arrow for every link within a page. Again, leaving this button deselected (the default) reduces the complexity of a site diagram.

The filter buttons

There are six "filter" buttons on the right side of the Link View toolbar. These toggle buttons display or hide, from left to right:

✦ **HTML Pages** — standard HTML files, including .HTM, .ASA and .ASP

✦ **Multimedia Files** — audio or video (animation) files such as .AVI and .WAV

✦ **Document Files** — embedded objects in standard application file formats, such as a Microsoft Word .DOC file HTML page or an Excel .XLS file

✦ **Executable Files** — in practice, standard image files (.JPG and .GIF). In theory, this button is supposed to toggle files such as .EXE programs, scripts, batch files, and other executables.

✦ **Other Protocols** — any other kind of file

✦ **External Files** — files that are not located within the current Web site. Links to external files might include an absolute URL to a graphic on your hard drive outside your Web application's directory, or a URL to a different server or a location on the Internet other than your own server.

Link View currently boasts 20 different icons which represent these kinds of files: active layouts; Active Server Pages (*.ASP); audio files; conditional range headers; data commands; data connections; data range headers; executable files; generic designer controls; GLOBAL.ASA files; HTML pages; images; image maps; Mail to; Microsoft Excel spreadsheets; Microsoft PowerPoint files; Microsoft Word documents; news; other applications; and other text files.

Using Local Files

When you work with others on a project, they can add new files or make changes to the master Web application that are not yet reflected in your local application. You'll sometimes need to see these changes. To do this, you *refresh* your local application.

It can be useful to work locally because you can customize your environment. You can assign your favorite editor to a particular file type. Then, when you open that file in Project Explorer, your choice of working environment pops up containing the file. You can open a file type with a particular editor a single time, or assign the editor as the default for this kind of file. To open a Web page to your choice of editor, right-click the filename in Project Explorer, then click Open With. Choose the editor you want, add a new editor to the list, or set an editor as the default, as shown in Figure 24-12.

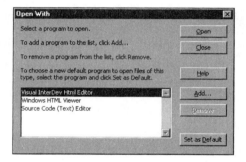

Figure 24-12: You can use custom editors on local files.

If you decide you want to see the latest version of a file from the master server, refresh your project. Just select the project you want to refresh in the Project Explorer, and in the Project menu, choose Web Project followed by Refresh Project View. To synchronize only some local files (as opposed to the entire project), select the project in Project Explorer, and in the Project menu, choose Web Project followed by Synchronize Files.

Tip   If you merely want to check to see how a local file compares to the master copy of that file, right-click the filename in Project Explorer and select Compare to Master Web.

Site Deployment

When you're happy with all your efforts and you consider your Web site finished, it's time to let others on your company's intranet, or the world on the Internet, enjoy the fruits of your labors. In other words, it's time to deploy your site to a public server—to move it from your local server. In VI, deployment is accomplished by copying the entire site, support files and all, to the public server.

Copying a site

If you want to copy an entire Web site from one production location to another, or from your personal workstation to a master server, VI makes the job easy. The job has several options, including copying only updated files, creating a second site on the same server with a different name, or creating an entirely new site.

Tip   Once a project has been copied to a new location (or name), developers working on the copy will be required to create projects for the copy. You can add a copied project to an existing project using the Web Project Wizard. Select New Project from the VI File menu and double-click the New Web Project icon.

To copy a Web site, follow these steps:

1. Select the project you want to copy in the Project Explorer.

2. From the Project menu, choose Web Project and Copy Web Application. You'll see the dialog shown in Figure 24-13.

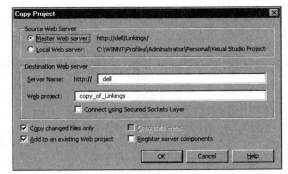

Figure 24-13: VI makes it easy to "instantly publish" a Web site.

3. Enter the destination server name in the text field marked http://. If the destination server is the same as the source server (as in Figure 24-13), the Web site will be located in a new virtual root directory on the same server.

4. The Connect using Secured Sockets Layer option is deselected by default. If the new server requires it, you must check this box to enable encrypted communications.

5. If you check the box marked Copy changed files only, the target site is updated, in the same manner that a disk drive backup can selectively archive only those files that have changed since the previous backup.

6. Choosing Add to an existing Web project causes your source project's files to be merged with the existing files in the destination site.

7. Finally, the Register server components option causes any components (ActiveX, .OCX, .DLL, or others) that require registration in the target server's Registry to be registered become usable.

8. When you've filled out the dialog, click OK, and VI will handle the job of copying for you. If you've created a new site on your local machine, you'll find it in the `INetPub/WWWRoot` folder.

Registering components

If you've attached to your site ActiveX or other objects that require registration, the Copy Web Application tool automatically registers your components on the server. If this doesn't happen, adjust your permission level on the server to permit you to register components. To enable registration, the Register Server Components option in the Copy Project dialog must be checked (see Figure 24-13).

Deployment Checklist

When you put your Web site out there for all to see, the assumption is that you've tested it, and that you have looked over the link diagrams to be sure everything is there, is navigable, and is sensibly organized. You might find this checklist useful, just as a final check before you go into the world and make your formal debut.

1. Have you checked all the hyperlinks in all the pages to make sure they are all referring to active, existing objects?

2. Are you sure that all the files required to support your project are updated on the master server? Has someone been working locally and not provided the latest version to the master server?

3. Be sure that support files (such as graphics) are also included in the master server.

4. Ensure that your data connection, if there is one, correctly points to the production database.

Note   Are the FrontPage Server Extensions installed on the production server? If not, you need the NT4 Option Pack, which is available for download from www.microsoft.com. The Option Pack includes Service Pack 3, though the files that comprise SP3 may also be downloaded separately. Versions of NT sold subsequent to January 1998 include the Option Pack. This enhancement (and bug fix) includes Internet Information Server (IIS) 4, which itself includes Microsoft's FrontPage Server Extensions.

If you're satisfied that these four issues have been adequately dealt with, go ahead with deployment by following the instructions described earlier in "Copying a Site."

Summary

This chapter complements Chapter 5, where you learned how to design a Web site using the Site Designer. Here, you used a similar tool, Link View, to review the links between your pages and see if they, after all is said and done, make sense from a user's point of view. You want visitors to find your site easily navigable and logical. You want their visits to your site to be pleasant and productive. In this chapter, you learned how to help make that happen:

✦ Reorganize a Web site

✦ Use Link View to condense or expand your site structure

✦ Repair broken links

✦ Automate repairs

✦ Recognize link symbols and scope

✦ Work with online, offline, master, and local files

✦ Understand content icons

✦ Use the Link View Toolbar filters

✦ Work with local files

✦ Copy a site to deploy it

✦ Register components

✦ Take a last look at everything, using a deployment checklist

✦   ✦   ✦

Exploring Security Issues

In This Chapter

Gauging how insecure the Internet truly is

Targets for Windows NT intruders

The critical role of permissions

Specific preventive measures for server intrusion

Certification and authentication

This chapter puts a realistic face on the issue of your Web server's security. The ideal Web application is crafted to interact plainly and directly with an innocent user. Those security measures that deal with what must happen should a user prove to be not so innocent are usually dealt with after the process of interacting with the ideal user has been perfected. Optimistically, this methodology is more convenient and allows you to concentrate on your application, rather than on security issues. But the topic of Internet security is not one that lends itself to as much optimism as we are accustomed to with other Microsoft products, where convenience is an expected option. Sometimes placing security at the bottom of the "to do" list proves to be a mistake. As a result, this chapter has its gloomy side—no doom, just a bit of gloom.

Because your Web application is designed specifically to be utilized by countless other people, many of whom are unknown to you, the security of your Web site is not an ancillary topic. Chances are that you'll use VI in conjunction with Windows NT Server 4.0 or Workstation 4.0, Internet Information Server (IIS) 4.0 (and thus Microsoft Transaction Server), and possibly FrontPage 98. Rarely will VI be deployed by itself, without any of these other components playing a role. Because security plays a role in the configuration of these other components, it is our view that security plays a role in Visual InterDev development.

There are measures that you can and should take to protect yourself and the users of your Web sites from unwarranted intrusion by a third party. These measures may not have anything directly to do with Visual InterDev and may have a bearing on NT Web servers that do not utilize VI at all; but this chapter will present these measures in detail.

For this chapter to give you a proper understanding of the nature of Web site intrusion and the preventative measures you should take beforehand, it must, unfortunately, give away some of the tricks with which intruders may break into your system. The decision to present this information was a difficult one on our part; after all, a chapter on preventing violence probably wouldn't go into detail as to the proper loading procedure for an automatic rifle. But interfering with the operations of a Web server remotely is shockingly simple. In some cases, the nature of the preventative process itself gives away the nature of the process it intends to prevent. We hope that a broader and more vivid understanding of this topic will not only help Web server administrators to take precautions now, but also help software manufacturers to not make intrusion so simple in the future.

Internet Security, and Other Oxymorons

At present, there is only one Internet with a capital "I." There are a handful of so-called "internetworking protocols," IP among them; but when we say a transaction takes place *on the Internet*, we truly are referring to one system. Every e-mail message, database query, poll response, request for subscription, and every single hyperlink ever clicked on from a Microsoft or Netscape browser, involves a transaction that takes place on this one single assembly of cables and processors.

As long as the Internet is not owned, in whole or in large part, by any one organization, no one organization is likely to ever undertake the task of securing the Internet as a whole. As a result, because the Internet is a public entity, users of the Internet are expected to regulate their own conduct, and servers of Web content are expected to secure themselves from those threats which the Internet as a whole is incapable of addressing. So, if you plan to conduct any formalized or important communications, business, or informational transactions on your Web site, it is solely your responsibility to ensure the safety, security, and secrecy of those transactions.

Whose transaction is it, anyway?

The only aspect of Internet communication that you — as Web server administrator (no matter who you or your company may be) — have direct control over is the *transaction*. Every legitimate access made by a Web user to your server is an encoded transaction. And every illegitimate access is a transaction as well, although it is generally cloaked to look like a legitimate one. The key to the success of the illegitimate access transaction is that it looks, to some part of your Web server, like a legitimate one, and thus gets passed through and executed while the other parts aren't looking. No intruder can send your server an electrical spike through the Internet; the only thing the intruder can send is *code* — which, like everything else that comes over the line, is digital. The illegitimate transaction is generally designed to take advantage of some bug or deficiency in your system, but it may also simply be doing harm that some part of your system was, albeit unknowingly, *designed* to do. (You'll read one amazing example of this later.) But no matter how it was designed, the illegitimate transaction must follow some protocol — and to some part of your Web server it will appear benign, or even benevolent.

To the programmer, a transaction is a coded request for access to, change to, or removal of some portion of data, or to submit new data. All relational databases are oriented around transactions; even though the newer ones such as Microsoft Access bill themselves as "transaction-oriented," in fact, Relational Database Management System (RDBMS) systems were always so. What makes the transaction scheme work for database systems is that those transactions are always very simple — some variation of just these four requests: access, change, remove, or add. The SQL language is pretty much summarized by these respective terms: SELECT, UPDATE, DELETE, and INSERT. While a database application is often quite complex, the terms behind its mechanism are just this simple. Visual InterDev Web applications are based on database transactions where these simple terms are employed.

Unfortunately, it is here — as well as anywhere else where simplicity of encoding is critical — that the Web application exposes itself to the greatest external threat. Because database dynamics were designed from the outset to be readily interpretable by both humans and machines, it becomes easy for an intruder to intuit or even *guess* the structure or schema of a relational database that supports a Web application. Most databases that contain people's names, for example, have a field or column whose name is LAST_NAME, or LASTNAME, or SURNAME. Even internationally, databases tend to be organized with English-language terms or phrases, mainly because the language and application used to build those databases are presented in English.

A major publisher of relational database systems (not Microsoft) has sold and installed thousands of copies of a Web gateway system with a horrible flaw: If a database query is attributed to an HTML form (<FORM> element), and instead of a number the Web user types a *SQL instruction* in a text box control in the form, the database manager will execute that instruction as a legitimate transaction. This is because the RDBMS sees the instruction not as a syntax error but as an "embedded instruction" — literally a *feature* rather than a mistake. Without saying much more about this (we don't want to give anyone bad ideas), imagine the damage that can be done by posing the simplest SQL instruction — for example, one which uses DELETE — as an ordinary criterion.

Can an open market be selectively closed?

While it is the open market that supposedly forms the crux of a democratic economy, most real-world business transactions take place under some shroud of confidence and secrecy. Even in a public market as open as the New York Stock Exchange, the details of every transaction that takes place on the floor are kept in confidence. The ticker only shows the values of stock trades and which issues were traded, but never who bought and never who sold. Trading specialists represent the buyer or the seller. The confidence these specialists place in each other's capacity to hold their transactions *in confidence* forms the foundations of this market. Open markets are thus not *exposed* markets.

The Internet is the most open transaction-processing system ever developed. Technically, it is the world's largest and most open market. Over the past few years, there has been considerable pressure to move existing markets in securities, bonds, commodities, currencies, options, futures, credit, and wholesale and retail goods onto this one immense virtual trading floor. But here — at least thus far — the specialists have not been the ones responsible for conducting legitimate transactions, but instead the ones responsible for ruining them. A cottage industry has emerged in working to make the Internet a more secure transaction system. But unlike every other aspect of computing, this industry has actually taken us *backward*; the Internet is a less secure system *today* than it was before the its retrofitting with security features was first undertaken. One reason is because it is impossible to present a fix without drawing attention to the flaw that requires it. But the primary reason is that Internet transactions are designed to be exposed; this is how TCP/IP packets get routed to their final destination. You cannot close an inherently open system.

What security there will ever be on the Internet can only come about if we perfect two categories of transaction-processing techniques: one is procedural and the other is mathematical. We can improve the way we organize material on our Web sites, so as to remove *confidential* material from prying eyes. And we can improve the way we encode our discrete transactions, so that that they appear meaningless, or at least *obfuscated*, to those individuals who are not supposed to know about them in the first place. While we wait for a more sensible internetworking scheme to emerge, we can work to open our business to the public in the world's most public of markets, inform those we choose to inform, and disinform everyone else.

Common Server Intrusions

Movies and popular media depict individuals breaking into network computers as a process of guessing the right password, or of using a telescope to spy on someone typing in the password, or of holding a gun to somebody's head and making him or her spit out the password. Because passwords themselves present formidable obstacles to breaking into computers, most intruders take an entirely different approach. The truth — although not very dramatic - is that intruders really don't break into computers much at all. More accurately, they *walk* in.

The Trojan horse

Any scholar of European history — or at least anyone who has seen the movie *Monty Python and the Holy Grail* — is familiar with the Trojan horse that was presented just outside the castle walls as a trophy. Historically, the gift has enveloped a fairly significant surprise in the form of an invading legion (the Monty Python "Trojan rabbit" case being the exception). On the Internet, a *Trojan horse* is generally a program uploaded to a server that opens a security gap that grants the uploader unauthorized access to that server.

Password exploitation

One of the most pervasive Trojan horse programs used over the past few years is in the form of a dynamic link library (DLL) that records additions and changes to the site's password list to an ordinary text file. An intruder uploads this DLL to an unsuspecting server, where it overwrites an existing DLL in the \WINDOWS\SYSTEM directory. The invading DLL runs in the background; and after a while, the intruder simply telnets back onto the server and FTP downloads the text file, where all the new passwords have been accumulated.

Solutions

Absolutely do not, under any circumstance, grant share permissions for the \WINDOWS or \WINDOWS\SYSTEM directories on the Web server.

Remove the Execute permission (X) from any directory where an Internet user is allowed to copy files (W). In other words, don't give an Internet user access to a directory where both X and W (write) permissions are enabled.

The rollback bomb

Perhaps the most dangerous — and in a dark sense, the most comical — case of Trojan horse attacks involves a utility program that is actually shipped with Windows NT. Although it's considered a Trojan horse, it doesn't have to be uploaded to the server because it's already there.

The command line utility ROLLBACK.EXE was designed so that people who *build* computers ("original equipment manufacturers," or OEMs) would have an easy way to revert the Windows Registry back to its default settings without reformatting the hard drive and reinstalling the operating system. The utility was inadvertently included on both the Server 4.0 and Workstation 4.0 CD-ROMs shipped to ordinary users. The innocent user, wondering "What does this do?" might double-click on ROLLBACK.EXE only to find it wipes the Registry clean *without any warning beforehand*. It's done, and there's no easy way back; not even the automatic backup SYSTEM.DA0 will kick in.

When the existence of this digital grenade was revealed, intruders began to take advantage of IIS' inherent capability to execute .EXE files from a client-supplied Uniform Resource Locator (URL), and simply issue the same ROLLBACK-laden URL to every server known to have IIS on-board.

Solutions

The chief fix for this problem is as simple as the problem itself: delete ROLLBACK.EXE from your server. You don't need it. However, the crafty intruder can still find ways to make the server administrator launch that program for some other reason. The intruder generally accomplishes this by uploading ROLLBACK.EXE to the system under some other name — say, PONG.EXE. If your method of testing uploads is double-clicking on them, placing this one in an empty directory first won't be nearly enough precaution.

The second solution is to closely monitor all uploads to your server, even those from individuals whom you have explicitly authorized. ROLLBACK.EXE is a very small utility. That, in and of itself, is one clue that it's not a Windows program. But if you want confirmation, go to Windows Explorer, right-click on the file in question, and select Properties. If the Properties dialog contains a Version tab, then the file follows Microsoft's New Executable File format. This means it is not a command line utility, and, therefore, is not ROLLBACK.EXE. But if the dialog comes up with tabs for setting how MS-DOS is to handle the program, chances are that you don't want it anyway. If the uploader gives you no explanation as to what the file is supposed to be, go ahead and delete it.

Finally, write permissions (W) should be removed from all major program directories — especially \WINDOWS and \WINDOWS\SYSTEM (also known as \WINNT and \WINNT\SYSTEM) — so that good files won't be replaced with renamed versions of bad files such as ROLLBACK.EXE. Such permissions pertaining to files are maintained by Windows NT (not by Windows 95 or Windows 98), and is discussed in further detail later.

Script incursion

One of the fundamental components of IIS architecture is Microsoft's Internet Server Application Program Interface (ISAPI) — essentially the native language of IIS. A program or script written using this language is called an Internet Server Application (ISA). In essence, an ISA, once compiled, is an interpreted program, like a Visual Basic program running within the VB environment. Unlike an ordinary compiled program written in C or C++, an interpreted program runs with the aid of a separate component which analyzes each instruction in the program as it comes across it, executing that instruction on the fly.

In IIS architecture, ISAs are offered as an alternative to the Common Gateway Interface (CGI) applications that are part of conventional UNIX-based Internet servers. Microsoft argues certain performance advantages over CGI — but, of course, they require IIS, which, in turn, requires Windows NT. While a CGI script is stored as an independent, text-based file interpreted in the conventional manner by what UNIX calls the "CGI process," an ISA script is fed into a C++ compiler, where it is compiled into a binary DLL. Windows NT recognizes this DLL as a compiled executable binary file — in other words, not a text file — but the ISAPI code within the compiled ISA still requires IIS to be present on the server as an interpreter when the DLL is run.

Exploiting ISAPI's covert nature

Because CGI is an independent process, the chances of it being able to interpret commands that do physical damage to the server is next to nil. But a compiled ISA (and here is the part that catches the attention of security experts) is capable of containing the same level of binary code that any other dynamic link library may contain. Keep this in mind for a moment.

A CGI script can be executed from a client request by the client's Web browser passing a URL to the server disclosing the name and location of that script on the server. It can be assumed that location is embedded within a hyperlink or form gadget. The front part of the URL is phrased like an ordinary resource locator path; but the tail part is generally appended with data tagged as input for the CGI script on the server end. This is an example CGI query where this very topic is passed to the AltaVista Web site:

```
http://altavista.digital.com/cgi-bin/query?
pg=aq&kl=XX&r=%22Internet+Information+Server+4.0
%22&search=Search&q=ISAPI+AND+security&d0=&d1=
```

An ISA is designed to be executed exactly the same way. In fact, if AltaVista used ISA scripts instead of CGI, conceivably this URL would not have to bear any difference (perhaps the cgi-bin subdirectory might be renamed for the sake of clarity). This URL would, in such a case, run a file called query.dll, and pass to it the same parameters listed here in exactly the same way.

Because an ISA's final form is that of a compiled DLL, which can be executed through IIS as a DLL, a URL can conceivably be phrased to execute any DLL available to the server processor, whether or not it's actually an ISA. Rephrased in English: Because an Internet Information Server script is made to look like any other executable Windows library, it is possible for the server to execute any other executable Windows library without regard to the possibility that it might not be proper to do so.

Solution

The only course of action that can stop IIS from being instructed to execute a DLL *by an ordinary user of the Web site* involves a detailed overhaul of the manner in which IIS grants permissions by default to ordinary users. You'll see this overhaul close-up in this chapter.

Permission reversion

Each remote user of an IIS Web server has certain permissions assigned to him or her by IIS (the details of which are discussed later). Every ISA runs under an account name that is designed to appear to the Web server as just another human user. This is part of the design of the IIS system, not some subterfuge.

For an ISA to work, it has to log on to the Web server just like any other user. But all ISAs are allowed to use — in fact, *directed* to use — a single account name, which is referred to within those scripts as IUSR_*MACHINENAME*, where *MACHINENAME* is the name of the server computer registered with Windows NT. The name itself literally means "the anonymous user of this server machine." So ISAs appear to the server to represent an administrator who has been assigned the same permissions as IUSR_*MACHINENAME*. But if one of these scripts contains the ISAPI method instruction RevertToSelf, the permissions given that script are instantly switched to those currently attributed to the SYSTEM account. It's not a diabolical instruction in and of itself, simply an innocent one that just happens to be fully loaded and ready to fire.

Note The formal documentation describes the role of the `RevertToSelf` method instruction as "terminating the impersonation" of a user begun by the ISA when it received permission to run. However, the method does not terminate the *script* — it's not like an `End` instruction in BASIC. The script can go on without any formal permissions assigned to it.

ISAPI instructions are not preinterpreted for possible destructive content, so `RevertToSelf()` gets passed just as easily as any other instruction. Once that's executed, the script can then go on to place system ( ) calls, which are the virtual equivalent of handing over your DOS prompt.

Solution

There is no easy solution to this problem. No ordinary user should be able to run just any program from your server, other than the server software itself. But even ordinary users may have to run *some* executable files by name, such as your ISAs, so you cannot simply deny a user all execution access to all DLLs in one fell swoop.

You can, however, apply restrictive share permissions that permit a general user only to execute files from a particular directory where you know in advance that safe ISAs are located. But don't grant a general user the right to copy or write files *anywhere*, even in this safe ISA directory. If your Web site does accept submissions of ISAs from the general public, *accept only the uncompiled source code*. An ISA cannot be run accidentally from a simple text file; it has to be compiled and made into a binary executable first. You can scan this text file for any occurrence of `RevertToSelf`, and either rewrite the script before compiling it or simply distrust it and junk it.

The one-two punch

Gaining direct access to the Access Control List on a server requires the permissions of an administrator. As you've just seen, giving an ordinary ISA program these permissions is not very difficult.

Passwords on nearly all servers for all operating systems are encoded somehow. But Windows NT doesn't actually store an *encrypted* password for each user, which would be the result of a code that obfuscates each bit of information in the password. Instead, NT stores *hash values*, which use fewer characters, and which represent the results of mathematical functions applied to information extracted from the password. When a user logs on to NT, the hash formula condenses the entry password into a hash value, which is then compared to the stored copy. If they match, the user is authenticated. It is possible that another password could yield an identical hash value, but it is unlikely.

Windows NT maintains two sets of passwords, one for logging on to the computer and another for logging on to the network resources used by that computer. The hash values for the latter set are obtained by an odd choice of methods, which many computer security experts have condemned as being too easy to crack. First, the 14-character form of the password is divided in two and both halves are encrypted. The hash values are generated from the encrypted forms of the password. Experts complain that it is far easier for a brute force algorithm to decrypt two 7-character segments than it is to decrypt one 14-character segment. And while the hash value for the main computer login password set is obtained using a far more trusted scheme, users generally adopt one password for both computer and network login, because it's easier to remember.

Because an administrator needs to perform system audits from time to time, it becomes necessary to discover the password for one of the users. But this list does not exist on the server computer; the hash values that are stored cannot possibly be used to obtain any one password, but only a list of possible passwords. Furthermore, the hash list is itself encrypted. So benevolent utility programs have been developed that temporarily remove the permissions and system attributes of the password hash files and then use a simple brute-force algorithm to decrypt those files to obtain the true hash values. The results from these utility programs are generally output to simple text files. Again, brute-force algorithms are applied to "guess" a user's password and to compare that guess against the hash value just as NT itself does during the logon procedure. While these algorithms require tens of thousands of attempts each time, today's fast processors have minimized the wait for the process to conclude.

If the hashing and encryption algorithms used for every NT server are the same, and this auditing utility program is widely available, what's the point of obfuscating the passwords in the first place? The answer is that such a utility should only be usable by an administrator — and that is the case. But as you've just seen, an automated ISA program can mimic an administrator with just one instruction. So it becomes possible for an intruder to log on normally under a standard guest account, upload the audit utility program to a particular directory on the server computer, execute that program with merely a URL (assuming IIS is present), and download the text file produced by the utility.

This intrusion capability takes advantage of two of Windows NT Server's most critical weak points: First, an ordinary user is given a Domain Users account, which by default grants that user permission to upload any kind of file. Second, because ISA scripts are DLLs, it is necessary to enable execution of binary files by way of an ordinary client-provided URL. Currently, there is no way to prescreen files for malicious content, and there will probably never be — how would it work? Further, if the administrator restricts uploads from general users to a particular directory, it only makes it easier for the intruder to remember where the uploaded executable file is, so that the intruder's URL can be phrased correctly the first time.

Solutions

When Windows NT is installed, it creates domain-local groups named Everyone and Power Users. Both of these groups have unnecessarily liberal permissions assigned to them. Often, stricter permissions are placed on smaller groups of users; as a result, the power of the Everyone group approaches that of an administrator. Conceivably, someone who is registered as just an Everyone could do more damage than someone who is more than just an Everyone. Using Windows NT's User Manager for Domains, remove the Everyone group entirely, along with the Power Users group. Few business-oriented networks need to grant "badges of honor" for users with greater-than-normal expertise; if there's anyone you should be more skeptical of, it is the expert user.

There is a more comprehensive solution to this security hole, which we discuss in depth in our discussion of permissions.

On Certificates, SSL, and Cookies

At the time of this writing, many security features intrinsic to the Visual InterDev/IIS/ASP combo are not functioning the way they are documented to function. Because this will probably not be the case permanently, we describe how things are working now.

In the optimum world of Internet communication, each party in every transaction is distinctly identified by a digital *certificate* — a type of code which is part license number, part cryptographic tool. The international standard number for Internet certificate technology today is X.509; thus, the name for the certificate currently in use is X.509. For certification through X.509 to be truly effective, every server and every client (browser) should be certified — today, a small percentage of IP hosts are certified. A certificate is used as a way of "signing" a transaction, so that the other party can be assured that the party that *completes* a transaction is the same party that *started* it. The way a certificate works, no one can steal it and use it as his or her own; someone else trying to send your certificate would send different data. When that data is checked against the certificate registry of a third party — called the *Certificate Authority* (CA), responsible for "signing" the certificate — the CA responds that the data is invalid.

The secret to this magic has to do with the bipartite nature of the certificate itself, which involves a type of math called *asymmetric cryptography*. The X.509 contains two keys: The *public key* is a code used to encrypt messages, but that key can be given away freely — in fact, the signature of an IP host on its own certificate is its public key. The *private key* is another code also used to encrypt messages, although it only resides on the computer where the X.509 originated. The two keys are interrelated by way of a formula known only to the CA.

When one party uses its private key to encrypt a message, then only its public key can be used to decrypt that message. Because everyone has access to the public key, that message can be easily decrypted. So the point of the encryption is not to make the message secret, but to help ensure its authenticity — that the party that says it originated the message actually did. The process then works in reverse: When another message is encrypted using the public key of the original sender, that new message can only be decrypted using the originator's private key. If the second, response message makes sense to the sender of the original message, then the original sender must truly be the sender.

But that only authenticates the sender to the sender. When the original sender sends the response message back to its source *unencrypted*, and *that* message matches the original response, then the respondent knows that the sender must be who it claims to be, because only that party could have possibly decrypted the response message.

In a HyperText Transmission Protocol (HTTP) transaction, Secure Sockets Layer (SSL) is used to assure that the two parties in any Web transaction are who they say they are, reducing, if not eliminating, the possibility of fraud. Netscape's implementation has added one step to the SSL process not mentioned thus far: After the two parties have authenticated each other, the server offers the browser client a new *session key*, different from all the other keys used thus far, and specific only to the current session of transactions. When the session ends, the session key is thrown out. This new key is used to encrypt all transactions that take place during the current session. Here is where things get sticky. SSL appears to take place even when the client browser does not have an X.509 certificate. This isn't supposed to happen, but it does everyday. The server, on discovering that the client is uncertified, does the Internet equivalent of saying, "Oh, what the heck!" So when it comes time for the server to generate the session key, it has to use the existing client public key to make sure the session key is different. On not finding a public key, it uses basically *nothing* as an aid in generating the session key. The result is that the session key isn't much of a key, which appears to have been the case in several SSL transactions involving Internet Information Server.

At the time of this writing, an article in Microsoft's online Knowledge Base states that SSL transactions have been taking place with uncertified clients, and implies that certification checking was not taking place even when the client *was* certified. You have the option to choose to use SSL in the first step of the New Project Wizard. However, until this problem is corrected, SSL won't provide the protection you seek.

What tipped Microsoft off to this problem has to do with *cookies*, which are small records of data. A Web server can send a client browser a cookie that is stored on the client side in a file called COOKIES.TXT in Netscape Navigator. If you are using IE, the cookie is a file that is stored in the cookies folder under the Windows directory. The server may later recall this record or file from the client. This way the Web site can personalize the site based on the information stored in the cookie, such as the client's user ID with respect to the server, or the client's profile or preferences.

The advent of cookies alerted security experts to the possibility that a server could retrieve records from the client side that were placed there by another server. While denials of this possibility still abound, the truth is, this happens every day. In fact, it's part of the engineering of the cookie system. When you click on an animated billboard on a commercial Web site, to take you to a Web page from an advertiser, that billboard is often placed there by a second site: an advertising site acting on behalf of its clients. When the initial site is using a cookie to "maintain state," to give that server some semblance of a session, the advertiser site has access to that cookie because its billboard is part of the same page. The advertiser uses this cookie to know who to pay for your having clicked on the billboard — because the billboard may appear on a number of sites and the entire point of the advertising enterprise is to be able to compensate Web sites for use of the ad. These sites are paid according to how many "click-throughs" the billboard receives, and one way to ascertain this number is by ascertaining session ID information from cookies.

If a session were indeed encrypted through SSL, then any cookies exchanged between server and client would be encrypted as well. Thus, a third party accessing a cookie from an SSL session would not be able to retrieve cookies created by other servers. Because they currently can, SSL is apparently not working the way it is designed to work. Consequently, until this issue is addressed, you shouldn't use cookies for sensitive information.

Server Harassment

The strange truth is that a majority of the intrusive behavior conducted over the Internet is not larceny but deliberate annoyance. Intruders take advantage of TCP/IP's inherent weaknesses, or Windows NT's incapability to adapt to TCP/IP's quirks, in order to make your system behave improperly or simply shut down. The examples cited here do not involve intrusive programs that take over your server, but instead are cunning methods for utilizing resources that are already present — ironically, methods that are part of the design of today's Internet protocols.

The dreaded "Ping of Death"

One of the most well-known forms of attacking a server probably acquired its fame for the simple reason that press writers, reporters, and authors are unable to resist the temptation of using this campy headline. The "Ping of Death" refers to an Internet process known as *ping*, the name having been taken from the term for the sound used by submarines to locate objects in their vicinity. On the Internet, one IP host can check for the presence and online status of another IP host by sending a "ping" packet assembled using Internet Control Message Protocol (ICMP). The proper response from the recipient IP host is a simple acknowledgment message, which itself comes in the form of an ICMP packet.

ICMP packets vary in size; but in the case of pinging, it's generally rather small. A ping packet whose length is 64K or greater can be sent to an unsuspecting Internet server (or even over a Windows-based LAN using TCP/IP as its transport protocol), causing that server's TCP/IP stack to be taken off-line. Although Windows is a multitasking system, there is only one incoming Internet line to a server (unless there is a separate, local TCP/IP stack). Incoming data is halted while Windows tries to make sense of this oddly sized packet. Meanwhile, the stack still trys to process the packet anyway, in order to give itself something to do while it's off line — which is a bit like trying to read a newspaper that's on fire. The ultimate result is the appearance of the Windows administrator's least favorite screen character, the ominous "blue screen of death."

Solution

Windows NT 4.0 editions published recently appear to be invulnerable to this form of attack. To be certain, download and install this patch file: `ftp://ftp.microsoft.com/bussys/winnt/winnt-public/fixes/usa/NT40/hotfixes-postSP3/teardrop2-fix`. NT 3.51 servers do require the most recent Service Pack to be installed, plus this patch file: *ftp://ftp.microsoft.com/bussys/winnt/winnt-public/fixes/usa/NT351/hotfixes-postSP5/icmp-fix*. Windows 95-based servers should have installed the file vipup11.exe, obtainable from the Microsoft Software Library.

Just the source code, period

One of the most notorious security holes in IIS — in unpatched versions up to 4.0 — is the capability of its clients to simply add a *period* (.) to the end of a valid URL and, instead of receiving properly parsed HTML code, receiving the Web page's *raw source code*. For an Active Server Page, this means that access to the server-side source code — which might even include such elements as default passwords and administrative secrets — is as easy as typing .asp. instead of .asp at the end of the URL. While Microsoft has released a patch to correct this problem on IIS, at the time of this writing Chili!Soft has not patched their ASP products.

Solution

For IIS users, even though a reliable patch is available on Microsoft's FTP site, the optimum solution is to *upgrade to the latest IIS version.* If you're running a Netscape server, at the time of this writing, you're in trouble. You might consider adopting IIS temporarily and switching back when the fix is available from Chili!Soft.

Caution

The GLOBAL.ASA file, as you learned earlier in this book, is the "autorun" Active Server Page that starts up when a user first accesses your Web site. The name GLOBAL.ASA is publicly known, especially to potential intruders. For this reason, until a full and reliable fix is provided to the source code sinkhole dilemma, you should not program any security measures into GLOBAL.ASA because an intruder is likely to see them. You may, instead, have to take the drastic measure of having GLOBAL.ASA call an ISAPI extension (ISA) DLL for handling user authentication processes. This is a difficult matter because the name of this file will be visible to intruders into GLOBAL.ASA. So your *real* startup ASP page will probably need to be one called by the ISA, whose filename is securely compiled in the binary code of the DLL.

Dumping on a file

IIS makes it possible for a client to run an executable file on the server side by simply naming that file's location and name in a URL. (This capability is also true for .BAT batch files.) With that in mind, the URL sent by the client Web browser to execute any command line utility can be crafted so that its output is redirected to another file. To accomplish this, the intruder need only attach a handful of characters to the end of the URL, such as those that appear in this example:

```
http://www.darkcloud.net/bin/utils/scan%0A%0D>\windows\system.ini
```

Here, the intruder is launching that most innocent of tools, SCAN.EXE, otherwise known as McAfee VirusScan. The URL is having the utility output its results to another text file that, obviously, should not be receiving any text from the outside world. No checks are performed on this URL prior to its execution; so unless SYSTEM.INI has been formally attributed with an -S flag using DOS' ATTRIB command (something that is not done automatically when Windows is installed), the SYSTEM.INI file will be overwritten without generating a backup. Next time the server tries to boot, it won't make it.

Solution

Your first course of action is to make SYSTEM.INI, and other initialization files like it, true "system" files. Under the NTFS file system, complex *shares* can be established which deny anonymous users, or any group of users, or any single user, access to designated files or directories. You'll see how this is accomplished later in this chapter.

The spoof flood

Although the Internet doesn't maintain closed circuits between client and server the way the telephone network maintains circuits between parties, an IP host server does maintain a session log for IP host clients that log on and make requests. For HTTP, the transport protocol that supports today's World Wide Web, a session lasts only a few seconds — just long enough for a browser to retrieve the components of a Web page. The session is then discontinued; but during the time when the browser was downloading page parts, the server did maintain a session for the browser's IP address in its log.

The architecture of TCP/IP contains no facilities whatsoever for tracing the IP address on a data packet to its attributed source. In the 1970s, when IP was designed and computers were kept under personal guard, it did not seem necessary to endow the protocol with security measures. After all, anyone caught tinkering with such a massive global network would certainly be guilty of a federal offense, and would be certain to spend a large portion of his or her life in prison. Security was a resource left to the law to handle, not to computer protocols.

So today it is possible for a crafty individual to build a program capable of sending a connection request packet to a server and signing that packet with a nonexistent IP address called a *spoof*. Whenever a server receives a connection request packet, it sends an acknowledgment signal back to the source address, but it then waits for a reacknowledgment back from that same address. TCP/IP doesn't specify what the server is supposed to do when it doesn't receive that reacknowledgment. So when the server sends an acknowledgment signal to a spoofed address and doesn't get a response, TCP/IP simply has the server try the signal again. And again. Windows NT, thankfully, stops trying after five attempts; but between each attempt, it waits for double the amount of time that it was set to wait for the last reacknowledgment. By the fifth attempt, the wait is 96 seconds; the total elapsed time is 3:09 minutes.

Because NT is a multitasking system, the server doesn't wait in limbo during this long period for the spoof address to miraculously come into existence — it continues processing other packets — which is why the prankster sends the targeted server not just one spoof packet, but several *thousand*, or tens of thousands. An unattended server could be put on hold for days processing spoof requests.

Solutions

For handling spoof requests, the patch for networks where NT 4.0 Service Pack 1 is installed can be downloaded from `ftp://ftp.microsoft.com/`

`bussys/winnt/winnt-public/fixes/usa/nt40/hotfixes-postSP1/syn-attack/syn40i.exe`. If you've installed a later service pack, you do not need this patch.

Pretending to be the domain name server

On all Web servers, certain numbered *ports* are reserved for designated services. Windows NT doesn't have any mechanism of its own to prevent an outside user from initiating a telnet connection (a direct terminal link) to any port number, even if that number isn't designated for terminal access. So an intruder can initiate a telnet connection with the NT port reserved for the Domain Name Server (DNS), which is the service that resolves how alphanumeric names are resolved against IP addresses. Once this connection is made, the intruder can simply type a few garbage characters into the terminal and force the server computer to hang tight while its DNS server tries, tries again, and tries again — unsuccessfully — to make sense of the garbage.

Solution

For dismissing telnet connections to reserved ports, the patches for networks where NT 4.0 Service Pack 3 is installed can be downloaded from `ftp://ftp.microsoft.com/bussys/winnt/winnt-public/fixes/usa/nt40/hotfixes-postSP3/dns-fix/dnsfix_a.exe` and `ftp://ftp.microsoft.com/bussys/winnt/winnt-public/fixes/usa/nt40/hotfixes-postSP3/dns-fix/dnsfix_i.exe`. By simply double-clicking on them, these patches automatically add corrective features to IIS. So far, these patches are capable of stopping the *known* methods for imitating DNS. Because new intrusive methods may be found, we recommend that you check Microsoft's FTP directory where these patches are located frequently, to see if the above patches have been supplemented.

Managing User Access

This section discusses the user security model for Windows NT, Internet Information Server, and Visual InterDev. You need to understand this model if you are to effectively wage combat against the almost inevitable intrusions to your Web server, especially the type of intrusions we've outlined thus far. At the end of this section, we present tips about how to use the IIS user security model to make your server safer.

Workstation domains

A Web site, from Windows NT's point of view, is not a bulletin board system. Its users are the users of Windows NT, and are, thus, classified in the same manner as any other user of the computer. That a Web server may have 10,000 or more users is of no more consequence to NT than the fact that a workstation may have just one user. So the administrator of an NT system and a person who logs on by simply having clicked on a hyperlink from someone else's Web page, are similar insofar as they are both users. One simply has a different set of permissions than the other.

It is academic to point out that an administrator is a person who has some permissions granted, as opposed to a general user who has permissions denied. Like many other volumes on the topic of Web sites, we could close this discussion right here, and proceed to a more appealing topic such as how to animate the bullets in tables of contents. But the process of managing how permissions are doled out is not nearly as simple as it appears on the surface.

NT maintains a *Network Environment Model*, which is smart for the reason that it effectively distinguishes *users* from their *computers*. However, this model is naïve because, in the initial stages of its design, it didn't account for the existence of the Internet. The NT network model has the administrator divide the pool of a network's workstations into one or more *domains* (not to be confused with the domains that comprise the Internet's Domain Name System). Generally, a network has at least two domains, in order to distinguish the workstations that administrators would normally use from those that general users may use. But many NT-based LANs establish their domain models so that they parallel the departments within their organization — for instance, R&D, Marketing, and Sales.

Simply dividing workstations into named domains does little to increase the overall security of the network. But as you'll see, a key distinction between different categories of domain users can make the difference between a secure network and one that's wide open.

User groups

While domains compartmentalize workstations or processors, *groups* compartmentalize users. On a small LAN, it might make sense for an administrator to grant permissions or restrictions only to individual users. But on a network that may have many users, an administrator cannot possibly have the time or inclination to grant permissions to each and every user individually. Besides, because of the way the Internet works, an administrator can't grant permissions to each requesting browser that comes over the line.

The permissions and restrictions applied to a group (restrictions being, in actuality, the *lack* of certain permissions) apply equally to each member assigned to that group. On an NT-based network where domains are employed, groups may be established whose permissions specify the extent to which members may have control over the resources in the network. These permissions are assigned using a component of NT called User Manager for Domains. There are two types of groups whose names you need to understand:

✦ A **domain-local group** specifies a set of permissions for user access to resources that reside within a designated domain.

✦ A **global group** specifies a set of special permissions that apply for users of computers in one domain who intend to access resources that belong to another domain.

On Windows NT, a user can be a member of both types of groups. For instance, on an ordinary LAN, a user whose base workstation resides in the Accounting domain, and who is a member of a domain-local group attributed to Accounting, might also be a member of an R&D-based global group, specifically adapted for situations where an accountant might need to check if research is going over budget.

It would seem to follow from this that an Internet user would have certain global group permissions that would apply when the user logs on to the local domain of the NT network running a TCP/IP stack. But this is not the case. When IIS is installed, it automatically creates a set of *domain-local groups* that represent remote users. The reason has to do partly with semantics and partly with network topology. Global groups specify the sharing permissions for *multiple* domains. When you build a Web site on your server, you will probably intend for the contents of that site to be centered on *one* server, or at least distributed amongst several adjoining servers. In any event, however many processors end up constituting your Web server from the point of view of your user, they will all reside within one NT domain. They have to, or else the Web server schematics won't work. Because the entirety of the Web server processors exists within one domain, all users of that server are local to that domain. The users themselves may be global, but the domain isn't.

The all-powerful anonymous user

All World Wide Web transactions utilize the Internet's HyperText Transfer Protocol (HTTP). In this protocol, whenever a client browser requests a resource from a server, the client introduces itself to the server, logs on, retrieves the resource, and then immediately logs off. There is no intervening session between browser client and Web server while the browser user is reading pages. HTTP does not utilize any form of user compartmentalization model; when it logs on to a server, it expects to either retrieve the requested resource (or more accurately, retrieve something in response to the request for this resource) or to retrieve nothing. So the Web server treats all HTTP requests as having originated from so-called *anonymous users*.

The fact that HTTP users are, by definition, anonymous throws a big monkey wrench in Windows NT's plans to subdivide all users into their appropriate groups. Internet Information Server's response to this problem is to give, in effect, the monkey wrench a name. IIS creates a special account to represent all anonymous users. This is the IUSR_*MACHINENAME* account mentioned in our earlier discussion of how intruders get around permission restrictions. The account is supposed to be enrolled as a member of a domain-local group called Guests. In actuality, the account is registered as a member of the far more powerful Domain Users group, which is a global group that has a domain-local representative called Users by default in all domains of the local NT network. So all *ordinary* URLs that the IIS server may receive (we discuss nonordinary URLs momentarily) may as well come from the same source — one big user rather than ten thousand little ones. And this one user ends up being very powerful.

The solution—and there is one—is a bit complex and involves resetting the permissions given to shared *resources* in the network.

Permissions

We've mentioned permissions several times, so it's time that we showed you exactly what permissions are. IIS recognizes two sets of permissions. First, IIS applies permissions to designated domain-local groups and to individual users. Second, IIS recognizes the existing permissions that the NT administrator has applied to specific resources on the network.

User-oriented permissions

The limits to what any remote user is capable of accessing or executing on the server side are spelled out by the permissions granted by IIS to the anonymous user account. IIS recognizes three levels of access for any group member who utilizes the designated Internet resources of a network:

✦ **Administer** access is basically defined as the lack of restrictions placed on an account. A user with administer access may create new files, delete files, create subdirectories, delete subdirectories, rename any resources, and remove all Internet-designated resources. Furthermore, administer access allows one to call up IIS' Access Control List to allocate permissions to other users or groups.

✦ **Author** access is granted by the administrator to those responsible for the upkeep and maintenance of Internet resources on the network. A user with author access is not restricted with regard to designated Internet resources; however, the user may still be restricted with regard to any other content on the network. The NT network administrator uses NT's User Manager for Domains tool to determine such restrictions.

✦ **Browse** access is the lowest level, basically giving the user read-only rights with regard to the designated Internet content. The user may not delete, move, or rename resources, or copy those resources to other points on the server.

Resource-oriented permissions

As Windows NT administrator, you determine the accessibility of resources and files on your entire network (rather than just the Internet-designated portion) through the Windows NT Explorer program, by right-clicking the resource in the hierarchical list and selecting Sharing from the popup menu. This begins the process of designating the item as a shared resource. A collection of these resources is called a *share*. In the Share Name box in the Sharing dialog, enter a name that will identify the share, and then click the Permissions button. The Access Through Share Permissions dialog shows you the levels of access NT applies to a share:

✦ **No Access** prevents any user other than an administrator from being able to see the resource.

✦ **Read** makes the resource visible to and executable by all users, though only an administrator can rename, change, or remove the resource.

✦ **Change** allows users the capabilities of Read access, plus the ability to append information to a resource (for example, adding to a word processor document), and even delete that resource.

✦ **Full Control** (*default*) grants all users all rights to manage, maintain, and delete the resource, plus the ability to define permissions for that resource.

With a share having been created, and access permissions automatically defined for it, you assign these shares to designated domain-local groups. First, click the Add button in the Access Through Share Permissions dialog, then choose the groups that will be assigned the share from the list in the Add Users and Groups dialog. Again, the terminology used here can be deceptive. A share may just as easily define those resources that are not to be shared as it can define those resources that are to be shared. For instance, you can create a share named Admin_Only which designates No Access permissions to certain resources, and then assign that share to those groups or users whom you do not want accessing these resources.

Resource-oriented permissions are important to Web server administration for one critical reason: When Windows NT is installed, it creates a domain-local group called Everyone. By definition, Everyone is . . . well, everyone, known and unknown users, even if they belong to other groups simultaneously. Whenever you create a new share, by default (unless you specify otherwise) it is assigned to Everyone, and whenever you make a network resource visible to Everyone, you make it potentially accessible to the anonymous user account IUSR_MACHINENAME—the account that represents the ordinary Internet user.

File/directory-oriented permissions

The NT File System (NTFS) associates permissions with files and directories in much the same way that DOS' older File Allocation Table (FAT) associates attributes with files and directories. These permissions' names are largely self-explanatory: Read (R), Write (W), Execute (X), Delete (D), Change Permissions (P), and Take Ownership (O). This latter permission deals with the capability of an enabled user to associate himself or herself with a given file so that no other general users may have undue access to that file.

Caution

Shares granted to a user or group regarding a *directory* (folder) tend to override stricter permissions regarding a file within that directory. For example, if a group is assigned a share which gives that group Full Control for a directory, and a file is placed in that directory whose permissions have been reduced to just Read (R), then the group will still be able to *delete* the file regardless of its permissions. However, if a user has no permissions assigned to the user's account or group with regard to that read-only file, then that user cannot delete the file. In short, *shares override file/directory permissions*.

Designating Internet resources

Earlier we used the term "designated Internet resources" to refer to content that is made visible to remote Internet users. The term Microsoft uses is "web," with a small "w." This term comes from the realm of Microsoft FrontPage 98. There's an interesting reason for that.

Visual InterDev and Internet Information Server both borrow the security model created for FrontPage. In fact, VI requires that the FrontPage server extensions be installed on any server where a Web application created with VI is made available through IIS. In the Microsoft parlance, a *server extension* is a program designed to function as an accessory to the existing Web server, so that the server may be able to utilize special functionality developed by Microsoft. With server extension architecture in place, Web site administrators can use both Microsoft and non-Microsoft servers to deliver FrontPage's exclusive functionality.

So the Internet resources your IIS server will expose to the outside world are the same as the "web" created from within Visual InterDev and/or FrontPage 98. A FrontPage web is comprised of a directory and its subdirectories designated on the server computer as shared resources. FrontPage perceives the central directory of this shared resource as the root directory of its web. The home page (say, INDEX.HTM or DEFAULT.ASP) is generally found in this directory. By default, this directory is entitled \WEBSHARE\WWWROOT.

With the FrontPage Server Extensions installed, the server is capable of amending the NT security model applied to domain-local groups with two tiers applied to the IUSR_*MACHINENAME* account:

✦ **Unrestricted browsing** is the default security setting for all new users, new groups, and all anonymous users. Basically, no restrictions are placed on which files belonging to the FrontPage web can be requested by the client browser.

✦ **Restricted browsing** allows you to designate a subdirectory of the root web directory — or what FrontPage calls a *sub-web* — as off-limits to the designated user or group. In effect, this establishes a share that designates No Access permission for the user or group.

Caution

FrontPage recognizes one *root web* belonging to the Web server at any one time. If there is more than one Web *site* maintained by the same server, then FrontPage will recognize these sites' directories as sub-webs of its root web. The permissions given to users with regard to the root web are by default inherited by users of any sub-web. Conceivably, a separate Web site may be rooted in a sub-web, while the main Web site is centered on the root web. So be careful that registering a user on one Web site on your server doesn't improperly register that user on some other Web site.

Giving identity to your users

One of Internet Information Server's primary tasks is to manage the accounts of registered users contacting an NT-based Web server via the Internet. A registered user of the root web is, and must always be, a registered user of the NT server. The permissions that apply to this user come either from a personal account, or by way of the user group or groups to which that user belongs. You use NT's User Manager for Domains to attribute each registered user either to an account or to a group. When you restrict access to all or part of your web (again, small "w") to certain registered users, you make those users officially members of your NT network domain.

In the terminology of Internet Information Server, the process of logging a registered Internet user on to a server is called *authentication*. This term covers the procedures undertaken by the Web server to identify the user and to determine that user's level of access or permissions.

IIS supports two methods for user authentication:

✦ **Basic** — The first, which is simply called *Basic* (not to be confused with the programming language), presents the user with a dialog box to which the user responds with a username and password. Sometimes to log on to an NT server with multiple domains, the user might prefix the username with a domain name, separated by a backslash (\). Both Netscape and Microsoft Web browsers can be remotely instructed by IIS to bring up this dialog box and to submit the results as an HTTP request.

✦ **Challenge/Response** — The second method assumes the browser user is also running Windows NT on the user's own workstation. The *Challenge/Response* method allows the server to periodically silently poll the client browser for the username and password with which the user logged on to the user's own Windows NT workstation. The poll message is encrypted, so only the real registered client and not an impostor can properly respond. The response is itself encrypted, so the user's password never travels the Internet in an unencrypted state. The user never sees this poll message or the browser's response to it — it all takes place in the background. While certainly more technically adept than the Basic method, Challenge/Response assumes that the username and password that the user submits to the Web server will be the same pair that registers the user on the user's own workstation, which probably resides on a separate network altogether. In one sense, this creates a convenience for the user, who only has to log in once; in another sense, it widens the impact of any security breach by making any domain-local impostor an Internet impostor as well.

Note

If you use a database in your Web application, you can define what authentication to use during design-time and run-time in the data connection. For design-time authentication, individual developers accessing the database can be prompted for an ID and password by Database Management Systems (DBMSs) such as SQL Server. For databases such as Microsoft Access that do not support authentication, you'll want to set file-sharing permissions, which are described in the next section. For run-time authentication, you do not want the database to attempt to prompt the Web user, because they will not be able to respond. Instead, you need to use an application-specific user account defined in the DBMS to control a user's privileges. Check your specific DBMS for information on how to define these user accounts.

To enable the Authentication methods for a Web site, do the following:

1. In the Internet Service Manager tool of IIS, right-click on the name of the web in the list, and from the pop-up menu select Properties.

2. In the properties page, under Password Authentication (there's that other word), are check boxes marked Basic and Windows NT Challenge/Response. Check the methods you intend your Web server to use.

3. To restrict access to your Web site only to registered users, thus locking out all anonymous users (and making the IUSR_*MACHINENAME* account moot), on this same Properties page, uncheck the box marked Allow Anonymous. By default, this box is checked; unchecking it means that any HTTP access of your Web site will be greeted with the Basic login dialog and/or a Challenge/Response message, whichever of the two is enabled, in that order. If neither are enabled, *no one* but you can access your Web site. This may be what you want while your Web site is under construction.

4. Click on OK to finalize your choices and close the Properties page.

There are permissions, and then there are permissions

When a registered user logs on to your Web server, the degree of accessibility the user has to the root web on that server is determined by the local permissions managed by the FrontPage Server Extensions. But the degree of accessibility the user has to the server computer is determined by the broader permissions maintained by Windows NT's Access Control List.

A Web page is not a terminal, so it's impossible for a browser to bring up something as live or sensitive as a DOS prompt via HTTP. But as you've seen, users have ways of bending the rules and getting messages out to the operating system. Visual InterDev includes sample Web pages that you can use to have new users formally register as members of your Web site. But the moment that Windows NT registers a new user on a server, it grants that user the permissions assigned to the global group Domain Users. Because this is a global group, it spans all domains in the NT network. For members of a global group to be members of a domain-local group, the global group is enrolled by name as a member of the domain-local group. (A rare case of the small fish swallowing the big fish.) By default, the Domain Users global group is enrolled in every Users domain-local group in every domain. As a result, you cannot use domains as a way to guarantee that remote Internet users do not have access to certain workstations in your network.

Until you change the permissions for the Domain Users group yourself, the permissions include the capability to launch programs. This is potentially the most lethal permission there is for a Windows NT Web server; almost every major form of incursion involves an intruder's capability to plant an executable file on the server and then execute it using a URL as the trigger. To further complicate matters, Microsoft suggests that, for the maximum level of flexibility, permissions be delegated to groups at the domain-local level only.

Because you want new users of your local network to have permissions by default that you wouldn't dare grant to a newly registered remote Internet user, it's important that new local users be made Domain Users, just as NT was designed to do. If your Web site is a fully restricted intranet application, then this default designation is convenient. But it is dangerous to grant these conveniences to a newly registered, though still unknown, Internet-based user.

Solution to the anonymous user dilemma and the "one-two punch"

Now that you know something more about permissions, you have a better understanding of what to do about the IUSR_*MACHINENAME* account being automatically given the broad permissions of the Domain Users group. From NT, bring up User Manager for Domains. Right-click on the account name (remember to look for the registered name of your own machine, to the right of IUSR_). From the pop-up menu, select Properties. Then from the User Properties dialog click on the Groups button at the bottom. In the Group Memberships dialog are two lists. On the left are those groups to which this account *does* belong; on the right are those groups to which this account *does not* belong. Choose Domain Users on the left and click on Remove. That shifts Domain Users to the right-side list. Now choose Guests (not Domain Guests) from the right-side list and click on Add. That puts Guests in the left-side list, where it should be the only group listed. Click on OK and then click on OK again. The problem is now solved.

Now, any anonymous user that logs on will be treated with the stricter permission settings of the Guests group. Also note that Guests is a domain-local group. This means that the anonymous user's reach will not extend to workstations on the network in domains other than that of the server.

Assigning Web permissions

To designate the browsing rights of users or groups within the content of your Web site, you designate Web-level permissions to a registered domain-local group. The procedure is as follows:

1. From Visual InterDev's Project menu, select Web Project, followed by Web Permissions. VI will bring up the Permissions dialog shown in Figure 25-1.

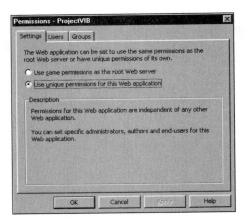

Figure 25-1: The Permission dialog box is used to maintain Web permissions.

2. By default, VI borrows its set of permissions for the current web from those currently assigned to the root web (where IIS maintains the home page of the Web site). To have VI instead keep a separate set of permissions for this web, set the option marked Use unique permissions for this Web application.

3. To show the list of registered groups, click on the Groups tab.

4. Initially, the list of groups is empty, regardless of how many groups are accessible to the network. To add a group to this list — even if NT already recognizes this group — click on the Add button. VI will bring up the Add Groups dialog shown in Figure 25-2.

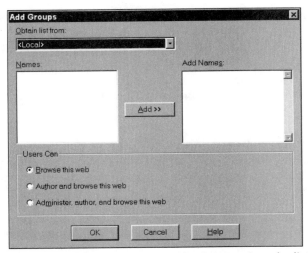

Figure 25-2: To move NT-recognized groups into the list of VI groups, you use the Add Groups dialog.

5. The default choice in the list box marked Obtain list from is <Local>. To choose a domain accessible from this workstation, click on the down-arrow, and then click on that domain in the list. The names of groups associated with the chosen domain will appear in the list marked Names.

6. To choose one or more groups to which new permissions will apply, choose those groups in the Names list, then click on the Add>> button. The names will be copied to the list marked Add Names.

7. The Browse, Author, and Administer permissions are represented by option buttons in the frame marked Users Can. Choose a permission from this frame.

8. To finalize your assignment of permissions to these groups, click on OK.

9. To continue assigning permissions to other groups, go back to Step 3. Otherwise, to conclude assigning permissions to groups, in the Permissions dialog, click on OK.

Design-Time Security During Web Construction

Windows NT's security system may be linked to the security features of Visual InterDev, so that certain domain-local groups of users are given specific permissions with regard to web files. In so doing, Microsoft suggests that you create two groups specifically for access to the Development Environment: one for administrators and the other for authors. It's probably a good idea to give these groups unique names that other individuals won't be able to guess — in other words, not just "Administrators" and "Authors." These groups will show up in VI's Permissions dialog box. From here, you may grant Administer or Author permissions to these NT groups.

Preventative strike measures

There are some measures that you can take to prevent unwarranted intrusions into your Web server:

Note

Many of the preventative measures presented here come from a 69-point checklist developed by veteran NT network administrator Bill Wall. Mr. Wall has made this checklist freely available on his personal Web site, which is one-half devoted to network security and the other half to. . . well, chess. You can find the entire checklist at http://www.txdirect.net/users/wall/ntcheck.htm.

✦ Two common extensions for executable files are .BAT (textual batch files) and .CMD (binary NT command files). Internet Information Sever is set to execute a file with either of these extensions. Because these types of files are of no use to a remote Internet user, the IIS file mappings for .BAT and .CMD files should be disabled.

✦ As an administrator, please don't name yourself administrator or admin. These are the two easiest usernames to guess for an intruder; everyday users have more difficult usernames. Instead, create a decoy account with the username administrator, but grant it very restrictive permissions. Then from your management console, watch the account to see who tries to access it.

✦ *Event auditing* is an optional feature of Windows NT where users logging on and off and accessing vital resources, and other noteworthy events, such as "blue screens of death" and changes to permissions and policies, are logged for future review. By default, this feature is turned off. Bring up User Manager for Domains and turn Audit on from the Policies menu.

✦ When an Emergency Repair Disk (ERD) is created, a copy of the system's System Accounts Manager password hash file is copied to it. Because the ERD is a floppy disk, it is accessible by default to the Everyone group (assuming you haven't removed that group). If an ERD is left in the floppy disk drive, an intruder can possibly FTP download the SAM file from that disk. Also, during the manufacturing procedure for the ERD, another copy of the SAM file is copied to the \WINDOWS\SYSTEM32\ERD subdirectory, and it, too, is accessible by Everyone. (See why "Everyone" must die?) This subdirectory is often left on the system after the ERD disk is created, leaving it to you to delete the subdirectory.

✦ Generally, when a user "logs on to" Windows NT with a null or blank password, the user's given some access to the system anyway — as much access as the Guest domain-local group allows. To protect the network both locally and remotely, blank passwords should be disallowed. Bring up User Manager for Domains, and from its Policies menu select Account. In the Account Policy dialog, *reset* the option marked Permit Blank Password. This will enable the field marked At Least x Characters, where a text box rests in place of x. Type a minimum number of characters in this box — no less than eight and no more than 14. Now, no restricted access can take place involving a user who submits a blank password to the client-side dialog.

✦ In this same Account Policy dialog, also set the option marked Account Lockout. In the frame below this option, set Lockout after x bad logon attempts so that the text box at x reads 4. Then set Reset count after x minutes so that the text box at x reads 30. This disables some brute-force algorithms from being capable of guessing a password an indefinite number of times.

Authenticode for Client-Side Security

If you're a veteran user of Internet Explorer, you encountered the *ActiveX control*. This is a component of a Web page that is actually run by a binary program on the client side, not the server side. ActiveX makes it possible for a client Web browser to download a binary program that defines a certain element of Web page functionality, and then apply that program in several places among several Web pages.

The fear that users have of ActiveX controls — a rational fear, as we discuss momentarily — is that they make it possible for unchecked and unsupervised program code to become instantaneously executed on the client side without the user having anything to say about it. Unrestricted, an ActiveX control could be programmed to do serious damage to a client computer. For this reason, Microsoft Internet Explorer gives users a way to tune its security options so that ActiveX controls are either only downloaded with user permission or not downloaded at all, rather than downloaded, installed, and executed without warning. Java applets that take advantage of native functions present the same security issues.

Can ActiveX controls be made secure?

ActiveX controls are actually binary code or, more to the point, installed components of the Object Linking and Embedding (OLE) system found in Microsoft Windows. Conceivably, Microsoft could have made it possible for the binary code of an ActiveX control to be embedded in a page, much the same way binary attachments are *uuencoded* (pronounced "you-you-encoded") and placed in the middle of e-mail messages and Usenet articles. Such a course of action, however, would have been architecturally unsound for several reasons.

First, even though the ActiveX control is brought to you in the form of a self-contained executable file, it is actually a component of the broader OLE process going on in the client system, and is entirely dependent on that process. The ActiveX control, in other words, is nothing by itself. For an ActiveX control to work within a downloaded Web page, the program code for that control has to be preinstalled on the client's computer, and a listing for the control must be entered in the client's local Windows Registry (this is done automatically, not by the user). If a page makes reference to an ActiveX control that is not yet installed on the client, an optional attribute of the <OBJECT> tag, CODEBASE, makes it possible for that control to be downloaded from the server of the person or company publishing that control. This way, if the client machine already has the control, the Web server need not download it again and again.

Second, delegating responsibility for transfer of the control to the server of the person or company that programmed the control increases at least the overall sense of security. Binary executable code — unlike anything your Java virtual machine might produce — can have extremely damaging effects on your computer. While only a virus-scanning utility can ultimately prevent such occurrences, ActiveX controls and Java applets that use native functions currently facilitate a system called Authenticode, which is designed to give you a reasonable degree of assurance that a reliable party is responsible for bringing you the control. Using Authenticode, a digital signature belonging to the control's publisher is mathematically verified with a list of such signatures on Authenticode's server. When the signature is verified, Internet Explorer presents an on-screen certificate stating verification is complete, and giving you the opportunity to browse the publisher's Web site to do some checking of your own before you download the control. IE also gives you the opportunity to cancel the download if for any reason you're uncertain.

When an ActiveX control referred to by an `<OBJECT>` element in a Web page does not include the CODEBASE attribute, Internet Explorer cannot initiate a download of that ActiveX component if it doesn't find its Globally Unique Identifier (GUID) in the System Registry. This means that the client must have already installed the control. Even then, by default, IE will interrupt the user to say it's about to activate an installed ActiveX control, and without one of those Authenticode certificates to verify it, there's no way for IE to tell in advance whether running the control is safe. Authenticode assumes the authenticated control is being distributed primarily over the Web, not through some development tool. So IE will generate a warning message whenever it encounters a new control, even if it's Microsoft's own product and it was already installed on the client system along with Visual InterDev, or some other component of Visual Studio. Because of the multitude of security issues generated — rather than solved — by Authenticode, you can expect the loading and execution of ActiveX-endowed Web pages never to be entirely automatic.

Clearing your control for distribution

If you're the programmer of an ActiveX control, and you wish to distribute it from your Web site, you need to enroll your Web server with a company called Verisign as a certified distributor of controls. There's a small fee involved; but once you're enrolled, you know what to enter for your control's <CODEBASE> attribute. Microsoft grants you a site certificate that will be used in designating to users that the code they are about to download is genuine. Even though other Web sites may use your control on their pages, when users download those pages, they end up downloading the control from *you*. So the client quizzes your Web site to see if the attributes it has ascertained from the Web page correspond to yours, which designate your site as the one authorized to distribute the control.

If you wish to use someone else's ActiveX control in your Web pages, and that control is freely distributed, you can simply include their <CODEBASE> attribute in your HTML source code for the `<OBJECT>` element that represents the control.

Authenticode actually does not make anything about an ActiveX control component more secure than any other type of binary executable file. Instead, it's a tool to be used by honorable people to help them stand behind their software product. An Authenticode certificate is designed to say to the browser user, "The following control is mine and I stand by it." A control that bears your Authenticode certificate is said to be *signed* by you. In turn, the authorized agent that dealt you the certificate, which is called the Certificate Authority (CA), signs your certificate. Verisign, Inc., an offshoot of one of the original developers of the X.509 certificate standard, is an official CA. You can apply for your Authenticode certificate online, through `http://digitalid.verisign.com`.

Summary

In this chapter, you learned that intruders gain remote access to a Web server via the path of least resistance. With Windows NT, such paths often circumvent the customary password barricade.

✦ One method for server intrusion takes advantage of a security hole in the Internet Server API. A script written using ISAPI, called an Internet Server Application (ISA), is compiled using a C++ compiler into a DLL. Embedded in this DLL, though, are remote procedure calls that are designed to be interpreted dynamically by IIS. Because the ISA is a DLL, it can contain any other type of binary code, including code that can inflict damage to the system. Such damage is generally averted because the access permissions of an ISA are quite restrictive, although an unchecked ISAPI command can be invoked which removes all permissions and grants the ISA unlimited access to the server computer.

✦ The most common form of server intrusion involves harassment, which is more annoying than it is destructive. Simple deficiencies in the TCP/IP protocol can be exploited, which cause the server to wait, perhaps forever, for a nonexistent IP address to return its call, or perhaps cause the server to crash or to reboot.

✦ Microsoft provides fixes for all of its known security flaws on its corporate Web site. But because there are probably more undiscovered flaws than there are discovered fixes, it is necessary for you, as the Web site administrator, to know how to manage the permissions systems for both Windows NT and FrontPage 98. IIS and Visual InterDev both rely on FrontPage 98 for their security model.

✦ In the Windows NT security model, groups of computers on a network are subdivided into domains, whereas groups of users are gathered together into what NT simply calls groups. A computer on the NT network is independent from its user, thus domains are initially independent from groups. This way, a user can log on to any machine in the network locally or remotely and still have his or her own access control scheme maintained.

✦ In NT, a share is a group of one or more shared resources on the network to which uniform permissions are applied. Once a share is defined, a group is associated with it, which defines the permissions that group has with regard to the shared resources. Some shares actually deny access to resources rather than grant access.

✦ IIS maintains an anonymous user account. Because most Web page accesses do not involve logon procedures, this anonymous account represents all users who may access the server without registration. The permissions applicable to this account are defined within a domain-local group.

✦ FrontPage Server Extensions must be installed on the IIS server to maintain permissions for designated Internet resources. FrontPage perceives such resources as its root web (small "w"). Within this web, certain subdirectories or sub-webs may be restricted from access. Web user permissions consist of Browse, Author, and Administer — verbs that define the extent to which a given user may act on the web. By joining these permissions with established Windows NT domain-local groups, it is possible to designate new NT users with permissions specific to Web site usage.

✦ Once a former anonymous user becomes registered, that user's username becomes part of NT's Access Control List, and that user becomes a user of the server just like any other user. By default, the newly registered user is considered a member of the Domain Users global domain, which grants that user overly broad permissions. Tightening the restrictions for Domain Users has the unwanted effect of burdening new users on the local network. One solution is to create an entirely new global domain for known, tangible, physical human beings who work in the same office or building, or at least for the same company, as the server administrator. Such new users may have their permissions switched from the default Domain Users group to the new, more relaxed group.

✦   ✦   ✦

Physical Design of the Sample Register Database

Chapter 19 discussed using the Database Designer to create a sample Microsoft SQL Server 6.5 database called Register. A copy of this database is located on the companion CD-ROM and instructions for installing the database are located in Chapter 18. The Register database is also used in Chapters 20 through 23.

The physical design for each of the eight tables in the Register database appear in the tables listed below:

Customer	Table A-1
CustomerToSession	Table A-2
Session	Table A-3
SpeakerToSession	Table A-4
Speaker	Table A-5
Form_of_Payment	Table A-6
Type_of_Session	Table A-7
Session_Focus	Table A-8

Chapter 19 has information on what each column in these tables means, as well as step-by-step instructions on how to use this information to create these tables, indexes, and constraints in Microsoft SQL Server, making use of the Visual Database Tools.

Table A-1
Physical Design for the Customer Table

Column Name	Datatype	Length	Precision	Identify Seed
Cust_ID	int			1
First_Name	char	25		
Last_Name	char	25		
Title	char	25		
Company	char	25		
Address_Line_1	char	25		
Address_Line_2	char	25		
City	char	25		
State	char	2		
Zip	char	5		
Phone	char	10		
Fax	char	10		
Email	char	50		
Form_of_Payment	tinyint			
Card_Number	char	16		
Expiration_Month	tinyint			
Expiration_Year	tinyint			
Amount_Received	smallmoney			

Column Name	Scale	Allow NULL	Default Value	Identify	Identify Increment
Cust_ID				yes	1
First_Name					
Last_Name					
Title		yes			
Company		yes			
Address_Line_1					
Address_Line_2					
City					
State					

Column Name	Scale	Allow NULL	Default Value	Identify	Identify Increment
Zip					
Phone		yes			
Fax		yes			
Email					
Form_of_Payment					
Card_Number		yes			
Expiration_Month	between 1 and 12	yes			
Expiration_Year	between 0 and 99	yes			
Amount_Received					

Column Name	Primary Key	Foreign Key	Index	Constraint
Cust_ID	yes		Pk	Pk
First_Name			1b	
Last_Name			1a	
Title				
Company				
Address_Line_1				
Address_Line_2				
City				
State				
Zip				
Phone				
Fax				
Email				
Form_of_Payment		Form_of_Payment		Fk
Card_Number				
Expiration_Month			C	
Expiration_Year			C	
Amount_Received				

Table A-2
Physical Design for the CustomerToSession Table

Column Name	Datatype	Length	Precision	Scale
Cust_ID	int			
Session_ID	int			

Column Name	Allow NULL	Default Value	Identify	Identify Seed	Identify Increment
Cust_ID					
Session_ID					

Column Name	Primary Key	Foreign Key	Index	Constraint
Cust_ID	yes	Customer	Pk	Fk
Session_ID	yes	Session	Pk	Fk

Table A-3
Physical Design for the Session Table

Column Name	Datatype	Length	Precision	Scale
Session_ID	int			
Title	char	50		
Room	char	20		
Start_DateTime	datetime			
Duration	decimal		5	2
Type_of_Session	tinyint			
Focus	tinyint			

Column Name	Allow NULL	Default Value	Identify	Identify Seed	Identify Increment
Session_ID			yes	1	1
Title					
Room		'TBA'			
Start_DateTime					
Duration					
Type_of_Session					
Focus					

Column Name	Primary Key	Foreign Key	Index	Constraint
Session_ID	yes		Pk	Pk
Title				
Room				
Start_DateTime				
Duration				
Type_of_Session		Type of Session		Fk
Focus		Session_Focus		Fk

Table A-4
Physical Design for the SpeakerToSession Table

Column Name	Datatype	Length	Precision	Scale
Speaker_ID	tinyint			
Session_ID	int			

Column Name	Allow NULL	Default Value	Identify	Identify Seed	Identify Increment
Speaker_ID					
Session_ID					

Column Name	Primary Key	Foreign Key	Index	Constraint
Speaker_ID	yes	Speaker	Pk	Fk
Session_ID	yes	Session	Pk	Fk

Table A-5
Physical Design for the Speaker Table

Column Name	Datatype	Length	Precision	Scale
Speaker_ID	tinyint			
First_Name	char	25		
Last_Name	char	25		
Company	char	25		

(continued)

Table A-5 *(continued)*

Column Name	Datatype	Length	Precision	Scale
Address_Line_1	char	25		
Address_Line_2	char	25		
City	char	25		
State	char	2		
Zip	char	5		
Phone	char	10		
Fax	char	10		
Email	char	50		
URL	char	150		
Specialty	char	25		

Column Name	Allow NULL	Default Value	Identify	Identify Seed	Identify Increment
Speaker_ID			yes	1	1
First_Name					
Last_Name					
Company	yes				
Address_Line_1					
Address_Line_2					
City					
State					
Zip					
Phone	yes				
Fax	yes				
Email	yes				
URL	yes				
Specialty		'TBA'			

Column Name	Primary Key	Foreign Key	Index	Constraint
Speaker_ID	yes		Pk	Pk
First_Name			1b	
Last_Name			1a	
Company				
Address_Line_1				
Address_Line_2				
City				
State				
Zip				
Phone				
Fax				
Email				
URL				
Specialty				

Table A-6
Physical Design for the Form_of_Payment Table

Column Name	Datatype	Length	Precision	Scale
Type	tinyint			
Description	char	25		

Column Name	Allow NULL	Default Value	Identify	Identify Seed	Identify Increment
Type					
Description					

Column Name	Primary Key	Foreign Key	Index	Constraint
Type	yes	Customer		PK
Description				

Table A-7
Physical Design for the Type_of_Session Table

Column Name	Datatype	Length	Precision	Scale
Type	tinyint			
Description	char	25		

Column Name	Allow NULL	Default Value	Identify	Identify Seed	Identify Increment
Type					
Description					

Column Name	Primary Key	Foreign Key	Index	Constraint
Type	yes	Session	PK	
Description				

Table A-8
Physical Design for the Session_Focus Table

Column Name	Datatype	Length	Precision	Scale
Focus	tinyint			
Description	char	25		

Column Name	Allow NULL	Default Value	Identify	Identify Seed	Identify Increment
Focus					
Description					

Column Name	Primary Key	Foreign Key	Index	Constraint
Focus	yes	Session	PK	
Description				

HTML 4.0 Reference

This appendix brings you up to date on HyperText Markup Language (HTML). The new version of the HTML standard, Version 4.0, extends the language in various ways. In this appendix are explanations with examples of the differences between HTML 3.2 and 4.0.

Note

If you would like a more complete reference on HTML 4.0, please see the *HTML 4 Bible* by Bryan Pfaffenberger and Alexis D. Gutzman, published by IDG Books Worldwide, Inc.

If we were forced to choose the one word that best describes HTML 4.0, it's *diversity*. The authors of the new version of HTML want to ensure that the World Wide Web will be truly worldwide. Documents created in HTML should communicate well with people using languages other than English, and with people who are physically challenged and who use the Web. For example, blind people should be well served if they are relying on a text-to-speech translation of Web documents. Also, HTML should be capable of embracing all kinds of embedded objects — from WebBot to movie players. The OBJECT element offers a way to accomplish this. Finally, HTML should be capable of expressing rich content on a variety of bandwidths using a variety of devices — including hand-held receivers and cell phones. In a word, the goal is to expand HTML to embrace as wide a variety of people and communications technologies as possible.

To achieve that goal, several general changes to HTML are proposed. Some elements are new, such as the new ACRONYM tag to identify abbreviations such as SPQR so a speech synthesizer won't try to pronounce it *spoker*. Other elements are now *deprecated,* which means they are to be played down (you should avoid using them). For example, the deprecated DIR element has been used to display multicolumn directory lists. You are urged to use the UL (unordered list) element instead to achieve the same effect. Deprecated elements (or attributes) can become obsolete in the future, and likely will. Finally, three elements — XMP, PLAINTEXT, and LISTING — are now described as *obsolete* and you should now use the PRE element to replace all of them. Broader changes are proposed for other components of HTML, in particular, several new features for forms, as you'll see later in this appendix. One major trend: a number of HTML formatting elements are now being moved out of the main HTML source code and into Cascading Style Sheets (see Chapter 13 for an in-depth discussion of Cascading Style Sheet features).

Tip

As HTML specifications have evolved over the years, certain conventions have arisen. Programmers commonly refer to HTML commands such as <BODY> as tags and associated tag modifiers such as the command BACKCOLOR in <BODY BACKCOLOR = "RED"> as arguments or parameters. However, the official HTML ruling group uses the term element for a tag and the term attribute for a modifying parameter. We use element and attribute in this appendix.

As is the usual case with computer languages, various kinds of illogic creep into the diction. For example, you can use the new COLGROUP to define aspects of groups of columns in a table. The equivalent HTML element for grouping *rows* in a table, however, is not ROWGROUP as you would expect. Instead, the term that was chosen is TBODY. It never seems to occur to computer language designers to invite grammarians, linguists, or even English majors to their planning discussions.

Note

You can reference the World Wide Web Consortium (W3C) organization's HTML 4.0 specification at http://www.w3.org/TR/1998/REC-html40-19980424.

New Elements

For simplicity, we use the term *browser* to mean any software that recognizes HTML and that is capable of translating HTML into useful information for the user. It is understood that a browser need not merely be software running in a typical computer. It can also be software supporting a speech synthesis/recognition device, a handheld device, or whatever other input/output machine that can handle HTML documents in whatever fashion. Some writers use the term *agent* (or *user agent*), thinking that this sufficiently distends the meaning of *browser*. However, *agent* is used in an entirely different sense in computing and, indeed, in discussions about the Internet and intranets. We feel that *agent* is more confusing than helpful in the effort to extend the meaning of *browser* beyond the classic keyboard/monitor input/output device pair.

ACROYNM

This new element is designed to set off acronyms such as NASA or BBC. Precisely what the display device does with this information depends on the browser software and the device's capabilities. However, it is assumed that one valuable benefit of tagging acronyms is that speech synthesizers won't attempt to pronounce them as a word, but will instead spell them out: B-B-C. Making a distinction between ordinary text and acronyms is also useful when spell-checking a document. HTML does not yet have an element to indicate abbreviations, such as *etc.*

Start and end tags are required:

```
<ACRONYM>UN</ACRONYM>
```

It's also sometimes useful to provide a translation of the acronym, which you do with the *title* attribute. The browser could then optionally spell out the acronym the first time it's used in a document (as is the common practice in magazines and books):

```
<ACRONYM title="United Nations">UN</ACRONYM>
```

You can also specify the language using the *lang* attribute. *En* means English:

```
<ACRONYM lang="en" title="United Nations">UN</ACRONYM>
```

These are the attributes that can be used with the ACRONYM element: CLASS, DIR, ID, LANG, ONCLICK, ONDBLCLICK, ONKEYDOWN, ONKEYPRESS, ONKEYUP, ONMOUSEDOWN, ONMOUSEMOVE, ONMOUSEOUT, ONMOUSEOVER, ONMOUSEUP, STYLE, and TITLE.

BUTTON

You're probably familiar with the BUTTON *attribute*, as in:

```
<INPUT type=BUTTON VALUE="Click this to see message."
NAME="Btn">
```

But what's new in HTML 4.0 is the BUTTON *element*:

```
<BUTTON name="submit" value="submit" type="submit">Send</BUTTON>
```

When you use a BUTTON with the TYPE="submit," it's quite similar to the older INPUT element with the TYPE attribute set to "submit." The INPUT submit button causes a FORM (in which the button is located) to be sent to the location indicated by the form's ACTION attribute.

However, the new BUTTON element has provisions for a fancier appearance; in particular, a button containing a graphic will look like a 3-D button and react to the user's click by displaying a second, "depressed" graphic. Where FORMs were previously restricted to two button types: SUBMIT and RESET, you can now use the BUTTON element to allow other kinds of button behaviors and appearances within FORMs.

Try the HTML source code in Listing B-1 to see the visual difference. When using the INPUT element, the graphic fills the entire button and there is no 3-D action when the button is clicked.

Listing B-1: **Graphic Button**

```
<html>
<head>
</head>

<body>

<INPUT type="image" name="submit" value="submit"
 src="buttn.gif" alt="No Visuals"></BUTTON>
<BR><BR>

<BUTTON name="submit" value="submit" type="submit">
 Send <IMG src="buttn.gif" alt="No Visuals"></BUTTON>


</body>
</html>
```

The effect, as you can see in Figure B-1, is still rather crude.

Figure B-1: The new BUTTON element allows you to place a graphic on a button, rather than covering the button (like the INPUT element above). The effect, however, is still limited and rather crude.

Tip

If you want to create attractive buttons, use Themes.

In practice, the BUTTON element isn't much of an improvement over the existing INPUT element. The starting and ending tags are required and you are urged to use the ALT attribute to provide a text explanation, such as this: alt="Picture of a dog," to those whose browsers cannot display an image.

The attributes that can be used with the BUTTON element are those: "forms.html" \l "adef-disabled"; NAME; "scripts.html" \l "adef-onblur"; "scripts.html" \l "adef-onclick"; "scripts.html" \l "adef-ondblclick"; "scripts.html" \l "adef-onfocus"; "scripts.html" \l "adef-onkeypress"; "scripts.html" \l "adef-onkeydown"; "scripts.html" \l "adef-onkeyup"; "scripts.html" \l "adef-onmousedown"; "scripts.html" \l "adef-onmouseover"; "scripts.html" \l "adef-onmousemove"; "scripts.html" \l "adef-onmouseout"; "scripts.html" \l "adef-onmouseup"; "forms.html" \l "adef-tabindex"; TYPE; "../struct/includes.html" \l "adef-usemap"; and VALUE.

COLGROUP

The COLGROUP element allows you to group sets of columns that have different width and alignment properties, as described by one or more COL elements. HTML has provisions for elaborate, sophisticated display of tabular data. Tables can include other tables, forms, figures, lists, paragraphs, and formatted text.

You need not use the COLGROUP element when creating a table. However, if you don't define any COLGROUPs, the table defaults to an implied, single column group that embraces all the columns in the table. For example, if you use the table definition tools in VI or FrontPage 98, COLGROUP isn't used by those utilities. You'll see all kinds of <TR>s and <TD>s but no COL or COLGROUP elements.

When you use the COL and COLGROUP elements, you provide browsers with important specifications for organization of the table. For example, the user could scroll the main table while the top row (containing titles for each column) remains static. The COL and COLGROUP elements also facilitate progressive display of tables, much the same way that some graphic images are gradually revealed as they arrive over the Internet.

COLGROUP works like this: Say that you're designing a table and you want the first column aligned left, the second column aligned in the center, and the final two columns aligned left. Here's the HTML to accomplish that action:

```
<COLGROUP align="left">
<COLGROUP align="center">
<COLGROUP align="left" span="2">
```

You can use COLGROUP to describe the default column alignments. Notice that the final COLGROUP uses the SPAN attribute to specify centering for the final three columns. (Recall that the equivalent of COLGROUP for *rows* is the TBODY element.) Listing B-2 shows the HTML source code that produces the results shown in Figure B-2.

Listing B-2: **Using COLGROUP**

```
<html>
<head>
</head>

<body>

<table border="3">
<COLGROUP align="center">
<COLGROUP align="left">
<COLGROUP align="center" span="3">
```

(continued)

Listing B-2 *(continued)*

```
<tr>
  <th>Primary Headers</th>
  <th>Your Name</th>
  <th>Your Address</th>
  <th>Your State</th>
  <th>Your Phone</th>
</tr>
<TBODY><tr>
  <td>First</td>
  <td>Second</td>
  <td>Third</td>
  <td>Fourth</td>
  <td>Fifth</td>
  </tr>
  <tr>
  <td>First</td>
  <td>Second</td>
  <td>Third</td>
  <td>Fourth</td>
  <td>Fifth</td>
 </tr>
 <tr>
  <td>First</td>
  <td>Second</td>
  <td>Third</td>
  <td>Fourth</td>
  <td>Fifth</td>
 </tr>
 </table>
</body>
</html>
```

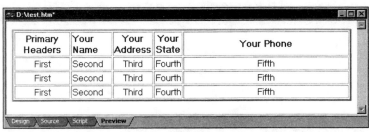

Figure B-2: The new COLGROUP element is used to define qualities for groups of columns.

SPAN

When using COLGROUP, the end tag </COLGROUP> is optional. The primary attribute used with COLGROUP is SPAN, which defines the number of columns in the group. Browsers, however, usually ignore the SPAN attribute if there are any COL elements within the group. SPAN defaults to 1. If you set the SPAN to any more than 1, that means the COLGROUP defines whatever number you've specified with SPAN. SPAN=4 means that four columns are in that COLGROUP.

SPAN can also be used with the COL element. If SPAN is set to anything greater than 1, the COL specification represents that number of columns. If you set SPAN=0, that COL then spans the remaining columns in the table.

The COL element works closely with the COLGROUP element, but COL doesn't define a group. COL can be used to define individual column qualities or to override a COLGROUP's default specifications, as in Listing B-3.

Listing B-3: **Using COL**

```
<TABLE>
<COLGROUP>
<COL width="50">
<COL width="35">
<COL width="35">
<COLGROUP align="center">
<COL width="40">
<COL width="40" align="right">

<THEAD> <TR>

. . .

</TABLE>
```

In this example, the first column is 50 pixels wide, followed by two columns that are 35 pixels wide. The entire second column group is defined as center-aligned, but the second column (defined by the second COL element) overrides the general (default) alignment specified by the COLGROUP, forcing a right-justified alignment in that second column. COL elements are not required in a COLGROUP.

WIDTH

The WIDTH attribute allows you to define a default width for a COLGROUP. If you do not use the % symbol, the width figure defaults to pixels. The % describes the width as a percentage of the available horizontal space in the row (between the margins on either side). Therefore, WIDTH="75" means make this column 75 pixels wide, whereas WIDTH="75%" means make this column apply the available horizontal space. Figure B-3 illustrates the various ways to express WIDTH. Listing B-4 shows the HTML source code that produces Figure B-3.

Listing B-4: **Using WIDTH**

```html
<html>
<head>
</head>

<body>

<table border="3">
<COLGROUP align="center">
<COLGROUP align="left">
<COLGROUP align="center" span="3">
<COL width="1*">
<COL width="35">
<COL width="50%">
<tr>
  <th>Primary Headers</th>
  <th>Your Name</th>
  <th>Your Address</th>
  <th>Your State</th>
  <th>Your Phone</th>
</tr>
<TBODY><tr>
  <td>First</td>
  <td>Second</td>
  <td>Third</td>
  <td>Fourth</td>
  <td>Fifth</td>
  </tr>
  <tr>
  <td>First</td>
  <td>Second</td>
  <td>Third</td>
  <td>Fourth</td>
  <td>Fifth</td>
  </tr>
  <tr>
  <td>First</td>
  <td>Second</td>
  <td>Third</td>
  <td>Fourth</td>
  <td>Fifth</td>
  </tr>
  </table>
</body>
</html>
```

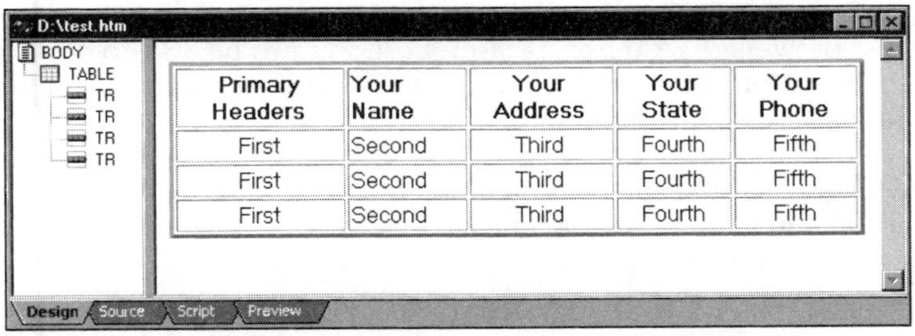

Figure B-3: Either absolute or relative measurements can be used for the WIDTH attribute of a COL element.

In that example, <COL width="50%"> causes the rightmost column to take up fully half of the space of the entire table width. The <COL width="*"> command means that the browser should assign only the minimum width necessary to hold that column's data. (You can also use "i*", where "i" is an integer, causing the browser to calculate a relative width for that column.) A browser first measures out any absolute widths (WIDTH="45" for example). Then the browser apportions the remaining space among any columns defined with relative widths such as i% or the i*. When you use the i* format, *each* column using the i* specification gets whatever space is available in proportion to the integer used with the "*" symbol. In other words, if 60 pixels were left over after all absolute column widths had been assigned, <COL width=V1*"> <COL width="2*"> would cause the browser to give the first column 20 pixels and the second column 40 pixels.

These attributes can be used with the COLGROUP element: ALIGN; CHAR; CHAROFF; CLASS; DIR; ID; LANG; ONCLICK; ONDBLCLICK; ONKEYDOWN; ONKEYPRESS; ONKEYUP; ONMOUSEDOWN; ONMOUSEMOVE; ONMOUSEOUT; ONMOUSEOVER; ONMOUSEUP; STYLE; TITLE; and VALIGN.

DEL and INS

This pair of elements allows browsers to indicate any editing that's been done to a document, much like the revision marks feature in word processors. As is so often the case with HTML, however, the key word is *allow* — it's up to each browser in each context as to what the browser actually *does* in response to the DEL and INS tags. In some situations, the browser will display the editing; in other situations, it will merely display the final result (or the original document). Similarly, which colors or other indicators are used to illustrate the marked-up text depends on the browser. Given the goal of allowing *users* to set up custom style sheets, specifying their own preferences, it's not hard to imagine browsers of the future giving the user control over when and how revisions are displayed, just as word processors allow you to toggle revision marks on and off.

Marking revisions is useful if various people are working to improve a document; like the interaction between a writer and editor, both want to be able to quickly see any changes (any insertions or deletions) without having to compare the before and after documents word by word.

INS indicates any new text that's been added to a document; DEL indicates deletions. Both start and end tags are required. The scope of a marked insertion or deletion can span anywhere from a single word to the entire document. These tags can also include tables, lists, and other HTML elements.

Let's assume you found a grammar error in a document you were asked to review. The following code shows how you could mark it, while Figure B-4 shows the results:

```
<DEL>We looks for two new employees</DEL>
<INS datetime="1994-11-05T08:15:30-05:00">
We look for two new employees
</INS>
```

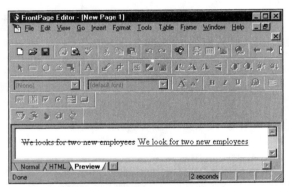

Figure B-4: FrontPage 98 indicates deletions and insertions (see the HTML) using strikeout and underlining.

DATETIME

To indicate when the editing was done, you can include the DATETIME attribute, as shown in the previous example.

CITE

To add reasons or explanations for your editing, you can provide a Uniform Resource Locator (URL) reference that contains this information:

```
<INS cite="reason.txt">
We look for two new employees
</INS>
```

Again, a browser can choose to display or conceal these citations.

The attributes that can be used with the DEL or INS elements are: "forms.html" \l "adef-disabled"; DIR; ID; LANG; "scripts.html" \l "adef-onclick"; "scripts.html" \l "adef-ondblclick"; "scripts.html" \l "adef-onkeypress"; "scripts.html" \l "adef onkeydown"; "scripts.html" \l "adef-onkeyup"; "scripts.html" \l "adef-onmousedown"; "scripts.html" \l "adef-onmouseover"; "scripts.html" \l "adef-onmousemove"; "scripts.html" \l "adef-onmouseout"; "scripts.html" \l "adef onmouseup"; STYLE; and TITLE.

FIELDSET and LEGEND

You can use the FIELDSET and LEGEND elements to assist people using nonvisual browsers. FIELDSET groups related controls into a single set. This kind of grouping can help to reveal the various logical zones of a document — what goes with what. For example, you might have some text describing a vacation package and several associated buttons the user can click for additional information about such things as cost, required inoculations, legal and medical information, and so on. Group all these buttons using the FIELDSET element to distinguish them from a different set of buttons that trigger displays of information about a cruise to Alaska. Some browsers — such as Internet Explorer — will *visually* group FIELDSETs, so you can see the several logical zones within the document (see Figure B-5).

This kind of grouping is also similar to the behavior of components collected together in a TabIndex, which is how controls can be ordered in a Visual Basic or Visual C application. When so ordered, pressing the Tab key cycles through the grouped controls. This same cycling through a group can be accomplished if the browser is based on a speech synthesizer rather than a visual output device. In this way, you can simplify things for people with disabilities.

The associated LEGEND element is how you add an explanatory caption to a FIELDSET. This explanation can make things clearer for those using a nonvisual browser. And for those who will view the set of components visually, you can use the ALIGN attribute to associate the LEGEND with the FIELDSET it describes. Listing B-5 shows the HTML for an example page that contains three FIELDSETs. The code in action is shown in Figure B-5.

Listing B-5: **An Example Page with Three FIELDSETs**

```html
<html>
<head>
</head>

<body>

<FORM method="post">
<FIELDSET>
<LEGEND align="top">Other Vacation Destinations</LEGEND>

<INPUT name="Japan" type="button" tabindex="1" width="42"
value="Japan"></INPUT>
<INPUT name="China" type="button" tabindex="2"
value="China"></INPUT>
<INPUT name="SSeas" type="button" tabindex="3"
value="South Seas"></INPUT>
</FIELDSET>

<FIELDSET>
<LEGEND align="top">Trip to Russia</LEGEND>

<INPUT name="Costs"
    type="button"
    value="Costs" tabindex="20"></INPUT>
<BR>
<INPUT name="Immune"
    type="button"
    value="immune" tabindex="21"></INPUT>
<BR>
<INPUT name="law"
    type="button"
    value="law" tabindex="22"></INPUT>

</FIELDSET>

<FIELDSET>
<LEGEND align="bottom">Alaska in the Spring</LEGEND>
<BR>
<INPUT name="Clothes"
    type="button"
    value="Clothes" tabindex="14"></INPUT>
<BR>
<INPUT name="gifts"
    type="button"
    value="gifts" tabindex="15"></INPUT>
</FIELDSET>
```

```
</FORM>


</body>
</html>
```

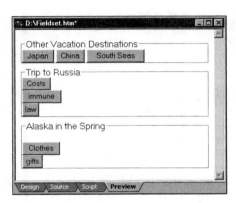

Figure B-5: The browser (VI's Preview mode) frames each FIELDSET, so the user can visually understand the logical zones within the document.

Of course, the buttons and other elements within the FIELDSETs illustrated in Figure B-5 would be considerably improved by the sophisticated formatting that is possible by adding a style sheet to this document. Also, the various buttons, when clicked, could trigger scripting that displays the information the user is requesting. In other words, the HTML code could include ButtonName_OnClick procedures so as to cause additional text to be displayed as required.

ALIGN

The ALIGN attribute (of the LEGEND element) can be specified as top, bottom, left, or right. It defines the position of the LEGEND text in relation to the body of the associated FIELDSET. LEGEND defaults to top. At the time of this writing, top is the *only* location a LEGEND is displayed in IE, regardless of the argument you give to the ALIGN attribute.

The attributes that can be used with the DEL or INS elements are: ACCESSKEY; ALIGN; "forms.html" \l "adef-disabled"; DIR; ID; LANG; "scripts.html" \l "adef-onclick"; "scripts.html" \l "adef-ondblclick"; "scripts.html" \l "adef-onkeypress"; "scripts.html" \l "adef-onkeydown"; "scripts.html" \l "adef-onkeyup"; "scripts.html" \l "adef-onmousedown"; "scripts.html" \l "adef-onmouseover"; "scripts.html" \l "adef-onmousemove"; "scripts.html" \l "adef-onmouseout"; "scripts.html" \l "adef-onmouseup"; STYLE; and TITLE.

Q

The new Q element is intended to indicate quoted material, text that is usually enclosed within quotation marks. However, because languages differ in the way that they handle punctuation, it is up to the browser, knowing the local rules of the "current" language enforced by the browser, to decide how or when to use quotation marks, single quotation marks (for nested quotes), or to leave them out entirely. Style sheets can also be used as a way of enforcing local punctuation rules (see the LANG attribute).

American English avoids quotation marks when long passages (paragraph or longer) are quoted. Instead, the long passage is indented, using the BLOCKQUOTE element, as shown in Figure B-6.

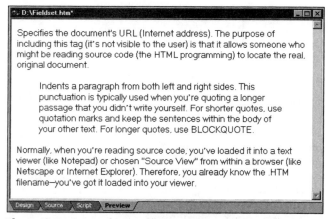

Figure B-6: Long pieces of quoted text are merely indented, with no quotation marks, in American English.

Listing B-6 shows the source code that generates the formatting shown in Figure B-6.

Listing B-6: **Using the BLOCKQUOTE Element**

```
Specifies the document's URL (Internet address). The
purpose of including this tag (it's not visible to the
user) is that it allows someone who might be reading
source code (the HTML programming) to locate the real,
original document.

<BLOCKQUOTE>
Indents a paragraph from both left and right sides. This
punctuation is typically used when you're quoting a
```

```
longer passage that you didn't write yourself. For
shorter quotes, use quotation marks and keep the
sentences within the body of your other text. For longer
quotes, use BLOCKQUOTE.
</BLOCKQUOTE>

Normally, when you're reading source code, you've loaded
it into a text viewer (such as Notepad) or chosen "Source
View" from within a browser (such as Netscape or Internet
Explorer). Therefore, you already know the .HTM filename-
-you've got it loaded in your viewer.
```

Because HTML is missing various kinds of formatting commands — such as indentation commands — many people have used the BLOCKQUOTE element as a way of indenting ordinary text (not a quotation). This use of BLOCKQUOTE is deprecated. You are urged to use a style sheet if you need to indent ordinary text.

CITE

Both BLOCKQUOTE and Q can make use of the CITE attribute to provide a URL that offers more information about the quoted material (its source, a footnote, whatever). Cite is also used with the DEL and INS elements, as just described. It is used with the Q and BLOCKQUOTE elements, like this:

```
<Q
cite="http://www.myhome.com/whitepapers/athens/sources.html">
Fair Greece! sad relic of departed worth! Immortal,
though no more! though fallen, great! </Q>
```

The attributes that can be used with the Q element are: CITE; "forms.html" \l "adef-disabled"; DIR; ID; LANG; "scripts.html" \l "adef-onclick"; "scripts.html" \l "adef-ondblclick"; "scripts.html" \l "adef-onkeypress"; "scripts.html" \l "adef-onkeydown"; "scripts.html" \l "adef-onkeyup"; "scripts.html" \l "adef-onmousedown"; "scripts.html" \l "adef-onmouseover"; "scripts.html" \l "adef-onmousemove"; "scripts.html" \l "adef-onmouseout"; "scripts.html" \l "adef-onmouseup"; STYLE; and TITLE.

Deprecated Elements

The following HTML elements are now deprecated. Recall that you should avoid deprecated elements and attributes because they can eventually be declared *obsolete* and not supported by browsers.

Align

The ALIGN attribute isn't entirely deprecated. What's deprecated is the use of ALIGN in the traditional way, like this:

```
<H1 align="right">This Headline Is Flush Right</H1>
```

Instead, you are supposed to use style sheets, like this:

```
<HEAD>
<STYLE>
H1 {text-align: right}
</STYLE>
</HEAD>
<BODY>
<H1>This Headline Is Flush Right</H1>
</BODY>
```

This same deprecation applies to the other arguments used with the ALIGN attribute: left, center, and justify. Instead of putting the alignment in the H1 or other element, like this deprecated version:

```
<H2 align="center">This Headline Is Centered</H1>
```

you define alignment in a style sheet, like this:

```
<HEAD>
<STYLE>
H2 {text-align: center}
</STYLE>
</HEAD>
<BODY>
<H2>This Headline Is Centered</H2>
</BODY>
```

Similarly, you would define the paragraph style in a style sheet, rather than using this deprecated version:

```
<P align="justify">
```

or this deprecated DIV version of the alignment attribute:

```
<DIV align="center">
```

Note   Center is handled the same way you handle align.

APPLET

All browsers that can handle Java recognize the APPLET element. However, you are asked to use the OBJECT element instead because it is more flexible. OBJECT can embrace many kinds of objects, ranging from simple text to ActiveX components.

Instead of this deprecated source code:

```
<APPLET code="Randomize.Class" width="200" height="300">
Java applet to randomize a dice throw.
</APPLET>
```

use this:

```
<OBJECT codetype="application/octet-stream"
    classid="java:Randomize.class"
    width="200" height="300">
Java applet to randomize a dice throw.
</OBJECT>
```

BASEFONT and FONT

BASEFONT specifies a basic (default) font size (using the size attribute) for a document. Thereafter, the FONT element can adjust the font size relative to this initially established base font size.

The BASEFONT and FONT elements — and the many attributes that modify them — are now deprecated. Instead, you should use style sheets to manipulate the appearance of text. Style sheets are more efficient (you need change a style in only one location, rather than many places throughout a document). Style sheets are also more flexible, permitting a greater variety of text effects.

This is a list of various font-related attributes that are now deprecated:

✦ STRIKE and S (display text with strikethrough)

✦ U (underlines text)

✦ SIZE (specifies the size of the font)

✦ COLOR (specifies the color)

✦ FACE (a list of alternative fonts, in order of preference, if the user's browser cannot display the requested font)

DIR

The DIR and the similar MENU elements are now deprecated. DIR was supposed to format text like multicolumn (DOS-style, with /W switch) directory lists, but some browsers arranged the list in vertical columns and some didn't. DIR wasn't of much use and wasn't used much. MENU was intended to create single column lists, similar to menu display. It, too, wasn't much used because most browsers didn't react to that element with any special formatting.

For example, IE renders the following with bullets in a single column:

```
<DIR>
<LI>General
<LI>Specific
<LI>Macro
<LI>Micro
<LI>Abstract
</DIR>
```

The only thing that happens when you use DIR in IE is that it creates a small left margin. MENU behaves exactly the same way as DIR.

Instead of DIR or MENU, you are urged to create lists with the UL element. UL stands for unordered list, and most browsers render this list with bullets, exactly the same way as the browsers render DIR and MENU data. UL provides bullets; the companion element, OL, provides a numbered list.

> **Note**
>
> MENU is handled the same way you handle DIR.

ISINDEX

The ISINDEX element is a strange bird. It provides a user-input text box and, by default, attaches the prompt text shown in Figure B-7.

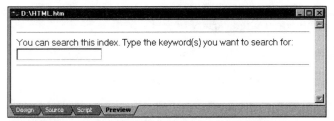

Figure B-7: The <ISINDEX> command automatically supplies this prompt.

You can use a PROMPT attribute to change the default prompt, but this ISINDEX element has been deprecated in favor of the far more flexible, general purpose INPUT element. What's more, ISINDEX is unnecessarily complex unless it can borrow its document's URL, which must be an HTTP URL. Besides, ISINDEX is functionally limited to the Latin-1 character set.

Instead of <ISINDEX>, use:

```
<FORM action="http://mysite.com/checkdata" method="post">
What do you want to search for? <INPUT type="text">
</FORM>
```

S, STRIKE, and U

The S and STRIKE elements specify that text should be rendered with strikethrough, and the U element specifies underlining. These elements have been deprecated, although we have been unable to locate a reason for this deprecation or the suggested alternative. Perhaps you should use the new INS and DEL elements, which, in Internet Explorer at least, display underlined and strikethrough text, respectively.

New Ways with FORMs

As HTML continues to attempt to reach the level of convenience, rich presentation, and efficiency available for years in word processors and graphical operating systems, a variety of initiatives have been introduced for both FORMs and TABLEs in HTML Version 4.0. The following are the primary new features of FORMs.

ACCESSKEY

The new ACCESSKEY attribute — which can currently be used with the LABEL, A (hyperlink), CAPTION, and LEGEND elements — is similar to the "hotkey" or "shortcut key" features of word processors and operating systems. In Windows, you can press Alt+Tab to switch between running applications. In most word processors, pressing Ctrl+F brings up a search (Find) dialog. In HTML, you can assign an access key to an element, allowing the user to send the focus to that element by pressing the special key. (Focus means that any subsequent keypresses will be accepted by the zone of the page that has the focus — a set of checkboxes will be selected or deselected, a text box will accept typed text, and so on.)

Unfortunately, the ACCESSKEY attribute is rather primitive (key combinations are Operating System-dependent, characters are case-insensitive, and there is a limit of four target elements). However, you can put a LABEL element in the same FORM as an INPUT device such as TYPE="text" or TYPE="button" and the focus will go to that "associated" input component. On devices running Windows, you are expected to press the Alt key in combination with the access key. However, this feature isn't yet working.

It's supposed to work like this:

```
<FORM>
<LABEL accesskey="U">
Please type in your favorite singer's last name</LABEL>
<INPUT type="text" name="fav">
</FORM>
```

If you attach an ACCESSKEY to a hyperlink (the A element), that link is *triggered* by the access keypress, just as if the user had clicked on the link.

DISABLED and READ-ONLY

In earlier versions of HTML, you couldn't make aspects of a FORM disabled (unresponsive to user keypress or mouse activity) by default at startup. You had to disable them after the document was loaded. Now you can use the DISABLED attribute to make elements unresponsive from the start. User input devices are, in some contexts, inappropriate. For example, you might want to disable a set of Medical History check boxes until the user has first agreed to reveal his or her history. This way, the user won't try to use input devices (such as check boxes) inappropriately. Disabling allows you to assist and control users' responses. A disabled element is not activated if the user is cycling through a group of elements by pressing Tab; a disabled element will not receive the focus in any fashion, nor will its data be submitted with a FORM.

You can use DISABLED as an attribute of these elements: BUTTON, INPUT, LABEL, OBJECT, OPTION, SELECT, and TEXTAREA. The next example illustrates how Internet Explorer indicates a disabled component. In Figure B-8, you can see that the disabled INPUT box on the left displays gray text while the enabled box on the right displays black text. Graying a component (not its contents) is the usual method of indicating a disabled state — but the reaction to the HTML DISABLED attribute is browser-dependent.

Figure B-8: An INPUT box grays its contents when disabled, but a TEXTAREA (shown above) looks the same enabled or disabled.

Here is the source code for Figure B-8:

```
<FORM method="post" ACTION="/cgi/res">

<TEXTAREA name="TheStory" rows="14" disabled>
</TEXTAREA>
</FORM>

<INPUT disabled value="Wait to enter your name">

<INPUT value="OK to enter your name">
```

The similar READONLY attribute also prevents the user from making any changes to an input component such as a text box. The primary difference between a DISABLED and a READONLY component is that the latter can receive the focus, be included in a tabbing cycle, and be submitted with its FORM. The user, however, cannot change the *contents* of an element with a READONLY attribute. Four elements utilize the READONLY attribute: INPUT, PASSWORD, TEXT, and TEXTAREA. As with DISABLED components, how a READONLY component makes its condition known visually (or otherwise) to a user depends on the browser.

ACCEPT and ACCEPT-CHARSET

The INPUT element now has the new ACCEPT attribute and the FORM element has an ACCEPT-CHARSET attribute.

The user is expected to send in a file when the INPUT element's attribute is TYPE="file". You can specify a list of file types (separated by commas) that your server can accept. This is a list of MIME types and the user's browser can check this list to prevent the submission of invalid filetypes by prompting the user during the file-selection process prior to submission.

Tip
MIME (Multimedia Internet Mail Extension) was originally used as a protocol for e-mail to permit more sophisticated formatting and content than plain text allows. Given that the Internet endeavors to embrace a wide variety of different operating systems and hardware, MIME was developed as a way of expressing content to all these diverse targets. MIME is now also used for other purposes, such as the file type list used with the ACCEPT attribute.

The ACCEPT-CHARSET attribute is a list of the character sets that a FORM's server is capable of dealing with. Commas or spaces can separate data on this list. The user's browser can employ this list to prompt the user or refuse to accept inappropriate characters.

✦   ✦   ✦

About the CD-ROM

The CD-ROM for Visual InterDev 6 Bible contains source code from the book's listings, an electronic copy of the book, a sample database, and Adobe Acrobat 3.01.

Source Code

Programmers naturally don't want to have to type out programming examples from a book. It's not only a wearing process in itself, but it's also all to easy to introduce typos that break the code. Then you have to debug. To avoid these problems, we've included all code listings in the book - script as well as HTML.

You'll find the source code in the folder on the CD-ROM named SourceCode. Each chapter containing a listing has its own file folder and each listing has its own text file. Therefore, if you wanted to copy and paste Listing 14-1, you'd find it on the CD-ROM in SourceCode\Chapter 14\14-1. The files are in .TXT format, so merely double-clicking on the filename will automatically load that chapter's code into Notepad.

Electronic Copy of This Book

PDF files of each chapter in this book have been provided so you may view the contents electronically. Each page appears in the same layout as the actual book. These files are located in the Book folder on this CD-ROM and must be viewed using Adobe Acrobat Reader 3.01 (or newer).

Utilities

Adobe Acrobat Reader

The Microsoft Windows 32-bit version of Adobe Acrobat Reader 3.01 is on the CD-ROM in the Applications directory. If you are running on any other operating system and want to read these electronic files, visit the Adobe Systems Web site (WWW.ADOBE.COM) to get the appropriate version of this reader.

Sample Database

You will also find a sample SQL Server database in the SourceCode/Ch18folder. The file's name is VIB_Sam.DAT. You will need it for Chapters 18, 19, 20, 21, 22, 23. Instructions for installing the database are in Chapter 18.

✦   ✦   ✦

Glossary

Absolute position HTML is usually relativistic. Font sizes, for example, are usually specified in such terms as small, bigger, biggest (or a range from 1 to 7), but what specific size that actually displays to a user depends on the size of the user's browser and the size of the user's monitor. Size and position of controls (such as buttons), text boxes, graphics, and other elements are difficult to deal with in classic HTML. Although HTML purports to be a page description language, it is remarkably weak in features that allow a programmer to easily define the location or size of an object on a page. Probably the easiest way to size and position visual components is to use the Layout object (see Chapter 12).

ActiveX Microsoft's name for what used to be called Dynamic Data Exchange (DDE) and, later, Object Linking and Embedding (OLE). The term *ActiveX* made its debut in December 1995 when Microsoft announced that it was repositioning itself in response to the exploding popularity of the Internet.

ActiveX is an umbrella term that covers the various concepts and technologies of DDE and OLE, and adds the idea that ActiveX Controls can also be embedded into traditional, and all-too-often dull and static, Web pages. ActiveX adds color, animation, sound, and, above all, efficient interactivity to Web pages. Microsoft is committed to ActiveX and all that the term *ActiveX* implies. It's a technology, a set of operating system features, a way of programming, and a collection of objects you can plug into your own programs or Web pages. ActiveX is, therefore, a general term that covers a variety of initiatives from Microsoft.

ActiveX component Previously called an ActiveX *control*, an ActiveX component is an object that may or may not have a visible user interface, and may or may not run as a server providing features to a client application. In practical terms, though, most ActiveX components are of the DLL type, meaning that they run in-process and act as servers (the second largest group of ActiveX components are UserControls). A Visual Basic control such as TextBox is an example of an ActiveX component. There are now several kinds of ActiveX components—ActiveX DLLs, ActiveX Exes, ActiveX Document DLLs, ActiveX Document Exes, and ActiveX control (UserControl). You can create all of these components easily using the Visual Basic language.

ActiveX DLL The commercial version of Visual Basic can produce several types of components that the Visual Basic Control Creation Edition (VBCCE) (a free ActiveX control creation version of Visual Basic; it's on this book's CD-ROM) cannot make. Full VB can produce these project types: ActiveX.EXE, ActiveX.DLL, ActiveX.Document DLL, ActiveX.Document EXE, Data project, IIS application, DHTML application, and Add-Ins. A DLL differs from other kinds of components in several ways. An ActiveX DLL component is always *in-process* meaning that it always resides within the address space and stack space of the client that's using it. A DLL component, therefore, loads fast when compared to an ActiveX EXE-style component (which is always out-of-process). The DLL doesn't have the overhead of causing other, *runtime* DLLs to be loaded. Also, messaging between the client and the DLL is faster. Procedures (methods) in a DLL can run as much as ten times faster than they would were they located in an out-of-process ActiveX EXE-type project.

ActiveX Document DLL An ActiveX Document is a disk file that contains an OLE link (or several). Once fired up, an ActiveX Document can manipulate data within its own file, or access other files. An ActiveX Document works within an ActiveX Document container (the client) that is capable of hosting an ActiveX Document. This technology used to be called Object Linking and Embedding, and was seen as a move toward *docucentric* computing. All of Microsoft's applications, such as Word and Excel, along with languages like Visual Basic, are capable of acting as ActiveX Document containers. Many other software houses have also made their applications capable of hosting ActiveX Documents. And, of course, Internet Browsers such as Internet Explorer can also host Document-style ActiveX components. The fundamental difference between an ordinary ActiveX DLL server and an ActiveX Document DLL is that the Document is specialized: it's designed to be activated within an Internet Browser or another container application such as Microsoft Word.

Active Server Pages *see* ASP

ActiveX Document EXE A Document-style version of ActiveX EXE components.

ActiveX EXE An ActiveX component designed to be run either as a server (but out-of-process with its client) or as a stand-alone Windows executable. In practice, people rarely find any use for ActiveX EXE-type components.

API Applications Programming Interface, the operating system's huge collection of functions (and a few subroutines) that you can tap into if a language such as Visual Basic doesn't have a feature you need, or does something too slowly. Windows 95 has an API, as does NT (they're quite similar, often identical). Java includes its own API in the form of a group of objects the programmer can access.

Application VI or FrontPage parlance, an application is made up of a collection of one or more projects that, collectively, comprise a finished Web site. The phrase *project group* refers to the same collection.

ASP Active Server Page, a page of HTML and script, such as VBScript or JavaScript, or an ActiveX component, that is to be executed on the *server* during an Internet transaction. ASP is a relatively new technology and endeavors to transfer the burden of computation to the bigger, faster computer (the server). Traditionally, a script language was intended for execution on the user's browser. Now, however, programming can be easily first executed by the server (and a resulting HTML document is then sent to the user). Microsoft's Internet Information Server (IIS) sees a file with the .ASP extension and knows that it should look for and execute any server script prior to sending the HTML (minus the server script) to the user's browser. The tags <% and %> delimit server script. ASP can also include objects, which are server-side components (such as a counter) intended to be executed server-side rather than downloaded to the user's hard drive (as is the case with traditional ActiveX components, or other components). For an in-depth discussion of all facets of ASP, see Chapters 16, 17, and 18.

Browser Internet Explorer and Netscape are the two giants among browsers. A browser is an application that can translate HTML into text and graphics that can be displayed. Browsers have additional capabilities as well, including the capability to locate addresses on the Internet (URLs), execute JavaScript or VBScript, handle some kinds of messaging, and display various multimedia. The capabilities of Browsers are expanding all the time and it's possible that in the future distinctions between an operating system and a browser will be academic or legalistic, not practical.

Cache A storage area. Operating systems often set aside some RAM in the computer to hold the most recently accessed files from the (slower-than-RAM) hard drive. Studies have shown that up to 80% of hard drive accesses are to files that were recently accessed. Therefore, if you can keep this data in a RAM cache, it will reappear within a requesting application much faster. Internet browsers cache the most recently visited Web documents — some to RAM and earlier ones to disk. If the user clicks the Back or Forward buttons, the cache (fast) is accessed rather than the hard drive (slow) or the Internet server (very slow).

Class A class is a template, a design, a list of qualities describing an object. You specify the qualities, features, and behaviors of an object when you write the programming that defines a class in the same way that an architect specifies the qualities, features, and behaviors of a building when the architect works up a blueprint. The blueprint is later used to create the actual, real building. Similarly, a running application or Web page can create an object (such as a particular text box) based on your specifications when you described the class in the source code of Visual Basic or another language that has the facilities for defining and instantiating (creating) classes.

Client script (or client-side script) A bit of programming (written in VBScript, JavaScript, Perl, or some other scripting language) that runs when a user's browser loads an HTML page containing the script. A scripting language is an abbreviated version of a larger language (JavaScript is a subset of Java, for example). Script languages don't have commands that can cause havoc in the wrong hands (they cannot access the hard drive, for example). Usually, a bit of script is triggered when the user interacts with a component (such as by clicking on an ActiveX Command Button). See Chapters 11 and 13 for more on this topic. A server script is the same thing, but it is executed on an Internet/intranet *server* machine when a user requests a page containing that script. Only after the script is executed by the server is the HTML then sent to the user's (client's) browser for execution (the server script portion is ignored and not sent to the user — it's already been executed). See Chapter 17.

Component This is another name for a *control*. (It can refer to a control with no visual interface, such as a WebBot, or to a Java or ActiveX object with or without a user interface.) Components are nearly always servers of the .DLL type. Microsoft prefers the term *component* to *control* given that there are several kinds of components of which only some are what most people think of as *controls* (UserControl or TextBox, Command Button, or CheckBox) or have a visible user interface. The term *control* suggests a visible interface, such as a text box. An ActiveX component might be simply a group of functions collected together into a library-like server, a .DLL (Dynamic Link Library).

Cookie A cookie is stored in a file on the user's hard drive. It's some data that an Internet/intranet site wants to remember after the user leaves the site. A cookie can, for example, provide information to your script about the user's previous visit to your site (so you can customize it for the user by remembering, in the cookie, the user's favorite font or address). Cookies are also a way to store truly global Variables. In fact, there are numerous situations where you might want to leave some information on the client side (a file in their hard drive), then later retrieve it. See Chapter 11.

Data connection This is a small list of specifications that describe how to access a database. It must include both the data source name (DSN) and the logon (and can also include passwords, the URL of the database's server, the user ID, and so on). A Data Connection is read each time that the user does something (such as clicking a Command Button that is intended to access the database) that makes it necessary for the program to open or access the database.

Data hiding *see* Encapsulation

Deployment When you finish a Web site, you make it publicly available to others in your office or around the world. Making it accessible to all comers is *deployment*. The process is sometimes referred to as *publishing* the site. In FrontPage, for example, you can click a toolbar button named Publish that will transfer all necessary files to the server you specify. Subsequent clicks on this button (when the same site is in the FrontPage Editor) will deploy that same Web to the previously specified server target, making editing and updating the Web quite simple. If you want to publish to a different server, choose Publish from FrontPage Explorer's File menu. For more about deployment, including a discussion of security issues, see Chapter 25.

DHTML Dynamic HTML. That this improvement to traditional HTML is called *dynamic* reveals that ordinary HTML is, for the most part, static. The DHTML proposal (from Microsoft) gives developers and programmers a way (through script languages) to move, instantiate (bring into existence), resize, and otherwise modify the elements and attributes of HTML. Internet Explorer 4.0 is DHTML-capable and contains various components (multimedia controls) that also reside within the user's computer as part of IE4. Both user-side scripting and the user-resident components make sophisticated audio and visual effects far more efficient than if the components (or the results of server-side scripting) had to be sent over the Internet. Even a static-still graphic image can take too long to traverse the narrow bandwidth of today's Internet. Ordinary HTML is sent to a user's browser with the intent that some data (text or pictures) be displayed. This display is basically hard-wired, inert, passive, and still. DHTML, however, changes the page-description language into a programming language, with all the interactivity, mutability, animation, and active, client-side processing that that implies.

Early binding When a client declares a new object, *by naming it directly*, that object is said to be early-bound (as opposed to using the generic command: *As Object*). For example, after you create a reference to Word's object library by this programming in Visual Basic

```
Dim objWord As Word.Application
```

you can then use a line of programming like this in Visual Basic to cause early binding:

```
Set objWord = New Word.application
```

The phrases *early* and *late binding* describe how a server is connected to a client when the server is first instantiated in the client.

When a client uses the *As Object* and *CreateObject* commands, an object is said to be late-bound:

```
Dim New_Object As Object
Set New_Object = CreateObject("excel.application")
```

With late binding, when Visual Basic compiles the project, the members of the object that your object variable points to cannot be checked. Reference to members (such as New_Object.Text) must be checked later, during runtime when the object is finally bound to your component. If your client can refer to objects using the early-bound technique, the server will perform more efficiently. An early-bound reference simply and directly codes a pointer to the object's member, eliminating the necessity of having to check the validity of that reference during runtime.

Encapsulation Encapsulation is a programming technique that refuses to allow outsiders — or even you, the programmer, or other objects in your own project — access to the Private variables or procedures within an object. This tactic, sometimes called *data hiding*, can decrease the number of bugs and increase the modularity of an object. *Modularity* involves not only subdivision (of a large program into smaller parts), but also the reusability of the objects (parts). If it's sufficiently modular, you or others should be able to easily plug an object into other, client programs, with no unexpected side effects. When you use the Visual Basic Private command to define a property or method, you limit access to that property or method to only those other procedures that are contained within the same module (or Form).

Technically, encapsulation means that the data (such as the value of the current BackColor property) within an object is never directly made available to a client. The data in an object is manipulated only within that object. Clients never know how the data is stored (all the variables within a class are Private) nor do clients know how the data is manipulated within the object. All a client needs to know is what members of the class have been made available (or *exposed* as it's sometimes called), what parameters they require, and what information they return, if any. (The term *members* means the properties, methods, and events, thought of collectively, of an object.)

Event A procedure in a client or control that is triggered when something outside happens — such as the user pressing a key or clicking the mouse. A developer or programmer can write programming within an Event procedure to specify a response — how the client or control should react if the user, for example, presses the Enter key while typing something into a text box.

Extranet A zone within an Internet Web site that cannot be accessed unless the user is registered (and therefore has permission to enter the restricted area).

GLOBAL.ASA A file with this name is created whenever you begin a new Web project in VI or FrontPage. The file includes event handlers that execute when a user initially contacts the Web site, and other event handlers that deal with what happens when the user exits from the site. A site's .ASA file resides on the IIS server and its scripts accomplish whatever housekeeping is appropriate for the site: initializing variables, connecting to a database, or depositing a cookie on the user's machine.

Global script Scripting that executes when a page is first loaded, because the script is not contained within a Function or Subroutine. In the following example, the alert will display as soon as this page is loaded in a user's browser:

```
<HTML>
<HEAD>

<SCRIPT LANGUAGE="VBScript">

alert "This page is loaded!"

</SCRIPT>

</HEAD>
```

```
<BODY>

</BODY>
</HTML>
```

whereas, in this next example, the Alert will never execute unless the user clicks on a button labeled Submit:

```
<HTML>
<HEAD>
<SCRIPT LANGUAGE="VBScript">

Sub Submit_OnClick
alert "This page is loaded!"
End Sub

</SCRIPT>
</HEAD>

<BODY>
<FORM NAME="MyForm">
Please type in your name:
<INPUT NAME="Text1" TYPE="TEXT" SIZE="42">
<INPUT NAME="Submit" TYPE="BUTTON" VALUE="Submit">
</FORM>
</BODY>

</HTML>
```

Global script is found only in client-side documents (.HTM pages that are loaded in a user's browser and intended to be interpreted locally on the user's computer). Another kind of procedureless script is called *in-line script* and is found in server-side files.

HTM A file ending in the .HTM extension contains HTML, and possibly scripting, and is intended to be displayed in a browser.

HTML HyperText Markup Language, the page-description language that is the basis of Internet/intranet documents. Web pages are described by HTML (telling a browser how to display text and graphics — their size, color, position, and so on). For action, multimedia, or other dynamic or computational behaviors, HTML is useless (although HTML is continually undergoing expansion via such proposals as Microsoft's DHTML — dynamic HTML). VBScript, ActiveX, or JavaScript can compute and add animation, instant feedback, and other benefits to Web pages. Similarly, objects such as ActiveX components can extend the capabilities of raw HTML.

Inheritance A class can provide its offspring (other "child" classes generated from a class) with its methods, events, and properties. *Subclassing* is another word for inheritance. Both terms mean that you take an existing class and modify it (usually making it more specialized). In this sense, when you subclass a generic TextBox control by modifying it to make it into a text box that accepts only passwords, you've created a more specialized form of the original, generic TextBox class.

Visual Basic doesn't permit "true" inheritance as defined by strict object-oriented programming (OOP) enthusiasts because there is no real parent-child relationship between the original class and the subclass. Many programmers are, however, grateful for this "lapse" because by ignoring that technical parent-child relationship, Visual Basic avoids certain problems inherent in strict OOP. In Visual Basic, for example, the original (or "parent") class is isolated from the subclass (or "child"). This means that if you change an original class, there is no way that you will cause problems in the subclass — they have no dynamic relationship in Visual Basic. That they don't is, all things considered, thought by many to be a blessing.

In-line script *see* Global script

In-process *see* Out-of-process

Instance *see* Instantiate

Instantiate When you create a class, it's a design, a set of specifications, for an object. A class is the assembly diagram, not the assembled barbecue cooker. The diagram or description of a class happens at design-time (while you're writing the program). When you (or a client) use that class to create an actual object, the object is said to be *instantiated*. This instantiating happens while your program runs (during runtime). Each object that's created is said to be an *instance* of the class that describes it. To put it simply: the assembly diagram is the class; the assembled barbecue is the instance.

Late binding *see* Early Binding

Layout In Visual InterDev, a layout is a template that specifies where navigation bars should be located on a Web page.

Local mode When you're working on a VI project and your changes are merely saved to your workstation, you're said to be in *local mode*. A special icon in VI's Project Explorer indicates local mode. This alerts you that your changes are not being saved to the master Web application. Contrast local mode with master mode in which changes are saved both to your computer (local workstation) as well as to the master files on the master Web server.

Local Web server This server resides on your computer and you can use it to test your VI application prior to posting it on the master Web server. The master Web server contains the final, official version of an application — all the pages of a document intended for use by the public via the Internet or within the company via an intranet. The local Web server is also known as the *staging* server (versus the *production server*).

Mapping This means borrowing the functionality of members of an existing component (see *Inheritance*). For example, if you're including an existing Visual Basic TextBox control in a new ActiveX component of your own creation, the TextBox has both a Text and a ForeColor property. You might want to pass the functionality of these properties through from the original Visual Basic TextBox to your new, subclassed ActiveX component. Borrowing existing features of original controls is called *mapping*.

Visual Basic and Visual Basic Control Creation Edition make mapping relatively painless because they include an ActiveX Control Interface Wizard that provides considerable help. It assists you by *writing the programming code* to map properties.

Master Mode *see* Local Mode

Master Web application This is the official version of a VI project and it resides on the master Web server. Contributing developers, designers, or others can modify it if they have permission. It is the final version of everyone's work, the pages that make up the document that will eventually (or is) exposed to the public on the Internet or the company on an intranet.

Master Web server *see* Local Web server

Members The properties, methods, and events of a particular object. Taken together, these three entities are referred to as an object's *members*.

Method A job that a component knows how to do. For example, a Visual Basic PictureBox has a Circle method because when you, the programmer, write its Circle method in your source code, the PictureBox knows how — during program execution — to draw circles and display them. You can also provide methods (behaviors) to components or classes you design — just write the programming code, for example, to calculate mortgage interest and put it into a Function or Subroutine. Then your component has a CalcMortgage Method — or whatever you decide to call it. Your component can do that job.

Navigation bar A design-time control that allows a user to click to move to different pages or other target locations within your site. To add one in VI, select the design-time controls tab in the VI Toolbox, then drag a *PageNavbar* object onto a Web page in the VI editor. The Navigation bar is a collection of links that reflects the parent/child relationships you've defined between your pages using the Site Designer. Select your project's name in the VI Project Explorer, thereby enabling the Add Item feature. Then, from the Project menu, choose Add Item and double-click Site Diagram. After you've added the control to a page, right-click on it and choose Properties to adjust the scope of the Navbar (where, in the parent/child hierarchy, the bar resides), its appearance, and other qualities of the Navbar.

Object-Oriented Programming (OOP) An approach to programming that stresses hiding data (encapsulation). OOP endeavors to enclose data, along with methods that process that data, into objects. OOP shifts the focus from the traditional procedure-oriented (Subroutines or Functions) programming style to an object-oriented style. Instead of merely listing the tasks that a program must accomplish, OOP asks that you then collapse (factor) those tasks into objects. Objects are identified as the *nouns* when you diagram the sentences in a task list:

1. Get the age of the **user** of this program.

2. Ask the annual salary of the **user** for the past ten years.

3. Calculate the **user's** probable Social Security compensation.

The object in this project is the user; it's the primary noun in each sentence (each task). So you make a class out of the User. In this User class, you create some properties and a method. The user has two properties: age and annual salary. The user has one method: calculating Social Security. You would build this project using OOP techniques by creating a User class (from which you can generate as many specific users as you might need). Then you would give this User class Age and Salary properties. Finally, you would include (in the User class) a CalcSS method that would check the Age and Salary properties, and look up the probable monthly Social Security check the user can expect at age 65.

Object A thing, an entity, a self-contained phenomenon. Fog, patriotism, the color blue, love, flying, and honey are not objects. They have no specificity, no discrete boundaries that distinguish them from other entities. Fog has a vague boundary; blue and love are nebulous, abstract concepts; honey flows. All these concepts are either abstract notions or something that has no particular start and end. An object is concrete. A specific stamp is an object and even a stamp collection enclosed within a stamp album is also an object. The abstract concept of stamps, though, isn't an object — it's an idea. Nor is a random sprinkling of stamps dumped on a carpet an object. In programming, when you define a class (an abstract plan), that class is capable of creating (concrete, specific) objects during runtime (when the program executes).

Out-of-process The term *out-of-process* means that a component is not running in the same address space or sharing a stack with its client application. UserControls and DLL-type components run in-process, simplifying and speeding things up when the client manipulates properties and methods in the server.

Polymorphism One of the three elemental characteristics of object-oriented programming (OOP) is called polymorphism, as in *polymorphous perverse*, one of Freud's more antic concepts. Literally, polymorphous means many forms, like a shape-shifter. (The other two elemental characteristics of OOP are *inheritance* and, most important of all, *encapsulation*).

But alas, as the word is used in computer programming, *polymorphism* is a more difficult idea to grasp than encapsulation or inheritance. Here's one way to understand polymorphism: Consider a drill sergeant saying "Fall in!" or mom saying "Everyone sit down for dinner, now." The command to fall in or sit down is a single command, a single idea — yet, in practice, various people do somewhat different things when they hear the command. Soldiers move to individual positions within the line; family members go to their chairs around the table. In OOP terms, several objects can be given the same command, but each object carries out that command in a way appropriate to it.

It's safe to assume that each family member is derived from the People Class and each member has inherited many behaviors from the original Class. However, each has modified some of those behaviors as necessary because each person is a *particular* object, a member of the BrotherBilly class, or the SisterSue class, or the DaddyJoe class. Each person has different chairs to go to when receiving the message to *sit*.

The ultimate benefit of this individualized polymorphic reaction to a single command (method) is that mom doesn't have to worry about what class each family member belongs to when making a request. Mom doesn't have to say, "Sue, sit in your chair over there and Brother Dan, go around the table until you find your usual chair there in the middle of the left side of the table...."

Translated into the idea of polymorphism in the programming world, a developer who uses your objects doesn't have to know each object's particular class when sending a command, that is, a message, to the object. *The object has the built-in sense to interpret the message correctly*, freeing the developer from worrying about the actual behavior. The developer merely wants all of the objects to fall in or sit down. The developer doesn't want to worry about the details of just how each object will accomplish the job in a way appropriate to its status and needs. You, the creator of an object, have given it the rudimentary intelligence needed to behave properly when it's requested to sit down or fall in.

Private file This file doesn't exist on the master Web server; it is only on your local computer, your "workstation." It has its own icon in the VI Project Explorer.

Project In general, this refers to a computer program. A project can mean the source code for an ActiveX component or for a full, large computer application, or the total source code (script, HTML, objects, images, whatever) that makes up a Web site. For some reason, Microsoft has decided to replace the traditional word *program* with the term *project*. The words are synonymous, except when referring to the source code for a Web site which is a project, and properly so called. In VI terminology, a project is a file or collection of related files that form a logical unit (a Web site might include several main projects and associated support projects). The complete Web site is called the *application* and is the total of the projects making up a *project group*. See *Application* for more on these definitions.

Program *see* Project

Property A quality of a component, like its color, fontsize, or width. A component's properties, methods, and events are called, collectively, its *members*.

Proxy server This server stands between your local network and the outside world, that is, the Internet. A proxy server prevents outside users from accessing information on your intranet.

Script Either VBScript or JavaScript. These are programming languages that can be embedded in HTML pages, and which allow you to make calculations, adjust aspects of the HTML that's being displayed (see DHTML), and, otherwise, *compute*.

Script is necessary because HTML is largely static, merely a page-description language that specializes in specifying font size, colors and other visual elements. It's most lively feature is the *link* which, when clicked, sends the user to a different location within the page, the site, or elsewhere on the Internet. Script programming can be embedded within documents sent to the user (client-side scripts) or script that executes on the Web site's server (server-side scripting, see *Active Server Page*). For more, see *Client Script*.

Scriptlet This is like any other script, except that it is saved in a separate .HTM file of its own and a reference to this file is embedded in a "container" HTML file as an OBJECT. Like objects, you can expose a scriptlet's members (see *Members*) to the outside world for programmatic manipulation. Or you can write the scriptlet so that it does things without requiring that any programming activate it, merely that it is an OBJECT in some HTML that is loaded in a browser. Scriptlets act like ActiveX objects or Java Applets: you can hide your source code and conveniently reuse scriptlets in other Web projects. For more on scriptlets, see Chapter 13.

Server script (or server-side script) This kind of script never makes it to the user's browser. Instead, the server executes it *before* the page is sent to the user's browser. The server script is removed from the HTML page before that page is sent to the user. Server script is most useful for looking up information in your database, processing information sent in by the user, or moving you to a different page on your Web. Also see *Client Script* and *Active Server Page*.

Session The time between when a user contacts your site and leaves it. There is a *session object* that you can access when you're writing ASP.

Style sheet A file that contains definitions of new elements, or redefinitions of existing HTML elements. The idea is that you can customize HTML tags or invent your own new tags, and these customizations can be global throughout an HTML document, reused as often as you want, or made quite local if you wish. In any case, it's efficient.

You've heard of Themes — pre-designed looks that you can add to a Web site in VI or FrontPage. Technically, a Theme is a set of Cascading Style Sheets (CSS) that include a coordinated group of elements (fonts, bullets, backgrounds, and so on), chosen because they are compatible. Cascading Style Sheets are lists of definitions for an HTML element (or several).

For example, you can redefine the qualities of <H1> (the first-level HTML headline) by specifying *changes* to the default qualities of its HTML element. Then, whenever you use that element in an HTML document — no matter how often — that element will display those changes, those new qualities you gave it in the style sheet. Style sheets are called *cascading* because there are several kinds (several levels of impact) of style sheets and each has its own order of precedence. You can adjust the focus of a CSS to make it apply to a single paragraph or an entire Web. See Chapter 10; it's mostly about CSS.

If you reference (name) a style sheet within one of your Web pages, you can permit all elements (tags) in your page that have corresponding entries in the style sheet to be automatically formatted according to the style sheet's specifications for that element.

You can use a built-in theme in Visual InterDev by selecting New Project from the File menu, then choosing New Web Project (double-click on its icon). This launches the Web Project Wizard. Answer the Wizard's questions and keep clicking the Next button until you get to the Instructions for selecting a theme.

Subclassing Deriving one thing from another. See *Inheritance.*

Template If you have to write a résumé for yourself, you can run Microsoft Word and load in the supplied example résumé. Then you can modify it to add the data that describes your working life. It's the same when you use a template in VI or FrontPage. A template is an .HTM or .ASP file or files that provide you with a predesigned page or pages. You can modify the contents to whatever degree is necessary to make the document work for your purposes, but with a template you don't have to start from scratch. Templates are useful for expediting the process of creating a consistent look and feel across an entire Web site, and also for making things easier for those who are challenged when asked to create attractive or coherent page designs. Templates and *themes* and some kinds of *wizards* are functionally quite similar. See *Style sheet.*

Theme *see* Style sheet

Transaction This is a group of actions (a job) that work or fail as a unit. There may be many steps involved — looking into a database, creating a report, responding to the user — but, taken as a whole, the entire job is called a *transaction.*

VBCCE Visual Basic Control Creation Edition. A fully functional programming environment that is very similar to the commercial versions of Visual Basic. The VBCCE, however, is only capable of producing compiled (runnable) ActiveX Controls (UserControls). It cannot create stand-alone Standard EXEs (typical Windows programs) or ActiveX Documents.

Wizard A utility that steps a user, programmer, or developer through the stages necessary to complete a task. Wizards can save a considerable amount of time and trouble (Visual Basic's Class Builder or Visual Basic Control Creation Edition's ActiveX Control Interface Wizard are enormously helpful) or be of quite limited usefulness (like the several Wizards that attempt to generate VBScript).

✦   ✦   ✦

Index

SYMBOLS

{ } (braces)
    in Cascading Style Sheets, 221
    in If Then constructs, 266
    in JScript, 259
: (colon), in VBScript statements, 260
<!—//—>, comment indicator, 259
( ) (parentheses)
    in arrays, 262
    in method names, 248
; (semicolon)
    in Cascading Style Sheets, 221
    in JScript statements, 260
    in method names, 248
& (ampersand)
    versus + (plus sign), 260
    in ASPs (Active Server Pages), 390
* (asterisk), in database diagrams, 486
" (double quote), in ASPs (Active Server Pages), 390
// (double slash), comment indicator, 259
= (equal sign)
    assigning values, 266
    equality testing, 266
== (equal signs), equality testing, 265–266
% (percent sign), in ASPs (Active Server Pages), 390
+ (plus sign)
    versus & (ampersand), 260
    in ASPs (Active Server Pages), 390
    concatenating text, 502
(pound sign), in Cascading Style Sheets, 227
? (question mark), in ASPs (Active Server Pages), 390
' (quote), comment indicator, 259
/ (slash), in ASPs (Active Server Pages), 390
<%...%> tags, 383–384

A

Absolute Mode option, 132
Absolute Positioning option, 131
Access Control Lists, 630–632
access restrictions. *See* user access
account information forms, 185–187
active HTML. *See* DHTML (Dynamic HTML)
Active Server Pages (ASPs). *See* ASPs
    (Active Server Pages)
ActiveX container, 237
ActiveX Control Interface Wizard
    API, 305

definition, 298–299
Graphical Device Interface, 305–308
private properties, 299–302
public properties, 299–302
ReadProperties procedure, 307–308
suppressing a properties window, 305
testing a control, 308
VBCCE source code, example, 302–304
ActiveX controls
    versus ActiveX, 234
    ActiveX container, 237
    adding to the toolbox, 249–251
    availability, 236–237
    browser support, 237
    building, 292–295
    compiling, 297
    DCOM (Distributed Component Object Model), 234
    definition, 234
    downloads, 235
    editing, 252–253
    inserting, 242–246, 251–252
    versus Java applets, 241
    performance, 236
    platform support, 235
    registering, 297–298
    versus scriptlets, 14
    security, 236, 649–650
    setting properties, 253–255
    sources for, 237
    strengths and weaknesses, 235
    testing, 296, 308
    toolbar button, 295–296
    VBCCE (Visual Basic Control Creation Edition), 292
    Web sites about, 235, 237
ActiveX Data Objects (ADO), 553
ActiveX Server components, creating
    your own, 425–426
Add a project... command, 83
Add Data Command option, 125
Add new projects... option, 89
Add outputs... command, 83
Add Project Outputs option, 125
add-ins, IDE, 133–134
Administer permission, 640
ADO (ActiveX Data Objects), 553
AdRotator component, 424
Advanced option, 121

(continued)

(continued)

(continued)

(continued)

(continued)

(continued)

(continued)

(continued)

IDG BOOKS WORLDWIDE, INC.
END-USER LICENSE AGREEMENT

4. **Restrictions on Use of Individual Programs.** You must follow the individual requirements and restrictions detailed for each individual program in the "About the CD-ROM" appendix of this Book. These limitations are also contained in the individual license agreements recorded on the Software Media. These limitations may include a requirement that after using the program for a specified period of time, the user must pay a registration fee or discontinue use. By opening the Software packet(s), you will be agreeing to abide by the licenses and restrictions for these individual programs that are detailed in the "About the CD-ROM" appendix and on the Software Media. None of the material on this Software Media or listed in this Book may ever be redistributed, in original or modified form, for commercial purposes.

5. **Limited Warranty.**

   (a) IDGB warrants that the Software and Software Media are free from defects in materials and workmanship under normal use for a period of sixty (60) days from the date of purchase of this Book. If IDGB receives notification within the warranty period of defects in materials or workmanship, IDGB will replace the defective Software Media.

   (b) **IDGB AND THE AUTHORS OF THE BOOK DISCLAIM ALL OTHER WARRANTIES, EXPRESS OR IMPLIED, INCLUDING WITHOUT LIMITATION IMPLIED WARRANTIES OF MERCHANTABILITY AND FITNESS FOR A PARTICULAR PURPOSE, WITH RESPECT TO THE SOFTWARE, THE PROGRAMS, THE SOURCE CODE CONTAINED THEREIN, AND/OR THE TECHNIQUES DESCRIBED IN THIS BOOK. IDGB DOES NOT WARRANT THAT THE FUNCTIONS CONTAINED IN THE SOFTWARE WILL MEET YOUR REQUIREMENTS OR THAT THE OPERATION OF THE SOFTWARE WILL BE ERROR-FREE.**

   (c) This limited warranty gives you specific legal rights, and you may have other rights that vary from jurisdiction to jurisdiction.

6. **Remedies.**

   (a) IDGB's entire liability and your exclusive remedy for defects in materials and workmanship shall be limited to replacement of the Software Media, which may be returned to IDGB with a copy of your receipt at the following address: Software Media Fulfillment Department, Attn.: *Visual InterDev 6 Bible*, IDG Books Worldwide, Inc., 7260 Shadeland Station, Ste. 100, Indianapolis, IN 46256, or call 1-800-762-2974. Please allow three to four weeks for delivery. This Limited Warranty is void if failure of the Software Media has resulted from accident, abuse, or misapplication. Any replacement Software Media will be warranted for the remainder of the original warranty period or thirty (30) days, whichever is longer.

(b) In no event shall IDGB or the authors be liable for any damages whatsoever (including without limitation damages for loss of business profits, business interruption, loss of business information, or any other pecuniary loss) arising from the use of or inability to use the Book or the Software, even if IDGB has been advised of the possibility of such damages.

(c) Because some jurisdictions do not allow the exclusion or limitation of liability for consequential or incidental damages, the above limitation or exclusion may not apply to you.

7. **U.S. Government Restricted Rights.** Use, duplication, or disclosure of the Software by the U.S. Government is subject to restrictions stated in paragraph (c)(1)(ii) of the Rights in Technical Data and Computer Software clause of DFARS 252.227-7013, and in subparagraphs (a) through (d) of the Commercial Computer — Restricted Rights clause at FAR 52.227-19, and in similar clauses in the NASA FAR supplement, when applicable.

8. **General.** This Agreement constitutes the entire understanding of the parties and revokes and supersedes all prior agreements, oral or written, between them and may not be modified or amended except in a writing signed by both parties hereto that specifically refers to this Agreement. This Agreement shall take precedence over any other documents that may be in conflict herewith. If any one or more provisions contained in this Agreement are held by any court or tribunal to be invalid, illegal, or otherwise unenforceable, each and every other provision shall remain in full force and effect.

my2cents.idgbooks.com

Register This Book — And Win!

Visit **http://my2cents.idgbooks.com** to register this book and we'll automatically enter you in our fantastic monthly prize giveaway. It's also your opportunity to give us feedback: let us know what you thought of this book and how you would like to see other topics covered.

Discover IDG Books Online!

The IDG Books Online Web site is your online resource for tackling technology — at home and at the office. Frequently updated, the IDG Books Online Web site features exclusive software, insider information, online books, and live events!

10 Productive & Career-Enhancing Things You Can Do at www.idgbooks.com

- Nab source code for your own programming projects.

- Download software.

- Read Web exclusives: special articles and book excerpts by IDG Books Worldwide authors.

- Take advantage of resources to help you advance your career as a Novell or Microsoft professional.

- Buy IDG Books Worldwide titles or find a convenient bookstore that carries them.

- Register your book and win a prize.

- Chat live online with authors.

- Sign up for regular e-mail updates about our latest books.

- Suggest a book you'd like to read or write.

- Give us your 2¢ about our books and about our Web site.

You say you're not on the Web yet? It's easy to get started with IDG Books' *Discover the Internet,* available at local retailers everywhere.

CD-ROM General Installation Instructions

Following are instructions for using materials located on this book's CD-ROM:

✦ You'll find the source code in the folder on the CD-ROM named SOURCECODE. Each chapter containing a listing has its own file folder and each listing has its own text file. Therefore, if you want to copy and paste Listing 14-1, you'd find it on the CD-ROM in SourceCode\Chapter 14\14-1.txt. The files are in .TXT format, so merely double-clicking on the filename will automatically load that chapter's code into Notepad.

✦ To copy applications and utilities, place the CD-ROM in your CD-ROM drive, run the setup program, and follow any instructions included.

✦ To install and run Adobe's Acrobat Reader and view the electronic version of this book, follow these steps:

1. Start Windows Explorer (if you're using Windows 95) or Windows NT Explorer (if you're using Windows NT), and then open the Acrobat folder.

2. Double-click ar32e30.exe and follow the instructions presented onscreen for installing the application.

3. After you've installed Adobe's Acrobat Reader, start Windows Explorer or Windows NT Explorer and open the Book folder on the CD-ROM.

4. Double-click the chapter or appendix file you would like to view. All documents in this folder end with a .PDF extension.

For more information on using the CD-ROM, please see this book's Appendix C.

✦   ✦   ✦